| 3rd edition |

GRE Writing

Analytical Essay

| 3rd edition |

GRE
Analytical Essay
WRITING

김문희 Michelle Seo 지음

한울
아카데미

들어가는 말

　이 책은 영어로 문장을 쓰려고 하면 생각이 꽉 막혀 글쓰기의 시작조차 어렵게 느끼는 학생이나 문법 지식이 다소 부족한 학생 모두 guided practice를 통해서 쉽게 고득점 이슈(issue) 에세이와 아규(argue) 에세이를 쓸 수 있도록 구성되었습니다. GRE 시험을 준비하는 사람뿐만 아니라 SAT, TOEFL Writing 시험에서 고득점을 희망하는 학생 또는 analytical 영어 에세이 쓰기를 배우고자 하는 모든 이들에게 유용한 책입니다. New GRE Writing을 통해 영작 실력을 한 단계 업그레이드할 수 있는 좋은 기회가 될 수 있습니다.

　무엇보다도 한국어로 먼저 떠오르는 아이디어를 유창한 영어로 집필할 수 있는 결정적인 노하우를 소개합니다. 예증 자료는 보편타당성을 입증할 풍부한 새로운 쓸 거리로 준비하였습니다. 논술 수사법과 전문 영어 표현으로 작성한 약 100편의 샘플 에세이와 더불어 부록에는 지난 10년간 합격한 다수 SOP 샘플도 부록으로 첨가하였습니다.

　이 책을 통해서 독자들이 자연스럽게 익힌 에세이 쓰기 습관은 장래 학업에 든든한 기초가 될 것입니다. 끝으로 GRE Writing의 출판을 위해 힘써주신 한울엠플러스(주) 여러분께 감사드립니다. 1판을 내고 2판 때 'New GRE Writing'으로 제목을 바꾸었으나, 본문 내용이 1판을 기본으로 하므로 제목을 1판 제목인 'GRE Writing'으로 회귀하고, 3판으로 출간하게 되었습니다.

IBTEDU.COM director

김문희(Michelle Seo)

A r g u e

Introduction

이슈란 무엇인가?

GRE 시험을 계획하고 준비하고자 하는 학생은 누구나 처음 GRE 시험을 주관하는 ETS가 공개하는 약 150개 topic을 대하게 되면 어떤 주제에서부터 어떻게 쓰기 학습을 시작해야 하나 하고 고심하게 된다. 하지만 통찰력을 가지고 ETS가 제시한 토픽 내용을 자세히 들여다보면 2가지 중요한 사실을 발견할 수 있다.

첫째는 같은 내용으로 작성할 수 있는 토픽이 다수 중복되어 있다는 점이며, 둘째는 다른 주제 토픽 내용 간에도 서로 유기적인 관계가 있다는 점이다. 그러므로 예증 다수의 토픽에 대해서 동일하게 사용할 수 있는 예증거리를 간추려 확보한다면, 최소 예증으로 다수 토픽을 커버할 수 있는 전략을 세울 수 있다. 다만 GRE 시험이 석박사 과정을 지원하는 학생에게 주어지는 시험인 만큼, 예증 내용과 표현은 학술적이고 전문적 지식을 바탕으로 이루어져야 한다. 전공지식인 지동설과 같은 역사적 사실 또는 미투운동과 같은 성차별에 관한 시사성 있는 사건을 예증으로 활용하는 것이 바람직하다.

> 예) NASA 예증은 143(interdisciplinary), 36(research), 45(competition), 1(technology)을
> Nicolas Copernicus의 지동설 예증은 34(controversy), 42(skepticism), 91(technology) 등
> 이슈 토픽 글거리로 아울러 쓸 수 있다.

이 책은 GRE 시험을 보고자 하는 학생들이 상대적으로 짧은 시간에 고득점을 할 수 있도록 전략적인 방법을 구조적이며, 체계적으로 고안했다. 149개 이슈 토픽을 우선 주제별로 분석해서 동일하거나 유사한 토픽을 가려낸 이후에 출제 가능성이 가장 많은 토픽만을 우선적으로 선정한 다음 방대한 토픽 주제들을 논리 순차로 정리해서 어떤 유형의 토픽이 나오더라도 수험생들이 자신감을 가지고 에세이를 쓸 수 있도록 강의노트를 구성했다. 또한 주장에 근거가 되는 예증들 간의 유기적 관계에 착안해서 최소한 예증으로 최다수 토픽을 아울러 쓸 수 있는 전략적 방법을 지도한다.

토픽 간에 유기적인 관계를 고려해서 12가지 그룹으로 추려낸 토픽을 중심으로 만든 기차표에 따라서 한 그룹 토픽당 예비지식을 다루는 강의노트와 샘플 에세이를 제공한다. 기차표 아래 빈 줄에 써넣은 토픽 예증 간 유기적인 관계를 중심으로 간추린 12가지 주제별로 작문 연습을 한

다면 실제 GRE 시험에서 어떤 토픽이든 무리 없이 쓸 수 있는 수준에 다다를 것이다.

이슈 에세이 질문

Write a response in which you discuss the extent to which you agree or disagree with the statement and explain your reasoning for the position you take. In developing and supporting your position, you should consider ways in which the statement might or might not hold true and explain how these considerations shape your position.

어떤 정도까지 동의하거나 반대하는지(your position)를 토론한 뒤 반대 또는 동의하는 자신의 주장의 이유(reasons)를 설명하는 답변을 작성하시오. 당신의 의견을 발전하고 지지하는 과정에서 위의 문제(statement)가 보편타당한지 아닌지를 고려해야 하며, 어떻게 이러한 타당성(might or might not hold true)이 당신의 주장을 근거(examples)하고 있는지를 설명하시오. 여기서 might or might not hold true는 반드시 반대 의견, 즉 마이너스 의견을 검토하라는 의미이다.

12 Categories in GRE issue topics

1. The Objectives and Methods of Education

2. Impacts of Technology on Society and Individuals

3. The Power of Technology, The Influence of Media

4. Heroes and Role Models

5. Leaders' Ethics

6. Values in History vs Culture

7. The Roles of Government

8. Conformity versus Individuality

9. Inspiration vs Perspiration

10. Politics and Laws

11. Environment

12. Knowledge & Research

사실상 대다수 이슈 에세이 토픽은 논지(agree or disagree)가 **평등한 민주사회 발전 방향**으로 결정되어 있다는 사실을 염두에 두고 글을 쓰는 것이 첫걸음이다. 그러므로 소수 토픽을 제외한 **대다수 에세이는 disagree**로 논쟁하도록 토픽이 쓰여 있다는 사실을 깨닫고 논지의 방향을 정해야 할 것이다. 효율적 내용 분석을 위해서 12가지 토픽의 카테고리를 만들고 가장 빈번하게 GRE 시험에 출제되는 **S급 주제**만을 선별해 샘플 모델링을 하였다. 주제 유형에 따라 **22문장 템플릿**을 착안해서 에세이를 써나간다면 ETS가 높게 평가하는 자연스러우면서 통일성 있는 에세이를 비교적 쉽게 작성할 수 있다.

3가지 고득점 자료

1. 설득력 있는 예시 Quotation, 수사법 등 주요 표현을 담은 강의노트
2. 논리적 사고의 흐름을 이어주는 signal word로 시작하는 22 문장 템플릿
3. 샘플 에세이 모델링이다.

6단계 쓰기 전략

1. ETS가 제공하는 토픽 안에 내포된 에세이 논지를 명확히 이해
2. partially agree 또는 partially disagree 입장 유형을 결정
3. 왜 동의 또는 반대하는지를 밝히는 내 주장 thesis 문장
4. 내 주장을 받쳐줄 보편타당한 글거리 예증을 선별 준비
5. 비법 템플릿 signal word를 사용한 내용 논리와 문장 연결구조 파악
6. 이슈 샘플 에세이의 전체적인 논지 흐름과 예증, 결론이 보여주는 보편타당성

4.0 에세이 평가 기준

만약에 누군가 어떻게 이슈 4.0 이상 득점을 확신하는가를 묻는다면 다음과 같이 답할 수 있다. 최소 4.0이라는 득점은 ETS가 사용하는 에세이 평가 채점표 기준을 근거로 한 것이다. 먼저 보편타당한 예증을 제시함으로써 content에서 1.0점, 템플릿을 사용해 일관성 있는 structure 와 organization에서 각각 0.75점과 1.0점을 취득해서 기본적으로 2.75점 취득이 가능하다. 그 외 다른 2가지 카테고리인 expression과 grammar 채점 영역인 적절한 어휘, 정확한 문법, 전문 용어 분야에서 최저 0.25씩 받는다고 가정하더라도 총점은 3.25점이 된다. 여기에 기본 점수 1.0을 더한다면 4.25점 취득이 가능하다. 아래의 ETS rubric(채점 기준표)을 참고해서 채점표 기준을 명확히 이해해야만 고득점을 취득할 수 있다는 전략이다. 구글 grammarly와 같은 도구를 사용해서 컴퓨터가 점수를 산정할 때 가장 한국인이 주로 틀리는 문법은 number agreement (수의 일치)와 불필요한 수동태라는 점을 명심해야 한다.

GRE 라이팅 점수 분포

5.0(93%), 4.5(82%), 4.0(60%), 3.5(42%), 3.0(17%)

ETS RUBIC

채점 기준	1.0	0.75	0.5	0.25
The essay develops a position on the issue through the use of incisive reasons and persuasive examples. (content)	×			
The essay's ideas are conveyed clearly and articulately. (structure)		×		
The essay maintains proper focus on the issue and is well organized. (organization)	×			
The essay demonstrates proficiency, fluency and maturity in its sentence structures, vocabulary, and idiom. (expression)				
The essay demonstrates an excellent command of the elements of standard written English, including grammar, word usage, spelling and punctuation, but may contain minor flaws in these areas. semicolon, colon, coma, capitalization (grammar and mechanics)				

Introduction

결론적으로 본 강의는 GRE 평가 기준서(rubric)에 의거해서 이슈 4.0 이상 글을 쓸 수 있도록 보편타당한 예시와 일관성 있는 글쓰기를 지도한다. 1) 토픽에 내재한 의미를 깊이 이해하고 분석해, 2) 유용한 예시를 선별할 수 있게 하며, 무엇보다도 3) **22문장 템플릿**을 바탕으로 signal words 사용해 머릿속에 떠오르는 아이디어를 논리적으로 정렬할 수 있는 방법을 소개한다.

ETS 평가 기준

1. 문단에 논점을 제시하는 서론 결론 문장과 논점을 제시하는 **명쾌한 이유**
2. 서론, 본론, 결론을 일관성 있게 연결하는 문단 구성과 적절한 **접속어 연결**
3. 본론에서 근거 있는 **보편타당한 예시**
4. 논지를 뒷받침하는 데 필요한 수사법과 **전문용어** 표현 사용
5. **올바른 문법**과 **Mechanics**(spelling, capitalization, punctuation).

GRE 논리구조

위에서 강조한 일관성 있는 글쓰기를 위해서는 접속사 사용이 매우 중요하다. 접속사는 독자들을 A 지점에서부터 B 지점까지 안내하기 위한 안내판 같은 역할을 한다.

논리 흐름을 연결하는 고리: 유용한 접속어

Transitional Words and Phrases	
Sequence 순차적인 연결	again, also, and, and then, finally, first, second, third, next, still, too, and so forth, afterward, subsequently, finally, consequently, previously, before this, simultaneously, concurrently
To add 첨가	besides, equally important, finally, further, furthermore, nor, lastly, what's more, moreover, in addition
To prove 증명	because, for, since, for the same reason, obviously, evidently, furthermore, moreover, besides, indeed, in fact, in any case, that is

To compare and contrast 비교 대조	whereas, but, yet, on the other hand, however, nevertheless, on the other hand, on the contrary, by comparison, where, compared to, up against, balanced against, vis a vis, but, although, conversely, meanwhile, after all, in contrast, although this may be true, still, though, yet, despite, as opposed to
Time 시간 순서	immediately, thereafter, soon, after a few hours, finally, then, later, previously, formerly, first (second, etc.), next, and then, as long as, as soon as
Cause-and-effect 원인 결과	as a result, because, consequently, for this purpose, so, then, therefore, to this end
Emphasis 강조	definitely, extremely, obviously, in fact, indeed, in any case, absolutely, positively, naturally, surprisingly, always, forever, perennially, eternally, never, emphatically, unquestionably, without a doubt, certainly, undeniably, without reservation
Exception 제외	yet, still, however, nevertheless, in spite of, despite, of course, once in a while, sometimes
Examples 예증	for example, for instance, in this case, in another case, on this occasion, in this situation, To summarize and
conclusion 요약 결론	in brief, on the whole, summing up, in conclusion, as I have shown, hence, therefore, accordingly, thus, as a result, consequently, as has been noted, as we have seen

* The above chart is provided by ETS iBT toefl.

논리적인 서론을 기술하는 논리 유형

Ⅰ. Partially disagree 유형

(1) 작가가 무엇 무엇이라고 말한다.
(2) 그러나 나는 작가 주장에 반대한다. [-]
(3) 왜냐하면 극단적 상황에서 토픽 주장에는 문제가 있기 때문이다.
(4) 그런 극심한 경우가 아니라면[otherwise] 작가 의견은 어느 정도 일리 있다. [+]

(1) The speaker claims so.
(2) However, I disagree with the speaker.
(3) Because in an undue case some problems occur.
(4) Otherwise, what the speaker asserts seems somewhat reasonable.

II. Prefer 유형

(1) 작가는 어떤 목적(교육)을 위해 A보다 B가 중요하다고 말한다.

(2) Of course, B의 장점이 있다.

(3) However, B의 단점이 있다.

(4) In contrast, A의 장점이 B의 단점보다 중요하다.

(5) Thus, A가 B보다 더 중요하지 않다.

(1) The speaker contents that A is more important than B.

(2) Of course, B has strength in X.

(3) However, B has its demerits in Y.

(4) In contrast, A is much more beneficial for Y.

(5) Thus, I think A is not so important as B.

꼬리를 무는 22문장 템플릿

이슈란 speaker가 주장하는 토픽에 대해서 동의하거나 반대하는 자신의 의견을 피력하고 설득하는 논설문(persuasive essay)이다. 미국 고등학교 현장에서 논설문 쓰기를 가르쳐본 경험에 따르면, 계속해서 본인의 소신을 밝히고자 토픽에 나오는 keyword에 대한 정의나 개념을 발전시키는 식으로 에세이를 쓰는 것이 아니라 적절한 예증으로 본문을 구성하고 서론에서 주장한 자기 의견이 맞다는 요지를 결론에서 다시 한번 마무리하는 양괄식으로 글을 끝맺는다. 이 형식을 지키지 않는다면 이슈 2.0이라는 아주 낮은 점수를 취득하게 된다. 중요한 것은 이른바 영미식 글쓰기라는 형식 틀을 지켜야만 고득점을 얻을 수 있다는 것이다. K-12(Kindergarten~12학년), 미국 공립 영어작문교과 과정에서 5 paragraph essay writing이 강조되는 것을 감안한다면, GRE Issue Essay는 대체로 5문단을 쓰는 것이 바람직하다. 하지만 내용의 예증에 따라서 본문(body) 부분을 2문단으로, 총 4문단 에세이라도 글의 수준이 높다면 5.0 이상도 무난히 득점할 수 있다. ETS가 바라는 6.0 이슈 에세이 채점 기준이 되는 다음과 같은 요소를 담고 있는 템플릿이 완전히 머릿속에 그려질 때 쓰기 연습을 할 것을 권고한다.

자세한 템플릿 구조 설명

Template의 구성은 전체적으로 5 paragraph essay로 되어 있다. 보통 여러분들이 analytical writing을 학생들에게 요구할 때는 five paragraph을 쓰는 것이 analytical essay의 전형이라는 것을 알아야 한다. 총 다섯 개의 문단 가운데 첫 문단은 서론 문단이며 둘째, 셋째, 넷째 문단은 본론인데, 두 번째 문단은 내 주장과 반대 방향인 마이너스 문단이라면 세 번째와 네 번째 문단은 플러스 문단이며, 그리고 마지막 문단은 결론 문단이다.

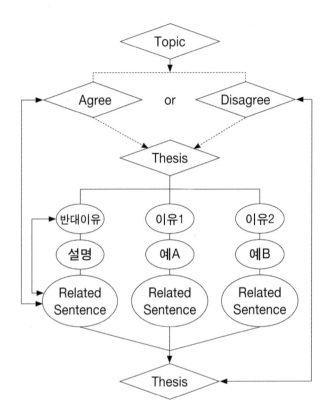

꼬리를 무는 22문장 템플릿

I. 서론

(1) Restate the topic.

(2) Some/Many may think that 나의 주장과 대조되는 의견과 이유

(3) However, I disagree with the speaker.

(4) because 이유 1 and 이유 2

(5) Ex A and Ex B best illustrate that 나의 주장

II. 본론

(6) Of course, the importance of 2번 주장 cannot be overlooked.

(7) 2번 주장을 세부 detail로 좀 더 develop한다.

(8) 7번 문장을 정리하고 더 발전시키는 문장

(9) 위의 두 문장을 토픽의 논지를 넣어 Related sentence를 만들어준다.

III. 본론

(10) Nevertheless, 나의 이유 1과 그 1로 인한 결과

(11) For example, 세부적 예증 A

(12) In contrast(unlike, while)로 위의 예증과 반의어 개념으로 대조하면서 설명

(13) 비교급을 사용해서 12번 문장을 한 번 더 정리한다.

(14) Related to the 8번 예증 to the key words of the given topic.

IV. 본론

(15) Another example(예증 2) that supports my claim (이유 2) is that ~

(16) Suppose, 세부적 설명 문제(problem) 제시

(17) 위의 상황에서 어떠한 harmful 결과(solution)를 주었나를 설명한다.

(18) 위의 문제 해결방법을 다시 한번 정리한다.

(19) Related to the 15번 예증 to the key words of the given topic.

V. 결론

(20) Clinch Sentence (Summary나 Quotation Sentence로) 마무리한다.

(21) As having seen in the above examples, 나의 주장

(22) 자기 말로 교훈적인 Highlight 또는 강조 문장(what you said in the above.)

Five paragraph essay의 각각의 문단은 5개의 문장으로 이루어진 서론과 4개의 문장으로 된 본문의 마이너스 문단, 그 뒤에 본론 바디 II와 바디 III가 되는 플러스 문단, 3가지 자기 자신의 주장을 받쳐주는 예증을 포함하는 문단이 따라온다. 위의 템플릿을 보면 문장 10~19번이 본론 중에 플러스 문단, 즉 나의 주장을 받쳐주는 두 가지 예증들을 적는 문단이다. 마지막 문단의 문장인 20번, 21번, 22번이 결론을 이루고 있다. 결론은 서론과 다소 닮은꼴이나 좀 더 인용문처럼 간결하면서도 교훈적인 의미를 지니는 하이라이트 문장으로 구성한다.

다시 전체적으로 보면 5, 4, 5, 5, 3의 문장 구성으로 에세이는 이루어지며, 서론은 5문장, 본론의 첫 문단이 "Of course"라고 해서 여기서는 나의 주장이 아니라 나와 대조되는 의견을 4문장 정도로 '마이너스 문단'을 작성한다. 여기서 유의해야 될 것은 나와 다른 의견을 같은 사람들의 주장과 근거를 써야 한다는 것이다. 유의할 점은 마이너스 문단을 4문장 이상 길게 쓰지 말라는 점이다, 당연히 내가 주장하는 예증이 제시되는 본문의 세 번째, 네 번째 문단을 더 길게 5문장씩 10문장 이상 길게 써야 자신의 주장을 위한 설명이 좀 더 자세히 쓸 수 있기 때문이다. 다시 말하

면, 10번에서부터 19번이니까 10개의 문장은 Nevertheless를 접속사로 시작 한 **5문장 예시**, 그리고 furthermore를 접속사로 한 **5문장 예시**로 구성하는 것을 기본으로 작성한다.

구체적으로 예증 내용을 위한 아이디어 mapping: 논리적 5형태 구조

Related S	Cause-Effect	Exemplification	Comparison / Contrast	Problem Solution

예증 문장을 논리적으로 쓰고자 하면 위에 열거한 다섯 가지 방법으로 기본 아이디어 mapping 논리를 이해해야 한다. Related Sentence(General Sentence)는 다음 문장에 보여 줄 자신의 예증의 타당성을 적는다. 이때 argument(주장)은 인과관계로 일반적이면서 포괄적인 첫 문장으로 시작한다.

본론은 서론에서 주장한 이유 1 + 이유 2를 받쳐주는 근거로 예증 A와 B를 예시화한다. 아이디어를 방법 **예증 A는 비교급**을 사용해서 비교, 대조로 구성하고 **예증 B는 'suppose'로 시작하는 가정법 문장**을 사용해서 자신의 논지와 반대의 경우에 발생하는 문제를 야기한 뒤, 그 해결책을 논의하는 세부적 문장이 뒤따라오는 문법적 전략까지 활용한다면 고득점 analytical essay로 평가 받을 수 있다.

결론을 쓰기 위해서는 quotation같이 간결하면서 강한 메시지를 줄 수 있는 하이라이트 문장으로 20번 문장을 생성한다. 20번 문장은 위에 쓴 모든 내용 전체를 포괄적으로 표현하는 것이 매우 중요하다. 21번은 As having seen above, 위에 본 바와 같이 나의 주장이 맞다라고 쓰고, 마지막으로 다시 22번은 20번 문장과 같은 성격의 문장으로 다시 한번 20번 문장 내용을 확장하면 된다.

1. 서론 다시 보기

토픽이 질문하는 의도를 분명하게 파악하기 위해서 토픽 문장에 보이는 정도부사가 가지고 있는 극단적인 폐해를 생각한 다음에 자신의 논지, 즉 partially agree인지 partially disagree인지를 정해야 한다. 요지를 파악할 때 유의해야 하는 것은 빈도부사에 따라서 논리가 뒤집힐 수 있다는 사실이다. 예를 들면 거의 모든 GRE topic은 "always, little, only"와 같은 빈도부사나 all, any, every와 같이 일반화할 수 있는 quantifier가 강조하는 내용에 근거해서 글의 논지를 결정해야만 논리적인 글을 완성할 수 있다. Off topic 에세이는 보편타당한 사고나 상식에 벗어나게 된다. 결과적으로 논지의 발전이 설득력이 없는 우왕좌왕 에세이를 작성하게 되며 이러한 에세이는 평가에서 1.0이라는 낮은 점수를 받게 된다. 다음 ETS 평가 기준을 명확하게 이해해야만 고득점 GRE essay를 쓸 수 있다.

무엇보다도 독자들이 토픽을 알고 있으리라는 전제로 토픽을 서론에 언급하지 않고 에세이를 시작하는 경우를 종종 본다. 종종 있다. 그러나 토픽에 대한 설명이 없는 서론은 구조에 있어서 첫 단추를 잘못 끼워 셔츠를 입는 것과 같다. 그리고 다른 한 가지는 동의하거나 반대하는 입장을 반드시 쓴다. 그리고 자신의 주장과 반대 의견을 모두 일관적 구성(−−−나 +++형)으로 본론을 구성하는 경우까지도, 서론(템플릿 둘째 문장)에서 자신의 의견과 상반되는 의견을 거론해야 한다. 그래서 템플릿 2번 문장은 주로 작가 자신의 결론이나 주장과는 달리 있을 수 있는 의견이나 생각에 대해서 짚어 보는 문장으로 구성한다. 다시 말해서 자신 의견에 대한 반론까지 고려해 보았다는 사려 깊은 에세이라는 인식을 주어야 한다.

a) 토픽 statement를 언급하여 audience(독자)에게 토픽이 무엇인지 환기시킨다.

ex) The speaker(statement) contends that ~

b) 본인의 입장과 반대 입장을 간단히 피력한다.

ex) Some(Many) people believe that ~

c) 자신의 입장, 즉 동의하는지 반대하는지를 독자에게 알린다.

ex) I disagree that~ (어느 정도까지)

d) 서론에 쓸 예증 2가지를 근거로 자신이 왜 이러한 주장을 하는지 이유를 적는다. 이유를 쓸 때 토픽의 key words의 definition 정도는 우선적으로 이해하고 있어야 자신의 주장을 펼치기가 쉽다. 본인의 주장을 더욱 강화할 수 있는 thesis문장(이유)을 한 번 더 강조하는 방향으로 쓴다.

2. 본론 다시 보기

본론에서는 서론에서 주장한 논지를 뒷받침할 수 있는 예증을 제시해야 한다. 이때 신문기사나 문학 작품, 과학자들 이야기나 역사적 사실들을 사용하는 것이 바람직하다. 하나의 예증을 다섯 가지 문장으로 구성하는 것이 요령이다. 본문의 첫 문장은 이유 1을 뒷받침해 줄 커다란 카테고리 예시 문장을 소개하고, 두 번째 문장은 for example을 사용해서 세부적인 예를 제시한다. 셋째 문장은 둘째 예시의 background 지식을 설명한다. 넷째 문장은 배경 지식 부연 설명을 하며, 다섯째 문장은 위의 예와 서론에서 밝힌 자기주장과의 관계를 정립, 정리한다. 이렇게 본문의 다른 2가지 근거도 다섯 문장으로 구성한다.

a. 3개나 4개 문단으로 본론에 쓸 보편타당한 예증을 찾는다. 이때 전공 지식을 활용한다.

b. 서론에서 밝힌 자신의 논지를 받쳐줄 보편타당성 있는 예증으로 작성해야 한다. 하나의 글 전체를 독자가 쉽게 이해할 수 있도록, 즉 통일성을 지키는 구조적인(coherent) 글은 완벽한 근거 자료인 예증으로 완성할 수 있기 때문이다.

c. 문단 통일성을 위해서 마지막 문장을 한 번씩 related sentence로 마무리한다. Related sentence란 위 예증과 서론 셋째 문장인 자신의 주장과 관계성을 보여주는 마무리 문장이다.

d. 서론에 쓴 자신의 주장을 부연하는 예증(examples)은 보편타당성과 설득력이 있어야 한다. 자신의 경험, 학문적 이론, 뉴스, 상식을 활용한다. 논지를 받쳐주는 점수에 결정적인 영향을 미친다는 것을 알아야 한다. 본론에 등장하는 예증들은 개인적인 측면은 물론, 사회적 perspective를 고려해야만 한다.

e. 영어로 예증 자료를 찾아 읽는다. (도움이 되는 link)
www.google.com, www.naver.com, http://wikipedia.com, www.answers.com, www.cnn.com, www.koreaherald.co.kr

3. 결론 다시 보기

결론은 본론에 적은 예들을 볼 때, 서론에서 주장한 내 의견이 맞다라고 끝맺음을 하는 문단이다. 결론의 첫 문장은 전체적으로 위에 적은 내용을 요약, 정리하는 결론적인 문장을 쓴다. 이 때 Quotation이나 간략한 에피소드를 적는 것도 한 방법이다. 전형적인 템플릿 용어인 As having seen from the foregoing examples …과 같은 문구를 사용해서 서론 (3)번 문장에서 자신의 주장을 다시 한번 반복한다. 다만 새로운 예증을 장황하게 소개하지는 말고 본인의 주장을 강조할 수 있는 문장이나 교훈적 메시지를 담을 수 있는 문장으로 에세이를 마감한다.

a. 서론과 본론의 동일한 내용을 압축 요약해서 쓰되 다소 표현을 바꾸어서 쓴다. 이때 동의어를 사용하면 쉽게 작성할 수 있다.
b. 서론의 주장을 약화하거나 본론에 없는 내용은 절대 쓰지 않는다.
c. 가능하다면 교훈적인 메시지를 주는 내용으로 마무리한다.
d. 새로운 예증은 소개하지 않는다.

7가지 GRE Writing 고득점 전략

ETS 채점 기준 5개 항목: 유의점	1.0	.75	.50	.25
Content Use incisive reasons and persuasive examples. 자기주장을 support 하는 이유 2가지와 예증 2가지가 필요하다. • 자기 자신의 주장과 대조되는 의견의 예증은 절대 쓰지 말 것				
Structure 논리적 접속사를 적절하게 쓰면서 전체적 문단의 흐름 관계를 rhetoric expression으로 잡아준다. • 적절한 논리 고리는 접속사와 수사법적 표현이 결정함				
Organization 5 sentence reasoning에 맞도록 쓴다. General Sentence, For example, Compare and Contrast, Detailed Sentence, Related Sentence이거나, suppose, if so, harmful effects, solutions for better results가 들어가도록 문단을 구성한다. • 5-4-5-5-4 문장 형식이 바람직함				
Expression Rhetorical expression(Academic English에서 사용하는 수사법적 표현)과 토픽의 분야 전문 용어(terms)를 쓴다.				
Grammar & Mechanics 문법, 타이프 오류, 문장부호 규칙에 맞게 사용한다. • 대문자 남발이나 부적절한 콤마(comma)는 감점의 중요한 이유이다.				

(1) 아이디어 흐름을 논리적으로 이해할 수 있는 논리고리인 접속사를 바르게 작성해야 한다. 이런 오류를 범하지 않기 위해서 머릿속에 글의 구조와 논리를 그리며 글을 쓰는 습관을 기른다. 즉, 템플릿이란 글의 논리 구성을 머릿속에 그릴 수 있는 구체적인 **아이디어 논리 그림**이다.

(2) Analytical essay를 쓰기 위한 **rhetoric expressions**로만 문장을 만들어야 한다. 다시 강조하자면, 국어를 직역한 듯한 자기 자신만의 영어 표현은 절대 사용해서는 안 된다는 뜻이다. 예를 들면, A가 B를 기인했다고 할 때, "A contributes to B 또는 A is responsible for B"이런 식으로 써야 rhetoric terms로 말하는 것이다. 하지만 많은 한국 학생들이 이러한 표현을 생략하고 쓰거나 after A, B occurred 나 A is very good for B 나 A is bad for B와 같은 유치한 표현구나 부적절한 표현을 마구 사용하는 오류로 인해서 2.0 이라는 낮은 점수를 받을 수 있다. 다시 정리하자면 **인과관계 문장**을 시간차(the order of time)로 작성하는 문장 논리 오류를 범해서는 아니 된다는 것이다.

(3) 동사가 내포하는 핵심적 의미를 깊이 파악한 다음 내가 쓰고자 하는 문장의 주어와 목적어의 관계가 논리적으로 연결되어 있는 문장들을 작성했는가를 보는 것 또한 논리적 글을 작성하는 데 있어서 매우 중요하다. GRE essay는 **삼인칭 대명사나 명사로 주어를 사용**하는 것이 객관적인 에세이를 쓸 때 지켜야 하는 중요한 요령이다. 특히 이인칭 대명사인 'you'는 절대 사용하지 말아야 한다. 주로 people, society, education과 같은 3인칭 명사를 주어로 설정한다. 일인칭 대명사 I는 I agree / disagree할 때만 사용한다.

(4) 서론에서 밝혀준 Thesis sentence(주장)와 본론에서는 이를 받쳐줄 예증을 2개 이상을 근거 자료로 써야 한다. 그리고 반드시 **자신의 주장과 대조되는 의견**을 피력해야 한다. 즉, GRE는 **partially** agree but disagree나 **partially** disagree but agree의 논리로 써야 한다. 예증은 역사적 사실이나 current events(시사)에서 가져다 쓰는 것이 고득점에 유리하다. 개인적인 에피소드를 사용은 자제해야 한다. 자칫 잘못하면 개인의 경험을 바탕으로 해서 "내 말, 내 경험을 보니 내 말이 맞다"라는 잘못을 범하게 되기 때문이다.

(5) 한국어를 모국어로 하는 학생들이 이슈에세이를 쓸 때 가장 많이 하는 오류는 내 주장과 다른 의견을 집어 줄 때 'because'를 사용하는데 'because'는 22문장 템플릿에서처럼 서론에 I partially disagree because ~ 구문에만 한 번만 사용하기를 권고한다. **'because, for example, suppose' 등의 접속사는 내 주장**을 피력하는데 만 사용하는 것이 바람직하다. Rhetorics는 내가 사용한 **주어와 동사가 collocation 위치**에 올 수 있는 가? 다시 말해서 어떤 주어의 위치에 온 단어와 함께 사용 가능한 동사, 동사 형태, 목적어, 관계대명사가 무엇인지를 확인하고 표현해야 한다. 또한 지나치게 감성적인 표현은 글을 설득력 있기 보다는 모호하게 만드는 경향이 있으므로 이슈는 논리적인 글임으로 만연체 스타일의 문장 생성은 피해야 한다.

(6) **문법 오류**가 없고 적절한 **Mechanics**(punctuation+capitalization)을 사용하는 것 또한 고득점 취득을 위한 요건 중 간과할 수 없는 매우 중요한 점이라는 것을 명심해야 한다. 책명, 고유 명사는 반드시 대문자화해야 한다. Mechanics에는 Capitalization과 Punctuation이 있다. Capitalization의 기본 법칙은 첫 머리에 오는 관사를 제외한 모든 관사와 전치사 이외에는 모든 단어를 첫 자는 대문자로 써야 한다.

Ex) The Lord of the Ring, The Pride and Prejudice, A Street Car Named Desire, Oliver Twist.

(7) **세미콜론**(Semicolon)은 기본적으로 접속사이다. And, but, however, therefore, 이런 단어 대신에 사용한다. 또한 세미콜론이 **문장의 middle position**에 올 때는 세미콜론+접속사+콤마(; however, / ; on the other hand,)의 순서로 적는다. 반면에 콜론(, colon)은 뒤에 오는 아이디어를 정리하고자 하는 기능이 있다. 그러므로 콜론 뒤에는 animals: cats, dogs and birds와 같이 동물의 종류를 열거하거나 인용구, 또는 콜론 앞에 오는 문장을 summary하는 기능이 있다. 미들 포지션 세미콜론은 논술에서 접속어를 간략하게 줄이는 표현으로 자주 등장한다. 다시 말하자면 논술이나 논문에서 콜론과 세미콜론을 자주 사용하는데 기본적으로 콜론 다음에는 명사 리스트, quotation, summary가 오고 세미콜론은 'however'과 같은 역접접속사나 'because' 와 같은 인과관계 접속이거나 아래보기 f)와 같이 긴 리스트를 간략하게 정리하는 연결접속사 'and' 대신 사용한다.

a) Use a colon to introduce a list:

- There are three countries in North America: Mexico, the USA and Canada.
- We can see many things in the sky at night: the moon, stars, planets, comets, planes and even satellites.

b) Actually, you can use a colon to introduce a single item, especially when you want to emphasize the item.

- We were all waiting for the hero of the evening: John.
- There is one thing that he will not accept: stupidity.
- The job of the colon is simple: to introduce.

c) Use a colon to introduce direct speech or a quotation:

- He stood up and said loudly: "Ladies and Gentlemen, please be seated."
- John whispered in my ear: "Have you seen Andrea?"
- As Confucius once wrote: "When words lose their meaning, people lose their freedom."

d) Use a colon to introduce an explanation:

- We had to cancel the party: too many people were sick.
- There is no need to rush: the meeting will be starting one hour late.

e) Use a semicolon in the place of conjunctions:

- Terry always slept with the light on; he was afraid of the dark.

f) Use a semicolon in complicated lists to sort out a complicated list containing many items, many of which themselves contain commas.

- In the meeting today we have Professor Wilson, University of Seoul; Dr. Watson, University of Korea in Seoul; Colonel Custard, Metropolitan Police and Dr. Mable Syrup, University of Otago, New Zealand.

에세이 쓰기

토픽 내용이 질문하고 있는 주요 어휘(key words)를 분석적으로 명확하게 이해한 다음에 머릿속휘젓기(brainstorming)를 한다. 머릿속휘젓기는 대략적인 에세이의 커다란 그림을 그려보는 단계를 말한다. 그런데 GRE를 준비하는 많은 학생들은 brainstorming과 outlining을 혼동하는 경우를 종종 본다. outlining은 brainstorming을 바탕으로 구체적으로 서론, 본론, 결론에 내용의 주요한 프레임을 만드는 작업을 말한다. 일반적으로 어떤 종류의 에세이든지 다음의 다섯 단계로 작성된다.

(1) Brainstorming → (2) Outlining → (3) Writing → (4) Editing → (5) Revising

Brainstorming

머릿속에 다음과 같은 그림을 그린 다음 동그라미 안에 자신이 생각하는 keyword를 적어 넣어본다.

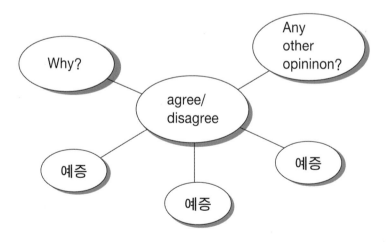

Introduction

Outlining

다음 논리 구조 아웃라인에 맞게 더 구체적으로 아이디어를 발전시킨다.

I	Some other people's opposite opinion. agree/disagree? disagree why reason 1 for exA, reason 2 for exB
II	contradictory opinion for my reasons
III	exA for reason 1 Does this example support my reason?
IV	exB for reason 2 Does this example support my reason?
V	Thus, I disagree.

문법과 표현

이슈는 Rhetoric usages: 명제 제시, 인과관계, 정보나 사건 기술(descriptive), 추론적 귀결 (derived conclusion)에 맞는 수사법만을 사용해 문장을 완성해야 한다. 불필요한 표현은 과감하게 삭제하고 문장을 장황하게 만드는 형용사나 부사 사용도 피해야 한다. 동의어를 활용하되 반의어적 표현을 익힌다면 좀 더 다채로운 문장을 생성할 수 있다. 그리고 문법 오류를 내지 않기 위해서 능동태와 수동태형의 동사를 올바르게 사용에도 주위를 기우려야 한다. 자동사를 타동사로 쓰는 문법적 오류를 범하지 말아야 한다. 또한 '정도부사'는 극단적인 표현을 제어하는 즉 나의 주장이나 논리를 무리하지 않는 톤으로 설득력 있게 만들어준다. 그리고 There is/are과 같은 장소부사로 시작하는 문장은 이슈 에세이 톤을 모호하게 하므로 피해야 하는 표현이다.

Editing

　문단을 표시하는 들여쓰기는 **tab key**를 한 번 누르거나 **space bar**를 세 번 치고 네 번째 칸부터 타이프를 한다. 다만 주의 할 점은 첫 번째 문단은 들여쓰기를 할 필요가 없다. 이는 누구나 첫 문단이라는 것이 너무 명백하기에 글쓰기 경제법칙에 의해서 불필요한 편집은 하지 않기 때문이다.

　문법오류를 줄이기 위해 반드시 다음 세 가지 agreements를 매 문장마다 확인하는 습관을 들인다: 1) number agreement, 2) tense agreement, 3) pronoun agreement, 그리고 spelling, punctuation과 capitalization 오류와 같은 편집의 가장 기본이 되는 규칙을 어겨서는 절대 안 된다.

　영어를 접근할 때 가장 흔한 오류는 정관사와 부정관사인 'a'와 'the'이다. 숫자 개념은 영어 논리에서 매우 중요한 개념임으로 확신이 안 설 때에는 **가급적 복수로** 쓰는 것이 감점의 요인을 미리 제거할 수 있는 좋은 방편이다.

Revising

　시간이 허락하는 한 **관사**, **주어동사일치**, **대명사일치**, **시제일치**, **spelling**, **capitalization**, **문장부호**를 꼼꼼하게 확인한다.

　New GRE Writing이 기존시험과 달라진 점은 **이슈**가 **시험시간** 45분에서 **30분**으로 단축되었다는 점이다. 토픽 질문은 거의 기존의 문제와 비슷한 틀을 유지하고 있으며 소수의 새로운 에세이가 첨가되었다. 아규도 기존 문제 유형과 틀을 비슷하게 유지했으나 문제의 key words, 즉 tackling(문제점을 야기하는) words들이 다소 바뀐 것들이 있다. **아규** 작성 시간은 종전과 마찬가지로 **30분**이다. 하지만 이슈는 15분이 단축되었다. 이슈의 시간이 단축된 것은 한국 수험생들에는 다소 유리하게 작용할 것으로 보인다. native speaker들에게 45분은 충분한 내용을 적고 수정까지 할 수 있는 시간이므로 15분이 짧아진 30분 안에 자신의 실력을 발휘하기 위해 좀 더 철저한 준비만 한다면 native writer와 경쟁력 있는 에세이 작성이 가능하다.

Introduction

기차표(영역별 1순위 이슈)

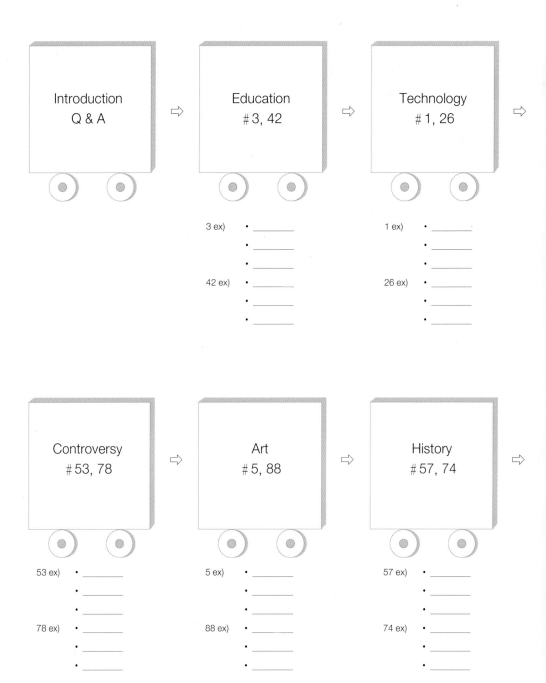

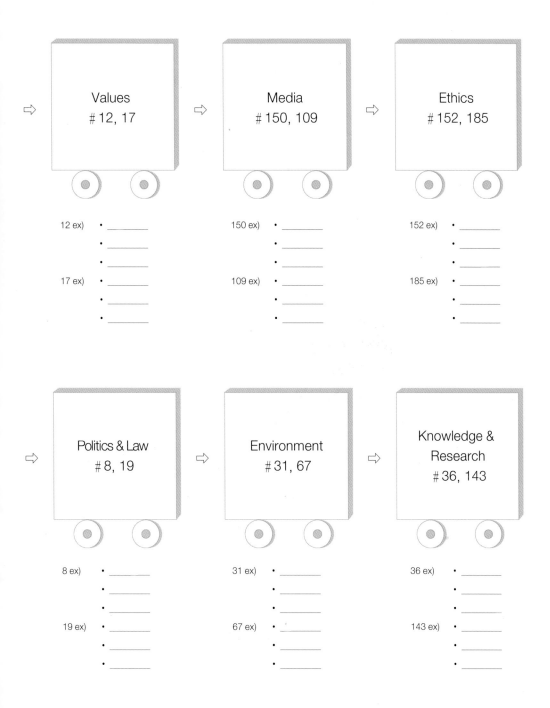

Lecture 1
Introduction

영역별 간략한 이슈 아이디어

다음은 150개 주제의 내용을 포괄적으로 정리해 놓은 것으로, 이슈 질문을 key word로 간략하게 줄여 과연 GRE Topic은 어떤 것인가를 이해하기 위한 것이다.

Education

The merits of the same national curriculum for schools.

Should college faculty also work at the practical field?

Should colleges emphasize courses in popular culture?

Should schools focus more on students' emotional development than intellectual development?

Is college education mainly for occupational training?

Should we monitor every student's progress with the use of measurement?

Should students be skeptical about what they learn in school?

Should all parents and communities participate in education?

Should education devote itself to enriching only our personal lives?

Is society responsible for identifying children with special talents?

Is the best way of education praising positive actions and ignoring negative ones?

Should colleges allow students to make their own decisions in selecting a major?

Technology

Do luxuries prevent our being strong and independent?

Should society place more emphasis on the intellect?

Has technology failed to help humanity progress?

Does technology impact on our leisure time?

Will human always be superior to machines?

Does technology threaten our quality of life?

Are we facing increasingly complex and challenging problems with technology?

Do technologies interfere with real learning? Image / Media

Is visual image often deceptive?

Is image more important than the truth behind?

Do high speed communication media make our life better?

Is media scrutiny of society's heroes reliable all the time?

From whom do our leading voices come? (publicity)

Are scandals always useful?

Ethics / Role Models

Should political leaders withhold information from the public?

Should public figures expect to lose their privacy?

Should successful leadership always meet the ethical and moral standards?

Is there a boundary which defines cooperate executive's responsibilities (CEO)?

Should effective leadership always be committed to particular principles?

Is complete honesty a useful virtue in politics?

Is morality necessary to succeed in politics?

Do worthy ends justify any means?

Can a person be committed to a policy and idea yet be critical of it?

Does a culture perpetuate its prevailing ideas?

Do a society's heroes or heroines reflect its character?

Should we pursue ideals or a reasonable consensus?

Can we make progress thorough discourse among people?

Introduction

Government

Should government preserve cultural traditions?

Should government give funds to scientific research?

Should government support artists even in economic crisis?

Environment

Is it our responsibility to save endangered species?

Is society better off when many people question authority?

Is welfare the surest indication of a great nation?

The proper use of public resources

History

Historic buildings-preservation vs. Practicality

Can only history determine an individual greatness?

Is history relevant our daily lives?

Studying the past to help us live in the present

What society has thought to be a success turns into the great discontent?

Do we have to choose tradition or modernization?

The chief benefit of the study of history

Is moderation in all things poor advice?

Controversy

Do we learn the more from those whose views contradict our own?

Is People's behavior largely determined by the society they belong?

Inspiration vs. Perspiration

Memorizing facts should supersede understanding ideas.

Imaginative works vs. factual accounts

Imagination vs. Experience

Original ideas come from common things

Individual vs. Society

The motivation of research: idiosyncratic or societal devotion

Teamwork as the key to productivity and benefits of competition

Pragmatic vs. Idealistic behavior

Defining ourselves by identifying with social groups

Setting research priorities

Is the absence of choice a rare circumstance?

Does personal economic success require conformity?

Does personal intellectual inquiry best serve the public good?

The impetus for innovation: individual enterprise or teamwork?

Do young people's behaviors reveal society's ideas and values?

Introduction

Law

Is our duty to disobey unjust laws?

Should laws be rigid or flexible?

Is it possible to make moral behavior legislated?

Do people prefer constraints to absolute freedom?

Research

Should we invest in controversial research?

As acquiring more knowledge, things become more flexible.

Recognizing the limit of research

Art

Do the arts reveal society's hidden ideas and impulses?

Is it necessary for art to be widely understood to have merit?

Value

Is practicality our idol in today's world?

Is welcoming new ideas are easier than accepting innovations and new ideas?

Is loyalty always a positive force?

Should all so called facts be mistrusted?

자가 진단 평가 Q&A GRE : True or False Question

(1) GRE 에세이는 형식은 이슈, 아규 모두 서론 본론 결론의 형식을 지키는 것이 고득점에 유리하다.

(2) GRE 에세이는 5문단으로 작성하는 것이 가장 바람직하다.

(3) 자신의 논지와 주장을 마지막 문단에서 밝히는 것이 고득점에 유리하다.

(4) 자신의 주장과 대조되는 문단인 마이너스 문단에 for example을 사용한다.

(5) 결론의 문단은 서론과 닮은꼴로 작성하되 강조 되는 하이라이트 문장으로 맺는다.

(6) 이슈와 아규 에세이 문체에는 별반 다를 것이 없다.

(7) 아규 에세이에는 분명하게 다른 오류를 3가지 이상 반박해야 한다.

(8) 이슈 에세이 글자 수가 450자 이상 쓰는 것이 고득점 가능성이 높다.

(9) 아규 에세이 글자 수도 450자 이상 쓰는 것이 고득점 가능성이 높다.

(10) 이슈와 아규 에세이 토픽은 2개 중 하나 선택이 가능하다.

(11) 아규, 이슈 에세이 시험 시간은 모두 30분씩이다.

(12) 시험장 컴퓨터에 copy paste 기능은 있으나 single copy만 가능하다.

(13) 아규는 정답을 찾는 사람들이 거의 동일한 오류를 찾아야 한다.

(14) 이슈 에세이의 논지는 partially agree but disagree나 partially disagree but agree로 쓴다.

(15) 토픽을 그대로 반복해서 쓰는 것을 되도록 피하고 paraphrase를 한다.

(16) 일인칭 대명사나 이인칭 대명사가 문장의 주어가 되게 쓰도록 한다.

(17) 한국인을 나타내는 예증은 고득점에 불리하다.

(18) 확실한 문장을 만들기 위해서 국어로 생각하고 영어로 번역한다.

(19) 창의적으로 쓰기 위해서 자신의 아이디어를 어떤 사회적 현상이나 학문적 지식에서 쓴다.

(20) 문단 들여 쓴 뒤(indenting)에 다시 한 줄을 띄우는 중복적 문단 표시는 감점된다.

답) T T F F T   F T T T F   T T T T T   F F F T T

Introduction

Score 6 Issue Essay

In addressing the specific task directions, a 6 response presents a cogent, well-articulated analysis of the issue and conveys meaning skillfully.

A typical response in this category:

- articulates a clear and **insightful position** on the issue in accordance with the assigned task
- develops the position fully with **compelling reasons and/or persuasive examples**
- sustains a **well-focused, well-organized analysis, connecting ideas logically**
- conveys ideas fluently and precisely, using **effective vocabulary and sentence variety**
- demonstrates facility with **the conventions of standard written English** (i.e., grammar, usage and mechanics), but may have minor errors

Understanding the Context for Writing : Purpose and Audience

The Issue task is an exercise in critical thinking and persuasive writing. The purpose of this task is to determine how well you can develop a compelling argument supporting your own perspective on an issue and to effectively communicate that argument in writing to an academic audience. Your audience consists of college and university faculty who are trained as GRE readers to apply the scoring criteria identified in the scoring guide for "Present Your Perspective on an Issue".

To get a clearer idea of how GRE readers apply the Issue scoring criteria to actual responses, you should review scored sample Issue essay responses and readers' commentaries. The sample responses, particularly at the 5 and 6 score levels, will show you a variety of successful strategies for organizing, developing, and communicating a **persuasive argument**. The readers' commentaries discuss specific aspects of analysis and writing, such as the use of **examples, development and support**, organization, **language fluency**, and **word choice**. For each response, the commentary points out **aspects that are particularly persuasive as well as any that detract from the overall effectiveness of the essay.**

이슈 에세이 작성 준비 단계

Because the issue task is meant to assess the persuasive writing skills that you have developed throughout your education, it has been designed neither to require any particular course of study nor to advantage students with a particular type of training.

Many college textbooks on composition offer advice on persuasive writing that you might find useful, but even this advice might be more technical and specialized than you need for the Issue task. You will not be expected to know specific critical thinking or writing terms or strategies; instead, you should be able to use reasons, evidence, and examples to support your position on an issue. Suppose, for instance, that an issue topic asks you to consider whether it is important for government to provide financial support for art museums.

If your position is that government should fund art museums, you might support your position by discussing the reasons art is important and explain that museums are public places where art is available to anyone. On the other hand, if your position is that government should not support museums, you might point out that, given limited governmental funds, art museums are not as deserving of governmental funding as are other, more socially important, institutions. Or, if you are in favor of government funding for art museums only under certain conditions, you might focus on the artistic criteria, cultural concerns, or political conditions that you think should determine how and whether art museums receive government funds. It is not your position that matters so much as the critical thinking skills you display in developing your position.

WRITING STEPS

1. Decide what position on the issue you want to take and defend. Remember you are free to agree or disagree completely or to agree with some parts or some applications but not others.

2. Decide what compelling evidence (reasons and examples) you can use to support your position. Remember that this is a task in critical thinking and persuasive writing. Therefore, you might find it helpful to explore the complexity of a claim in one of the topics by asking yourself the following questions:
   - What, precisely, is the central issue?
   - Do I agree with all or with any part of the claim? Why or why not?
   - Does the claim make certain assumptions? If so, are they reasonable?
   - Is the claim valid only under certain conditions? If so, what are they?
   - Do I need to explain how I interpret certain terms or concepts used in the claim?
   - If I take a certain position on the issue, what reasons support my position?
   - What examples, either real or hypothetical, could I use to illustrate those reasons and advance my point of view?
   - Which examples are most compelling?

3. Once you have decided on a position to defend, consider the perspective of others who might not agree with your position. Ask yourself :
   - What reasons might someone use to refute or undermine my position?
   - How should I acknowledge or defend against those views in my essay?

4. To plan your response, you might want to summarize your position and make brief notes about how you will support the position you're going to take. When you've done this, look over your notes and decide how you will organize your response.

5. Then write a response developing your position on the issue. Even if you don't write a full response, you should find it helpful to practice with a few of the issue topics and to sketch out your possible responses.

6. After you have practiced with some of the topics, try writing responses to some of the topics within the 30 minute time limit so that you have a good idea of how to use your time in the actual test.

It would probably be helpful to get **some feedback on your response** from an instructor who teaches critical thinking or writing or to trade papers on the same topic with other students and discuss one another's responses in relation to the scoring guide. Try to determine how each paper meets or misses the criteria for each score point in the guide.

Comparing your own response to the scoring guide will help you see how and where you might need to improve.

템플릿 기본 구조

You are free to organize and develop your response in any way that you think will effectively communicate your ideas about the issue. Your response may, but need not, incorporate particular writing strategies learned in English composition or writing-intensive college courses. GRE readers will not be looking for a particular developmental strategy or mode of writing in fact, when GRE readers are trained, they review hundreds of Issue responses that, although highly diverse in content and form, display similar levels of critical thinking and persuasive writing.

Readers will see, for example, some issue responses at the 6 score level that begin by briefly summarizing the writer's position on the issue and then **explicitly announcing the main points to be argued**. They will see others that lead into the writer's position by **making a prediction, asking a series of questions, describing a scenario, or defining critical terms in the quotation**.

Look at the sample issue responses, particularly at the 5 and 6 score levels, to see how other writers have successfully developed and organized their arguments. You should use as many or as few paragraphs as you consider appropriate for your argument; for example, you will probably need to create a new paragraph whenever your discussion shifts to a new cluster of ideas. What matters is not the number of examples, the number of paragraphs, or the form your argument takes but, rather, **the cogency of your ideas about the issue and the clarity and skill with which you communicate those ideas to academic readers**.

주제별 이슈 분석표

EDUCATION	3	Educational institutions have a responsibility to dissuade students from pursuing fields of study in which they are unlikely to succeed. [35] 교육기관들은 학생들이 성공하지 못할 것 같은 연구 분야의 공부를 추구하는 것을 막을 책임이 있다.

3   Educational institutions have a responsibility to dissuade students from pursuing fields of study in which they are unlikely to succeed. [35]
교육기관들은 학생들이 성공하지 못할 것 같은 연구 분야의 공부를 추구하는 것을 막을 책임이 있다.

6   A nation should require all of its students to study the same national curriculum until they enter college. [14/96/116]
국가는 모든 학생들이 대학에 들어가기 전까지는 동일한 국정 교과과정으로 공부할 수 있도록 이를 의무화해야 한다.

12   Governments should offer free university education to any student who has been admitted to a university but cannot afford the tuition. [25]
정부는 대학에 입학허가를 받았으나 등록금을 낼 수 없는 학생들에게 무상교육을 제공해야 한다. [VALUE와 연계되는 토픽]

13   Universities should require every student to take a variety of courses outside the student's field of study. [46/70/102/112/140]
대학은 학생들이 자신의 전공 외 분야 학과목을 이수하도록 의무화해야 한다.

15   Educational institutions should actively encourage their students to choose fields of study that will prepare them for lucrative careers. [135]
교육기관은 학생들이 수입이 높은 직업이 보장되는 분야를 공부할 수 있도록 북돋아 주어야 한다.

17   Formal education tends to restrain our minds and spirits rather than set them free. [68]
공교육은 우리들의 정신과 영혼을 자유롭지 않도록 제한하는 경향이 있다. [VALUE와 연계된 토픽]

20   Some people believe that college students should consider only their own talents and interests when choosing a field of study. Others believe that college students should base their choice of a field of study on the availability of jobs in that field. [32/129]
어떤 사람들은 대학생들이 자신의 재능과 관심을 고려해서 전공 분야를 선택해야 한다고 생각한다. 다른 사람들은 고용의 기회를 선택 기준으로 삼아야 한다고 한다.

29   The best way to teach — whether as an educator, employer, or parent — is to praise positive actions and ignore negative ones. [24/52]
교육의 최상의 방법은 가르치는 사람이 누구든 — 교육자이든, 고용주이든, 부모이든 — 간에 긍정적 행위는 칭찬하고 부정적 행위는 아는 척하지 말아야 한다는 것이다.

37   Society should identify those children who have special talents and provide training for them at an early age to develop their talents.

사회는 특별한 재능을 가진 아이들을 발굴해서 그들이 조기에 재능을 개발할 수 있도록 훈련 시켜야 한다.

39   College students should be encouraged to pursue subjects that interest them rather than the courses that seem most likely to lead to jobs.
대학생들은 그들이 직업을 얻을 가능성이 있는 과목보다 관심이 있는 과목을 택하도록 고무 되어야 한다.

40   When planning courses, educators should take into account the interests and suggestions of their students.
학과목을 계획할 때, 교육자들은 자신의 학생들의 제안과 관심을 고려해야만 한다.

42   Students should always question what they are taught instead of accepting it passively.
학생들은 자신들이 배운 것에 대해 수동적으로 받아들이기보다는 항상 의문을 가져야 한다.

45   Competition for high grades seriously limits the quality of learning at all levels of education. [138]
고득점을 위한 경쟁은 모든 수준의 교육에 있어서 양질의 교육을 저해한다. [VALUE와 연계]

46   Universities should require every student to take a variety of courses outside the students' field of study. [13/70/102/112/140]
대학은 모든 학생들이 의무적으로 자신의 전공 외에도 다양한 과목들을 수강하도록 해야 한다.

47   Educators should find out what students want included in the curriculum and then offer it to them.
교육자들은 학생들이 원하는 것을 찾아서 그것을 교과과정에 포함시키고 학생들에게 제공 해야 한다.

51   Young people should be encouraged to pursue long term, realistic goals rather than seek immediate fame and recognition. [71]
젊은 사람들은 즉각적인 명성이나 인정보다는 장기적, 현실적 목표를 추구하도록 격려되어 야 한다.

54   In order to become well-rounded individuals, all college students should be required to take courses in which they read poetry, novels, mythology, and other types of imaginative literature.
모든 대학생들은 원만한 인격을 형성하기 위해서 시, 소설, 신화 그리고 여타의 창작 문학 작품들을 읽을 수 있는 과목들을 반드시 택하도록 해야 한다. [ART와 연계된 토픽]

58   Learning is primarily a matter of personal discipline; students cannot be motivated by school or college alone.
배움은 근본적으로 개인적 과제이다. 그러므로 학생은 단지 학교나 대학에서만 동기를 부여 받을 수는 없다.

68 Some people believe that the purpose of education is to free the mind and the spirit. Others believe that formal education tends to restrain our minds and spirits rather than set them free. [17]
어떤 사람들은 교육의 목적이 마음과 영혼을 자유롭게 하는 데 있다고 믿는다. 다른 사람들은 공교육이 우리들의 마음과 영혼을 자유롭게 하기보다는 억누른다고 믿는다. [VALUE와 연계]

73 Colleges and universities should require all faculty to spend time working outside the academic world in professions relevant to the courses they teach.
대학은 모든 교수들이 의무적으로 자신이 가르치는 전공 분야 외에서도 연구를 하도록 해야 한다.

81 All parents should be required to volunteer time to their children's schools. [95]
모든 학부모들은 자신의 아이들의 학교에서 의무적으로 자원봉사를 해야만 한다.

82 Colleges and universities should require their students to spend at least one semester studying in a foreign country. [97/100/124]
대학은 학생들이 의무적으로 적어도 한 학기는 다른 나라에서 공부를 하도록 해야 한다.

83 Teachers'salaries should be based on the academic performance of their students. [30]
교사들의 월급은 그들이 가르친 학생들의 학업성취도에 근거를 두어야 한다.

92 Educators should base their assessment of students' learning not on students' grasp of facts but on the ability to explain the ideas, trends, and concepts that those facts illustrate.
교육자들은 학생들의 사실 파악 능력이 아니라 그 사실이 설명하고 있는 아이디어, 경향, 개념을 설명할 수 있는 능력으로 학생들의 성취도를 평가해야 한다.

98 Educational institutions should actively encourage their students to choose fields of study in which jobs are plentiful. [136]
교육기관들은 그 학생들이 직업이 풍부한 전공 분야를 선택하도록 적극 권장해야 한다.

101 Although innovations such as video, computers, and the Internet seem to offer schools improved methods for instructing students, these technologies all too often distract from real learning.
비디오, 컴퓨터, 인터넷 같은 발명들이 학교가 학생들을 지도하는 데 발전된 방법들을 제공하는 것처럼 보이지만 이러한 기술들은 모두 언제나 진정한 배움에 방해가 된다. [TECHNOLOGY와 연계된 토픽]

138 Some people believe that competition for high grades motivates students to excel in the classroom. Others believe that such competition seriously limits the quality of real learning. [45]
어떤 사람들은 높은 학점을 받기 위한 경쟁은 학생들이 수업에서 최선을 다 하도록 동기를 부여한다고 믿는다. 다른 사람들은 그러한 경쟁은 진정한 배움의 질을 저해한다고 믿는다.

Lecture 1

Introduction

142   Claim : Colleges and universities should specify all required courses and eliminate elective courses in order to provide clear guidance for students.

주장: 대학원 학생들에게 좀 더 구체적인 지도를 하기 위해서는 모든 필수과목을 특화하고 선택과목들은 없애야 한다.

Reason : College students — like people in general — prefer to follow directions rather than make their own decisions.

이유: 대학생들은 — 일반 대중처럼 — 스스로 결정하는 것보다는 지침을 따르는 것을 선호한다.

TECHNOLOGY   1   As people rely more on technology to solve problems, the ability of humans to think for themselves will surely deteriorate.

사람들은 문제를 해결하기 위해 점점 테크놀로지에 의존하기 때문에 스스로 생각하는 인간의 능력은 분명히 파괴될 것이다.

26   The luxuries and conveniences of contemporary life prevent people from developing into truly strong and independent individuals.

현대 생활의 호사성과 편리성은 강하고 독립적인 개인으로 성장하는 것을 저해한다.

43   The increasingly rapid pace of life today causes more problems than it solves.

급속도로 빠른 현대 생활은 더 많은 문제를 해결하기보다는 더 많은 문제를 만든다.

64   The human mind will always be superior to machines because machines are only tools of human minds.

인간의 정신은 기계보다 우수하다. 기계는 단지 인간이 사용하는 도구이기 때문이다.

91   The primary goal of technological advancement should be to increase people's efficiency so that they have more leisure time.

기술발전의 목적은 사람들의 효율성을 증대시켜 더 많은 여가 시간을 갖게 하는 데 있다.

101   Although innovations such as video, computers, and the Internet seem to offer schools improved methods for instructing students, these technologies all too often distract from real learning.

비디오, 컴퓨터, 인터넷 같은 발명들이 학교가 학생들을 지도하는 데 발전된 방법들을 제공하는 것처럼 보이지만 이러한 기술들은 모두 언제나 진정한 배움에 방해가 된다.

132   Some people believe that our ever-increasing use of technology significantly reduces our opportunities for human interaction. Other people believe that technology provides us with new and better ways to communicate and connect with one another.

어떤 사람들은 점점 증가하는 기술의 사용이 새로운 상호 인간관계를 만들 기회를 현저하게 줄여준다고 믿는다. 다른 사람들은 기술이 새롭고 더 나은 소통과 관계를 서로에게 가져다준다고 믿는다.

VALUES	12	Governments should offer free university education to any student who has been admitted to a university but cannot afford the tuition. [25] 정부는 대학에 입학허가를 받았으나 등록금을 낼 수 없는 학생들에게 무상 교육을 제공해야 한다. [교육과 연계되는 토픽]
	17	Formal education tends to restrain our minds and spirits rather than set them free. [68] 공교육은 우리들의 정신과 영혼을 자유롭지 않도록 제한하는 경향이 있다. [교육과 연계되는 토픽]
	45	Competition for high grades seriously limits the quality of learning at all levels of education. [138] 고득점을 위한 경쟁은 모든 수준의 교육에 있어서 양질의 교육을 저해한다. [교육과 연계되는 토픽]
	68	Some people believe that the purpose of education is to free the mind and the spirit. Others believe that formal education tends to restrain our minds and spirits rather than set them free. [17] 어떤 사람들은 교육의 목적이 마음과 영혼을 자유롭게 하는 데 있다고 믿는다. 다른 사람들은 공교육이 우리들의 마음과 영혼을 자유롭게 하기보다는 억누른다고 믿는다. [교육과 연계되는 토픽]
	83	Teachers' salaries should be based on the academic performance of their students. [30] 교사들의 월급은 그들이 가르친 학생들의 학업성취도에 근거를 두어야 한다. [교육과 연계되는 토픽]
MEDIA	4	Scandals are useful because they focus on our attention on problems in ways that no speaker or reformer ever could. 스캔들은 유용하다. 어떤 연설가나 혁신자도 할 수 없는 방법으로 사람들의 관심을 문제에 집중시키기 때문이다.
	44	Claim : It is no longer possible for a society to regard any living man or woman as a hero. 주장: 우리 사회는 더 이상 생존해 있는 사람을 영웅이라고 여길 수가 없게 되었다. Reason : The reputation of anyone who is subjected to media scrutiny will eventually be diminished. 이유: 미디어 검증 대상이 되는 사람의 평판은 결국은 사라질 것이다. [75/84/122]
	93	Unfortunately, in contemporary society, creating an appealing image has become more important than the reality of truth behind that image. 불행하게도 현대 사회에서는 호소력 있는 이미지를 만드는 것이 현실이나 이미지 뒤에 담긴 진실보다 더 중요하게 되었다.

Introduction

ETHICS	22	The best way to understand the character of a society is to examine the character of the men and women that the society chooses as its heroes and its role models. [122] 주장: 한 사회의 성격은 그 사회의 구성원들이 선택한 영웅이나 귀감이 되는 인물들을 보면 이해할 수 있다. Reason : Heroes and role models reveal a society's highest ideals. 이유: 영웅들이나 모범이 되는 사람들은 그 사회가 추구하는 최고의 가치를 나타낸다.
	69	Some people believe it is often necessary, even desirable, for political leaders to withhold information from the public. Others believe that the public has a right to be fully informed. 어떤 사람들은 정치지도자가 정보를 알려 주지 않는 것은 필요할 뿐만 아니라 심지어 바람직하다고 믿는다. 다른 사람들은 대중은 모든 정보를 알권리가 있다고 믿는다.
	77	The most effective way to understand contemporary culture is to analyze the trends of its youth. 현대 문화를 이해하기 위한 가장 효과적인 방법은 젊은 사람들의 경향을 분석하는 것이다.
	104	To be an effective leader, a public official must maintain the highest ethical and moral standards. [16/107] 위대한(효과적인) 지도자가 되기 위해서 공무원은 최고의 윤리적, 도덕적 수준을 지켜야만 한다.
	130	Some people believe that corporations have a responsibility to promote the well-being of the societies and environments in which they operate. Others believe that the only responsibility of corporations, provided they operate within the laws is to as much money as possible. 어떤 사람들은 대기업이 사회복지와 그들이 유용하고 있는 환경을 증진시킬 책임이 있다고 믿는다. 다른 사람들은 법의 테두리 안에서 운영을 하는 한, 대기업의 유일한 책무는 이윤을 창조하는 것이라고 믿는다.
CONTROVERSY	11	People's behavior is largely determined by forces not of their own making. [99] 사람들의 행위는 자신이 스스로 결정하는 것이 아니라 외부의 힘에 의해서 결정된다.
	17	Formal education tends to restrain our minds and spirits rather than set them free. [68] 공교육은 우리들의 정신과 영혼을 자유롭게 하기보다는 제약하는 경향이 있다.
	22	The best way to understand the character of a society is to examine the character of the men and women that the society chooses as its heroes and its role models. [122] 주장: 한 사회의 성격은 그 사회의 구성원들이 선택한 영웅이나 귀감이 되는 인물들을 보면

이해할 수 있다
Reason : Heroes and role models reveal a society's highest ideals.
이유: 영웅들이나 모범이 되는 사람들은 그 사회가 추구하는 최고의 가치를 나타낸다.

27 In a field of inquiry, the beginner is more likely than the expert to make important contribution.
어떠한 연구 분야에서든, 초보자가 전문가보다 더 중요한 기여를 하는 것 같다.

34 In any situation, progress requires discussion among people who have contrasting points of view.
어떠한 상황에서도, 진보는 대조적 견해를 갖고 있는 사람들 간의 토론을 통해서 이루어진다.

38 It is primarily through our identification with social groups that we define ourselves.
자신이 누구인가는 우리가 함께 어울려 다니는 소셜 그룹의 아이덴티티를 보면 알 수 있다.

41 The greatness of individuals can be decided only by those who live after them, not by their contemporaries.
한 개인의 위대함은 동시대 사람이 아니라 그의 사후에 후대 사람들에 의해서 결정된다.

45 Competition for high grades seriously limits the quality of learning at all levels of education. [138]
고득점을 위한 경쟁은 모든 수준의 교육에 있어서 양질의 교육을 저해한다.

49 Claim : We can usually learn much more from people whose views we share than from those whose views contradict our own. [76/118]
주장: 우리는 다른 의견을 가진 사람들보다 같은 의견을 가진 사람들로부터 더 많은 것을 배운다.
Reason : Disagreement can cause stress and inhibit learning.
이유: 의견의 차이는 스트레스를 유발하고 배움을 저해한다.

53 If a goal is worthy, then any means taken to attain it are justifiable.
목적이 가치가 있다면 그것을 성취하기 위해서 취한 어떠한 방법도 정당화될 수 있다.

61 People should undertake risky action only after they have carefully considered its consequences.
사람들은 오로지 모험의 결과를 조심스럽게 고려한 다음에 어떤 행동을 해야 한다.

77 The most effective way to understand contemporary culture is to analyze the trends of its youth.
현대 문화를 이해하기 위한 가장 효과적인 방법은 젊은 사람들의 경향을 분석하는 것이다.

78 People's attitudes are determined more by their immediate situation or surroundings than by society as a whole.
사람들의 태도는 자신이 당면한 상황이나 환경보다는 사회 전체에 의해서 결정된다.

Introduction

79   Claim : The best test of an argument is its ability to convince someone with an opposing viewpoint. [146]

주장: 논쟁 능력을 시험하는 가장 적절한 방법은 반대 관점을 가진 다른 사람을 설득해보는 것이다.

Reason : Only by being forced to defend an idea against the doubts and contrasting views of others does one really discover the value of that idea.

이유: 오로지 남과 다른 아이디어를 방어하는 과정에서만 그 아이디어의 진가를 발견할 수 있기 때문이다.

108   Critical judgment of work in any given field has little value unless it comes from someone who is an expert in that field. [110]

어떤 분야든지 비판적 판단은 그 분야의 전문가로부터 나오지 않는 한 그 가치가 없다.

123   The best way for a society to prepare its young people for leadership in government, industry or other fields is by instilling in them a sense of cooperation, not competition. [128]

젊은이들이 정부, 산업 또는 다른 전문 분야에서 리더십을 기르기 위해서는 경쟁보다는 협동의 개념을 고무해야 한다.

130   Some people believe that corporations have a responsibility to promote the well-being of the societies and environments in which they operate. Others believe that the only responsibility of corporations, provided they operate within the laws is to as much money as possible.

어떤 사람들은 대기업이 사회복지와 그들이 유용하고 있는 환경을 증진시킬 책임이 있다고 믿는다. 다른 사람들은 법의 테두리 안에서 운영을 하는 한, 대기업의 유일한 책무는 이윤을 창조하는 것이라고 믿는다.

138   Some people believe that competition for high grades motivates students to excel in the classroom. Others believe that such competition limits the quality of real learning. [45]

어떤 사람들은 높은 학점을 받기 위한 경쟁은 학생들이 수업에서 최선을 다 하도록 동기를 부여한다고 믿는다. 다른 사람들은 그러한 경쟁은 진정한 배움의 질을 저해한다고 믿는다.

144   True success can be measured primarily in terms of the goals one sets for oneself.

진정한 성공은 주로 스스로 설정하는 목표로서 평가될 수 있다.

ART   2   To understand the most important characteristics of a society, one must study its major cities.

한 사회의 성격을 이해하기 위해서는 우리는 반드시 (그 사회가 만든) 대도시를 이해해야만 한다.

5   Claim : Governments must ensure that their major cities receive the financial support they need in order to thrive. [117]

주장: 정부들은 그들의 대도시가 번영하기 위해 필요한 재정적 지원을 받는 것을 보장해야만 한다.

Reason : It is primarily in cities that a nation's cultural traditions are preserved and generated.

이유: 한 국가의 문화 전통이 생성되고 보존되는 곳은 대부분 도시이기 때문이다.

7   Some people believe that government funding of the arts is necessary to ensure that the arts can flourish and be available to all people. Others believe that government funding of the arts threatens the integrity of the arts.

어떤 사람들은 정부는 예술이 번영하고 모든 사람들이 즐길 수 있도록 예술 자금을 지원해야 할 필요가 있다고 믿는다. 다른 사람들은 정부 자금은 예술의 순수성을 위협한다고 믿는다.

54   In order to become well-rounded individuals, all college students should be required to take courses in which they read poetry, novels, mythology, and other types of imaginative literature.

모든 대학생들은 원만한 인격을 형성하기 위해서 시, 소설, 신화 그리고 여타의 창작 문학 작품들을 읽을 수 있는 과목들을 반드시 택하도록 해야 한다.

55   In order for any work of art — for example, a film, a novel, a poem, or a song — to have merit, it must be understandable to most people.

영화, 소설, 시나 노래 같은 예술작품들이 가치를 가지려면 반드시 대중이 이해할 수 있는 것들이어야만 한다.

80   Nations should suspend government funding for the arts when significant numbers of their citizens are hungry or unemployed.

국가가 상당수 국민들이 빈곤하거나 실직했을 때 예술을 위한 자금 지원을 보류하는 것은 당연하다.

88   Claim : Nations should suspend government funding for the arts when significant numbers of their citizens are hungry or unemployed.

주장: 국가가 상당수 국민들이 빈곤하거나 실직했을 때 예술을 위한 자금 지원을 보류하는 것은 당연하다.

Reason : It is inappropriate — and, perhaps, even cruel — to use public resources to fund the arts when people's basic needs are not being met.

이유: 국민의 기본적 요구가 충족되지 않을 때 공적인 자원을 예술 자금 지원에 쓴다는 것은 부적절할 뿐만 아니라 심지어 잔인하기까지 하다.

HISTORY   57   The main benefit of the study of history is to dispel the illusion that people living now are significantly different from people who lived in earlier times.

역사학의 유익한 점은 현대 인간은 과거의 인간과 다르다는 환상을 깨는 것이다.

74   Knowing the past cannot help people to make important decisions today.
      [133, 134]
      과거를 아는 것은 현재의 결정에 도움이 되지 않는다.

119   When old building stand on ground that modern planners feel could be better
      used for modern purposes, modern development should be given
      precedence over the preservation of historic buildings.
      현재의 이익을 추구하며 더 유용하게 쓰기 위해서 오래된 건물을 보존하는 것보다 현대적
      발전을 중시해야 한다.

133   Claim : Knowing about the past cannot help people to make important
      decisions today.
      주장: 과거를 아는 것은 현재의 결정에 도움이 되지 않는다.
      Reason : The world today is significantly more complex than it was even in the
      relatively recent past. [134]
      이유: 오늘날 세상은 근대 생활보다 더 복잡하기 때문이다.

POLITICS &   8   Claim : In any field — business, politics, education, government — those in
LAW   power should step down after five years. [111, 149]
                   주장: 비즈니스, 정치, 교육, 정부 등 어느 분야에서든 권력을 가진 사람은 5년 후에는 사임해
                   야만 한다.
                   Reason : The surest path to success for any enterprise is revitalization
                   through new leadership.
                   이유: 어떤 조직에서든 성공에 이르는 확실한 길은 새로운 지도력을 통해서 재활성화하는 것이다.

              16   Some people believe that in order to be effective, political leaders must yield
                   to public opinion and abandon principle for the sake of comprise. Others
                   believe that the most essential quality of an effective leader is the ability to
                   remain consistently committed to particular principles and objectives.
                   [104/107]
                   어떤 사람들은 효율적이 되기 위해서 정치지도자들은 여론을 따르고 타협을 위해서 원칙을
                   희생해야 한다고 믿는다. 다른 사람들은 효율적 지도자의 가장 중요한 자질은 특정 원칙과
                   목적에 전념하는 능력이라고 믿는다.

              18   The well-being of a society is enhanced when many of its people question
                   authority.
                   한 사회의 복지는 많은 사람들이 권위에 도전할 때 강화된다.

              19   Government should focus on solving the immediate problems of today rather
                   than on trying to solve the anticipated problems of the future.
                   정부는 미래에 예측되는 문제들을 푸는 것보다 오늘날의 긴급한 문제를 해결하는 데 집중적
                   으로 노력해야 한다.

21 Law should be flexible enough to take account of various circumstances, times and places.
법은 다양한 환경, 시간과 장소를 고려할 정도로 유연해야 한다.

28 The surest indicator of a great nation is represented not by the achievements of its rulers, artists, or scientists, but by the general welfare of its people. [113/120/121/127/145]
위대한 국가의 명확한 척도는 지도자, 예술가 또는 과학자들이 성취한 과업에 나타나는 것이 아니라 그 나라 국민의 전체적인 복지 상태로 결정된다.

50 Government officials should rely on their will rather than unquestioningly carry out the will of the people they serve. [86/115]
고위 공무원은 무조건적으로 민중의 뜻을 수행하기보다 자신의 의지에 근거해야 한다.

60 Politicians should pursue common ground and reasonable consensus rather than elusive ideals.
정치가는 허황된 아이디어보다는 대중적 합의와 합리적 동의를 추구해야 한다.

62 Leaders are created by the demands that they are placed on them.
지도자는 그들이 처해진 시대적 요구에 의해서 탄생한다.

66 People who are the most deeply committed to an ideal or policy are also the most critical of it.
어떤 정책이나 아이디어에 가장 충실하게 헌신하는 사람들이 바로 그런 정책과 아이디어에 가장 비판적이다.

85 Some people believe that in order to thrive, a society must put its overall success before the well-being of its individual citizens. Others believe that the well-being of a society can only be measured by the general welfare of all its people.
어떤 사람들은 한 사회가 번영하기 위해서는 개개인의 복지가 그 사회 전체의 성공보다 우선 시되어야 한다고 믿는다. 다른 사람들은 한 사회의 성공적인 척도는 오로지 모든 사람들의 복지로만 측정된다고 말한다.

86 Some people believe that government officials must carry out the will of the people they serve. Others believe that officials should base their decisions on their own judgment. [50/115]
어떤 사람들은 공무원은 민중의 뜻을 수행해야 한다고 생각한다. 다른 사람들은 공무원들이 내리는 결정은 스스로의 판단에 근거해야 한다고 생각한다.

89 Claim : Many problems of modern society cannot be solved by laws and the legal systems.
주장: 현대 사회의 많은 문제들은 법이나 사법제도로 해결될 수 없다.
Reasons: Laws cannot change what is in people's hearts or minds.
이유: 법은 사람들의 마음과 양심을 바꿀 수 없기 때문이다.

94   The effectiveness of a country's leader is best measured by examining the well-being of that country's citizens. [147]
한 나라의 지도자가 얼마나 효과적으로 나라를 이끌고 있는지 알아보기 위한 가장 좋은 방법은 그 나라 국민들의 복지 수준을 측정하는 것이다.

139   Claim : Major policy decisions should always be left to politicians and other government Experts.
주장: 주요한 정책 결정은 정치인과 다른 정부 전문가에게 맡겨야 한다.
Reasons: Politicians and other government officials are more informed and thus have better Judgment and perspective than do members of the general public.
이유: 정치인이나 다른 정부 전문가들은 더 많은 정보를 소유하기 때문에 일반 대중보다 더 나은 판단과 견해를 가질 수 있다.

141   It is more harmful to compromise one's own beliefs than to adhere to them.
자신의 소신에 매달리는 것보다 자기 자신의 소신에 타협하는 것이 더 해롭다

ENVIRONMENT

10   Nations should pass laws to preserve any remaining wilderness areas in their natural state, even if these areas could be developed for economic gain. [125/148]
아직 남아 있는 야생지역들이 경제적 이득을 위해서 개발될 수 있는 지역이라 하더라도, 국가는 이 지역들을 자연 상태로 보존하기 위한 법들을 통과시켜야만 한다.
국가는 비록 남은 자연 상태의 야생지역을 경제적 이득을 위해서 개발할 수 있다고 하더라도, 자연지역 보호를 위해서 법을 통과해야만 한다.

31   Society should make efforts to save endangered species only if the potential extinction of those species is the result of human activities. [63/67]
종의 멸종이 인간 활동의 결과로 인한 경우에 한해서 사회는 멸종될 위기에 처한 종들을 구하기 위한 노력을 해야 한다.
우리 사회는 인간 활동의 결과에서 기인한 동식물 멸종을 막기 위해 노력해야만 한다.

63   There is little justification for society to make extraordinary efforts — especially at a great cost in money and jobs — to save endangered animal or plant species.
우리 사회가 멸종위기에 처한 동식물의 종들을 보호하기 위해 지나친 노력 — 특히 많은 돈과 일이 드는 — 을 하는 것은 별로 정당성이 없다.
돈이나 고용으로 인한 이익을 포기하고 멸종 동물을 보호하기 위한 우리 사회의 상당한 노력은 별로 정당성은 없다.

67   Some people believe that society should try to save every plant and animal species, despite the expense to humans in effort, time, and financial well-being. Others believe that society need not make extraordinary efforts, especially at a great cost in money and jobs, to save endangered species.

어떤 사람들은 우리 사회가 인간에 쓰는 노력, 시간, 재정적 풍요를 지불해서라도 모든 동식물의 종들을 보존해야 한다고 믿는다. 다른 사람들은 우리 사회가 멸종위기에 처한 종들을 보호하기 위한 상당한 노력을 — 특히 많은 돈과 노력을 드는 — 할 필요가 없다고 믿는다. 어떤 사람들은 노력, 시간, 재정적 풍요를 포기하고도 모든 동식물종을 보존해야 한다고 믿고 있다. 다른 사람들은 돈이나 고용으로 인한 이익을 포기하고 멸종 동식물을 보호하기 위한 우리 사회의 상당한 노력은 별로 정당성은 없다고 한다.

125   Some people claim that a nation's government should preserve its wilderness areas in their natural state. Others argue that these areas should be developed for potential economic gain.
어떤 사람들은 자연 상태의 야생지역을 보호해야 한다고 한다. 다른 사람들은 잠재적인 경제 이익을 위해서 개발해야 한다고 한다.

148   Nations should pass laws to preserve any remaining wilderness areas in their natural state.
국가들은 아직 자연 상태로 남아 있는 야생지역을 보호하기 위해서 법을 통과시켜야만 한다.

KNOWLEDGE & RESEARCH

9   In any field of endeavor, it is possible to make a significant contribution without first being strongly influenced by past achievements within that field.
어떠한 연구 분야든 그 분야가 이룬 과거 업적에서 지대한 영향을 받지 않고 위대한 업적을 이루는 것은 불가능하다.

36   Governments should not fund any scientific research whose consequences are unclear. [72]
정부는 결과가 불분명한 것에 대한 연구를 위한 자금을 지원하지 않아야 한다.

56   Many important discoveries or creations are accidental: it is usually while seeking the answer to one question that we come across the answer to another.
대부분의 발견이나 발명은 우연으로 인한 것이다. 다른 하나의 문제에 대한 답변을 찾는 중에 우연히 얻게 되는 것이다.

59   Scientists and other researchers should focus their research on areas that are likely to benefit the greatest number of people.
과학자나 연구자들은 많은 사람들이 이익을 받게 될 것 같은 연구 분야에만 집중해야 한다.

72   Governments should not fund any specific research whose consequences are unclear. [36]
정부는 결과가 불분명한 것에 대한 연구를 위한 자금을 지원하지 않아야 한다.

87   Claim : Any piece of information referred to as a fact should be mistrusted, since it may well be proven false in the future.
주장: 사실이라고 알려진 어떤 정보도 의심을 해야 한다. 그 정보가 미래에 허위라고 증명될 가능성이 있기 때문이다.

Reason : Much of the information that people assume is factual actually turns out to be inaccurate.
이유: 우리가 사실이라고 가정하고 있는 많은 정보는 사실상 부정확한 것으로 드러난다.

103 The best ideas arise from a passionate interest in commonplace things.
가장 위대한 아이디어는 평범한 것들에 대한 열정적 관심으로부터 탄생한다.

106 Claim : Imagination is a more valuable asset than experience.
주장: 상상력은 경험보다 더 가치가 있는 자산이다.
Reason : People who lack experience are free to imagine what is possible without the constraints of established habits or studies.
이유: 경험이 부족한 사람들은 확립된 습관이나 태도의 제한 없이 자유로운 상상을 할 수 있기 때문이다.

109 Some people believe that scientific discoveries have given us a much better understanding of the world around us. Others believe that science has revealed to us that the world is infinitely more complex than we ever realized.
어떤 사람들은 과학적 발견이 우리가 세상을 더 잘 이해할 수 있도록 해 주었다고 믿는다. 다른 사람들은 과학이 세상을 우리가 알던 것보다 무한히 더 복잡하게 만들었다고 한다.

131 Claim : Researchers should not limit their investigations to only those areas in which they expect to discover something that has an immediate, practical application.
주장: 연구원들은 즉각적이고 현실적 적용이 기대되는 분야의 연구에만 국한해서는 안된다.
Reason : It is impossible to predict the outcome of a line of research with any certainty.
이유: 확신을 가지고 연구 결과를 예측하는 것은 불가능하기 때문이다.

143 No field of study can advance significantly unless it incorporates knowledge and experience from outside that field.
다른 분야의 지식과 경험을 통합하지 않고 발전할 수 있는 학문은 없다.

Issue Topics

Each Issue topic consists of an issue statement or statements followed by specific task instructions that tell you how to respond to the issue. The wording of some topics in the test might vary slightly from what is presented here. Also, because there may be multiple versions of some topics with similar or identical wording but with different task instructions, it is very important to read your test topic and its specific task directions carefully and respond to the wording as it appears in the actual test.

① 실제 시험에 나오는 토픽 단어들의 표현이 다를 수도 있다.

② 동일한 토픽이라 할지라도 실제 시험에서는 비슷한 표현으로 구성된 다양한 형태로 물어볼 수 있기 때문에 토픽에 관한 에세이를 쓰기 위해서는 토픽이 내포하는 표현의 의미와 세부 지시 사항을 정확하게 파악하는 것이 매우 중요하다.

새로운 GRE-writing test는 "wording"이 아래 샘플과 다를 수 있다는 점을 시사하고 있다. 이 책은 수험생들이 시험장에서 토픽의 의미를 제대로 파악할 수 있는 훈련을 할 수 있도록 만들어졌다. [ ] 안에 있는 번호는 동일하거나 유사한 주제 번호이다.

샘플 에세이는 기본 템플릿의 논리를 따라 많은 부분을 작성함으로써 처음 GRE 에세이를 연습하고자 하는 학생들이 쉽게 아이디어 map의 흐름을 견지할 수 있도록 했다. 반면에 에세이를 좀 더 다양하고 독창적으로 쓰고자 하는 학생들을 위해서 좀 더 다양하고 modify한 에세이들도 수록했다. 처음으로 영어 에세이 쓰기를 하려면 우선 기본 템플릿의 논리대로 글을 연습하는 것이 단기간에 고득점을 할 수 있는 효과적 방법이다. 이 책에 실린 에세이는 『New GRE Writing』에 실린 것과는 달리 새롭게 작성된 에세이가 다수이다.

1   As people rely more and more on technology to solve problems, the ability of humans to think for themselves will surely deteriorate.

사람들은 문제를 해결하기 위해 점점 테크놀로지에 의존하기 때문에 스스로 생각하는 인간의 능력은 분명히 파괴될 것이다.

Write a response in which you discuss the extent to which you agree or disagree with the statement and explain your reasoning for the position you take. In developing and supporting your position, you should consider ways in which the statement might or might not hold true and explain how these considerations shape your position.

2   To understand the most important characteristics of a society, one must study its major cities.

한 사회의 성격을 이해하기 위해서는 우리는 반드시 (그 사회가 만든) 대도시를 이해해야만 한다.

Write a response in which you discuss the extent to which you agree or disagree with the statement and explain your reasoning for the position you take. In developing and supporting your position, you should consider ways in which the statement might or might not hold true and explain how these considerations shape your position.

3   Educational institutions have a responsibility to dissuade students from pursuing fields of study in which they are unlikely to succeed. [35/137]

교육기관들은 학생들이 성공하지 못할 것 같은 연구 분야 공부를 추구하는 것을 막아야 할 책임이 있다.

Write a response in which you discuss the extent to which you agree or disagree with the claim. In developing and supporting your position, be sure to address the most compelling reasons and/or examples that could be used to challenge your position.

4   Scandals are useful because they focus our attention on problems in ways that no speaker or reformer ever could.

스캔들은 유용하다. 어떤 연설가나 혁신자도 할 수 없는 방법으로 사람들의 관심을 문제에 집중시키기 때문이다.

Write a response in which you discuss the extent to which you agree or disagree with the claim. In developing and supporting your position, be sure to address the most compelling reasons and/or examples that could be used to challenge your position.

5   Claim : Governments must ensure that their major cities receive the financial support they need in order to thrive. [117]

주장: 정부들은 그들의 대도시가 번영하기 위해 필요한 재정적 지원을 받는 것을 보장해야만 한다.

Reason : It is primarily in cities that a nation's cultural traditions are preserved and generated.

이유: 한 국가의 문화 전통이 생성되고 보존되는 곳은 대부분 도시이기 때문이다.

Write a response in which you discuss the extent to which you agree or disagree with the claim and the reason on which that claim is based.

6   A nation should require all of its students to study the same national curriculum until they enter college. [96/116]

국가는 모든 학생들이 대학에 들어가기 전까지는 동일한 국정 교과과정으로 공부할 수 있도록 이를 의무화해야 한다.

Write a response in which you discuss the extent to which you agree or disagree with the recommendation and explain your reasoning for the position you take. In developing and supporting your position, describe specific circumstances in which adopting the recommendation would or would not be advantageous and explain how these examples shape your position.

7   Some people believe that government funding of the arts is necessary to ensure that the arts can flourish and be available to all people. Others believe that government funding of the arts threatens the integrity of the arts.
어떤 사람들은 정부는 예술이 번영하고 모든 사람들이 즐길 수 있도록 예술 자금을 지원해야 할 필요가 있다고 믿는다. 다른 사람들은 정부 자금은 예술의 순수성을 위협한다고 믿는다.
Write a response in which you discuss which view more closely aligns with your own position and explain your reasoning for the position you take. In developing and supporting your position, you should address both of the views presented.

8   Claim : In any field — business, politics, education, government — those in power should step down after five years.
주장: 비즈니스, 정치, 교육, 정부 등 어느 분야에든 권력을 가진 사람은 오년 후에는 사임해야만 한다.
Reason : The surest path to success for any enterprise is revitalization through new leadership. [111/149]
이유: 어떤 조직에서든 성공에 이르는 확실한 길은 새로운 지도력을 통한 재활성화이다.
Write a response in which you discuss the extent to which you agree or disagree with the claim and the reason on which that claim is based.

9   In any field of endeavor, it is impossible to make a significant contribution without first being strongly influenced by past achievements within that field.
어떠한 연구 분야든 그 분야가 이룬 과거 업적에서 지대한 영향을 받지 않고 위대한 업적을 이루는 것은 불가능하다.
Write a response in which you discuss the extent to which you agree or disagree with the statement and explain your reasoning for the position you take. In developing and supporting your position, you should consider ways in which the statement might or might not hold true and explain how these considerations shape your position.

10 Nations should pass laws to preserve any remaining wilderness areas in their natural state, even if these areas could be developed for economic gain. [125/148]
아직 남아 있는 야생지역들이 경제적 이득을 위해서 개발될 수 있는 지역이라 하더라도, 국가는 이 지역들을 자연 상태로 보존하기 위한 법들을 통과시켜야만 한다.
Write a response in which you discuss your views on the policy and explain your reasoning for the position you take. In developing and supporting your position, you should consider the possible consequences of implementing the policy and explain how these consequences shape your position.

11　People's behavior is largely determined by forces not of their own making. [99]
사람들의 행위는 자신이 스스로 결정하는 것이 아니라 외부의 힘에 의해서 결정된다.
Write a response in which you discuss the extent to which you agree or disagree with the statement and explain your reasoning for the position you take. In developing and supporting your position, you should consider ways in which the statement might or might not hold true and explain how these considerations shape your position.

12　Governments should offer a free university education to any student who has been admitted to a university but who cannot afford the tuition. [25]
정부는 대학에 입학허가를 받았으나 등록금을 낼 수 없는 학생들에게 무상 교육을 제공해야 한다.
Write a response in which you discuss your views on the policy and explain your reasoning for the position you take. In developing and supporting your position, you should consider the possible consequences of implementing the policy and explain how these consequences shape your position.

13　Universities should require every student to take a variety of courses outside the student's field of study. [46/70/102/112/140]
대학은 학생들이 자신의 전공 외 분야 학과목을 이수하도록 의무화해야 한다.
Write a response in which you discuss the extent to which you agree or disagree with the claim. In developing and supporting your position, be sure to address the most compelling reasons and/or examples that could be used to challenge your position.

14　A nation should require all of its students to study the same national curriculum until they enter college. [6/96/116]
국가는 모든 학생들이 대학에 들어가기 전까지는 동일한 국정 교과과정으로 공부할 수 있도록 이를 의무화해야 한다.
Write a response in which you discuss your views on the policy and explain your reasoning for the position you take. In developing and supporting your position, you should consider the possible consequences of implementing the policy and explain how these consequences shape your position.

15　Educational institutions should actively encourage their students to choose fields of study that will prepare them for lucrative careers. [135]
교육기관은 학생들이 수입이 높은 직업이 보장되는 분야를 공부할 수 있도록 북돋아 주어야 한다.
Write a response in which you discuss the extent to which you agree or disagree with the claim. In developing and supporting your position, be sure to address the most compelling reasons and/or examples that could be used to challenge your position.

16　Some people believe that in order to be effective, political leaders must yield to public opinion and abandon principle for the sake of compromise. Others believe that the most essential quality of an effective leader is the ability to remain consistently committed to particular principles and objectives. [104/107]

어떤 사람들은 효율적이 되기 위해서 정치지도자들은 여론을 따르고 타협을 위해서 원칙을 희생해야 한다고 믿는다. 다른 사람들은 효율적 지도자의 가장 중요한 자질은 특정 원칙과 목적에 전념하는 능력이라고 믿는다.

Write a response in which you discuss which view more closely aligns with your own position and explain your reasoning for the position you take. In developing and supporting your position, you should address both of the views presented.

---

17   Formal education tends to restrain our minds and spirits rather than set them free. [68]

공교육은 우리들의 정신과 영혼을 자유롭지 않도록 제한하는 경향이 있다.

Write a response in which you discuss the extent to which you agree or disagree with the statement and explain your reasoning for the position you take. In developing and supporting your position, you should consider ways in which the statement might or might not hold true and explain how these considerations shape your position.

---

18   The well-being of a society is enhanced when many of its people question authority.

한 사회의 복지는 많은 사람들이 권위에 도전할 때 강화된다.

Write a response in which you discuss the extent to which you agree or disagree with the statement and explain your reasoning for the position you take. In developing and supporting your position, you should consider ways in which the statement might or might not hold true and explain how these considerations shape your position.

---

19   Governments should focus on solving the immediate problems of today rather than on trying to solve the anticipated problems of the future.

정부는 미래에 예측되는 문제들을 푸는 것보다 오늘날의 긴급한 문제를 해결하는 데 집중적으로 노력해야 한다.

Write a response in which you discuss the extent to which you agree or disagree with the recommendation and explain your reasoning for the position you take. In developing and supporting your position, describe specific circumstances in which adopting the recommendation would or would not be advantageous and explain how these examples shape your position.

---

20   Some people believe that college students should consider only their own talents and interests when choosing a field of study. Others believe that college students should base their choice of a field of study on the availability of jobs in that field. [32/129]

어떤 사람들은 대학생들이 자신의 재능과 관심을 고려해서 전공 분야를 선택해야 한다고 생각한다. 다른 사람들은 고용의 기회를 선택 기준으로 삼아야 한다고 한다.

Write a response in which you discuss which view more closely aligns with your own position and explain your reasoning for the position you take. In developing and supporting your position, you should address both of the views presented.

21   Laws should be flexible enough to take account of various circumstances, times, and places.
        법은 다양한 환경, 시간과 장소를 고려할 정도로 유연해야 한다.
        Write a response in which you discuss the extent to which you agree or disagree with the
        statement and explain your reasoning for the position you take. In developing and supporting
        your position, you should consider ways in which the statement might or might not hold true
        and explain how these considerations shape your position.

22   Claim : The best way to understand the character of a society is to examine the character of the
        men and women that the society chooses as its heroes or its role models.
        주장: 한 사회의 성격은 그 사회의 구성원들이 선택한 영웅이나 귀감이 되는 인물들을 보면 이해할 수 있다.
        Reason : Heroes and role models reveal a society's highest ideals. [44/75/84/122]
        이유: 영웅들이나 모범이 되는 사람들은 그 사회가 추구하는 최고의 가치를 나타낸다.
        Write a response in which you discuss the extent to which you agree or disagree with the claim
        and the reason on which that claim is based.

23   Governments should place few, if any, restrictions on scientific research and development.
        정부는 과학연구와 개발을 최소한으로 규제해야 한다.
        Write a response in which you discuss the extent to which you agree or disagree with the
        recommendation and explain your reasoning for the position you take. In developing and
        supporting your position, describe specific circumstances in which adopting the recommendation
        would or would not be advantageous and explain how these examples shape your position.

24   The best way to teach is to praise positive actions and ignore negative ones. [29/52]
        교육하는 데 최상의 방법은 긍정적 행위는 칭찬하고 부정적 행위는 아는 척하지 말아야 한다는 것이다.
        Write a response in which you discuss the extent to which you agree or disagree with the
        statement and explain your reasoning for the position you take. In developing and supporting
        your position, you should consider ways in which the statement might or might not hold true
        and explain how these considerations shape your position.

25   Governments should offer college and university education free of charge to all students. [12]
        정부는 모든 학생들에게 무상 대학교육을 제공해야 한다.
        Write a response in which you discuss the extent to which you agree or disagree with the
        recommendation and explain your reasoning for the position you take. In developing and
        supporting your position, describe specific circumstances in which adopting the recommendation
        would or would not be advantageous and explain how these examples shape your position.

26   The luxuries and conveniences of contemporary life prevent people from developing into truly
        strong and independent individuals.
        현대 생활의 호사성과 편리성은 강하고 독립적인 개인으로 성장하는 것을 저해한다.
        Write a response in which you discuss the extent to which you agree or disagree with the
        statement and explain your reasoning for the position you take. In developing and supporting

your position, you should consider ways in which the statement might or might not hold true and explain how these considerations shape your position.

27 In any field of inquiry, the beginner is more likely than the expert to make important contributions.

어떠한 연구 분야에서든, 초보자가 전문가보다 더 중요한 기여를 하는 것 같다.

Write a response in which you discuss the extent to which you agree or disagree with the statement and explain your reasoning for the position you take. In developing and supporting your position, you should consider ways in which the statement might or might not hold true and explain how these considerations shape your position.

28 The surest indicator of a great nation is represented not by the achievements of its rulers, artists, or scientists, but by the general welfare of its people. [85/113/120/121/127/145]

위대한 국가의 명확한 척도는 지도자, 예술가 또는 과학자들이 성취한 과업에 나타나는 것이 아니라 그 나라 국민의 전체적인 복지 상태로 결정된다.

Write a response in which you discuss the extent to which you agree or disagree with the statement and explain your reasoning for the position you take. In developing and supporting your position, you should consider ways in which the statement might or might not hold true and explain how these considerations shape your position.

29 The best way to teach — whether as an educator, employer, or parent — is to praise positive actions and ignore negative ones. [24/52]

교육의 최상의 방법은 가르치는 사람이 누구 — 교육자이든, 고용주이든, 부모이든 — 든 간에 긍정적 행위는 칭찬하고 부정적 행위는 아는 척하지 말아야 한다는 것이다.

Write a response in which you discuss the extent to which you agree or disagree with the claim. In developing and supporting your position, be sure to address the most compelling reasons and/or examples that could be used to challenge your position.

30 Teachers' salaries should be based on their students' academic performance. [83]

교사들의 월급은 그들이 가르친 학생들의 학업성취도에 근거를 두어야 한다.

Write a response in which you discuss the extent to which you agree or disagree with the claim. In developing and supporting your position, be sure to address the most compelling reasons and/or examples that could be used to challenge your position.

31 Society should make efforts to save endangered species only if the potential extinction of those species is the result of human activities. [63/67]

종의 멸종이 인간 활동의 결과로 인한 경우에 한해서 사회는 멸종될 위기에 처한 종들을 구하기 위한 노력을 해야 한다.

Write a response in which you discuss your views on the policy and explain your reasoning for the position you take. In developing and supporting your position, you should consider the possible consequences of implementing the policy and explain how these consequences shape your position.

32   College students should base their choice of a field of study on the availability of jobs in that
      field. [20/129]
      대학생들은 고용의 기회를 전공의 선택 기준으로 삼아야 한다.
      Write a response in which you discuss the extent to which you agree or disagree with the claim.
      In developing and supporting your position, be sure to address the most compelling reasons
      and/or examples that could be used to challenge your position.

33   As we acquire more knowledge, things do not become more comprehensible, but more
      complex and mysterious.
      더 많은 지식을 습득할수록 사물이 더 이해되는 것이 아니라 더 복잡해지고 모호해진다.
      Write a response in which you discuss the extent to which you agree or disagree with the
      statement and explain your reasoning for the position you take. In developing and supporting
      your position, you should consider ways in which the statement might or might not hold true
      and explain how these considerations shape your position.

34   In any situation, progress requires discussion among people who have contrasting points of
      view.
      어떠한 상황에서도, 진보는 대조적 견해를 갖고 있는 사람들 간의 토론을 통해서 이루어진다.
      Write a response in which you discuss the extent to which you agree or disagree with the
      statement and explain your reasoning for the position you take. In developing and supporting
      your position, you should consider ways in which the statement might or might not hold true
      and explain how these considerations shape your position.

35   Educational institutions should dissuade students from pursuing fields of study in which they
      are unlikely to succeed. [3/137]
      교육기관들은 학생들이 성공하지 못할 것 같은 연구 분야 공부를 추구하는 것을 막아야한다.
      Write a response in which you discuss your views on the policy and explain your reasoning for
      the position you take. In developing and supporting your position, you should consider the
      possible consequences of implementing the policy and explain how these consequences
      shape your position.

36   Governments should not fund any scientific research whose consequences are unclear. [72]
      정부는 결과가 불분명한 것에 대한 연구를 위한 자금을 지원하지 않아야 한다.
      Write a response in which you discuss the extent to which you agree or disagree with the
      recommendation and explain your reasoning for the position you take. In developing and
      supporting your position, describe specific circumstances in which adopting the
      recommendation would or would not be advantageous and explain how these examples shape
      your position.

37　Society should identify those children who have special talents and provide training for them at an early age to develop their talents.

사회는 특별한 재능을 가진 아이들을 발굴해서 그들이 조기에 재능을 개발할 수 있도록 훈련시켜야 한다.

Write a response in which you discuss the extent to which you agree or disagree with the recommendation and explain your reasoning for the position you take. In developing and supporting your position, describe specific circumstances in which adopting the recommendation would or would not be advantageous and explain how these examples shape your position.

38　It is primarily through our identification with social groups that we define ourselves.

자신 자신이 누구인가는 우리가 함께 어울려 다니는 소셜 그룹의 아이덴티티를 보면 알 수 있다.

Write a response in which you discuss the extent to which you agree or disagree with the statement and explain your reasoning for the position you take. In developing and supporting your position, you should consider ways in which the statement might or might not hold true and explain how these considerations shape your position.

39　College students should be encouraged to pursue subjects that interest them rather than the courses that seem most likely to lead to jobs.

대학생들은 직업에 필요할 것 같은 과목들보다는 그들이 관심이 있는 과목을 택하도록 권장되어야 한다.

Write a response in which you discuss the extent to which you agree or disagree with the recommendation and explain your reasoning for the position you take. In developing and supporting your position, describe specific circumstances in which adopting the recommendation would or would not be advantageous and explain how these examples shape your position.

40　Claim : When planning courses, educators should take into account the interests and suggestions of their students.

주장: 교과 과정을 계획할 때, 교육자들은 자신의 학생들의 제안과 관심을 고려해야만 한다.

Reason : Students are more motivated to learn when they are interested in what they are studying.

이유: 학생들은 그들이 공부하는 것에 관심이 있을 때 공부에 더 의욕을 가진다.

Write a response in which you discuss the extent to which you agree or disagree with the claim and the reason on which that claim is based.

41　The greatness of individuals can be decided only by those who live after them, not by their contemporaries.

한 개인의 위대함은 동시대 사람이 아니라 그의 사후에 후대 사람들에 의해서 결정된다.

Write a response in which you discuss the extent to which you agree or disagree with the statement and explain your reasoning for the position you take. In developing and supporting your position, you should consider ways in which the statement might or might not hold true and explain how these considerations shape your position.

42   Students should always question what they are taught instead of accepting it passively.
학생들은 자신들이 배운 것에 대해 수동적으로 받아들이기보다는 항상 의문을 가져야 한다.
Write a response in which you discuss the extent to which you agree or disagree with the statement and explain your reasoning for the position you take. In developing and supporting your position, you should consider ways in which the statement might or might not hold true and explain how these considerations shape your position.

43   The increasingly rapid pace of life today causes more problems than it solves.
급속도로 빠른 현대 생활은 더 많은 문제를 해결하기보다는 더 많은 문제를 만든다.
Write a response in which you discuss the extent to which you agree or disagree with the statement and explain your reasoning for the position you take. In developing and supporting your position, you should consider ways in which the statement might or might not hold true and explain how these considerations shape your position.

44   Claim : It is no longer possible for a society to regard any living man or woman as a hero.
주장: 우리 사회는 더 이상 생존해 있는 사람을 영웅이라고 여길 수가 없게 되었다.
Reason : The reputation of anyone who is subjected to media scrutiny will eventually be diminished. [22/75/84/122]
이유: 미디어 검증 대상이 되는 사람의 평판은 결국 사라질 것이다.
Write a response in which you discuss the extent to which you agree or disagree with the claim and the reason on which that claim is based.

45   Competition for high grades seriously limits the quality of learning at all levels of education. [138]
고득점을 위한 경쟁은 모든 수준의 교육에 있어서 양질의 교육을 저해한다.
Write a response in which you discuss the extent to which you agree or disagree with the statement and explain your reasoning for the position you take. In developing and supporting your position, you should consider ways in which the statement might or might not hold true and explain how these considerations shape your position.

46   Universities should require every student to take a variety of courses outside the student's field of study. [13/70/102/112/140]
대학은 모든 학생들이 의무적으로 자신의 전공 외에도 다양한 과목들을 수강하도록 해야 한다.
Write a response in which you discuss the extent to which you agree or disagree with the recommendation and explain your reasoning for the position you take. In developing and supporting your position, describe specific circumstances in which adopting the recommendation would or would not be advantageous and explain how these examples shape your position.

47   Educators should find out what students want included in the curriculum and then offer it to them.
교육자들은 학생들이 원하는 것을 찾아서 그것을 교과과정에 포함시키고 학생들에게 제공해야 한다.

Write a response in which you discuss the extent to which you agree or disagree with the recommendation and explain your reasoning for the position you take. In developing and supporting your position, describe specific circumstances in which adopting the recommendation would or would not be advantageous and explain how these examples shape your position.

48   Educators should teach facts only after their students have studied the ideas, trends, and concepts that help explain those facts. [92]
교육자들은 학생들이 사실을 설명하는 데 도움이 되는 아이디어, 경향, 개념을 공부한 후에만 그 사실을 가르쳐야 한다.
Write a response in which you discuss the extent to which you agree or disagree with the recommendation and explain your reasoning for the position you take. In developing and supporting your position, describe specific circumstances in which adopting the recommendation would or would not be advantageous and explain how these examples shape your position.

49   Claim : We can usually learn much more from people whose views we share than from those whose views contradict our own.
주장: 우리는 다른 의견을 가진 사람들보다 같은 의견을 가진 사람들로부터 더 많은 것을 배운다.
Reason : Disagreement can cause stress and inhibit learning. [76/118]
이유: 의견의 차이는 스트레스를 유발하고 배움을 저해한다.
Write a response in which you discuss the extent to which you agree or disagree with the claim and the reason on which that claim is based.

50   Government officials should rely on their own judgment rather than unquestioningly carry out the will of the people they serve. [86/115]
고위 공무원은 무조건적으로 민중의 뜻을 수행하기보다 자신의 의지에 근거해야 한다.
Write a response in which you discuss the extent to which you agree or disagree with the recommendation and explain your reasoning for the position you take. In developing and supporting your position, describe specific circumstances in which adopting the recommendation would or would not be advantageous and explain how these examples shape your position.

51   Young people should be encouraged to pursue long-term, realistic goals rather than seek immediate fame and recognition. [71]
젊은 사람들은 즉각적인 명성이나 인정보다는 장기적, 현실적 목표를 추구하도록 격려되어야 한다.
Write a response in which you discuss the extent to which you agree or disagree with the recommendation and explain your reasoning for the position you take. In developing and supporting your position, describe specific circumstances in which adopting the recommendation would or would not be advantageous and explain how these examples shape your position.

52   The best way to teach is to praise positive actions and ignore negative ones. [24/29]
      교육하는 데 최상의 방법은 긍정적 행위는 칭찬하고 부정적 행위는 아는 척하지 말아야 한다는 것이다.
      Write a response in which you discuss the extent to which you agree or disagree with the
      recommendation and explain your reasoning for the position you take. In developing and
      supporting your position, describe specific circumstances in which adopting the
      recommendation would or would not be advantageous and explain how these examples shape
      your position.

53   If a goal is worthy, then any means taken to attain it are justifiable.
      목적이 가치가 있다면 그것을 성취하기 위해서 취한 어떠한 방법도 정당화될 수 있다.
      Write a response in which you discuss the extent to which you agree or disagree with the
      statement and explain your reasoning for the position you take. In developing and supporting
      your position, you should consider ways in which the statement might or might not hold true
      and explain how these considerations shape your position.

54   In order to become well-rounded individuals, all college students should be required to take
      courses in which they read poetry, novels, mythology, and other types of imaginative literature.
      모든 대학생들은 원만한 인격을 형성하기 위해서 시, 소설, 신화 그리고 여타의 창작 문학 작품들을 읽을 수 있는
      과목들을 반드시 택하도록 해야 한다. [Art와 연계된 토픽]
      Write a response in which you discuss the extent to which you agree or disagree with the
      recommendation and explain your reasoning for the position you take. In developing and
      supporting your position, describe specific circumstances in which adopting the
      recommendation would or would not be advantageous and explain how these examples shape
      your position.

55   In order for any work of art — for example, a film, a novel, a poem, or a song — to have merit,
      it must be understandable to most people.
      영화, 소설, 시나 노래 같은 예술작품들이 가치를 가지려면 반드시 대중이 이해할 수 있는 것들이어야만 한다.
      Write a response in which you discuss the extent to which you agree or disagree with the
      statement and explain your reasoning for the position you take. In developing and supporting
      your position, you should consider ways in which the statement might or might not hold true
      and explain how these considerations shape your position.

56   Many important discoveries or creations are accidental: it is usually while seeking the answer to
      one question that we come across the answer to another.
      대부분의 발견이나 발명은 우연으로 인한 것이다. 다른 하나의 문제에 대한 답변을 찾는 중에 우연히 얻게 되는
      것이다.
      Write a response in which you discuss the extent to which you agree or disagree with the
      statement and explain your reasoning for the position you take. In developing and supporting
      your position, you should consider ways in which the statement might or might not hold true
      and explain how these considerations shape your position.

57   The main benefit of the study of history is to dispel the illusion that people living now are significantly different from people who lived in earlier times.

역사학의 유익한 점은 현대 인간은 과거의 인간과 다르다는 환상을 깨는 것이다.

Write a response in which you discuss the extent to which you agree or disagree with the statement and explain your reasoning for the position you take. In developing and supporting your position, you should consider ways in which the statement might or might not hold true and explain how these considerations shape your position.

58   Learning is primarily a matter of personal discipline; students cannot be motivated by school or college alone.

배움은 근본적으로 개인적 과제이다. 그러므로 학생은 단지 학교나 대학에서만 동기를 부여받을 수는 없다.

Write a response in which you discuss the extent to which you agree or disagree with the statement and explain your reasoning for the position you take. In developing and supporting your position, you should consider ways in which the statement might or might not hold true and explain how these considerations shape your position.

59   Scientists and other researchers should focus their research on areas that are likely to benefit the greatest number of people.

과학자나 연구자들은 많은 사람들이 이익을 받게 될 것 같은 연구 분야에만 집중해야 한다.

Write a response in which you discuss the extent to which you agree or disagree with the recommendation and explain your reasoning for the position you take. In developing and supporting your position, describe specific circumstances in which adopting the recommendation would or would not be advantageous and explain how these examples shape your position.

60   Politicians should pursue common ground and reasonable consensus rather than elusive ideals.

정치가는 허황된 아이디어보다는 대중적 합의와 합리적 동의를 추구해야 한다.

Write a response in which you discuss the extent to which you agree or disagree with the recommendation and explain your reasoning for the position you take. In developing and supporting your position, describe specific circumstances in which adopting the recommendation would or would not be advantageous and explain how these examples shape your position.

61   People should undertake risky action only after they have carefully considered its consequences.

사람들은 오로지 모험의 결과를 조심스럽게 고려한 다음에 행동을 해야 한다.

Write a response in which you discuss the extent to which you agree or disagree with the recommendation and explain your reasoning for the position you take. In developing and supporting your position, describe specific circumstances in which adopting the recommendation would or would not be advantageous and explain how these examples shape your position.

---

62   Leaders are created by the demands that are placed on them.

지도자는 그들이 처해진 시대적 요구에 의해서 탄생한다.

Write a response in which you discuss the extent to which you agree or disagree with the statement and explain your reasoning for the position you take. In developing and supporting your position, you should consider ways in which the statement might or might not hold true and explain how these considerations shape your position.

---

63   There is little justification for society to make extraordinary efforts — especially at a great cost in money and jobs — to save endangered animal or plant species. [31/67]

우리 사회가 멸종위기에 처한 동식물의 종들을 보호하기 위해 지나친 노력 — 특히 많은 돈과 일이 드는 —을 하는 것은 별로 정당성이 없다.

Write a response in which you discuss the extent to which you agree or disagree with the statement and explain your reasoning for the position you take. In developing and supporting your position, you should consider ways in which the statement might or might not hold true and explain how these considerations shape your position.

---

64   The human mind will always be superior to machines because machines are only tools of human minds.

인간의 정신은 기계보다 우수하다. 기계는 단지 인간이 사용하는 도구이기 때문이다.

Write a response in which you discuss the extent to which you agree or disagree with the statement and explain your reasoning for the position you take. In developing and supporting your position, you should consider ways in which the statement might or might not hold true and explain how these considerations shape your position.

---

65   Every individual in a society has a responsibility to obey just laws and to disobey and resist unjust laws.

사회의 모든 개인은 정당한 법은 준수하고 악법은 배척하며 저항해야 할 책무가 있다.

Write a response in which you discuss the extent to which you agree or disagree with the claim. In developing and supporting your position, be sure to address the most compelling reasons and/or examples that could be used to challenge your position.

---

66   People who are the most deeply committed to an idea or policy are also the most critical of it.

어떤 정책이나 아이디어에 가장 충실하게 헌신하는 사람들이 바로 그런 정책과 아이디어에 가장 비판적이다.

Write a response in which you discuss the extent to which you agree or disagree with the statement and explain your reasoning for the position you take. In developing and supporting your position, you should consider ways in which the statement might or might not hold true and explain how these considerations shape your position.

---

67   Some people believe that society should try to save every plant and animal species, despite the

expense to humans in effort, time, and financial well-being. Others believe that society need not make extraordinary efforts, especially at a great cost in money and jobs, to save endangered species. [31/63]

어떤 사람들은 우리 사회가 인간에 쓰는 노력, 시간, 재정적 풍요를 지불해서라도 모든 동식물의 종들을 보존해야 한다고 믿는다. 다른 사람들은 우리 사회가 멸종위기에 처한 종들을 보호하기 위한 상당한 노력을 – 특히 많은 돈과 노력을 들일 필요가 없다고 믿는다.

Write a response in which you discuss which view more closely aligns with your own position and explain your reasoning for the position you take. In developing and supporting your position, you should address both of the views presented.

68   Some people believe that the purpose of education is to free the mind and the spirit. Others believe that formal education tends to restrain our minds and spirits rather than set them free. [17]

어떤 사람들은 교육의 목적이 마음과 영혼을 자유롭게 하는 데 있다고 믿는다. 다른 사람들은 공교육이 우리들의 마음과 영혼을 자유롭게 하기보다는 억누른다고 믿는다.

Write a response in which you discuss which view more closely aligns with your own position and explain your reasoning for the position you take. In developing and supporting your position, you should address both of the views presented.

69   Some people believe it is often necessary, even desirable, for political leaders to withhold information from the public. Others believe that the public has a right to be fully informed.

어떤 사람들은 정치지도자가 정보를 알려 주지 않는 것은 필요할 뿐만 아니라 심지어 바람직하다고 믿는다. 다른 사람들은 대중은 모든 정보를 알권리가 있다고 믿는다.

Write a response in which you discuss which view more closely aligns with your own position and explain your reasoning for the position you take. In developing and supporting your position, you should address both of the views presented.

70   Claim : Universities should require every student to take a variety of courses outside the student's major field of study. [13/46/102/112/140]

주장: 대학은 모든 학생들이 의무적으로 자신의 전공 외에도 다양한 과목들을 수강하도록 해야 한다.

Reason : Acquiring knowledge of various academic disciplines is the best way to become truly educated.

이유: 다양한 분야의 지식을 습득하는 것이 진정한 교육을 받는 것이기 때문이다.

Write a response in which you discuss the extent to which you agree or disagree with the claim and the reason on which that claim is based.

71   Young people should be encouraged to pursue long-term, realistic goals rather than seek immediate fame and recognition. [51]

젊은 사람들은 즉각적인 명성이나 인정보다는 장기적, 현실적 목표를 추구하도록 격려되어야 한다.

Write a response in which you discuss the extent to which you agree or disagree with the statement and explain your reasoning for the position you take. In developing and supporting your position, you should consider ways in which the statement might or might not hold true and explain how these considerations shape your position.

72   Governments should not fund any scientific research whose consequences are unclear. [36]
정부는 결과가 불분명한 것에 대한 연구를 위한 자금을 주지 말아야 한다.
Write a response in which you discuss your views on the policy and explain your reasoning for the position you take. In developing and supporting your position, you should consider the possible consequences of implementing the policy and explain how these consequences shape your position.

73   Colleges and universities should require all faculty to spend time working outside the academic world in professions relevant to the courses they teach.
대학은 모든 교수들이 의무적으로 자신이 가르치는 전공 분야 외에서도 연구를 하도록 해야 한다.
Write a response in which you discuss your views on the policy and explain your reasoning for the position you take. In developing and supporting your position, you should consider the possible consequences of implementing the policy and explain how these consequences shape your position.

74   Knowing about the past cannot help people to make important decisions today. [133/134]
과거를 아는 것은 현재의 결정에 도움이 되지 않는다.
Write a response in which you discuss the extent to which you agree or disagree with the statement and explain your reasoning for the position you take. In developing and supporting your position, you should consider ways in which the statement might or might not hold true and explain how these considerations shape your position.

75   In this age of intensive media coverage, it is no longer possible for a society to regard any living man or woman as a hero. [22/44/84/122]
언론 보도가 극심한 시대에, 우리 사회는 더 이상 생존해 있는 사람을 영웅이라고 여길 수가 없게 되었다.
Write a response in which you discuss the extent to which you agree or disagree with the statement and explain your reasoning for the position you take. In developing and supporting your position, you should consider ways in which the statement might or might not hold true and explain how these considerations shape your position.

76   We can usually learn much more from people whose views we share than from people whose views contradict our own. [49/118]
우리는 일반적으로 다른 의견을 가진 사람들보다 같은 의견을 가진 사람들로부터 더 많은 것을 배울 수 있다.
Write a response in which you discuss the extent to which you agree or disagree with the statement and explain your reasoning for the position you take. In developing and supporting your position, you should consider ways in which the statement might or might not hold true and explain how these considerations shape your position.

77   The most effective way to understand contemporary culture is to analyze the trends of its youth.

현대 문화를 이해하기 위한 가장 효과적인 방법은 젊은 사람들의 경향을 분석하는 것이다.

Write a response in which you discuss the extent to which you agree or disagree with the statement and explain your reasoning for the position you take. In developing and supporting your position, you should consider ways in which the statement might or might not hold true and explain how these considerations shape your position.

78   People's attitudes are determined more by their immediate situation or surroundings than by society as a whole.

사람들의 태도는 자신이 당면한 상황이나 환경보다는 사회 전체에 의해서 결정된다.

Write a response in which you discuss the extent to which you agree or disagree with the statement and explain your reasoning for the position you take. In developing and supporting your position, you should consider ways in which the statement might or might not hold true and explain how these considerations shape your position.

79   Claim : The best test of an argument is its ability to convince someone with an opposing viewpoint.

주장: 논쟁을 시험하는 데 가장 적절한 방법은 반대 관점을 같은 다른 사람을 설득하는 것이다.

Reason : Only by being forced to defend an idea against the doubts and contrasting views of others does one really discover the value of that idea. [146]

이유: 오로지 남과 다른 아이디어를 방어하는 과정에서만 그 아이디어의 진가를 발견할 수 있기 때문이다.

Write a response in which you discuss the extent to which you agree or disagree with the claim and the reason on which that claim is based.

80   Nations should suspend government funding for the arts when significant numbers of their citizens are hungry or unemployed. [88]

국가가 상당수 국민들이 빈곤하거나 실직했을 때 예술을 위한 자금 지원을 보류하는 것은 당연하다.

Write a response in which you discuss the extent to which you agree or disagree with the recommendation and explain your reasoning for the position you take. In developing and supporting your position, describe specific circumstances in which adopting the recommendation would or would not be advantageous and explain how these examples shape your position.

81   All parents should be required to volunteer time to their children's schools. [95]

모든 학부모들은 자신의 아이들의 학교에서 의무적으로 자원봉사를 해야만 한다.

Write a response in which you discuss the extent to which you agree or disagree with the recommendation and explain your reasoning for the position you take. In developing and supporting your position, describe specific circumstances in which adopting the recommendation would or would not be advantageous and explain how these examples shape your position.

82   Colleges and universities should require their students to spend at least one semester studying in a foreign country. [97/100/124]

대학은 학생들이 의무적으로 적어도 한 학기는 다른 나라에서 공부를 하도록 해야 한다.

Write a response in which you discuss the extent to which you agree or disagree with the recommendation and explain your reasoning for the position you take. In developing and supporting your position, describe specific circumstances in which adopting the recommendation would or would not be advantageous and explain how these examples shape your position.

83   Teachers' salaries should be based on the academic performance of their students. [30]

교사들의 월급은 그들이 가르친 학생들의 학업성취도에 근거를 두어야 한다.

Write a response in which you discuss the extent to which you agree or disagree with the recommendation and explain your reasoning for the position you take. In developing and supporting your position, describe specific circumstances in which adopting the recommendation would or would not be advantageous and explain how these examples shape your position.

84   It is no longer possible for a society to regard any living man or woman as a hero. [22/44/75/122]

우리 사회는 더 이상 생존해 있는 사람을 영웅이라고 여길 수가 없게 되었다.

Write a response in which you discuss the extent to which you agree or disagree with the claim. In developing and supporting your position, be sure to address the most compelling reasons and/or examples that could be used to challenge your position.

85   Some people believe that in order to thrive, a society must put its own overall success before the well-being of its individual citizens. Others believe that the well-being of a society can only be measured by the general welfare of all its people.

어떤 사람들은 한 사회가 번영하기 위해서는 개개인의 복지가 그 사회 전체의 성공보다 우선시되어야 한다고 믿는다. 다른 사람들은 한 사회의 성공적인 척도는 오로지 모든 사람들의 복지로만 측정된다고 말한다.

Write a response in which you discuss which view more closely aligns with your own position and explain your reasoning for the position you take. In developing and supporting your position, you should address both of the views presented.

86   Some people believe that government officials must carry out the will of the people they serve. Others believe that officials should base their decisions on their own judgment. [50/115]

어떤 사람들은 공무원은 민중의 뜻을 수행해야 한다고 생각한다. 다른 사람들은 공무원들이 내리는 결정은 스스로의 판단에 근거해야 한다고 생각한다.

Write a response in which you discuss which view more closely aligns with your own position and explain your reasoning for the position you take. In developing and supporting your position, you should address both of the views presented.

87   Claim : Any piece of information referred to as a fact should be mistrusted, since it may well be proven false in the future.

주장: 사실이라고 알려진 어떤 정보도 의심을 해야 한다. 그 정보가 미래에 허위라고 증명될 가능성이 있기 때문이다.

Reason : Much of the information that people assume is factual actually turns out to be inaccurate.

이유: 우리가 사실이라고 가정하고 있는 많은 정보는 사실상 부정확한 것으로 드러난다.

Write a response in which you discuss the extent to which you agree or disagree with the claim and the reason on which that claim is based.

88   Claim : Nations should suspend government funding for the arts when significant numbers of their citizens are hungry or unemployed.

주장: 국가가 상당수 국민들이 빈곤하거나 실직했을 때 예술을 위한 자금 지원을 보류하는 것은 당연하다.

Reason : It is inappropriate — and, perhaps, even cruel — to use public resources to fund the arts when people's basic needs are not being met. [80]

이유: 국민의 기본적 요구가 충족되지 않을 때 공적인 자원을 예술 자금 지원에 쓴다는 것은 부적절할 뿐만 아니라 심지어 잔인하기까지 하다.

Write a response in which you discuss the extent to which you agree or disagree with the claim and the reason on which that claim is based.

89   Claim : Many problems of modern society cannot be solved by laws and the legal system.

주장: 현대 사회의 많은 문제들은 법이나 사법제도로 해결될 수 없다.

Reason : Laws cannot change what is in people's hearts or minds.

이유: 법은 사람들의 마음과 양심을 바꿀 수 없기 때문이다.

Write a response in which you discuss the extent to which you agree or disagree with the claim and the reason on which that claim is based.

90   Educators should take students' interests into account when planning the content of the courses they teach.

교육자들은 가르치는 교과 내용을 계획할 때 학생들의 관심을 고려해야만 한다.

Write a response in which you discuss the extent to which you agree or disagree with the recommendation and explain your reasoning for the position you take. In developing and supporting your position, describe specific circumstances in which adopting the recommendation would or would not be advantageous and explain how these examples shape your position.

91   The primary goal of technological advancement should be to increase people's efficiency so that they have more leisure time.

기술발전의 목적은 사람들의 효율성을 증대시켜 더 많은 여가 시간을 갖게 하는 데 있다.

Write a response in which you discuss the extent to which you agree or disagree with the statement and explain your reasoning for the position you take. In developing and supporting your position, you should consider ways in which the statement might or might not hold true

and explain how these considerations shape your position.

92   Educators should base their assessment of students' learning not on students' grasp of facts but on the ability to explain the ideas, trends, and concepts that those facts illustrate. [48]

교육자들은 학생들의 사실 파악 능력이 아니라 그 사실이 설명하고 있는 아이디어, 경향, 개념을 설명할 수 있는 능력으로 학생들의 성취도를 평가해야 한다.

Write a response in which you discuss the extent to which you agree or disagree with the recommendation and explain your reasoning for the position you take. In developing and supporting your position, describe specific circumstances in which adopting the recommendation would or would not be advantageous and explain how these examples shape your position.

93   Unfortunately, in contemporary society, creating an appealing image has become more important than the reality or truth behind that image.

불행하게도 현대 사회에서는 호소력 있는 이미지를 만드는 것이 현실이나 이미지 뒤에 담긴 진실보다 더 중요하게 되었다.

Write a response in which you discuss the extent to which you agree or disagree with the statement and explain your reasoning for the position you take. In developing and supporting your position, you should consider ways in which the statement might or might not hold true and explain how these considerations shape your position.

94   The effectiveness of a country's leaders is best measured by examining the well-being of that country's citizens. [147]

한 나라의 지도자가 얼마나 효과적으로 나라를 이끌고 있는지 알아보기 위한 가장 좋은 방법은 그 나라 국민들의 복지 수준을 측정하는 것이다.

Write a response in which you discuss the extent to which you agree or disagree with the claim. In developing and supporting your position, be sure to address the most compelling reasons and/or examples that could be used to challenge your position.

95   All parents should be required to volunteer time to their children's schools. [81]

모든 학부모들은 자신의 아이들의 학교에서 의무적으로 자원봉사를 해야만 한다.

Write a response in which you discuss the extent to which you agree or disagree with the claim. In developing and supporting your position, be sure to address the most compelling reasons and/or examples that could be used to challenge your position.

96   A nation should require all of its students to study the same national curriculum until they enter college. [6/14/116]

국가는 모든 학생들이 대학에 들어가기 전까지는 동일한 국정 교과과정으로 공부할 수 있도록 이를 의무화해야 한다.

Write a response in which you discuss the extent to which you agree or disagree with the claim. In developing and supporting your position, be sure to address the most compelling reasons and/or examples that could be used to challenge your position.

97   Colleges and universities should require their students to spend at least one semester studying in a foreign country. [82/100/124]

대학은 학생들이 의무적으로 적어도 한 학기는 다른 나라에서 공부를 하도록 해야 한다.

Write a response in which you discuss the extent to which you agree or disagree with the claim. In developing and supporting your position, be sure to address the most compelling reasons and/or examples that could be used to challenge your position.

98   Educational institutions should actively encourage their students to choose fields of study in which jobs are plentiful. [136]

교육기관들은 그 학생들이 직업이 풍부한 전공 분야를 선택하도록 적극 권장해야 한다.

Write a response in which you discuss your views on the policy and explain your reasoning for the position you take. In developing and supporting your position, you should consider the possible consequences of implementing the policy and explain how these consequences shape your position.

99   People's behavior is largely determined by forces not of their own making. [11]

사람들의 행위는 자신이 스스로 결정하는 것이 아니라 외부의 힘에 의해서 결정된다.

Write a response in which you discuss the extent to which you agree or disagree with the claim. In developing and supporting your position, be sure to address the most compelling reasons and/or examples that could be used to challenge your position.

100   Colleges and universities should require their students to spend at least one semester studying in a foreign country. [82/97/124]

대학은 학생들이 의무적으로 적어도 한 학기는 다른 나라에서 공부를 하도록 해야 한다.

Write a response in which you discuss your views on the policy and explain your reasoning for the position you take. In developing and supporting your position, you should consider the possible consequences of implementing the policy and explain how these consequences shape your position.

101   Although innovations such as video, computers, and the Internet seem to offer schools improved methods for instructing students, these technologies all too often distract from real learning.

비디오, 컴퓨터, 인터넷 같은 발명들이 학교가 학생들을 지도하는 데 발전된 방법들을 제공하는 것처럼 보이지만 이러한 기술들은 모두 언제나 진정한 배움에 방해가 된다.

Write a response in which you discuss the extent to which you agree or disagree with the statement and explain your reasoning for the position you take. In developing and supporting your position, you should consider ways in which the statement might or might not hold true and explain how these considerations shape your position.

102   Universities should require every student to take a variety of courses outside the student's field of study. [13/46/70/112/140]

대학은 모든 학생들이 의무적으로 자신의 전공 외에도 다양한 과목들을 수강하도록 해야 한다.

Write a response in which you discuss your views on the policy and explain your reasoning for the position you take. In developing and supporting your position, you should consider the possible consequences of implementing the policy and explain how these consequences shape your position.

103   The best ideas arise from a passionate interest in commonplace things.
가장 위대한 아이디어는 평범한 것들에 대한 열정적 관심으로부터 탄생한다.

Write a response in which you discuss the extent to which you agree or disagree with the statement and explain your reasoning for the position you take. In developing and supporting your position, you should consider ways in which the statement might or might not hold true and explain how these considerations shape your position.

104   To be an effective leader, a public official must maintain the highest ethical and moral standards. [16/107]
위대한(효과적인) 지도자가 되기 위해서 공무원은 최고의 윤리적, 도덕적 수준을 지켜야만 한다.

Write a response in which you discuss the extent to which you agree or disagree with the claim. In developing and supporting your position, be sure to address the most compelling reasons and/or examples that could be used to challenge your position.

105   Claim : Imagination is a more valuable asset than experience.
주장: 상상력은 경험보다 더 가치가 있는 자산이다.

Reason : People who lack experience are free to imagine what is possible without the constraints of established habits and attitudes.
이유: 경험이 부족한 사람들은 확립된 습관이나 태도의 제한 없이 자유로운 상상을 할 수 있기 때문이다.

Write a response in which you discuss the extent to which you agree or disagree with the claim and the reason on which that claim is based.

106   In most professions and academic fields, imagination is more important than knowledge. [126]
대부분의 전문 분야와 학문 분야에서, 상상력이 지식보다 더 중요하다.

Write a response in which you discuss the extent to which you agree or disagree with the statement and explain your reasoning for the position you take. In developing and supporting your position, you should consider ways in which the statement might or might not hold true and explain how these considerations shape your position.

107   To be an effective leader, a public official must maintain the highest ethical and moral standards. [16/104]
효과적인 지도자가 되기 위해서 공무원은 최고의 윤리적, 도덕적 수준을 지켜야만 한다.

Write a response in which you discuss the extent to which you agree or disagree with the statement and explain your reasoning for the position you take. In developing and supporting your position, you should consider ways in which the statement might or might not hold true

and explain how these considerations shape your position.

108   Critical judgment of work in any given field has little value unless it comes from someone who is an expert in that field. [110]

어떤 분야든지 비판적 판단은 그 분야의 전문가로부터 나오지 않는 한 그 가치가 없다.

Write a response in which you discuss the extent to which you agree or disagree with the statement and explain your reasoning for the position you take. In developing and supporting your position, you should consider ways in which the statement might or might not hold true and explain how these considerations shape your position.

109   Some people believe that scientific discoveries have given us a much better understanding of the world around us. Others believe that science has revealed to us that the world is infinitely more complex than we ever realized.

어떤 사람들은 과학적 발견은 우리가 세상을 더 잘 이해하도록 해 주었다고 믿는다. 다른 사람들은 과학이 세상을 우리가 알던 것보다 무한히 더 복잡하게 만들었다고 한다.

Write a response in which you discuss which view more closely aligns with your own position and explain your reasoning for the position you take. In developing and supporting your position, you should address both of the views presented.

110   Critical judgment of work in any given field has little value unless it comes from someone who is an expert in that field. [108]

어떤 분야든지 비판적 판단은 그 분야의 전문가로부터 나오지 않는 한 그 가치가 없다.

Write a response in which you discuss the extent to which you agree or disagree with the claim. In developing and supporting your position, be sure to address the most compelling reasons and/or examples that could be used to challenge your position.

111   In any profession — business, politics, education, government — those in power should step down after five years. [8/149]

비즈니스, 정치, 교육, 정부 등 어느 분야에서든 권력을 가진 사람은 5년 후에는 사임해야만 한다.

Write a response in which you discuss the extent to which you agree or disagree with the claim. In developing and supporting your position, be sure to address the most compelling reasons and/or examples that could be used to challenge your position.

112   Requiring university students to take a variety of courses outside their major fields of study is the best way to ensure that students become truly educated. [13/46/70/102/140]

대학이 학생들에게 전공 분야 외에 다양한 분야의 과목들을 택하도록 요구하는 것이 학생들에게 진정한 교육을 받도록 하는 최선의 방법이다.

Write a response in which you discuss the extent to which you agree or disagree with the statement and explain your reasoning for the position you take. In developing and supporting your position, you should consider ways in which the statement might or might not hold true and explain how these considerations shape your position.

Introduction

113   Claim : The surest indicator of a great nation is not the achievements of its rulers, artists, or scientists.

주장: 위대한 국가의 명확한 척도는 지도자, 예술가 또는 과학자들이 성취한 과업에 나타나는 것이 아니라 그 나라 국민의 전체적인 복지 상태로 결정된다.

Reason : The surest indicator of a great nation is actually the welfare of all its people. [28/120/121/127]

이유: 위대한 국가인지 알 수 있는 분명한 척도는 그 나라 모든 국민의 실질적 복지이다.

Write a response in which you discuss the extent to which you agree or disagree with the claim and the reason on which that claim is based.

114   Any leader who is quickly and easily influenced by shifts in popular opinion will accomplish little.

여론의 변화에 쉽고 빨리 영향을 받는 지도자는 제대로 된 성과를 얻지 못할 것이다.

Write a response in which you discuss the extent to which you agree or disagree with the statement and explain your reasoning for the position you take. In developing and supporting your position, you should consider ways in which the statement might or might not hold true and explain how these considerations shape your position.

115   Government officials should rely on their own judgment rather than unquestioningly carry out the will of the people whom they serve. [50/86]

공무원들은 무조건적으로 민중의 뜻을 수행하기보다 자신의 의지에 근거해야 한다.

Write a response in which you discuss the extent to which you agree or disagree with the statement and explain your reasoning for the position you take. In developing and supporting your position, you should consider ways in which the statement might or might not hold true and explain how these considerations shape your position.

116   A nation should require all of its students to study the same national curriculum until they enter college. [6/14/96]

국가는 모든 학생들이 대학에 들어가기 전까지는 동일한 국정 교과과정으로 공부할 수 있도록 이를 의무화해야 한다.

Write a response in which you discuss the extent to which you agree or disagree with the statement and explain your reasoning for the position you take. In developing and supporting your position, you should consider ways in which the statement might or might not hold true and explain how these considerations shape your position.

117   It is primarily in cities that a nation's cultural traditions are generated and preserved. [5]

한 국가의 문화 전통이 생성되고 보존되는 곳은 주로 도시이다.

Write a response in which you discuss the extent to which you agree or disagree with the statement and explain your reasoning for the position you take. In developing and supporting your position, you should consider ways in which the statement might or might not hold true and explain how these considerations shape your position.

118   We can learn much more from people whose views we share than from people whose views contradict our own. [49/76]

우리는 일반적으로 다른 의견을 가진 사람들보다 같은 의견을 가진 사람들로부터 더 많은 것을 배울 수 있다.

Write a response in which you discuss the extent to which you agree or disagree with the statement and explain your reasoning for the position you take. In developing and supporting your position, you should consider ways in which the statement might or might not hold true and explain how these considerations shape your position.

119   When old buildings stand on ground that modern planners feel could be better used for modern purposes, modern development should be given precedence over the preservation of historic buildings.

현재의 이익을 추구하며 더 유용하게 쓰기 위해서 오래된 건물을 보존하는 것보다 현대적 발전을 중시해야 한다.

Write a response in which you discuss the extent to which you agree or disagree with the statement and explain your reasoning for the position you take. In developing and supporting your position, you should consider ways in which the statement might or might not hold true and explain how these considerations shape your position.

120   Claim : The surest indicator of a great nation must be the achievements of its rulers, artists, or scientists.

주장: 위대한 국가의 명확한 척도는 틀림없이 그 나라의 지도자, 예술가 또는 과학자들이 성취한 업적이다.

Reason : Great achievements by a nation's rulers, artists, or scientists will ensure a good life for the majority of that nation's people. [28/113/121/127]

이유: 한 나라의 지도자, 예술가 또는 과학자들이 성취한 업적은 대부분의 국민들의 행복한 생활을 보장할 것이다.

Write a response in which you discuss the extent to which you agree or disagree with the claim and the reason on which that claim is based.

121   Some people claim that you can tell whether a nation is great by looking at the achievements of its rulers, artists, or scientists. Others argue that the surest indicator of a great nation is, in fact, the general welfare of all its people. [28/113/120/127]

어떤 사람들은 한 국가의 위대성은 그 나라의 지도자, 예술가 또는 과학자들을 봄으로써 알 수 있다고 주장한다. 다른 사람들은 위대한 국가의 확실한 척도는 실제로 국민들의 복지라고 주장한다.

Write a response in which you discuss which view more closely aligns with your own position and explain your reasoning for the position you take. In developing and supporting your position, you should address both of the views presented.

122   The best way to understand the character of a society is to examine the character of the men and women that the society chooses as its heroes or its role models. [22]

한 사회의 성격을 이해하기 위한 최선책은 그 사회의 구성원들이 선택한 영웅이나 귀감이 되는 인물들의 성격을 살펴보는 것이다.

Write a response in which you discuss the extent to which you agree or disagree with the claim. In developing and supporting your position, be sure to address the most compelling reasons and/or examples that could be used to challenge your position.

123   The best way for a society to prepare its young people for leadership in government, industry, or other fields is by instilling in them a sense of cooperation, not competition.
젊은이들이 정부, 산업 또는 다른 전문 분야에서 리더십을 기르기 위해서는 경쟁보다는 협동의 개념을 고무해야 한다.
Write a response in which you discuss the extent to which you agree or disagree with the claim. In developing and supporting your position, be sure to address the most compelling reasons and/or examples that could be used to challenge your position.

124   All college and university students would benefit from spending at least one semester studying in a foreign country. [82/97/100]
모든 대학생들은 적어도 한 학기는 다른 나라에서 공부를 함으로써 이득을 볼 것이다.
Write a response in which you discuss the extent to which you agree or disagree with the statement and explain your reasoning for the position you take. In developing and supporting your position, you should consider ways in which the statement might or might not hold true and explain how these considerations shape your position.

125   Some people claim that a nation's government should preserve its wilderness areas in their natural state. Others argue that these areas should be developed for potential economic gain. [10/148]
어떤 사람들은 자연 상태의 야생지역을 보호해야 한다고 한다. 다른 사람들은 잠재적인 경제 이익을 위해서 개발해야 한다고 한다.
Write a response in which you discuss which view more closely aligns with your own position and explain your reasoning for the position you take. In developing and supporting your position, you should address both of the views presented.

126   In most professions and academic fields, imagination is more important than knowledge. [106]
대부분의 전문 분야와 학문 분야에서, 상상력이 지식보다 더 중요하다.
Write a response in which you discuss the extent to which you agree or disagree with the claim. In developing and supporting your position, be sure to address the most compelling reasons and/or examples that could be used to challenge your position.

127   The surest indicator of a great nation is not the achievements of its rulers, artists, or scientists, but the general well-being of all its people. [28/113/120/121]
위대한 국가의 명확한 척도는 지도자, 예술가 또는 과학자들이 성취한 과업에 나타나는 것이 아니라 그 나라 국민의 전체적인 복지 상태로 결정된다.
Write a response in which you discuss the extent to which you agree or disagree with the claim. In developing and supporting your position, be sure to address the most compelling reasons and/or examples that could be used to challenge your position.

128   Some people argue that successful leaders in government, industry, or other fields must be highly competitive. Other people claim that in order to be successful, a leader must be willing and able to cooperate with others. [123]

어떤 사람들은 정부, 산업 또는 다른 전문 분야에서 훌륭한 지도자는 상당히 경쟁력이 있어야 한다고 주장한다. 다른 사람들은 성공하기 위해서 지도자는 반드시 다른 사람들과 협력하려는 의지와 능력이 있어야 한다고 주장한다.

Write a response in which you discuss which view more closely aligns with your own position and explain your reasoning for the position you take. In developing and supporting your position, you should address both of the views presented.

129   College students should base their choice of a field of study on the availability of jobs in that field. [20/32]

대학생들은 고용의 기회를 전공의 선택 기준으로 삼아야 한다.

Write a response in which you discuss the extent to which you agree or disagree with the recommendation and explain your reasoning for the position you take. In developing and supporting your position, describe specific circumstances in which adopting the recommendation would or would not be advantageous and explain how these examples shape your position.

130   Some people believe that corporations have a responsibility to promote the well-being of the societies and environments in which they operate. Others believe that the only responsibility of corporations, provided they operate within the law, is to make as much money as possible.

어떤 사람들은 대기업이 사회복지와 그들이 유용하고 있는 환경을 증진시킬 책임이 있다고 믿는다. 다른 사람들은 법의 테두리 안에서 운영을 하는 한, 대기업의 유일한 책무는 이윤을 창조하는 것이라고 믿는다.

Write a response in which you discuss which view more closely aligns with your own position and explain your reasoning for the position you take. In developing and supporting your position, you should address both of the views presented.

131   Claim : Researchers should not limit their investigations to only those areas in which they expect to discover something that has an immediate, practical application.

주장: 연구원들은 즉각적이고 현실적 적용이 기대되는 분야의 연구에만 국한해서는 안 된다.

Reason : It is impossible to predict the outcome of a line of research with any certainty.

이유: 확신을 가지고 연구 결과를 예측하는 것은 불가능하기 때문이다.

Write a response in which you discuss the extent to which you agree or disagree with the claim and the reason on which that claim is based.

132   Some people believe that our ever-increasing use of technology significantly reduces our opportunities for human interaction. Other people believe that technology provides us with new and better ways to communicate and connect with one another.

어떤 사람들은 점점 증가하는 기술의 사용이 새로운 상호 인간관계를 만들 기회를 현저하게 줄여준다고 믿는다. 다른 사람들은 기술이 새롭고 더 나은 소통과 관계를 서로에게 가져다준다고 믿는다.

Write a response in which you discuss which view more closely aligns with your own position and explain your reasoning for the position you take. In developing and supporting your position, you should address both of the views presented.

---

133   Claim : Knowing about the past cannot help people to make important decisions today.
주장: 과거를 아는 것은 현재의 결정에 도움이 되지 않는다.
Reason : The world today is significantly more complex than it was even in the relatively recent past. [74/134]
이유: 오늘날 세상은 근대 생활보다 더 복잡하기 때문이다.
Write a response in which you discuss the extent to which you agree or disagree with the claim and the reason on which that claim is based.

---

134   Claim : Knowing about the past cannot help people to make important decisions today.
주장: 과거를 아는 것은 현재의 결정에 도움이 되지 않는다.
Reason : We are not able to make connections between current events and past events until we have some distance from both. [74/133]
이유: 우리는 두 사건 사이에 어느 정도 간격이 없다면 현재의 사건과 과거의 사건을 연결시킬 수 없다.
Write a response in which you discuss the extent to which you agree or disagree with the claim and the reason on which that claim is based.

---

135   Educational institutions should actively encourage their students to choose fields of study that will prepare them for lucrative careers. [15]
교육기관은 학생들이 수입이 높은 직업이 보장되는 분야를 공부할 수 있도록 적극 권장해야 한다.
Write a response in which you discuss your views on the policy and explain your reasoning for the position you take. In developing and supporting your position, you should consider the possible consequences of implementing the policy and explain how these consequences shape your position.

---

136   Educational institutions should actively encourage their students to choose fields of study in which jobs are plentiful. [98]
교육기관들은 그 학생들이 직업이 풍부한 전공 분야를 선택하도록 적극 권장해야 한다.
Write a response in which you discuss the extent to which you agree or disagree with the claim. In developing and supporting your position, be sure to address the most compelling reasons and/or examples that could be used to challenge your position.

---

137   Educational institutions have a responsibility to dissuade students from pursuing fields of study in which they are unlikely to succeed. [3/35]
교육기관들은 학생들이 성공하지 못할 것 같은 연구 분야 공부를 추구하는 것을 막아야 하는 책임이 있다.
Write a response in which you discuss the extent to which you agree or disagree with the statement and explain your reasoning for the position you take. In developing and supporting your position, you should consider ways in which the statement might or might not hold true

and explain how these considerations shape your position.

138 Some people believe that competition for high grades motivates students to excel in the classroom. Others believe that such competition seriously limits the quality of real learning. [45]
어떤 사람들은 높은 학점을 받기 위한 경쟁은 학생들이 수업에서 최선을 다 하도록 동기를 부여한다고 믿는다. 다른 사람들은 그러한 경쟁은 진정한 배움의 질을 저해한다고 믿는다.
Write a response in which you discuss which view more closely aligns with your own position and explain your reasoning for the position you take. In developing and supporting your position, you should address both of the views presented.

139 Claim : Major policy decisions should always be left to politicians and other government experts.
주장: 주요한 정책 결정은 정치인과 다른 정부 전문가에게 맡겨야 한다.
Reason : Politicians and other government experts are more informed and thus have better judgment and perspective than do members of the general public.
이유: 정치인이나 다른 정부 전문가들은 더 많은 정보를 소유하기 때문에 일반 대중보다 더 나은 판단과 견해를 가질 수 있다.
Write a response in which you discuss the extent to which you agree or disagree with the claim and the reason on which that claim is based.

140 Some people believe that universities should require every student to take a variety of courses outside the student's field of study. Others believe that universities should not force students to take any courses other than those that will help prepare them for jobs in their chosen fields. [13/46/70/102/112]
어떤 사람들은 대학이 학생들에게 반드시 전공 분야 외에 다양한 분야의 과목들을 택하도록 해야 한다고 생각한다. 다른 사람들은 대학이 학생들이 선택한 분야의 직업에 도움이 되는 과목 이외의 과목들을 강요해서는 안 된다고 믿는다.
Write a response in which you discuss which view more closely aligns with your own position and explain your reasoning for the position you take. In developing and supporting your position, you should address both of the views presented.

141 It is more harmful to compromise one's own beliefs than to adhere to them.
자신의 소신에 매달리는 것보다 자기 자신의 소신에 타협하는 것이 더 해롭다
Write a response in which you discuss the extent to which you agree or disagree with the statement and explain your reasoning for the position you take. In developing and supporting your position, you should consider ways in which the statement might or might not hold true and explain how these considerations shape your position.

142 Claim : Colleges and universities should specify all required courses and eliminate elective courses in order to provide clear guidance for students.
주장: 대학들은 학생들에게 명확한 지침을 제공하기 위해서 모든 필수과목들 구체적으로 명시하고 선택과목들은 없애야 한다.

Reason : College students — like people in general — prefer to follow directions rather than make their own decisions.
이유: 대학생들은—일반 대중처럼—스스로 결정하는 것보다는 지침을 따르는 것을 선호한다.
Write a response in which you discuss the extent to which you agree or disagree with the claim and the reason on which that claim is based.

143   No field of study can advance significantly unless it incorporates knowledge and experience from outside that field.
다른 분야의 지식과 경험을 통합하지 않고 발전할 수 있는 학문은 없다.
Write a response in which you discuss the extent to which you agree or disagree with the statement and explain your reasoning for the position you take. In developing and supporting your position, you should consider ways in which the statement might or might not hold true and explain how these considerations shape your position.

144   True success can be measured primarily in terms of the goals one sets for oneself.
진정한 성공은 주로 스스로 설정하는 목표로서 평가될 수 있다.
Write a response in which you discuss the extent to which you agree or disagree with the statement and explain your reasoning for the position you take. In developing and supporting your position, you should consider ways in which the statement might or might not hold true and explain how these considerations shape your position.

145   The general welfare of a nation's people is a better indication of that nation's greatness than are the achievements of its rulers, artists, or scientists. [28/113/120/121/127]
그 국가의 지도자들, 예술가들 또는 과학자들의 업적보다는 일반 국민들의 복지 상태가 한 국가의 위대성을 측정하는 더 나은 척도이다.
Write a response in which you discuss the extent to which you agree or disagree with the claim. In developing and supporting your position, be sure to address the most compelling reasons and/or examples that could be used to challenge your position.

146   The best test of an argument is the argument's ability to convince someone with an opposing viewpoint. [79]
논쟁 능력을 시험하는 가장 적절한 방법은 반대 관점을 가진 다른 사람을 설득해보는 것이다.
Write a response in which you discuss the extent to which you agree or disagree with the statement and explain your reasoning for the position you take. In developing and supporting your position, you should consider ways in which the statement might or might not hold true and explain how these considerations shape your position.

147   The effectiveness of a country's leaders is best measured by examining the well-being of that country's citizens. [94]
한 나라의 지도자가 얼마나 효과적으로 나라를 이끌고 있는지 알아보기 위한 가장 좋은 방법은 그 나라 국민들의 복지 수준을 측정하는 것이다.

Write a response in which you discuss the extent to which you agree or disagree with the statement and explain your reasoning for the position you take. In developing and supporting your position, you should consider ways in which the statement might or might not hold true and explain how these considerations shape your position.

148   Nations should pass laws to preserve any remaining wilderness areas in their natural state. [10/125]
국가들은 아직 자연 상태로 남아 있는 야생지역을 보호하기 위해서 법을 통과시켜야만 한다.
Write a response in which you discuss the extent to which you agree or disagree with the claim. In developing and supporting your position, be sure to address the most compelling reasons and/or examples that could be used to challenge your position.

149   In any field — business, politics, education, government — those in power should be required to step down after five years. [8/111]
비즈니스, 정치, 교육, 정부 등 어느 분야에서든 권력을 가진 사람은 5년 후에는 사임해야만 한다.
Write a response in which you discuss your views on the policy and explain your reasoning for the position you take. In developing and supporting your position, you should consider the possible consequences of implementing the policy and explain how these consequences shape your position.

Lecture 2

Education

Education Topic Analysis

교육에 관한 토픽 유형은 2가지 key 개념을 비교 대조하면서 쓰는 방법을 익혀나가야 한다. 교육에 대한 토픽이 가장 많은 숫자를 차지하고 있다는 사실은 교육의 중요성을 시사한다. 모든 에세이를 partially agree but disagree나 partially disagree but agree로 쓸 때 반드시 토픽 안에서 비교 대조의 개념을 끌어내어 쓰도록 한다.

즉, 개념 암기 vs 개념 이해, 협동 vs 경쟁, 직업교육 vs 교양교육, 직업교육 vs 재능교육, 가치관 교육(역사) vs 실리적 교육, 선택과목 vs 필수과목, 지역사회에 맞는 교육 vs 국가적 국민교육 등의 내용이 있으며 재능교육에 관한 토픽은 아동교육을 초점으로 하는 질문이다.

교육에 관한 토픽에 답변을 할 때에는 무엇보다 중요한 것은 토픽이 묻고 있는 학교가 초등학교인지 중고등학교인지 또는 대학교인지를 먼저 파악해야 한다는 것이다.

또한 교육과 가치관에 대해서 묻는 토픽이 있으나 이 부분은 Values chapter에서 다시 설명한다. 가치관의 맥락으로 모든 부모들은 자녀들의 학교에서 자원봉사를 해야 하는가?, 무상 대학교육 vs 유상 대학교육 등을 다루고 있다.

101번처럼 Technology와 연계되어서 기자재 사용이 교육의 질을 높이느냐고 묻는 질문과 Art와 연계해서 예술 과목을 반드시 대학교육에 포함해야 하느냐 등이 있다.

Lecture 2
Education

42   Students should always question what they are taught instead of accepting it passively.

학생들은 자신들이 배운 것에 대해 수동적으로 받아들이기보다는 항상 의문을 가져야 한다.

Write a response in which you discuss the extent to which you agree or disagree with the statement and explain your reasoning for the position you take. In developing and supporting your position, you should consider ways in which the statement might or might not hold true and explain how these considerations shape your position.

강의노트   42번 이슈는 'always'라는 빈도부사 때문에 partially disagree 방향으로 작성해야 한다. 대조되는 개념으로 암기 훈련이 수동적 배움의 필요한 적절한 예증이다. 결론적으로 수동적 배움 없이 효율적으로 이루어지지 못한다. 빈도 부사를 사용해서 always가 아니라 occasional question은 필요하나 frequently는 불가하다고 주장한다.

(1) 의문문으로 토픽을 restate한다.

(2) 다른 사람의 의견: 배우는 것을 질문한다의 장점을 적는다.

(3) However, I partially disagree that 〈topic〉 because 수동적 배움의 장점

(4) always question이 가져오는 또 다른 단점을 적는다.

(5) In this way, (5)번 방법으로 효과적 교육이 가능하다고 서론을 맺는다.

(6) Of course, 교사는 학생이 질문하기를 두려워하게 만들면 안 된다.

(7) 창의적 에세이는 비판적 사고에서 시작한다. [암기와 대조되는 경우]

(8) 바로 이런 비판적 사고는 질문으로부터 시작된다.

(9) For this reason, 교사는 학생이 자유롭게 질문할 수 있는 수업 분위기를 만든다.

(10) However, 암기 훈련은 지식을 축적하는 데 유용한 수동적 배움이다.

(11) While 개념 이해를 위해서 학생은 질문해야 하지만, 암기 훈련도 중요하다.

(12) For example, unlike 암기하지 않은 학생과 달리 화학주기표를 암기하는 학생은 화학 반응 방정식 풀기 다음 단계로 쉽게 갈 수 있다.

(13) 암기한 정보를 바탕으로 화학 반응 방정식 배울 때 혼란이 적다.

(14) 그러므로 학생은 항상 질문하기보다는 수동적으로 배워야 한다.

(15) Another 예증은 50개 주나 capital 이름은 반복을 통해서 암기한다.

(16) Imagine 암기하지 않는다고 하면, 학습 시간이 더 길어질 것이다.

(17) Rote memorization은 개념 이해에 관한 질문과는 연관이 없는 skills이다.

(18) 그러나 암기한 지식을 바탕으로 학생들은 더 많은 지식을 쌓을 수 있다.

(19) 그러므로 수동적 배움이 항상 질문하는 것 보다 중요하다.

(20) In sum, as having seen in the above, 암기와 질문하는 걸 혼합한 교과가 효율적 교육이다.

(21) 암기 훈련이 안 되는 short-term memory에 의거하는 교육은 비효율적이다.

(22) 더욱이 학생이 너무 자주하는 질문으로 인해서 다른 학생 배움에도 지장이 된다.

Do students need to question always what they are taught rather than accepting it passively? Some may think students should be allowed to ask a question anytime to stimulate discussion so they can promote dynamics in class instead of absorbing knowledge silently. However, in my opinion more effective learning happens when students gain essential knowledge by following their instructions based on the curriculum syllabus and textbook. They are supposed to ask questions occasionally only with the teacher's permission not to disturb others. In this way, they can develop the ability to deepen their understanding of matters and the world more effectively than by constantly questioning what they are learning all the time.

Of course, teachers should encourage students to raise questions about the content they are learning. Instead of passive learning, they are more likely to learn how to develop critical thinking skills and creative writing skills through questions. In this sense, teachers should promote a classroom atmosphere where students feel comfortable asking some questions.

However, passive learning is more effective for the integration of knowledge. For example, teachers give a quiz to find students who can memorize all the names of the chemical elements in the Periodic Table before moving to the advanced level of chemical reactions. Also, students' memorization of the multiplication tables help them carry out more speedy calculations. Suppose some student persistently questions the numbers in the timetable chart in a math class. If so, it would disturb others' building

Education

the fast computation skill. Those who mechanically memorize them would feel easy to solve more complex multiplication and fraction problems. Thus, students should be encouraged to accept knowledge passively without raising questions too often.

Another compelling example is memorizing the 50 states' names and their capitals. Students should learn them by repetition without comprehending information or facts in detail about a particular state or city. Imagine students are supposed to solve multiplication or fraction problems without rote memorization; if so, it might save valuable instruction time. Rote memory generally entails material without much reference to the meaning, seemingly irrelevant to the question. However, more effective learning occurs when students integrate the information they remember to advance knowledge.

In sum, students can learn better when teachers use a curriculum that combines critical thinking skills with memorization drills. Most professionals understand that poor short-term memory can make it difficult to master language and math concepts; therefore, they train students to absorb knowledge by repetition. Moreover, a student's frequent questions can be disturbing behaviors. [425]

81

All parents should be required to volunteer time to their children's schools.

모든 학부모들은 자신의 아이들의 학교에서 의무적으로 자원봉사를 해야만 한다.

(1) Although 자원봉사는 중요하지만

(2) 모든 부모에게 요구해서는 안 된다.

(3) Thus, 그러므로 I disagree

(4) Because unfair policy이기 때문이다.

(5) 부모가 감옥에 있거나 암에 걸린 부모에게 이런 자원봉사 정책은 이는 "교육 기회 평등"의 문제를 야기한다.

(6) Of course, 부모 참여는 자원봉사로 교육의 질을 높여준다.

(7) 그래서 어떤 교장은 학부모 조직을 중요시 여긴다.

(8) In addition, 교육은 학부모의 참여로 지역사회와 학교를 연결하는 통로가 된다.

(9) Of course, 학부모 참여로 인한 유익을 간과해서는 안 된다.

(10) However, 모든 학부모 참여가 강요되어서는 안 된다.

(11) For instance, ill parents

(12) 참여하고 싶어도 일을 해야 하는 ill mothers는 불만을 품는다.

(13) 참여하는 부모와 참여 못하는 부모 대조

(14) Thus, 우리 지역사회를 둘로 나누는 부정적인 결과를 가져 온다.

(15) Another example은 감옥에 있는 한 부모다.

(16) 무엇보다도 force하는 policy는 자원봉사 정신에 위배된다.

(17) 만약에 참여할 수 없는 부모가 반드시 와야 한다면

(18) 학생은 모멸감으로 힘들 것이다.

(19) Thus, 자원봉사 정신을 위배하므로 불평등 정책에 반대한다.

(20) Without question~ 자원봉사는 교육의 질을 어느 정도 높인다.

(21) Nevertheless, 마이너리티를 배려하지 않는 정책은 오히려 해로울 수 있다.

(22) Moreover, 이러한 정책은 타자를 배려하는 커뮤니티 정신을 왜곡한 것이다.

Lecture 2
Education

81   All parents should be required to volunteer time to their children's schools.

모든 학부모들은 자신의 아이들의 학교에서 의무적으로 자원봉사를 해야만 한다.

Write a response in which you discuss the extent to which you agree or disagree with the recommendation and explain your reasoning for the position you take. In developing and supporting your position, describe specific circumstances in which adopting the recommendation would or would not be advantageous and explain how these examples shape your position.

강의노트   토픽이 all parents라고 했기 때문에 partially disagree로 작성한다. '경제적인 이유나 신체적으로 불편한 부모들은 봉사활동을 강요하는 정책은 불평등 정책이기 때문이다.

Although all parents are welcome to be involved in volunteer activities for local schools, requiring all parents to do so is not a fair educational policy. Thus, I disagree with the statement. Impartial school policies fail to provide pleasant learning environments to all students by excluding those in the marginal area. Few would doubt the benefits that local schools can have with volunteer. The more parents are involved in volunteer activities, the better they promote the quality of education at local schools. Nonetheless, a mandatory policy that excludes students with a parent in prison or illnesses is unfair.

Of course, the benefits that local schools can receive from parent volunteers are significant. Parent volunteers have played a pivotal role in supporting school programs in various ways to the extent that promotes the quality of education at local schools. Moreover, parent volunteers can develop meaningful connections with other community members by exchanging information and building mutual relationships.

However, the mandatory policy may frustrate students and their parents who are too sick to participate in a volunteer program. For example, unlike healthy parents, ill parents might suffer from a terminal disease like cancer. While some students could benefit from the policy, others might have to bear disadvantages in evaluations with this discriminatory policy. As a result, this policy leads to a social divide between students with healthy parents and those with illnesses.

Another compelling example is the students with incarcerated parents. Due to the impartial policy, such students would go through unbearable frustration, which may grow into humiliation. Their stressful feelings prevent them from concentrating on what they are learning. This policy also tarnished the volunteer spirit of sharing others' pain and difficulties.

Without question, many parents' participation in their children's schools will surely increase the quality of education at the local schools by supporting professional educators. Nonetheless, the possible disadvantages of the policy weigh greater than its benefits.

In short, most compulsory rules end up emphasizing the justification of compulsory obedience. Mandatory policies can work adversely against promoting a fair educational atmosphere in our schools and communities. [365]

Lecture 2
Education

EDUCATION	3	Educational institutions have a responsibility to dissuade students from pursuing fields of study in which they are unlikely to succeed. [35] 교육기관들은 학생들이 성공하지 못할 것 같은 연구 분야의 공부를 추구하는 것을 막을 책임이 있다.

3 Educational institutions have a responsibility to dissuade students from pursuing fields of study in which they are unlikely to succeed. [35]
교육기관들은 학생들이 성공하지 못할 것 같은 연구 분야의 공부를 추구하는 것을 막을 책임이 있다.

6 A nation should require all of its students to study the same national curriculum until they enter college. [14/96/116]
국가는 모든 학생들이 대학에 들어가기 전까지는 동일한 국정 교과과정으로 공부할 수 있도록 이를 의무화해야 한다.

12 Governments should offer free university education to any student who has been admitted to a university but cannot afford the tuition. [25]
정부는 대학에 입학허가를 받았으나 등록금을 낼 수 없는 학생들에게 무상 교육을 제공해야 한다. [VALUE와 연계되는 토픽]

13 Universities should require every student to take a variety of courses outside the student's field of study. [46/70/102/112/140]
대학은 학생들이 자신의 전공 외 분야 학과목을 이수하도록 의무화해야 한다.

15 Educational institutions should actively encourage their students to choose fields of study that will prepare them for lucrative careers. [135]
교육기관은 학생들이 수입이 높은 직업이 보장되는 분야를 공부할 수 있도록 북돋아 주어야 한다.

17 Formal education tends to restrain our minds and spirits rather than set them free. [68]
공교육은 우리들의 정신과 영혼을 자유롭지 않도록 제한하는 경향이 있다. [VALUE와 연계된 토픽]

20 Some people believe that college students should consider only their own talents and interests when choosing a field of study. Others believe that college students should base their choice of a field of study on the availability of jobs in that field. [32/129]
어떤 사람들은 대학생들이 자신의 재능과 관심을 고려해서 전공 분야를 선택해야 한다고 생각한다. 다른 사람들은 고용의 기회를 선택 기준으로 삼아야 한다고 한다.

29 The best way to teach — whether as an educator, employer, or parent — is to praise positive actions and ignore negative ones. [24/52]
교육의 최상의 방법은 가르치는 사람이 누구—교육자이든, 고용주이든, 부모이든—든 간에 긍정적 행위는 칭찬하고 부정적 행위는 아는 척하지 말아야 한다는 것이다.

37 Society should identify those children who have special talents and provide training for them at an early age to develop their talents.
사회는 특별한 재능을 가진 아이들을 발굴해서 그들이 조기에 재능을 개발할 수 있도록 훈련시켜야 한다.

39 College students should be encouraged to pursue subjects that interest them rather than the courses that seem most likely to lead to jobs.
대학생들은 그들이 관심이 있는 과목보다 직업을 얻을 가능성이 있는 과목들을 택하도록 고무되어야 한다.

40 When planning courses, educators should take into account the interests and suggestions of their students.
학과목을 계획할 때, 교육자들은 자신의 학생들의 제안과 관심을 고려해야만 한다.

42 Students should always question what they are taught instead of accepting it passively.
학생들은 자신들이 배운 것에 대해 수동적으로 받아들이기보다는 항상 의문을 가져야 한다.

45 Competition for high grades seriously limits the quality of learning at all levels of education. [138]
고득점을 위한 경쟁은 모든 수준의 교육에 있어서 양질의 교육을 저해한다. [VALUE와 연계]

46 Universities should require every student to take a variety of courses outside the students' field of study. [13/70/102/112/140]
대학은 모든 학생들이 의무적으로 자신의 전공 외에도 다양한 과목들을 수강하도록 해야 한다.

47 Educators should find out what students want included in the curriculum and then offer it to them.
교육자들은 학생들이 원하는 것을 찾아서 그것을 교과과정에 포함시키고 학생들에게 제공해야 한다.

51 Young people should be encouraged to pursue long term, realistic goals rather than seek immediate fame and recognition. [71]
젊은 사람들은 즉각적인 명성이나 인정보다는 장기적, 현실적 목표를 추구하도록 격려되어야 한다.

54 In order to become well-rounded individuals, all college students should be required to take courses in which they read poetry, novels, mythology, and other types of imaginative literature.
모든 대학생들은 원만한 인격을 형성하기 위해서 시, 소설, 신화 그리고 여타의 창작 문학 작품들을 읽을 수 있는 과목들을 반드시 택하도록 해야 한다. [ART와 연계된 토픽]

58 Learning is primarily a matter of personal discipline; students cannot be motivated by school or college alone.
배움은 근본적으로 개인적 과제이다. 그러므로 학생은 단지 학교나 대학에서만 동기를 부여받을 수는 없다.

68 Some people believe that the purpose of education is to free the mind and the spirit. Others believe that formal education tends to restrain our minds and spirits rather than set them free. [17]
어떤 사람들은 교육의 목적이 마음과 영혼을 자유롭게 하는 데 있다고 믿는다. 다른 사람들은 공교육이 우리들의 마음과 영혼을 자유롭게 하기보다는 억누른다고 믿는다. [VALUE와 연계]

Education

73 Colleges and universities should require all faculty to spend time working outside the academic world in professions relevant to the courses they teach.
대학은 모든 교수들이 의무적으로 자신이 가르치는 전공 분야 외에서도 연구를 하도록 해야 한다.

81 All parents should be required to volunteer time to their children's schools. [95]
모든 학부모들은 자신의 아이들의 학교에서 의무적으로 자원봉사를 해야만 한다.

82 Colleges and universities should require their students to spend at least one semester studying in a foreign country. [97/100/124]
대학은 학생들이 의무적으로 적어도 한 학기는 다른 나라에서 공부를 하도록 해야 한다.

83 Teachers'salaries should be based on the academic performance of their students. [30]
교사들의 월급은 그들이 가르친 학생들의 학업성취도에 근거를 두어야 한다.

92 Educators should base their assessment of students' learning not on students' grasp of facts but on the ability to explain the ideas, trends, and concepts that those facts illustrate.
교육자들은 학생들의 사실 파악 능력이 아니라 그 사실이 설명하고 있는 아이디어, 경향, 개념을 설명할 수 있는 능력으로 학생들의 성취도를 평가해야 한다.

98 Educational institutions should actively encourage their students to choose fields of study in which jobs are plentiful. [136]
교육기관들은 그 학생들이 직업이 풍부한 전공 분야를 선택하도록 적극 권장해야 한다.

101 Although innovations such as video, computers, and the Internet seem to offer schools improved methods for instructing students, these technologies all too often distract from real learning.
비디오, 컴퓨터, 인터넷 같은 발명들이 학교가 학생들을 지도하는 데 발전된 방법들을 제공하는 것처럼 보이지만 이러한 기술들은 모두 언제나 진정한 배움에 방해가 된다.
[TECHNOLOGY와 연계된 토픽]

138 Some people believe that competition for high grades motivates students to excel in the classroom. Others believe that such competition seriously limits the quality of real learning. [45]
어떤 사람들은 높은 학점을 받기 위한 경쟁은 학생들이 수업에서 최선을 다 하도록 동기를 부여한다고 믿는다. 다른 사람들은 그러한 경쟁은 진정한 배움의 질을 저해한다고 믿는다.

142 Claim : Colleges and universities should specify all required courses and eliminate elective courses in order to provide clear guidance for students.
주장: 대학원 학생들에게 좀 더 구체적인 지도를 하기 위해서는 모든 필수과목을 특화하고 선택과목들은 없애야 한다.
Reason : College students — like people in general — prefer to follow directions rather than make their own decisions.
이유: 대학생들은 — 일반 대중처럼 — 스스로 결정하는 것보다는 지침을 따르는 것을 선호한다.

Sample essay

3   Educational institutions have a responsibility to dissuade students from pursuing fields of study in which they are unlikely to succeed.
교육기관들은 학생들이 성공하지 못할 것 같은 연구 분야 공부를 추구하는 것을 막아야 하는 책임이 있다.
Write a response in which you discuss the extent to which you agree or disagree with the claim. In developing and supporting your position, be sure to address the most compelling reasons and/or examples that could be used to challenge your position.

강의노트   3번 토픽은 교육이 직업교육을 강조해야 하는가라는 것을 묻는 질문이다. 이 토픽을 읽고 Occupational education vs. exploration of individual talents or interests라는 대조 개념으로 작성한다. Disagree 방향이다.

The speaker contends that educational institutions have a responsibility to dissuade students from pursuing the field of study in which they are unlikely to succeed. Some may think educational institutions should provide a variety of courses in which students can explore their interests and talents. However, college programs should be designed in ways to train students to be productive workers in their respective fields of study. Although college is mainly for occupational education, I disagree with the speaker because it should be students themselves who have to decide to drop out from a course or program in which they are unlikely to succeed, not professors or the department office.

Many professors in engineering schools think they have to train students to be productive engineers, so they are obliged to help students find a job in a large organization or research institute upon graduation. Although they need to evaluate their student's academic performances, the decision whether the students transfer to another major or program in consideration of their possible failure in obtaining an engineering job should leave to individual students. Colleges can give some advice to students whose academic performances barely meet the criteria. Even so, they are not supposed to discourage them.

College students are mature enough to make their career decisions. For example, being a college dropout, Steve Jobs emphasized the importance in focusing more on exploring one's interests instead of following the established curricula. He also mentioned students should study the subjects they are passionate about. In other words, it should be the students who have to decide whether they fulfill the requirements for the degree in their respective fields of study.

In addition, universities measure students' capabilities or performances with tests. But tests sometimes fail to reflect one's potential for career success. The episode about Steve Jobs tells us that English and calligraphy courses helped him to become an innovative CEO. College education should be considered the platform on which students develop knowledge and skills, but not the final step to one's career success.

In short, career decisions should be left to individual students' decisions, not to an educational institution. Professors should not prevent students from pursuing their career goals and give them sufficient time for their academic progress. [379]

---

6   A nation should require all of its students to study the same national curriculum until they enter college.
국가는 모든 학생들이 대학에 들어가기 전까지는 동일한 국정 교과과정으로 공부할 수 있도록 이를 의무화해야 한다.
Write a response in which you discuss the extent to which you agree or disagree with the recommendation and explain your reasoning for the position you take. In developing and supporting your position, describe specific circumstances in which adopting the recommendation would or would not be advantageous and explain how these examples shape your position.

강의노트   6번도 national curriculum vs. local curriculum이라는 대조 개념을 파악해야 한다. local community 산업이나 문화적 특성에 따라서 curriculum은 수정되는 것이 합리적이다. 3번 에세이와 비슷한 포인트는 직업교육의 중요성을 포함하고 있다는 점이다. 이 토픽은 고등학교를 예증으로 선택한다.

The speaker emphasizes the importance of the national curriculum in secondary education unduly. Few would deny the benefits of a national curriculum. The national curriculum nurtures students with the basic knowledge related to develop common sense. However, I disagree that the same national curriculum should be the graduation requirement for secondary school because a variety of courses reflecting the characters of a local community would better serve the purpose of education. Local high schools can educate students to become skillful workers and generous community members.

Of course, the national curriculum in secondary schools are designed to train students to become productive workers. Students learn basic yet broad academic knowledge and skills so they can advance to a college education, and a core curriculum encourage students to recognize the value of citizenship. Almost all public high schools require students to take a US history course to learn good citizenship by deepening their understanding of national values and the social norm.

In addition, the national curriculum would disserve its local industries and the nation. For example, many secondary schools in Silicon Valley modify their curriculum to meet the needs of their local computer industry, while those in Las Vegas provide courses related to serendipity business to serve their local tourism business. Schools should support the local industry by training students to fit into appropriate jobs upon graduation. In short, the local high school curriculum should reflect the characteristics to supply a skillful workforce to local industries and businesses.

Moreover a modified curriculum should reflect the students' cultural identities. By learning their history they can build positive identities. A compelling example is the secondary schools in China Town in San Francisco City. High schools in the area provide not only US History courses but also Chinese History courses so local students can develop a positive image of their self-identity as Chinese descendants. They also celebrate Chinese holidays along with other national holidays. On the other hand, high schools near the University of Southern California offer a variety of music and art courses to discover young artists in the region. These examples show that the Department of Education should allow local high schools to modify their curricula to educate students to become healthy and dynamic individuals instead of imposing the values of conformity through the national curriculum.

In short, implementing the national curriculum without considering the characteristics of a local community is detrimental to increasing national productivity. Educating all students with the same curriculum instead of a modified curriculum will lead to a divided society where a third choice cannot be an option. Thus, I disagree with the statement that a nation should impose a "one size fits all" education on all its students. [447 words]

---

20   Some people believe that college students should consider only their own talents and interests when choosing a field of study. Others believe that college students should base their choice of a field of study on the availability of jobs in that field.
어떤 사람들은 대학생들이 자신의 재능과 관심을 고려해서 전공 분야를 선택해야 한다고 생각한다. 다른 사람들은 고용의 기회를 선택 기준으로 삼아야 한다고 한다.
Write a response in which you discuss which view more closely aligns with your own position and explain your reasoning for the position you take. In developing and supporting your position, you should address both of the views presented.

강의노트 대조되는 key 단어는 students' talents and interests 와 the availability of jobs이며 위의 3번 에세이와 유사한 예증을 활용할 수 있다. 다만 20번은 대학생은 직업을 얻게 위한 것임을 강조한다.

While some people think college students should explore their talents and interests by taking courses, others say students should be trained to find a job. In my view, college students should declare their major in consideration of employment opportunities. A large number of graduates from engineering schools and business schools best support my opinion.

Of course, some college students are interested in exploring their talents in art. They practice painting or playing instruments in college years to express or articulate their imagination or ideas while seeking the greater good of humanity instead of high-salary jobs. In this sense, we cannot say that college education should be designed to train students to meet the needs of local industries or businesses.

However, most students are eager to have their diplomas to have a well-paying job upon graduation. The number of students studying computer engineering and material engineering, which is bigger than that of art and history majors, is the evidence showing why students receive occupational training in college. Engineers will work together to operate, maintain and develop the systems of industries, hospitals, banks, or research organizations. As our society needs professionals such as engineers, mechanics, and analysts, students should tale the courses required to train them to obtain specific skills. If colleges fail to educate students to meet the need in the field of engineering engineers, the entire industry would suffer from a lack of professional employees. In short, the number of jobs available on the job market affects college student' choices of a field of study.

As the global market has rapidly grown along with technological development, obtaining a business administration degree has become more popular than before. College students who took a series of courses related to accounting and finance as well as statistics in business school, have a better chance to have a high-salary job than those who studied liberal arts. Like this business schools contribute to producing financial specialists and analysts to meet the need in the finance market.

In conclusion, the primary goal of a college education is to train students to be

Education

productive workers to meet the needs of the communities or industries. From the individual student's perspective, being financially independent to support themselves and their families can be the most important reason for them to pursue a college diploma. Most students are prone to choose a field of study that is more likely to allow them to obtain a job with a decent annual income. [415]

---

29   The best way to teach — whether as an educator, employer, or parent— is to praise positive actions and ignore negative ones.
교육의 최상의 방법은 가르치는 사람이 누구 ― 교육자이든, 고용주이든, 부모이든 ― 든 간에 긍정적 행위는 칭찬하고 부정적 행위는 아는 척하지 말아야 한다는 것이다.
Write a response in which you discuss the extent to which you agree or disagree with the statement and explain your reasoning for the position you take. In developing and supporting your position, you should consider ways in which the statement might or might not hold true and explain how these considerations shape your position.

강의노트   29번은 훈육 방법에 관한 에세이다. 미국 교육 제도는 체벌은 범죄 행위로 간주한다. 떠드는 학생들은 교실 문 밖에 약 5분 정도 세워두거나 detention room(훈육실)로 보내 기회를 박탈하는 방식으로 잘못된 행동에 따라서 어떤 대가를 치르게 한다.

"Spare the rod or spoil your children!" This rule was common in schools in the past, but today corporal punishment has been banned from most schools as educators recognize its harmful effects on the development of psychology. Once we understand physical punishment can model aggressive behavior creating a violent environment, today's teachers tend to pay more attention to praising positive actions than before. Then, what should we do to discipline today's disrespectful youth when necessary spanking is not allowed?

Although praising positive action is an effective way to encourage those without behavioral problems, it is less likely to correct those with misbehaviors. Unless students understand the consequences that they will encounter because of their unruly behaviors, they may keep doing the same misconduct. To provide a safe and pleasant learning environment to all students, schools usually set up conduct rules and impose punishment accordingly to the degree of negative behavior when a student brings about troubles on campus. Thus, I disagree with the speaker. Instead of ignoring students' negative actions, disciplinary actions should be taken by taking away their privileges rather than corporal punishment.

Admittedly, domestic education requires children to be well-disciplined by restraining their negative actions. Parents ignoring their children's unruly behaviors is detrimental to developing a sense of moral accountability. When a child uses a fist to take a toy from his younger brother or sister, parents should discipline them by taking it away from that child and making him grounded for a while. To make them understand the consequences they will encounter, parents should explain why forcefully taking their brother's toy is improper. In this way, parents should prevent another possible violent behavior against younger siblings. By scolding negative behaviors instead of neglecting them, parents can educate their children better to grow to be mature citizens.

When it comes to company, self-disciplinary behaviors are closely related to its productivity and profits. Imagine your boss ignores an affirmative duty to disclose sexual harassment claims and resolve the problem under the table. If so, it will create an unpleasant and insecure working environment. Low employee morale is a silent killer of workplace productivity and performance. What is more, low employee morale is contagious.

In sum, regardless of a company, school, or home, negative behavior should be punished accordingly. Children should learn behavior codes for socializing, and it contributes to building their moral senses. Otherwise, the entire society has to pay a lot more cost necessary to promote social well-being. [418]

Lecture 2
Education

37   Society should identify those children who have special talents and provide training for them at an early age to develop their talents.

사회는 특별한 재능을 가진 아이들을 발굴해서 그들이 조기에 재능을 개발할 수 있도록 훈련시켜야 한다.

Write a response in which you discuss the extent to which you agree or disagree with the recommendation and explain your reasoning for the position you take. In developing and supporting your position, describe specific circumstances in which adopting the recommendation would or would not be advantageous and explain how these examples shape your position.

강의노트   37번 또한 3, 6, 20번과 같은 맥락의 토픽이다. 유의해야 할 표현은 at an early age라는 어구이다. 예체능 과목에 재주가 있는 학생들은 어린 시절부터 그 재주를 발견하고 교육해야 하나 대다수 일반 과목 교육은 재주가 있는가를 아는 것도 중학교나 고등학교 정도가 되어야 알 수 있다는 점을 생각하고 에세이 논지를 발전시킨다.

Should society train children with talents to improve their skills and abilities? Some may think that whether gifted children become world-class stars in their respective fields of profession or not depends on their parents' support. However, I agree that society should support gift children's training because the entire human race can benefit from their extraordinary abilities. Some public schools provide magnet programs to find and train high-achievement students at an early age.

Gifted children are eager to learn and show passion for reading, writing, and numbers. To make a better society, schools and communities should strive to support them to develop their potential to the fullest extent, not lose valuable human resources in the future.

Some educators think of acceleration as an all-or-nothing proposition in which some little socially awkward kid skips grades and goes to school in a den of big kids, and misses everything of childhood. For this reason, public schools provide magnet programs to train brilliant students to fully develop their capabilities considering the psychological difficulties that gifted children might go through in school.

To support prodigies in poverty, many teachers sometimes collaborate with social workers. For example, Khadijah Williams could finally find a home at Harvard University. Although she was a homeless child, she continued to develop her voice for the disadvantaged through the public school system.

Intensive training in music and sports begins when children are as little as four or five years old. Some prodigy musicians started playing an instrument as little as three years old. For example, a famous violinist, Sarah Chang, began playing songs with a quarter size violin when she was only three years old, and she was lucky to have a violinist father and composer mother.

Public schools should provide special programs in which dancing, painting, singing, acting, and photography classes are all on the menu for children nationwide. To ensure equal educational opportunities, schools and communities should participate in discovering and training gifted children at an early age.

While gifted children enhance their knowledge and skills, they can have feelings of accomplishment society can benefit from their legendary work; as a result, they contribute to humanity's progress, let alone boost national pride and the economy. Thus, we should discover and support talented children to develop their potential to the extent that others can benefit from their talents. [392]

42　　Students should always question what they are taught instead of accepting it passively.
　　　학생들은 자신들이 배운 것에 대해 수동적으로 받아들이기보다는 항상 의문을 가져야 한다.
　　　Write a response in which you discuss the extent to which you agree or disagree with the statement and explain your reasoning for the position you take. In developing and supporting your position, you should consider ways in which the statement might or might not hold true and explain how these considerations shape your position.

Lecture 2
Education

강의노트 42번 이슈는 partially agree 방향으로 앞에 쓴 42번 에세이와 방향이 반대로 쓰여 있다. 여기서도 빈도 부사 always를 중심으로 논리를 틀어야 한다. 의구심을 같은 사람만이 세상을 바꾸는 일을 했다는 사실을 이유로 thesis 문장을 쓸 때 세상을 바꾼 방법 2가지에 대해서 과학적 발명과 사회적 혁신이라는 2가지 세부 이유를 바탕으로 쓰는 것이 바람직하다.

Should students always question what they are taught instead of accepting it passively? Confucian virtue teaches that learning passively is common, so students should show their loyalty to great teachers. However, I agree with the speaker because the progress of humanity and science has been possible with the contributions of those who dared to question the existing authority and prevailing ideas. Leading voices came from those who refused to accept conventional ideas with blind credulity in all areas of human endeavor. Thus, teachers should encourage students' questions but not always.

In the past constant questions about what they are taught were considered a challenge to the teachers' authority. Such behaviors are not still tolerated in some schools today since they may deter others' learning. Particularly in a public education setting, where the ratio between teachers and students is high, persistently raising questions about what students are taught is improper. In contrast, those who possibly learn by memorizing all the contents without too many questions tend to receive higher grades.

Nevertheless, skepticism has been the propelling power for discoveries and innovation. For example, "Revolutions on the Celestial Bodies"was published by Nicolas Copernicus' students. Had it not been for their courage to disagree with the Geocentric theory, the progress of science could have been much delayed. Without questioning the Geocentric Theory of the leading scholar group of Ptolemy at that time, Copernicus might not shed light on Heliocentric Theory. Revolutionary ideas came from those who dared to accept what they were taught.

Furthermore, social reform was made by those who questioned what they learned in schools. For instance, Martin Luther King Jr's rejection of the Segregation Laws, which were predominant in the 1950s of American society, paved the way for the Civil Rights Movement. By questioning the fairness and relevance of the laws in the early 1950s, he appealed to the public running the Civil Rights Movement, which led to the abolition of Segregation Laws. Thus, students should be encouraged to question the fallacious assumptions hidden in the textbooks.

Once, Wilson Mizner said, "I respect faith but doubt is what gets you an education". To educate students to be another innovator or reformers, they should be encouraged to ask questions to teachers instead of blindly accepting whatever they are learning. [40]

---

68   Some people believe that the purpose of education is to free the mind and the spirit. Others believe that formal education tends to restrain our minds and spirits rather than set them free. 어떤 사람들은 교육의 목적이 마음과 영혼을 자유롭게 하는 데 있다고 믿는다. 다른 사람들은 공교육이 우리들의 마음과 영혼을 자유롭게 하기보다는 억누른다고 믿는다.
Write a response in which you discuss which view more closely aligns with your own position and explain your reasoning for the position you take. In developing and supporting you position, you should address both of the views presented.

강의노트   12번과 동일한 예증으로 68번을 작성했다. 이는 독자들이 동일한 예증으로 다른 에세이를 쓸 때 어떤 점이 달라지는지를 보이기 위해서 작성했다. Related sentence를 유의 깊게 비교 대조해 보면 좀 더 논리적으로 아이디어를 mapping하는 법을 연습할 수 있다.

Does formal education tend to restrain our minds and spirits rather than set them free? Some may say that public education contributes to reducing prejudice and discrimination. However, formal education shaped young minds in a way preferable to the few in power. Thus, I agree with the statement.

Lecture 2
Education

History tells us that wealth and power inherit over generations through public education. History textbooks tend to fetter our minds and spirits by indoctrinating a certain ideal preferable to the few in power. Confucian virtues and the pride of the homogeneous race of Han perpetuate students in the public school system so they could sustain their life within the boundaries set up by the status quo.

A striking example of using education as a tool of idolization is in North Korean public education system. It employs Juche Ideology that emphasizes independence. This political principle justifies the Iron Gate policy that made the military dictatorship of the Kim family possible. Public education has been an effective tool for indoctrination in North Korea's education system.

When it comes to South Korea's public education, few would doubt that it encourages young students to have free minds so they can and will challenge the status quo. However, when closely examining history textbooks, we can find the intention hidden in the texts to produce citizens who are submissive and loyal to their nation or society. Confucian virtues taught in school have played a pivotal role in maintaining the norm of patriarchy. The fact that only two heroines appear in the textbook, Shinsaimdang and Yoo Gwan-shun clearly shows gender discrimination. Without acknowledging women's contributions to the progress of Korea in the past, whoever learned with the current Korean history textbooks would tarnish their spirits with gender discrimination.

Another bias deeply rooted in young students' minds is the national pride of being a homogeneous race. Koreans learn to have pride in the Han race to boost nationalism. They overlook the importance of diversity; instead, they foster prejudice against other people by promoting hostile feelings toward non-Koreans. This shows that the rigid ethnocentricity imposed on South Korea's public education fettered students' minds with nationalism rather than liberating them.

In short, the above examples of gender discrimination and nationalism weaved in the Korean history textbook show public education has fettered young minds instead of freeing them. Thus, I disagree with the given statement. [402]

73　Colleges and universities require all faculty to spend time working outside the academic world in professions relevant to the courses they teach.
대학은 모든 교수들이 의무적으로 자신이 가르치는 전공 분야 외에서도 연구를 하도록 해야 한다.
Write a response in which you discuss your views on the policy and explain your reasoning for the position you take. In developing and supporting your position, you should consider the possible consequences of implementing the policy and explain how these consequences shape your position.

강의노트　73번은 위의 교육 정책의 결과에 대해서 논하라는 점을 이해하고 글을 써야 한다. 'require'라는 동사는 all policy, 즉 impartial policy이기 때문에 반대 방향으로 쓴다. 미술이나 문학을 가르치는 교수와 대조해야 한다. 공과대학 교수나 경영학과 adjunct 교수가 아닌 경우에는 기업에서 일할 필요는 없다.

The answer to the question as to whether colleges and universities require all faculty to affiliate with an organization related to their job field outside of school can be varied depending on the characteristics of the field of study. Although there are adjunct professors in engineering schools, many full-time professors focus on teaching students the professional knowledge and skills necessary to work in the industry upon graduation. Moreover, professors help students conduct to advance their research in their labs on campus.

Let us examine how the English Department train students to become teachers or journalists. Of course, Journalism major students can benefit from a Communication and Journalism internship to have real-life experience in newsrooms, TV stations, or Internet companies.

Lecture 2
Education

On the other hand, professors in the English Literature or Linguistics Department should spend more time discussing how to develop and refine their new ideas and expressions in literature writing. Some students are eager to master writing skills to become a writer. Although the author of "Jungle", Upton Sinclair worked as a disguised worker in the meat industry to find out the wrong-doings of the managers or owners, requiring professors in humanity to work in the field would rather deprive their time; otherwise, they could spend more time to show how to write books for publication. In Theoretical Linguistics professors should focus more on teaching how to analyze texts to find grammar rules in the surface sentence structure by understanding of the logic in the deep structure instead of wasting time working in the newspaper company.

Today, the importance of academic training has been overshadowed by occupational training. For this reason, there has been a great misconception that the goal of a college education is solely for having well-paying jobs. And adding the lines of field experiences on the resume has been considered more important than anything else. However in college years, students should focus on intellectual growth without worrying too much about their financial success. [400]

---

82   Colleges and universities should require their students to spend at least one semester studying in a foreign country.
대학은 학생들이 의무적으로 적어도 한 학기는 다른 나라에서 공부를 하도록 해야 한다.
Write a response in which you discuss the extent to which you agree or disagree with the recommendation and explain your reasoning for the position you take. In developing and supporting your position, describe specific circumstances in which adopting the recommendation would or would not be advantageous and explain how these examples shape your position.

강의노트   all과 같은 빈도부사는 없으나 동사에서 should require이란 뜻은 거의 의무적이라고 해석해야 한다. 그럼으로 경제적으로 어려운 학생이나 외국에 가지 않아도 할 수 있는 전공을 수학하고자 하는 학생들은 제외되어야 한다고 에세이를 발전시키는 것이 바람직하다.

Due to globalization, many colleges and universities have provided study abroad programs to encourage students to avoid developing a myopic view in understanding international affairs, diverse cultures, and languages. Although students should spend at least one semester studying in a foreign country, making it a mandatory requirement for graduation should be carefully reviewed in that this policy can substantially accrue the expense of college education that is already too high to be affordable. Moreover, the speaker overlooks alternative ways in which students can deepen their understanding of others' cultures and languages without physically traveling to the country of their interests.

Admittedly, it would be great if all college students could spend a semester in a foreign country through study abroad programs. Those in international studies would benefit a lot from the policy. In many cases, students can learn English more effectively when they live in English-speaking countries.

However, this requirement may create an unfair educational environment that would prevent poor students from receiving college diplomas. For example, the fee for taking three credit units in colleges in the United Kingdom is much higher than taking the same amount of credits from local universities or colleges. Due to the difference in the two nations' educational costs, if some students have to do extra work to pay for the study abroad program, they have to do more work to meet the qualification required for a BA diploma. Thus, the mandatory policy of studying in a university in a foreign country is more likely to be an extra burden to the students who cannot afford a studying abroad program. And it leads to widening the gap between those who have and those who have not.

Furthermore, the policy requiring spending at least one semester in another country underestimates the ability to learn through indirect experiences such as reading and writing. Although directly experiencing what we have learned is effective for advancing one's knowledge, there are plenty of cases in which students can obtain specific skills by reading books or exploring the Internet. Moreover, today students can learn about foreign cultures and their languages by visiting various websites. Without attending a foreign college, students can have a somewhat similar or better understanding of different cultures and languages; therefore, it is unreasonable to require all students to spend time in a foreign country. In short, a mandatory policy often leads to impartial education.

College education should ensure equal opportunities with those from the socio-economically disadvantaged class. Any policy likely to create an unfair learning environment should be banned. [400]

---

92 Educators should base their assessment of students' learning not on students' grasp of facts but on the ability to explain the ideas, trends, and concepts that those facts illustrate.
교육자들은 학생들의 사실 파악 능력이 아니라 그 사실이 설명하고 있는 아이디어, 경향, 개념을 설명할 수 있는 능력으로 학생들의 성취도를 평가해야 한다.
Write a response in which you discuss the extent to which you agree or disagree with the recommendation and explain your reasoning for the position you take. In developing and supporting your position, describe specific circumstances in which adopting the recommendation would or would not be advantageous and explain how these examples shape your position.

강의노트 이 토픽은 객관식 시험보다는 주관식 시험을 잘 볼 수 있도록 학생들 가르쳐야 하는 것을 질문한다. 어느 정도는 객관식 시험으로 학생들의 지식의 수준을 확인할 수 있다. 하지만 주관식, 즉 에세이 시험에서 학생들은 자신이 새롭게 지식을 integrate할 수 있는 능력을 기를 수 있기 때문에 개념 파악을 중시하는 것이 중요하다는 식으로 글을 쓰는 것이 중요하다.

There has been great concern about which method would be the most appropriate to evaluate students' academic performance. Although mechanical memorization can accelerate students' learning, they would accomplish little toward developing research abilities and ideas. Reading comprehension or vocabulary tests are important to a certain degree to measure students' abilities to develop their ideas, but writing essays are more appropriate to assess students' creatively and their actual ability to convince others. Thus, I agree with the speaker.

Of course, it would take more time to figure out the main ideas, concepts, or trends without memorizing historical events. Korean history teachers use chanting to memorize the years and names of the kings in reign in a dynasty so students can develop a better picture of the sequence of historical events. Similarly, high school students drill to memorize a new list of vocabulary everyday week to develop writing skills.

Nonetheless, effective learning happens when students understand details or facts illustrated to support the main ideas. For example, by simply checking whether the students understood many pieces of detailed information like the name of the literacy group of writers, it is inappropriate to evaluate how much and how well students learned it. To better assess students' understanding of the core concepts and main ideas or inferences, essay writing tests are more effective than multiple-choice tests.

Without understanding the concepts of chemical changes, students could experience difficulty in solving problems in chemical coordination and integration. Instead of rote memorization of the names of chemical elements, if students understand the essence of chemical traits of chemical elements and their reaction to other chemicals, they can better understand the processes of chemical changes. To assess their students' learning progress, teachers should test their ability to explain why and how some chemical reactions do not work.

The GRE verbal section tests consist of reading, sentence completion tests, and writing tests. The benefit of multiple questions is that evaluators can save time in measuring how much their students have made progress in learning. However, students can better address their opinions and ideas by writing essays in which they can utilize what they have learned creatively. [397]

---

138   Some people believe that competition for high grades motivate students to excel in the classroom. Others believe that such competition seriously limits the quality of real learning.
어떤 사람들은 높은 학점을 받기 위한 경쟁은 학생들이 수업에서 최선을 다 하도록 동기를 부여한다고 믿는다. 다른 사람들은 그러한 경쟁은 진정한 배움의 질을 저해한다고 믿는다.
Write a response in which you discuss which view more closely aligns with your own position and explain your reasoning for the position you take. In developing and supporting your position, you should address both of the views presented.

강의노트   교육은 학생들에게 협동과 경쟁의 가치를 밸런스에 맞도록 가르치는 것이라고 해야 한다. 그런 의미로 본다면 학점은 과열 경쟁만 되지 않는다고 하면 분명 스스로의 발전을 확인할 수 있는 도구로서 자신의 발전을 도모하는 긍정적인 경쟁의식, 즉 동기 부여가 될 수 있다. 여러 상황에서 경쟁과 협동의 가치가 우리 사회에 미치는 긍정적 부정적 영향을 묻는다.

Although few colleges or universities adopt the "Pass or Non-pass" grading system, most high schools adopt a letter grade system to measure their students' performance. The most crucial reason students are eager for high grades is the college admission decisions that mainly rely on As and Bs. Many teachers assume that competition is more likely to motivate students to excel in the classroom; however, in my view, schools should endeavor to provide a less competitive educational environment where the quality of real learning can be of more concern.

As the administration of public schools has become systemized, students' evaluation methods have become standardized; as a result, students came to line up by their academic abilities from the highest grade A to the lowest grade F. However, this competitive method of assessing young students' progress in learning has brought out more problems than the old education system, in which slow learners were not considered special children.

Although a grading system is necessary to evaluate students' performances, it rather prevents students from advancing learning at their own pace. According to the Ministry of Education, academic stress resulted in an increase in the number of high school dropouts. This example shows that the current grading system negatively affects the healthy development of the "self"; therefore, administrators and teachers should provide an alternative method to measure students' performance instead of a numeric or alphabetic evaluation.

Top students contributed to the progress of science or social changes less than those who concentrated on working on imagination or ideas. Albert Einstein's anecdote best illustrates that competition is little to do with fostering creativity in young students' minds. The 7-year-old Thomas Edison was not a good fit for the school system so the teacher sent his parents a recommendation letter of expulsion. This clearly shows that the public school system fails to recognize prodigies. Interestingly, what motivates students to learn is not a competition to win over others but the self-motivation to learn together in a safe and inclusive environment. Students should have sufficient time to explore their interests instead of making them frustrated with grades.

In short, I disagree that real learning can be motivated by competition for high grade. The quality of education will increase when more discussions or readings are encouraged in the class instead of many quizzes or ongoing tests to evaluate how much they have learned. Moreover, the school system should support self-motivated students by providing various programs that reflect their talents and interests. [489]

Technology

Technology Topic Analysis

Technology 유형은 Media와 연계되어서 쓸 수 있는 토픽이다, 왜냐하면 Technology 토픽은 Communication technology를 예증으로 써야 하기 때문이다. Technology 토픽은 예증을 반드시 지난 세기에 발전한 기술로 쓰도록 한다. Transportation technology와 Communication technology가 이 2가지 기술을 뜻하는 자동차, 비행기, TV, 컴퓨터 등이 예증이 돼야 한다.

기본적으로 기술의 발전에 인간의 삶을 안락하게 했는가, 아니면 나약한 인간을 만들게 했는가 등의 질문, 즉 기술이 사회에 끼치는 긍정적인 영향과 부정적인 결과에 대해서 생각을 정리하고 써야 한다. 작은 개념에서 본다면 물론 해를 끼친 점도 많다. 그러나 기술의 발전은 인간의 창의적 정신의 결실이며 문제 해결을 위한 노력의 대가라고 해야 한다. 여기에서도 빈도 부사에 따라서 반대나 찬성 방향이 달라질 수 있다.

급속도로 성장하는 기술은 소수 약자의 사회참여 기회를 제공하여 민주화에 기여했으나 기술의 폐해로는 컴퓨터 중독이나 환경문제 등이 야기되었다.

Quotation:

"The spectacular improvements in our lives over the past century have not come without cost."

"Technology is dominated by two different types of people: those who do understand what they do not manage and those who do manage what they do not understand." — Putt's Law

"The chief obstacle of human race is the human race on Marquis."

Lecture 3
Technology

1   As people rely more on technology to solve problems, the ability of humans to think for themselves will surely deteriorate.
사람들은 문제를 해결하기 위해 점점 테크놀로지에 의존하기 때문에 스스로 생각하는 인간의 능력은 분명히 파괴될 것이다.

26   The luxuries and conveniences of contemporary life prevent people from developing into truly strong and independent individuals.
현대 생활의 호사성과 편리성은 강하고 독립적인 개인으로 성장하는 것을 저해한다.

43   The increasingly rapid pace of life today causes more problems than it solves.
급속도로 빠른 현대 생활은 더 많은 문제를 해결하기보다는 더 많은 문제를 만든다.

64   The human mind will always be superior to machines because machines are only tools of human minds.
인간의 정신은 기계보다 우수하다. 기계는 단지 인간이 사용하는 도구이기 때문이다.

91   The primary goal of technological advancement should be to increase people's efficiency so that they have more leisure time.
기술발전의 목적은 사람들의 효율성을 증대시켜 더 많은 여가 시간을 갖게 하는 데 있다.

101   Although innovations such as video, computers, and the Internet seem to offer schools improved methods for instructing students, these technologies all too often distract from real learning.
비디오, 컴퓨터, 인터넷 같은 발명들이 학교가 학생들을 지도하는 데 발전된 방법들을 제공하는 것처럼 보이지만 이러한 기술들은 모두 언제나 진정한 배움에 방해가 된다.

132   Some people believe that our ever-increasing use of technology significantly reduces our opportunities for human interaction. Other people believe that technology provides us with new and better ways to communicate and connect with one another.
어떤 사람들은 점점 증가하는 기술의 사용이 새로운 상호 인간관계를 만들 기회를 현저하게 줄여준다고 믿는다. 다른 사람들은 기술이 새롭고 더 나은 소통과 관계를 서로에게 가져다준다고 믿는다.

Sample essay

1   As people rely more and more on technology to solve problems, the ability of humans to think for themselves will surely deteriorate.
사람들은 문제를 해결하기 위해 점점 테크놀로지에 의존하기 때문에 스스로 생각하는 인간의 능력은 분명히 파괴될 것이다.
Write a response in which you discuss the extent to which you agree or disagree with the statement and explain your reasoning for the position you take. In developing and supporting your position, you should consider ways in which the statement might or might not hold true

and explain how these considerations shape your position.

Despite the spectacular advancement of technology, I disagree that the ability of humans to think for themselves will surely deteriorate. Today our organizations, economies, and societies get better results by being more data-driven. Even so, the ability of machines will not surely supersede that of humans because human intuition contributes to providing creative solutions to mechanical problems. The examples of a CEO's decision-making process and a writer's creative writing skills best support my stance.

Admittedly, when it comes to speedy processing, humans cannot compete with machines that process an enormous amount of data in a relatively short time. Speedy data analysis helps CEOs save time to plan and carry out projects, thus increasing profits. Autocorrect typing makes writers free from typos or grammar mistakes. As such, algorithms may assist humans to process a large amount of data and to reduce grammar and mechanics errors.

However, it is the person who should be center stage, not the machine, helping and advising in the line of business understanding of what data means and how to use it. Other than simply reading the results from the data, the top management of a business should decide how its organization will go through the wrenching changes needed to make better ones. For example, IBM or Apple make their business decisions based on an expert's judgment instead of solely relying on the results driven by the software. This clearly shows that machines are merely an assistant to humans, and therefore we

Technology

cannot say that humans will lose their intuitive and creative minds at the cost of adopting technology in business.

Another compelling example that shows human's superiority to machines is creative writing. Grammarly Tools developed by Google can prevent writers from minor mistakes through auto-correction tools; however, it is less likely to create stories as much innovative as human writers. While AI writing helps human writers to some degree, it is far from perfect, so AI writers superior to professional writers are an unlikely imagination.

In short, although some asserts AI technology sails perilously close to a situation where algorithm machines always seem better than humans who cannot avoid making clumsy mistakes, I disagree that machines will perform better than the humans, who invent them for their convenience. [359]

---

26   The luxuries and conveniences of contemporary life prevent people from developing into truly strong and independent individuals.
현대 생활의 호사성과 편리성은 강하고 독립적인 개인으로 성장하는 것을 저해한다.
Write a response in which you discuss the extent to which you agree or disagree with the statement and explain your reasoning for the position you take. In developing and supporting your position, you should consider ways in which the statement might or might not hold true and explain how these considerations shape your position.

강의노트   토픽은 technology의 발전으로 인한 호사스러운 생활로 현대인이 더 유약한 사람으로 변화했느냐는 것을 묻는다. 예증으로는 transportation technology 중 하나인 자동차나 비행기의 발명이나 communication technology의 하나인 컴퓨터, cellular phone으로 글을 써야 한다. 이러한 속뜻을 알고서 이 토픽을 써야만 고득점이 가능하다.

Today we no longer need to ride a horse to travel over the Silk Road to reach the far west tip of Europe. Such convenience can be credited to the turbo engine of luxurious automobiles that made a group of travelers move around conveniently and more safely to their destination. Another remarkable innovation of communication technology contributed to extending women's social boundary to be equal to men's. In my view, these two technologies innovated in the past century, indeed, helped people to be stronger and more independent individuals, and therefore I agree with the speaker.

While driving habits made us exercise less to the extent of having feeble muscles, the lazy mind relying on the ability of fast and accurate mechanical calculation of computers prevents us from critical thinking skills. Although some problems occur due to the misuse of technology, it contributed to help women overcome their physical weakness and thus reduce gender discrimination.

Modern-day people navigate over the sky with airplanes. Ever since Write Brothers maneuver airplanes to quickly land across the oceans, human's exploration of space has developed to the extent to venture the Moon and Mars. So we cannot say today's astronauts are weaker than boat padders.

In the past, women were bounded by housekeeping jobs, and but today they are equal to men in terms of social opportunity. For example, the first astronaut who traveled to space as a Korean is a woman scientist, Kim So-yeon. This fact clearly shows that modern technology contributed to accomplishing gender equality. As a result, today's women became more responsible for social change than before.

As having seen in the above, today's people are much stronger and more independent in light of their minds or abilities. Today's technology plays a pivotal role in fostering more independent individuals and democratic citizens. [350]

Technology

43   "The increasingly rapid pace of life today causes more problems than it solves."
급속도로 빠른 현대 생활은 더 많은 문제를 해결하기보다는 더 많은 문제를 만든다.

Even though technology helps us to enjoy conveniences and comforts by saving time and effort, the issue of whether the increasingly rapid pace of life has been helpful to our lives is still controversial. The speaker affirms that technology leads to the debasement of human quality producing more problems than it solves. Although it is undeniable that the spectacular development of technology over the past century contributed to reducing labor and time, it brought about health problems and global warming.

The innovation of automobiles and airplanes allows people to travel quickly and to access places that would otherwise be difficult to reach. Further, advanced transportation technology made trade and commerce more convenient and faster, thus promoting the economy. The development of Robots and AI technology contributes to accessing more information at the tip of users' fingers. This illustrates that technologies well serve people to the extent that they enjoy a more luxurious and comfortable life.

Despite the advantages and conveniences facilitated by technology, people encountered more problems. When we thought we solved one problem thoroughly, at the next moment, another problem arises with a more serious quest. For instance, today, almost all societies struggle with the responsibility to take care of nuclear waste and incinerated coals. Medical science has also engineered mutant viruses, immune to casual treatment. As such, people suffer from greenhouse effects and health problems. In this respect, we cannot say technology contributes to solving problems.

Finally, the issue of whether technology plays a pivotal role in increasing the quality of human life needs to be addressed from various perspectives. Happiness is a subjective criterion, so one cannot conclude that a maid of the Medieval times spent a relatively less miserable life than the workers today. For example, cellphones bound them to remain responsible for 24 hours. It would harm psychoanalytic health by the lack of refreshment needed to relieve the stress from people today.

In conclusion, technology is a double-edged sword asking people not to misuse it. However, humans undermined its harmful effects and thus caused environmental, pathological, and mental problems. The indispensability of technology has become a core part of our daily routine, so we should be more cautious about using technology wisely. [420]

91　The primary goal of technological advancement should be to increase people's efficiency so that they have more leisure time.
기술발전의 목적은 사람들의 효율성을 증대시켜 더 많은 여가 시간을 갖게 하는 데 있다.
Write a response in which you discuss the extent to which you agree or disagree with the statement and explain your reasoning for the position you take. In developing and supporting your position, you should consider ways in which the statement might or might not hold true and explain how these considerations shape your position.

강의노트　기술의 목적이 편안한 삶을 가져오기 위함만은 아니다. 사람은 본질적으로 탐구하고자 하는 마음을 가지고 있다. 창의적 발전을 위해서 노력해야 하는 것, 즉 지식의 발전을 위해서 노력하고자 하는 창의적 마음 때문에 사람들은 기술을 발전하고자 하며, 여가는 부수적으로 기술의 발전을 저절로 따라 오는 것이라고 에세이를 발전해야 한다.

Should the primary goal of technology be to have more leisure time? Do scientists work solely to meet this end? Before answering these questions, we'd better examine what people want to do in their leisure time. While most people want to travel to a fancy resort on vacation, some scientists prefer to take a break from their work to

Technology

devote themselves to realizing their ideas. In my opinion, the primary goal of technology is not more leisure time but, it is something good for the entire human race. Scientists pursue human flourishing by providing solutions to problems and uncovering the mysteries of nature. Thus, I disagree that the primary goal of technology is to have more leisure time.

The development of transportation and communication technologies provided people with sufficient leisure time. Today robots replaced many human jobs in factories and restaurants, thus reducing the number of overtime employees. Moreover, adventurous travelers became more confident in exploring the South Pole with Google Maps and reducing their risks in danger. The use of electrical devices allows us to have more meaningful activities in our leisure time.

Although smartphones have been a necessity for tourists to look for information, how to use technology and what to do in our free time depends on an individual's preference or job. Some scientists left their work temporarily to concentrate on studying the research questions in their minds with a group of other scientists. Cutting-edge equipment helps them conduct experiments fast and accurately, so they can collect more data. NASA astronauts, scientists, and engineers collaborate to break barriers to achieve the seemingly impossible, and it is inevitable to use advanced technology to carry out such tasks.

Other professionals who have become much busier with smartphones and computers are those in the international business market. Due to globalization, businessmen cannot be relaxed because they pay closer attention to the changes in the market trends over weekends, so they can avoid any possible risk that may lead to reduced profits. Instead of seeking more leisure time, they need to fly to another country for meetings with their global partner while making notes of their ideas necessary to persuade their counterpart CEOs. Some workaholic executives take classes online to learn how to use the newly developed software.

As seen above, considering leisure time is free time in which people are not working so they can not only relax but also do things they like, we cannot say the goal of technology is to have more leisure time. [419]

---

132 Some people believe that our ever-increasing use of technology significantly reduces our opportunities for human interaction. Other people believe that technology provides us with new and better ways to communicate and connect with one another.
어떤 사람들은 점점 증가하는 기술의 사용이 새로운 상호 인간관계를 만들 기회를 현저하게 줄여준다고 믿는다. 다른 사람들은 기술이 새롭고 더 나은 소통과 관계를 서로에게 가져다준다고 믿는다.
Write a response in which you discuss which view more closely aligns with your own position and explain your reasoning for the position you take. In developing and supporting your position, you should address both of the views presented.

강의노트   기술 발전으로 인한 사람들의 상호 관계는 긍정적이기도 하고 부정적이기도 하다. 다만 기술이 긍정적인 결과를 가져올 수 있느냐는 것은 기술을 어떻게 써야 하느냐는 점에 달려 있다. 칼날의 양면성과 같이 칼을 사용하는 사람이 어떠한 목적으로 어떻게 기술을 이용하느냐는 점을 바탕으로 해서 에세이를 쓰는 것이 보편타당한 것이다.

The statement questions if the use of communication technology has promoted human interaction. Although social media and mobile phones may harm developing children and teenagers, communication technology has made life more comfortable, convenient, and enjoyable. Without online communication available during the crisis of the Covid pandemic, businesses and enterprises might experience more difficulties in increasing profits. Digital communication contributes to promoting interactions and improvements in business and jobs.

What matters is the overuse of electronic devices can be addicting, and the overuse of digital device often harm our health by causing insomnia, eyestrain, and increased

Technology

anxiety and depression. Instead of interacting with family members, many children prefer to play online games or watch Youtube. Quite a few people are socially isolated, and in-person contact is no longer the dominant form of communication.

However, digital technology succeeded in diffusing information through social media, thus constructing a more transparent society. For example, it increased employment opportunities by recruiting better-fit workers through social media sites like Linkedin. The open communication between employers and employees also increased work efficiency by sharing feedback and questions online. Like this, digital transparency contributes to efficient hiring and communication transactions in business administration. Equality can be promoted not only by politicians but also scientists and engineers developing digital tools for advanced communication technology.

Digital users can now upload stories, reports, polls, and post updates on social media platforms such as Instagram and Youtube. These media platforms provide them with a cyber site, so they can fully engage in discussing the topics of their interest. For example, audiences can form a collective opinion by creating a pool on which side their views would like to vote. The results of the polls often affect public opinion. Another useful digital tool is the digital camera implemented on the cellular phone. Passengers often provide evidence showing a predator's sexual harassment crime by running a video tool on their mobile phones.

Moreover, social media let us have more fun by connecting us to those with similar interests or talents. The great hit of BTS could have been possible due to a fandom so-called "army". Thus in my view, the advantages of digital communication outweigh its disadvantages. [374]

Values

Values Topic Analysis

가치관에 관한 토픽은 교육과 많이 연계되어 있다. New GRE 시험에서 가치관은 크게 2가지로 정리할 수 있다. 하나의 그룹은 교육이 우리의 영혼을 자유롭게 하는가를 묻는다. 교육이 우리의 영혼을 자유롭게 하기는커녕 오히려 소수 지배 계급에게 유리한 사상을 심는 도구로 사용되어 온 것이 현실이다. 불행하게도 이데올로기를 세뇌하기 위해서 북한의 공교육은 김 씨 삼부자 우상화에 열을 올린다.

그렇다고 해서 일본이나 우리나라와 같은 국가들이 하는 공교육이 우리의 영혼을 결코 자유롭게 하는 것은 아니다. 일본은 우익 사상과 절대적 국가에 대한 충성을 요구하는 교육을 단행하고 있기 때문에 왜곡된 역사 교과서를 사용하는 것을 나라를 위하는 길이라 믿고 있다. 우리나라도 좌편향 교과서, 우편향 교과서라는 말이 나오는 것은 정권을 잡은 세력들이 진실보다는 자신의 정치구도에 유리한 쪽으로 국사 교과서를 편찬하기 때문이다.

다른 한 가지 토픽 그룹은 경쟁과 협동이라는 개념을 파악해야 하며, 이 2가지 개념은 정반대의 개념이 아니며 서로가 서로를 보완하는 개념으로 받아들여야 한다. 예를 들면 학교 교육에서 스포츠가 중요하게 생각되는 것은 게임을 통해 학생들이 자연스럽게 경쟁에서 이기려면 어떻게 협동해야 하는가를 배울 수 있기 때문이다.

Lecture 4
Values

12   Governments should offer free university education to any student who has been admitted to a university but cannot afford the tuition. [25]
정부는 대학에 입학허가를 받았으나 등록금을 낼 수 없는 학생들에게 무상 교육을 제공해야 한다. [교육과 연계되는 토픽]

17   Formal education tends to restrain our minds and spirits rather than set them free. [68]
공교육은 우리들의 정신과 영혼을 자유롭지 않도록 제한하는 경향이 있다. [교육과 연계되는 토픽]

45   Competition for high grades seriously limits the quality of learning at all levels of education. [138]
고득점을 위한 경쟁은 모든 수준의 교육에 있어서 양질의 교육을 저해한다. [교육과 연계되는 토픽]

68   Some people believe that the purpose of education is to free the mind and the spirit. Others believe that formal education tends to restrain our minds and spirits rather than set them free. [17]
어떤 사람들은 교육의 목적이 마음과 영혼을 자유롭게 하는 데 있다고 믿는다. 다른 사람들은 공교육이 우리들의 마음과 영혼을 자유롭게 하기보다는 억누른다고 믿는다. [교육과 연계되는 토픽]

83   Teachers' salaries should be based on the academic performance of their students. [30]
교사들의 월급은 그들이 가르친 학생들의 학업성취도에 근거를 두어야 한다. [교육과 연계되는 토픽]

Sample essay

12   Governments should offer college and university education free of charge to all students.
정부는 모든 학생들에게 무상 대학교육을 제공해야 한다.
Write a response in which you discuss the extent to which you agree or disagree with the recommendation and explain your reasoning for the position you take. In developing and supporting your position, describe specific circumstances in which adopting the recommendation would or would not be advantageous and explain how these examples shape your position.

강의노트   12번은 all policy 유형이다. 교육토픽이나 사회적 불평등에 focus를 맞추어야 한다. 대학교육은 사회적으로 엘리트 교육인 만큼 어느 정도까지는 개인이 자신의 교육비용에 대해서 책임을 저야 한다고 논리를 발전하는 것이 보편타당하다. 현재 미국 대학교육은 저소득 자녀들에게 삼분의 일을 각각 정부보조금,

정부 보장 loan과 work study라고 해서 학교에서 일거리를 주고 임금에서 세금을 제하지 않고 주는 식으로 학비와 생활비를 4년간 주정부 주재로 마련하도록 지원한다.

Should the government offer college and free university education to all students? Some advocate free college education considering the students suffer a mountain of debt before they have a chance to get their first paycheck. In the past decade, student loan debt has risen more than three times while public college costs twice more. Then, who pays for universities, students or taxpayers? If we want to train students to be more responsible for their social costs as taxpayer, students should understand their financial responsibility. They are obliged to pay back what they owe to society as elite members of that society.

Of course, college education contributed to supplying well-trained employees and thus promoting the national economy. A welfare state assumes funding college education leads to increasing the number of productive workers and professionals and thus accomplishing high long-term social and economic public returns. Indeed, a free college education is an upfront investment that ensures a state's financial abundance with higher income taxes and lower social security expenses.

However, we should question: Why does everyone have to go to college? Why a college degree that is subject to higher lifetime earnings? It seems unfair for those who seek the-job training or other forms of noncollege education. Should all taxpayers pay for the educational expenses accrued from those seeking more professional education? The government's funding for higher education is a taxpayer's money risk, which is a reverse distribution of social wealth from the poor to the rich, thus dwindling social equality. In light of fair redistribution, college education has to be paid for by individuals who want to enhance their skills for higher lifetime incomes.

In addition, students who seek financial aid to pay for their college tuition and other associated expenses can receive grants, scholarships, and loans. If they want to reduce the loan amount, they can also participate in work-study programs that help them have relevant experiences while taking courses. Through work-study students also learn how to play their role in the campus community.

In short, the government should provide financial aid program to ensure equitable and transparent funding for the students from low income families. In turn, high public returns on the state's investment need to support taxpayers without college degrees. [405]

---

17   Formal education tends to restrain our minds and spirits rather than set them free.
공교육은 우리들의 정신과 영혼을 자유롭지 않도록 제한하는 경향이 있다.
Write a response in which you discuss the extent to which you agree or disagree with the statement and explain your reasoning for the position you take. In developing and supporting your position, you should consider ways in which the statement might or might not hold true and explain how these considerations shape your position.

강의노트   17번은 공교육은 지배 계급이 선호하는 사상을 그대로 학생들이 답습할 수 있도록 한다는 뜻이다. 역사 교과서를 편찬할 때 기득권 세력과 세상을 혁신적으로 보려는 학자들 사이에 갈등을 야기하는 것이 모두 공교육이 학생들의 영혼을 자유롭게 하는 것이 아니라 그들을 기득권자들이 선호하는 가치관으로 교육하고 자 하는 도구로 쓰여 왔다는 사실을 지적해야 한다. 성차별 의식, 단일 민족 사상은 영혼을 자유롭게 하는 것이 아니라 구속하는 가치관이며, 남아 선호 사상과 배타적 국수주의 사상의 결과로 보아야 한다.

Few would question that education plays a pivotal role in producing individuals' free minds and spirits. However, when closely scrutinizing what we are taught from history text books, it is easy to notice that formal education is designed to implement a certain idea that is favorable to the dominant class. Thus, I agree that formal education tends to restrain our minds and spirits rather than set them free.

Every society builds schools to teach their children essential knowledge to survive, advance and flourish in their life. They also teach what is a normal or abnormal attitude, and which values have to be upheld. History textbooks are written in a way to boost national ideals or conventional virtues. The stories of the legendary characters and their contributions to society affect forming individual identity and the collective goal of people in a society.

In this way, public school education prevents individuals from having liberal or skeptical minds. For example, a Korean history book introduces Sinsaimdang whose portrait is also imprinted on the 50,000 won bill as an exemplary woman. To restrain the flexible mind of students, submissiveness has been accepted as an important value over generations. In addition, the fact that the Korean history textbooks include only a few heroines in the past two thousand years of its history best illustrates that gender-biased idea was deeply rooted in the patriarchal system. Thus, those who receive such an education from schools tend to restrain his/her minds and spirits in the framework of patriarch.

Another conventional idea that fettered Korean students' minds and spirits is the notion of homogeneity of the Great Han race. This nationalism idea hinders them from understanding multicultural values which is essential for Koreans to have global leadership in the dynamically changing modern society. Unfortunately, the distorted content in Korean textbooks infuses national propaganda by overstating the supremacy of the Korean cultural heritage. To free the minds and spirits of Korean students, public schools should teach the values of diversity to embrace diverse populations rather than that of conformity.

We should understand that wealth and power have inherited over generations through public education. We should educate young students to have more flexible

Values

minds to challenge the propaganda and to discrete gender bias or nationalistic values hidden in the history textbooks. [400]

---

83   Teachers' salaries should be based on the academic performance of their students.

교사들의 월급은 그들이 가르친 학생들의 학업성취도에 근거를 두어야 한다.

Write a response in which you discuss the extent to which you agree or disagree with the recommendation and explain your reasoning for the position you take. In developing and supporting your position, describe specific circumstances in which adopting the recommendation would or would not be advantageous and explain how these examples shape your position.

강의노트   학업 성취도에 근거해서 월급을 지불한다면 교육 현장이 너무 경쟁의 가치를 부추기는 결과를 가져올 것이다. 더불어 협동적으로 살아가는 건전한 사회를 이루기 위한 교육이라면 당연히 교사 월급을 성취도에 따라서 지불한다는 것에 반대해야 한다.

The incentive policy that teachers' salary increases as the score of their students' national or state-wide exams can cause several detrimental effects on the quality of education in the K to 12. Too much emphasis on the student's academic performance on teacher evaluation leads to fostering a competitive learning atmosphere. This may promote jealousy or hostile feelings, which would adversely affect on developing well-rounded and generous personalities necessary for leadership. Thus, I disagree with the statement because it only accounts for the importance of academic performance.

In past decades, the Department of Education of South Korea has been running an "Education Reform Policy" to enhance the knowledge in core subjects such as languages, math, and science. To cope with the policy, many public schools employed many academically outstanding high school teachers with incentives. Although this policy seemed beneficial to increase college admission rates, it was counterproductive for those in the occupational program, thus reducing the number of high school graduates ready to work in the industry. This policy also failed to boost the academic motivation of even those in the college prep program.

In addition, this policy encountered teachers' complaints. Kangnam school districts that paid an incentive to the teachers with their students' high performances were the teachers of the core subjects. In contrast, teachers for elective courses such as art or history and physical education expressed their honest feeling of being treated as second-degree teachers. Thus, an incentive policy based on the student's performance may cause problems in segregating non-core subject teachers from core subject teachers. If unhappy teachers quit their teaching job and transfer to take another occupation, it would make districts struggle with a shortage of teachers.

Moreover, the current salary scales that all teachers from elementary to high schools should be paid by the years they serve schools shows that fostering undue competition is not beneficial for both students and teachers. Undue competition for higher grades can promote selfish attitudes that eventually prevent students from developing healthy minds. Schools should be a place where many students learn more about the values of cooperation, in conclusion, teachers' salary scales based on their students' performance is not recommended.

In short, it is important to compensate teachers based on their performance not on their student's performance. Students cannot work to their potential when they are so much frustrated to get high grades. [489]

Lecture 5

Media

Media Topic Analysis

여러 토픽 가운데 매우 중요한 토픽이 Media이다 이는 정치, 법, 가치관 그리고 기술에 모두 연관 지어서 쓸 수 있는 토픽이기 때문이다. 각각의 토픽이 그룹이 지어져 있어도 사실을 모두 함께 종합해서 자기 자신의 독창적인 에세이를 쓸 수 있어야 하겠다.

우리는 visual image 시대를 살아가고 있다. 언어보다는 이미지를 중시하는 시대라는 뜻이다. 다른 기술과 마찬가지로 미디어가 보여주는 강력한 이미지는 사람들의 생각에 지대한 영향을 끼친다. 대통령 선거란 이미지 메이킹이라는 말이 성행하고 아름다운 이미지의 인기 배우들의 이미지를 이용한 화장품 선전 등은 사람들이 가치관을 뒤바꾸어 놓는 결과를 가져왔다. 외모지상주의, 즉 lookism, materialism이 만연한 사회가 되고 말았다.

물론 미디어가 민주주의 발전에 기여한 점을 간과해서는 안 된다. 정치 스캔들이야말로 어떠한 개인도 혁신할 수 없는 사회적 정의를 이루는 데 기여한다. 미디어가 다수 대중을 향해서 효과적으로 어떤 아이디어나 정보를 퍼트릴 수 있는 도구라는 점을 이해한다면 이것이 사회적 가치관을 좌우하는 도구라고 정의할 수 있다. 미디어 폐해로 왜곡하는 진실과 증거 없는 폭로성, 프라이버시 침해로 간주해야 한다.

Lecture 5
Media

4   Scandals are useful because they focus on our attention on problems in ways that no speaker or reformer ever could.
스캔들은 유용하다. 어떤 연설가나 혁신자도 할 수 없는 방법으로 사람들의 관심을 문제에 집중시키기 때문이다.

44   Claim : In this age of intensive media coverage, it is no longer possible for a society to regard any living man or woman as a hero.
주장: 우리 사회는 더 이상 생존해 있는 사람을 영웅이라고 여길 수가 없게 되었다.
Reason : The reputation of anyone who is subjected to media scrutiny will eventually be diminished.
이유: 미디어 검증 대상이 되는 사람의 평판은 결국은 사라질 것이다.
[75/84/122]

93   Unfortunately, in contemporary society, creating an appealing image has become more important than the reality of truth behind that image.
불행하게도 현대 사회에서는 호소력 있는 이미지를 만드는 것이 현실이나 이미지 뒤에 담긴 진실보다 더 중요하게 되었다.

Sample essay

4   Scandals are useful because they focus on our attention on problems in ways that no speaker or reformer ever could.
스캔들은 유용하다. 어떤 연설가나 혁신자도 할 수 없는 방법으로 사람들의 관심을 문제에 집중시키기 때문이다.
Write a response in which you discuss the extent to which you agree or disagree with the claim. In developing and supporting your position, be sure to address the most compelling reasons and/or examples that could be used to challenge your position.

강의노트   4번 토픽은 미디어의 힘에 관한 질문이다. 20세기 민주주의 발전은 미디어라는 새로운 소통의 방법으로 급진적 발전이 가능하게 되었다. 예증으로는 Water Gate scandal과 최순실 scandal의 결과를 논해야 한다. 특히 이러한 스캔들이 민주사회 발전에 혁신적 개인의 목소리보다 여론 조성에 효과적이다라고 대조한다.

Is the media more influential than a reformers? I agree with the statement if scandals are for the public's welfare. Why might scandals be good for democracy? It is because scandals have a positive effect on promoting institutional accountability and voter attentiveness.

Given today's social media privacy issues and concerns, scandals have made negative impacts. The security of personal information has risen to a critical problem. Some scandal coverage makes the individual who is involved in that scandal take suicide. In this regard, scandals have been detrimental rather than beneficial. In addition, political scandals are frequently treated as a stain on the political system, resulting from poor personal judgment, lax rule enforcement, or bald political corruption. Media coverage treats these as sensational events.

However, scandals may also help to change public discourse about issues and candidates. For example, the Watergate scandal revealed that the Nixon presidency was involved in critical manipulation and abuse of power for years. And this investigation led to his resignation in Aug 1974. The Watergate scandal proved that democracy continues to work and that not even the president is above the law and the United States Constitution. In this way, the media contributed to forming a public opinion that was powerful enough to give pressure on the president in power. The War Power Act requires presidents to consult with Congress before American troops are sent into combat abroad and to withdraw them after 60 days unless Congress approves their stay. As such, the media contribute to reforming the abuse of power.

Another compelling example that shows scandals as a collective public power is the disclosure of Choi Sun-sil's influence paddling scandal. President Park Keun-hye was indicted on charges relating to abuse of power in her role as president. Embezzlement and influence paddling scandals report the misuse of political leaders acting for selfish gains. Scandals play a pivotal role in increasing the quality of public discourse about political issues.

In sum, viewers tend to be more attentive to the politics behind the scandals when informed by the media about the players and their schemes. Scandals have promoted

Lecture 5
Media

democracy by increasing the quality of public discourse about corruption and wrongdoings more effectively than a speaker or reformer. [420]

---

44   Claim : It is no longer possible for a society to regard any living man and woman as a hero.
주장: 우리 사회는 더 이상 생존해 있는 사람을 영웅이라고 여길 수가 없게 되었다.
Reason : The reputation of anyone who is subjected to media's scrutiny will eventually be diminished.
이유: 미디어 검증 대상이 되는 사람의 평판은 결국은 사라질 것이다.
Write a response in which you discuss the extent to which you agree or disagree with the claim and the reason on which that claim is based.

강의노트   미디어의 검증으로 히어로로 여겨지는 사람의 수는 점점 줄게 되었다. 그러나 오늘날도 미디어 조사와 무관하게 본보기가 되는 삶을 살아가는 히어로들이 있다. 미디어가 유명인을 비판하는 경향은 있으나 동시대 모든 영웅이 미디어 조사로 인해서 살아진다는 논리에는 반대한다. 예증으로 Michael Jackson과 Malala Yousafzai를 제시했다.

Is it no longer possible to regard any woman or man as a hero today? Some may think no one can pass the media's scrutiny. However, I disagree because the media often discover new heroes while rebroadcasting the legendary achievements of our heroes in the past. Although media tend to defame our heroes, they look for heroes who did something beneficial to the world or the betterment of the entire human race.

Many people imagine a hero must be a person who holds a noble profession, a nurse or a firefighter. However, the uniform of these people does not necessarily elevate an individual to the status of a hero. Unlike the New York City firefighters and police who showed courageous acts of heroism during the 9/11 terrorist attack on the Twin Trade Towers and the Pentagon, the media uncovered the LAPD cops' ruthless beating of Rodney King while arresting him. The media play a pivotal role in revealing who to be villains or heroes and thus make our society more transparent and safe.

However, viewers are confused by media presenting different images of the same individual, sometime as an angel and another time as a criminal. For example, television and the Internet broadcast Michael Jackson's child molestation repeatedly. Although some media maliciously dug into Michael Jackson's privacy, he was acquitted of all criminal charges later. Nonetheless, he was considered a hero because of the achievement he made. He fought for racial barriers in the music industry while helping others through his humanitarianism, and music lasted forever. He was a one-of-a-kind performer who demolished what the stereotypical performer was supposed to be. As such, he is still considered one of the most legendary people in history.

Moreover, heroic characters dare to step forward to advocate beliefs rejected by their contemporaries. For example, the media reported that Malala Yousafzai, a 15-year-old Pakistani girl, was shot in the head by the Taliban, but she never gave up criticizing the Taliban's actions against women. Malala believed that all girls should have the opportunities to learn in school, standing up for girls and women's rights everywhere. Now wherever she goes, the media's lens follows her to keep her from the Taliban's threats.

Once it is said that no one does not get dust by shaking it off . However, the reputation of heroes cannot be tarnished by gossip or scandals played by mass media. [421]

93   Unfortunately, in contemporary society, creating an appealing image has become more important than the reality of truth behind that image.
불행하게도 현대 사회에서는 호소력 있는 이미지를 만드는 것이 현실이나 이미지 뒤에 담긴 진실보다 더 중요하게 되었다.
Write a response in which you discuss the extent to which you agree or disagree with the

statement and explain your reasoning for the position you take. In developing and supporting your position, you should consider ways in which the statement might or might not hold true and explain how these considerations shape your position.

강의노트   visual image의 influence에 대해서 묻는 질문이다. 예증으로는 대통령 선거에 이미지 making이랑 광고에 대중들이 좋아하는 인물들을 발탁해서 선전효과를 늘이고자 하는 이미지를 이용한 매출 증대 효과에 대해서 적었다. 미디어 시대에 deceptive images에 현혹될 수 있는 오늘날 세태에 대해서 말하고 있다. 토픽을 동의하는 방향으로 글을 작성한다.

The speaker contends that an appealing image is now more important than the reality of the truth behind that image. Few would doubt that truth is more important than images. However, I disagree with the speaker because what determines public opinion and consumer decisions is a deceptive image, not the truth behind that image. When viewers are easily blind to the truth behind that image especially when they are obsessed with an attractive image.

Of course, we should check possible lies hidden in extravagant images. Both Democratic Party and Conservative Party spend quite a lot of money to create great political campaign photos of their candidates by shaping their appearance. Some smart voters discuss their leadership qualities and possible lies with neighbors and online users. And they pay more attention to the public discourse not to be fooled by misleading images.

However, voters tend to pay more attention to the illusive image than the content of the candidates' policies or promises. Whoever advertises handsome yet innocent looks is more likely to succeed in persuading voters. Using a computer for political activities has been crucial for running a campaign, so creating a predominant image for the candidate has become more important to win the race. Viewers exercise their votes in favor of the candidate who succeeded in creating a dominant image in the advertisement. Most customers choose a familiar product frequently shown on TV.

For example, American actress Margaret Qualley's look for the Chanel brand advertisement leads customers to purchase. Wishing to be like her, consumers foster loyalty toward a specific brand whose delusive images hone in on a consumer's attitude toward a brand-name product.

This made them fanatic to the degree that they are no longer concerned about the worth of materials in the brand name product. In a society where lookism and materialism are predominant, many young workers assume shaping their appearance is more important than building their personalities or qualities. Companies tend to interview applicants to check their looks in advance. As a result, delusive images hone in on a consumer's attitude toward a brand-name product.

In short, image-making has become more important to build public opinion and fashion trends today than ever before. Thus, voters should discrete the quality of candidates and make choices based on the reality of the truth. [390]

Lecture 6

Ethics

Ethics Topic Analysis

Ethics 토픽은 정치적 지도자 학자 또는 대기업 사장과 같은 사회적 지도자, 즉 일반 대중으로부터 존경받는 부러움의 대상인 role model이 보여주어야 할 사회적 책임에 관해서 묻는 토픽이다.

지도자는 만인에게 본보기가 되는 윤리적 책임감이 있다는 것을 강조하면서 써야 한다. 기업인의 사회적 책임 또한 정치나 사회운동가 못지않다는 것을 알고 글을 적어야 한다.
또한 공무원들의 임기는 5년마다 바뀌어야 한다는 뜻의 leadership change의 개념은 사회적으로 매우 중요한 것을 뜻한다. 민주주의 근간은 새로운 리더십을 선택하는 데 있다는 사실이다. 새로운 시대를 이끌고 나아갈 새로운 리더를 선택할 수 있는 국민이야말로 선진 국민이라 할 수 있다.

특히 69번이 말하는 정치인의 confidentiality와 대중의 알아야 할 권리와의 관계는 역사적 변천을 겪어왔다. 특히 미디어의 발전으로 인해서 점점 국민의 알권리는 강화되어 왔다. 국가 안보를 위한 중대한 사항 이외에 정보를 남용하는 사례는 정치권에서 더 이상 관용되어서는 안 된다는 추세이다.

Ethics 토픽은 Politics & Law와 연결해서 써가는 것이 바람직하다.

Lecture 6
Ethics

22　The best way to understand the character of a society is to examine the character of the men and women that the society chooses as its heroes and its role models. [122]
주장: 한 사회의 성격은 그 사회의 구성원들이 선택한 영웅이나 귀감이 되는 인물들을 보면 이해할 수 있다.
Reason : Heroes and role models reveal a society's highest ideals.
이유: 영웅들이나 모범이 되는 사람들은 그 사회가 추구하는 최고의 가치를 나타낸다.

69　Some people believe it is often necessary, even desirable, for political leaders to withhold information from the public. Others believe that the public has a right to be fully informed.
어떤 사람들은 정치지도자가 정보를 알려 주지 않는 것은 필요할 뿐만 아니라 심지어 바람직하다고 믿는다. 다른 사람들은 대중은 모든 정보를 알권리가 있다고 믿는다.

77　The most effective way to understand contemporary culture is to analyze the trends of its youth.
현대 문화를 이해하기 위한 가장 효과적인 방법은 젊은 사람들의 경향을 분석하는 것이다.

104　To be an effective leader, a public official must maintain the highest ethical and moral standards. [16/107]
위대한(효과적인) 지도자가 되기 위해서 공무원은 최고의 윤리적, 도덕적 수준을 지켜야만 한다.

130　Some people believe that corporations have a responsibility to promote the well-being of the societies and environments in which they operate. Others believe that the only responsibility of corporations, provided they operate within the laws is to as much money as possible.
어떤 사람들은 대기업이 사회복지와 그들이 유용하고 있는 환경을 증진시킬 책임이 있다고 믿는다. 다른 사람들은 법의 테두리 안에서 운영을 하는 한, 대기업의 유일한 책무는 이윤을 창조하는 것이라고 믿는다.

Sample essay

22　Claim : The best way to understand the character of a society is to examine the character of the men and women that the society chooses as its heroes or its role models.
주장: 한 사회의 성격은 그 사회의 구성원들이 선택한 영웅이나 귀감이 되는 인물들을 보면 이해할 수 있다.
Reason : Heroes and role models reveal a society's highest ideals.
이유: 영웅들이나 모범이 되는 사람들은 그 사회가 추구하는 최고의 가치를 나타낸다.
Write a response in which you discuss the extent to which you agree or disagree with the claim and the reason on which that claim is based.

강의노트 22번 에세이는 기본 템플릿에서 약간 벗어나게 쓰여 있다. 혹 다른 형태로 쓰고자 하는 분들을 위한 샘플이다. 그러므로 혹 동일한 line of reasoning을 보려고 하면 혼동될 수 있다는 점을 감안하며 읽어야 한다. 독자들 가운데 좀 다른 형태의 에세이를 쓰고자 하는 분들을 위해서 약간 변형을 주는 형식이 사용되었다.

Do heroes represent the character of a society? If someone asks South Koreans about their role model, their answers can be varied. However, if the same question asks to North Koreans, they unanimously say it is their beloved supreme leader, Kim Jong-il. This contrast clearly shows that the best way to understand the characters of a society is to examine who is the most admirable person in that society.

Of course, the fashion style of young people or their popular culture represents the cultural trend of society to a certain extent. Many Iranian young women think wearing hijabs is to identify themselves as Muslim and to show their cultural pride, while college students in North Korea show their pride in the communist uniform. What controls society is the value system that manipulate people in a way favorable to the few in power.

In this sense, it is efficient to investigate the essence of leadership that society reveres. Considering the fact the only hero in North Korea is Kim's family under the justification of Juche ideology, we can imagine how North Koreans suffer from being restrained by the political frame of oppression that has been dominant in the last three scores in that society. For example, when the first leader of North Korea, Kim Il-sung, died, North Korean people mourned days and nights while crying and hitting their heads and chests aside. These awkward behaviors are accepted as the most loyal gesture. The picture of North Koreans mourning their deceased supreme leader at the funeral clearly shows the oppressed social structure.

In contrast, when South Koreans are interviewed about their heroes, their responses

Lecture 6
Ethics

can be varied. Some would say they admire Kim Dae-jung, a former president, while others would admire the great leadership of Cardinal Kim Su-whan, who devoted his life to the oppressed and the disadvantaged. Another would consider BTS band artists who reached number one on the Billboard Hot 100 charts. The various features of the heroes upheld in South Korea best reflect its liberal and individualistic characters.

Public high schools in California celebrate Martin Luther King Jr.'s Day instead of Columbus Day. Like this, the progress of humanity can be identified in the changes in national holidays.

---

69   Some people believe it is often necessary, even desirable, for political leaders to withhold information from the public. Others believe that the public has a right to be fully informed.
어떤 사람들은 정치지도자가 정보를 알려 주지 않는 것은 필요할 뿐만 아니라 심지어 바람직하다고 믿는다. 다른 사람들은 대중은 모든 정보를 알권리가 있다고 믿는다.
Write a response in which you discuss which view more closely aligns with your own position and explain your reasoning for the position you take. In developing and supporting your position, you should address both of the views presented.

강의노트   대통령이 정보를 제공하지 않을 권리에 대해서 설득력 있는 에세이를 쓰려면 political scandals을 예증으로 쓰는 것이 좋다. 국가적 위기 상황에서 국가 안보에 관한 경우가 아닌 경우에는 정보를 제공해야 한다. 미디어의 발전으로 점점 더 정치인들은 자신의 정보를 제공해야 하는 추세이다. 예증으로는 water gate scandal과 Chaney 스캔들을 들었다.

Although there has been growing concern for the public's rights to know, historically, presidents have claimed the right of executive privilege when they have the information they want to keep confidential, either because it would jeopardize national security or because disclosure would be contrary to the interests of the executive branch. It is justifiable for executive officers to withhold information in case of a national emergency, but if it is used to abuse power, it should be discrete.

During the presidency of Dwight D. Eisenhower, the power of president enhanced in the area of national security. The Military may refuse to divulge requested information when national security is at stake. While warning that such requests could not be simply left to the "caprice of executive officers," people believed that the compulsion of the evidence will expose military matters which cannot be divulged in the interest of national security. For this, presidents can withhold confidential information for national prosperity.

However, the use of executive privilege decreased during the 1960s when a constitutional crisis occurred by Watergate, a series of scandals involving President Richard Nixon and his associates. When Congress sought to obtain White House tapes containing Oval Office conversations, Nixon refused to turn them over, claiming that the tapes were subject to absolute executive privilege asserting that the judiciary had no authority to order their production or inspection. This case was brought to the court. Although it affirmed the officer's executive privilege, the U.S. people's rights to full disclosure outweighed the president's right to secrecy. This momentous decision soon led to Nixon's resignation.

Another compelling example is that a federal judge ordered officials in the Bush administration to release information in an investigation of an energy task force led by Vice President Richard B. Cheney. The release of the information under the Freedom of Information Act was stalled by administrators. Although the case against Cheney's energy group was later dismissed, several liberal and conservative interest groups criticized the Bush administration for controlling information.

Due to the media's scrutiny, it has become much more challenging for executive officers to withhold information from the public. However, in a crisis, the public's demand to know about confidential information may lead to panic. The Constitution

Lecture 6
Ethics

does not enumerate the president's right to executive privilege, but the concept has evolved over the years as presidents have claimed it. [414]

---

104 To be an effective leader, a public official must maintain the highest ethical and moral standards. [16/107]
위대한(효과적인) 지도자가 되기 위해서 공무원은 최고의 윤리적, 도덕적 수준을 지켜야만 한다.
Write a response in which you discuss the extent to which you agree or disagree with the claim. In developing and supporting your position, be sure to address the most compelling reasons and/or examples that could be used to challenge your position.

강의노트 언뜻 보면 agree라고 쓰기 쉬운 토픽이다. 그러나 이 토픽은 반드시 disagree로 전개해야만 한다. 시민을 위해서 일하는 공공의 지도자는 판단 능력이 있어서 어려운 위기를 예견하고 당면한 문제를 해결할 수 있는 능력을 겸비해야 하기 때문이다. 이 토픽에 답변하게 위해서는 대통령의 직무에 관한 기본 상식이 있어야 한다.

Although the highest ethical standard that can be exemplary to the people is crucial for judging effective leadership, it is not the only measurement for his/her followers. What makes a great leader is the ability to make a best possible decision by reducing risks. Thus, I disagree with the statement. A public official's maintaining the highest ethical standard is a must, but the Senate adjudged that Clinton is not guilty in the first article of impeachment.

Integrity is an important aspect to judge a president's leadership qualities. A president involved in scandals is more likely to harm people or defame the nation. President Nixon single-handedly destroyed his presidency and his place in history with the Watergate scandal. President Clinton stained his career with many personal scandals, including lying to the public. Without demonstrating the virtue of integrity, no president can be considered a great leader.

However, a capable president should be able to mobilize public opinion to take initiative with Congress. The president has to know how to negotiate with assemblymen and women when dealing with Congress. If he is pushy and takes an unskilled approach, Congress may be offended, as a result, he is unlikely to be successful. If a president is willing to lobby Congress and bargain a deal with its members, he can be very successful. George H. Bush saw most of his legislation pass, even though opposing Democrats controlled both houses of Congress. The president's negotional skills lead Congress to pass the bills that are credited to helping people.

Another critical factor for judging a president's abilities is crisis management skills. Presents are held responsible for the political and economic climate, whether a time is good or bad. A successful president has to have a program or policy ready to stimulate the economy if necessary. For instance, Jimmy Carter and George H. Bush are recent presidents who lost their bids for reelection due to economic decline. At the same time, a booming economy can get a president reelected though his fame was tarnished because of the Lewinsky scandal, as Bill Clinton demonstrated in 1996.

Along with integrity, several other crucial abilities are required to be an effective leader. Respect from foreign nations is as important as the qualifications that are discussed above. In short, US presidents should ensure that the international community can see the US in a credible and positive light. [440]

---

130   Some people believe that corporations have a responsibility to promote the well-being of the societies and environments in which they operate. Others believe that the only responsibility of corporations, provided they operate within the laws is to as much money as possible.
어떤 사람들은 대기업이 사회복지와 그들이 유용하고 있는 환경을 증진시킬 책임이 있다고 믿는다. 다른 사람들은 법의 테두리 안에서 운영을 하는 한, 대기업의 유일한 책무는 이윤을 창조하는 것이라고 믿는다.
Write a response in which you discuss which view more closely aligns with your own position and explain your reasoning for the position you take. In developing and supporting your position, you should address both of the views presented.

Lecture 6
Ethics

강의노트   130번은 기업인의 사회적 책임에 대해서 묻는 질문이다. 이 토픽은 some people vs other people로 물어보고 있다. 이러한 유형의 토픽은 Introduction에 있는 템플릿의 두 번째 문장에 자기 자신의 주장과 반대되는 의견을 쓰고 자신과 동의하는 의견을 However, 다음의 세 번째 문장에 적으면 글의 논리가 정연하게 된다. 템플릿을 떠나지 않고 쓰는 것이 바람직하다.

Every company or business usually starts with its own set agenda, which varies from one to another. Corporations can be successful, if it provides a needed service to a community, nation, or the world. In this sense, corporations have social responsibility not only to its shareholders and the world it trades but also to the people whether they are clients or not.

In its most basic terms, corporate social responsibilities can come down to the ethics of a business. Each company has its own set of core values that also affect everyone with whom the business is associated. For example, the investment decision of the Hyundai corporation to the Keumgang Mountain tourism instigated the reunion of the separated families due to the division of Korea. Hyundai Corporation could have made more profits if it chose to invest in the telecommunication market like other companies such as SK or LG. Unlike them its founding CEO, Jeong Ju-young took risks in developing the Keumgang mountain tourism for the sake of the two Koreas' reconciliation. His crossing the Freedom Bridge with a herd of cattle has been a symbolic action for the reconciliation of the two Koreas. This clearly shows that a company's investment decisions are closely associated with a nation's prosperity.

There are a set of laws that companies had to be adhered with regards to financial and social responsibilities; nonetheless, corporate responsibility has to account for all people on a much larger scale. Today labor laws have legislated to prevent the exploitation of workers in the 3rd world countries. Executive officials should concern about environment protection to prevent the rainforest from disappearing. Thus, the responsibility of corporations is greater than simply creating profits within the legal boundary.

Technology has changed how we produce and connect to increase workers' mobility and thus reduce the costs and risks of innovation. In the globalized market, the corporation's social responsibility has become more important than in the past. A company's sustainable development strategy should focus on action plans that are created based on social and environmental concerns rather than legal obligation.

In sum, it is more important for companies to carry out work in an exemplary way. Ethics education is an exceptional tool for promoting moral conduct, and thus making ethical decisions. Ethical operations can boost a company's reputation and its brand name image. [480]

Lecture 7

Controversy

Controversy Topic Analysis

Controversy 토픽은 주로 개인과 사회의 관계를 묻는다. 즉, 개인은 사회적 제약으로부터 자유로울 수 있는가? Values 토픽과 연관지어 볼 수 있는 토픽들이다. 그리고 사회를 개혁하는 데 용기를 가지고 일어나는 개인들의 헌신에 대해서도 잘 이해하고 있어야 한다. 우리 사회는 획일성보다는 다양성을 인정해야 한다는 것은 Value와 동일한 맥락이라 하겠다.

또한 우리는 같은 생각을 하는 동질적인 사람으로부터 더 배우는가 아니면 이질적인 사람으로부터 더 배우느냐는 토픽들이 있다. 기존 아이디어와 세력에 대해서 저항하는 사람들이 세상을 발전 혁신해왔다는 역사적 사실을 근거로 해서 쓰면 바람직한 토픽이다. GRE 시험을 보는 학생들이 가장 많이 쓴 위인은 Martin Luther Jr. King이고 과학의 발전을 위해 다른 의견을 제시한 위인의 예로는 Nicolas Copernicus를 들 수 있다.

성공에 대한 정의에 관해서 묻는 토픽도 중요하다. 53번은 목적을 위한 어떠한 방법도 정당화될 수 없다고 써야 하며 144번은 사회적 인정이 진정한 성공의 목표가 되는 것이 개인의 만족을 위한 성공보다 가치가 있다고 써야 한다. 61번은 모험을 택하는 사람만이 성공할 수 있지만 그 모험이 어떤 결과를 가져오는지를 알고 모험을 택해야 한다고 논지를 펴야 한다. 모든 위인들을 불분명한 결과가 나온다 할지라도 자신의 의지대로 모험을 선택해서 세상을 바꾸는 일들을 했기 때문이다.

Lecture 7
Controversy

11   People's behavior is largely determined by forces not of their own making. [99]
사람들의 행위는 자신이 스스로 결정하는 것이 아니라 외부의 힘에 의해서 결정된다.

17   Formal education tends to restrain our minds and spirits rather than set them free. [68]
공교육은 우리들의 정신과 영혼을 자유롭게 하기보다는 제약하는 경향이 있다.

22   The best way to understand the character of a society is to examine the character of the men and women that the society chooses as its heroes and its role models. [122]
주장: 한 사회의 성격은 그 사회의 구성원들이 선택한 영웅이나 귀감이 되는 인물들을 보면 이해할 수 있다
Reason : Heroes and role models reveal a society's highest ideals.
이유: 영웅들이나 모범이 되는 사람들은 그 사회가 추구하는 최고의 가치를 나타낸다.

27   In a field of inquiry, the beginner is more likely than the expert to make important contribution.
어떠한 연구 분야에서든, 초보자가 전문가보다 더 중요한 기여를 하는 것 같다.

34   In any situation, progress requires discussion among people who have contrasting points of view.
어떠한 상황에서도, 진보는 대조적 견해를 갖고 있는 사람들 간의 토론을 통해서 이루어진다.

38   It is primarily through our identification with social groups that we define ourselves.
자신이 누구인가는 우리가 함께 어울려 다니는 소셜 그룹의 아이덴티티를 보면 알 수 있다.

41   The greatness of individuals can be decided only by those who live after them, not by their contemporaries.
한 개인의 위대함은 동시대 사람이 아니라 그의 사후에 후대 사람들에 의해서 결정된다.

45   Competition for high grades seriously limits the quality of learning at all levels of education. [138]
고득점을 위한 경쟁은 모든 수준의 교육에 있어서 양질의 교육을 저해한다.

49   Claim : We can usually learn much more from people whose views we share than from those whose views contradict our own. [76/118]
주장: 우리는 다른 의견을 가진 사람들보다 같은 의견을 가진 사람들로부터 더 많은 것을 배운다.
Reason : Disagreement can cause stress and inhibit learning.
이유: 의견의 차이는 스트레스를 유발하고 배움을 저해한다.

53   If a goal is worthy, then any means taken to attain it are justifiable.
목적이 가치가 있다면 그것을 성취하기 위해서 취한 어떠한 방법도 정당화될 수 있다.

61   People should undertake risky action only after they have carefully considered its consequences.
사람들은 오로지 모험의 결과를 조심스럽게 고려한 다음에 어떤 행동을 해야 한다.

77 The most effective way to understand contemporary culture is to analyze the trends of its youth.
현대 문화를 이해하기 위한 가장 효과적인 방법은 젊은 사람들의 경향을 분석하는 것이다.

78 People's attitudes are determined more by their immediate situation or surroundings than by society as a whole.
사람들의 태도는 자신이 당면한 상황이나 환경보다는 사회 전체에 의해서 결정된다.

79 Claim : The best test of an argument is its ability to convince someone with an opposing viewpoint. [146]
주장: 논쟁 능력을 시험하는 가장 적절한 방법은 반대 관점을 가진 다른 사람을 설득해보는 것이다.
Reason : Only by being forced to defend an idea against the doubts and contrasting views of others does one really discover the value of that idea.
이유: 오로지 남과 다른 아이디어를 방어하는 과정에서만 그 아이디어의 진가를 발견할 수 있기 때문이다.

108 Critical judgment of work in any given field has little value unless it comes from someone who is an expert in that field. [110]
어떤 분야든지 비판적 판단은 그 분야의 전문가로부터 나오지 않는 한 그 가치가 없다.

123 The best way for a society to prepare its young people for leadership in government, industry or other fields is by instilling in them a sense of cooperation, not competition. [128]
젊은이들이 정부, 산업 또는 다른 전문 분야에서 리더십을 기르기 위해서는 경쟁보다는 협동의 개념을 고무해야 한다.

130 Some people believe that corporations have a responsibility to promote the well-being of the societies and environments in which they operate. Others believe that the only responsibility of corporations, provided they operate within the laws is to as much money as possible.
어떤 사람들은 대기업이 사회복지와 그들이 유용하고 있는 환경을 증진시킬 책임이 있다고 믿는다. 다른 사람들은 법의 테두리 안에서 운영을 하는 한, 대기업의 유일한 책무는 이윤을 창조하는 것이라고 믿는다.

138 Some people believe that competition for high grades motivates students to excel in the classroom. Others believe that such competition limits the quality of real learning. [45]
어떤 사람들은 높은 학점을 받기 위한 경쟁은 학생들이 수업에서 최선을 다 하도록 동기를 부여한다고 믿는다. 다른 사람들은 그러한 경쟁은 진정한 배움의 질을 저해한다고 믿는다.

144 True success can be measured primarily in terms of the goals one sets for oneself.
진정한 성공은 주로 스스로 설정하는 목표로서 평가될 수 있다.

Lecture 7
Controversy

11   People's behavior is largely determined by forces not of their own making.
      사람들의 행위는 자신이 스스로 결정하는 것이 아니라 외부의 힘에 의해서 결정된다.
      Write a response in which you discuss the extent to which you agree or disagree with the
      statement and explain your reasoning for the position you take. In developing and supporting
      your position, you should consider ways in which the statement might or might not hold true
      and explain how these considerations shape your position.

강의노트   Controversy 11번은 사회적 규범이나 관습에 얽매어 있는 개인들은 진정한 의미의 선택권이 없다는
        것을 말하고 있다. 이 토픽은 society vs. individual의 관계를 논하라는 의미로 적혀있다. 아이러니
        하게도 개인은 조직이나 정부와 같은 기관이 만든 법이나 rule은 물론 관습적인 가치관으로도 자신의
        의지대로 선택할 수 있는 자유를 구속받고 있다.

The speaker contends that people's behavior is largely determined by forces, not of their own making. While the recent upsurge of the "Me Too" movement in South Korea has been pervasive, its force has been mainly emotional and subjective rather than intellectual and persuasive because people rarely question the forces behind the ideologies of the present socio-political institutions. Do we understand that the institutional mechanism is working in the social context? Do we know our gender and ethnicity determine how we behave and build relationships?

Young children are happy to go to school where they make friends and memories. They learn how to perceive others and what and how to do to be accepted by teachers and friends. School is the place where young students learn about the stereotypical girl style and White dominant culture. As they receive education, their mind and behaviors are fixed in a frame that the dominant class of people set up in their preference.

As seeing movies, young people might question why so few woman protagonists appear in big movies. For example, Lord of the Rings would have been less successful if Frodo was a girl. The male superheroes are male fantasies of who they'd like to be.

By creating male superheroes like Superman and Spiderman, the Hollywood industry gained an astronomical amount of profit from the movies by reconfirming that our superheroes are men, not women. Like this, the media have played a key role in enhancing the patriarchal system.

The recent upsurge of feminist activity in this country contributed to reforming our society with gender equality to a certain degree. However, as John Stuart Mill suggested, we tend to accept whatever is natural, which is just as true in the realm of academic investigation as it is in our social arrangements. The very position of women is outsider, and in reality, the White-male position is considered natural. "He" as the subject of all scholarly predicate is a decided advantage.

Although feminism has become more active than the past, the glass ceiling is still something women face today. Many women and minority workers still struggle in the social context that prevents them from promoting to top positions in management. As seen above, people's behavior is primarily determined by the social environment, not by their own will. Thus, I agree with the statement. [381]

---

38   It is primarily through our identification with social groups that we define ourselves.
      자신이 누구인가는 우리가 함께 어울려 다니는 소셜 그룹의 아이덴티티를 보면 알 수 있다.
      Write a response in which you discuss the extent to which you agree or disagree with the statement and explain your reasoning for the position you take. In developing and supporting your position, you should consider ways in which the statement might or might not hold true and explain how these considerations shape your position.

강의노트   38번 에세이의 중요한 점은 social groups의 의미를 바르게 이해해야 한다는 점이다. Social groups이란 정당, 봉사활동단체, 사교클럽 등을 예증으로 들어야 한다. Sports group이나 orchestra 등은 부적절한 예증이다. 적절한 예증을 선택해야만이 off topic 에세이가 되지 않는다.

We do not need to look any further than an old saying, "The same flocks gather together." To understand that one's social identification can be easily discovered when viewing his or her surroundings. Thus, I agree with the speaker that it is primarily through our identification with social groups that we define ourselves because we prefer to associate with those of similar ideas or values. It is certainly easy to get along and be influenced by someone who shares similar traits and beliefs than with someone who differs in opinion, as it may be a recipe for conflict.

Of course, in terms of personality or character, membership in a social group such as the community bicycle club cannot define or generalize all members' social identification. Personality or taste can be quite different from one to another according to their lifestyle or occupation. Considering the range of ages of a sports club, we can easily tell that it is difficult to portray certain distinctive characters as a single type of group that share identical values.

However, when it comes to political parties, we can tell much about one's identity. By investigating the policies for member supports we can understand one's attitude toward social changes. For example, in South Korea, many of progressive politicians are members of the Democratic Party while the People Power Party claims conservatism as their political principle. It is common for a politician to ally with those who share similar political ideas and political vision.

Another compelling example that shows how people define themselves by way of sharing a common goal is volunteer groups. Although most people mainly seek their selfish goal some value giving and sharing what they have with others so they collaborate in a charity organization. Instead of seeking more wealth or power, these people feel happier and more fulfilled when they receive social recognition in the form of praise and respect. In contrast, many people want to associate with the high-class people. The distinctive characters of two different social groups explicitly show that people associate with those with similar interests or desires.

How to educate young students to find their own identities and enhance them has been one of the most important educational goals. Individual identities are formed in the socio-economic context, so undeniably, it is primarily through our identification with social groups that we define ourselves.

53　If a goal is worthy, then any means taken to attain it are justifiable.
　　목적이 가치가 있다면 그것을 성취하기 위해서 취한 어떠한 방법도 정당화될 수 있다.
　　Write a response in which you discuss the extent to which you agree or disagree with the statement and explain your reasoning for the position you take. In developing and supporting your position, you should consider ways in which the statement might or might not hold true and explain how these considerations shape your position.

강의노트　목적을 이루기 위한 정당한 방법을 강조하는 에세이 토픽이다. 결과론적인 행위보다는 어떤 행위의 의도 또한 중요하게 평가해야 하는 사회를 이루어야만 한다. 이러한 에세이는 만약에 어떤 학생이 agree한다면 서론에서부터 실격이 되는 에세이를 작성하는 오류를 범한다.

From a consequentialist standpoint, euthanasia can be just because they believe a morally right act is the one that will produce a good outcome, which would reduce the suffering of a dying patient. Although one intends to help the beloved one free from pain, assisting in killing another human being and ending their existence is immoral. When it comes to justice, the intrinsic cause is a more important thing to account for than the impacts of consequence. Thus, I disagree with the statement that supports the consequentialist viewpoint.

Of course, even when one's intention is innocent if the results harm others, the one is responsible for the action that he /she took. For accidental murder, one must be punished accordingly; however, all good consequences cannot be praised or acknowledged. In many cases, seemingly beneficial results can turn out to be the

Lecture 7
Controversy

cause of evil decisions.

Professor Michael Sandal'lecture on Utilitarianism begins with a question as to whether it can be a justifiable action if one can spare the lives of five on a trolley car that is about to rack at the end of the track by flipping over the fat man leaning over the by-pass bridge so he can be used to act as a heavy object that would stop it from running. We know such behavior is not morally acceptable even when more people can benefit from sacrifice.

Another compelling example can be seen in an officer's violation of due process when arresting a criminal. Due process is the regulation that the court reviews when they question the enforcement of laws. In any case, public officers' vow to uphold should not justify an act of breaking the law as an excuse to enforce them. A Miranda warning has to be done to prevent prophylactic crimes by requiring law enforcement to protect an individual in custody and subject to direct questioning. Some cops' ruthless beating in arresting a black motorist outraged the LA riot in 1992 and a chain of events followed the incident. Our society honors those who accomplished their goal through fair play rather than using double standards.

Without practicing due process, our society dooms into chaos caused by corruption or abusive behaviors. The court makes a sentence, they look into the cause of crime more importantly than its result. The motives in crimes are the most significant determining whether a defendant is guilty or not. [449]

---

78 People's attitudes are determined more by their immediate situation or surroundings than by society as a whole.
사람들의 태도는 당면한 상황이나 환경에 의해서 지배되는 것이 아니라 사회 전체의 통념으로 지배되는 것이다.
Write a response in which you discuss the extent to which you agree or disagree with the

statement and explain your reasoning for the position you take. In developing and supporting your position, you should consider ways in which the statement might or might not hold true and explain how these considerations shape your position.

개인의 행위는 사회적 통념에 지배된다. 즉, 사회적 가치관의 영향으로 개인들은 자신이 선택할 수 있는 자유를 상실하는 경우가 종종 있다. 파시즘에 광란했던 독일 사회나 회교도 사회를 볼 때 우리는 개인의 권리와 욕구는 거대한 통치 이념과 종교적 가치관에 억눌리게 되었다는 것을 쉽게 알 수 있다. 개인의 자유와 사회적 제약, 이 2가지 대조되는 개념을 이해하고 글을 써나가야 한다.

People's actions and attitudes are greatly influenced by their immediate situation or surrounding because the impacts are often more personal and apparent. It is human nature to value self-motivation, which motivates us to take action for everything we deem necessary for survival. However, political campaigns can spark mass movements and change attitudes by informing or convincing society to act upon collective ideals. Thus, I agree with the speaker because people's attitudes are not free from ideals or values hidden in the social context.

Most people are preoccupied with a busy life structure consisting of daily jobs, chores, family, and friendships. The status of each factor has a significant impact on well-being, and it affects the personal lives of people. This would determine their attitude and course of action as a change in one or the other requires proper adaptation to ensure personal well-being. For instance, if a person is laid-off from the workplace, acquiring a source of income becomes a priority. Such situations prompt immediate action since it is difficult to live without the ability to purchase necessities.

Furthermore, where you live determines your qualify of life. Some areas may have a secure and safe environment but, other sectors are high in crime and poverty. Those who live in such areas are more likely to be involved in crime because of the insecure social or familiar environment. A poor sector of a metropolis is often plagued with much more crime than upscale communities. Individual needs can surely affect a

Controversy

society's collective opinion in these circumstances, therefore determining the attitudes of the poor residents.

On the other hand, history shows that politics and the media stirs the public to act upon the propaganda. For example, the Nazi Party of Germany quickly changed popular opinion towards anti-Semitic beliefs by political control and propaganda. The promise of a better society from a Fascist regime seemed appealing enough to control public attitudes in Germany as a whole to accept the idea of discrimination and aggressive expansion. From this point of view, the political climate of a society contributes to shaping the attitudes of its citizens.

Though a decline in society can often change the situations and surroundings of people, hardships can still exist without such circumstances. When societal pressure is low, attending to one's personal life is of utmost importance. Therefore, people's attitudes are determined not by what is happening immediately, but by the socio-political norm, which creates a collective action when being promoted in specific manners. [430]

Lecture 8

Art

Art Topic Analysis

ART 토픽과 대조되는 개념은 과학과 기술이다. 비현실적으로 보이는 예술이 우리들에게 끼치는 영향을 깊이 이해하고 토픽에 접근해야 한다. 그러므로 교육과 연계되는 토픽으로 대학생들에 반드시 예술과 관계되는 과목을 가르쳐야 되는지를 묻는다. 실용적인 학문만이 인기 있는 요즘 대학의 추세에서 예술의 중요성을 언급하면 된다.

예술의 산물은 대도시이다. 그러므로 정부는 소도시나 농촌지역보다는 대도시 삶을 더 지원해야 한다. 대도시는 문화를 생산하는 장소이기 때문이다. 이처럼 문화라는 것과 대도시의 중요성을 부각해서 에세이를 발전시키는 것이 매우 중요하다. 즉, 예술이 없는 사회는 문화가 없는 사회가 될 수 있다는 위험 부담이 있다.

아주 실리적인 면에서만 사회를 바라보는 사람들은 예술의 지원은 너무 사치스러운 일이라고 생각한다. 그러므로 이들은 정부가 예술을 지원하는 것보다 가난하고 고통받는 사람들을 위한 지원을 하는 것을 급선무로 하고 있다. 그러나 예술가들이 우리 사회 지도자라고 볼 때 그들은 현실적인 방법이 아니라 우리의 영혼에 호소하는 방법으로 때로는 경각심을 주고 때로는 상상력을 풍부하게 만들어줌으로써 사회 발전에 기여한다.

2 To understand the most important characteristics of a society, one must study its major cities.
한 사회의 성격을 이해하기 위해서는 우리는 반드시 (그 사회가 만든) 대도시를 이해해야만 한다.

5 Claim : Governments must ensure that their major cities receive the financial support they need in order to thrive. [117]
정부들은 그들의 대도시가 번영하기 위해 필요한 재정적 지원을 받는 것을 보장해야만 한다.
Reason : It is primarily in cities that a nation's cultural traditions are preserved and generated.
이유: 한 국가의 문화 전통이 생성되고 보존되는 곳은 대부분 도시이기 때문이다.

7 Some people believe that government funding of the arts is necessary to ensure that the arts can flourish and be available to all people. Others believe that government funding of the arts threatens the integrity of the arts.
어떤 사람들은 정부는 예술이 번영하고 모든 사람들이 즐길 수 있도록 예술 자금을 지원해야 할 필요가 있다고 믿는다. 다른 사람들은 정부 자금은 예술의 순수성을 위협한다고 믿는다.

54 In order to become well-rounded individuals, all college students should be required to take courses in which they read poetry, novels, mythology, and other types of imaginative literature.
모든 대학생들은 원만한 인격을 형성하기 위해서 시, 소설, 신화 그리고 여타의 창작 문학 작품들을 읽을 수 있는 과목들을 반드시 택하도록 해야 한다.

55 In order for any work of art — for example, a film, a novel, a poem, or a song — to have merit, it must be understandable to most people.
영화, 소설, 시나 노래 같은 예술작품들이 가치를 가지려면 반드시 대중이 이해할 수 있는 것들이어야만 한다.

80 Nations should suspend government funding for the arts when significant numbers of their citizens are hungry or unemployed.
국가가 상당수 국민들이 빈곤하거나 실직했을 때 예술을 위한 자금 지원을 보류하는 것은 당연하다.

88 Claim : Nations should suspend government funding for the arts when significant numbers of their citizens are hungry or unemployed.
주장: 국가가 상당수 국민들이 빈곤하거나 실직했을 때 예술을 위한 자금 지원을 보류하는 것은 당연하다.
Reason : It is inappropriate — and, perhaps, even cruel — to use public resources to fund the arts when people's basic needs are not being met.
이유: 국민의 기본적 요구가 충족되지 않을 때 공적인 자원을 예술 자금 지원에 쓴다는 것은 부적절할 뿐만 아니라 심지어 잔인하기까지 하다.

Sample essay

5   Claim : Governments must ensure that their major cities receive the financial support they need
      in order to thrive.
      주장: 정부들은 그들의 대도시가 번영하기 위해 필요한 재정적 지원을 받는 것을 보장해야만 한다.
      Reason : It is primarily in cities that a nation's cultural traditions are preserved and generated.
      이유: 한 국가의 문화 전통이 생성되고 보존되는 곳은 대부분 도시이기 때문이다.
      Write a response in which you discuss the extent to which you agree or disagree with the claim
      and the reason on which that claims is based.

강의노트   ART 5번 주제는 토픽 question과 2가지 이유인 cultural traditions are preserved and generated라는
            이유를 주고서 논하라는 토픽이다. 역사적으로 대도시가 예술과 문화의 산물을 생성하고 보존하는 것이라는
            사실을 잘 이해하고 써야 한다. 그러므로 답변은 agree이다.

The speaker claims that governments must financially support large cities to thrive because it is primarily in cities that a nation's cultural traditions are preserved and generated. Some would say it is unfair to provide major cities funds rather than rural areas where more traditional ways of life and culture are pervasive. Nevertheless, I agree with the speaker because it is primarily large cities where many artists collaborate to produce artwork. Museums and galleries are open to the public so more people can participate in various cultural activities.

Of course, governments should ensure some budget to preserve cultural traditions in the small cities or rural areas to pass down traditional songs, customs, and rituals to the future generation. Without the government's financial support, cultural heritage would disappear.

Nevertheless, the government should provide more funds to the Center of Arts and Culture. Major cities are cultural places where many artists are associating to generate new art culture by expressing their ideals, which leads to a new trend in the center for artist performances or exhibitions. For example, many tourists visit New York City knows because of its eclectic features; scores of diverse cultural influences are evident everywhere. Thus, governments should impose a policy supporting cultural agendas for personal and collective development.

Another compelling argument in favor of the speaker's position is that art should be available to all people, so governments should build more museums and performance halls in their major cities so audiences can appreciate concerts, operas, and exhibitions with a reasonable ticket price. Indeed, art can enrich our life by removing stress from the strenuous daily workload of cities with the dynamics that art generates, and this energy will lead to forming a new cultural wave or trend by connecting us through cultural diffusion. Without preserving the legacy of physical artifacts and intangible yet valuable attributes of a society, a nation would accomplish little toward promoting cultural heritage.

In conclusion, Rome is the trace of the Roman Empire while Seoul is 600 years of Korea. In fact, the best way to understand a culture or civilization of a group of people is to examine cultural centers and artistic activities in which art and cultures can thrive over generation. [410 words]

7   Some people believe that government funding of the arts is necessary to ensure that the arts can flourish and be available to all people. Others believe that government funding of the arts threatens the integrity of the arts.
어떤 사람들은 정부는 예술이 번영하고 모든 사람들이 즐길 수 있도록 예술 자금을 지원해야 할 필요가 있다고 믿는다. 다른 사람들은 정부 자금은 예술의 순수성을 위협한다고 믿는다.
Write a response in which you discuss which view more closely aligns with your own position and explain your reasoning for the position you take. In developing and supporting your position, you should address both of the views presented.

강의노트   ART 7번 토픽은 2가지 견해를 some people과 others로 제시하고 나서 당신의 의견은 어떠한가를 묻는 형식으로 되어 있다. 예술이 정치의 수단이 되어서는 안 되고, 도시는 우리사회에 절대적으로 필요한 창의적인 예술가들의 활동은 물론 일반 대중들도 great art work에 다가갈 수 있는 기회를 주어야 한다고 논리를 편다. 모든 사람들이 예술을 감상할 수 있는 권한이 주어지는 사회야말로 평등한 사회이기 때문이다.

The effects of government funding of the arts have long been controversial. Some would claim that the government fund for art should not be used as a tool for propaganda or the pleasure of the few in power. However, the government should provide sufficient funds not only for the realization of artistic inspiration of young artists but also to allow the public to access artworks or performances. Thus, the salutary effects of art on society cannot be overlooked at the cost of pragmatic pursuits.

In communist nations, artists have been considered as the tool of the idolization of their supreme leader using artists to serve the few in power. History witnessed that art has in possession of those who have the privilege to enjoy an extravagant lifestyle. Since most artists' income sources were from the wealthy and powerful, their integrity of art has been frequently questioned.

Over the past century, due to the development of technology, the values of art education have been overshadowed by engineering and technician education. Many high schools already replaced art classes with other subjects related to engineering or business. However, a lack of prominent artists would suffer the absence of creative energy that plays a key role in boosting innovation. We should remember that consumers want to buy a product with good design instead of a durable but heavyweight Without the government's funding for art education, students have difficulties in developing their sense of beauty, and this will lead to economic failure in the near future. Thus, governments should support art education so it can contribute to raising future artists.

Furthermore, art is an indispensable commodity for mental relief and expression of thought. Therefore, any other practical field of study cannot overshadow art. Those who may argue that there are better ways for the government to spend money is for the welfare of people. However, to increase public access to art, the government should provide sufficient funds to public facilities such as museums and performance halls so they can facilitate more art programs. True democracy can be accomplished when the government is ready to support artists and audiences.

In this materialistic age, even art forms are not free to enjoy. Thus, governments should provide a substantial amount of funds so that everyone can benefit from the cultural heritage. [500]

---

88 Claim : Nations should suspend government funding for the arts when significant numbers of their citizens are hungry or unemployed.
주장: 국가가 상당수 국민들이 빈곤하거나 실직했을 때 예술을 위한 자금 지원을 보류하는 것은 당연하다.
Reason : It is inappropriate — and, perhaps, even cruel — to use public resources to fund the arts when people's basic needs are not being met.
이유: 사람들이 기본적인 생필품마저 공급받지 못할 때 예술을 지원한다는 것은 부적절할 뿐 아니라 잔인한 일이기 때문이다.
Write a response in which you discuss the extent to which you agree or disagree with the recommendation and explain your reasoning for the position you take. In developing and supporting your position, describe specific circumstances in which adopting the recommendation would or would not be advantageous and explain how these examples shape your position.

강의노트 88번은 claim과 reason이 함께 주어지는 유형의 토픽이다. 토픽을 paraphrase하는 skills로는 비교급을 사용하는 것이 가장 바람직하다. 토픽을 restate하는 기법으로 다음과 같이 간결한 비교급 의문문으로 paraphrase 구문으로 에세이를 시작하는 방법이 바람직하다. 이 토픽은 예술가에게 정부가 주는 fund보다는 가난에 고통 받는 사람들을 도와야 하느냐고 묻는다. 당연히 disagree를 해야 한다. 예술가 또한 우리 사회 발전에 기여하는 중요한 역할을 하기 때문이다.

Is supporting people in need more important than giving funds to artists? To pragmatists, funding for the arts is secondary to the immediate needs of the suffering population from poverty. For this reason, when the local government announces its new plan to construct a somewhat luxurious city hall building, they organize a protest to stop it from spending money for useless purposes. However, if our world is full of pragmatists, no great civilization could have been constructed or advanced. Artists can generate the inspiration necessary for promoting artistic creation and cultivating altruistic minds in the heart of people. Without such creative and philanthropic minds, our society would accomplish less toward constructing monuments.

Most governments look after a devastated population suffering from the shortage of basic needs such as food and a more secure and safe social environment. Of course, when a whole society is devastated by political turmoil, economic crisis, or natural disasters, the government should focus on solving immediate problems.

We should understand that the contributions of the artists are second to none, though our society is not giving due importance to their work of creation. A nation that weighs the cultural aspects of art can better flourish in its economy. For example, countries like France and the U.S. allotted annual budgets to support art so more tourists and audiences are invited to their museums or art performances, thus, leading to creating more revenues in tourist industries and businesses. With the income generated by tourism, the whole economy of a nation can be better, and at the core of such cultural activities is the great work of artists.

Ironically, those in need of financial support can be better helped by artists with philanthropic minds. It is well known that a pop star, Michael Jackson, holds a world record for most charities with monetary donations through sponsorship of the non-profit organization. Fundraising art performances are frequent in the major cities where benevolent artists collaborate to generate otherwise hidden impulses of society, and they play a pivotal role in the moral awakening by enhancing humanistic values.

Art

In short, artists contribute to our society by boosting altruistic spirits instead of merely pursuing their reputations.

The statement that it is inappropriate — and, perhaps, even cruel — to use public resources to fund the arts when people's basic needs are not being met is generated from a myopic view to understand interactions between artists and the general public. I would say artists are the ones who support society instead of entertaining those of the privileged class. Moreover, solutions to social problems should not be provided with the dichotomy of the haves and have-nots.

History

History Topic Analysis

역사 분야에서는 과거가 현재의 거울이 될 수 있는가를 묻는 질문이다. 과거와 현재를 동일한 역사 발전 선상에 보지 않고 과거는 그저 쓸모없는 물건이라고 보는 경향이 있다. 그러나 과거 없는 현재는 결국 과거로부터 미래로 가는 것이라는 요지를 파악해야 한다. 주의해야 할 점은 예증을 문화에서 가려내어 쓰는 것이다.

119번은 현재의 이익을 추구하며 더 유용하게 쓰기 위해서 오래된 건물을 보존하는 것보다 현대적 발전을 중시해야 하는지를 묻는다. 건물은 문화유산이기 때문에 국가의 자존심이며 문화유산이라는 점을 명시하고 이러한 유산이 현재의 우리는 다른 문화와 식별할 수 있게 만든다는 사실을 알아야 한다.

또한 역사가 한 시대가 다른 시대와 다른 점을 연구한다는 이 토픽은 비교 대조라는 기본 연구 방법을 안다면 당연히 누구나 쉽게 동의한다로 글을 풀어갈 수 있다. 비교 대조를 통해서 한 시대가 어떻게 다른 시대로 변화해 갔느냐를 알 수 있는 분야이다.

Lecture 9
History

HISTORY	57	The main benefit of the study of history is to dispel the illusion that people living now are significantly different from people who lived in earlier times. 역사학의 유익한 점은 현대 인간은 과거의 인간과 다르다는 환상을 깨는 것이다.
	74	Knowing the past cannot help people to make important decisions today. [133, 134] 과거를 아는 것은 현재의 결정에 도움이 되지 않는다.
	119	When old building stand on ground that modern planners feel could be better used for modern purposes, modern development should be given precedence over the preservation of historic buildings. 현재의 이익을 추구하며 더 유용하게 쓰기 위해서 오래된 건물을 보존하는 것보다 현대적 발전을 중시해야 한다.
	133	Claim : Knowing about the past cannot help people to make important decisions today. 주장: 과거를 아는 것은 현재의 결정에 도움이 되지 않는다. Reason : The world today is significantly more complex than it was even in the relatively recent past. [134] 이유: 오늘날 세상은 근대 생활보다 더 복잡하기 때문이다.

Sample essay

57

The main benefit of the study of history is to dispel the illusion that people living now are significantly different from people who lived in earlier times.
역사학의 유익한 점은 현내 인간은 과거의 인간과 다르다는 환상을 깨는 것이다.
Write a response in which you discuss the extent to which you agree or disagree with the statement and explain your reasoning for the position you take. In developing and supporting your position, you should consider ways in which the statement might or might not hold true and explain how these considerations shape your position.

강의노트 57번 토픽은 과연 역사학이란 무엇인가에 대해서 묻는 질문이다. 역사학이란 비교 대조를 통해서 한 시대가 다른 시대로 어떻게 변해 가는지에 대해서 묻는 질문이다. 예를 들면 역사학자들은 동일한 사람이라 할지라도 중세 시대에는 농노, 근대에는 자영 농민, 현재는 시민이라 불린다. 동시대 사람이라 할지라도 사회구조가 공산주의면 인민, 민주주의면 시민이라 불리는 이러한 개념을 비교 대조라는 방법론을 통해서 역사학을 연구한다.

Few would deny that knowledge across all disciplines has been developed by the analysis of compare and contrast. Anyone who fails to figure out analogous reasoning

Without understanding how to make an analogy, no one is likely to contribute to the progress of knowledge. It is not an illusion that people living today are significantly different from people who lived in the past. Subjects in the past look up to a master, but citizens are so far equal in that none have hereditary rights superior to others today. The people today and yesterday live in a different social context. Different social structures made them placed in different political and economic circumstances. Historians endeavor to reveal past stories to compare those of today so they can show how civilizations or cultures have evolved to today's modern era. Thus, I disagree with the speaker's contention.

From the view of biological features, most modern humans are very similar to those who lived in earlier times. There is not much difference in the life of mankind in that all human beings have to face personal and social conflicts. As there are ongoing wars or natural disasters today, people in the past also suffered from such events as there have always been political conflicts and hostilities between and among nations. It may seem true that people today are somewhat similar to those of the past when investigating the two groups of people in terms of human suffering.

The quality of life revealed between today's people and those of the past shows that history is not an illusion. For example, much has changed in the social status of subjects in the past and that of today's citizens. Unlike the peasants who were enslaved to be obedient to a lord, today's citizens have the responsibility to elect their leader by voting, and they can challenge leaders' wrongdoings by the collective power of organizing street rallies. The role of historians is to portray distinctive social characters across ages in the objective description.

Furthermore, historians established an imaginary line between historically meaningful events to establish a chronicle that gives a clearer picture of the long

Lecture 9
History

history. For example, the modern era of Korean history begins with the development of human-centered values due to the introduction of Western technology. Considering the fact there was a big difference in lifestyles of the people and their rights, it is undeniable that the study of history is not to dispel the illusion that people living now are not the same as those who lived in the earlier time but to reveal why and how social changes affect paradigm shifts in society.

In conclusion, the main benefits of history are not to dispel the illusion that today's people are different from those from the past. More importantly, history on a large scale across long time frames and epochs through a multi-disciplinary approach has been beneficial for the development of arts and science. Technology has been dramatically developed in the past century, so today's people come to live more convenient but busier life with advanced communication and transportation technologies than in the past. [450]

---

74 Knowing the past cannot help people to make decisions today.
과거를 아는 것은 현재의 결정에 도움이 되지 않는다.
Write a response in which you discuss the extent to which you agree or disagree with the statement and explain your reasoning for the position you take. In developing and supporting your position, you should consider ways in which the statement might or might not hold true and explain how these considerations shape your position.

강의노트 과거를 아는 것, 즉 역사를 공부하는 것은 지난날의 잘못을 배움으로써 같은 잘못을 반복하지 않아야 한다는 점을 강조해야 한다. 예증으로는 과거 역사적 관계를 알아야만 현재 외교 정책을 수립하는 데 도움이 되며, 또한 투자에 있어서도 과거에 어떤 이유로 손해를 보았다면 동일한 실수를 하지 않기 위해서 과거를 거울삼아야 한다고 써야 한다.

It is foolhardy to make important decisions today without understanding past events related to current events or issues. Since all decision-making processes involve risk, it is imperative to investigate similar incidents in the past to identify alternative and optimal choices, especially in political or diplomatic decisions of today. Understanding past events should be precedent in solving today's problems. Thus, I think the speaker's notion that knowing the past cannot help people to make decisions today is unpersuasive.

Some may say that even if we know about the past, we tend to make decisions based on impulse or immediate and short-term satisfaction. Thus, pondering past stories little help us today. However, such a view is short of references and data, so it would accomplish little toward making optimal decisions.

Those who can understand current issues in the historical context can make better decisions for their nation. Lessons from history diplomatic policies to avoid making a similar mistake in the past. College students majoring in Political Science or History study past international relationships at the state level. For example, Kim Dae-jung, a former South Korean president, imposed the "Sunshine Policy" on North Korea to promote peace in the Korean Peninsula. To maintain the two Koreas' closer and more friendly relationships, he signed the Keumkang mountain tourism.

It is common to see investors who are fooled by a hoax. Their investment decisions that are seemingly reliable assets but later turn out to be an illusion. Regret and resentment are soon to follow. They could have avoided financial loss they conducted accurate research to the minutest detail regarding the history of the companies. In short, sensible investors examine not only the current business situation but also the history behind the seemingly profitable investments. By learning from failures in the past, people can preserve wealth by making less risky investments. Whoever invests their assets without knowing about the past fluctuating stock market trend or the history of the companies is less likely to be a successful business investor.

Lecture 9
History

Today is a reflection of the past: thus, understanding when and why past events occurred and finding who solved the problem how would help today's people not to repeat the same mistakes in the past. [429]

Politics & Law

Politics & Law Topic Analysis

정치인으로서 자기 자신의 소신에 매달려야 하느냐는 토픽은 소신보다 더 중요한 것은 민중의 합의라는 점을 잘 이해하고 써야 한다. 민주주의 근간은 미국의 초대 대통령이 George Washington의 "Great Compromise"의 의미를 알고 있어야 이 토픽을 제대로 이해한다.

공무원(정치인)들이 의사를 결정할 때 물론 여론을 반영해야 한다. 그러나 포퓰리즘에 의거 한 정치는 희망이 없는 징치가 될 수 있다는 점을 잊어서는 안 된다. 또한 정부의 기능에 관한 토픽은 정부는 미래의 재난을 방지하기 위해서 부단히 노력하는 기관이라는 것일 잘 알고 써야 한다.

사회복지가 잘 된 나라와 위대한 과학자나 예술가, 정치인들을 배출한 국가가 강대국이냐고 묻는 이 토픽은 개개인이 사회에 기여하는 기여도에 대해서 묻고 있다. 한 개인의 성공, 즉 발명이나 사회적 혁신은 사회복지 환경에 기여했고, 개인의 성과를 무시하는 북한과 같은 폐쇄적인 사회는 결국 사회복지도 약화되었다.

법 분야에서는 법이 우리를 도덕적으로 만드느냐는 것과 법은 시간과 장소에 따라서 유연하게 적용되어야 하느냐는 질문이 나온다. 시간과 공간에 따라서 변화하는 법이 예증을 들어 설명해야 한다.

Lecture 10
Politics & Law

POLITICS &
LAW

8   Claim : In any field — business, politics, education, government — those in power should step down after five years. [111, 149]
주장: 비즈니스, 정치, 교육, 정부 등 어느 분야에서든 권력을 가진 사람은 5년 후에는 사임해야만 한다.
Reason : The surest path to success for any enterprise is revitalization through new leadership.
이유: 어떤 조직에서든 성공에 이르는 확실한 길은 새로운 지도력을 통해서 재활성화하는 것이다.

16 Some people believe that in order to be effective, political leaders must yield to public opinion and abandon principle for the sake of comprise. Others believe that the most essential quality of an effective leader is the ability to remain consistently committed to particular principles and objectives. [104/107]
어떤 사람들은 효율적이 되기 위해서 정치지도자들은 여론을 따르고 타협을 위해서 원칙을 희생해야 한다고 믿는다. 다른 사람들은 효율적 지도자의 가장 중요한 자질은 특정 원칙과 목적에 전념하는 능력이라고 믿는다.

18 The well-being of a society is enhanced when many of its people question authority.
한 사회의 복지는 많은 사람들이 권위에 도전할 때 강화된다.

19 Government should focus on solving the immediate problems of today rather than on trying to solve the anticipated problems of the future.
정부는 미래에 예측되는 문제들을 푸는 것보다 오늘날의 긴급한 문제를 해결하는 데 집중적으로 노력해야 한다.

21 Law should be flexible enough to take account of various circumstances, times and places.
법은 다양한 환경, 시간과 장소를 고려할 정도로 유연해야 한다.

28 The surest indicator of a great nation is represented not by the achievements of its rulers, artists, or scientists, but by the general welfare of its people. [113/120/121/127/145]
위대한 국가의 명확한 척도는 지도자, 예술가 또는 과학자들이 성취한 과업에 나타나는 것이 아니라 그 나라 국민의 전체적인 복지 상태로 결정된다.

50 Government officials should rely on their will rather than unquestioningly carry out the will of the people they serve. [86/115]
고위 공무원은 무조건적으로 민중의 뜻을 수행하기보다 자신의 의지에 근거해야 한다.

60 Politicians should pursue common ground and reasonable consensus rather than elusive ideals.
정치가는 허황된 아이디어보다는 대중적 합의와 합리적 동의를 추구해야 한다.

62 Leaders are created by the demands that they are placed on them.
지도자는 그들이 처해진 시대적 요구에 의해서 탄생한다.

66   People who are the most deeply committed to an ideal or policy are also the
     most critical of it.
     어떤 정책이나 아이디어에 가장 충실하게 헌신하는 사람들이 바로 그런 정책과 아이디어에
     가장 비판적이다.

85   Some people believe that in order to thrive, a society must put its overall
     success before the well-being of its individual citizens. Others believe that the
     well-being of a society can only be measured by the general welfare of all its
     people.
     어떤 사람들은 한 사회가 번영하기 위해서는 개개인의 복지가 그 사회 전체의 성공보다 우선
     시되어야 한다고 믿는다. 다른 사람들은 한 사회의 성공적인 척도는 오로지 모든 사람들의 복
     지로만 측정된다고 말한다.

86   Some people believe that government officials must carry out the will of the
     people they serve. Others believe that officials should base their decisions on
     their own judgment. [50/115]
     어떤 사람들은 공무원은 민중의 뜻을 수행해야 한다고 생각한다. 다른 사람들은 공무원들이
     내리는 결정은 스스로의 판단에 근거해야 한다고 생각한다.

89   Claim : Many problems of modern society cannot be solved by laws and the
     legal systems.
     주장: 현대 사회의 많은 문제들은 법이나 사법제도로 해결될 수 없다.
     Reasons: Laws cannot change what is in people's hearts or minds.
     이유: 법은 사람들의 마음과 양심을 바꿀 수 없기 때문이다.

94   The effectiveness of a country's leader is best measured by examining the
     well-being of that country's citizens. [147]
     한 나라의 지도자가 얼마나 효과적으로 나라를 이끌고 있는지 알아보기 위한 가장 좋은 방법
     은 그 나라 국민들의 복지 수준을 측정하는 것이다.

139 Claim : Major policy decisions should always be left to politicians and other
     government Experts.
     주장: 주요한 정책 결정은 정치인과 다른 정부 전문가에게 맡겨야 한다.
     Reasons: Politicians and other government officials are more informed and thus
     have better Judgment and perspective than do members of the general public.
     이유: 정치인이나 다른 정부 전문가들은 더 많은 정보를 소유하기 때문에 일반 대중보다 더
     나은 판단과 견해를 가질 수 있다.

141 It is more harmful to compromise one's own beliefs than to adhere to them.
     자신의 소신에 매달리는 것보다 자기 자신의 소신에 타협하는 것이 더 해롭다

Sample essay

8   In a field of — business, politics, education, government — those in power should step down after five years.
Reason : The surest path to success for any enterprise is revitalization through new leadership.
주장: 비즈니스, 정치, 교육, 정부 등 어느 분야에든 권력을 가진 사람은 5년 후에는 사임해야만 한다.
이유: 어떤 조직에서든 성공에 이르는 확실한 길은 새로운 지도력을 통한 재활성화이다.
Write a response in which you discuss the extent to which you agree or disagree with the claim and the reason on which that claim is based.

강의노트   리더십을 바꾸는 것은 대체로 4, 5년마다 한 번씩 이루어지는 것이 민주주의의 기본이다. 새로운 리더십은 새로운 변화를 가져온다고 써야 한다. 특히 정치나 교육과 같이 대중을 위해서 일하는 기관에서 장기간의 리더십은 부작용을 가져다준다. 하지만 기업의 경우는 애플 사에 기여한 Steve Jobs 의 경우를 보면 innovative 한 아이디어를 가진 CEO에 한해서는 5년 만에 물러나야 한다는 법칙은 합리적이 아니라고 쓴다. 예로는 비즈니스, 정치, 교육, 정부에서 다양하게 입증한다.

Steve Jobs led the Apple company successfully for 14 years as CEO, but a long-term leadership seems exceptional even in the business sector. When it comes to the leadership that serves the general public, leadership should change regularly to prevent corruption and abuse of power. Nevertheless, it is questionable whether it is necessary to change our leaders every five years. Thus, I disagree with the statement.

Five years short-term of the presidency should not be applied to the business arena where profitability should be the most important concern. As mentioned earlier, we cannot undermine the talents that a brilliant CEO Steve Jobs demonstrated. Thus, as long as a CEO is healthy enough to contribute to the profitable operation of a company, multiple terms or appointments to the chief executive position should be allowed.

History tells how much people struggled to achieve the right to elect their leader. Some of them were arrested, tortured, or killed in the process of toppling a military dictator. For example, Park Jung-hee's 17-year dictatorship halted the development of democracy in South Korea. After he was assassinated during a dinner at the Korean

CIA, another military dictator, Jeon Du-hwan staged a coup and held power through an indirect election of the electoral college whose members were selectively favorable to him. The May 18th democratic uprising led to forcing him to resign after seven years. And the constitutional court in Kim Young-sam's government, the first people's government, mandated the presidential term to five years.

In the case of superintendents or government high officers, the serving time should be restricted to five years, especially for board members with professional careers in the field of education. Unlike the business sector where the leadership has played a crucial role in increasing profits and thus benefiting its success that leads to higher employment in turn, leadership for public service should change regularly so new dynamics can boost the motivation for better diversification and quality in education. Every five years election would encourage more community members to participate in local school programs, which will determine future development.

In short, the restriction on the five-year term should apply to political leaders or government officers who serve the public based on the democratic constitution. Although a CEO's long term service can be more effective for business operations and beneficial for business success. [380]

---

16   Some people believe that in order to be effective political leaders must yield to public opinion and abandon principle for the sake of compromise. Others believe that the most essential quality of an effective leader is the ability to remain consistently committed to particular principles.
어떤 사람들은 효율적이 되기 위해서 정치지도자들은 여론을 따르고 타협을 위해서 원칙을 희생해야 한다고 믿는다. 다른 사람들은 효율적 지도자의 가장 중요한 자질은 특정 원칙과 목적에 전념하는 능력이라고 믿는다. Write a response in which you discuss which view more closely aligns with your own position and explain your reasoning for the position you take. In developing and supporting your position, you should address both of the views presented.

Lecture 10
Politics & Law

강의노트   민주주의의 근본은 타협이다. 물론 지도자가 생각하는 아이디어나 원칙이 민주주의나 인본주의에 근간을 둔 것이라면 그 원칙을 지키고자 지도자 자신이 부단히 노력해야 할 것이다. 그러나 여론에 기우리지 않고 자신만의 원칙을 고수하는 것은 사회 전체적으로 비생산적일 수 있다. 근거 자료로는 세금 납부자로서 국민의 권리와 불만족한 대중은 사회적 혼란을 야기할 수 있다는 것을 제시한다.

Yielding to the public for the sake of compromise is necessary for the effective political leadership. If public opinion is overshadowed by the name of the political ideal or principles, it will spark protests in an accumulative manner. When the public displays discontent and civil disobedience towards the ideal unfavorable to the taxpayer, commerce decreases, and thus, further escalation towards uprising becomes inevitable. Thus, I disagree with the statement.

Generally, it is taxpayers who pay for political campaigns and government operations. Political leaders are elected and financed by the people on the promise of serving the public good. From this point of view, politicians should strive to represent the public opinion rather than persistently to uphold the principle unless they lean on populism.

Furthermore, compromise is the desirable form of diplomacy in which cooperation should be highly valued and practiced. Committing to principles unwaveringly is a recipe for vigorous opposition as people naturally differ in opinions, especially within politics. Discontent and rebellious attitudes quickly grow to strong disagreements, thus further harm society with social unrest or war.

Finally, in many cases, political leaders use principles to achieve selfish gains while convincing the general public to believe in their benefits. Through isolated education systems and propaganda in the form of media, freedom of choice is often stripped away to absolutely dominate social structures. For example, North Koreans are oblivious to current events occurring in the rest of the world and only have access to selective information. Juche Ideology has been used to indoctrinate North Koreans to worship the mortal leaders of Kim's family as god-like beings.

Though holding a particular principle can enhance power, what matters more is how to adopt and use the principle. Sacrificing liberty to force a principle without public concurrence often turns in a resentful population. Therefore, effective political leaders should converse and compromise with the citizens they are supposed to serve instead of posing their political principle unconditionally. [425]

---

18   The well-being of a society is enhanced when many of its people question authority.
한 사회의 복지는 많은 사람들이 권위에 도전할 때 강화된다.
민주주의 사회에서는 시위 형태의 항쟁이라는 집단 궐기 형태로 여론을 관철한다. 그러나 때때로 소수 집단의 이기적인 목적으로 시위가 진행되는 경우가 있다. 그러므로 시위 단체의 의도에 따라서 복지의 향상, 즉 민주주의 사회의 발전에 긍정적 또는 부정적으로 작용할 수 있다고 쓴다.

Write a response in which you discuss the extent to which you agree or disagree with the statement and explain your reasoning for the position you take. In developing and supporting your position, you should consider ways in which the statement might or might not hold true and explain how these considerations shape your position.

Whether the well-being of a society is enhanced when many of its people question authority or not can be determined by the characteristics of the people's collective action. If the likely-minded people are united to protest their interests such as NIMBY, it could be detrimental to society as a whole. However, if street rallies stop government wrongdoings, they will promote transparency and accountability in the public sector.

A new word, NIMBY is an abbreviation for "not in my backyard." This coinage points out the selfish behaviors of a group of people who stubbornly refuse to build an unfavorable public facility such as a crematorium in their neighborhood. This type of collective action of some people would rather cause inconvenience and frustration to others.

In contrast, when South Koreans stood up against the military power violating human rights, democracy was bolstered. For example, the June Gwangju civil unrest brought about an uprising against the oppressive rule of the military government. Without the civil unrest organized to challenge the authority of Chun Du-hwan's power, more innocent people could have been killed or imprisoned.

Another compelling example is vigil protests in South Korea to address political dissent in a manner combating injustice peacefully. They organized to force Park Geun-hye to step down from the presidency. Approximately more than one million people gathered to use the collective power to reveal the truth behind Choi Sun-sil's scandal in interventions to the presidency. The collective power of the public contributed to changing ill policies or authority, thus promoting equality and justice to increase the quality of life.

Due to the development of communication technology, more people are capable of being aware of ongoing domestic and international issues, increasing participation in government affairs compared to the past. Nonetheless, we cannot say all protests organized to challenge authority is not always beneficial for people. Illegal boycotts of the transportation workers would rather harm society. [500 words]

---

19   Governments should focus on solving the immediate problems of today rather than on trying to solve the anticipated problems of the future.
정부는 미래에 예측되는 문제들을 푸는 것보다 오늘날의 긴급한 문제를 해결하는 데 집중적으로 노력해야 한다.
Write a response in which you discuss the extent to which you agree or disagree with the

recommendation and explain your reasoning for the position you take. In developing and supporting your position, describe specific circumstances in which adopting the recommendation would or would not be advantageous and explain how these examples shape your position.

강의노트　　정부는 미래의 문제를 예측하고 계획해야 하는 책임이 있다. 정부는 조직이기 때문에 현재 당면한 문제도 정부 기관을 통해서 해결해 나아가야 한다. 정부는 그때그때 일어난 어려운 문제를 해결하기 위해서 서둘러서는 안 된다. 자연재해나 경제적 위기도 잘 이겨 나갈 수 있는 기관을 조직하는 능력이 있어야 한다. 예증으로는 코비드 팬데믹 대처를 정부기관인 재난 본부가 하는 것과 우주 탐사 기관인 NASA를 들었다.

Most people think the government should focus on solving illegal immigration and poverty issues rather than space exploration. This statement overlooks the important jobs of government organizations designed to plan, budget, and administrate policies. This will lead to not only preventing a future crisis but also prospering economy. When we closely investigate ongoing problems that we experience today, some of them could have been prevented if the government planned and prepared more carefully in advance.

Of course, governments should respond immediately during a national emergency to reduce the degree of catastrophic damage and the number of deaths. When Hurricane Katrina swept the seashores and lawlessness followed, the US government quickly dispatched crews of the Federal Emergency Management Organization to the disaster area. It took immediate actions to rescue victims and to contain the spread of destruction.

The death number and impacts of the Coronavirus of 2019 were unprecedented and the most costly and devastating pandemic that reached a death toll of about 7 million worldwide. The U.S. government carried out the comprehensive health and welfare administration to minimize its impacts on health and the loss of life, mental health, and well-being by issuing stimulus checks to stabilize the economy, so it will continuously

Politics & Law

work to reduce social inequalities toward the long-term plan of the 2030 Agenda for Sustainable Development.

The government should prepare for all possible problems and disasters in advance to prevent future crises. For this, governments organized subsidiary departments and offices under the federal government. The national disaster agency dispatched people to help victims in the disaster area. For example, when the Los Angeles riot occurred in 1992, The Federal Emergency Management Agency provided medical and economic support to the people in the disaster area. Considering that government is a system in which many organizations work to provide a safer and more secure environment, it should endeavor to prevent future problems more than immediate problems. Only well planned and prepared policies can reduce the size of damage and loss.

Many people oppose government's spending money on the exploration of space. NASA's launching satellites might seem too costly and extravagant to those who need immediate relief on Earth. But the government should provide funds to scientists to uncover mysteries in the universe in preparation for cosmic disasters and the depletion of resources on our planet. Although some people are reluctant towards public expenditures on seemingly less urgent matters, experts in various fields serving the public should work to predict future problems with convincing evidence so they can reduce the size of damage and support victims and their recoveries as well as financial loss.

Governments should work for their immediate needs correlating to long-term plans if they intend to improve public services. It is often too late to respond to epidemics when leashed. Therefore, governments need to act as an organization to prepare for emergencies by way of solving the anticipated problems of the future. [550 words]

Laws should be flexible enough to take account of various circumstances, times, and places.
법은 다양한 환경, 시간과 장소를 고려할 정도로 유연해야 한다.
Write a response in which you discuss the extent to which you agree or disagree with the statement and explain your reasoning for the position you take. In developing and supporting your position, you should consider ways in which the statement might or might not hold true and explain how these considerations shape your position.

강의노트 법은 시간에 따라 변해왔다는 사실을 근거로 법의 유연성을 논해야 한다. 법이 모든 사람 앞에서 평등해야 하지만 시대의 변화나 상황적 근거 또한 사회적 가치관에 따라서 서로 다른 법을 적용하고 있는 국가들은 볼 때 agree로 쓰는 것이 타당하다.

Although it is unusual to give a minimum sentence to a criminal who committed a crime with malicious intention, it is pretty common to give a generous reduction of the charge to an insane convict who accidentally killed someone. The shocking news that John Hinckley Jr. shot Ronald Reagan in an attempt to kill the president shook the world; however, the court's decision that he was sentenced to be treated at a psychic ward instead of serving a jail time was more stunning. The law and social regulations should be flexible enough to take account of various circumstances, times, and places.

Societies uphold different cultural values and religious beliefs. As outrageous as it might appear to European women, Muslim women think requiring them to wear hijab in public is their tradition. However, such practice can be viewed as discrimination against women in European countries. Once Fox News showed the clash between the Muslim Orthodox population and the French cops. French Law prohibits wearing women's head covering in public places. This example shows that rigid laws contributed to civil discontent and protests.

Moreover, tax laws need to be modified to accommodate fluctuating market trends. The capital gain tax needs to be lowered when the housing market is frozen. When house sales were on the down slope to the extent of paralyzing economic activity last year, the legislative of South Korea legislated a new bill to lower the property sales tax rate. By doing so, policymakers contribute to changing laws to increase the volume of the housing market.

Moreover, history tells us that social progress has been marked many times through amendments to constitutional laws. The abolition of the Segregation Laws contributed to correcting the unfair, discriminated social order through the 14th Amendment. This revolutionary reform could be possible with the civil rights movement led by Martin Luther King Jr. If law cannot account for the democratic justification, they are not legal agreements but a tool for oppression.

As seen above, rigid laws may lead to social unrest and economic crises. In conclusion, laws should be lenient to maintain our collective sense of circumstantial equity, thus preventing future possible crises. [362]

---

28   The surest indicator of a great nation is represented not by the achievements of its rulers, artists, or scientists, but by the general welfare of its people.
위대한 국가의 명확한 척도는 지도자, 예술가 또는 과학자들이 성취한 과업에 나타나는 것이 아니라 그 나라 국민의 전체적인 복지 상태로 결정된다.
Write a response in which you discuss the extent to which you agree or disagree with the statement and explain your reasoning for the position you take. In developing and supporting your position, you should consider ways in which the statement.

강의노트   20세기 초 대부분 공산주의 국가들은 자신은 복지 제도가 강력한 국력을 대변한다고 말했다. 그러나 과학자, 작가와 같은 개개인이 기여하지 않는 사회는 생산력이 떨어질 수밖에 없다. 한 위대한 개인의 창의적 아이디어나 혁신적 리더십은 오히려 복지제도의 강화를 가져올 수 있다는 점을 고려해서 에세이를 작성한다.

Most socialist states tend to monitor artists to find whether the subjects of their artworks are against their political principle. In my opinion, a society that hardly values individual achievements is more likely to fail in boosting economic growth, let alone enhance its welfare system. Totalitarian leadership often argues in favor of this statement undermining the significance of individual achievements at the cost of nationalistic control over the entire society based on equal distribution. Great nations support the excellence of artists, scientists, and rulers it produces to realize their innovative ideas.

History tells us that any society that fetters the freedom of artistic expression is bound to perish. Talented artists offer an enormous amount of social dynamics to the other fields of professionals by awakening them with impulses for creation and initiatives for social reform. Their productions of creative entertainment contributed to increasing national profits. According to the entertainment and media industry, the sales volume of South Korean pop music and movies has been dramatically growing due to several young artists' popularity across the globe. In short, a nation without artists is more like a country without intrigue.

When it comes to scientists, even communist nations strive to encourage their young people to study science in hopes of using their intelligence to develop cutting-edge technology. No one can deny that the revolutionary ideas of scientists contributed to changing the whole paradigm of the modern era. For example, computer technology contributed to providing a better quality of social service to people who need public support. Welfare receivers no longer need to worry about their missing checks lost in delivery with the online public service. It shows a nation's better public service is closely related to advancing technology.

Few would deny that both public health and national security can also be enhanced by brilliant leadership that solves difficult problems under economic or military pressure. For this reason, electing the most desirable leader who protects its population is very important in a democracy. In contrast, the welfare system is

Politics & Law

emphasized as mere propaganda for the idolization of its supreme leader. Thus, we should investigate the qualities of its leaders to judge if a nation is great or not.

General welfare is the byproduct of individual achievements. Innovative accomplishments benefit the whole world beyond their national boundaries by setting examples of excellence and intrigue that is worthy of emulation. [423]

---

89   Claim : Many problems of modern society cannot be solved by laws and the legal systems.
주장: 현대 사회의 많은 문제들은 법이나 사법제도로 해결될 수 없다.
Reasons : Laws cannot change what is in people's hearts or minds.
이유: 법은 사람들의 마음과 양심을 바꿀 수 없기 때문이다.

I agree that laws and the legal system cannot solve many problems today because moral behavior cannot be legislated. When we look at the many stagnant social problems caused by the absence of self-awareness, it is obvious that laws are not the only solution to crimes and violations. Although laws prohibit discrimination to prevent the exploitation of labor and illegal abortions, there are still many business executives who violate minimum wage regulations for more profit and pregnant women who undergo illegal abortions. To build a morally healthy society, we should invest more money and time in ethical education rather than legislating new laws. This is because even harsh laws cannot prevent capital crimes. As our society changes rapidly and diversely with the development of technology, it requires further discussion on moral boundaries and issues.

Even though laws prohibit discrimination by offering equal opportunities to all persons regardless of their race, sex, or color, it is not difficult to find unfair opportunities in our society. For example, Hispanic and African-American activists alerted the University of California that banning affirmative action resulted in a decline of minorities on the campuses of the University of California. Ward Connerly, the UC regent who led the fight to drop race and gender preferences in admissions, contends that the elementary and high school system is not preparing black and Latino students to compete for college admissions. This clearly shows that laws cannot legislate discrimination rooted in our educational system.

The minimum wage is legalized to protect working youth. Nonetheless, many employers are more concerned with creating profits than providing educational opportunities for children. According to an article on illegal abortions, 46 million abortions worldwide each year, among them 20 million take place in countries where abortion is prohibited by law. When the babies are unintended, or even more cruelly, found to be female, they end up being aborted. Although laws attempt to legislate moral behavior, it is unlikely to control people's greed and selfishness through the legal system.

A law is valuable not because it is law, but because it is righteous. As we have seen above, instead of legislating moral behavior, we need to educate our citizens to choose the right course of action. Because the goal of our legal system is to maintain social fairness and security by accomplishing justice and equality, the government should put more effort and time into educating people about the significance of righteousness before it enforces laws to solve the problems of modern society. [480]

---

94   The effectiveness of a country's leaders is best measured by examining the well-being of that country's citizens.
한 나라의 지도자가 얼마나 효과적으로 나라를 이끌고 있는지 알아보기 위한 가장 좋은 방법은 그 나라 국민들의 복지 수준을 측정하는 것이다.
Write a response in which you discuss the extent to which you agree or disagree with the claim.

Lecture 10
Politics & Law

In developing and supporting your position, be sure to address the most compelling reasons and/or examples that could be used to challenge your position.

강의노트   한 국가의 리더십은 자국 국민의 복지 능력에 따라서 결정되는 것보다 국제 사회에서 그 리더십에 대해서 인정받는 것이 중요하다고 논리를 발전해야 한다. 물론 자국의 복지의 수준이 올라가면 자국민의 행복 지수는 올라갈 것이다. 그러나 위대한 지도력은 무역과 상업이 활성화될 뿐 아니라 이민자들까지도 평등하게 살아갈 수 있는 균등한 사회적 지위를 부여할 수 있어야 한다.

A country with a strong middle-class and a high standard of living reflects effective leadership to a great extent. Well-being is a measurement of the happiness and satisfaction of all people, and it is a significant factor in determining the qualities of leaders of a country. It also shows a country's production, trade capacity, and social security. However, good leadership is something to be emulated by the rest of the world. Thus, I disagree with the statement because the effectiveness of a country's leaders can be best measured by investigating the well-being of that country's citizens and its world image.

An effective leader needs to keep the happiness of a country's population at satisfying levels to maintain order and stability. It is fundamental to exercise decision-making skills to provide citizens with fully supportive policies that determine their level of happiness. If citizens are discontent with their lifestyle, impeachment or uprising will soon follow social disturbance, as seen in the June Gwangju Uprising. From this point of view, leaders need to promote transparency and justice to make effective governance possible in a country.

When wealth is sufficient in one's country, it reflects the overall product and trade capabilities. It is almost impossible to maintain a good living standard without producing goods and trading them to accumulate wealth. For example, the volume of common-goods for trade of developing countries is less than that in industrialized nations. Production and commerce are a key factor in measuring the national wealth.

However, a leader's diplomacy is another important factor in determining effective leadership. A country where prosperity is distributed equally to the citizens is highly respected, and it represents a land of opportunity. For example, the United States of America regarded as the land of the free and home of the brave. It was a place where hard work compensated with a good chance at prosperity, even for those who migrated over with absolutely nothing could have an affluent life. This shows that effective leaderships ensure even immigrant populations in pursuit of a better life.

Though the effective leaders should promote the domestic economy, their reputation around the world cannot be overlooked at the cost of the well-being of their citizens. Effective leaders should ensure a life of liberty and happiness to not only for citizens but also for the global community. They should also be an example in the eyes of the global community. [550]

Environment

Environment Topic Analysis

환경에 관한 토픽은 국가는 노력, 시간, 재정적 풍요를 포기하고도 모든 동식물종을 보존해야 한다고 생각하는가에 대한 질문을 한다. 우리는 경제적인 발전을 명분으로 많은 동식물이 멸종 하게 되었다는 사실을 알고 있다. 이러한 동식물의 감소나 멸종은 결국 자연의 한 부분인 인류 의 생존에도 위협적인 존재가 되기 때문에 법으로 자연을 보호해야 한디는 논지를 펴야 한다.

경제적 성장을 위한 개발이 이미 포화상태라는 사실을 이해하고 이 토픽을 접해야 한다. 자연 보호를 위해 부단히 노력해야만 현재 우리가 겪고 있는 이산화탄소 배출로 인한 대기 오염을 줄일 수 있다는 것과 온실효과에 관한 우려를 적어야 한다.

환경 보호를 위해서 무엇을 할 것인지를 고민해 봐야 하며 중요한 점은 경제적 발전과 환경 보호라는 대조되는 이 두 개념을 잘 비교하면서 써야 한다는 것이다.

Lecture 11
Environment

10   Nations should pass laws to preserve any remaining wilderness areas in their natural state, even if these areas could be developed for economic gain. [125/148]

아직 남아 있는 야생지역들이 경제적 이득을 위해서 개발될 수 있는 지역이라 하더라도, 국가는 이 지역들을 자연 상태로 보존하기 위한 법들을 통과시켜야만 한다.

국가는 비록 남은 자연 상태의 야생지역을 경제적 이득을 위해서 개발할 수 있다고 하더라도, 자연지역 보호를 위해서 법을 통과해야만 한다.

31   Society should make efforts to save endangered species only if the potential extinction of those species is the result of human activities. [63/67]

종의 멸종이 인간 활동의 결과로 인한 경우에 한해서 사회는 멸종될 위기에 처한 종들을 구하기 위한 노력을 해야 한다.

우리 사회는 인간 활동의 결과에서 기인한 동식물 멸종을 막기 위해 노력해야만 한다.

63   There is little justification for society to make extraordinary efforts — especially at a great cost in money and jobs — to save endangered animal or plant species.

우리 사회가 멸종위기에 처한 동식물의 종들을 보호하기 위해 지나친 노력 — 특히 많은 돈과 일이 드는 — 을 하는 것은 별로 정당성이 없다.

돈이나 고용으로 인한 이익을 포기하고 멸종 동식물을 보호하기 위한 우리 사회의 상당한 노력은 별로 정당성은 없다.

67   Some people believe that society should try to save every plant and animal species, despite the expense to humans in effort, time, and financial well-being. Others believe that society need not make extraordinary efforts, especially at a great cost in money and jobs, to save endangered species.

어떤 사람들은 우리 사회가 인간에 쓰는 노력, 시간, 재정적 풍요를 지불해서라도 모든 동식물의 종들을 보존해야 한다고 믿는다. 다른 사람들은 우리 사회가 멸종위기에 처한 종들을 보호하기 위한 상당한 노력을 — 특히 많은 돈과 노력을 드는 — 할 필요가 없다고 믿는다.

어떤 사람들은 노력, 시간, 재정적 풍요를 포기하고도 모든 동식물종을 보존해야 한다고 믿고 있다. 다른 사람들은 돈이나 고용으로 인한 이익을 포기하고 멸종 동물을 보호하기 위한 우리 사회의 상당한 노력은 별로 정당성은 없다고 한다.

125   Some people claim that a nation's government should preserve its wilderness areas in their natural state. Others argue that these areas should be developed for potential economic gain.

어떤 사람들은 자연 상태의 야생지역을 보호해야 한다고 한다. 다른 사람들은 잠재적인 경제 이익을 위해서 개발해야 한다고 한다.

148   Nations should pass laws to preserve any remaining wilderness areas in their natural state.

국가들은 아직 자연 상태로 남아 있는 야생지역을 보호하기 위해서 법을 통과시켜야만 한다.

31   Society should make efforts to save endangered species only if the potential extinction of those species is the result of human activities.
Write a response in which you discuss your views on the policy and explain your reasoning for the position you take. In developing and supporting your position, you should consider the possible consequences of implementing the policy and explain how these consequences shape your position.

강의노트   31번 에세이는 다양한 스타일의 에세이 샘플을 소개하기 위해서 서론에 소개한 템플릿 프레임을 따르지 않고 작성했다. 마이너스 문단이 본론 마지막 문단, 즉 4문단에 배치되었다는 점이 특징이다.

Whether society should implement policies to protect endangered species from human activities depends on the value of how it contributes to nature and our well-being. Certain plants and animals produce consumer goods such as herbal medicine or coffee, respectively. Such unique properties serve to benefit our society in many ways so it is necessary to preserve it. If there is nothing to harvest to satisfy the needs of society, protecting such species would only be a liability in terms of cost.

Herbs or plant-derived medicines are often used to treat illnesses across the world. Protecting endangered plants with natural healing properties such as herbal antacids are beneficial for humans. Remedies produced by a natural process are often cheaper to maintain than a production lab as it would require far fewer resources to operate. It also gives us more choices in choosing medicine that work for a particular individual or case. Because of the potential benefit these plants provide, preserving them would be significant in improving living conditions.

Furthermore, some animals have special characteristics that produce high-quality consumer goods such as the Kopi Luwak coffee. It is known to be the world's finest coffee bean, and it comes from a civit-like animal called the Luwak. It would be a good idea to preserve their existence and the products from these animals stimulate human economies through import and export. Harvesters can profit from its production while consumers can enjoy a high-quality good that satisfies their needs. This serves to be beneficial to human society as it promotes trade and satisfaction, therefore they should be protected.

However, other plants and animals may serve no purpose to nature or human society. These species only consume resources and there is nothing to harvest or benefit from their existence. Therefore, as long as there are no catastrophic consequences that would undermine our ecosystem upon their extinction, protecting them would only cost money and labor because it requires substantial efforts for keeping them alive. In this case, endangered species should be allowed to go extinct even if it is caused by human activities.

Since certain endangered species can have positive or negative consequences on nature and society, political action should depend on their impact. While there is much to gain from protecting some, others may only deplete valuable resources. It is important to determine such distinctions to make proper decisions because it will influence life on earth. [411]

---

67   Some people believe that society should try to save every plant and animal species, despite the expense to humans in effort, time, and financial well-being. Others believe that society need not make extraordinary efforts, especially at a great cost in money and jobs, to save endangered species.

어떤 사람들은 우리 사회가 인간에 쓰는 노력, 시간, 재정적 풍요를 지불해서라도 모든 동식물의 종들을 보존해야 한다고 믿는다. 다른 사람들은 우리 사회가 멸종위기에 처한 종들을 보호하기 위한 상당한 노력을-특히 많은 돈과 노력을 들일 필요가 없다고 믿는다.

Write a response in which you discuss which view more closely aligns with your own position and explain your reasoning for the position you take. In developing and supporting your position, you should address both of the views presented.

환경에 관한 토픽에 대해서는 자연 환경의 파괴는 곧 인류의 멸종을 의미할 수 있기 때문에 자연 환경을 훼손하는 모든 행위는 제재되어야 한다. 예증으로는 4대강 개발이 가져올 수 있는 동식물의 멸종과 더불어 식물이 의약품의 원료로 쓰이는 점을 지적했다.

Researchers pointed out that soil polluted by heavy metals, pesticides, and plastics has adversely affected human health. They also warn to reduce the amount of emission gas to prevent climate change. If we do not work for sustainable development to preserve the ecosystem, humans will encounter catastrophic consequences from the destruction of mother nature. Plants and animals are so important to maintain the natural cycle of life keeping the balance in the ecosystem. The ecological collapse will eventually lead to human extinction.

Decisions on saving natural resources are seldom made by the risk of survival. Over-exploitation of natural resources harms the ecosystem and the well-being of people. The polluted earth threatens human life with toxins released by factories, oil spills, and wars are often extremely harmful to all species on the planet.

Nevertheless, some politicians promised a bright future with the development of housing and transportation. For instance, the Four Great Rivers development in South Korea spearheaded by the previous South Korean government of Lee Myung-park caused water pollution and floods. The project destroyed the river line inhabited by wild animals and plants.

Furthermore, herbs or plants derived medicines are often used to treat illnesses across the world. Protecting endangered plants that hold natural healing properties such as herbal antacids provides many benefits to humans. Remedies produced by a natural process are often cheaper to maintain than a production lab as they would require fewer resources to operate. It also gives us more choices in choosing medicine that works for a particular individual or case. Because of the potential benefit these

Environment

plants can provide, preserving them is crucial for improving health conditions.

"Sustainability" has emerged in the last decade in fear of irrecoverable destructions in nature. In the past five decades, the issues of economic growth have been considered more important than environmental preservation. Without solving the problems of contaminated soils, polluted air, and sick animals, the human species is doomed to extinction. Thus, we should put more effort into the perseverance of nature before everything is too late to preserve nature and its ecosystem. [350]

Lecture **12**

Knowledge & Research

Knowledge & Research Topic Analysis

지식에 관한 토픽은 지식의 이해와 한계에 대해서 묻는다. '새로운 지식의 습득으로 우리는 더 혼란을 겪는가 아니면 과거보다 더 많은 것들에 답변할 수 있는가?'에 관한 지식의 한계를 질문하는 토픽에는 우리 지식의 반경이 넓어졌기 때문에 점점 더 어려운 문제에 당면하게 되었다고 주장한다. 또한 발명이나 발견은 평범한 것을 관찰하고 상상력을 발휘할 때 가능한 것이다. "아인슈타인은 복잡하게 만드는 것보다 가장 간단하게 만드는 용기가 있어야 한다"고 말했다.

어떠한 연구 분야든 그 분야가 이룬 과거 업적에서 지대한 영향을 받지 않고 위대한 업적을 이루는 것은 불가능하다. 오늘날 각각의 학문 분야가 매우 세분화되었기 때문에 여러 분야가 서로 협동을 하지 않고서는 발전해 나갈 수 없다고 쓰는 것이 바람직하다. 각 대학에서도 교차전공(Interdisciplinary)로 학위를 수여하는 것을 보면 알 수 있다.

과학자나 연구자들은 많은 사람들이 이익을 받게 될 것 같은 연구 분야에만 집중해야 한다. 정부는 결과가 불분명한 연구에는 funding을 주어서는 안 된다는 주장과 즉각적으로 사용 가능한 연구만을 지원해야 하느냐는 질문에 대한 예증으로는 long term research를 적는다.

Knowledge & Research

9   In any field of endeavor, it is possible to make a significant contribution without first being strongly influenced by past achievements within that field.
어떠한 연구 분야든 그 분야가 이룬 과거 업적에서 지대한 영향을 받지 않고 위대한 업적을 이루는 것은 불가능하다.

36   Governments should not fund any scientific research whose consequences are unclear. [72]
정부는 결과가 불분명한 것에 대한 연구를 위한 자금을 지원하지 않아야 한다.

56   Many important discoveries or creations are accidental: it is usually while seeking the answer to one question that we come across the answer to another.
대부분의 발견이나 발명은 우연으로 인한 것이다. 다른 하나의 문제에 대한 답변을 찾는 중에 우연히 얻게 되는 것이다.

59   Scientists and other researchers should focus their research on areas that are likely to benefit the greatest number of people.
과학자나 연구자들은 많은 사람들이 이익을 받게 될 것 같은 연구 분야에만 집중해야 한다.

72   Governments should not fund any specific research whose consequences are unclear. [36]
정부는 결과가 불분명한 것에 대한 연구를 위한 자금을 지원하지 않아야 한다.

87   Claim : Any piece of information referred to as a fact should be mistrusted, since it may well be proven false in the future.
주장: 사실이라고 알려진 어떤 정보도 의심을 해야 한다. 그 정보가 미래에 허위라고 증명될 가능성이 있기 때문이다.
Reason : Much of the information that people assume is factual actually turns out to be inaccurate.
이유: 우리가 사실이라고 가정하고 있는 많은 정보는 사실상 부정확한 것으로 드러난다.

103   The best ideas arise from a passionate interest in commonplace things.
가장 위대한 아이디어는 평범한 것들에 대한 열정적 관심으로부터 탄생한다.

106   Claim : Imagination is a more valuable asset than experience.
주장: 상상력은 경험보다 더 가치가 있는 자산이다.
Reason : People who lack experience are free to imagine what is possible without the constraints of established habits or studies.
이유: 경험이 부족한 사람들은 확립된 습관이나 태도의 제한 없이 자유로운 상상을 할 수 있기 때문이다.

109   Some people believe that scientific discoveries have given us a much better understanding of the world around us. Others believe that science has revealed to us that the world is infinitely more complex than we ever realized.
어떤 사람들은 과학적 발견이 우리가 세상을 더 잘 이해할 수 있도록 해 주었다고 믿는다. 다른 사람들은 과학이 세상을 우리가 알던 것보다 무한히 더 복잡하게 만들었다고 한다.

131 Claim : Researchers should not limit their investigations to only those areas in which they expect to discover something that has an immediate, practical application.
주장: 연구원들은 즉각적이고 현실적 적용이 기대되는 분야의 연구에만 국한해서는 안 된다.
Reason : It is impossible to predict the outcome of a line of research with any certainty.
이유: 확신을 가지고 연구 결과를 예측하는 것은 불가능하기 때문이다.

143 No field of study can advance significantly unless it incorporates knowledge and experience from outside that field.
다른 분야의 지식과 경험을 통합하지 않고 발전할 수 있는 학문은 없다.

Sample essay

36 Governments should not fund any scientific research whose consequences are unclear.
정부는 결과가 불분명한 것에 대한 연구를 위한 자금을 지원하지 않아야 한다.
Write a response in which you discuss the extent to which you agree or disagree with the recommendation and explain your reasoning for the position you take. In developing and supporting your position, describe specific circumstances in which adopting the recommendation would or would not be advantageous and explain how these examples shape your position.

강의노트 연구의 결과가 명확한 것은 현실적으로 어렵다. 그래서 사회 전체로서 윤리를 파멸이라는 도덕적 문제를 야기하지 않는 한 결과가 모호해도 정부는 연구를 지원해야 한다고 써야 한다. 예증으로는 우주개발이나 Manhattan Project를 든다.

Should governments disapprove any scientific research whose consequences are not promising? Some may think government's funding for uncertain research projects would be a waste of the public money. However, I disagree with the speaker because it is not so easy to predict the results of all scientific research in advance. Unless researches are ethically controversial, governments should provide funds to researchers whose consequences are uncertain. Tesla intuitively deduced that the commutator was unnecessary and that AC could be harnessed without this equipment. In that time, the professor dismissed Tesla's idea.

Knowledge & Research

Funding for ethically challenging research should be disapproved based on a high moral standard. If governments fail to establish the guideline to prevent possible ethical problems, it may lead to moral hazard. The stem cell research regulation can prevent researchers from using human products to advance bioengineering as they wish.

However, few would know whether the results of the research would be promising in advance. For example, quantum mechanics could not have been developed to the extent that we understand today if the US government disapproved of Albert Einstein's research. Unlike electrical engineering research whose results are immediate to the real-world application, Albert Einstein had serious theoretical issues with quantum mechanics and took many years to disprove or modify it. Some theoretical research requires more time and effort than mechanical engineering. In short, scientific research should not be merely a matter of practicality, though its utility is an important consideration.

Furthermore, space exploration led to many technological developments that we now take for granted. When it comes to investments in space technology, many Koreans are skeptical about funding research claiming that there are many more urgent things to be taken care of on the earth to promote the welfare of the general public. In the past, space engineering was considered costly research that only the two leading nations U.S. and the Soviet Union could afford. Now many more governments are eager to participate in this venture. Unless the government effort to elucidate uncertain knowledge by solving unsolved problems, space engineering could not have been advanced as is now.

Uncertainty is a part of science: all scientific research is subject to uncertainty. As seen in the above examples, if policymakers are reluctant to invest in a research project due to the uncertainty of the consequence of research, their nation would eventually fail to become a great nation. [430]

---

103   The best ideas arise from a passionate interest in commonplace things.
      가장 위대한 아이디어는 평범한 것들에 대한 열정적 관심으로부터 탄생한다.
      Write a response in which you discuss the extent to which you agree or disagree with the recommendation and explain your reasoning for the position you take. In developing and supporting your position, describe specific circumstances in which adopting the recommendation would or would not be advantageous and explain how these examples shape your position.

강의노트   예증을 고를 때 평범한 사물을 관찰하거나 평범한 사물로부터 영감을 받아서 발명을 한 과학자들을 예증으로 해야 한다. "things"란 발명품을 일컫는 말이다. 샘플 에세이에는 라이트 형제의 나는 물건의 꿈이나 멘델의 유전 법칙은 Pea, 즉 평범한 파란 콩을 관찰함으로서 밝힌 예를 근거로 했다.

The speaker contends that the best ideas arise from a researcher's passionate interest in commonplace things. History tells us innovative ideas came from the scrutiny of the simple things around us, which most people took it for granted.; Thus, I agree with the speaker because seemingly complicated phenomena could have a better explanation by understanding conceptual ideas or core principles. Inventors' fervent desire with persistent investigations of commonplace objects shed light on the development of knowledge.

Unfortunately, as we require more advanced technology, the importance of observation was overshadowed by data analysis. However, inspiration from common behaviors contributes to the revolutionary search engine that Larry Page and Sergey Brin, graduate students at Stanford University founded Google while they were Ph.D students at Stanford University in California. Unlike conventional search engines that count how many times the search terms appeared on the page, they theorized about a better system that analyzed the relationships among websites by analyzing people's interacting behaviors.

Knowledge & Research

Many technological innovations are derived from the archetype created by nature. Wright brothers told their experience with the toy airplane was the initial spark of their interest in flying. This shows how seeing common objects from different angles plays a pivotal role in the development of aeronautical technology.

When it comes to the development of biology, it was also through commonplace observations that Gregory Johann Mendel gained posthumous fame as the figurehead of the new science of genetics for his study of the inheritance of certain traits in pea plants. By simply observing the inheritance traits of the peas, he proved particular laws of the inheritance applicable to mankind. Thus, keen observations of common objects around us shed light on Mendel's laws.

Once, Einstein said that anyone can make things bigger and more complex, but what requires more is effort and courage in the opposite direction that makes things as simple as possible. As seen above, keen observations of mechanical or natural phenomena lead to revolutionary ideas and discoveries. [350]

---

109 Some people believe that scientific discoveries have given us a much better understanding of the world around us. Others believe that science has revealed to us that the world is infinitely more complex than we ever realized.
어떤 사람들은 과학적 발견은 우리가 세상을 더 잘 이해하도록 해주었다고 믿는다. 다른 사람들은 과학이 세상을 우리가 알던 것보다 무한히 더 복잡하게 만들었다고 한다.
Write a response in which you discuss which view more closely aligns with your own position and explain your reasoning for the position you take. In developing and supporting your position, you should address both of the views presented.

강의노트　과학이 발전하면 할수록 지식의 반경이 확대되기 때문에 some people이 아니라 others에 agree하는 방향으로 에세이를 발전시킨다. 예증으로는 Google의 search engine, DNA 연구들을 사용했다.

As we require more knowledge, things do not become more comprehensible, but more complex and mysterious. As advancement in computer technology advances in the past decades, our understanding of the world became much broader. The development of genetics broadened our horizons far beyond what we knew in the past, ironically, we now come to be placed in a more incomprehensible world.

The worldwide Internet infrastructure has created a global community in which we need to put more effort to construct, maintain, use, and develop the computer system. As a result, a large pool of scientist is needed to properly operate the computer system, and as it becomes part of our life, they have to challenge more complex problems. For example, Google gained a reputation for developing a faster and more effective search engine technology, but they encountered even more problems needed to be tackled to satisfy users.

The flood of innovation over the past century allowed us to comprehend what we have not understood before. On one hand, the discovery of the double helix of DNA deepened our understanding of genetics, and as a result, doctors can give better answers to the unsolved problems of life. On the other hand, every step of progress in the study of physics ranging from Newton's mechanism to quantum mechanics contributed to the comprehension of the universe. Although the quantum mechanical description of black holes is still in its fantasy, it does involve advanced mathematics. The more knowledge we require, the more new discoveries and innovations could be possible.

Science has risen to the challenge of our quest for true understanding, leading us to solve puzzles that would otherwise remain unsolved. In search of answers to deepen our understanding of the universe, many scientists are conducting pioneer research to provide answers to the unsolved mysteries of the universe or life.

Lecture 12
Knowledge & Research

We now live in a much more complex world today though we have advanced knowledge and technology. We are bound to face more questions when going forward. The reality is that it is impossible to comprehend all things around us. When we achieve our exploration of new knowledge, ironically we become more perplexed with new problems, seemingly more complicated than before. [420]

---

143   No field of study can advance significantly unless it incorporates knowledge and experience from outside that field.
다른 분야의 지식과 경험을 통합하지 않고 발전할 수 있는 학문은 없다.
Write a response in which you discuss the extent to which you agree or disagree with the statement and explain your reasoning for the position you take. In developing and supporting your position, you should consider ways in which the statement might or might not hold true and explain how these considerations shape your position.

강의노트   143번은 interdisciplinary 교육의 장점에 대해서 논하면 된다. 편리상 각각의 전공 분야를 나누어 놓았으나 학문은 서로 다른 분야에 영향을 주면서 발전해 나아갔다는 사실을 잊어서는 안 된다. 현실적으로 많은 대학에서 교차 학과 지원이라는 프로그램이 점점 늘어가는 추세이다.

According to the development of knowledge, a field of study has become divided into several different specializations, and therefore, without expertise from various fields it has become more difficult to make a significant advancement in a specialized research area. Moreover, the seemingly irrelevant field of study can be an inspiration from other fields of study because all fields of study can be better understood in the context of multi-disciplines. The most compelling examples that pertinently illustrate this point involve the interchangeable knowledge and experiences in the fields of physics and modern art. In addition, the fact that psychology has been based on the fields of business and education proves that no field of study can advance significantly, unless they integrate knowledge across the disciplines.

The current university education system is designed to produce more specialists rather than generalists. The amount of accumulated knowledge has been much greater than ever before. It is important to see the whole picture of diverse phenomena when it comes to the advance of knowledge in science. Thus, no area of intellectual inquiry can be advanced without understanding the interplay between and among different fields.

By learning how Thomas Kuhn published "The Structure of Scientific Revolutions" we can easily understand the fact that expertise in a field of study contributes to integrating the knowledge and experiences of other fields. He obtained his B.S. M.S. and Ph.D. degrees from Harvard University in physics but later he switched his research from physics to history and philosophy of science. The new word coined on the basis of his theory of "paradigm shift" has been widely employed in a variety of studies including social science.

The most representative study of modern days that has affected other fields of study is Psychology. Psychologists and economists collaborated to explain why people buy both lottery tickets and insurance. This question was answered by the psychological dilemma between fear and hope. Like this, psychological studies have also provided many solutions to the controversial debates in the field of education. Erikson's developmental psychology theory was adopted to construct primary and secondary school curricula.

Although a field of study can develop independently, there are overlapping areas between the vague boundary of two different majors or departments, thus the development of a field of study is likely to be dependent on other fields of study. [409]

Argue

Introduction

Argue란 무엇인가?

아규는 speaker가 주장하는 바를 읽고 그 주장의 잘못된 점, 즉 오류들을 발견하고 speaker 주장을 support하는 speaker의 assumption들이 이러이러한 이유로 틀리다고 자신의 반박 주장을 펴나가는 에세이이다.

6.0 아규는 논쟁에 사용하는 어법(rhetorical words and phrases)을 사용해서 오류를 정확하게 명시해야 한다. 아규의 서론과 결론은 Rhetoric usage는 그대로 사용해도 무방하며, 본론에서 오류를 반박할 때 반드시 다음 네 단계가 포함되어야 한다.

(1) 작가의 assumption(오류)를 지적한다: conclusion과 assumption이 동일한 경우는 correlation error이다.

(2) 오류 세 가지 종류를 지적한다: A false cause and effect relationship, analogy error, sampling error.

(3) 작가가 증거로 제시하는 조건이나 경우가 아닌 경우의 예(counter-examples)를 제시하며 세 가지 오류를 조목조목 반박한다.

(4) 그러므로 (3)번의 경우가 생기지 않기 위해서는 자료나 필요조건을 보완해야 한다고 해결책을 제시한다.

상투적인 어법을 사용하는 아규는 비영어권 학생일지라도 고정적인 템플릿을 사용해서 상투적인 표현을 쓰기 때문에 5.0 이상 고득점 얻기는 이슈보다 상대적으로 쉽다. 또한 아규가 점수 취득이 용이한 또 다른 이유는 아규 문제의 해답이, 다시 말해서 오류를 반박할 수 있는 tackling words가 지문 안에 모두 들어 있다는 점이다. 그러나 아규도 종류에 따라서는 주어진 내용에 관한 기본적인 지식이 있어야만 반론을 제기할 수 있는 경우도 있다.

Argue 분석 요령

(1) speaker의 주장이 무엇인가를 지문 안에서 정확하게 찾아 밑줄을 친다. 주장은 대개 suggest, claim, assert, recommend, should 등의 동사 뒤에 오거나 부사인 therefore, thus, since, however, but, clearly 등 부사 뒤에 위치한다.

(2) speaker가 전제로 하고 있는 premises가 있는지를 확인한다. 대다수 아규 문제는 premises 없이 evidence만 있는 유형이다.

(3) speaker가 어떤 문제점이 있는 주장을 어떤 증거 자료들을 근거로 하고 있는지를 파악한 다음 각각 근거에 번호를 매긴다. 문제에 따라서 다르나 evidence가 여러 개 있는 문제와 단 하나의 evidence가 있는 경우나 아예 증거 없이 모호하게 주장하는 경우도 있다.

(4) 아규 오류 유형은 다음과 같은 세 가지 유형 가운데 어떤 타입인지 분석한다.

   1) false cause and effect assumption : X caused Y

   2) weak analogy assumption: A and B are similar.

   3) fallacious sampling assumption: The study is a representative sample
   sampling 오류는 다음과 같은 종류로 세분화할 수 있다.
   statistical problem(no number),

      survey problem(respondent or questions),

      group-member problem(nationwide, local, throughout, region),

      time-shift problem(five years ago, last year, the past year, other most
      months.)

아규 Rhetoric usages

다음 문장들은 아규에 사용하는 논쟁 어법을 아규하고자 하는 의도에 따라 세분화한 것이다. 다음 영어 표현을 사용함으로 아규 에세이의 본질적 특성인 논리적인 설득력을 갖출 수 있다.

- Assumption이 틀리다고 할 때

  It might be caused by some other reason …

  There could be an alternative explanation.

  It is unfair that the different condition leads to the same result.

  X does not necessarily mean

- Analogy 오류

  The argument assumes falsely that the same effect would result from the different condition.

  It falsely assumes that the current trends will continue in the future.

  The speaker overlooks the difference between A and B

- 샘플 오류를 말할 때 …

  The smaller sample size, the less reliable results

  The sample is insufficient to represent the overall population of ….

  It is unfair that all conditions have not changed over the … (period).

  It is false that the sample represents all over workers. (residents …)

- …이 부족하다고 반박할 때

  However, it is possible that ~, it is equally possible that ~

  Perhaps, Or Perhaps, Maybe, Or maybe

  Lacking details on survey, it is not reliable to

  Lacking such evidence, it is impossible

  However, it is not possible, Perhaps,

  Without ruling out

  Without considering,

  Without having further information …

• Supply and demand를 반박할 때

   ... values are a function of supply and demand.

   The increase could be explained by ...

의도에 따라 사용하는 아규 어휘

• 주장

   Assert, state, affirm, claim, conclude, recommend, maintain

• 추론

   Assume, suppose, presume, think, imagine, believe, imply

• 근거

   evidence, fact, report, study, last month

• 가정이나 조건을 할 때

   assuming that, considering that, although

• speaker의 말을 인용할 때

   speaker cites, or asserts, or points out, indicate

• 입장이나 관점의 증거 자료를 제시할 때

   promote, facilitate, provide, serve to, further, accomplish, achieve, demonstrate,

   suggest, show

   * 동사 prove, infer, deduct 사용하지 말 것.

- 서론에서 입장이나 관점에 대한 반박을 시작할 때

  However, closer scrutiny reveals that the speaker's assumption is erroneous.

  A more thorough analysis proves that the speaker's evidence(s) lends little credible support for his assertion.

  Further observation shows that the speaker should provide another supporting details to make his assumptions more credible.

  When viewed more closely, the speaker's assumptions lend no credible support to his assertion.

  When viewed from another perspective, the speaker's assumption is erroneous.

- 문제점을 지적하며 반론할 때

  however, nevertheless, yet, still, despite, of course

- 작가 주장이 틀리다고 할 때

  serious misleading, problematic, countervailing factors, weak, poor, unsound, poorly reasoned, poorly supported, dubious, specious (assumptions), unsubstantiated, questionable, improvable

  * 주의할 점: don't use true or false, correct and incorrect

- 결론을 불충분한 근거를 반대하는 의견을 제시할 때

  work against, undermines, thwarts, defeats, runs contrary to,

  fails to achieve (promote, accomplish), is inconsistent with, impedes

- 마지막으로 결론적 입장을 제시하고자 할 때

  on balance, on the whole, all things considered, in the final analysis

- 주장한 결론이 타당하지 않다고 할 때

  unjustified, indefensible, unsupported, improbable, weak, unlikely

서론 부분

- 위에서 누구누구는 이러해야 한다고 주장한다.

  In this argument, the ⟨director, editor, Onega University dean⟩
  recommends (concludes) that …

- 작가의 주장이 그럴 듯하게 보이지만

  Although it might appear credible at first glance that ⟨작가 주장: 아규 points⟩
  At first glance it would seem convincing that ⟨작가 주장: 아규 points⟩

- 자세한 검토는 그의 주장이 여러 가지 불충분한 가설(assumptions)임을 밝힌다.

  Closer scrutiny of this argument (these evidences) reveals that it rests on a series
  of unsubstantiated assumptions, and is therefore unpersuasive as it stands.
  I find this argument specious on several grounds.

본론 부분

- 접속어

  first, second, third, fourth, finally, in sum/First and foremost, assuming, even
  assuming, besides, in conclusion

- 자세한 검토는

  upon closer examination, when viewed more closely, when viewed from another
  perspective, further observation shows

- 반드시 …라는 것을 제시하지 않는다. (필요충분조건)

  ⟨evidence: 반박할 단어⟩ does not necessarily indicate that … would be

- 2가지 또는 3가지 반박점을 명시할 때

  …도 제시하지 않고 …도 제시하지 않는다. 또한 …도 정당한 이유가 아니다.

  … does not necessarily indicate that neither X nor Y … unreasonable ….

- 아마 … 했을지도 모르고 또 …했을는지도 모른다.

  perhaps … happens to be …, or

- 그러한 이유로 아마도 … 기인한지도 모른다.

  for that reason (matter), perhaps … are due to

  are due to

- 다른 가능한 증거 없이 …그 증거를 근거로, speaker는 나에게 확신을 주지 못한다.

  Without providing other possible evidences (reasons) for …, the speaker cannot

  convince me on the basis of them that 〈어떤 증거〉.

- 단지 …라 하는 것으로

  let alone that 〈주장하는 결과〉.

- …라는 경우라도 … 주장하는 이는 that 이하의 사실을 지나치게 가정한다.

  설사 작가 주장한 첫 주장이 맞더라도 두 번째(further) 주장은 문제가 있다.

  even if …, the speaker assumes further that …

- 그러한 근거 없이

  Lacking such evidence

- 사실상 아마도,

  in fact, perhaps …

- 보장하기에 충분하지 않은 숫자일수도 있다.

  (these members) might be insufficient in number to (ensure profit).

- assumptions을 강화하지 않으면 나는 확신하지 못한다.

  Until the speaker substantiate assumptions, I am (remain) unconvinced that ....

- 다른 조건이 …한 결과를 가져왔을는지 모른다.

  other factors were instead possible for the (increase, profit, success)

- 아규 주장을 받쳐주지 못한다.

  … does not support the argument.

결론 부분

- 결론적으로 아규 주장은 틀리다.

  In sum, the recommendation relies on certain doubtful assumptions that render it unconvincing as it stands.

- 나는 명확한 조건이나 증거 없이 아규를 받아들일 수 없다는 결론에 도달했다.

  Without having clear evidence or survey or study, I became to conclude that I cannot accept the speaker's assertions.

- 나는 …과 같은 증거가 필요하고 …한 증거가 필요하다.

  I would need to know why .... Also (besides) I would need to know ....

아이디어를 연결하고자 할 때 필요한 접속어

- 부가적 아이디어를 연결할 때

  and, again, and then, besides, equally important, finally, further, furthermore, or(nor), too, next, lastly, accordingly

- 점층법으로 아이디어를 연결할 때

  furthermore, additionally, in addition, also, moreover, more importantly

- 부사를 사용한 연결

  significantly, consequently, simultaneously, concurrently, accordingly, admittedly, finally, lastly

- 비교나 대조를 하고자 할 때

  but, although, on the contrary to, conversely(반대로), in contrast, on the other hand, whereas, otherwise, notwithstanding, opposite to, while, meanwhile, but, except,

  by comparison, where, when, compared to

- 이유, 즉 … 때문에로 연결할 때

  because, for , since, for the same reason

- 재확인을 할 때

  obviously, evidently, indeed, that is obvious

- 예외적인 조건을 명시할 때

  yet, still, however, nevertheless, in spite of, despite, of course, occasionally, sometimes, in rare instances, in few instances, in any case

- 시간이나 논리의 순차적 또는 동시 다발적 연결

  first, second(ly), third(ly),

- 예를 들고자 할 때

  for example, for instance, perhaps, consider, take the case of, to demonstrate, to illustrate, as an illustration, one possible scenario, in this case, in another case, on this occasion, in this situation

- 무엇도 아니고 무엇도 아니다 라고 연결할 때

  either … or, neither … nor, both … and … not, not only … but also

- 전제를 이유로 결론을 내리고자 할 때

  therefore, thus, hence, accordingly, as a result, it follows that, therefore, in turn

- 결론을 맺을 때

  in sum, in the final analysis, in brief, summing up, in conclusion, to conclude

대명사를 사용할 때 유의해야 할 점

대명사를 쓸 때는 선행하는 명사와 일치하는 대명사의 인칭을 선택, 사용해야 한다. 즉, he를 선택하면 his로 she를 선택하면 her를 일관적으로 사용해야 한다. 또한 긴 구절이 선행사와 명사 사이에 올 때는 선행사를 지시하는 대명사보다 명사를 그대로 다시 반복해서 명시하는 것이 좋다.

- 반론하는 자신을 지칭하는 주어는 I나 We로 서론과 본론에서 자신의 주장을 반박할 때 쓴다.

  I agree with ….

  In my view, ….

  Without additional evidence, we cannot assume that ….

- 주장하는 이를 명시할 때 쓰는 대명사 일치

  The speaker argues … her argument is …, but she overlooks ….

  The manager cites … in support of his argument …. He then recommends ….

  To strengthen its conclusion, the editorial must …, It must also ….

- 지문에 명시된 주장을 지시할 때

  this statement, this claim, this assertion

- 주장을 지시하는 구체적인 명사는

  claim, assertion, recommendation, editorial, memo, letter, article

- 주장을 지시하는 전체적인 명사

  argument

- 지문을 주장하는 사람을 일반적으로 명시할 때

  the speaker, author

- 지문에 소개되는 직책을 구체적으로 쓸 때

  the vice president, this Omni, Inc. Omega University

논리적인 글을 쓸 때 주의할 점

1. 가장 중요한 point는 오류라고 생각하는 문장을 짧고 간결하게 쓴다.
2. 여러 가지 사항을 대조나 비교할 때는 동일한 문장 구조를 대칭이 되게 쓰는 것이다.
3. 같은 뜻의 문장을 반복하지 않는다.
4. 의문문을 사용해서 오류가 의심스럽다는 점을 지적할 수 있으나 직접의문문보다 간접의문문의 형태를 유지한다.
5. 2개의 절을 역접이나 순접으로 연결하고자 할 때는 ;을 사용하기도 하고 ; and ; but처럼 함께 사용할 수 있다.

6. 주절과 종속절 주어나 목적어가 요지를 전달하는 논리 순서로 구성되어 있는지를 파악한다.

7. 불필요한 콤마를 유의하되 콜론과 세미콜론을 적절한 장소에 사용한다.

오류별 아규 표현을 이용한 템플릿

서론

speaker가 이렇게 주장한다고 할 때

(1) The speaker(주장하는 이) asserts(recommends) that _____.

speaker의 증거 자료를 제시할 때

(2) To support the assertion he provides the following evidence;

처음 볼 때는 그럴 듯하나 자세히 보면 작가 주장이 설득력이 없다고 할 때

(3) At first glance, his assertion would seem convincing; however, scrutiny of his argument reveals that it lacks substantiated evidence and is therefore unpersuasive as it stands.

본론

Analogy 오류를 말할 때

(4) First, the speaker made a false analogy between A and B.

(5) The speaker compared the condition of A to that of B.

(6) Perhaps 다른 경우 설명. A에서 일어났던 일이 반드시 B에서 일어나지 않는다.
   What happened in A does not necessarily happen in B.
   Sampling 오류를 말할 때
   정확한 숫자가 없다고 할 때

(7) Second, the speaker's assumption is not based on specific numbers or data.

(8) He did not include the specific number indicating "(high consumption)" or the number (indicating) a "(substantial amount)".

(9) Perhaps 주어지지 않은 숫자에 따라서 다른 상황이 될 수 있다. The speaker's assertion is based on scant evidence.

Survey에 대한 정보가 불확실하다고 할 때

(10) Third the survey that the speaker provided is not convincing because it lacks the detailed information needed to make a decision.

(11) The speaker's survey information is insufficient.

(12) It is possible that 응답자의 연령, 건강, 성별, 환경에 따라서 다를 수도 있다.

Time Shift를 말할 때

(15) Fourth, he made a time shift error comparing those of (A time) and those of (B time).

(16) Without reflecting the time shift between those of (A time) and those of (B time).

(17) Perhaps the conditions of (A time) might have changed for l (B time).

Generalization 오류

(18) Fifth, the author commits an error of generalization by assuming that ____.

(19) Therefore, if the sampling group in the study cannot represent the entire (something population), this suggestion may not work as expected.

(20) Maybe ....

(21) This could be a problematic assumption.

결론

결론을 말할 때

(22) In sum, the argument is not well-supported and reasonably concluded.

(23) Strengthen it, the author must provide further evidence such as _____.

8 Steps for Writing the Argument Essay

아규 문제는 다음 단계에 따라서 순차적으로 분석하며, 오류를 지적하고, 그 오류 종류가 무엇인지 파악해야 한다.

1. Read the Argument thoroughly.

2. Find the Conclusion: thus, in conclusion, predict, recommend, clearly

3. Find out if there is any given premise.

   (전제 조건: 34번과 같은 유형은 전제 조건이 있는 아규 문제이다. 전반적으로 아규 문제는 전제가 없다.)

4. And find out evidence(증거).

5. Identify the problems: causal, analogy, and sampling

6. sampling 오류에는 세부적으로 어떤 오류가 있는지 분석한다.

7. Figure out the counterexamples: specific alternate explanations

   (설득력 있는 반박을 한다.)

8. Organize body paragraphs and write: at least 3 body paragraphs

   (즉, 3가지 major 이유와 2개 정도 minor 이유를 쓰는 것이 바람직하다.)

3가지 오류 종류와 4 steps 분석 방법

Argument type: Causal

(1) Assumption: A causes B

(2) Maybe something else caused B

그리고 다음과 같은 질문을 스스로 해본다.

(3) Ques) Does A necessarily cause B?

Maybe an alternative explanation is possible. Perhaps there are(is) another reasons for [speaker's 주장], such as p, q, r.

Argument type: Analogy

- Two places or times(A and B) are compared.
- Maybe A and B are not equal in some way.

  그리고 다음과 같은 질문을 스스로 해본다.

- Ques) Are A and B really equal?

  Will what happened in A necessarily happen in B?

  Are the situation at the A and B equal? If the situation is not similar, there is the possibility that [the same result] will not happen again. If something is different, then maybe this is a bad analogy.

Argument type : Sampling

- A survey or study(research) about a sampling group is applied to a bigger group or a small size group.
- A survey assumes that the people in the survey will do what they said they would.
- A study assumes that two separate events occurred at the same time, and the author makes an assumption that there is the relationship between these two events.
- Maybe a small group represents a large one by overgeneralization.
- 그리고 다음과 같은 질문을 스스로 해본다.

  Ques) Do the people in the sampling group really represent the people in the bigger group?

Easier way to figure out errors:

오류 분석을 할 때 다음과 같은 Key words로 오류 종류를 가려낸다.

False Cause / Time Shift / No Number / Location / Different Condition / Analogy /

Generalization / Supply and Demand / Respondents / Questions

4 steps to write body paragraphs .

(1) You point out the unsubstantiated assumption with scant evidence.

(2) And then the reason why the speaker's assumption is erroneous.

(3) After that you make a refute using "perhaps, maybe, it is possible that".

(4) At last, you provide solutions to resolve the problems you pointed out above.

   Consequently, thus, therefore

다음 4단계로 작성한다.

1. 작가 증거(잘못된 가정) → 2. 오류 종류 → 3. 반박예증 → 4. 구체적인 오류 보완 대안

  1) State the assumption.

       ~ the argument assumes that ~

       ~ another assumption is that ~(두 가지 speaker의 assumptions)

  2) Mention the problem there could be another explanation.

  3) Give a counterexample (perhaps, maybe) : 최대 2가지 반박만 필요

  4) Explain why the conclusion is vulnerable to criticism if the assumption is false.

    (if, then)

종류별 대표적 아규 표현 정리

Assumption	Expression
X causes Y	The speaker assumes that X contributed to Y. But there might be an alternative explanation for ….
Time shift	The speaker fails to show whether the increase in A can be applicable to B. Whether the condition of the past … years is indicative enough to be similar to the present or the future.

Analogy	Maybe B are not similar with A. Even though in A …. happened, … will not happen in B.
Sampling Numbers	A part of B cannot represent B or Nationwide average is not applicable to ….
Sampling survey	Respondents might behave differently from what they said they would ….
Negative effects	If something does not happen, something worse will happen ….
Vague numbers	It is not clear what they mean by "a high number or low".
Lack of evidence	It does not provide appropriate (evidence, proof) or specific time to support the argument.

한눈에 보는 아규 서론, 본론, 결론 구조

서론

The speaker concludes that ….

To support the argument he provides the following evidence ….

At first glance, the argument would seem persuasive; however, the argument overlooks alternative explanations that may refute the speaker's assertion.

본론

First,

(1) assumption

(2) 오류 판단

(3) 반박 자료

(4) 위의 자료 없이는 작가의 주장은 오류이다.

Second, Repeat the above steps for Analogy error

(1) bad analogy assumption

(2) 오류 지적

(3) 반박 근거

(4) ~ 없이는 작가의 주장에 동의할 수 없다.

Third, Repeat the above steps for Sampling errors

(1) a sweeping generalization

(2) 오류 지적

(3) 반박 제시

(4) ~ 없이는 작가의 주장은 bias이다.

결론

In sum, the argument has several loopholes in its reasoning. To bolster it, the author must prove that ....

And the argument should also provide evidence that ... to be acceptable.

Argue

유형별 분석

Argue

BUSINESS / new store opening 유형

아규 9번 문제를 읽은 뒤에 다음 템플릿을 이용해서 다음과 같은 5단계로 분석 정리한 후에 아규 9번을 써 보도록 하자. ① 문제를 면밀하게 읽고, Speaker가 누구이며 무슨 결론을 내렸는가를 파악한 다음 물결 밑줄을 긋는다. ② evidence를 모두 찾아 밑줄을 긋고 증거 자료가 아규 9번처럼 여러 개일 경우에는 각각의 근거에 번호를 매긴다(여기서는 3가지). ③ 각각 한 가지 증거에 하나 또는 2가지의 반박 근거를 찾는다. ④ 모든 vague terms에다 가는 동그라미 또는 하이라이트를 그려 표시한다. ⑤ 이러한 반박 의문을 해소할 수 있는 보충 요건, 즉 해답은 무엇인가를 답한다. 아규 문제를 분석할 때, 원인과 결과 X and Y, 그리고 유사관계 similar between A and B, 마지막을 일반화 오류를 암시하는 clue words를 찾아야만 한다.

분석하기

1. The following appeared in a memorandum written by the vice president of Nature's Way, a chain of stores selling health food and other health-related products.

Nature's Way, a chain of stores selling health food and other health-related products, is opening its next franchise in the town of Plainsville. The store should prove to be very successful: Nature's Way franchises tend to be most profitable in areas where residents lead healthy lives, and clearly Plainsville is such an area. Plainsville merchants report that sales of running shoes and exercise clothing are at all-time highs. The local health club has more members than ever, and the weight training and aerobics classes are always full. Finally, Plainsville's schoolchildren represent a new generation of potential customers: these schoolchildren are required to participate in a fitness-for-life program, which emphasizes the benefits of regular exercise at an early age.

* 대명사 전환: 해답을 작성할 때는 대명사 we를 they로 바꾸어야 한다.

fc / ts / no lo / con / S&D / ana / gen / res / Q /

(sampling 오류 분석 key words 약자를 사용해서 분석하기)

false cause	근거	(1) 운동화나 운동복 판매가 증가한다고 반드시 건강보조식품이 반드시 잘 팔리지 않을 것이다.
	반박	아니다. 스포츠웨어가 유행이기 때문에 건강보조식품이 잘 팔렸을 것이다.
location		헬스클럽에서 멀리 떨어진 Plainsville 외곽에 NW 가게가 위치한다면 bad analogy이다.
Sampling	근거	(3) 새로운 세대가 고객이 될 것이다.
	반박	아니다. 학생들이 초등학교 저학년이라면 너무 어려서 고객이 되려면 너무 오랜 시간을 기다려야 할 것이다. 또는 가격이 비싸서 어린 학생들은 못 살 것이다. 또는 학교에서 필수로 요구해서 운동하는 학생들은 별로 건강을 위한 제품에는 관심이 없을 것이다
Sampling	오류	no sufficient data, vague terms

아규 1번 유형 템플릿

(1) In this memo the speaker concludes that CONCLUSION

(2) To support his claim he provides the following evidence; 1) EVIDENCE

(3) ; and 2) EVIDENCE

(4) ; and 3) EVIDENCE

(5) At first glance it would seem convincing; however, closer scrutiny reveals that it

lacks substantial evidence or support and is, therefore, problematic as it stands.

CAUSAL ERROR

(6-1) First, the speaker cites that 1) EVIDENCE

(6-2) However, 1) EVIDENCE does not necessarily mean that 작가 CONCLUSION

(6-3) It is possible that COUNTER-EXAMPLE (다른 결과가 발생할 경우)

(6-4) Without ruling out this possibility the speaker's conclusion would be false.

ANALOGY

(7-1) Second, the speaker assumes that health food store is located at the area where its purchasing power is somewhat similar with that of the local health club.

(7-2) However, If ~~~

(7-3) Perhaps COUNTER-EXAMPLE (다른 결과가 발생할 경우)

(7-4) Thus, the speaker should provide more detailed information on REASON'S OF 2) EVIDENCE to convince me. Otherwise the speaker's argument is erroneous.

SAMPLING ERROR

(8-1) Last, the speaker's conclusion is based on vague terms and no data.

(8-2) It is difficult to make a business decision on the vague terms such as

(8-3) Moreover, the speaker's assumptions are based on a biased sample that may not represent the whole population of

(8-4) In order to make the argument credible the speaker should clarify the terms with more detailed information and reliable data.

(8-5) Without having more information and data, it would not be so easy to make a confident decision.

결론

(9-1) In sum, the argument is not well-developed to support the speaker's assumptions.

(9-2) To strengthen it, the speaker should provide sufficient evidence that will eliminate all the above doubts and questions.

(9-3) To better assess the recommendation the speaker should provide further evidence such as solution 1)_____, solution 2) and solution 3).

Argue

그림으로 보는 아규 논리 개념

서론

(1) CONCLUSION

TO SUPPORT HIS ARGUMENT HE PROVIDES 　　1) ⬭

　　2) ⬭

　　3) ⬭

(2) AT FIRST GLANCE, IT WOULD SEEM CREDIBLE; HOWEVER, CLOSER SCRUTINY REVEALS THAT IT LACKS SUBSTANTIAL EVIDENCE AND THEREFORE IT IS PROBLEMATIC AS IT STANDS

본론

(3) EVIDENCE: X did not cause Y

(4) EVIDENCE: A and B are different.

(5) SAMPLING ERROR

결론

(6) IN SUM, THE SPEAKER'S ARGUMENT IS NOT WELL SUPPORTED.

(7) TO STRENGTHEN IT THE SPEAKER SHOULD PROVIDE FURTHER EVIDENCE THAT WILL ELIMINATE THE ABOVE DOUBTS AND QUESTIONS.

(8) TO BETTER ASSESS THE RECOMMENDATION THE SPEAKER PRO VIDE FURTHER EVIDENCE SUCH AS _____.

SOLUTION OF 1) ⬭

2) ⬭

3) ⬭

여기서 solution이라고 하는 것은 위 템플릿이 지적한 문제에 대한 해답을 뜻하는 것이다. 6-2·3, 7-2·3, 8-2·3문장에서 지적하는 문제점을 해결하려면 무엇무엇이 필요하다고 써야 한다. 이때 필요한 사항을 명사구나 wh question으로 답할 수 있다.

예) The number of potential health food buyers or how many buyers will actually purchase ....

Sample

서론

(1) In this memo the speaker concludes that their next NW store will be successful in Plainsville in which many health concerned residents live. (2) To support his claim he provides the following evidence; 1) Plainsville merchants report that sales of running shoes and exercise clothing are at all-time highs.

(3) ; and 2) the local health club, which nearly closed five years ago due to lack of business, has more members than ever, and the weight training and aerobics classes are always full.

(4) ; and 3) We can even anticipate a new generation of customers: Plainsville's schoolchildren are required to participate in a 'fitness for life' program, which emphasizes the benefits of regular exercise at an early age.

(5) At first glance it would seem convincing; however, closer scrutiny reveals that it lacks substantial evidence or support and is therefore problematic as it stands.

본론

CAUSAL ERROR

(6-1) First, the speaker cites that 1) Plainsville merchants report that sales of running shoes and exercise clothing are at all-time highs.

(6-2) However, 1) EVIDENCE does not necessarily mean that NW store will be successful in Plainsville.

(6-3) It is possible that year round high sales volume of running shoes and exercise clothing is due to their relatively inexpensive price comparing other clothing types. Or perhaps that may be caused by a temporary fashion trend.

(6-4) Without ruling out this possibility the speaker's conclusion would be false.

ANALOGY

(7-1) Second, the speaker assumes that in terms of location, the next Plainsville is also located in an area where purchasing power is equal to that of a local health club.

(7-2) This assumption can be problematic if healthy club members are not interested in buying health food products.

(7-3) If health club members' ages are much younger than those of Plainsville customers, high sales that the speaker anticipates is unlikely to occur.

(7-4) Without investigating whether the health club members are interested in purchasing health foods that Plainsville store sells, it is difficult to conclude that its business at the new location will be profitable.

SAMPLING ERROR

(8-1) Third, the speaker points out that 3) we can even anticipate a new generation of customers: Plainsville's schoolchildren are required to participate in a 'fitness for life' program, which emphasizes the benefits of regular exercise at an early age.

(8-2) But 3) the schoolchildren's required 'fitness for life' program at an early age will not cause higher demand for health food products of NW.

(8-3) Perhaps the children are too young to buy NW products that are most likely to be a high price. Or maybe the children who are required to exercise are not interested in their health life at all.

(8-4) Lacking sufficient evidence it is not credible that NW store can even anticipate a new generation of customers in Plainsville.

SAMPLING ERROR

(9-1) Last, the speaker's conclusion is based on vague terms and no data.

(9-2) It is difficult to make a business decision on vague terms such as highly concerned, all-the-time high, always full, and at an early age. Moreover, the speaker's assumptions are based on a merchant report, a health club, and a local school that may not represent the whole population of Plainsville.

(9-3) To make the argument credible the speaker should clarify the terms with more detailed information and reliable data.

(9-3) Without having more information and data, it would not be so easy to make a confident decision.

결론

(10) In sum, the argument is not well-supported to make the speaker's assertions persuasive.

(11) To strengthen it, the speaker should provide sufficient evidence that will eliminate all the above doubts and questions.

(12) To better assess the recommendation the speaker should provide further evidence such as solution 1) market trends, solution 2) the number of potential health product buyers, solution 3) further detailed business analysis of N.W.

Argue

부동산 / variable X 유형

4. The following appeared in a letter from a homeowner to a friend.

"Of the two leading real estate firms in our town — Adams Realty and Fitch Realty — Adams Realty is clearly superior. Adams has 40 real estate agents; in contrast, Fitch has 25, many of whom work only part-time. Moreover, Adams' revenue last year was twice as high as that of Fitch and included home sales that averaged $168,000, compared to Fitch's $144,000. Homes listed with Adams sell faster as well: ten years ago I listed my home with Fitch, and it took more than four months to sell; last year, when I sold another home, I listed it with Adams, and it took only one month. Thus, if you want to sell your home quickly and at a good price, you should use Adams Realty."

1) 문제를 명확하게 파악한다. 이때 Tackling words, 즉 false cause, weak analogy, time shift, biased sample, poorly defined terms 등을 찾아내야 한다.

2) 원인과 결과 X is responsible for Y. 풀어 쓰면 more numbers of agents is a clear indication for Adam's quality service

3) 유사 관계: A and B are similar. 풀어 쓰면, the conditions or price ranges of the houses that Fitch Realty sold and that of the house that Adam Realty sold are equally in good condition.

4) 샘플링: scant evidence: no other data was given other than the average sales prices for both realtors.

sample essay

In the forum, the speaker recommends using Adams realty because it will sell any house more quickly and at a good price than Fitch realty. To support his suggestion, he provides the following evidence: (1) Adams has 40 real estate agents; however,

Fitch has 25 employees, and most of them are part-time workers; (2) Adams 'revenue last year was twice as high as Fitch's; and (3) his personal experience that Adams sold one of his houses in one month last year whereas Fitch did in four months 10 years ago. At first glance, his argument would seem persuasive; however, closer scrutiny reveals that it lacks convincing proof or support and is therefore erroneous as it stands.

First, the speaker depends on the false assumption that 1)_____ agents will sell a home more quickly and at a good price. Common sense tells us that the capabilities of the agents cannot be solely measured by 2)_____. It is possible that Fitch's agents are more experienced with more knowledge of real estate transactions. Moreover, the speaker provides detailed information with regard to the abilities of the part-time employees in both realtors. Without knowing 3)_____ of the full-time employees of both realtors and their contributions to the promotion of sales, this argument is erroneous.

Second, the speaker also cites that Adam's revenue last year was twice 4)_____ that of Fitch's. However, he undermines the possibility that after the deduction of the expense, Fitch's profits may be greater than Adams. If Adam's sold a few expensive estates such as mansions or luxurious condos in town and this mainly contributed to increasing the average of sales. If so, the average home sales price can be higher regardless of the number of homes they sold last year. Adams might have only a few rich customers whereas Fitch might have many medium-price range homeowners. In addition, from the client's perspective, the vicinity is another 5)_____ to hire an agent. It is a common practice that most clients would find a realtor that is located near the area in which they live. Therefore, without scrutinizing the price range and similar conditions of the houses sold by both agents, it is difficult to conclude that Adams is superior to Fitch.

Third, reflecting on his personal experiences last year with Adams and 10 years ago with Fitch, the speaker concludes that Adams will sell a home faster than Fitch at a good price. However, 6)_____ last year, the market trends could have changed from a buyer's market to a seller's market. Or, the houses listed with Adams last year might be better condition at a reasonable price to be sold than the ones sold by Fitch ten years ago. In short, he fails to provide real estate market trends over the ten years and the conditions of the two houses when sold.

Last, aside from no numbers the speaker's assumption is based on vague terms such as "quickly, good, and most". 7)_____ Adams sold a seller's house at a higher price, if its sales commission rate is much higher than that of Fitch's, the client's net profit would be less than the time when she contracts with Fitch. Without knowing the exact price with which the two houses were sold and the commission rate, it is difficult to rely on the speaker's assertion.

In sum, the argument is not well-supported. To bolster it, the speaker should provide sufficient evidence that will eliminate all the above doubts and questions. To better evaluate the recommendation the speaker should provide further evidence: the quality and abilities of the agents of the two realtors, the vicinity to the client's house, reliable data showing the average price sold per agent, price ranges of the real estate mostly sold at Adams and Fitch, conditions of the two houses sold and the market trends over the ten years as well as the commission rates.

1) the average number of sales

2) as high as

3) Perhaps

4) numbers of real estate agents

5) failed to

6) important factor to be considered is

7) Even if

8) the sales volumes

Answer keys   4 1 8 2 6 3 7

HEALTH 유형

40. Milk and dairy products are rich in vitamin D and calcium — substances essential for building and maintaining bones. Many people therefore say that a diet rich in dairy products can help prevent osteoporosis, a disease that is linked to both environmental and genetic factors and that causes the bones to weaken significantly with age. But a long-term study of a large number of people found that those who consistently consumed dairy products throughout the years of the study have a higher rate of bone fractures than any other participants in the study. Since bone fractures are symptomatic of osteoporosis, this study result shows that a diet rich in dairy products may actually increase, rather than decrease, the risk of osteoporosis. [Old version 34]

Write a response in which you discuss what specific evidence is needed to evaluate the argument and explain how the evidence would weaken or strengthen the argument.

우유와 유지방 제품에는 뼈를 형성시키고 강화시키는 데 아주 중요한 역할을 히는 비타민 D와 칼슘이 많다. 이 때문에 많은 사람들이 유지방이 풍부한 식이요법을 하면, 환경 및 유전적 요인에 의한 손상과, 노화에 의해 뼈가 심각하게 손상을 입는 질병인 골다공증을 억제하는 데 도움이 된다고 믿고 있다. 그러나 상당수의 사람을 대상으로 한 장기간 실험을 통해서 볼 때, 이들 대상자 중 실험기간 동안 유제품을 꾸준히 섭취한 사람들은 그렇지 않은 사람에 비해 훨씬 높은 골절현상을 보였다. 골절증상은 골다공증이 원인이기 때문에, 이러한 실험 결과는 우유제품을 많이 섭취하는 것은 골다공증을 줄이기보다는 오히려 증가시킨다는 것을 보여준다."

40번은 문제를 읽을 때 premises가 있는 유형인 아규 문제라는 것을 알아야만 한다. "Milk and dairy products are rich in vitamin D and calcium. Substances essential for building and maintaining bones."라고 전제하는데 이것은 결론과 상반(contradictory)되는 내용임을 알

아야 한다. 또한 작가 결론을 받쳐주는 증거를 약하게 하는 "Many people believe that osteoporosis is a disease in which the bones weaken significantly with age and that is linked to both environmental and genetic factors." 이 문장에서 우리는 respondents 환경이나 유전적 요소를 고려해 봐야 한다는 반박자료를 제공하고 있다는 것을 파악해야 한다. 모든 health 유형의 샘플링에 들어가는 표현은 공통적이다.

분석하기

원인과 결과 : X is responsible for Y vitamin D and Calcium is responsible for
weakening bones

유사 관계 : bone fractures 환자 group이랑 정상 환자 그룹이랑 동일하다.

샘플링 오류 : health records 없이 왜 뼈에 금이 갔는지 알 수 있는 정보가 없다.

다음 문제를 풀어 보며 아규용 표현을 연습해 보도록 하자.

A series of deductions in this argument are placed on a line which begins with the evidence of a long-term study of a number of people and ends with a conclusion that However, closer scrutiny reveals that the speaker concludes through 1)_____. In addition, there is scant evidence to support the conclusion.

The most crucial mistake that the speaker made in this argument is that he assumes the pool of subjects from which he developed a conclusion is 2)_____. Based on the result of a long-term study he established between the regular consumption of dairy products and weakening bones. To support this assumption he states that the bone fracture risks of the group of regular milk consumers are greater than that of those who do not so. Unless the speaker enhances the argument with more detailed information such as health history : ages and genders, asserting "regularly" taking milk contributes to increasing the risks of osteoporosis is susceptible to criticism.

Another hasty assumption that the speaker inferred from scant evidence is that the two groups of subjects who are sampled 3)_____. He overlooks the possibility that the bone density of one group of subjects is genetically much weaker than that of the other group. If so, the reason why the regular milk-consuming group experienced more bone fractures can be explained simply by genetic reasons. In order to make this argument to be convincing the speaker should further 4)_____.

5)_____ that both groups of sampled subjects were equally healthy and young, if more bone fractures occurred as the result of active sports activities, we cannot lend credit to regularly taking milk consumption for strengthening bones. Since athletes tend to have high risks of bone fractures during games, the conclusion that dairy products rather increase than decrease the risks of osteoporosis suffers from the absence of evidence. 6)_____ the participants' occupation, blindly trusting the speaker's conclusion will result in weakening bones 7)_____.

In short, the recommendation is neither well-supported nor soundly reasoned. To persuade readers that the speaker's suggestion would achieve the desired outcome, the author would have to assure that there were no 8)_____ for bone fractures, in the health condition of the two groups of subjects sampled, and 9)_____ that would provide 10)_____ including as gender, age as well as medical history. After that I will consider the speaker's assertion.

1) a representative sample

2) a hasty process of deduction

3) a diet rich in dairy products may actually increase the risks of osteoporosis

4) lacking sufficient information with regards to

5) have equally healthy bones

6) investigate as to whether both groups of subjects are in completely health conditions

7) even if were to agree

8) a mere correlation

9) and thus increasing risks of osteoporosis.

10) alternative reasons

11) have no difference

12) health records

13) and substantial evidence

Answer keys   2 1 11 6 7 4 9 10 13 12

54. Humans arrived in the Kaliko Islands about 7,000 years ago, and within 3,000 years most of the large mammal species that had lived in the forests of the Kaliko Islands had become extinct. Yet humans cannot have been a factor in the species' extinctions, because there is no evidence that the humans had any significant contact with the mammals. Further, archaeologists have discovered numerous sites where the bones of fish had been discarded, but they found no such areas containing the bones of large mammals, so the humans cannot have hunted the mammals. Therefore, some climate change or other environmental factor must have caused the species' extinctions. [Old version 202]

Write a response in which you examine the stated and/or unstated assumptions of the argument. Be sure to explain how the argument depends on these assumptions and what the implications are for the argument if the assumptions prove unwarranted.

인간은 약 7000년 전에 Kaliko섬으로 왔고, 3000년 사이에 Kaliko섬 숲속에 살았던 대부분의 거대한 포유류 종들이 멸종되었다. 그래도 인간이 멸종의 주요 원인은 아니다. 인간이 이들 포유류들과 어떠한 중요한 접촉이 있었다는 증거가 전혀 없기 때문이다. 더욱이 고고학자들은 어류의 뼈들이 버려진 여러 장소들을 발견했으나 이들 지역에서 포유류의 뼈는 발견되지 않았으니, 인간이 포유류를 사냥하지 않았을 것이다. 그러므로 어떤 기후변화나 다른 환경 요소로 인해 포유류가 멸종했을 것이다.

분석하기

X cannot be the cause of Y: Humans cannot be the cause of the mammals' extinction:
A and B are similar: The areas investigated in the forests and other areas of the Kaliko

Island

Lack of evidence: there is no evidence to substantiate this assumption.

This argument claims that human the extinction of large mammal species in the Kaliko islands 3,000 years ago. To support this assertion, the speaker emphasizes that no evidence exists that humans hunted or had another significant contact with these mammals. He also pointed out scattered fish bones were found but not the mammal bones there. However, when I closely examine this assertion, I found it unpersuasive: the argument is full of 1)_____ based on scant evidence.

First, the speaker mistakenly assumes that 2)_____ of human contact with mammals shows that humans could not have hunted mammals. Perhaps the mammal's bones 3)_____ as material for tools or ornaments due to its durability unlike, the fish bones. Without ruling out this alternative explanation for the disappearance of these species from the Kaliko Islands, the speaker fails to justify the conclusion that humans are solely responsible for their extinction from the islands but the climate changes.

Secondly, the speaker's assumption that as the numerous sites that archaeologists investigated there are 4)_____ humans' hunting activities in other areas of the Kaiko Islands is inferred from a bad analogy. If the Kailiko Islands are huge, the speaker needs to investigate other areas than the forest areas of the islands. Even assuming there is no evidence in other areas of the islands if human activities caused the migration of mammal species to 5)_____ that were excluded from the several sites that the speaker provided as evidence, it is still humans who are responsible for the extinction of mammals.

Lastly, the speaker's conclusion relies on scant evidence : 6)_____ that some climate change or other environmental factors were instead the cause of the mammal species' extinctions at Kaliko islands.

Without any evidence substantiating the assumption that no human activities would be discovered in all other areas, the speaker's conclusion is fallacious.

In conclusion, the argument is unconvincing as it stands. To bolster it, the speaker must provide further explanations by exploring more regions of the Kaliko islands. He 7)_____ about the human activities on the islands and possible climate changes. After that, I will accept the speaker's contention.

1) also needs to provide information

2) fallacious assumptions

3) the absence of evidence

4) no evidence showing

5) were not a factor

6) might have been used

7) other areas

8) It is possible that

9) vulnerable to criticism

10) could not have been possible

Answer keys　　2 3 6 4 7 8 1

Argue

Samples

1. Woven baskets characterized by a particular distinctive pattern have previously been found only in the immediate vicinity of the prehistoric village of Palea and therefore were believed to have been made only by the Palean people. Recently, however, archaeologists discovered such a "Palean" basket in Lithos, an ancient village across the Brim River from Palea. The Brim River is very deep and broad, and so the ancient Paleans could have crossed it only by boat, and no Palean boats have been found. Thus it follows that the so-called Palean baskets were not uniquely Palean. (37)

Write a response in which you discuss what specific evidence is needed to evaluate the argument and explain how the evidence would weaken or strengthen the argument.

특이한 무늬의 대나무 바구니는 Palea족이 거주하던 선사시대 마을 인근에서만 발견되어 왔기 때문에, Palea족에 의해서만 만들어졌다고 여겨졌었다. 그러나 최근 들어 고고학자들은 Lithos에서 이러한 "Palean" 바구니를 발견했는데, 이 고대 마을은 Palea과 Brim강으로 막혀 있다. 이 강은 수심이 아주 깊고 강폭이 넓어서, 고대의 Palea인들은 배를 이용해서만 강을 건널 수 있었을 것이나 Palean족의 배는 발견된 적이 없다. 따라서 이른바 Palean 바구니는 Palea족의 전유물이라고 볼 수 없다.

❙ Argument   Palean baskets were not uniquely Palean.

강의노트   이 아규는 archaeology type의 아규임을 알고 쓰는 것이 중요하다. 평상적인 marketing 유형보다는 유연한 영어 표현으로 3가지 오류(인과관계, 유사관계, 샘플 사이즈 오류)를 설명할 수 있어야 한다. Bold로 표시된 부분은 반드시 반박에서 걸고 넘어가야만 하는 중요한 tackling words이다. 이러한 오류를 정답에 포함할 때만 고득점이 가능하다.

The speaker's conclusion that Palean baskets were not uniquely Palean is inherently flawed. The reasoning behind his or her argument is not convincing, and there are several loopholes in the line of its reasoning. In addition, the scant evidence with poorly defined terms from which it is drawn lends little credence to this argument. To make this argument credible, further investigation is necessary.

First, the speaker's assumption that the Brim River acted as a barrier that blocked trade between the peoples of Palea and those in Lithos is invalid. Perhaps the river froze in the winter and thus allowed Palean baskets to move to Lithos without boats. Or, maybe there was an inland route from Palea, which detours to Lithos. Lacking such evidence and concluding that Palean baskets were not unique is unpersuasive because trades between these two peoples could have been through other means.

Second, the speaker fails to provide important information such as the existence of people who had learned weaving skills from Palea people and moved Palean baskets to the Lithos area after boats could have been made many centuries later. The speaker's argument continues to fall apart because it is based on the premise that the Palean people were the only people who could make bamboo baskets in prehistoric times. This premise is unlikely to be true when considering the interactions that occurred in history. Unless the speaker provides more information about the people who ever contacted the people of the Palea area, the assertion is vulnerable to criticism.

Third, pointing out "a basket", the speaker hastily concludes that a basket is strong evidence that Lithos people produced somewhat similar bamboo baskets that Lithos made. If the Litho people also weaved the same pattern of bamboo baskets and used them for their daily use, the baskets could have been found in numerous areas in a larger quantity. One basket cannot be strong evidence that Lithos people did not develop similar weaving skills that Palean had at that time, and scant evidence shows that the Lithos people were not the crafters of the bamboo baskets. Without sufficient details on how these two people developed their direct or indirect relationships, this argument is problematic as it stands.

To remedy this argument, the speaker should further collect more evidence that will eliminate all the doubts discussed above. Without a more advanced archaeological study of these two people's trading histories, it is more likely that the argument is invalid. [450]

2. The following appeared as part of a letter to the editor of a scientific journal.

"A recent study of eighteen rhesus monkeys provides clues as to the effects of birth order on an individual's levels of stimulation. The study showed that in stimulating situations (such as an encounter with an unfamiliar monkey), firstborn infant monkeys produce up to twice as much of the hormone cortisol, which primes the body for increased activity levels, as do their younger siblings. Firstborn humans also produce relatively high levels of cortisol in stimulating situations (such as the return of a parent after an absence). The study also found that during pregnancy, first-time mother monkeys had higher levels of cortisol than did those who had had several offspring." [New]

Write a response in which you discuss one or more alternative explanations that could rival the proposed explanation and explain how your explanation(s) can plausibly account for the facts presented in the argument.

다음 내용은 한 과학 잡지의 편집자에게 보낸 편지의 일부이다.

18마리의 붉은털원숭이에 대한 최근의 한 연구는 출산 순서가 각자의 흥분 수준에 영향을 미친다는 단서를 주고 있다. 흥분된 상태에서 (잘 모르는 원숭이끼리의 대치 같은), 맨 처음 태어난 원숭이들은 동생 원숭이에 비해 거의 2배에 가까운 cortisol 호르몬을 분비하는데, 이 호르몬으로 몸의 활동량이 증가한다. 먼저 태어난 인간도 흥분된 상황 속에서 (부모가 외출에서 돌아오는 것 같은) 상대적으로 많은 cortisol을 분비한다. 연구는 출산을 처음 한 원숭이들은 여러 번 출산을 한 원숭이들보다 임신 기간 중에 더 많은 cortisol을 분비한다는 것도 밝혀냈다.

Argument The birth order effects on an individual's levels of stimulation.

강의노트 Health 유형으로 분류될 수 있으며, 유사관계를 꼭 집어서, 즉 인간과 쥐와는 생물적으로 다르다는 반박을 포함할 때 좋은 점수를 얻을 수 있다.

The argument that there is a correlation between high levels of cortisol and the effects of birth order on an individual's level of stimulation based on f a recent study of eighteen rhesus monkeys is not logically convincing. It also made a false analogy between monkeys and humans that underestimates possible differences between their biological systems. Unless the author provides more solid evidence that will rule out all other possible explanations, this argument is vulnerable to criticism.

First and foremost, the author asserts that the production of high levels of cortisol is the production of the firstborn monkey's more active response in stimulated situations. This assertion has loops in its reasoning. It is possible that firstborn monkeys might have shown more active behaviors due to another cause like ingesting high concentrations of cholesterol, a precursor for hormone synthesis. Perhaps the firstborn monkeys used in this study were simply more stressed or ill in comparison to siblings and therefore produced higher levels of cortisol in stimulated situations. Without considering alternative explanations the author's claim is too weak to be persuasive.

Second, the author's implication that human and monkey are similar in their biology rests on a weak analogy. It is a crucial mistake to interchangeably associate the responses of these two very different mammalian species, especially under different circumstances. Unlike the monkeys that showed discomfort due to the presence of an unfamiliar monkey, firstborn human children may have been more active because of the experience involving the return of their parents rather than being pre-disposed for increased cortisol levels. From this point of view, the speaker failed to support his argument by making assumptions and lacking detail.

Last but not least, the 18 monkeys that contributed to the sample could represent an exceptional case. Based on a biased sample, the speaker hastily concluded that cortisol levels correlate with the birth order. In addition, without specific data, the conclusion was drawn from vague terms such as "twice as much as", in some cases, even twice an the amount of cortisol can be a meager amount of hormone to affect a certain reaction or behavior.

In general, this argument provides insufficient information with specific data, which is crucial for drawing any general inferences about the effects of the firstborn monkeys on individual stimulation levels. To better evaluate, the author should provide more information that would prove the sameness between humans and monkeys along with other possible factors that may affect the firstborn monkeys' reactions to the stimulus situation.

As it is written, the argument is inherently flawed. The entire argument could be redeemed if the author removed unsubstantiated assumptions and instead point out explanations for other possible causes, differences in biological conditions, and at the area validity of the represented sample. [480]

5. The following appeared in a letter to the editor of the Balmer Island Gazette.

"On Balmer Island, where mopeds serve as a popular form of transportation, the population increases to 100,000 during the summer months. To reduce the number of accidents involving mopeds and pedestrians, the town council of Balmer Island should limit the number of mopeds rented by the island's moped rental companies from 50 per day to 25 per day during the summer season. By limiting the number of rentals, the town council will attain the 50 percent annual reduction in moped accidents that was achieved last year on the neighboring island of Seaville, when Seaville's town council enforced similar limits on moped rentals."

Write a response in which you discuss what questions would need to be answered in order to decide whether the recommendation is likely to have the predicted result. Be sure to explain how the answers to these questions would help to evaluate the recommendation.

다음은 Balmer Island Gazett 편집인에게 보낸 서신 내용이다.

"Balmer Island에서는 모페드가 인기 있는 교통수단이고 여름철에는 인구가 십만 명으로 늘어난다. 시 의회는 Moped와 보행자 간 사고를 줄이기 위해 여름에 대여업체들이 대여하는 모페드 대여 수를 하루 50대에서 25대로 제한해야 한다. 대여 숫자를 줄임으로써 시 의회는, 지난해 이웃 Seaville섬에서 이와 동일한 규제를 시행해서 50%나 사고를 줄인 것처럼 연간 모페드 사고 50% 감소라는 목표를 달성할 수 있을 것이다."

Recommendation	The town council of Balmer Island should limit the number of mopeds rented by the island's moped rental companies from 50 per day to 25 per day during the summer season.

The author of this editorial suggests that restricting the number of moped rentals available per day would reduce the number of accidents involving mopeds and pedestrians. To support this recommendation, the author states that the neighboring island of Seaville reduced its accident rate to 50 % by enforcing a similar policy. In the following, I will investigate what other information is needed to give answers to the questions before agreeing with the author.

First of all, the author incorrectly assumes that the usage of mopeds is the only factor influencing collision rates involving mopeds and pedestrians. There is a possibility that unsafe roads helped reduce the number of accidents. Perhaps the neighboring island, Seaville might have a more sophisticated transportation system, which caused the decrease in the number of accidents. Although decreasing the number of moped rentals may lower accident rates by simply restricting its usage, the speaker's expectation of a similar outcome to that of a neighboring island based on a single factor is a far-stretched assumption. Blind acceptance of the speaker's argument may fail to achieve the desired intention and instead, only hinder the moped rental business.

Furthermore, another assumption that the weather condition of Balmer Island is somewhat similar to Seaville is erroneous. If Balmer Island gets more rainy days annually than Seaville, it is possible that the rate of accidents might be due to bad weather rather than the number of mopeds traveling on roads. If moped transportation is preferable in Balmer Island, more signs or signals could be more helpful for preventing crashes. Without investigating other possibilities, the author's assertion accomplishes little toward the conclusion.

Additionally, the author fails to provide details and the number of moped and pedestrian accidents. The number of moped-pedestrian accidents is unknown, and a 50 % decrease can be relatively insignificant depending on the total amount. If the number of accidents at Seaville is as small as five or six, a 50 % reduction is too meager to justify the assertion. If so, the author fails to place the argument into a larger perspective by relying on too scant evidence to support her claim.

In short, the recommendation is neither well-supported nor soundly reasoned. To persuade readers that the speaker's suggestion would achieve the desired outcome, the author needs to assure what else can be responsible for the decrease in the number of moped-pedestrian accidents at Seaville Island and whether the environmental conditions are similar between Balmer Island and Seville Island, and the argument is based on a representative sample. [497]

7. The following is a recommendation from the Board of Directors of Monarch Books.

"We recommend that Monarch Books open a café in its store. Monarch, having been in business at the same location for more than twenty years, has a large customer base because it is known for its wide selection of books on all subjects. Clearly, opening the café would attract more customers. Space could be made for the café by discontinuing the children's book section, which will probably become less popular given that the most recent national census indicated a significant decline in the percentage of the population under age ten. Opening a café will allow Monarch to attract more customers and better compete with Regal Books, which recently opened its own café."

Write a response in which you discuss what questions would need to be answered in order to decide whether the recommendation is likely to have the predicted result. Be sure to explain how the answers to these questions would help to evaluate the recommendation.

다음은 Monarch 서점 이사진의 권고 사항이다.

"우리 Monarch 서점이 매장 내에 카페를 열 것을 권한다. 한 장소에서 20년 이상 영업을 해온 Monarch 서점은, 모든 주제에 관한 다양한 책들을 취급하기 때문에 많은 고객층이 다양하다. 카페를 열면, 분명히 더 많은 고객을 끌 수 있을 것이다. 아동도서 코너를 폐지해서 필요한 공간을 확보할 수 있는데, 10세 이하 어린이들이 현저하게 줄어든다는 것을 보여주는 가장 최근의 전국인구 통계조사를 고려한다면 이 코너는 점점 인기가 없어질 것이다. 카페의 개장으로 Monarch 서점은 더 많은 고객을 끌 것이고, 최근에 카페를 연 Regal 서점과 경쟁을 더 잘할 수 있을 것이다."

Recommendation   We recommend that Monarch Books open a café in its store to compete Regal Books.

The board of Monarch bookstore recommends that Monarch Bookstore should open a café in the area where they are now selling children's books to attract more coffee consumers. At first glance, it might seem appropriate to accept their recommendation immediately. However, a closer examination reveals it suffers from several spurious assumptions: a mere correlation, a bad analogy, and sampling errors. Unless they strengthen it with sufficient and appropriate data, it is unpersuasive as it stands.

First, the board of Monarch Bookstore assumes that opening a café in the area where they are now selling children's books would lead to increasing profit. Taking the fact that Monarch bookstore was able to maintain its reputation in the area with the variety of selection of books into consideration, accepting the recommendation without filtering uncertainty would lead to making a negative effect on producing more profits. This assumption is problematic because Monarch Bookstore will lose profit at the cost of opening a café in the children's book section if it fails to attract parent customers with their children. Without eliminating the possibility that opening a café might make its customers dissatisfy and thus turn them away from the Monarch bookstore, it is premature to agree with them.

Second, the board of Monarch's assumption that Monarch bookstore and Regal bookstore are somewhat similar in the demand for coffee is fallacious. There is a possibility that the Regal bookstore could be the only café available in the area; but, Monarch Bookstore is located right next to the Starbucks coffee shop. If so, Monarch bookstore customers would prefer drinking coffee from Starbucks to the Monarch bookstore's café. It is also possible that Monarch Bookstore customers prefer reading books in a quiet environment to enjoying coffee. Without ruling out these possibilities, their recommendation is vulnerable to criticism.

Last but not least, the entire argument is based on a biased sample with insufficient data. The fact that the competent Regal Bookstore recently opened its café little indicates that it succeeded in gaining more profits since its opening café. Without sufficient data with specific numbers such as a profit and loss statement, accepting the board's recommendation blindly will result in decreases in the number of customers and lead to a lot of loss of profits.

To bolster the recommendation, the board members should consider if there could be other possible factors that might affect an increase in sales volume and profits and if Monarch Bookstore and Regal Bookstore are equal in the demands of coffee consumers. In addition, they should make their recommendation based on specific numbers or data; otherwise, it would little accomplish toward it. [433]

고유명사만 다른 유사한 토픽

유사한 내용의 토픽이 약간 다르게 출제되므로 반드시 문제를 읽어보고 작성한다.

98. The following is a recommendation from the business manager of Monarch Books.

"Since its opening in Collegeville twenty years ago, Monarch Books has developed a large customer base due to its reader-friendly atmosphere and wide selection of books on all subjects. Last month, Book and Bean, a combination bookstore and coffee shop, announced its intention to open a Collegeville store. Monarch Books should open its own in-store café in the space currently devoted to children's books. Given recent national census data indicating a significant decline in the percentage of the population under age ten, sales of children's books are likely to decline. By replacing its children's books section with a café Monarch Books can increase profits and ward off competition from Book and Bean."

Write a response in which you examine the stated and/or unstated assumptions of the argument. Be sure to explain how the argument depends on these assumptions and what the implications are for the argument if the assumptions prove unwarranted.

다음은 Monarch 서점 사업부장의 권고 사항이다.

"20년 전 Collegeville에 매장을 연 이래, 독자들이 편한 환경과 모든 영역에 관한 폭넓은 도서를 취급해서 Monarch 서점은 두터운 독자층을 형성해 왔다. 지난달 커피점과 서점을 혼합한 Book and Bean이 Collegeville에 매장을 열겠다는 의도를 밝혔다. Monarch 서점은 현재 아동도서 코너로 이용되는 공간에 매장 내 카페를 열어야 한다. 10세 이하 어린이들이 현저하게 줄어든다는 것을 보여주는 최근의 전국인구 통계조사를 고려한다면, 아동도서의 판매는 감소할 것 같다. 아동도서 코너를 카페로 바꿔서 Monarch 서점은 수익도 올리고 Book and Bean과 경쟁도 피할 수 있을 것이다."

Argument Monarch Books should open its own in-store café in the space currently devoted to children's books.

8. The following appeared in a memo from the director of student housing at Buckingham College.

"To serve the housing needs of our students, Buckingham College should build a number of new dormitories. Buckingham's enrollment is growing and, based on current trends, will double over the next 50 years, thus making existing dormitory space inadequate. Moreover, the average rent for an apartment in our town has risen in recent years. Consequently, students will find it increasingly difficult to afford off-campus housing. Finally, attractive new dormitories would make prospective students more likely to enroll at Buckingham." [Old version 240]

Write a response in which you discuss what specific evidence is needed to evaluate the argument and explain how the evidence would weaken or strengthen the argument.

다음은 Buckingham College 학생 주거 담당 책임자의 메모 내용이다.

"Buckingham College는 우리 학생들의 주거 수요를 충족시키기 위해 새로운 기숙사를 건축해야 한다. 등록이 증가하고 있고 현재의 추세로 보면, 앞으로 50년 동안 학생 수가 2배로 늘 것이므로, 기존의 기숙사 시설로는 불충분하다. 더군다나 이곳의 아파트 평균 임대 비용도 최근에 올라가고 있다. 결과적으로 학생들은 학교 밖에서 집을 구하는 것이 상당히 어렵게 되었다. 결국은 새로운 기숙사가 예비 학생들이 우리 대학을 더 지원하도록 만들 것이다."

Argument   To serve the housing needs of our students, Buckingham College should build a number of new dormitories. [9/88/90]

In this memo, the director of student housing at Buckingham College argues that he suggested constructing new dormitories to attract more students to the college. To support this suggestion, he points out the current trends of growing enrollment and its projection that it will double over the next 50 years and that the average rent for an apartment in their town has risen in recent years. Although his assertion sounds plausible at first glance, careful examination reveals that it rests on groundless assumptions derived from poor information.

First, it is possible that the director may be mistaken about the cause and effect relating to the need for new housing at Buckingham College. Perhaps the increase in the average rent for an apartment can be a temporal problem. If a lot more apartments are constructed in the following 50 years, the average rent off-campus would be a lot cheaper due to an increased supply. Simply counting recent years to make long-term predictions fails to account for other possible outcomes. Unless further evidence supports the director's assertion, costly investment into more dormitories carries a high risk and is rather unwarranted. To enhance this argument, the director should further investigate if the students still prefer on- campus housing to off-campus housing even when the off-campus housing is available at a reasonable price.

Furthermore, the director states that attractive new dormitories would increase in the number of students enrolling at Buckingham. This notion is problematic because it assumes a constant rise in enrollment while ignoring reasons behind prospective the speaker overlooks the possibility that the number of students will decrease in the forthcoming years. Perhaps it is a good education system supported by excellent professors that is responsible for the high enrollment trend. In this case, assuring growth through the maintenance of proper education deserves more focus before considering expensive construction projects. Overlooking alternative factors that may influence investment outcomes are a critical mistake that needs to be addressed. Therefore, the director should conduct a more in depth study that guarantees consistent enrollment growth instead of wasting Buckingham's financial resources on new dormitories that may lead to financial shortage.

Finally insufficient information about town size and the cost of rent among different neighborhoods further weakens the argument. Averaging rent of an entire town that is considered quite large could be a generalized point of view as various districts may offer affordable housing to compete new on-campus apartments. The director fails to provide specific comparable data and therefore his or her case rests on a generalized view based on poor assumptions.

In sum, the director's conclusion has several holes in its reasoning. To strengthen it, he should provide sufficient evidence that will rule out all the above doubts and questions. Further research relating to student preference, rental markets, and investment risk analysis should be precedent to claim such needs at Buckingham College. In sum, the director's conclusion has several loopholes in its reasoning. To remedy such a conclusion, he should provide further evidence to rule out all the above doubts and questions. Before agreeing to the claim emphasizing such needs at Buckingham College, further research is needed to find more detailed information such as students' preference on their housing facilities, rental market trend and risk analysis in the housing investment. [474]

10. The following appeared in a memo from the director of student housing at Buckingham College.

"Twenty years ago, Dr. Field, a noted anthropologist, visited the island of Tertia. Using an observation-centered approach to studying Tertian culture, he concluded from his observations that children in Tertia were reared by an entire village rather than by their own biological parents. Recently another anthropologist, Dr. Karp, visited the group of islands that includes Tertia and used the interview-centered method to study child-rearing practices. In the interviews that Dr. Karp conducted with children living in this group of islands, the children spent much more time talking about their biological parents than about other adults in the village. Dr. Karp decided that Dr. Field's conclusion about Tertian village culture must be invalid. Some anthropologists recommend that to obtain accurate information on Tertian child-rearing practices, future research on the subject should be conducted via the interview-centered method."

Write a response in which you discuss what questions would need to be answered in order to decide whether the recommendation and the argument on which it is based are reasonable. Be sure to explain how the answers to these questions would help to evaluate the recommendation.

Write a response in which you discuss what questions would need to be answered in order to decide whether the recommendation and the argument on which it is based are reasonable. Be sure to explain how the answers to these questions would help to evaluate the recommendation.

20년 전, 한 저명한 인류학자였던 Field 박사는 Tertia섬을 방문했다. Tertian의 문화를 연구하기 위해서 관찰 중심 접근법을 사용한 후, 그의 관찰에서 그는 Tertia섬의 어린이들은 생물학적 부모에 의해 양육을 받은 것이 아니고 집단 공동체에 의해서 양육되었다는 결론을 내렸었다.

최근 또 다른 인류학자인 Dr. Karp는 Tertia 군도를 방문해서, 아이들의 양육법을 연구하기 위해서 인터뷰 중심 방법을 사용했다. Dr. Karp가 이 군도에 사는 아이들과 실시한 인터뷰에서, 아이들은 마을의 다른 어른들에 대한 이야기보다 그들의 생물학적 부모에 대한 이야기를 더 많이 했다. Dr. Karp는 Tertian 마을에 관한 Dr. Field의 결론이 근거가 없다고 보았다. 일부 인류학자들은 Tertian의 아이 양육법에 관한 정확한 정보를 얻기 위해서는 인터뷰 중심법을 통해서 미래 연구가 이루어져야 한다고 권고한다.

> **Recommendation** To obtain accurate information on Tertian child-rearing practices, future research on the subject should be conducted via the interview-centered method.

In this article, Dr. Karp concludes that Dr. Field's research conducted twenty years ago is invalid because Dr. Karp interview method showed contradicting results. Though Dr. Karp's study consisted of several islands including Tertia, interview method research should not overshadow the results obtained from an observation study. An observation study can be more valid than the interview method and it may be more proper to combine both methods to find out the rearing custom at Tertia.

The argument's chief problem is that the speaker believes that an interview method is somehow more accurate than observation research. However, it appears reasonable that actively watching the daily routine of children would surely reflect a degree of social rearing occurring in their life. Third-party observation can be better for viewing the ordinary life in Tertia and thus provides a realistic account. On the other hand, an interview may often stress or discomfort children with personal question. Such a study could produce misleading results because its validity is entirely based on honesty, which may not be a virtue upheld by every interviewee. From this point of view, it is unjustifiable to claim that an observation-centered method is invalid when it seems more appealing as it studies rearing culture in a natural state.

Furthermore, twenty years have elapsed since Dr. Field's study, and rearing culture could have changed during this relatively long time frame. Perhaps the once collectivist mindset of Tertian society decided to adopt a family-oriented policy that emphasizes rearing by biological parents. This invites much criticism to Dr. Karp's conclusion as it fails to address the possibility of cultural changes within a dynamic society.

And finally, Dr, Karp conducted his interviews in a group of islands that included Tertia. There is no information regarding the sample size of each island or the surveys used for his/her study. The absence of important detail brings out skepticism because the research would be biased if the collected sample size of Tertia was much smaller than the other islands. And since it is Tertian culture that is under debate, it would be logical to focus on Tertia rather than surrounding islands that may vary in rearing culture and thus insignificant to the study.

These issues must be addressed to create a more reasonable argument as a claim based on assumptions and possibly irrelevant data is very difficult to defend. To justify the statement, convincing evidence supporting the accuracy of interview-centered methods over observation must be presented. In addition, all other explanations need to be ruled out and detailed information regarding research should be included.

11. The council of Maple County proposed restrictions on housing development to prevent it from being overdeveloped.

"The council of Maple County, concerned about the county's becoming overdeveloped, is debating a proposed measure that would prevent the development of existing farmland in the county. But the council is also concerned that such a restriction, by limiting the supply of new housing, could lead to significant increases in the price of housing in the county. Proponents of the measure note that Chestnut County established a similar measure ten years ago, and its housing prices have increased only modestly since. However, opponents of the measure note that Pine County adopted restrictions on the development of new residential housing fifteen years ago, and its housing prices have since more than doubled. The council currently predicts that the proposed measure, if passed, will result in a significant increase in housing prices in Maple County." [109 유사토픽]

Write a response in which you discuss what questions would need to be answered in order to decide whether the prediction and the argument on which it is based are reasonable. Be sure to explain how the answers to these questions would help to evaluate the prediction.

County의 지나친 개발을 우려하는 Maple County 의회는 county 내 기존 농지의 개발을 금지하고자 하는 제안을 토론하고 있다. 그러나 의회는 이러한 규제가, 신규 주택의 공급 제한으로, 상당한 주택 가격 상승을 가져올 수 있다는 점도 우려하고 있다. 제안에 찬성하는 사람들은 Chestnut County가 10년 전에 비슷한 조치를 취했지만, 그 후 주택 가격은 완만하게 올라갔다는 점을 지적했다. 하지만 그 조치에 반대하는 사람들은 Pine County가 15년 전에 신규주택개발을 제안하는 정책을 시행한 이래로 주택 가격이 2배 이상 뛰었다는 점을 지적하고 있다. 의회는 현재, 이 안이 가결된다면, Maple County에서 상당한 주택가격 상승이 있을 것이라고 예상하고 있다.

Argument   The proposed measure that would prevent the development of existing farmland in the county will result in a significant increase in housing prices in Maple County.

The Council of Maple County proposes that the effect of imposing restrictions on the development of farmland for housing development will not lead to an increase in housing prices. To support the proposition they pointed out that an increase in Chestnut County housing prices was minor since it adopted the same measure ten years ago. However, a close examination of their proposition shows that it is more likely to lead to soaring housing prices in Maple County. Without enhancing the proposition with sufficient information and specific data, which will clear all the following questions, it would be too hasty to vote in favor of the proposition.

First, the Council of Maple County assumes that limiting the supply of new housing would accomplish little toward increases in housing prices, so they recommend imposing restrictions on the housing development plan on the farmland. This assumption is problematic because a shortage in the supply of new houses is responsible for increasing housing prices. There is a possibility that a population influx to Maple County could have been due to the growth in jobs. If so, it might cause an increase in the demand for houses. There is another possibility that the lower mortgage interest rate might lead to a booming seller's market. Without making a thorough analysis of the housing market in the function of supply and demand, blindly supporting their proposal would result in a housing market crash. Unless the Council of Maple County studies alternative factors that might cause an increase in housing prices and, if we accept their proposition unconditionally, it would make, let alone the housing prices, Maple County's entire economy paralyzed. To avoid such a crisis, they should examine other possible factors that may affect the housing prices in Maple County.

Second, the Council of Maple County's assumption that what happened in Chestnut County in the past 10 years ago will also occur in their county is flawed. Maybe the housing market was a buyer's market in the past 10 years but if the housing market shifted from a downturn to a hike as happened in Pine County in the past five years,

Maple County will encounter soaring housing prices in the forthcoming five years. Or maybe Chestnut County is located far from the metropolitan cities while Maple County is in the vicinity of large cities. Moreover, there is counter-evidence that the opponents addressed to turn down the proposal. There is a possibility that Maple County is somewhat similar to Pine County in terms of convenience in transportation. If so, Maple County's housing prices would experience soaring housing prices as did Pine County in the near future. Before we support the Council of Maple County, we need to investigate if Maple County is analogous to Chestnut County or Pine County with regard to the housing market and job availability, otherwise, it is premature to agree with them.

Last but not least, the Council of Maple County's assertion is based on poor evidence without specific numbers or data. When carrying out a housing development project, Maple County has to review more detailed information with sufficient data. We do not know the housing market demand and the number of jobs newly created, or transportation route changes and so on.

Without accounting for other possible factors, fallacious analogous relationships, and hasty generalization based on a biased sample, supporting the restrictions on the development of farmland will make an adverse impact on the supply of houses. [575]

12. Omega University should terminate student evaluation of professors to increase higher graduates' employment rate.

"Fifteen years ago, Omega University implemented a new procedure that encouraged students to evaluate the teaching effectiveness of all their professors. Since that time, Omega professors have begun to assign higher grades in their classes, and overall student grade averages at Omega have risen by 30 percent. Potential employers, looking at this dramatic rise in grades, believe that grades at Omega are inflated and do not accurately reflect student achievement; as a result, Omega graduates have not been as successful at getting jobs as have graduates from nearby Alpha University. To enable its graduates to secure better jobs, Omega University should terminate student evaluation of professors." [9 유사토픽]

Write a response in which you discuss what specific evidence is needed to evaluate the argument and explain how the evidence would weaken or strengthen the argument.

15년 전, Omega 대학은 학생들이 교수들의 교습 효과를 평가하도록 권장하는 새로운 조치를 시행했다. 이후, 교수들은 학생들에게 높은 학점을 주었으며, 그에 따라 Omega 학생들의 전체 평점이 30%나 올랐다. 이런 급격한 학점 인상을 바라보는 잠재적 고용주들은 Omega 대학의 학점이 부풀려져서 학생들의 실력을 제대로 반영하지 않았다고 믿는다. 그 결과 Omega 대학의 졸업생들이 인근 Alpha 대학 졸업자들보다 취업을 잘 하지 못하고 있다. Omega 대학의 졸업생들이 좋은 직업을 가지려면 교수에 대한 학생 평가를 중단해야만 한다.

> **Argument** To enable its graduates to secure better jobs, Omega University should terminate student evaluation of professors.

This memo suggests that Omega terminate student evaluations of professors because it encourages inflated grades. In turn, employers are less likely to hire graduates from a certain university that carries such inflationary symptoms. However, other reasons might probably be responsible for less hiring of its graduates. The presentation of such evidence could severely weaken the claim that student evaluations are associated with the employment rate of graduates.

First, the speaker hastily assumes that the low hiring rate of Omega University students is a direct effect of inflated grades caused by student evaluations. This assumption overlooked other possible explanations that might be responsible for it. Perhaps students at Alpha University might receive more career training in relation to job interviews and resumes. If so, a higher graduate employment rate may be more closely associated with students' preparation for interviews rather than inflated grades.

Another assumption is that the characteristics of Omega and n University are similar in terms of professional fields. Omega might be known for its education in Liberal Arts while Alpha is for Engineering. From this point of view, graduates' employment rates could be different according to the types of jobs available. If engineers are in higher demand than artists, then it would appear reasonable for students from Alpha to find more jobs regardless of inflate grades.

Finally, the absence of data from the student evaluations is critical to finding its actual effect on professors assigning grades. The rise of 30 % could be insignificant if the given total number of students with a job upon graduation is too small. Even if I was to agree the 30% rise in the average grades inflated, it could have been possible due to the recent change made from the relative evaluation to the absolute evaluation.

In sum, the line of reasoning of this argument is poorly developed from scant evidence. There are many alternative explanations that can produce a similar outcome, which weakens the argument as it stands. To determine an appropriate strategy, additional information should be examined before making a hasty decision about changing policy.

13. The speaker recommends Prunty County's slower speed limit on highways be back to 55 miles per hour.

"In an attempt to improve highway safety, Prunty County last year lowered its speed limit from 55 to 45 miles per hour on all county highways. But this effort has failed: the number of accidents has not decreased, and, based on reports by the highway patrol, many drivers are exceeding the speed limit. Prunty County should instead undertake the same kind of road improvement project that Butler County completed five years ago: increasing lane widths, resurfacing rough highways, and improving visibility at dangerous intersections. Today, major Butler County roads still have a 55 mph speed limit, yet there were 25 percent fewer reported accidents in Butler County this past year than there were five years ago." [18 유사토픽]

Write a response in which you discuss what specific evidence is needed to evaluate the argument and explain how the evidence would weaken or strengthen the argument.

고속도로의 안선을 향상시기기 위한 시도로, Prunty County는 작년에 모든 County 고속도로의 제한속도를 55마일에서 45마일로 낮추었다. 그러나 이러한 노력은 실패했다. 사고건수는 줄지 않았고, 고속도로 경찰의 보고에 따르면 많은 운전자들은 제한속도를 초과하고 있다. 그 대신 Prunty County는, Butler County가 5년 전에 끝낸, 차선 확장, 파손된 고속도로 노면 재포장, 그리고 위험한 진출입로의 시야 개선 작업 같은 계획을 시행해야 한다. 현재도 Butler County의 도로 제한속도는 여전히 55마일이나 5년 전에 비해 금년에는 사고율이 25%나 감소했다고 보고되었다.

| Argument | To improve highway safety, Prunty County should undertake the road improvement project that Butler County completed five years ago. |

Punity County contends despite the enforcement on the lower speed limit of 45 miles an hour, most collision accidents happen when least expected due to the lack of visibility, reckless driving, or neglecting the road and its surroundings. For Prunty County to push for effective changes exemplified by Butler County, sufficient evidence is needed to strengthen its argument.

First, the speaker concludes that speed limits are difficult to enforce as terrain, weather, and other road situations may slow or hasten the velocity of an automobile. From this point of view, accidents might occur due to reckless driving instead of slight exceeds in speed limits. Prunty County should investigate whether drivers in Butler County also exceed the set speed limit of 55mph. Evidence as such true would further support the notion that minor changes in speed limits are insignificant to reducing the number of accident occurrences.

In addition, weather conditions are as significant for safety as flooded or frozen roads when driving. Therefore, comparing the weather environment between Prunty and Butler would be valuable in assessing the level of road safety. Evidence showing similar weather forecasts throughout the past, present, and future would eliminate the possible influence weather has on accident rates and therefore emphasize the importance of good road infrastructure.

Furthermore, to determine whether the improvements in road infrastructure contributed to the decrease in the number of accidents, the speaker should compare relating to the number of cars and their driving distance and roads during heavy traffic hours in both counties. If the evidence indicates that the numbers of drivers in Prunty and Butler are similar, then it would further support the notion that proper signals, lane width, and improved visibility promote safe road conditions to deter accidents.

In conclusion, scant evidence makes the entire assertion vulnerable to criticism. While accident prevention is an important issue, wasting investment funds in pursuit of insignificant changes can be detrimental. Therefore, providing further information mentioned above would certainly strengthen the argument. [385]

14. The following appeared as part of an article in a business magazine.

"A recent study rating 300 male and female Mentian advertising executives according to the average number of hours they sleep per night showed an association between the amount of sleep the executives need and the success of their firms. Of the advertising firms studied, those whose executives reported needing no more than 6 hours of sleep per night had higher profit margins and faster growth. These results suggest that if a business wants to prosper, it should hire only people who need less than 6 hours of sleep per night." [New]

Write a response in which you examine the stated and/or unstated assumptions of the argument. Be sure to explain how the argument depends on these assumptions and what the implications are for the argument if the assumptions prove unwarranted.

하루 평균 잠자는 시간에 따라 남녀 300명의 Mentian 광고사의 임원을 평가한 최근의 한 연구 결과는 임원들이 필요로 하는 수면 시간과 그들 부서(회사)의 성과 사이에 관련이 있음을 보여주고 있다. 조사된 광고회사 중, 단지 6시간의 수면만 필요하다고 보고된 임원들의 회사가 수익도 더 내고 성장도 빨랐다. 이 결과는, 사업에서 성공을 원한다면, 하루에 6시간 미만을 자는 사람들만 고용해야 한다는 것을 시사한다.

Argument If a business wants to prosper, it should hire only people who need less than 6 hours of sleep per night.

The author attempts to associate the amount of sleep required with business profit margins by citing a study suggesting that sleeping less than 6 hours per night equates to faster growth. However, this argument appears rather far-fetched because the amount of sleep one needs has more to do with an individual's body clock but little to do with intellect and executive leadership.

First of all, it is absurd to correlate the sleeping hours of executives with business profit and growth. This assumption is fallacious because the amount of sleep needed is an unlikely indicator of leadership capabilities. There can be alternative explanations for the reason that certain advertising firms happened to be successful. Perhaps the study might be conducted during the heyday of some advertisement firms rather than the entire industry. As companies generally have busy and non-busy periods per year, it is conceivable that company executives sleep less than 6 hours when business is booming. As the argument fails to mention the atmosphere and time frame in which the study is performed, it seems unreasonable to enforce draconian hiring policies purely based on how much one sleeps.

Secondly, the speaker assumes that the characters of a business industry are identical to others. Even if the quality of work improved in the advertising sector as a result of having less than 6 hours of sleep, to say that the same would occur in the consulting industry is unreasonable because the skills and characteristics needed for the jobs are different. As a consultant, an individual would certainly need sufficient sleep to maximize concentration during business meetings instead of dozing off due to fatigue. From this point of view, having more than 6 hours of sleep would increase company productivity by allowing workers to be highly focused. It is necessary to compare different skills in various jobs, otherwise, the assertion that less sleep generates higher profits is unlikely to be true.

Thirdly, the recent study rating 300 male and female Mentian advertising executives provides little support for the speaker's assertion. As the study is limited to only one particular area, it fails to account for the overall executive population of other regions or towns. This severely limits the study because the sample size is inadequate to represent all the industries in operation. If executives from other cities sleep more than 6 hours and run firms that are more profitable than those of Mentian, the argument would completely fall apart. Little information provided in the study regarding other competitive markets is open to skepticism. Therefore, a decision that is driven by unclear terms would be unreliable.

In conclusion, the speaker fails to persuade me that there is an absolute relationship between the hours of sleep and business success. Further investigation is needed, otherwise comparing Mentian advertising executives to other business firms is unpersuasive as it stands. In addition, the speaker should clarify the difference between hard work and dedication with fewer hours of sleep, as both are independent factors that can often co-exist with one another. [485]

15. The following memorandum is from the business manager of Happy Pancake House restaurants.

"Butter has now been replaced by margarine in Happy Pancake House restaurants throughout the southwestern United States. Only about 2 percent of customers have complained, indicating that 98 people out of 100 are happy with the change. Furthermore, many servers have reported that a number of customers who ask for butter do not complain when they are given margarine instead. Clearly, either these customers cannot distinguish butter from margarine or they use the term 'butter' to refer to either butter or margarine. Thus, to avoid the expense of purchasing butter and to increase profitability, the Happy Pancake House should extend this cost-saving change to its restaurants in the southeast and northeast as well." [182]

다음은 Happy Pancake House 식당 사업부장의 메모이다.

"최근, 미국의 남서부 전역에 걸쳐 있는 Happy Pancake House에서 버터가 마가린으로 대체되고 있다. 그렇지만, 이러한 변화는 우리 고객들한테 거의 영향이 없다. 실제로, 단지 2%의 고객만이 불평하는 것으로 봐서 100명 중 평균 98명은 이런 변화에 호의적임을 보여준다. 더욱이 많은 종업원들은 버터를 찾는 상당수의 고객들에게 대신 마가린을 주어도 불평하지 않는다고 전했다. 분명히, 고객들은 버터와 마가린을 구분하지 못하거나 아니면 그들은 '버터'라는 용어를 버터 혹은 마가린을 뜻하는 것으로 사용한다."

> **Argument** Either customers do not distinguish butter from margarine or they use the term 'butter' to refer to either butter or margarine.

The business manager's argument that serving only margarine to all customers at Happy Pancake House restaurants will contribute to increasing their profits is inherently flawed. The argument reasoning is not persuasive as it stands, and therefore there are several loopholes in s the line of reasoning, which need to be addressed. In the following, I will expose three main erroneous points to suggest the argument be made more dependable.

The manager argues that more profits will be created if they use margarine instead of butter. While this may be technically true, a closer look reveals that it is incredibly one-sided. Of course, the profits of the Pan Cake House restaurants will be greater due to the lower cost of margarine. However, just because a customer doesn't report a complaint, does not mean a customer is satisfied. The customer who got margarine instead of butter may simply refuse to return rather than take tedious measures to report a complaint. In this way, the loss of customers may actually decrease profits despite saving money by the use of margarine.

The manager argues that the use of margarine in place of butter will lead to more profits. While this may be technically true, a close look reveals that it is incredibly one-sided. Of course, the Pan Cake House restaurants will have more profits due to the lower cost of margarine. However, just because the fact that a customer doesn't report a complaint does not mean a customer is satisfied. A customer who receives margarine when asking for butter may disapprove of such dishonest business may lead to simply refusing to return rather than taking tedious measures to report a complaint. In this way, the loss of customers may decrease profits despite saving money by using margarine.

In addition, concluding that the restaurant has a 98 percent satisfaction rate is a tremendous exaggeration. It is unlikely that every single customer would take the time to report whether they are satisfied with the food served. Measuring satisfaction should include other details showing such as how many times the same customer returns to the restaurant. If evidence shows that there is no loyal customer, it indicates that everyone who had dinner at the restaurant would be very displeased with the service they received.

Moreover, the sample population used in the supportive study included customers only in the Southwestern area. The argument assumes that the two populations are identical in terms of customer preferences However, if the customer preferences were different in the Northeast, adopting such a change uniformly may be a grave mistake.

In conclusion, the flaws in the line of reasoning in the manager's argument make it logically unconvincing. The postulation that the manager induced from the poor evidence is unlikely to be accepted by readers. It is impossible to improve the argument without enhancing it with sufficient information with specific data. [375]

19. The station manager of KICK in Medway recommends that KICK include more call-in advice programs.

"Two years ago, radio station WCQP in Rockville decided to increase the number of call-in advice programs that it broadcast; since that time, its share of the radio audience in the Rockville listening area has increased significantly. Given WCQP's recent success with call-in advice programming, and citing a nationwide survey indicating that many radio listeners are quite interested in such programs, the station manager of KICK in Medway recommends that KICK include more call-in advice programs in an attempt to gain a larger audience share in its listening area." [New]

Write a response in which you discuss what questions would need to be answered in order to decide whether the recommendation and the argument on which it is based are reasonable. Be sure to explain how the answers to these questions would help to evaluate the recommendation.

2년 전, Rockville에 있는 라디오 방송국 WCQP는, 방송 중인 전화상담 프로그램의 회수를 늘이기로 결정했고, 그 후 Rockville 청취 지역에서 라디오 청취자 점유율이 상당히 늘어났다. WCQP의 전화상담 프로그램의 최근 성공을 고려하고, 많은 라디오 청취자들이 그런 프로그램에 많은 흥미를 가지고 있다는 전국적인 조사를 인용하면서, Medway에 있는 KICK 방송국 책임자는 KICK가 청취 지역에서 높은 점유율을 확보하기 위해서는 더 많은 전화상담 프로그램을 편성해야 한다고 권한다.

Argue   Samples

> **Recommendation**   KICK should include more call-in advice programs in an attempt to gain a larger audience share in its listening area.

강의노트   Marketing 유형

Argue 문제에 Bold로 표시된 부분은 반드시 이 문제에서 다루어야만 하는 problematic words이다. 모든 아규 문제에 공통적으로 있는 ① 원인과 결과, ② 유사관계, ③ 샘플링 사이즈 오류, ④ 모호한 단어 사용을 지적해야 한다.

Despite the ostensible validity of the speaker's claim, there are quite a few possible fallacies in his or her argument that require further clarification in the following advice. Although the logic behind this argument may seem sound at first glance, more information should be required before initiating any course of action.

First and foremost, the speaker employs vague and ambiguous words to gauge instead of statistical data, by saying "a large size of" or "many". From a business perspective, the exact increase in the number of viewers is critical because it would help determine whether an investment in additional programs would generate the necessary profit to continue running a radio business. To strengthen the argument, the evidence that indicates an influx in WCQP revenue following call-in advice programs are a lot bigger. This shows that the increase in the number of viewers is significant enough to maintain additional radio broadcasting operations.

The argument also fails to consider the possibility that the KICK audience may have a different preference from the nationwide survey and WCQP listeners. If so, then call-in advice programs would not attract more KICK listeners because it fails to target the audience's interest. From this point of view, a preference survey should be conducted to reflect the radio listeners' voice in Medway rather than relying on national opinion. Evidence that shows the popularity of call-in advice programs in Medway would further enhance the argument.

Finally, the speaker assumes that an audience is attracted by only the theme of a program not by any other factor. A radio program host plays an extremely important role in captivating the intended audience. In this way, a program can be successful because of the host's popularity. To strengthen the argument, there must be evidence that indicates that the host has nothing to do with attracting a particular audience.

At best, this argument evokes the need for a skeptical analysis of its contents. It uses vague and ambiguous terms to define essential data, thus making a hasty conclusion that fails to account for other possible factors that may influence the outcome. More research is necessary to take a course of action. [400]

22. All colleges should adopt an honor code to prevent student's cheating.

"According to a recent report, cheating among college and university students is on the rise. However, Groveton College has successfully reduced student cheating by adopting an honor code, which calls for students to agree not to cheat in their academic endeavors and to notify a faculty member if they suspect that others have cheated. Groveton's honor code replaced a system in which teachers closely monitored students under that system, teachers reported an average of thirty cases of cheating per year. In the first year the honor code was in place, students reported twenty-one cases of cheating; five years later, this figure had dropped to fourteen. Moreover, in a recent survey, a majority of Groveton students said that they would be less likely to cheat with an honor code in place than without. Thus, all colleges and universities should adopt honor codes similar to Groveton's in order to decrease cheating among students." [242]

Write a response in which you discuss what questions would need to be answered

in order to decide whether the recommendation and the argument on which it is based are reasonable. Be sure to explain how the answers to these questions would help to evaluate the recommendation.

최근의 한 보고에 따르면 대학생들 사이에서 부정행위가 증가하고 있다. 하지만 Groveton 대학은 아너코드를 도입해서 부정행위를 하는 학생을 성공적으로 감소시켰는데, 이것은 학생들에게 부정행위를 하지 않을 것에 동의하고 만일 다른 학생이 부정행위를 했다는 의심이 드는 경우 교직원에게 알리는 것을 요구하는 것이다. Groveton의 아너코드는 교사들이 가까이서 학생들을 감시하는 구제도를 대체했는데, 그 제도하에서 교사들은 연간 평균 30건의 부정행위를 보고했다. 아너코드가 시행된 시행 첫 해에 학생들은 21건의 부정행위를 보고했고 5년 후에는 이 수치가 14건으로 감소했다. 더욱이 최근 조사에서 Groveton 학생 대다수는 아너코드가 있을 때가 없을 때보다 부정행위를 덜하게 하는 것 같다고 말했다. 그러므로 모든 대학들은 학생들 사이에서 부정행위를 줄이기 위해 Groveton의 것과 유사한 아너코드를 도입해야 한다.

Recommendation   All colleges and universities should adopt honor codes similar to Groveton's to decrease cheating among students.

In this article, the speaker claims that the honor code is effective in reducing the number of cheating, and thus all other universities should also adopt it. At first glance, it would sound reasonable. However, a close examination reveals that it overlooks an alternative explanation for the drop in the number of cheating at Groveton College and the total number of student enrollment over the past five years. In addition, the entire argument is based on scant evidence without specific data.

First and foremost, the argument assumes that the number of cheating incidences dropped because of the establishment of an honor code that replaced a monitoring system. However, maybe there was a reduction in reports filed as a result of students being monitored less. An honor code could actually encourage cheating rather than deter it, as it lowers the risk of students being caught. This assumption might not be credible if fewer students reported, although there were actually more students with complaints. There is a possibility that the honor code encouraged cheating rather than deter it, as it lowers the risk of being caught. Students are more likely to cooperate to achieve a common goal of good grades if it is easy to cheat others. Without accounting for these possibilities, the speaker's recommendation is unlikely to be reliable as it fails to address the motivation behind cheating.

Building on this implication, the speaker mistakenly assumes that over a five year period, all conditions possibly affecting the reported incidence of cheating at Groveton remained unchanged. If the number of students also declined during this time then a reduction in cheating incidences may be no surprise. In this case, the decline in the numbers of cheating cases is attributable to the decreased number of students who were subjected to tests at Groveton. Scant information weakens the argument and without sufficient data, it can be only a bold claim about the effectiveness of an honor code.

Last but not least, the speaker fails to verify whether the survey questions are fair enough to provide a representative sample. If the students intended to give unreliable answers to avoid returning to the old monitoring system, it would be a hasty generalization to recommend that all schools should implement the honor code. Without data showing the conscience of the respondents, relying on such a survey for important decisions is doomed to weaken the students' morale.

In conclusion, this recommendation is unlikely to be a way to deter cheating from occurring. To prove the effectiveness of the honor code system, the speaker should further investigate a representative sample and the correlation between cheating and the honor code. [383]

24. Salicylates are useful for Mentia's residents' reducing headaches.

"A recently issued twenty-year study on headaches suffered by the residents of Mentia investigated the possible therapeutic effect of consuming salicylates. Salicylates are members of the same chemical family as aspirin, a medicine used to treat headaches. Although many foods are naturally rich in salicylates, food-processing companies also add salicylates to foods as preservatives. The twenty-year study found a correlation between the rise in the commercial use of salicylates and a steady decline in the average number of headaches reported by study participants. At the time when the study concluded, food-processing companies had just discovered that salicylates can also be used as flavor additives for foods, and, as a result, many companies plan to do so. Based on these study results, some health experts predict that residents of Mentia will suffer even fewer headaches in the future."

Write a response in which you discuss what questions would need to be answered in order to decide whether the prediction and the argument on which it is based are reasonable. Be sure to explain how the answers to these questions would help to evaluate the prediction.

최근에 발표된 Mentia 주민들이 겪고 있는 두통에 관한 20년간의 연구는 살리실산염 섭취의 치료적 효과에 대한 가능성을 조사했다. 살리실산염은 아스피린과 같은 동일 화학물질 계열로써, 두통을 치료하는 데 사용되는 의약품이다. 많은 음식에 살리실산염이 풍부하게 함유되어 있지만, 식품 가공업체들 역시 식품에 살리실산염을 방부제로 첨가해 왔다. 20년간의 연구는 살리실산염의 상업적 이용 증가와 연구에 참여한 사람들에 의해서 보고된 평균 두통 횟수의 꾸준한 감소 사이에 상관관계가 있음을 밝혀냈다. 연구 결과와 더불어, 식품가공 회사들은 살리실산염이 식품의 향료 첨가물로 사용될 수도 있음을 발견했고, 그 결과 많은 회사들이 살리실린을 사용할 계획이다. 이 연구 결과를 바탕으로, 일부 건강 전문가들은 Mentia 주민들이 앞으로는 두통을 덜 겪게 될 것이라고 예측한다.

With this new use for salicylates, residents of Mentia will suffer even fewer headaches in the future.

In this memo, the speaker predicts that the rise in the commercial use of salicylates will bring about a steady decline in the average number of headaches of Mentia residents. To support this prediction, he pointed out a 20-year study of the Mentia residents' headaches. I find this prediction problematic for several reasons.

Firstly, the speaker's inherent assumption that there is a correlation between the rise of the commercial use of salicylates and a lower average number of headaches is unlikely to be convincing because other factors might have contributed to the decline in the average number of headaches of the Mentia residents. Perhaps instead of salicylates increased numbers of the younger and healthier population who moved into Mentia might be responsible for the lower average number of headaches of the Mentia residents. If this is the case, the speaker's suggestion is flawed as it stands.

In addition, the speaker implies that there would be no difference in the quality or amount of salicylates naturally contained in foods and its commercial use. If the commercial use of salicylates are harmful for its side effects when overused, yielding to the speaker's suggestion will cause more health problems to the Mentia residents. Further analysis is required to provide answers to the question regarding the harmful effects of commercial salicylates.

Lastly, the 20-year study that showed the decline in the number of headaches of the Mentia residents is ripe with unclear terms. The speaker's assumptions are more likely to be fallacious. Without a particularly given number, "average" can be a meager number that cannot be very helpful for deciding the harmful effects of salicylates. In addition, the speaker fails to provide information about the demographic changes at

Mentia. Without sufficient information with specific data, many questions arise about the sampling pool.

In short, the speaker's unsubstantiated conclusion gives rise to several crucial questions: What other factors are responsible for the lower average of headaches of the Mentia residents? What difference can there be in the effects of salicylates contained in foods and those for commercial use? Can "average" be a meaningful term to measure the seriousness of headaches that the Mentia residents are suffering? After the speaker provides answers to these questions, I would consider taking his advice into consideration. [403]

25. The following was written as a part of an application for a small-business loan by a group of developers in the city of Monroe.

"A jazz music club in Monroe would be a tremendously profitable enterprise. Currently, the nearest jazz club is 65 miles away; thus, the proposed new jazz club in Monroe, the C-Note, would have the local market all to itself. Plus, jazz is extremely popular in Monroe: over 100,000 people attended Monroe's annual jazz festival last summer several well-known jazz musicians live in Monroe; and the highest-rated radio program in Monroe is 'Jazz Nightly,' which airs every weeknight at 7 P.M. Finally, a nationwide study indicates that the typical jazz fan spends close to $1,000 per year on jazz entertainment." [Old version 6]

Write a response in which you discuss what specific evidence is needed to evaluate the argument and explain how the evidence would weaken or strengthen the argument.

다음은 Monroe시에 있는 한 개발업자 그룹의 중소기업 대부 신청서 일부에 기록된 내용이다.

"Monroe시에 있는 재즈 클럽은 엄청나게 수익성이 좋은 사업이다. 현재, 가장 가까운 클럽은 65마일 밖에 있다. 그래서 Monroe에 제안된 새로운 재즈 클럽, C-Note는, 그 자체로 지역상권을 석권할 것이다. 더구나 재즈는 Monroe에서 아주 인기가 있다. 10만 명 이상의 사람들이 지난 여름 Monroe의 연례 재즈 축제에 참석했고, 몇몇 유명한 재즈 음악가들이 Monroe에 살고 있으며, Monroe에서 최고 시청률의 라디오 프로그램은 매일 주중 오후 7시에 방영되는 'Jazz Nightly'이다. 마지막으로 전국 조사에서도 일반적인 재즈 팬들은 재즈 오락물에 연간 1,000달러 가까이 지출하고 있는 것으로 보고되고 있다."

In this loan packet, the developer maintains that Monroe would be a profitable venture. To substantiate this claim, the developer states the fact that Monroe has no other jazz clubs. He also indicates other evidence that jazz is popular at Monroe based on a national survey.

The first assumption that the speaker inferred from the evidence is that the closest jazz club is 65 miles away from Monroe. Although he interpreted this fact as supportive evidence, it is less likely to be true. The reason why there is no other jazz club in Moroe may indicate that the demand for jazz in the town is insignificant. Without investigating the actual numbers of jazz fans, predicting the profitability of the new jazz club at Monroe is unlikely.

The popularity of Monroe's annual jazz festival and its nightly jazz radio program seems to lend credit to the developer's assertion. However, he undermines the possibility that the great summer festival's success was due to the visitors from other towns. He also overlooks the scenario that radio listeners prefer staying home rather than go out to a jazz club. Moreover, the characteristics of the residents near C note can be quite different from those in Monroe City. If the Monroe residents are not interested in spending money at the jazz club at all, opening a jazz club in Monroe will be a business failure. Without eliminating all these possible negative consequences, yielding to the developer's suggestion will lead to losing money.

Finally, the nationwide survey showing the average jazz fan spends $1,000 a year on jazz entertainment would support the speaker's claim only if Monroe residents typify fans nationwide. Since the nationwide size is too large, it is unlikely to apply to a local area. Besides, the developer's claim rests on unclear terms to determine a business decision.

In conclusion, the developer's argument gives rise to several problems: a mere correlation, weak analogy, and hasty generalization. Thus yielding to his assertion would amount to losing money instead of generating profits. To bolster it, the developer needs to provide a representative sample. [400]

27. The following appeared in a letter to the editor of a local newspaper.

"Commuters complain that increased rush-hour traffic on Blue Highway between the suburbs and the city center has doubled their commuting time. The favored proposal of the motorists' lobby is to widen the highway, adding an additional lane of traffic. But last year's addition of a lane to the nearby Green Highway was followed by a worsening of traffic jams on it. A better alternative is to add a bicycle lane to Blue Highway. Many area residents are keen bicyclists. A bicycle lane would encourage them to use bicycles to commute, and so would reduce rush-hour traffic rather than fostering an increase." [Old version 55]

Write a response in which you discuss what specific evidence is needed to evaluate the argument and explain how the evidence would weaken or strengthen the argument.

다음은 한 지역 신문사 편집장에게 보낸 편지의 내용이다.

"통근자들은 Blue Highway상 교외 지역과 시내 중심 사이에서의 러시아워 교통량이 그들의 통근 시간을 2배로 만든다고 불평한다. 운전자들의 압력단체가 선호하는 제안은 고속도로의 폭을 확장해서 추가 차선을 만드는 것이다. 그러나 작년에 근처의 Green Highway에 증설한 추가 차선으로 그곳의 교통체증은 더 나빠졌다. 더 나은 대안은 Blue Highway에 자전거 전용로를 추가하는 것이다. 많은 지역 주민들은 자전거 애호가들이다. 자전거 전용도로는 그들이 자전거를 타고 통근을 하도록 유도할 것이고, 그래서 러시아워 교통체증을 조장하기보다는 줄일 것이다."

> **Argument** To reduce rush-hour traffic on Blue highway, a bicycle lane should be added instead of a traffic lane.

Although the author advised adding a bike lane to reduce the congestion during the traffic hours on Blue Highway instead of an additional lane, this advice is more likely to aggravate the current traffic jams on Green Highway. To show adding a bike lane is a plausible solution to this traffic problem, the author pointed out the fact that the Green Highway suffered more traffic when they added a car lane. He also emphasized another fact that there are many bicycle riders in the areas that are connected to Blue Highways. Closer scrutiny of the author's claim reveals that it suffers from scant evidence and is therefore unpersuasive, as it stands.

First and foremost, without understandable reasons, the author claimed that the additional lane at Green Highways worsened the traffic jams. This assumption is problematic if dramatically increased numbers of automobiles cause a booming automobile market. An additional lane was effective for faster traffic flows even though the surplus of cars on Green Highways might have still caused the traffic jams. An ineffective signal system can be an alternative cause that rises to the traffic jams on Green Highways. Without carefully investigating further evidence that shows the reasons for aggravating traffic jams at Green Highways, recommending a bike lane to reduce traffic jams on Blue Highways is problematic.

Another problematic point of the developer's recommendation is that it is inferred from an inherent assumption that the essence of the traffic problems of Blue Highways would be somewhat similar to that of Green Highways. He mistakenly overlooked possible dissimilarities between these two highway routes. Unlike Green Highways if Blue Highways consume a lot more cars in traffic hours, using a bike lane would rather leads to increasing congestion than helping the traffic flow move faster. Scant evidence accepting the recommendation will worsen the traffic on Green Highways.

Furthermore, no specific number was given as evidence to support the developer's claim. Although he indicated that many bike riders use the interjunction to Blue Highways, it is uncertain if those bike riders would use bikes for commuting. If they prefer to use their bikes for leisure over weekends, the developer's claim of adding a bike lane to reduce traffic jams is vulnerable to criticism. In this respect, the evidence lends little credible support for the argument.

In sum, without additional information, the construction of a bike lane to Blue Highways should refrain from following the developer's advice. To better assess the soundness of this advice, it would be helpful to know the following: (1) the demographic profile of drivers who will take Blue Highways for commuting in traffic hours; (2) the extent to which bike riders would actually prefer using a bike lane on Blue Highways to an additional traffic lane. [460]

29. The following appeared as a recommendation by a committee planning a ten-year budget for the city of Calatrava.

"The birthrate in our city is declining: in fact, last year's birthrate was only one-half that of five years ago. Thus, the number of students enrolled in our public schools will soon decrease dramatically, and we can safely reduce the funds budgeted for education during the next decade. At the same time, we can reduce funding for athletic playing fields and other recreational facilities. As a result, we will have sufficient money to fund city facilities and programs used primarily by adults, since we can expect the adult population of the city to increase." [New]

Write a response in which you discuss what specific evidence is needed to evaluate the argument and explain how the evidence would weaken or strengthen the argument.

In this memo, the committee recommends that Calatrava invest more money in adult facilities instead of school education during the next decade based on the dramatically reduced birth rate last year. At first glance, it would seem persuasive; however, a close examination reveals that this recommendation is vulnerable to criticism because of inherent assumptions. Unless they provide further evidence that would eliminate all the following issues, it suffers from a mere correlation, a bad analogy, and a biased sample. If we accept their advice hastily, Calatrava citizens will experience a budget deficit in their children's education.

First, the author assumes that last year's low birth rate is the only indicator determining the educational budget. This assumption is erroneous if there is a growing number of students or a substantial number of students in Calatrava city, and this trend continues in the forthcoming decade. Without considering the educational budget for

K to 12 students, bluntly reducing the budgets for athletic fields and other recreational facilities will dissatisfy students and their parents to the extent that they decide to move to another city. If Calatrava gains its reputation as an educational city, there can be a considerable number of parents who will leave the city for a better quality of education.

Second, It may not be valid that the number of students in other types of schools also reduced. Private schools may experience an increase in the number of students enrolled in private schools. If this is true, Calatrava should not allocate fewer funds for the facilities for young students. Unless the committee provides further evidence, accepting the recommendation would fail to ensure that young students receive a quality education. Without eliminating the possibility that other types of schools might have had more students last year, blindly supporting the committee would lead to a decrease in the quality of life of the Calatrava residents.

Lastly, the committee should present a representative sample from sufficient data and detailed information to make their argument more reliable. Establishing the ten-year budget based on last year's reduced birth rate rests on a sweeping generalization. Perhaps last year can be aberrant. Observing a relatively short period to enforce long-term city plans is a hasty decision. Planning a city usually requires long-term research before it is approved. Evidence showing a rise in birth rates within the past 20 years would severely weaken the claim as it may suggest that there will be more children in the future rather than fewer. Following its suggestion is highly open to criticism and needs more supportive information before pushing for drastic changes.

Unless the committee enhances the argument with more information, it will turn out to be an economic failure and may lead to forcing the young population to move out of Calatrava. To enhance it they should account for other indicators for fewer budgets for education programs and facilities, the enrollment numbers of students in all students, and long-term research for a representative sample. For these reasons, the author's suggestion is highly open to criticism and needs a lot more supportive information before pushing for drastic changes. Presentation of evidence mentioned above would discredit the argument and prove that such changes are unreasonable. [537]

31. The following appeared in a letter to the editor of Parson City's local newspaper.

"In our region of Trillura, the majority of money spent on the schools that most students attend — the city-run public schools — comes from taxes that each city government collects. The region's cities differ, however, in the budgetary priority they give to public education. For example, both as a proportion of its overall tax revenues and in absolute terms, Parson City has recently spent almost twice as much per year as Blue City has for its public schools — even though both cities have about the same number of residents. Clearly, Parson City residents place a higher value on providing a good education in public schools than Blue City residents do." [Old version 214]

Write a response in which you discuss what specific evidence is needed to evaluate the argument and explain how the evidence would weaken or strengthen the argument.

다음은 Parson City의 지역신문사 편집장에게 보낸 편지 내용이다.

"우리 Trillura 지역에서, 대부분 학생들이 다니는 학교—시립학교들—에 쓰는 돈의 대부분은 각 시 정부가 거두는 세금에서 나온다. 하지만 그들이 공교육에 쓰는 예산의 우선순위는 지역의 시마다 다르다. 예를 들어 두 시의 주민 수는 거의 비슷한데도 전체적인 세수에서 차지하는 비율과 절대치 모두에서, Parson City는 연간 Blue City가 공교육에 쓰는 돈의 거의 2배를 썼다. 확실히 Parson City의 주민들이 Blue City의 주민들보다 질 좋은 공교육을 제공하는 데 더 높은 가치를 두고 있다."

Argument   Parson City residents place a higher value on providing a good education in public schools than Blue City residents do.

In this memo, the editor of Parson City's local newspaper concludes that Parson City provides a better education than Blue City. To support this conclusion, he points out that Parson City has recently spent almost twice as much per year as Blue City has for its public school. However, a close examination reveals that the argument is flawed because it develops from a series of unsubstantiated assumptions based on scant evidence.

In the first place, implicit in the editor's conclusion is inferred from the assumption that the amount of funds is an indicator that can effectively measure the residents' desire for education. This assumption involves a mere correlation between the funds spent on public education and the residents' primary concern. Even if the residents of Blue City valued the importance of public education, they might have invested more money in constructing more educational infrastructures such as museums and public parks. If so, it is too hasty to conclude that residents of Parson City value public education more than those of Blue City.

Next, the editor assumes that Parson City residents are more passionate about public education than Blue City because twice as many funds were collected even though there is about the same number of residents. However, unlike Blue City, if there are twice as many young students at its public schools, the funding amount per individual student would be equal to that of Parson City. Without providing an education budget for each student, it is difficult to conclude that Parson City residents have more concern for their public education. To further evaluate the justification of this argument, the editor should investigate how much money both cities allot for each student's education per year.

Last, the editor's line of reasoning is that since a majority of funds for education come from city taxes, the quality of both cities in the Trillura area's education can be measured by the amount of educational funds that both cities spend for public schools. This reasoning can be problematic because it is based on poorly defined terms. "A majority of funds" means slightly over 50% of the total tax money. If this is the case, it is unreasonable that Parson City residents have more concern about public education. "A proportion of overtax can be too vague to indicate how much percent of the total revenue of city taxes Parson City invested in education. Unless the poorly defined terms are clear with specific numbers, the editor's assertion accomplishes little toward the conclusion.

In short, the argument is neither well-supported nor soundly reasoned. To make it reliable, the editor needs to provide more supplementary information including the total tax revenues of the two cities, educational funds for each student of both cities, and an evaluation of the quality of education provided to students in these two cities. With scant information the assertion is unlikely to be true. [543]

32. The following appeared in a memo from a vice president of Quiot Manufacturing.

"During the past year, Quiot Manufacturing had 30 percent more on-the-job accidents than at the nearby Panoply Industries plant, where the work shifts are one hour shorter than ours. Experts say that significant contributing factors in many on-the-job accidents are fatigue and sleep deprivation among workers. Therefore, to reduce the number of on-the-job accidents at Quiot and thereby increase productivity, we should shorten each of our three work shifts by one hour so that employees will get adequate amounts of sleep." [Old version 12]

Write a response in which you examine the stated and/or unstated assumptions of the argument. Be sure to explain how the argument depends on these assumptions and what the implications are for the argument if the assumptions prove unwarranted.

다음은 Quiot 제조업체 부사장의 메모에 있는 내용이다.

"지난해 동안, Quiot 제조사는 인근 Panoply Industries보다 업무상 재해가 30%나 더 많았는데, Panoply Industries는 교대시간이 우리보다 1시간 짧다. 전문가들은 대부분 업무상 재해에 있어서 가장 중요한 요인은 근로자들의 과로와 수면 부족이라고 한다. 따라서 Quiot에서 높은 산업 재해율을 줄이고, 그렇게 함으로써 생산성을 높이기 위해서는, 근로자들이 적당한 수면을 취할 수 있도록 각 3교대의 (근무) 시간을 1시간씩 줄여야 한다."

Argument To reduce the number of on-the-job accidents at Quiot, we should shorten each of our three work shifts by one hour.

The proposition that the vice-president of Quiot manufacturing company is that they should shorten each of their three work shifts by one hour and thus increase profits. To support this claim, he points out that the rate of on-job accidents at the Panoply Industries plant is 30 % smaller than that of the Quiot manufacturing company. I find this claim problematic for several reasons.

First and foremost, the vice-president of Quiot manufacturing company believes reducing its working hours from one hour will cause less fatigue and thus leads to fewer job accidents. This prediction is problematic because it involves a mere correlation between the rate of accidents and fewer working hours. Perhaps the decrease in accidents at Panoply might have been due to the less work they had to handle during working hours. Even though I would agree that seven-hour work shift was effective for reducing accidents at the Panoply manufacturing plant, whether seven-hour shifts that Quiot adopted would be effective is still questionable. A further assumption that the seven-hour working shifts would bring more profits to Quiot is tenable. Due to the seven-hour shifts, if Quiot needs to hire some part-time employees, this may result in more difficulty for employees' working hour management. Unless he accounts for all these cases that might work adversely toward increasing profits, it is too hasty to accept the vice president's advice.

Next, the vice president's assumption is inherent because he rests on a weak analogy between two manufacturing companies assuming the working environments are similar. Perhaps the work environment of Quiot manufacturing company might be much safer than that of Panoply, even when adopting the less working hour shift; the rate of on-the-job accidents will not drop at all. Without comparing the characteristics of work given to employees at both Quiot manufacturing company and Panoply manufacturing plant, hastily assuming fewer working hours would contribute to reducing on-job accidents is unconvincing.

Last but not least, last year can be an aberration. The Quiot manufacturing company might have had fewer accident rates than Panoply in other years than the past year. Due to too many surplus orders, Quiot might have hired many times more workers at the company. A series of problems with the argument arises from the scant statistical information on which it relies. In comparing the number of accidents at both business entities, the vice president should further investigate the total number of employees working at these two businesses.

In short, the argument for emulating Panoply's less working-hour shift policy is unconvincing. Before I agree with the vice president, I would need to know if the shortened work shift length was responsible for the decreased accident rate at Panoply; and statistical information on the job accidents at both businesses. The vice president must also provide further evidence to support his conclusion that a lower accident rate would increase overall worker productivity. [480]

34. The vice president of human resources at Climpson Industries sent the following recommendation to the company's president.

"In an effort to improve our employees' productivity, we should implement electronic monitoring of employees' Internet use from their workstations. Employees who use the Internet from their workstations need to be identified and punished if we are to reduce the number of work hours spent on personal or recreational activities, such as shopping or playing games. By installing software to detect employees' Internet use on company computers, we can prevent employees from wasting time, foster a better work ethic at Climpson, and improve our overall profits." [Old version 127]

Write a response in which you examine the stated and/or unstated assumptions of the argument. Be sure to explain how the argument depends on these assumptions and what the implications are for the argument if the assumptions prove unwarranted.

Climpson Industries의 인사부 부사장이 회사 사장에게 보낸 권고 내용이다.

"당사 종업원들의 생산성을 향상시키기 위한 일환으로, 직원들이 작업장에서 인터넷을 사용하는 것에 대해 전자 감시를 실시해야 합니다. 쇼핑과 게임 같은 개인적 또는 오락 활동에 낭비되는 작업 시간을 줄이려면, 자기 자리에서 인터넷을 사용하는 직원들을 확인해서 제재를 해야 합니다. 회사 컴퓨터에 인터넷 사용을 감시하는 소프트웨어를 설치해서, 직원들이 시간을 낭비하는 것을 막을 수 있고, 근무 윤리를 고무할 수 있으며, 전체적인 수익도 향상시킬 수 있습니다.”

Argument In an effort to improve our employees' productivity, we should implement electronic monitoring of employees' Internet use from their workstations.

The recommendation that the vice president of human resources at Climpson Industries sent to the company's president asserts that the prevention of employees' using the Internet for personal use will ensure more profits for the company. This claim is unconvincing because it is inferred from several unsubstantiated assumptions without evidence. To bolster the argument, the vice president should investigate further evidence that shows a clear correlation between the employees' Internet use and productivity; otherwise, it is vulnerable to criticism.

The first problematic point of the vice president's assumption is that inhibiting employees from using Internet will promote work ethics by installing a machine that will detect the Internet use at the workstation. While it may be true that retraining employees from the personal use of the Internet at the workstation, perhaps there are quite a few negligent employees, and most of the employees at Climpson are mature enough to complete their job assignments regardless of monitoring. In this case, installing software on all computers at the working station will be a waste of money, thus decrease profits instead of increasing profits. Since installation of new tools can cost time and money, before implementing a new device, the vice president should conduct a cost and benefit analysis based on sufficient data.

Another seriously inherent assumption that the vice president made is that negative disciplinary rules would boost the employees' motivation, which will amount to increasing productivity. However, it is not negative enforcement but a positive one that will encourage workers to do their best. This simple rule clearly shows that the installation of monitoring software will adversely influence profits. At the same time, the vice president overlooked positive enforcement that would contribute to boosting profits. Instead of regulating employees from the use of the Internet, it would be much better to pay an incentive or to give a special award to the employees who contribute to the increase in productivity. Without considering other ways of boosting profits, insisting on the use of monitoring software to deter the workers from the use of the Internet may have a negative impact on productivity.

Another weakness of this assumption rests on insufficient data. We do not know how many employees are using the Internet for private use for how long a day. In addition, from the information given above, we cannot also understand what kind of jobs the employees are performing. If their job requires frequent uses for online work, limiting the Internet use is more likely to promote an unpleasant working atmosphere that will work negatively toward increasing profits. To examine the validity of the vice president's argument, we would need sufficient information with specific data relevant to productivity.

In conclusion, the assertion is too weak for several reasons. The vice president failed to reasonably develop the argument based on poor assumptions that suffer from scant evidence. To enhance this argument, he should further investigate why the employees are using the Internet, and how many are actually using the Internet for personal business. Moreover, he should take other possible factors that will help to boost employees' motivation to work. Considering all these the president should recommend the implementation of detecting software for the Internet use. [564]

35. The following appeared in a letter from the owner of the Sunnyside Towers apartment complex to its manager.

"One month ago, all the shower heads in the first three buildings of the Sunnyside Towers complex were modified to restrict maximum water flow to one-third of what it used to be. Although actual readings of water usage before and after the adjustment are not yet available, the change will obviously result in a considerable savings for Sunnyside Corporation, since the corporation must pay for water each month. Except for a few complaints about low water pressure, no problems with showers have been reported since the adjustment. I predict that modifying shower heads to restrict water flow throughout all twelve buildings in the Sunnyside Towers complex will increase our profits even more dramatically." [Old version 185]

Write a response in which you discuss what questions would need to be answered in order to decide whether the prediction and the argument on which it is based are reasonable. Be sure to explain how the answers to these questions would help to evaluate the prediction.

다음은 Sunnyside Towers 아파트의 소유주가 관리인에게 보낸 편지 내용이다.

"한 달 전, Sunnyside Towers 단지 중 우선 3개 동의 모든 샤워 꼭지가 원래의 1/3 정도 수압으로 제한되도록 조정이 되었다. 아직 조정 전후의 실제 물 사용 계량 수치는 알 수 없으나 회사가 매달 수도료를 납부해야 하기 때문에, 이 조정으로 Sunnyside 회사는 분명히 상당한 비용절감을 할 것이다. 낮은 수압에 대한 소수의 불만을 제외하고는, 이 변경 후 샤워기에 대한 문제점이 보고된 적은 없었다. Sunnyside Towers 단지 내 12개 동 전체에 수압을 제한하도록 샤워 꼭지를 조정한다면, 우리의 수익도 급격하게 늘 것이다."

> **Prediction** Modifying shower heads to restrict water flow throughout all twelve buildings in the Sunnyside Towers complex will increase our profits even more dramatically.

A threshold problem with the speaker's argument arises from the assumption that simply changing the shower heads of the Sunnyside Towers will contribute to reducing water bills and thus, increasing profits. This assumption is vulnerable to criticism because it has several loopholes in its line of reasoning. Moreover, the speaker concluded based on the sample collected from the three buildings that cannot be the representative sample for all twelve buildings.

First, the speaker overlooks other factors that will contribute to increasing profits. There could be an alternative explanation for increasing profits. Maybe future tenants pay more attention to kitchen or bathroom renovation than the water-conserving shower heads despite paying more expensive monthly rent. Or advertising one-month discount coupon instead of spending money for new shower heads and their installation will contribute to attracting more tenants. Without ruling out these possibilities, blindly following the speaker's recommendation will accomplish little toward increasing profits.

Even if I were to agree that the tenants in the first three buildings are happy with water-conserving shower heads, we do not know if those in the other nine buildings would like the shower heads to restrict maximum water flow to one-third of what it used to be. The speaker's assertion is inferred from a weak analogy that what happened to the first three buildings will also happen in the other nine buildings. Unless the speaker enhances the argument with more evidence showing the similarity between the first three buildings and the other nine buildings, it is too premature to accept the speaker's suggestion.

Last, the entire argument develops from vague terms such as "a few complaints and low flow." Moreover, no data or numbers were provided to support the speaker's argument. If there were a lot of tenants' complaints, but they were busy making immediate reports, the entire argument suffers from a biased sample. Unless the speaker enhances it with sufficient data and information, blindly accepting the suggestion will lead to decreasing profits.

In short, the speaker's conclusion develops from several hasty assumptions; a mere correlation, weak analogy, and sweeping generalization. I need to review more evidence such as a cost-benefit analysis, profit and loss statement, and survey. After that, I will determine if the speaker's assertions are credible. [380]

36. The following report appeared in the newsletter of the West Meria Public Health Council. [38/162/165]

"An innovative treatment has come to our attention that promises to significantly reduce absenteeism in our schools and workplaces. A study report that in nearby East Meria, where fish consumption is very high, people visit the doctor only once or twice per year for the treatment of colds. Clearly, eating a substantial amount of fish can prevent colds. Since colds represent the most frequently given reason for absences from school and work, we recommend the daily use of Ichthaid — a nutritional supplement derived from fish oil — as a good way to prevent colds and lower absenteeism."

Write a response in which you discuss what specific evidence is needed to evaluate the argument and explain how the evidence would weaken or strengthen the argument.

다음은 서부 Meria Public Health 의회 신문에 실린 내용이다.

"학교와 직장에서의 잦은 결석과 결근을 상당히 줄일 것 같은 획기적인 치료법이 우리의 이목을 끌고 있습니다. 한 연구 조사에서, 생선 소비가 아주 높은 인근 동부 Meria 지역 주민들은 감기를 치료하기 위해 단지 연간 1~2회 정도 병원을 가는 것으로 나타났습니다. 분명히 상당한 양의 생선을 먹는 것은 감기를 예방할 수 있습니다. 감기는 학교나 직장에서 결석이나 결근의 가장 잦은 이유가 되기 때문에, 감기를 예방하고 잦은 결석을 줄일 수 있는 좋은 방법으로, 생선 기름에서 추출한 건강 보충제인 Ichthaid를 매일 섭취할 것을 권장합니다."

Prediction Modifying shower heads to restrict water flow throughout all twelve buildings in the Sunnyside Towers complex will increase our profits even more dramatically.

강의노트 Health 유형
Argue 문제에 Bold로 표시된 부분은 반드시 이 문제에서 다루어야만 하는 problematic words이다. 모든 아규 문제에 공통적으로 있는 ① 원인과 결과, ② 유사관계, ③ 샘플링 사이즈 오류, ④ 모호한 단어 사용을 지적해야 한다. 이 문제의 특이점은 2가지 결과가 있다는 점이다. 즉, to prevent colds and lower absenteeism이 있다. 그리고 비교 대상인 West Meria가 지문 위에 있는 메모에 있다.

The West Meria Public Health Council suggests taking Ichthaid fish oil contributes to reducing absenteeism. To support this suggestion, he indicates that East Meria people's fewer number of their doctor's visits is strong evidence. This argument is problematic as it stands. Further analyses reveal that there are several loopholes in its line of reasoning. The council undermines the possibilities derived from a mere correlation, the climate difference between East Meria and West Meria, and scant evidence.

First, the author assumes that consuming fish oil is solely responsible for reducing absenteeism. Maybe the East Mercia people might have caught fewer colds not because of fish oil but because of their healthy lifestyle. Maybe, the East Meria people's fewer visits to the hospital can be explained by their improved immunity developed from regular exercise. Or, they might have taken antibiotics to combat common colds instead of visiting doctors. Without eliminating these possibilities, it is too premature to consider the West Meria council's suggestion.

Second, the assumption that the climate in East Meria is similar to that of West Meria is problematic. Even if the weather of East Meria is milder than that of West Meria, if the average age of West Meria is much older than that of East Meria, a similar method of fish consumption is less likely to reduce the number of visits to the hospital cold are possible. Such a difference between these two areas would make the argument vulnerable to criticism.

Last but not least, this assertion is based on a biased sample without data or details of the study report near East Meria. If the study investigates healthy workers or, if a sample size is too small to be representative, it is not reliable.

Without sufficient information to rule out all the doubts listed above, the council's argument is vulnerable to criticism. Following their advice to eat fish is unlikely to reduce cold and/or absenteeism in West Meria. [404]

37. The following appeared in a recommendation from the planning department of the city of Transopolis.

"Ten years ago, as part of a comprehensive urban renewal program, the city of Transopolis adapted for industrial use a large area of severely substandard housing near the freeway. Subsequently, several factories were constructed there, crime rates in the area declined, and property tax revenues for the entire city increased. To further revitalize the city, we should now take similar action in a declining residential area on the opposite side of the city. Since some houses and apartments in existing nearby neighborhoods are currently unoccupied, alternate housing for those displaced by this action will be readily available." [Old version 230]

Write a response in which you discuss what specific evidence is needed to evaluate the argument and explain how the evidence would weaken or strengthen the argument.

다음은 Transopolis시의 기획국에서 권장 사항이다.

"10년 전, 포괄적 도시 재개발 프로그램의 일부로, Transopolis시는 고속도로 근처의 넓은 열악한 주택지역을 산업용도로 전용했다. 그 후, 여러 공장들이 그곳에 건설되었으며, 이 지역 범죄율도 줄어들었으며, 전체 도시의 재산세 수입이 증가했다. 더욱 시를 재활성화하기 위해, 도시 반대편에 있는 주거 감소 지역에 유사한 조치를 취해야 한다. 인근 지역에 있는 일부 집들과 아파트들이 현재 비어 있기 때문에, 이 조치로 인한 철거민들을 위한 대체 주택을 쉽게 사용할 수 있을 것이다."

| Argument | We should adapt for industrial use in a declining residential area on the opposite side of the city.

In this argument, the planning department of Transopolis City proposes to convert some areas on the opposite side of the city for industrial use and relocate residents from the currently available apartments nearby. As a supporting ground, the planners in the state implemented a similar project ten years ago near a freeway, which was a great success because the crime rate declined and the average property tax revenue increased.

First, the planners mistakenly assume that the conversion of the slum area caused the decline in crime rates, which amounts to an increase in the property price. This assumption is fallacious because the freeway area conversion may be due to a lower crime rate in the city. If these two events are a sequence of two temporal events, it is vulnerable to criticism. For the same reason, the planners also assume that the conversion plan is responsible for the average property tax revenue increase. This assumption also involves a relation between two coincidental events. If the cause of the increased property tax revenue was due to the booming real estate market ten years ago, lending the whole credit to the city conversion plan at Transopolis City ten years ago is unconvincing. Perhaps the number of property tax revenue increased from the converted area could be about the same or smaller. In contrast, property taxes elsewhere in the city contributed to the rise of the average property tax revenue. Without ruling out these alternative scenarios, the city planner's claim is problematic.

Even though the previous two assumptions prove to be realistic, the planners' projection that the proposed conversion would also lead to the same result in the foreseeable future at the opposite side of the freeway ten years later may be dubious. If there are differences between the two areas, the same effect that occurred ten years ago will not happen now on the opposite side of the freeway of Transopolis. While the converted area ten years ago at Transopolis was a multiple housing zone, if the area in the new conversion is a single-resident zone consisted of middle-upper income class, it may decrease the property taxes because of the unpleasant atmosphere of the industrial zones. Considering that the city must have been changed over ten years, expecting the same outcome as what happened ten years ago is dubious. The changes made over the ten years to carry out another conversion plan on the opposite side of the city is more likely to lead to an unrealistic suggestion.

Although the planners pointed out some houses available for the residents in the area of the new conversion plan, scant information is provided to support their conclusion. If the number of homes is insufficient for displaced residents, the city will encounter a more severe housing problem. Unless the planners ensure that all displaced residents will find their housing in the city with data, the new conversion plan will adversely impact the development of Transopolis City. In fact, with the uncertainty of data, the new conversion plan seems skeptical.

In sum, further research needs to be done to eliminate alternative causes for the reduction of crime and the increase in property taxes, different zoning, and housing risks, otherwise, accepting the planners' proposition will not bring about their anticipated results. The city's conversion in the area on the opposite side will accomplish little toward their anticipated results. [569]

40. Milk and dairy products are rich in vitamin D and calcium — substances essential for building and maintaining bones. Many people therefore say that a diet rich in dairy products can help prevent osteoporosis, a disease that is linked to both environmental and genetic factors and that causes the bones to weaken significantly with age. But a long-term study of a large number of people found that those who consistently consumed dairy products throughout the years of the study have a higher rate of bone fractures than any other participants in the study. Since bone fractures are symptomatic of osteoporosis, this study result shows that a diet rich in dairy products may actually increase, rather than decrease, the risk of osteoporosis. [Old version 34]

Write a response in which you discuss what specific evidence is needed to evaluate the argument and explain how the evidence would weaken or strengthen the argument.

"우유와 유지방 제품에는 뼈를 형성시키고 강화시키는 데 아주 중요한 역할을 하는 비타민 D 와 칼슘이 많다. 이 때문에 많은 사람들이 유지방이 풍부한 식이요법을 하면, 환경 및 유전적 요 인에 의한 손상과, 노화에 의해 뼈가 심각하게 손상을 입는 질병인 골다공증을 억제하는 데 도움 이 된다고 믿고 있다. 그러나 상당수의 사람을 대상으로 한 장기간 실험을 통해서 볼 때, 이들 대 상자 중 실험 기간 동안 유제품을 꾸준히 섭취한 사람들은 그렇지 않은 사람에 비해 훨씬 높은 골 절 현상을 보였다. 골절증상은 골다공증이 원인이기 때문에, 이러한 실험 결과는 우유 제품을 많 이 섭취하는 것은 골다공증을 줄이기보다는 오히려 증가시킨다는 것을 보여준다."

Argument   Since bone fractures are symptomatic of osteoporosis, this study result shows that a diet rich in dairy products may actually increase, rather than decrease, the risk of osteoporosis.

The speaker concludes that dairy products are responsible for increasing the risk of osteoporosis based on a long-term study. However, closer scrutiny reveals that the speaker's conclusion is derived from erroneous inferences. In addition, there is scant evidence to support the conclusion.

The most crucial mistake that the speaker made in the argument is that he assumes the pool of subjects from which he developed a conclusion can be a representative sample. He established a mere correlation between the regular consumption of dairy products and weakening bones. Unless the speaker enhances the argument with a representative sample, which includes health history, age, and gender, the speaker's assertion that milk contributes to increasing the risks of osteoporosis is susceptible to criticism.

Another hasty assumption that the speaker inferred from scant evidence is that the two groups of sampling subjects have equally healthy bones. He overlooks the possibility that the bone density of one group of subjects is genetically weaker than that of the other group. If so, the reason why the milk-consuming group experienced more bone fractures can be explained simply by their genetically weak bones. To make this argument convincing, the speaker should further investigate whether both groups of subjects have similar health conditions with bone density.

Even if I were to agree that both groups of sampled subjects were equally healthy and young, if more bone fractures occurred because of active sports activities, we cannot lend credit to milk consumption for healthy bones. Since athletes tend to have high risks of bone fractures while playing games, the conclusion that dairy products decrease the risk of osteoporosis has the problem of a weak analogy. Without ruling out other reasons for the bone fractures, blindly trusting the speaker's conclusion cannot ensure reducing the risk of osteoporosis.

In short, the recommendation is not well-supported or soundly reasoned. To persuade readers that the speaker's suggestion would achieve the desired outcome, the author should provide further information: Alternative reasons for bone fractures and similarities and differences in the health conditions of the two groups. Moreover, more detailed information such as, gender, age, and medical history is necessary. After that, I will reconsider the speaker's assertion. [385]

41. The following appeared in a health newsletter.

"A ten-year nationwide study of the effectiveness of wearing a helmet while bicycling indicates that ten years ago, approximately 35 percent of all bicyclists reported wearing helmets, whereas today that number is nearly 80 percent. Another study, however, suggests that during the same ten-year period, the number of bicycle-related accidents has increased 200 percent. These results demonstrate that bicyclists feel safer because they are wearing helmets, and they take more risks as a result. Thus, to reduce the number of serious injuries from bicycle accidents, the government should concentrate more on educating people about bicycle safety and less on encouraging or requiring bicyclists to wear helmets." [Old version 120]

Write a response in which you examine the stated and/or unstated assumptions of the argument. Be sure to explain how the argument depends on these assumptions and what the implications are for the argument if the assumptions prove unwarranted.

다음은 한 보건 신문에 실린 내용이다.

"자전거를 탈 때 헬멧을 쓰는 효과에 관한 10년간의 전국적인 연구조사에서, 10년 전에는 자전거를 타는 사람들의 35%가 헬멧을 썼다고 한 데 반해, 오늘날에는 그 수가 거의 80%라고 한다. 하지만 또 다른 연구에서는 같은 10년 동안 자전거 관련 사고는 200% 증가했다고 한다. 이 결과는 자전거를 타는 사람들이 헬멧을 착용했기 때문에 더 안전하다고 느끼고, 그 결과 더 위험을 감수한다는 것을 보여준다. 따라서 자전거 사고로부터 심각한 부상자 수를 줄이기 위해서는, 정부는 자전거의 안전성에 대한 교육에 더 집중하고, 자전거를 타는 사람들에게 헬멧 착용을 권장하거나 강제하지 말아야 한다."

> **Argument** The government should concentrate more on educating people about bicycle safety and less on encouraging or requiring bicyclists to wear helmets.

The article concludes that the doubled bicycle-related accidents in the past ten years show that requiring helmets for bicycle riders has been ineffective in reducing bicycle-related accidents, so the author recommends that city safety education is better to reduce the number of bicycle accidents. To substantiate this recommendation, the author points out two studies that show increased bicycle accidents over ten years.

However, it depends on several unwarranted assumptions with scant evidence.

First, the author's assumption rests on a mere correlation between the rate of bicycle accidents and the helmet-wearing requirement. The author undermines the possibility that more people used bicycles if so, it might have been responsible for double bicycle accidents over the ten years. This assumption is not tenable because it fails to consider all possible factors that might have caused the increase in the rate of bicycle accidents over the past ten years. Perhaps increases in the number of reckless automobile drivers or pedestrians were responsible for double bicycle accidents. If so, the author's belief that wearing a helmet accomplished little in reducing the number of bicycle accidents is unwarranted. Without further investigation, accepting the claim is more likely to lead to a higher rate of bicycle accidents.

Another inherent assumption is that the two studies were done in a similar area or condition. What if they were carried out in different places? It is possible that while one study was for bicycle accidents nationwide study, the other was in the local area. If so, the author's conclusion is derived from a weak analogy. Unless he reveals more information about the areas where the samples of both studies were collected in these comparative studies, blindly agreeing with the speaker's assertion can be a mistake.

Maybe in the past, there could be more bicycle accidents but it was not reported while today 80 % of the accidents were reported. If there were unreported bicycle accidents in the past, it is difficult to judge if the helmet-wearing requirement has been effective. In addition, if the number of bicycle users increased a lot more than 200 %, the bicycle-related accidents could be interpreted as an effective measure to prevent accidents. Moreover, the author's argument is based on vague terms.

In short, the argument is full of unsubstantiated assumptions with scant evidence. To justify it, the speaker should enhance it with sufficient information and specific details which will remove all the doubts discussed above. [384]

47. The following appeared in a memorandum from the owner of Movies Galore, a chain of movie-rental stores.

"Because of declining profits, we must reduce operating expenses at Movies Galore's ten movie-rental stores. Raising prices is not a good option, since we are famous for our low prices. Instead, we should reduce our operating hours. Last month our store in downtown Marston reduced its hours by closing at 6:00 p.m. rather than 9:00 p.m. and reduced its overall inventory by no longer stocking any DVD released more than five years ago. Since we have received very few customer complaints about these new policies, we should now adopt them at all other Movies Galore stores as our best strategies for improving profits." [Old version 213]

Write a response in which you discuss what specific evidence is needed to evaluate the argument and explain how the evidence would weaken or strengthen the argument.

다음은 비디오 대여점 체인인 Movies Galore의 주인이 한 메모 내용이다.

"수익이 줄고 있기 때문에, 우리는 Movies Galore 10개 체인점의 운영 비용을 줄여야만 한다. 우리는 저가로 유명하기 때문에, 가격을 올리는 것은 좋은 방안이 아니다. 그 대신, 영업시간을 줄여야 한다. 지난달 Marston 시내에 있는 가게가 저녁 9시가 아닌 6시에 문을 닫아 시간을 줄이고, 출시된 지 5년 이상 된 DVD들을 더 이상 비치하지 않음으로써 전체 재고를 줄였다. 이러한 새 정책에 대해서 극히 일부 고객들로부터 불평을 접수했으므로, 수익을 늘리기 위한 최상의 전략으로 이제 나머지 모든 Movies Galore 가게에서도 이 정책을 도입해야 한다."

Argument   We should reduce our operating hours at all Movies Galore stores as our best strategies for improving profits.

In this memo, the owner of a chain of movie rental stores suggested reducing the evening business hours and some old inventory thus increasing profits based on the Downtown Marston store's success last month. At first glance, it would seem convincing; however, closer scrutiny reveals that it rests on several unsubstantiated assumptions and therefore is problematic as it stands.

The first hasty assumption that the owner made is that reducing the expense will contribute to improving profits. However, the correlation between these two factors can be a dubious one. A more common practice for a business to increase profits is offering low prices which is the chain stores' current marketing strategy. Downtown Marston store's increased profits last month can be simply explained by a new release movie that was a great hit last month. Without considering alternative explanations for why the Downtown Marston store showed a rise in sales last month, the owner's conclusion is problematic.

Another inherent assumption that derives from a weak analogy is that the owner undermined the possible different conditions between the Downtown Marston store and all other stores. If all other stores are located in residential zones instead of commercial zones, closing early in the evening would negatively affect the promotion of profits. The video rental customers in all other areas may be much older residents, they are prone to borrow old movies popular in the past. Unless the owner further provides the demographic information, which proves the same customer preferences between the downtown store and all other stores, I will not accept the assertion. In short, what happened in the downtown Marston store last month does not apply to all stores.

Another questionable point in the owner's argument is the evidence of "few complaints". He failed to provide detailed information with specific data to prove the increase in profit at the downtown store. Few complaints do not necessarily mean increased business profits. To take the conclusion more seriously, I will need to investigate the profit and loss statement of the Marston store for at least several years. Without providing the balance sheets of all chain stores, the owner's argument is not dependable.

In sum, the argument is not substantially supported by business data or soundly developed. To strengthen it, the owner should investigate detailed information; otherwise, blindly accepting it is more likely to lose profits. [399]

66. The following appeared in a memo from the owner of a chain of cheese stores located throughout the United States.

"For many years all the stores in our chain have stocked a wide variety of both domestic and imported cheeses. Last year, however, all of the five best-selling cheeses at our newest store were domestic cheddar cheeses from Wisconsin. Furthermore, a recent survey by Cheeses of the World magazine indicates an increasing preference for domestic cheeses among its subscribers. Since our company can reduce expenses by limiting inventory, the best way to improve profits in all of our stores is to discontinue stocking many of our varieties of imported cheese and concentrate primarily on domestic cheeses."

Write a response in which you discuss what specific evidence is needed to evaluate the argument and explain how the evidence would weaken or strengthen the argument.

다음은 미국 전역에 있는 한 치즈 체인점 주인의 메모 내용이다.

"수년 동안, 우리 체인점은 국내산 및 수입산 치즈를 상당량 확보해 놓았다. 그러나 지난해 신규로 개장한 체인점에서 최고로 잘 팔리는 5가지 치즈들은 모두 위스콘신산 국산 체다 치즈였다. 더욱이, 세계의 치즈라는 잡지의 최근 조사에서, 구독자들 가운데 국내산 치즈에 대한 선호도가 증가하고 있다고 나타났다. 우리 회사는 재고를 줄여서 비용을 절감할 수 있기 때문에, 모든 우리 가게들이 이익을 늘릴 수 있는 최상의 방법은 다양한 수입산 치즈의 비축을 중단하고 주로 국산 치즈를 확보하는 것이다."

Recommendation The best way to improve profits in all of our stores is to discontinue stocking many of our varieties of imported cheese and concentrate primarily on domestic cheeses.

In this memo, the speaker recommends that discontinuity in stocking many varieties of foreign cheese and concentration on domestic cheeses will reduce the company's cost of inventories and thus increase sales. He points out the recent survey by Cheeses of the World magazine supports his recommendation. At first glance, it would seem credible; however, closer investigation reveals that there are several loopholes in the line of reasoning into a logical conclusion. In addition, this argument is based on scant evidence.

First, the speaker mistakenly assumes that stocking domestic cheddar cheeses from Wisconsin is responsible for an increase in sale in their newest store. This assumption is flawed in that it confuses a mere correlation as a necessary relationship. There is a strong possibility that the improved sales are due to a seasonal increase in cheddar cheese consumption in Wisconsin. It is equally possible that the varieties of domestic and foreign cheeses are the cause of increased sales. Without eliminating these possibilities, the speaker's recommendation is vulnerable to criticism.

Second, the speaker's assumption that the company's newest store and other stores are similar in terms of consumers' preferences is unwarranted; however, it involves a weak analogy. The speaker overlooks the possibility that consumers' preferences between their newest store and other stores are different. Unlike the consumers of the newest stores, the consumers of many other stores might not be in favor of domestic cheeses. Even if I were to agree with the speaker's argument that the consumers of the newest store prefer domestic cheeses, if the consumers of other stores like foreign cheeses more, the sale of the company will decrease. To strengthen this argument, the speaker should further investigate the similarity in the characters of both consumers.

Third, this assertion could be based on a biased sample: a recent survey by Cheese of the World magazine. Perhaps the subscribers of the magazine cannot be a representative sample for the company's consumers, and therefore the speaker's argument based on an inappropriate sample size is flawed. Although more domestic cheese sale was possible at the newest store last year, this can be an aberration. Moreover, it suffers from poorly defined terms without specific data. Without sufficient information, this argument is too weak to draw a reasonable conclusion.

In sum, the speaker's recommendation is neither strongly supported by evidence nor reasonably developed to a conclusion. To justify it, he should further verify other possible explanations, differences in consumer preferences, and the validity of the sampling size.

83. The following is a letter to the editor of an environmental magazine.

"In 1975 a wildlife census found that there were seven species of amphibians in Xanadu National Park, with abundant numbers of each species. However, in 2002 only four species of amphibians were observed in the park, and the numbers of each species were drastically reduced. There has been a substantial decline in the numbers of amphibians worldwide, and global pollution of water and air is clearly implicated. The decline of amphibians in Xanadu National Park, however, almost certainly has a different cause: in 1975, trout — which are known to eat amphibian eggs — were introduced into the park." [150]

Write a response in which you discuss what specific evidence is needed to evaluate the argument and explain how the evidence would weaken or strengthen the argument.

다음은 한 환경잡지 편집장에게 보낸 편지이다.

"1975년 야생동물 조사에 의하면 제나두 국립공원에는 7종류의 양서류가 있었고, 각 종의 개체수도 많았다. 하지만 2002년도에는 겨우 4종류의 양서류만이 목격되었고, 각 종의 개체수도 급격하게 줄었다. 전 세계적으로 양서류들의 수가 현저하게 줄어들고 있는데, 이는 분명히 세계적인 물과 공기의 오염이 그 원인으로 보인다. 하지만 제나두 국립공원에서 양서류가 감소하는 것은 다른 원인이 있음이 거의 확실하다: 즉 1975년에 송어—양서류의 알을 먹는 것으로 알려진—가 이 공원에서 발견되었기 때문이다."

Argument   The decline of amphibians in Xanadu National Park has a different cause because trout — which are known to eat amphibian eggs — were introduced into the park.

Although it may be true that trout is responsible for the decline in the number of amphibians, the author's argument fails to support the cause of the decline between 1975 and 1992. It is plausible that trout can be a reason for the decline; however, closer scrutiny shows that it lacks sufficient evidence that substantiates that trout is solely responsible for the reduced number of amphibians. This argument is full of hasty assumptions and is therefore weak to criticism as it stands.

First and foremost, the speaker implies that global pollution cannot be the real reason for the decline in the number of amphibians between 1975 and 1992. This problematic implication fails to provide other possible explanations for it. The speaker overlooks the possibility that global pollution is instead responsible for the decline in the number of amphibians. There is a possibility that sudden climate changes between 1975 and 1992 might contribute to the reduced number of amphibians.

Second, the implication in the argument is that the location investigated in 1975 is similar to that of 1992. This argument is scant information that shows whether the samplings of amphibians are in a similar location or not. Even assuming the investigations were carried out in a similar area, if samplings collect from the two different seasons of the year, the decline in the number of amphibians in 1992 can be explained due to hibernation in winter. If this is the case, the speaker's explanation is defenseless to criticism. Unless the speaker bolsters the argument with further evidence that shows the exact time and location, it is too weak to be conclusive.

Last, the argument fails to provide data or detailed information to support the speaker's assertions. Unless he removes the ambiguity with specific research data, it is difficult to conclude that trout is solely responsible for the decline between 1975 and 1992 at Xanadu National Park. To make this argument more plausible, the author should further investigate other areas than Xandadu Park. If the only sample of Xandadu Park is biased, it can not substantiate his argument.

Although there is a possibility that trout is responsible for the decline in the number of amphibians at Xanadu National Park, before the author blames trout for such a cause, he should further examine alternative explanations for it. In addition, otherwise, we know whether samplings were taken from similar locations or in the same season, the author's assertion is too weak to persuade readers that it is trout, not the global pollution, contributed to the decline in the number of amphibians.

91. Three years ago, because of flooding at the Western Palean Wildlife Preserve, 100 lions and 100 western gazelles were moved to the East Palean Preserve, an area that is home to most of the same species that are found in the western preserve, though in larger numbers, and to the eastern gazelle, a close relative of the western gazelle. The only difference in climate is that the eastern preserve typically has slightly less rainfall. Unfortunately, after three years in the eastern preserve, the imported western gazelle population has been virtually eliminated. Since the slight reduction in rainfall cannot be the cause of the virtual elimination of western gazelle, their disappearance must have been caused by the larger number of predators in the eastern preserve. [New]

Write a response in which you discuss what specific evidence is needed to evaluate the argument and explain how the evidence would weaken or strengthen the argument.

3년 전, Western Palean 야생동물 보호지역의 홍수로, 100마리의 사자와 100마리의 서부 영양이, 서부 보호지역에서 발견되는 대부분의 동일종들이 사는 East Palean 보호구역으로 옮겨졌는데, 이곳은 서부 영양과 비슷한 종인 동부 영양들이 많이 살고 있다. 기후의 차이는 단지 동부 보호지역의 강우량이 일반적으로 다소 적다는 것이다. 유감스럽게도 3년 후, 옮겨진 서부 영양이 동부 보호지역에서 거의 사라졌다. 서부 영양이 없어진 이유가 근소한 강우량의 감소 때문은 아닐 것이므로, 이들이 사라진 이유는 틀림없이 동부 보호지역에 사는 수많은 천적들 때문일 것이다.

The disappearance of western gazelle must have been caused by the larger number of predators in the eastern preserve.

The argument concludes that it must have been the large number of predators that resulted in the distinction of gazelles at the East Palean Preserve in three years. To substantiate this argument, the speaker emphasizes that there is little difference in the climate between Western Palean and East Palean areas other than slightly less rainfall in West Palean. However, this argument is unconvincing as it stands.

The first assumption of the argument is that since there is no difference in the environment between East Paelan and West Palean, only the increase in the number of predators can be the reason for the virtual elimination of western gazelles. However, the speaker undermines the possibility that the outgrown number of western gazelles caused a lack of food. Unconditionally following the speaker's assertion can mislead us to an unreliable conclusion. To substantiate this argument, the speaker should compare the number of predators.

The second assumption is that eastern gazelles and western gazelles are similar in terms of size and eating habits mentioning that gazelles that moved to Western Palean were a close relative to eastern gazelles. However, it overlooks the possibility western gazelles have larger stomachs than eastern gazelles. To substantiate this argument, the speaker should compare the amount of food western gazelles and eastern gazelles consume daily. Unlike eastern gazelles if the western gazelles moved to the Western Palean Preserve suffered a lack of grass due to drought, it is possible that starvation might contribute to the western gazelle's disappearance.

Lastly, the argument presents cloudy terms that cannot fully support the speaker's assertion. In addition, except for the disappearance of gazelles at West Palea, little information has been known besides that Western Paelan is "home to the most same species". Moreover, the argument failed to provide information about the lions that moved to West Palea along with gazelles. If all the 100 lions also disappeared, we cannot say that the outgrown number of predators is solely responsible for the western gazelle's disappearance in Western Palean. Without providing more detailed information about the number of all kinds of predators, it is difficult to blame the increase in the number of predators for the gazelle's extinction.

To justify this argument, the author should further substantiate it with further evidence to find who or what was responsible for the disappearance of gazelles. And supplementary information regarding the ecosystem in Western Palea that might give a clue to the elimination of gazelles at West Palea is needed. [400]

92. Workers in the small town of Leeville take fewer sick days than workers in the large city of Masonton, 50 miles away. Moreover, relative to population size, the diagnosis of stress-related illness is proportionally much lower in Leeville than in Masonton. According to the Leeville Chamber of Commerce, these facts can be attributed to the health benefits of the relatively relaxed pace of life in Leeville. [234]

Write a response in which you discuss one or more alternative explanations that could rival the proposed explanation and explain how your explanation(s) can plausibly account for the facts presented in the argument.

소도시 Leeville에 사는 근로자들이 50마일 떨어진 대도시 Masonton에 사는 근로자들보다 병가를 덜 낸다. 더구나 인구에 비해서, 스트레스 관련 질병의 진단은 Leeville이 Masonton보다 훨씬 적다. Leeville 상공회의소에 따르면, 이런 사실은 Leeville에서의 상대적으로 여유로운 생활에서 오는 건강상의 이점 때문이라고 한다.

The fewer sick days and the lower diagnosis of stress-related illness in Leeville can be attributed to the health benefits of the relatively relaxed pace of life in Leeville.

In this memo, the speaker concludes that the health benefits of Leeville residents are greater than those of Mansoton based on the following facts: 1) workers in the small town of Leeville take fewer sick days than workers in the large city of Masonton; 2) concerning population size, the diagnosis of stress-related illness is proportionally much lower in Leeville than in Masonton. This conclusion is derived from a series of unsubstantiated assumptions, which renders it unpersuasive as it is.

First, the speaker assumes that fewer sick days reported by the Leeville workers dictates that the residents in Leeville have more relaxed life than those of Masonton. This assumption is problematic because a direct correlation between fewer sick days and the relatively relaxing pace of life does not necessarily prove that the former is the result in the latter. Perhaps, the average age of Leeville workers might be much younger. In addition, the lower number of diagnoses can be due to the essence of the work in which Leeville workers are engaged. Without considering alternative explanations possible, the speaker cannot justifiably conclude that relaxed lifestyle is a contributing cause.

Even assuming the workers in both areas are equally healthy and young, we know little about the environment of Leeville, if it is equal to that of Masonton. With scant evidence to the contrary, fewer diagnoses of the stress of the Leeville workers is more likely to occur due to factors that have nothing to do with a relaxed lifestyle. Common sense tells us that comparing a small city life with a large city, one must include their environment in terms of air or water pollution.

Additionally, the speaker provides no evidence for the argument that fewer sick days reported by the Leeville workers than those of Masonton are a clear indication. The speaker must also show data for the total number of populations as the exact number of sick reports made in both cities. With scant evidence to support the speaker's assumptions, this argument is dubious at best.

To strengthen it, the author must assure me with sufficient information with specific data that will contribute to removing all the doubts discussed above. After that, I will consider his assertion. [404]

97. The following appeared in an e-mail sent by the marketing director of the Classical Shakespeare Theatre of Bardville.

"Over the past ten years, there has been a 20 percent decline in the size of the average audience at Classical Shakespeare Theatre productions. In spite of increased advertising, we are attracting fewer and fewer people to our shows, causing our profits to decrease significantly. We must take action to attract new audience members. The best way to do so is by instituting a 'Shakespeare in the Park' program this summer. Two years ago the nearby Avon Repertory Company started a 'Free Plays in the Park' program, and its profits have increased 10 percent since then. If we start a 'Shakespeare in the Park' program, we can predict that our profits will increase, too." [New]

Write a response in which you discuss what questions would need to be answered in order to decide whether the recommendation is likely to have the predicted result. Be sure to explain how the answers to these questions would help to evaluate the recommendation.

다음은 Bardville의 Classical Shakespeare 극장의 영업부장이 보낸 이메일 내용이다.

"지난 10년간, Classical Shakespeare 극장의 평균 관람객 수가 20%나 줄었다. 광고를 늘렸음에도 불구하고 우리 쇼를 찾는 사람들은 점점 줄고 있고 그래서 수익도 상당히 줄어들었다. 우리는 새로운 관객들이 흥미를 느낄 만한 조치를 취해야만 한다. 최선의 방법은 이번 여름에 'Shakespeare in the Park' 프로그램을 시작하는 것이다. 2년 전, 근처의 Avon Repertory 회사가 'Free Plays in the Park' 프로그램을 시작했는데, 그 후로 이 회사의 이익이 19%나 늘었다. 우리가 'Shakespeare in the Park' 프로그램을 시작한다면, 우리 수익도 늘 것으로 전망된다."

| Recommendation | The best way to do so is by instituting a 'Shakespeare in the Park' program this summer. |

In this email, the marketing director of the Classical Shakespeare Theatre of Bardville suggested that it implement 'Shakespeare in the Park' program this summer to reverse the decline in profits. To support the claim he points out that Avon Repertory Company launched a 'Free Plays in the Park' program two years ago and, as a result, it has increased 10 percent in profits. However, I find it depends on several unsubstantiated assumptions and is therefore, unpersuasive as it stands.

First of all, the marketing director suggests that the Classical Shakespeare Theatre of Bardville show 'Shakespeare in the Park' program to compete with the nearby Avon Repertory Company, which instituted 'Free Plays in the Park' program two years ago. This suggestion involves a mere correlation error. The director overlooks the possibility that the Avon Repertory Company's profit increase by 10 percent might have been due to its offering a free program, which succeeded in attracting more young viewers in Bardville. If so, the Classical Shakespeare Theatre will not attract new audiences by offering 'Shakespeare in the Park' program, thus losing even more profits. The speaker even said advertising was ineffective in attracting more audiences. Without ruling out this possibility, accepting the director's advice will accomplish little toward its increasing profits.

Another question that the director must consider if the Classical Shakespeare Theatre and the nearby Avon Repertory Company are the only entertainment companies in competition at Bardville. If another entertainment company opens close to the Classical Shakespeare Theater in the near future, both the Classical Shakespeare Theatre and the Avon Repertory Company will lose profits. To eliminate this scenario, the director should further investigate if there will be more demands for the 'Shakespeare in the Park' program.

Another assumption that both companies target audiences with a similar interest. There is a possibility the old audiences preferred the Classical Shakespeare Theatre while young audiences liked those of the Avon Repertory Company. If so, accepting the manager's advice will end up losing profit.

Last, the speaker's assertion is based on vague terms without specific numbers. It is unreasonable to conclude from the scant evidence without understanding why the Classical Shakespeare Theatre experienced a decrease in profit over the past two years. To make the argument credible the speaker should substantiate it with reliable data: otherwise, accepting the director's claim is too risky.

As is stated, the suggestion that the Classical Shakespeare Theatre launch a summer program to increase profit is inherently flawed. The entire argument could be redeemed if the director enhances it with further evidence that will contribute to removing all the questions listed above. [414]

98. The following is a recommendation from the business manager of Monarch Books.

"Since its opening in Collegeville twenty years ago, Monarch Books has developed a large customer base due to its reader-friendly atmosphere and wide selection of books on all subjects. Last month, Book and Bean, a combination bookstore and coffee shop, announced its intention to open a Collegeville store. Monarch Books should open its own in-store café in the space currently devoted to children's books. Given recent national census data indicating a significant decline in the percentage of the population under age ten, sales of children's books are likely to decline. By replacing its children's books section with a café Monarch Books can increase profits and ward off competition from Book and Bean." [44]

Write a response in which you discuss what specific evidence is needed to evaluate the argument and explain how the evidence would weaken or strengthen the argument.

다음은 Monarch 서점 사업부장의 권고 사항이다.

"20년 전 Collegeville에 매장을 연 이래, 독자들이 편한 환경과 모든 영역에 관한 폭넓은 도서를 취급해서 Monarch 서점은 두터운 독자층을 형성해 왔다. 지난달 커피점과 서점을 혼합한 Book and Bean이 Collegeville에 매장을 열겠다는 의도를 밝혔다. Monarch 서점은 현재 아동도서 코너로 이용되는 공간에 매장 내에 카페를 열어야 한다. 10세 이하 어린이들이 현저하게 줄어든다 것을 보여주는 최근의 전국인구 통계조사를 고려한다면, 아동도서의 판매는 감소할 것 같다. 아동도서 코너를 카페로 바꿔서 Monarch 서점은 수익도 올리고 Book and Bean과 경쟁도 피할 수 있을 것이다."

| Argument | Monarch Books should open its own in-store café in the space currently devoted to children's books. |

The manager's argument that opening a café at Monarch Bookstore would allow them to attract more customers and increase profits is not logically convincing. To support his argument, he pointed out the profit increase of Book and Bean last month. I found the evidence is too weak to draw a reasonable conclusion for several reasons.

The manager maintains that opening a café in the current children's book section will bring more profits to Monarch Books at Collegeville, which ward off competition from Book and Bean planning to open a Collegeville Store. This assertion rests on a weak analogy because the manager fails to see differences in the sales trend between these two stores. If Monarch Books has its reputation for a quiet reading environment and its wide selection of books, especially children's books, blindly accepting the manager's advice would lead to losing its current reputation and, thus, reduce its profitability. To bolster this argument, the manager should enhance it with further evidence that customers would like to spend more money at the in-store coffee shop at the cost of removing its current benefit of a wide selection of books. Scant evidence shows that the manager's claim is vulnerable to criticism.

In addition, the manager pointed out the recent increase in the profits of Book and Bean to support his assertion. However, he overlooks the possibility that the last month could be aberrant. If so, the manager's assertion ends up with a hasty generalization. Moreover, one month is too short to grasp the trend of profit increase. In short, the manager's conclusion develops from poorly defined terms. Without sufficient evidence, the assertion is unconvincing as is.

Even assuming the in-store coffee shop is a popular trend that will contribute to a temporary increase in profit if Bean and Books opened its next store in Collegeville soon, an additional café at Collegeville would result in a surplus in the supply of coffee shops. If this is the case, the surplus supply in the book cafés at Collegeville will lead to decrease profit. Another scenario is if more than half of Monarch Books' customers are children, contrary to the national survey, removing the children's book section will adversely impact profitability. Without providing clear evidence that an in-store café in place of the children's book section will bring more profits to Monarch Books, the director's suggestion is too risky.

In conclusion, the argument unfairly assumes that correlation is tantamount to causation. It also fails to provide a convincing survey that is suitable for the local region of Collegeville. Another hasty assumption is that the characteristics of Collegeville are similar to those of the Bean and Book area. [479]

142. Hospital statistics regarding people who go to the emergency room after roller-skating accidents indicate the need for more protective equipment. Within that group of people, 75 percent of those who had accidents in streets or parking lots had not been wearing any protective clothing (helmets, knee pads, etc.) or any light-reflecting material (clip-on lights, glow-in-the-dark wrist pads, etc.). Clearly, the statistics indicate that by investing in high-quality protective gear and reflective equipment, roller skaters will greatly reduce their risk of being severely injured in an accident. [New]

Write a response in which you examine the stated and/or unstated assumptions of the argument. Be sure to explain how the argument depends on these assumptions and what the implications are for the argument if the assumptions prove unwarranted.

롤러스케이트를 타가다 사고가 나서 응급실을 찾는 사람들에 대한 병원 통계는 더 많은 보호 장비가 필요하다는 것을 보여준다. 이 사람들 중, 길거리나 주차장에서 사고를 낸 사람들의 75% 가 아무런 보호복(헬멧, 무릎 보호대 등)이나 빛 반사용 기구(클립식 라이트, 야광 손목 보호대 등)를 착용하지 않았다. 분명히, 이 통계는 질 좋은 보호 장비와 반사용 기구에 투자를 함으로써, 롤러 스케이트를 타는 사람들이 사고 시 심한 부상을 당하는 위험을 상당히 줄일 것이라는 점을 시사한다.

> **Argument** Roller skaters will greatly reduce their risk of being severely injured in an accident by investing in high-quality protective gear and reflective equipment.

The notion that protective gear and reflective equipment contributed to reducing the number of injuries suffered in accidents would seem convincing at first glance. However, careful investigation disappoints us because this conclusion that investing in high-quality protective gear and reflective equipment will reduce the risk of being severely injured in an accident is more likely to mask other potentially more significant causes of injuries based on a biased sample in addition to committing a poor analogy to provoke customers with impulsive purchases of such products.

First and foremost, the speaker mistakenly assumes the cause of skate roller accidents is not wearing protective gear. This assumption is too weak to be persuasive because it does not consider other explanations that may affect the accident rate. Perhaps the old pavement with curvy roads might be responsible for the accidents. If so, the speaker's assumption is unlikely to be convincing. Unless he investigated other alternative reasons for the lower rate of incidents of those who use a protective gear, it could be a poorly stated assumption.

In addition, the argument assumes that there is no difference in the physical conditions between unhealthy skaters who did not wear a protective gear and those who were healthy but wore helmets with reflective equipment. The skaters who wore gear may be less likely to be involved in accidents than those who use reflective equipment and those who do not use such gear or equipment. Thus, the speaker's assumption undermines a fallacious analogy that would critically weaken it.

Furthermore, the statistics above are based entirely on the streets and parking lots which are relatively dangerous places to skate in the first place. More safety-conscious people (and therefore more likely to wear gear) may choose safer skating areas such as parks or backyards. The statistics fail to differentiate the severity of injuries. The conclusion that safety gear prevents severe injuries suggests that people come to the emergency room only with severe injuries based on little evidence ensuring that reflective equipment prevents injuries.

After all, the stated assumptions are vulnerable to criticism without sufficient evidence proving the effectiveness of protective gear in reducing the rate of incidents. [404]

151. The following appeared in a memo to the board of directors of Bargain Brand Cereals.

"One year ago we introduced our first product, Bargain Brand breakfast cereal. Our very low prices quickly drew many customers away from the top-selling cereal companies. Although the companies producing the top brands have since they tried to compete with us by lowering their prices and although several plans to introduce their own budget brands, not once have we needed to raise our prices to continue making a profit. Given our success in selling cereal, we recommend that Bargain Brand now expand its business and begin marketing other low-priced food products as quickly as possible." [171]

Write a response in which you discuss what questions would need to be answered in order to decide whether the recommendation and the argument on which it is based are reasonable. Be sure to explain how the answers to these questions would help to evaluate the recommendation.

다음은 Bargain Brand Cereals 회사의 이사회에 보낸 메모이다.

"1년 전 우리 회사는 우리의 첫 제품인 Bargain Brand라는 아침식사용 시리얼을 출시했었다. 이 제품의 값싼 가격 때문에 가장 잘 팔리는 시리얼 회사들의 고객들을 단번에 끌어왔다. 그간 최고 제품을 가지고 있던 이 회사들이 가격을 낮추면서 우리와 경쟁을 해왔고, 심지어 수차례에 걸쳐 저가 상품을 출시했으나 지속적인 수익을 내기 위해서 한 번도 가격을 올릴 필요는 없었다. 성공적인 시리얼 판매에 따라서 이제 Bargain Brand의 사업을 확장하고, 가능한 또 다른 저가 식품을 빨리 출시해야 한다."

In this memo, the board director suggests that the Bargain Cereal company expand its bargain brand productions to other food products. To support this suggestion, he points out that its Bargain Brand cereal has made profits for a year even in competition with the top-selling brand companies. However, the director's suggestion is dubious on several grounds.

First, even if the Bargain Brand cereal made profits for the past year, whether the Bargain Brand company will continue making profits with the Bargain Brand cereals or not is questionable. Unlike in the past, if there is a shortage in grain supply this year, the company should raise the cereal prices inevitably. It is also possible that customers may turn away from low-priced products in the economic cycle is going upbound. Without considering the possible changes in the cereal market in light of the function of supply and demand, it is too risky to follow the director's advice that the company expand the Bargain Brand cereal to other food products.

Another problematic assumption is that as Bargain Brain achieved its business success in a low-priced cereal, it will also gain a similar business success in other products as well. Although Bargain Brand gained its reputation as a low-priced cereal in the market, there is a possibility that it might not be successful with other food products. While cereal products gained its reputation, if the other Bargain Brand foods are not as good as other companies, it will end up with gaining an insignificant market share. If so, Bargain Brand might need to file Chapter 11 to avoid bankruptcy.

The last question regarding the director's suggestion is if the one-year sales trend of Bargain Brand cereal will continue to bring profits to it. Since all markets can be affected by the function of Demand and Supply, the director must investigate if the market economy will be in a slump during which customers tend to look for cheaper brands in general. However, if the national economy turns to a booming cycle, even best-selling Bargain Brand will experience decreases in sales. In addition, the director's conclusion draws from scant evidence. Unless the director enhances this conclusion with more detailed information with specific data, it is premature to follow the director's assertion.

In short, the director's suggestion is ripe with hasty assumptions. To better the argument it is necessary to have more evidence showing how Bargain Brand would overcome difficulties in competing with other companies in both the cereal market and the other product markets. Until the director finds possible solutions to the question above, he should withdraw his recommendation to expand its line of budget-priced foods. [509]

156. The following appeared in a memo from the marketing director of Top Dog Pet Stores.

"Five years ago Fish Emporium started advertising in the magazine Exotic Pets Monthly. Their stores saw sales increase by 15 percent after their ads began appearing in the magazine. The three Fish Emporium stores in Gulf City saw an even greater increase than that. Because Top Dog Pet Stores is based in Gulf City, it seems clear that we should start placing our own ads in Exotic Pets Monthly. If we do so, we will be sure to reverse the recent trend of declining sales and start making a profit again." [New]

Write a response in which you examine the stated and/or unstated assumptions of the argument. Be sure to explain how the argument depends on these assumptions and what the implications are for the argument if the assumptions prove unwarranted.

In this memo, the marketing director of Top Dog Pet stores asserts that their advertisement at Exotic Pets Monthly will reverse the recent trend of declining sales, thus increasing profits. This assertion that Fish Emporium stores experienced a sales increase of 15 % due to the advertisement at Exotic Pets Monthly is fallacious. He points out three Fish Emporium stores in Gulf City increased profits. Although the assertion would seem convincing at first glance, a closer scrutiny reveals that the director's conclusion is developed from a mere correlation and a bad analogy. Moreover, it is unsubstantiated with scant evidence.

To begin with, while it may be true that advertising at Exotic Pets Monthly would bring Top Dog Pet stores in Gulf City an increase in profits, it is skeptical that it will lead to the result that the director of Top Dog Pet stores anticipated. There can be alternative explanations for why Fish Emporium increased its sales by 15 %. Perhaps it might promote fish sales during the advertising period. Or, perhaps the Fish Emporium store might have launched a daily newspaper with discount coupons.

Secondly, the director's assumption that all subscribers of Exotic Pets Monthly are equally interested in both tendering fish and caring for dogs infers from the paucity of evidence. This assumption is unconvincing as is because of a weak analogy between Top Dog Pat Store and Fish Emporium assuming that the subscribers of Exotic Pet Monthly are also the clients of Fish Emporium. If dog owners are not interested in subscribing to a magazine, advertising at Exotic Pets Monthly will lead to only a waste of money. Without investigating the customers' characteristics of Top Dog Pat Store and Fish Emporium, following the director's will lead to a decrease in profit.

Lastly, the assumption all pet stores in Gulf City will increase their sales if they advertise at Exotic Pets Monthly is a hasty generalization. Although Fish Emporium benefited from its advertisement at Exotic Pets Monthly, there is a possibility that Gulf City is a commercial zone where silent pets are only permitted but not barking dogs. Without accounting for the regulations on pets, anticipating the sales of Top Dog Pet stores in Gulf City will rise in sales is not tenable.

Even assuming that Fish Emporium stores enjoyed increased sales by 15 percent, if the total amount of their previous sales was too small, it could be a meager amount. To enhance this argument, the director should investigate specific data that would remove the uncertainty of increased sales volume at Fish Emporium stores due to the advertisement they made at Exotic Pets Monthly five years ago. The director also undermined the possibility that the increase could explain the booming economic cycle playing a more pivotal role than pet purchases at Fish Emporium stores.

In short, the director's assertion is inferred from hasty assumptions. To justify this argument, he should further investigate other possible reasons for the increased sales of Fish Emporium stores and more detailed data proving the characteristics of the Exotic Pets Monthly subscribers. Insufficient data and uncertain terms made the argument susceptible to criticism. [535]

다음은 Amburg 상공회의소 회장의 권고이다.

"지난 10월, Belleville시는 중심 상업지역에 고강도 조명을 설치했고, 기물파손 행위는 즉시 줄어들었다. 반면, Amburg시는 최근 상업지역에 자전거 순찰을 시작했다. 그러나 기물파손 행위는 여전했다. 고강도 조명은 확실히 범죄와의 전쟁에서 가장 효과적인 방법이기 때문에, 현재 자전거 순찰에 쓰는 돈을 Amburg시 전체에 이러한 조명등을 설치하는 데 사용할 것을 건의한다. 우리가 이런 고강도 조명등을 설치한다면, Amburg시에서의 범죄율은 상당히 감소할 것이다."

Recommendation We should use the money that is currently being spent on bicycle patrols to install such lighting throughout Amburg to reduce crime rates.

Amburg's Chamber of Commerce president asserts that high-intensity lighting in its central business district is responsible for reducing crime and revitalizing city neighborhoods. In support of the assertion, the president states that when Belleville started police patrols on bicycles in its business district, vandalism was pervasive. However, the speaker's contention is problematic because it is induced from is induced from unsubstantiated evidence and is therefore unpersuasive as it stands.

First, the argument rests on the unsupported assumption that the only reason for the decrease in crimes in Belleville City is because the president gives credit only to the intensity of lightning without considering other possible causes. Perhaps a more active neighborhood-watching program in Belleville City might prevent vandalism. Or perhaps, almost all the criminals who had committed vandalism around the city might be arrested on the last day of September. If so, the number of vandalism recorded in October might have been fewer than in the previous months. Without eliminating other feasible explanations for the decline, the president's argument is too weak to reasonably conclude that the intensity of lightning contributes to diminishing the rate of vandalism at Amburg.

Second, the speaker's assumption that the traits of the ongoing crimes accompanied by vandalism in both cities are somewhat similar is more likely flawed. Unlike Belleville City, if there is a higher rate of felony crimes in Amburg City, it would be better for them to enhance the current police patrol. Perhaps, other changes, a demographic shift or economic downfall, might be served to increase vandalism at Amburg. Without investigating such changes, the speaker cannot conclude that high-intensity lighting would be more effective for deterring vandalism.

Finally, even if high-intensity lighting would be Amburg's best way of reducing crime in this central business district, the speaker's further assertion that reducing crime in this area would surely result in fewer crimes is not credible. The recommendation is not fully supported to convince me. I would need further evidence that will remove all the questions above.

In sum, the argument is poorly developed from scant evidence, thus making it questionable. To bolster it, the speaker must show further evidence that intensive lighting is more effective for preventing vandalism than police patrol. After that, I would agree with the speaker. [371]

168. The following is a letter that recently appeared in the Oak City Gazette, a local newspaper.

"The primary function of the Committee for a Better Oak City is to advise the city government on how to make the best use of the city's limited budget. However, at some of our recent meetings we failed to make important decisions because of the foolish objections raised by committee members who are not even residents of Oak City. People who work in Oak City but who live elsewhere cannot fully understand the business and politics of the city. After all, only Oak City residents pay city taxes, and therefore only residents understand how that money could best be used to improve the city. We recommend, then, that the Committee for a Better Oak City vote to restrict its membership to city residents only. We predict that, without the interference of non-residents, the committee will be able to make Oak City a better place in which to live and work."

Write a response in which you discuss what questions would need to be answered in order to decide whether the recommendation is likely to have the predicted result. Be sure to explain how the answers to these questions would help to evaluate the recommendation.

다음은 한 지역 신문인 Oak City Gazette지에 최근 실린 글이다.

"Better Oak시 위원회의 주 기능은 한정된 시의 예산을 어떻게 쓰는 것이 최선인지에 대해서 시 정부에 자문을 하는 것이다. 하지만 최근의 회의에서 Oak시의 주민도 아닌 위원회 위원들이 제기한 어리석은 반대로 우리는 중요한 결정을 내리지 못했다. Oak시에서 근무를 하지만 Oak시에 살지 않는 사람들은 시의 사업과 정치를 완전하게 이해할 수 없다. 결국, Oak시의 주민들만 시의 세금을 내기 때문에, 주민들만이 시를 발전시키기 위해서 어떻게 그 돈을 써야 하는지 알 수 있다. 그래서 우리는 Better Oak시의 위원회가 그 회원 자격을 시의 주민들에 한정하는 투표를

할 것을 권한다. 우리는 비주민들의 간섭 없이, 이 위원회가 Oak시를 살기 좋고 일하기 좋은 곳
으로 만들 것이라고 믿는다."

<blockquote>
Recommendation The Committee for a Better Oak City vote to restrict its membership to city residents only.
</blockquote>

강의노트   local tax는 지방세로 재산세를 말하면, sales tax는 부가가치세를 일컫는다.
부가가치세는 유동인구가 물건을 구입할 때 내는 세금을 말한다.

In this memo, the Oak City committee recommends residents be required to
participate in the meetings to make it a better place for workers and residents. This
recommendation would seem credible at first glance; however, closer examination
reveals that it infers from a series of erroneous assumptions: a mere correlation, weak
analogy, and sweeping generalization. Unless the speaker enhances it with further
evidence, the city government's acceptance of their advice will lead to a reduction in
the volume of sales tax, thus doomed to a budget deficit.

To begin with, the Oak City committee's advice is questionable because it did not
recognize the volume of the sales tax collected from daytime workers' economic
activities. If the sales tax amount is more than that of the property tax collected from
the homeowners, following this advice will lead to making its economy shrink. If the
committee excludes non-resident members, they tend to make decisions only
preferable to residents without hearing the voice of the daytime consumers
contributing to the economic growth in Oak City. Or if the companies in the city pay
a lot of corporate tax, their exclusive policy will make them move to another place. If
so, they will lose a substantial amount of income resources and, therefore, suffer from
a budget deficit. Without ruling out this possibility, blindly accepting the committee's
suggestion will make it a worse place instead of a better place.

Another inherent assumption is that the business tax amount is at least equal to or less than the property tax. This assumption is problematic if the commercial tax amount is much more than the property tax collected from residents. Even in a worse scenario, if most business owners are non-residents and their opinions are unlikely to be reflected in the city government's administration, they will also consider leaving Oak City. If it consists of more commercial zones than resident zones, it will suffer from a shortage of budgets.

Moreover, this letter provides scant evidence. We rarely know about how much resident tax amount and commercial tax amount are collected annually. In further support of the recommendation, the author pointed out some non-resident members' interruptions to the meetings held in the townhouse at Oak City. This evidence fails to fully support his claim because there can be other non-resident members who gave helpful ideas to provide a better way to increase the city budgets. Based on scant evidence concluding that all non-residents are not interested in city affairs and thus excluding them from Oak City meetings is more likely a sweeping generalization.

In conclusion, Oak City Commerce will disappoint with this exclusive recommendation considering the benefits and profits created by the non-resident daytime workers and business owners. It is unlikely to have the predicted result, and it may lead to a budget deficit in the Oak City government. Even if he tries to enhance it with more evidence, the recommendation develops its reasoning based on a biased sample of a few disturbing members. In short, it will encounter more opposition than proposition. [505]

170. The following appeared in a memo from the vice president of a company that builds shopping malls around the country.

"The surface of a section of Route 101, paved just two years ago by Good Intentions Roadways, is now badly cracked with a number of dangerous potholes. In another part of the state, a section of Route 40, paved by Appian Roadways more than four years ago, is still in good condition. In a demonstration of their continuing commitment to quality, Appian Roadways recently purchased state-of-the-art paving machinery and hired a new quality-control manager. Therefore, I recommend hiring Appian Roadways to construct the access roads for all our new shopping malls. I predict that our Appian access roads will not have to be repaired for at least four years." [233]

Write a response in which you discuss what questions would need to be answered in order to decide whether the recommendation is likely to have the predicted result. Be sure to explain how the answers to these questions would help to evaluate the recommendation.

다음은 전국에 걸쳐 쇼핑몰을 건설하는 회사 부사장 메모 내용이다.

"Good Intentions Roadways가 겨우 2년 전에 포장한, 101번 도로 구간의 표면이, 심하게 금이 가면서 위험한 작은 웅덩이들이 생겼다. 4년 전 Appian Roadways사가 포장한, 주의 다른 쪽 40번 도로 구간은 여전히 상태가 좋다. 변함없는 품질 보장을 보여주는 방편으로, Appian Roadways사는 최근 최고의 포장 기계를 구매했고 새로운 품질관리 담당자를 고용했다. 그러므로 나는 우리의 신규 쇼핑몰 진입로 건설에 Appian Roadway사를 고용할 것을 추천한다. 나는 Appian이 건설한 진입로가 최소한 4년간은 보수가 필요 없을 것이라고 예측한다."

Recommendation   We should hire Appian Roadways to construct the access roads for all our new shopping malls.

Argue

강의노트 tacking words 중에서 another로 analogy의 key를 잡아서 쓰도록 한다.

    The vice president of the construction company recommends Appian Roadways to construct the access roads for all our new shopping malls rather than Good Intentions Roadways. To substantiate this recommendation, he states the following facts: (1) a section of Route 40 paved by Appian Roadways lasted more than four years ago in good condition, and (2) Appian Roadways recently purchased state-of-the-art paving machinery and hired a new quality-control manager. However, closer examination shows that this argument is vulnerable to criticism because there are several loopholes in developing its line of reasoning, thus making it dubious as it stands.

    About the first piece of evidence given, it is difficult to agree with the vice president's recommendation because his assumption develops based on the fact that a section of Route 40 by Appian Roadways lasted two years longer than a section of Route 101 by Good Intentions Roadways. This assumption involves false causation and result. The traffic amount on Route 101 may be ten times greater than on Route 40. If so, the damages made on Route 101 might be due to the heavier use of cars. It is also possible that the weather on Route 40 is a lot tougher than that on Route 101. Without ruling out these possibilities, this recommendation is an ill-advised suggestion.

    Even assuming that the quality of Appian Roadways's construction is better than that of Good Intentions Roadway, it is still unclear if Appian Roadways' biting price of the access roads to the shopping malls can be cheaper. The vice president assumes that the skills for paving the local road are equal to those for highway construction. If the engineering for highway road construction might require much more difficult time and expense, it lends too much credit to Appian Roadways for the access roads and expressways. Unless we compare the equal competencies in a similar section of the highways both constructed and the prices between the two companies, particularly for building the access roads to the shopping mall, I would not recommend Appian Roadways.

Lastly, the vice president emphasizes that new machines and the recent capable managers' hiring would ensure a better quality of constructing access roads to the mall. These two factors are not critical measures for building access roads. What to know is how skillful the workers who are subject to laying the access roads, not new equipment or the quality of the manager. Similarly, the four years term guarantee can be a relatively short term for the duration of access roads. Based on poorly defined terms such as "a section of the route and access roads", it is premature to accept the recommender's assertion.

In conclusion, the argument consists of dubious assumptions. The vice president should clarify all the doubts on what other possible reasons caused faster damage on a section of Route 101 than Route 40, which specific skills both companies have for building the access roads, how much it would cost them, and how well the workers will do. Providing all the answers to these questions will make it more reliable. [498]

Argue

Groups

Argue Groups

Instruction Sets

- Write a response in which you discuss what specific evidence is needed to evaluate the argument and explain how the evidence would weaken or strengthen the argument.

- Write a response in which you examine the stated and/or unstated assumptions of the argument. Be sure to explain how the argument depends on these assumptions, and what the implications are for the argument if the assumptions prove unwarranted.

- Write a response in which you discuss what questions would need to be answered in order to decide whether the recommendation and the argument on which it is based are reasonable. Be sure to explain how the answers to these questions would help to evaluate the recommendation.

- Write a response in which you discuss what questions would need to be answered in order to decide whether the advice and the argument on which it is based are reasonable. Be sure to explain how the answers to these questions would help to evaluate the advice.

- Write a response in which you discuss what questions would need to be answered in order to decide whether the prediction and the argument on which it is based are reasonable. Be sure to explain how the answers to these questions would help to evaluate the prediction.

- Write a response in which you discuss one or more alternative explanations that could rival the proposed explanation and explain how your explanation(s) can plausibly account for the facts presented in the argument.

- Write a response in which you discuss what questions would need to be addressed in order to decide whether the conclusion and the argument on which it is based are reasonable. Be sure to explain how the answers to the questions would help to evaluate the conclusion.

Topics by Groups

New	Old	Claim / Recommendation / Advice
1	37	Palean baskets were not uniquely Palean.
2	New	The birth order effects on an individual's levels of stimulation.
3, 171	227	To bring business back in Central Plaza, the city should prohibit skateboarding in Central Plaza.

4	4	If you want to sell your home quickly and at a good price, you should use Adams Realty.
5, 159, 173	20	To reduce the number of accidents involving mopeds and pedestrians, the town council of Balmer Island should limit the number of mopeds rentals.
6	45	We can conclude that the purported decline in deer populations is the result of the deer's being unable to follow their age-old migration patterns across the frozen sea.
7, 98	44	We recommend that Monarch Books open a café in its store.
8	240	To serve the housing needs of our students, Buckingham College should build a number of new dormitories.
9, 88, 90	1	The next franchise store opening in the town of Plainsville should prove to be very successful.
10, 21, 23	36	Some anthropologists recommend that to obtain accurate information on Tertian child-rearing practices, future research on the subject should be conducted via the interview-centered method.
11	109	The council currently predicts the proposed measure that would prevent the development of existing farmland in the county will result in a significant increase in housing prices in Maple County.
12	9	To enable its graduates to secure better jobs, Omega University should terminate student evaluation of professors.
13	18	To improve highway safety, Prunty County should undertake the road improvement.
14, 118	New	If a business wants to prosper, it should hire only people who need less than 6 hours of sleep per night.
15, 51, 130, 131, 133	182	Either customers do not distinguish butter from margarine or they use the term 'butter' to refer to either butter or margarine.
16	137	The city government should devote more money in this year's budget to riverside recreational facilities.
17, 19, 93, 109, 110	235, 97	1) To reverse a decline in listener numbers, we should change to a news and talk format, a form of radio that is increasingly popular in our area. 2) KICK should include more call-in advice programs in an attempt to gain a larger audience share in its listening area.
18, 20	135	1) In order to attract more viewers to our news programs and to avoid losing any further advertising revenues, we should expand our coverage of weather and local news on all our news programs.
22, 119, 120, 138	242	1) All colleges and universities should adopt honor codes similar to Groveton's in order to decrease cheating among students. 2) Academic honor codes are far more successful than are other methods at deterring cheating among students at colleges and universities.

24, 26, 28	35	With this new use for salicylates, residents of Mentia will suffer even fewer headaches in the future.
25, 100, 102, 164	6	1) A jazz music club in Monroe would be a tremendously profitable enterprise. 2) The C Note, our proposed club, cannot help but make money.
27, 29	55	To reduce rush-hour traffic on Blue highway, a bicycle lane should be added instead of a traffic lane.
30	New	We should reduce the funds budgeted for education during the next decade and increase the money to fund city facilities and programs used primarily by adults.
31	214	Parson City residents place a higher value on providing a good education in public schools than Blue City residents do.
32, 104, 105, 106, 167	12	1) To reduce the number of on-the-job accidents, we should shorten each of our three work shifts by one hour. 2) Panoply's superior safety record can therefore be attributed to its shorter work shifts.
33	208	Since our three electric generating plants in operation for the past twenty years have always met our needs, construction of new generating plants will not be necessary.
34, 58, 94	127	1) In an effort to improve our employees' productivity, we should implement electronic monitoring of employees' Internet use from their workstations. 2) Installing software to monitor employees' Internet use will allow us to prevent employees from wasting time, thereby increasing productivity and improving overall profits.
35, 52, 128, 129	185	1) Modifying shower heads to restrict water flow throughout all twelve buildings in the Sunnyside Towers complex will increase our profits further. 2) Restricting water flow throughout all the twenty floors of Sunnyside Towers will increase our profits further.
36, 163, 166	38	1) The daily use of Ichthaid is a good way to prevent colds and lower absenteeism. 2) We recommend the daily use of a nutritional supplement derived from fish oil.
37	230	We should adapt for industrial use in a declining residential area on the opposite side of the city.
38, 95, 96	21	1) We should resume production of alpaca overcoat. 2) Sartorian's alpaca overcoats will be more profitable than ever before.
39, 174	23	The new Captain Seafood restaurant that specializes in seafood should be quite popular and profitable.
40	34	Since bone fractures are symptomatic of osteoporosis, this study result shows that a diet rich in dairy products may actually increase, rather than decrease, the risk of osteoporosis.
41, 123, 125	120	1) The government should concentrate more on educating people about bicycle safety and less on encouraging or requiring bicyclists to wear helmets. 2) The government should launch an education program that concentrates on the factors other than helmet use that are necessary for bicycle safety.

42	152	In order to stop the erosion, we should charge people for using the beaches.
43	11	Because of our town's strong commitment to recycling, the available space in our landfill should last for considerably longer than predicted.
44	141	Environmental disasters can be prevented if consumers simply refuse to purchase products that are made with CCC's copper unless the company abandons its mining plans.
45, 49	39	Humana University should begin immediately to create and actively promote online degree programs both to increase its total enrollment and solve its budget problems.
46	48	Fitness levels will improve in Corpora when the economy does.
47, 111, 112	213	1) We should reduce our operating hours at all Movies Galore stores as our best strategies for improving profits. 2) In order to stop the recent decline in our profits, we must reduce operating expenses at Movies Galore's ten movie-rental stores.
48	216	Clearview should be a top choice for anyone seeking a place to retire.
50	167	The study proves that lavender cures insomnia within a short period of time.
53, 144, 151	201	1) The citizens of Forsythe have adopted more healthful lifestyles. 2) The obesity rate in Benton City will soon be well below the national average.
54, 165	202	1) Some climate change or other environmental factor must have caused the species' extinctions in the Kaliko Islands. 2) The only clear explanation is that humans caused the extinction of the various mammal species through excessive hunting.
55	147	The sales of Whirlwind video games are likely to increase dramatically in the next few months.
56, 57, 82	111	We can increase our profits by discontinuing use of the Endure manufacturing process.
59	94	To boost sales and profits, we should increase the size of the family rooms and kitchens in all the homes we build and should make state-of-the-art kitchens a standard feature.
60, 150, 154, 155/145, 146/76	66/15	1) We predict an increased demand for heating oil and recommend investment in Consolidated Industries, one of whose major business operations is the retail sale of home heating oil. 2) We can safely predict that this region will experience an increased demand for heating oil during the next five years.
61, 139, 141, 143, 162	68	1) Some city commissioners recommend that funding for the symphony be eliminated from next year's budget. 2) Increased revenue from larger audiences and higher ticket prices will enable the symphony to succeed without funding from the city government. 3) Now that the symphony has succeeded in finding an audience, the city can eliminate its funding of the symphony.
62, 121, 122, 124	98	To prevent serious patient infections, we should supply UltraClean at all hand-washing stations throughout our hospital system.

63	206	Parkville should discontinue organized athletic competition for children under nine.
64	56	The life-size sculptures will decrease in value while the miniatures increase in value.
65	63	If Stanley Park is ever to be as popular with our citizens as Carlton Park, the town will obviously need to provide more benches, thereby converting some of the unused open areas into spaces suitable for socializing.
66, 107, 108	65	The best way to improve profits in all of our stores is to discontinue stocking many of our varieties of imported cheese and concentrate primarily on domestic cheeses.
67	43	If the Rialto intends to hold on to its share of a decreasing pool of moviegoers, it must offer the same features as Apex.
68	129	Sherwood Hospital should form a partnership with Sherwood Animal Shelter to institute an adopt-a-dog program to reduce the incidence of heart disease in the general population.
69, 70, 115	93	We recommend using Zeta rather than Alpha for our new building project, even though Alpha's bid promises lower construction costs.
71	119	To solve traffic problem in Waymarsh, it would be better to implement a policy that rewards people who share rides to work, giving them coupons for free gas.
72	143	The article that the majority of competent workers who have lost jobs as a result of downsizing face serious economic hardship is undermined.
73	172	The Mozart School of Music should be the first choice for parents considering enrolling their child in music lessons.
74, 147, 148, 149, 156	174	1) The president of Grove College has recommended that the college abandon its century-old tradition of all-female education and begin admitting men. 2) Grove College should preserve its century-old tradition of all-female education.
75	10	To prevent farmers from continuing to receive excessive profits on an apparently increased supply of milk, the Batavia government should begin to regulate retail milk prices.
77, 169	25	The best way to improve Hopewell's economy — and generate additional tax revenues — is to build a golf course and resort hotel similar to those in Ocean View.
78, 114, 116, 117	41	1) Our best means of saving money is to return to Buzzoff for all our pest control services. 2) This difference in pest damage is best explained by the negligence of Fly-Away.
79	173	The magazine curtail its emphasis on politics to focus more exclusively on economics and personal finance.
80, 97	New	Super Screen should therefore allocate a greater share of its budget next year to reaching the public through advertising.
81	165	Promofoods concluded that the canned tuna did not, after all, pose a health risk.
83, 84	150	1) The decline of amphibians in Xanadu National Park has a different cause because trout — which are known to eat amphibian eggs — were introduced into the park. 2) The decline of amphibians in Xanadu National Park was caused by the introduction of trout into the park's waters, which began in 1975.

85, 87	161	It can be concluded that the respondents in the first study had misrepresented their reading habits.
86, 89	241	The proposal for using Walsh Personnel Firm in place of Delany would be a mistake.
91	New	The disappearance of western gazelle must have been caused by the larger number of predators in the eastern preserve.
92, 101, 103	234	1) The fewer sick days and the lower diagnosis of stress-related illness in Leeville can be attributed to the health benefits of the relatively relaxed pace of life in Leeville. 2) People seeking longer and healthier lives should consider moving to small communities.
113, 126, 127, 161	180	1) To improve productivity, Acme should require all of our employees to take the Easy Read course. 2) Acme would benefit greatly by requiring all of our employees to take the Easy Read course.
132, 134, 136	175	All students should be required to take the driver's education course at Centerville High School.
135, 137, 140	193	Teachers in our high schools should assign homework no more than twice a week.
142	New	Roller skaters will greatly reduce their risk of being severely injured in an accident by investing in high-quality protective gear and reflective equipment.
152, 153	171	Bargain Brand now should expand its business and begin marketing other low-priced food products as quickly as possible.
157, 158	New	We should start placing our own ads in Exotic Pets Monthly to reverse the recent trend of declining sales and start making a profit again.
160, 172	205	1) We should use the money that is currently being spent on bicycle patrols to install such lighting throughout Amburg to reduce crime rates. 2) We should install high-intensity lighting throughout Amburg to revitalize the declining neighborhoods in our city.
168	177	The Committee for a Better Oak City vote to restrict its membership to city residents only.
170	233	We should hire Appian Roadways to construct the access roads for all our new shopping malls.

1. Woven baskets characterized by a particular distinctive pattern have previously been found only in the immediate vicinity of the prehistoric village of Palea and therefore were believed to have been made only by the Palean people. Recently, however, archaeologists discovered such a "Palean" basket in Lithos, an ancient village across the Brim River from Palea. The Brim River is very deep and broad, and so the ancient Paleans could have crossed it only by boat, and no Palean boats have been found. Thus it follows that the so-called Palean baskets were not uniquely Palean. [Old version 37]

Write a response in which you discuss what specific evidence is needed to evaluate the argument and explain how the evidence would weaken or strengthen the argument.

특이한 무늬의 대나무 바구니는 Palea족이 거주하던 선사시대 마을 인근에서만 발견되어 왔기 때문에, Palea족에 의해서만 만들어졌다고 여겨졌었다. 그러나 최근 들어 고고학자들은 Lithos에서 이러한 "Palean" 바구니를 발견했는데, 이 고대 마을은 Palea과 Brim 강으로 막혀 있다. 이 강은 수심이 아주 깊고 강폭이 넓어서, 고대의 Palea인들은 배를 이용해서만 강을 건널 수 있었을 것이나 Palean족의 배는 발견된 적이 없다. 따라서 소위 말하는 Palean 바구니는 Palea족의 전유물이라고 볼 수 없다.

❚ Argument   Palean baskets were not uniquely Palean.

2. The following appeared as part of a letter to the editor of a scientific journal.

"A recent study of eighteen rhesus monkeys provides clues as to the effects of birth order on an individual's levels of stimulation. The study showed that in stimulating situations (such as an encounter with an unfamiliar monkey), firstborn infant monkeys produce up to twice as much of the hormone cortisol, which primes the body for increased activity levels, as do their younger siblings. Firstborn humans also produce relatively high levels of cortisol in stimulating situations (such as the return of a parent after an absence). The study also found that during pregnancy, first-time mother monkeys had higher levels of cortisol than did those who had several offspring." [New]

Write a response in which you discuss one or more alternative explanations that could rival the proposed explanation and explain how your explanation(s) can plausibly account for the facts presented in the argument.

다음 내용은 한 과학 잡지의 편집자에게 보낸 편지의 일부이다.

"18마리의 붉은털원숭이에 대한 최근의 한 연구는 출산 순서가 각자의 흥분수준에 영향을 미친다는 단서를 주고 있다. 흥분된 상태에서 (잘 모르는 원숭이끼리의 대치 같은), 맨 처음 태어난 원숭이들은 그의 동생 원숭이에 비해서 거의 2배에 가까운 cortisol 호르몬을 분비하는데, 이 호르몬으로 몸의 활동량이 증가한다. 먼저 태어난 인간도 흥분된 상황 속에서 (부모가 외출에서 돌아오는 것 같은) 상대적으로 많은 cortisol을 분비한다. 연구는 첫 출산을 한 원숭이들은 출산을 여러 번 한 원숭이들보다, 임신 기간 중에 더 많은 cortisol을 분비한다는 것도 밝혀냈다."

▌Argument The birth order effects on an individual's levels of stimulation.

3. The following appeared as a letter to the editor from a Central Plaza store owner.

"Over the past two years, the number of shoppers in Central Plaza has been steadily decreasing while the popularity of skateboarding has increased dramatically. Many Central Plaza store owners believe that the decrease in their business is due to the number of skateboard users in the plaza. There has also been a dramatic increase in the amount of litter and vandalism throughout the plaza. Thus, we recommend that the city prohibit skateboarding in Central Plaza. If skateboarding is prohibited here, we predict that business in Central Plaza will return to its previously high levels." [Old version 227]

Write a response in which you discuss what questions would need to be answered in order to decide whether the recommendation is likely to have the predicted result. Be sure to explain how the answers to these questions would help to evaluate the recommendation.

다음은 Central Plaza의 한 상인이 편집인에게 보낸 편지의 일부이다.

"지난 2년간 Central Plaza에서 스케이트보드의 인기는 급속하게 늘고 있는 반면, 쇼핑객은 지속적으로 줄고 있다. 상당수의 Central Plaza 상인들은 그들의 영업 감소가 plaza에서 스케이트보드를 타는 사람들 수 때문이라고 믿고 있다. 또한 plaza 전체에 걸쳐 쓰레기와 기물파손도 현저히 늘고 있다. 그러므로 우리들은 시가 Central Plaza에서 스케이트보드를 타는 것을 금지해 줄 것을 촉구한다. 만약 이곳에서 스케이트보드가 금지된다면 우리는 장사가 예전 수준으로 회복될 것으로 예상한다."

Recommendation To bring business back in Central Plaza, the city should prohibit skateboarding in Central Plaza.

171. The following appeared as a letter to the editor from the owner of a skate shop in Central Plaza.

"Two years ago the city voted to prohibit skateboarding in Central Plaza. They claimed that skateboard users were responsible for the litter and vandalism that were keeping other visitors from coming to the plaza. In the past two years, however, there has only been a small increase in the number of visitors to Central Plaza, and litter and vandalism are still problematic. Skateboarding is permitted in Monroe Park, however, and there is no problem with litter or vandalism there. In order to restore Central Plaza to its former glory, then, we recommend that the city lift its prohibition on skateboarding in the plaza."

Write a response in which you discuss what questions would need to be answered in order to decide whether the recommendation and the argument on which it is based are reasonable. Be sure to explain how the answers to these questions would help to evaluate the recommendation.

다음은 Central Plaza 내에 있는 스케이트 가게 주인이 편집인에게 보낸 편지 내용이다.

"2년 전 시는 Central Plaza 내에서 스케이트보드를 타는 것을 금지시키는 법을 통과시켰다. 시는 쓰레기 투기가 스케이트보드 사용자들의 책임이고 사람들이 플라자에 오지 않는 것은 밴달리즘 때문이라고 주장한다. 하지만 지난 2년 동안 Central Plaza를 찾는 사람들은 겨우 약간 늘었고, 쓰레기 투기와 밴달리즘은 아직도 문제이다. Monroe Park에서는 스케이트보드를 타는 것이 허용되지만, 거기서는 쓰레기 투기와 밴달리즘 문제가 없다. 그래서 Central Plaza의 옛 명성을 되찾기 위해서, 우리는 시가 플라자 내에서 스케이트보드 타는 것을 금지하는 법을 폐지할 것을 권고한다."

| Recommendation   The city lift should its prohibition on skateboarding in the plaza.

4. The following appeared in a letter from a homeowner to a friend.

"Of the two leading real estate firms in our town — Adams Realty and Fitch Realty — Adams Realty is clearly superior. Adams has 40 real estate agents; in contrast, Fitch has 25, many of whom work only part-time. Moreover, Adams' revenue last year was twice as high as that of Fitch and included home sales that averaged $168,000, compared to Fitch's $144,000. Homes listed with Adams sell faster as well: ten years ago I listed my home with Fitch, and it took more than four months to sell; last year, when I sold another home, I listed it with Adams, and it took only one month. Thus, if you want to sell your home quickly and at a good price, you should use Adams Realty." [Old version 4]

Write a response in which you examine the stated and/or unstated assumptions of the argument. Be sure to explain how the argument depends on these assumptions and what the implications are for the argument if the assumptions prove unwarranted.

다음은 한 주택소유자가 친구에게 보낸 편지의 일부이다.

"우리 동네의 두 유명한 부동산 회사 — Adams Realty와 Fitch Realty — 중에서 Adams가 분명히 우수하다. Adams에는 40여 명의 중개인이 있는 반면, Fitch는 25명만 있고, 이들 중 상당수는 정규 직원이 아니다. 더구나 Adams의 지난해 총매출액은 Fitch보다 2배나 많았으며, 평균 주택매매 가격이 Fitch는 144,000달러인 데 반해, Adams는 168,000달러였다. 또한 Adams에 내놓은 주택이 더 빨리 팔린다. 10년 전, Fitch 회사에 집을 내놓았는데, 파는 데 4개월 이상이 걸렸으나 지난해에 다른 집을 Adams에 내놨는데 한 달 만에 팔렸다. 그러므로 집을 좋은 가격에 빨리 팔려면 Adams 부동산을 이용해야 한다."

Argument   If you want to sell your home quickly and at a good price, you should use Adams Realty.

5. The following appeared in a letter to the editor of the Balmer Island Gazette.

"On Balmer Island, where mopeds serve as a popular form of transportation, the population increases to 100,000 during the summer months. To reduce the number of accidents involving mopeds and pedestrians, the town council of Balmer Island should limit the number of mopeds rented by the island's moped rental companies from 50 per day to 25 per day during the summer season. By limiting the number of rentals, the town council will attain the 50 percent annual reduction in moped accidents that was achieved last year on the neighboring island of Seaville, when Seaville's town council enforced similar limits on moped rentals."

Write a response in which you discuss what questions would need to be answered in order to decide whether the recommendation is likely to have the predicted result. Be sure to explain how the answers to these questions would help to evaluate the recommendation.

다음은 Balmer Island Gazett 편집인에게 보낸 서신 내용이다.

"Balmer Island에서는 모페드가 인기 있는 교통수단이고, 여름철에는 인구가 십만 명으로 늘어난다. Moped와 보행자 간 사고를 줄이기 위해, 시 의회는 여름에 대여업체들이 대여하는 모페드 대여 수를 하루 50대에서 25대로 제한해야 한다. 대여 숫자를 줄임으로써, 시 의회는, 지난해 이웃 Seaville섬에서 이와 동일한 규제를 시행해서 50%나 사고를 줄인 것처럼 연간 모페드 사고 50% 감소라는 목표를 달성할 수 있을 것이다."

Recommendation The town council of Balmer Island should limit the number of mopeds rented by the island's moped rental companies from 50 per day to 25 per day during the summer season.

159. The following appeared in a letter to the editor of the Balmer Island Gazette.

"The population on Balmer Island increases to 100,000 during the summer months. To reduce the number of accidents involving mopeds and pedestrians, the town council of Balmer Island plans to limit the number of mopeds rented by each of the island's six moped rental companies from 50 per day to 30 per day during the summer season. Last year, the neighboring island of Torseau enforced similar limits on moped rentals and saw a 50 percent reduction in moped accidents. We predict that putting these limits into effect on Balmer Island will result in the same reduction in moped accidents." [Old version 20]

Write a response in which you discuss what questions would need to be answered in order to decide whether the prediction and the argument on which it is based are reasonable. Be sure to explain how the answers to these questions would help to evaluate the prediction.

다음은 Balmer Island Gazett 편집인에게 보낸 서신 내용이다.

"Balmer Island 인구가 여름철에는 십만 명으로 늘어난다. Moped와 보행자 간 사고를 줄이기 위해, 시 의회는 6개의 자전거와 Moped 대여업체에게 이 기간 동안에는 대여 숫자를 하루 50대에서 30대로 제한하려고 한다. 지난해 이웃 Torseau 섬에서 이와 동일한 모페드 대여 규제를 시행해서 50%나 사고를 줄였다. Balmer Island도 이런 제한을 시행해서 모페드 사고를 50% 정도 줄일 수 있을 것으로 예상한다."

| Prediction | Putting limits on moped rentals into effect on Balmer Island will result in a 50 percent reduction in moped accidents. |

173. The following appeared in a letter to the editor of the Balmer Island Gazette.

"The population on Balmer Island doubles during the summer months. During the summer, then, the town council of Balmer Island should decrease the maximum number of moped rentals allowed at each of the island's six moped and bicycle rental companies from 50 per day to 30 per day. This will significantly reduce the number of summertime accidents involving mopeds and pedestrians. The neighboring island of Torseau actually saw a 50 percent reduction in moped accidents last year when Torseau's town council enforced similar limits on moped rentals. To help reduce moped accidents, therefore, we should also enforce these limitations during the summer months."

Write a response in which you examine the stated and/or unstated assumptions of the argument. Be sure to explain how the argument depends on these assumptions and what the implications are for the argument if the assumptions prove unwarranted.

다음은 Balmer Island Gazett 편집인에게 보낸 서신 내용이다.

"Balmer Island 인구는 여름철에는 2배로 늘어난다. 여름 동안, Moped와 보행자 간 사고를 줄이기 위해, Balmer Island 시 의회는 6개의 자전거와 Moped 대여업체에게 허용된 모페드의 최대 대여숫자를 하루 50대에서 30대로 줄여야만 한다. 이렇게 함으로서 여름철 모페드와 보행자 사고를 현저하게 줄일 수 있을 것이다. 실제로 지난해 이웃 Torseau시 의회는 이와 비슷한 모페드 대여 제한을 시행해서 모페드 사고를 50%나 줄였다. 그러므로 모페드 사고를 줄이기 위해서 우리도 여름철에 이런 제한을 시행해야만 한다."

Argument   To help reduce moped accidents, therefore, we should also enforce these limitations during the summer months.

6. Arctic deer live on islands in Canada's arctic regions. They search for food by moving over ice from island to island during the course of the year. Their habitat is limited to areas warm enough to sustain the plants on which they feed and cold enough, at least some of the year, for the ice to cover the sea separating the islands, allowing the deer to travel over it. Unfortunately, according to reports from local hunters, the deer populations are declining. Since these reports coincide with recent global warming trends that have caused the sea ice to melt, we can conclude that the purported decline in deer populations is the result of the deer's being unable to follow their age-old migration patterns across the frozen sea. [Old version 45]

Write a response in which you discuss what specific evidence is needed to evaluate the argument and explain how the evidence would weaken or strengthen the argument.

북극 사슴은 캐나다의 극지방에 산다. 이들은 일 년 내내 얼음 위로 섬들을 돌아다니며 먹이를 찾는다. 이들의 서식지는 이들이 먹는 초목식물이 자랄 수 있을 정도로 따뜻하고, 최소한 일 년 중 어느 정도는 서로 떨어져 있는 섬들 사이의 바다가 얼음으로 덮여 사슴들이 그 위로 이동할 수 있을 정도로 추운 지역에 한정되어 있다. 유감스럽게도 지역 사냥꾼들의 보고에 따르면, 사슴의 개체수가 줄어들고 있다고 한다. 이리한 소식이 최근 바다의 얼음을 녹이는 원인인 지구온난화 추세와 일치하는 점으로 보아, 알려진 사슴의 개체 수 감소는 사슴이 얼어붙은 바다를 건너서 이동하던 오래된 습성을 유지할 수 없기 때문에 생겨 난 결과라고 결론을 내릴 수 있다.

Argument	We can conclude that the purported decline in deer populations is the result of the deer's being unable to follow their age-old migration patterns across the frozen sea.

7. The following is a recommendation from the Board of Directors of Monarch Books.

"We recommend that Monarch Books open a café in its store. Monarch, having been in business at the same location for more than twenty years, has a large customer base because it is known for its wide selection of books on all subjects. Clearly, opening the café would attract more customers. Space could be made for the café by discontinuing the children's book section, which will probably become less popular given that the most recent national census indicated a significant decline in the percentage of the population under age ten. Opening a café will allow Monarch to attract more customers and better compete with Regal Books, which recently opened its own café."

Write a response in which you discuss what questions would need to be answered in order to decide whether the recommendation is likely to have the predicted result. Be sure to explain how the answers to these questions would help to evaluate the recommendation.

다음은 Monarch 서점 이사진의 권고 사항이다.

"우리는 Monarch 서점이 매장 내에 카페를 열 것을 권한다. 한 장소에서 20년 이상 영업을 해온 Monarch 서점은, 모든 주제에 관한 다양한 책들을 취급하기 때문에 많은 고객층이 다양하다. 카페를 열면, 분명히 더 많은 고객을 끌 수 있을 것이다. 아동도서 코너를 폐지해서 필요한 공간을 확보할 수 있는데, 10세 이하 어린이들이 현저하게 줄어든다는 것을 보여주는 가장 최근의 전국인구 통계조사를 고려한다면, 이 코너는 점점 인기가 없어질 것이다. 카페의 개장으로 Monarch 서점은 더 많은 고객을 끌 것이고, 최근에 카페를 연 Regal 서점과 경쟁을 더 잘할 수 있을 것이다."

| Recommendation   We recommend that Monarch Books open a café in its store.

98. The following is a recommendation from the business manager of Monarch Books.

"Since its opening in Collegeville twenty years ago, Monarch Books has developed a large customer base due to its reader-friendly atmosphere and wide selection of books on all subjects. Last month, Book and Bean, a combination bookstore and coffee shop, announced its intention to open a Collegeville store. Monarch Books should open its own in-store café in the space currently devoted to children's books. Given recent national census data indicating a significant decline in the percentage of the population under age ten, sales of children's books are likely to decline. By replacing its children's books section with a café Monarch Books can increase profits and ward off competition from Book and Bean."

Write a response in which you examine the stated and/or unstated assumptions of the argument. Be sure to explain how the argument depends on these assumptions and what the implications are for the argument if the assumptions prove unwarranted.

다음은 Monarch 서점 사업부장의 권고 사항이다.

"20년 전 Collegeville에 매장을 연 이래, 독자들이 편한 환경과 모든 영역에 관한 폭넓은 도서를 취급해서 Monarch 서점은 두터운 독자층을 형성해 왔다. 지난달 커피점과 서점을 혼합한 Book and Bean이 Collegeville에 매장을 열겠다는 의도를 밝혔다. Monarch 서점은 현재 아동도서 코너로 이용되는 공간에 매장 내 카페를 열어야 한다. 10세 이하 어린이들이 현저하게 줄어든다는 것을 보여주는 최근의 전국인구 통계조사를 고려한다면, 아동도서의 판매는 감소할 것 같다. 아동도서 코너를 카페로 바꿔서 Monarch 서점은 수익도 올리고 Book and Bean과 경쟁도 피할 수 있을 것이다."

Argument   Monarch Books should open its own in-store café in the space currently devoted to children's books.

99. The following is a recommendation from the business manager of Monarch Books.

"Since its opening in Collegeville twenty years ago, Monarch Books has developed a large customer base due to its reader-friendly atmosphere and wide selection of books on all subjects. Last month, Book and Bean, a combination bookstore and coffee shop, announced its intention to open a Collegeville store. Monarch Books should open its own in-store café in the space currently devoted to children's books. Given recent national census data indicating a significant decline in the percentage of the population under age ten, sales of children's books are likely to decline. By replacing its children's books section with a café Monarch Books can increase profits and ward off competition from Book and Bean." [Old version 44]

Write a response in which you discuss what specific evidence is needed to evaluate the argument and explain how the evidence would weaken or strengthen the argument.

[98]번과 동일한 지문이나 instruction이 다름.

| Argument | Monarch Books should open its own in-store café in the space currently devoted to children's books. |

8. The following appeared in a memo from the director of student housing at Buckingham College.

"To serve the housing needs of our students, Buckingham College should build a number of new dormitories. Buckingham's enrollment is growing and, based on current trends, will double over the next 50 years, thus making existing dormitory space inadequate. Moreover, the average rent for an apartment in our town has risen in recent years. Consequently, students will find it increasingly difficult to afford off-campus housing. Finally, attractive new dormitories would make prospective students more likely to enroll at Buckingham." [Old version 240]

Write a response in which you discuss what specific evidence is needed to evaluate the argument and explain how the evidence would weaken or strengthen the argument.

다음은 Buckingham College 학생 주거 담당 책임자의 메모 내용이다.

"Buckingham 대학은 우리 학생들의 주거 수요를 충족시키기 위해 새로운 기숙사를 건축해야 한다. 등록이 증가하고 있고 현재의 추세로 보면, 앞으로 50년 동안 학생 수가 2배로 늘 것이므로, 기존의 기숙사 시설로는 불충분하다. 더군다나 이곳의 아파트 평균 임대비용도 최근에 올라가고 있다. 결과적으로 학생들은 학교 밖에서 집을 구하는 것이 상당히 어려워졌다. 결국은 새로운 기숙사가 예비학생들이 우리 대학을 더 지원하도록 할 것이다."

| Argument | To serve the housing needs of our students, Buckingham College should build a number of new dormitories. |

9. Nature's Way, a chain of stores selling health food and other health-related products, is opening its next franchise in the town of Plainsville. The store should prove to be very successful: Nature's Way franchises tend to be most profitable in areas where residents lead healthy lives, and clearly Plainsville is such an area. Plainsville merchants report that sales of running shoes and exercise clothing are at all-time highs. The local health club has more members than ever, and the weight training and aerobics classes are always full. Finally, Plainsville's schoolchildren represent a new generation of potential customers: these schoolchildren are required to participate in a fitness-for-life program, which emphasizes the benefits of regular exercise at an early age.

Write a response in which you examine the stated and/or unstated assumptions of the argument. Be sure to explain how the argument depends on these assumptions and what the implications are for the argument if the assumptions prove unwarranted.

건강식품 및 건강 관련 제품을 파는 체인 스토아 Nature's Way는 Plainsville에 다음 체인점을 열었다. 이 가게는 반드시 성공할 것이다. Nature's Way 체인은 주민들이 건강한 생활을 하는 지역에서 가장 많은 수익을 내는 경향이 있고, 분명히 Plainsville은 그런 지역이다. Plainsville 지역 상인들은 역대 최고의 운동화와 운동복의 판매를 보고했다. 지역 헬스클럽도 그 어느 때보다 회원이 많고, 웨이트 트레이닝과 에어로빅 강좌도 항상 만원이다. 마지막으로, Plainsville의 학생들은 잠재적 고객의 새로운 세대라고 할 수 있다. 이 학생들은, 유년시절부터 정규적인 운동 습관의 이점을 강조하는, "Fitness-for-Life"라는 프로그램에 의무적으로 참여해야 한다.

▎Argument The store in the town of Plainsville should prove to be very successful.

88. The following appeared in a memorandum written by the vice president of Health Naturally, a small but expanding chain of stores selling health food and other health-related products.

"Our previous experience has been that our stores are most profitable in areas where residents are highly concerned with leading healthy lives. We should therefore build one of our new stores in Plainsville, which clearly has many such residents. Plainsville merchants report that sales of running shoes and exercise equipment are at all-time highs. The local health club, which nearly closed five years ago due to lack of business, has more members than ever, and the weight-training and aerobics classes are always full. We can even anticipate a new generation of customers: Plainsville's schoolchildren are required to participate in a program called Fitness for Life, which emphasizes the benefits of regular exercise at an early age." [Old version 1]

Write a response in which you discuss what specific evidence is needed to evaluate the argument and explain how the evidence would weaken or strengthen the argument.

다음은 건강식품과 건강 관련 제품을 파는, 작지만 성장하는 체인점인 Health Naturally의 부사장이 쓴 메모 내용이다.

"지난 경험으로 보아, 우리 가게들은 거주자들이 건강생활에 높은 관심을 지닌 지역에서 가장 많은 이익을 낸다. 따라서 이러한 주민들이 많이 거주하고 있는 Plainsville에 새로운 가게를 세워야 한다. 이 지역 상인들은 역대 최고의 운동화와 운동기구들 판매를 보고했다. 5년 전에는 장사가 안 되서 거의 폐업을 하려던 지역 헬스클럽에 그 어느 때보다 회원이 늘고, 웨이트 트레이닝과 에어로빅 강좌도 항상 만원이다. 심지어 새로운 고객층도 기대할 수 있다. 이 지역의 학생들은 유년시절부터 정규적인 운동 습관의 이 점을 강조하는 "Fitness for Life"라는 프로그램에 의무적으로 참여해야만 하기 때문이다."

| Argument We should therefore build one of our new stores in Plainsville.

90. The following appeared in a memorandum written by the vice president of Health Naturally, a small but expanding chain of stores selling health food and other health-related products.

"Our previous experience has been that our stores are most profitable in areas where residents are highly concerned with leading healthy lives. We should therefore build one of our new stores in Plainsville, which clearly has many such residents. Plainsville merchants report that sales of running shoes and exercise equipment are at all-time highs. The local health club, which nearly closed five years ago due to lack of business, has more members than ever, and the weight-training and aerobics classes are always full. We can even anticipate a new generation of customers: Plainsville's schoolchildren are required to participate in a program called Fitness for Life, which emphasizes the benefits of regular exercise at an early age."

Write a response in which you examine the stated and/or unstated assumptions of the argument. Be sure to explain how the argument depends on these assumptions and what the implications are for the argument if the assumptions prove unwarranted.

[88]번과 동일한 지문이나 instruction이 다름.

| Argument   We should therefore build one of our new stores in Plainsville.

10. Twenty years ago, Dr. Field, a noted anthropologist, visited the island of Tertia. Using an observation-centered approach to studying Tertian culture, he concluded from his observations that children in Tertia were reared by an entire village rather than by their own biological parents. Recently another anthropologist, Dr. Karp, visited the group of islands that includes Tertia and used the interview-centered method to study child-rearing practices. In the interviews that Dr. Karp conducted with children living in this group of islands, the children spent much more time talking about their biological parents than about other adults in the village. Dr. Karp decided that Dr. Field's conclusion about Tertian village culture must be invalid. Some anthropologists recommend that to obtain accurate information on Tertian child-rearing practices, future research on the subject should be conducted via the interview-centered method.

Write a response in which you discuss what questions would need to be answered in order to decide whether the recommendation and the argument on which it is based are reasonable. Be sure to explain how the answers to these questions would help to evaluate the recommendation.

20년 전, 저명한 인류학자였던 Field 박사는 Tertia섬을 방문했다. Tertian의 문화를 연구하기 위해서 관찰 중심 접근법을 사용한 후, 그의 관찰에서 그는 Tertia 섬의 어린이들은 생물학적 부모에 의해 양육을 받은 것이 아니고 집단 공동체에 의해서 양육되었다는 결론을 내렸었다.
최근 또 다른 인류학자인 Dr. Karp는 Tertia 군도를 방문해서, 아이들의 양육법을 연구하기 위해서 인터뷰 중심 방법을 사용했다. Dr. Karp가 이 군도에 사는 아이들과 실시한 인터뷰에서, 아이들은 마을의 다른 어른들에 대한 이야기보다 그들의 생물학적 부모에 대한 이야기를 더 많이 했다. Dr. Karp는 Tertian 마을에 관한 Dr. Field의 결론이 근거가 없다고 보았다. 일부 인류학자들은 Tertian의 아이 양육법에 관한 정확한 정보를 얻기 위해서는 인터뷰 중심법을 통해서 미래 연구가 이루어져야 한다고 권고한다.

Recommendation   To obtain accurate information on Tertian child-rearing practices, future research on the subject should be conducted via the interview-centered method.

21. The following appeared in an article written by Dr. Karp, an anthropologist.

"Twenty years ago, Dr. Field, a noted anthropologist, visited the island of Tertia and concluded from his observations that children in Tertia were reared by an entire village rather than by their own biological parents. However, my recent interviews with children living in the group of islands that includes Tertia show that these children spend much more time talking about their biological parents than about other adults in the village. This research of mine proves that Dr. Field's conclusion about Tertian village culture is invalid and thus that the observation-centered approach to studying cultures is invalid as well. The interview-centered method that my team of graduate students is currently using in Tertia will establish a much more accurate understanding of child-rearing traditions there and in other island cultures." [Old version 36]

Write a response in which you discuss what specific evidence is needed to evaluate the argument and explain how the evidence would weaken or strengthen the argument.

다음은 인류학자인 Karp 박사가 기고한 글의 내용이다.

"20년 전, 한 저명한 인류학자였던 Field 박사는 Tertia섬을 방문해서, 관찰을 통해 이 섬의 어린이들은 생물학적 부모에 의해 양육을 받은 것이 아니고 집단 공동체에 의해서 양육되었다는 결론을 내렸었다. 그러나 Tertia를 포함한 이곳 군도에 거주하는 아이들과 나눈 최근의 내 인터뷰는 이 아이들이 마을의 다른 어른들에 대해서보다는 그들 부모에 대한 이야기를 더 많이 한다는 것을 보여준다. 이러한 나의 연구는 Tertian 마을 문화에 관한 Field 박사의 결론이 근거가 없고, 그래서 문화 연구에 있어서 관찰 중심법 역시 옳지 않다는 것을 증명했다. 내 팀의 대학원생들이 Tertia에서 현재 이용하는 인터뷰 중심법이 이 섬과 다른 섬에서 아이들을 양육하는 관습을 훨씬 더 정확하게 이해하도록 해줄 것이다."

> Argument
> The interview-centered method that my team of graduate students is currently using in Tertia will establish a much more accurate understanding of child-rearing traditions there and in other island cultures.

23. The following appeared in an article written by Dr. Karp, an anthropologist.

"Twenty years ago, Dr. Field, a noted anthropologist, visited the island of Tertia and concluded from his observations that children in Tertia were reared by an entire village rather than by their own biological parents. However, my recent interviews with children living in the group of islands that includes Tertia show that these children spend much more time talking about their biological parents than about other adults in the village. This research of mine proves that Dr. Field's conclusion about Tertian village culture is invalid and thus that the observation-centered approach to studying cultures is invalid as well. The interview-centered method that my team of graduate students is currently using in Tertia will establish a much more accurate understanding of child-rearing traditions there and in other island cultures."

Write a response in which you examine the stated and/or unstated assumptions of the argument. Be sure to explain how the argument depends on these assumptions and what the implications are for the argument if the assumptions prove unwarranted.

[21]번과 동일한 지문이나 instruction이 다름.

Argument	The interview-centered method that my team of graduate students is currently using in Tertia will establish a much more accurate understanding of child-rearing traditions there and in other island cultures.

11. The council of Maple County, concerned about the county's becoming overdeveloped, is debating a proposed measure that would prevent the development of existing farmland in the county. But the council is also concerned that such a restriction, by limiting the supply of new housing, could lead to significant increases in the price of housing in the county. Proponents of the measure note that Chestnut County established a similar measure ten years ago, and its housing prices have increased only modestly since. However, opponents of the measure note that Pine County adopted restrictions on the development of new residential housing fifteen years ago, and its housing prices have since more than doubled. The council currently predicts that the proposed measure, if passed, will result in a significant increase in housing prices in Maple County. [Old version 109]

Write a response in which you discuss what questions would need to be answered in order to decide whether the prediction and the argument on which it is based are reasonable. Be sure to explain how the answers to these questions would help to evaluate the prediction.

County의 지나친 개발을 우려하는 Maple County 의회는 county 내 기존 농지의 개발을 금지하고자 하는 제안을 토론하고 있다. 그러나 의회는 이러한 규제가, 신규 주택의 공급 제한으로, 상당한 주택가격 상승을 가져올 수 있다는 점도 우려하고 있다. 제안에 찬성하는 사람들은 Chestnut County가 10년 전에 비슷한 조치를 취했지만, 그 후 주택가격은 완만하게 올라갔다는 점을 지적했다. 하지만 그 조치에 반대하는 사람들은 Pine County가 15년 전에 신규 주택개발을 제안하는 정책을 시행한 이래로 주택가격이 2배 이상 뛰었다는 점을 지적하고 있다. 의회는 현재 이 안이 가결된다면 Maple County에서 상당한 주택가격 상승이 있을 것이라고 예상하고 있다.

> Argument The proposed measure that would prevent the development of existing farmland in the county will result in a significant increase in housing prices in Maple County.

12. Fifteen years ago, Omega University implemented a new procedure that encouraged students to evaluate the teaching effectiveness of all their professors. Since that time, Omega professors have begun to assign higher grades in their classes, and overall student grade averages at Omega have risen by 30 percent. Potential employers, looking at this dramatic rise in grades, believe that grades at Omega are inflated and do not accurately reflect student achievement; as a result, Omega graduates have not been as successful at getting jobs as have graduates from nearby Alpha University. To enable its graduates to secure better jobs, Omega University should terminate student evaluation of professors. [Old version 9]

Write a response in which you discuss what specific evidence is needed to evaluate the argument and explain how the evidence would weaken or strengthen the argument.

15년 전, Omega 대학은 학생들이 교수들의 교습효과를 평가하도록 권장하는 새로운 조치를 시행했다. 이후, 교수들은 학생들에게 높은 학점을 주었으며, 그에 따라 Omega 학생들의 전체 평점이 30%나 올랐다. 이런 급격한 학점 상승을 바라보는 잠재적 고용주들은 Omega 대학의 학점이 부풀려져서 학생들의 실력을 제대로 반영하지 않았다고 믿는다. 있다. 그 결과, Omega대학의 졸업생들이 인근 Alpha 대학 졸업자들보다 취업을 잘 하지 못하고 있다. Omega 대학의 졸업생들이 좋은 직업을 가지려면 교수에 대한 학생평가를 중단해야만 한다.

| Argument | To enable its graduates to secure better jobs, Omega University should terminate student evaluation of professors. |

13. In an attempt to improve highway safety, Prunty County last year lowered its speed limit from 55 to 45 miles per hour on all county highways. But this effort has failed: the number of accidents has not decreased, and, based on reports by the highway patrol, many drivers are exceeding the speed limit. Prunty County should instead undertake the same kind of road improvement project that Butler County completed five years ago: increasing lane widths, resurfacing rough highways, and improving visibility at dangerous intersections. Today, major Butler County roads still have a 55 mph speed limit, yet there were 25 percent fewer reported accidents in Butler County this past year than there were five years ago. [Old version 18]

Write a response in which you discuss what specific evidence is needed to evaluate the argument and explain how the evidence would weaken or strengthen the argument.

고속도로의 안전을 향상시키기 위한 시도로, Prunty County는 작년에 모든 County 고속도로의 제한속도를 55마일에서 45마일로 낮추었다. 그러나 이러한 노력은 실패했다. 사고건수는 줄지 않았고, 고속도로 경찰의 보고에 따르면 많은 운전자들은 제한속도를 초과하고 있다. 그 대신 Prunty County는, Butler County가 5년 전에 끝낸, 차선 확장, 파손된 고속도로 노면 재포장, 그리고 위험한 진출입로의 시야 개선 작업 같은 계획을 시행해야 한다. 현재에도 Butler County의 도로 제한속도는 여전히 55마일이나 5년 전에 비해 금년에는 사고율이 25%나 감소했다고 보고되었다.

Argument To improve highway safety, Prunty County should undertake the road improvement project that Butler County completed five years ago.

14. The following appeared as part of an article in a business magazine.

"A recent study rating 300 male and female Mentian advertising executives according to the average number of hours they sleep per night showed an association between the amount of sleep the executives need and the success of their firms. Of the advertising firms studied, those whose executives reported needing no more than 6 hours of sleep per night had higher profit margins and faster growth. These results suggest that if a business wants to prosper, it should hire only people who need less than 6 hours of sleep per night." [New]

Write a response in which you examine the stated and/or unstated assumptions of the argument. Be sure to explain how the argument depends on these assumptions and what the implications are for the argument if the assumptions prove unwarranted.

"하루 평균 잠자는 시간에 따라 남녀 300명의 Mentian 광고사의 임원을 평가한 최근의 한 연구 결과는 임원들이 필요로 하는 수면 시간과 그들 부서(회사)의 성과 사이에 관련이 있음을 보여주고 있다. 조사된 광고회사 중, 단지 6시간의 수면만 필요하다고 보고된 임원들의 회사가 수익도 더 내고 성장도 빨랐다. 이 결과는, 사업에서 성공을 원한다면, 하루에 6시간 미만을 자는 사람들만 고용해야 한다는 것을 시사한다.

> Argument   If a business wants to prosper, it should hire only people who need less than 6 hours of sleep per night.

118. The following appeared as part of an article in a business magazine.

"A recent study rating 300 male and female advertising executives according to the average number of hours they sleep per night showed an association between the amount of sleep the executives need and the success of their firms. Of the advertising firms studied, those whose executives reported needing no more than six hours of sleep per night had higher profit margins and faster growth. On the basis of this study, we recommend that businesses hire only people who need less than six hours of sleep per night."

Write a response in which you discuss what questions would need to be answered in order to decide whether the recommendation and the argument on which it is based are reasonable. Be sure to explain how the answers to these questions would help to evaluate the recommendation.

[14]번과 거의 동일한 지문이나 instruction이 다름.

| Recommendation | Businesses should hire only people who need less than six hours of sleep per night. |

15. The following memorandum is from the business manager of Happy Pancake House restaurants.

"Recently, butter has been replaced by margarine in Happy Pancake House restaurants throughout the southwestern United States. This change, however, has had little impact on our customers. In fact, only about 2 percent of customers have complained, indicating that an average of 98 people out of 100 are happy with the change. Furthermore, many servers have reported that a number of customers who ask for butter do not complain when they are given margarine instead. Clearly, either these customers do not distinguish butter from margarine or they use the term 'butter' to refer to either butter or margarine."

Write a response in which you discuss one or more alternative explanations that could rival the proposed explanation and explain how your explanation(s) can plausibly account for the facts presented in the argument.

다음은 Happy Pancake House 식당 사업부장의 메모이다.

"최근, 미국의 남서부 전역에 걸쳐 있는 Happy Pancake House에서 버터가 마가린으로 대체되고 있다. 그렇지만, 이러한 변화는 우리 고객들한테 거의 영향이 없다. 실제로, 단지 2%의 고객만이 불평하는 것으로 봐서 100중 평균 98명은 이런 변화에 호의적임을 보여준다. 더욱이 많은 종업원들은 버터를 찾는 상당수의 고객들에게 대신 마가린을 주어도 불평하지 않는다고 전했다.
분명히, 고객들은 버터와 마가린을 구분하지 못하거나 아니면 그들은 '버터'라는 용어를 버터 혹은 마가린을 뜻하는 것으로 사용한다."

Argument   Either customers do not distinguish butter from margarine or they use the term 'butter' to refer to either butter or margarine.

51. The following memorandum is from the business manager of Happy Pancake House restaurants.

"Butter has now been replaced by margarine in Happy Pancake House restaurants throughout the southwestern United States. Only about 2 percent of customers have complained, indicating that 98 people out of 100 are happy with the change. Furthermore, many servers have reported that a number of customers who ask for butter do not complain when they are given margarine instead. Clearly, either these customers cannot distinguish butter from margarine or they use the term 'butter' to refer to either butter or margarine. Thus, to avoid the expense of purchasing butter and to increase profitability, the Happy Pancake House should extend this cost-saving change to its restaurants in the southeast and northeast as well." [Old version 182]

Write a response in which you discuss what questions would need to be answered in order to decide whether the recommendation is likely to have the predicted result. Be sure to explain how the answers to these questions would help to evaluate the recommendation.

[15]번과 거의 동일한 지문이나 instruction이 다름.

| Recommendation | The Happy Pancake House should extend this cost-saving change to its restaurants in the southeast and northeast as well. |

130. The following memorandum is from the business manager of Happy Pancake House restaurants.

"Butter has now been replaced by margarine in Happy Pancake House restaurants throughout the southwestern United States. Only about 2 percent of customers have filed a formal complaint, indicating that an average of 98 people out of 100 are happy with the change. Furthermore, many servers have reported that a number of customers who ask for butter do not complain when they are given margarine instead. Clearly, either these customers cannot distinguish butter from margarine or they use the term 'butter' to refer to either butter or margarine. Thus, to avoid the expense of purchasing butter, the Happy Pancake House should extend this cost-saving change to its restaurants throughout the rest of the country."

Write a response in which you examine the stated and/or unstated assumptions of the argument. Be sure to explain how the argument depends on these assumptions and what the implications are for the argument if the assumptions prove unwarranted.

[15]번과 거의 동일한 지문이나 instruction이 다름.

Argument To avoid the expense of purchasing butter, the Happy Pancake House should extend this cost-saving change to its restaurants throughout the rest of the country.

131. The following memorandum is from the business manager of Happy Pancake House restaurants.

"Butter has now been replaced by margarine in Happy Pancake House restaurants throughout the southwestern United States. Only about 2 percent of customers have complained, indicating that an average of 98 people out of 100 are happy with the change. Furthermore, many servers have reported that a number of customers who ask for butter do not complain when they are given margarine instead. Clearly, either these customers cannot distinguish butter from margarine or they use the term 'butter' to refer to either butter or margarine. Thus, we predict that Happy Pancake House will be able to increase profits dramatically if we extend this cost-saving change to all our restaurants in the southeast and northeast as well."

Write a response in which you discuss what questions would need to be answered in order to decide whether the prediction and the argument on which it is based are reasonable. Be sure to explain how the answers to these questions would help to evaluate the prediction.

다음은 Happy Pancake House 식당 사업부장의 메모이다.
"버터는 현재 남서부 전역에 걸쳐 있는 Happy Pancake House 식당에서 마가린으로 대체되고 있다.
단지 고객 중 2%만이 불평을 하는데, 이는 100중 평균 98명은 이 변화에 호의적이라는 것을 나타낸다. 더욱이 많은 종업원들은 버터를 찾는 상당수의 고객들에게 마가린을 줘도 불평하지 않는다고 전했다. 분명히, 고객들은 버터와 마가린을 구분하지 못하거나 아니면 '버터'라는 용어를 버터나 또는 마가린을 뜻하는 것으로 사용한다. 그러므로 이런 비용을 절감하는 변경을 남동부와 북동부에 있는 모든 식당으로도 확대한다면, Happy Pancake House는 수익을 급격하게 늘릴 수 있을 것이다."

> Prediction Happy Pancake House will be able to increase profits dramatically if we extend this cost-saving change to all our restaurants in the southeast and northeast as well.

Argue Groups

133. The following memorandum is from the business manager of Happy Pancake House restaurants.

"Butter has now been replaced by margarine in Happy Pancake House restaurants throughout the southwestern United States. Only about 2 percent of customers have complained, indicating that an average of 98 people out of 100 are happy with the change. Furthermore, many servers have reported that a number of customers who ask for butter do not complain when they are given margarine instead. Clearly, either these customers cannot distinguish butter from margarine or they use the term 'butter' to refer to either butter or margarine. Thus, to avoid the expense of purchasing butter and to increase profitability, the Happy Pancake House should extend this cost-saving change to its restaurants in the southeast and northeast as well."

Write a response in which you discuss what specific evidence is needed to evaluate the argument and explain how the evidence would weaken or strengthen the argument.

[51]번과 거의 동일한 지문이나 Instruction이 다름.

Argument To avoid the expense of purchasing butter and to increase profitability, the Happy Pancake House should extend this cost-saving change to its restaurants in the southeast and northeast as well.

396

16. In surveys Mason City residents rank water sports (swimming, boating, and fishing) among their favorite recreational activities. The Mason River flowing through the city is rarely used for these pursuits, however, and the city park department devotes little of its budget to maintaining riverside recreational facilities. For years there have been complaints from residents about the quality of the river's water and the river's smell. In response, the state has recently announced plans to clean up Mason River. Use of the river for water sports is, therefore, sure to increase. The city government should for that reason devote more money in this year's budget to riverside recreational facilities. [Old version 137]

Write a response in which you examine the stated and/or unstated assumptions of the argument. Be sure to explain how the argument depends on these assumptions and what the implications are for the argument if the assumptions prove unwarranted.

조사에서, Mason시 주민들은 좋아하는 오락활동 중에서 물놀이(수영, 보트 타기, 낚시)를 최고로 뽑았다. 시를 관통하는 Mason강은 이런 활동에 거의 이용되지 않지만, 시 공원국은 강변의 오락시설을 유지 관리하기 위한 예산을 거의 배정하지 않는다. 수년간 강의 수질과 냄새에 대한 주민들의 불평이 있어왔다. 이에 대응해 주 정부는 최근 Mason강을 청결하게 하려는 계획을 발표했다. 그러므로 수상 스포츠를 위한 강의 이용이 틀림없이 증가할 것이다. 따라서 시 정부도 올해는 강변의 오락시설에 예산을 배정해야 한다.

> Argument The city government should for that reason devote more money in this year's budget to riverside recreational facilities.

17. The following appeared in a memorandum from the manager of WWAC radio station.

"To reverse a decline in listener numbers, our owners have decided that WWAC must change from its current rock-music format. The decline has occurred despite population growth in our listening area, but that growth has resulted mainly from people moving here after their retirement. We must make listeners of these new residents. We could switch to a music format tailored to their tastes, but a continuing decline in local sales of recorded music suggests limited interest in music. Instead we should change to a news and talk format, a form of radio that is increasingly popular in our area." [Old version 235]

Write a response in which you discuss what specific evidence is needed to evaluate the argument and explain how the evidence would weaken or strengthen the argument.

다음은 WWAC 라디오 방송국 총 책임자의 메모 내용이다.

"청취자 수의 감소를 만회하기 위해서, 우리 사주는 현재의 록음악 방식의 WWAC의 음악프로그램을 바꾸어야 한다고 결정했다. 이런 (청취자) 감소는 우리 청취 지역에서 인구가 늘었음에도 불구하고 나타났지만, 그런 (인구의) 증가는 주로 은퇴 후 이곳으로 이사 오는 사람들 때문이다. 우리는 그들의 취향에 꼭 맞는 음악구성으로 바꿀 수 있지만, 지속적인 음반 판매의 감소는 음악에 대한 흥미에 한계가 있다는 것을 암시한다. 그 대신에 우리 지역에서 인기가 늘고 있는 라디오 형태인 뉴스와 토크 형식으로 바꾸어야만 한다."

Argument We should change to a news and talk format, a form of radio that is increasingly popular in our area.

19. Two years ago, radio station WCQP in Rockville decided to increase the number of call-in advice programs that it broadcast; since that time, its share of the radio audience in the Rockville listening area has increased significantly. Given WCQP's recent success with call-in advice programming, and citing a nationwide survey indicating that many radio listeners are quite interested in such programs, the station manager of KICK in Medway recommends that KICK include more call-in advice programs in an attempt to gain a larger audience share in its listening area. [Old version 97]

Write a response in which you discuss what questions would need to be answered in order to decide whether the recommendation and the argument on which it is based are reasonable. Be sure to explain how the answers to these questions would help to evaluate the recommendation.

2년 전, Rockville에 있는 라디오 방송국 WCQP는, 방송 중인 전화상담 프로그램의 회수를 늘이기로 결정했고, 그 후 Rockville 청취지역에서 라디오 청취자 점유율이 상당히 늘어나 왔다. WCQP의 전화상담 프로그램의 최근 성공을 고려하고, 많은 라디오 청취자들이 그런 프로그램에 많은 흥미를 가지고 있다는 전국적인 조사를 인용하면서, Medway에 있는 KICK 방송국 책임자는 KICK가 청취지역에서 청취자 높은 점유율을 확보하기 위해서는 더 많은 전화상담 프로그램을 편성해야 한다고 권한다.

Recommendation KICK should include more call-in advice programs in an attempt to gain a larger audience share in its listening area.

93. The following appeared in a memorandum from the manager of WWAC radio station.

"WWAC must change from its current rock-music format because the number of listeners has been declining, even though the population in our listening area has been growing. The population growth has resulted mainly from people moving to our area after their retirement, and we must make listeners of these new residents. But they seem to have limited interest in music: several local stores selling recorded music have recently closed. Therefore, just changing to another kind of music is not going to increase our audience. Instead, we should adopt a news-and-talk format, a form of radio that is increasingly popular in our area."

Write a response in which you discuss what questions would need to be answered in order to decide whether the recommendation and the argument on which it is based are reasonable. Be sure to explain how the answers to these questions would help to evaluate the recommendation.

다음은 WWAC 라디오 방송국 총 책임자의 메모 내용이다.

"우리 청취 지역에서 인구가 늘었지만 청취자 수는 줄어들기 때문에, WWAC는 현재의 록음악 방식의 프로그램을 바꾸어야만 한다. 인구의 증가는 주로 은퇴 후 이곳으로 이사 오는 사람들 때문이고, 우리는 이 새로운 주민들을 청취자로 만들어야 한다. 그러나 그들은 음악에 별 관심이 없는 듯하다: 즉 음반을 파는 지역 가게들이 최근 문을 닫고 있다. 그러므로 단지 다른 음악프로그램으로 바꾸는 것은 우리 청취자를 늘리지 못할 것이다. 그 대신에 우리 지역에서 점점 인기가 높아가는 라디오 형식인 뉴스와 토크쇼 방식을 도입해야 한다."

Recommendation   We should adopt a news-and-talk format, a form of radio that is increasingly popular in our area.

109. The following appeared in a memorandum from the general manager of KNOW radio station.

"Several factors indicate that radio station KNOW should shift its programming from rock-and-roll music to a continuous news format. Consider, for example, that the number of people in our listening area over fifty years of age has increased dramatically, while our total number of listeners has declined. Also, music stores in our area report decreased sales of recorded music. Finally, continuous news stations in neighboring cities have been very successful. The switch from rock-and-roll music to 24-hour news will attract older listeners and secure KNOW radio's future." [Old version 235]

Write a response in which you examine the stated and/or unstated assumptions of the argument. Be sure to explain how the argument depends on these assumptions and what the implications are for the argument if the assumptions prove unwarranted.

다음은 KNOW 라디오 방송국 총책임자의 메모 내용이다.

"라디오 방송국 KNOW는 프로그램을 로큰롤 음악에서 연속적인 뉴스 형식으로 바꾸어야만 한다는 것을 보여주는 몇 가지 요인이 있다. 예를 들어, 우리 청취 지역에서 50세 이상은 급격하게 증가하고 있으나 반면에 전체 청취자의 수는 감소하는 것을 고려해 보자. 또한, 우리 지역 음악 가게들은 감소된 음반 판매를 보고하고 있다. 끝으로, 인접 도시들의 뉴스 전문 방송국들은 아주 성공적이다. 록큰롤 음악에서 24시간 뉴스로의 전환은 노인 청취자들을 끌어들일 것이고 KNOW 라디오의 미래를 담보할 것이다."

Argument   Radio station KNOW should shift its programming from rock-and-roll music to a continuous news format.

110. The following appeared in a memorandum from the manager of KNOW radio station.

"Several factors indicate that KNOW radio can no longer succeed as a rock-and-roll music station. Consider, for example, that the number of people in our listening area over fifty years of age has increased dramatically, while our total number of listeners has declined. Also, music stores in our area report decreased sales of rock-and-roll music. Finally, continuous news stations in neighboring cities have been very successful. We predict that switching KNOW radio from rock-and-roll music to 24-hour news will allow the station to attract older listeners and make KNOW radio more profitable than ever."

Write a response in which you discuss what questions would need to be answered in order to decide whether the prediction and the argument on which it is based are reasonable. Be sure to explain how the answers to these questions would help to evaluate the prediction.

[109]번과 거의 동일한 지문이나 instruction이 다름.

Prediction | Switching KNOW radio from rock-and-roll music to 24-hour news will allow the station to attract older listeners and make KNOW radio more profitable than ever.

18. The following is a memorandum from the business manager of a television station.

"Over the past year, our late-night news program has devoted increased time to national news and less time to weather and local news. During this period, most of the complaints received from viewers were concerned with our station's coverage of weather and local news. In addition, local businesses that used to advertise during our late-night news program have canceled their advertising contracts with us. Therefore, in order to attract more viewers to our news programs and to avoid losing any further advertising revenues, we should expand our coverage of weather and local news on all our news programs." [Old version 135]

Write a response in which you examine the stated and/or unstated assumptions of the argument. Be sure to explain how the argument depends on these assumptions and what the implications are for the argument if the assumptions prove unwarranted.

다음은 한 TV 방송국 사업부장의 메모이다.

"지난 한 해 동안, 우리의 심야 뉴스 프로그램은 전국 뉴스에 많은 시간을 할애했고 날씨와 지역 뉴스는 적게 다루었다. 동 시간대에 시청자로부터 받은 대부분의 불만 사항은 날씨와 지역 뉴스의 보도와 관련된 것이었다. 게다가, 심야 뉴스 방송시간에 광고를 하던 지역 업체들이 광고계약을 해약했다. 따라서 뉴스 프로그램 시청자를 더 확보하고 더 이상의 광고 수익 손실을 막기 위해서는, 모든 뉴스 방송에서 날씨와 지역 뉴스의 보도를 늘여야 한다."

Argument   We should expand our coverage of weather and local news on all our news programs.

20. The following is a memorandum from the business manager of a television station.

"Over the past year, our late-night news program has devoted increased time to national news and less time to weather and local news. During this time period, most of the complaints received from viewers were concerned with our station's coverage of weather and local news. In addition, local businesses that used to advertise during our late-night news program have just canceled their advertising contracts with us. Therefore, in order to attract more viewers to the program and to avoid losing any further advertising revenues, we should restore the time devoted to weather and local news to its former level."

Write a response in which you discuss what specific evidence is needed to evaluate the argument and explain how the evidence would weaken or strengthen the argument.

[18]번과 거의 동일한 지문이나 instruction이 다름.

> Argument   We should restore the time devoted to weather and local news to its former level.

22. According to a recent report, cheating among college and university students is on the rise. However, Groveton College has successfully reduced student cheating by adopting an honor code, which calls for students to agree not to cheat in their academic endeavors and to notify a faculty member if they suspect that others have cheated. Groveton's honor code replaced a system in which teachers closely monitored students; under that system, teachers reported an average of thirty cases of cheating per year. In the first year the honor code was in place, students reported twenty-one cases of cheating; five years later, this figure had dropped to fourteen. Moreover, in a recent survey, a majority of Groveton students said that they would be less likely to cheat with an honor code in place than without. Thus, all colleges and universities should adopt honor codes similar to Groveton's in order to decrease cheating among students.

Write a response in which you discuss what questions would need to be answered in order to decide whether the recommendation and the argument on which it is based are reasonable. Be sure to explain how the answers to these questions would help to evaluate the recommendation.

최근의 한 보고에 따르면 대학생들 사이에서 부정행위가 증가하고 있다. 하지만 Groveton 대학은 아너코드를 도입해서 부정행위를 하는 학생을 성공적으로 감소시켰는데, 이것은 학생들에게 부정행위를 하지 않을 것에 동의하고 만일 다른 학생이 부정행위를 했다는 의심이 드는 경우 교직원에게 알리는 것을 요구하는 것이다. Groveton의 아너코드는 교사들이 가까이서 학생들을 감시하는 구제도를 대체했는데, 그 제도하에서 교사들은 연간 평균 30건의 부정행위를 보고했다. 아너코드가 시행된 시행 첫해에 학생들은 21건의 부정행위를 보고했고 5년 후에는 이 수치가 14건으로 감소했다. 더욱이 최근 조사에서 Groveton 학생 대다수는 아너코드가 있을 때가 없을 때보다 부정행위를 덜하게 하는 것 같다고 말했다. 그러므로 모든 대학들은 학생들 사이에서 부정행위를 줄이기 위해 Groveton의 것과 유사한 아너코드를 도입해야 한다.

Recommendation All colleges and universities should adopt honor codes similar to Groveton's in order to decrease cheating among students.

119. Evidence suggests that academic honor codes, which call for students to agree not to cheat in their academic endeavors and to notify a faculty member if they suspect that others have cheated, are far more successful than are other methods at deterring cheating among students at colleges and universities. Several years ago, Groveton College adopted such a code and discontinued its old-fashioned system in which teachers closely monitored students. Under the old system, teachers reported an average of thirty cases of cheating per year. In the first year the honor code was in place, students reported twenty-one cases of cheating; five years later, this figure had dropped to fourteen. Moreover, in a recent survey, a majority of Groveton students said that they would be less likely to cheat with an honor code in place than without.

Write a response in which you discuss one or more alternative explanations that could rival the proposed explanation and explain how your explanation(s) can plausibly account for the facts presented in the argument.

학생들에게 학업에서 부정행위를 하지 않겠다는 동의를 받고 만일 다른 학생이 부정행위를 했다는 의심이 드는 경우 교직원에게 알리는 것을 요구하는, 학업 아너코드가 대학생들 사이에서 부정행위를 근절시키는 방법으로서 훨씬 더 성공적이란 증거가 있다. 수년 전, Groveton 대학은 이런 코트를 도입하고 교사들이 가까이서 학생들을 감시하는 구제도를 폐지했다. 구제도하에서, 교사들은 연간 평균 30건의 부정행위를 보고했다. 아너코드가 시행된 시행 첫해에 학생들은 21건의 부정행위를 보고했고 5년 후에는 이 수치가 14건으로 감소했다. 더욱이 최근의 조사에서 Groveton 학생 대다수는 아너코드가 있을 때가 없을 때보다 부정행위를 줄이는 것 같다고 말했다.

Argument　Academic honor codes are far more successful than are other methods at deterring cheating among students at colleges and universities.

120. Several years ago, Groveton College adopted an honor code, which calls for students to agree not to cheat in their academic endeavors and to notify a faculty member if they suspect that others have cheated. Groveton's honor code replaced a system in which teachers closely monitored students. Under that system, teachers reported an average of thirty cases of cheating per year. The honor code has proven far more successful: in the first year it was in place, students reported twenty-one cases of cheating; five years later, this figure had dropped to fourteen. Moreover, in a recent survey, a majority of Groveton students said that they would be less likely to cheat with an honor code in place than without. Such evidence suggests that all colleges and universities should adopt honor codes similar to Groveton's. This change is sure to result in a dramatic decline in cheating among college students.

Write a response in which you discuss what questions would need to be answered in order to decide whether the recommendation is likely to have the predicted result. Be sure to explain how the answers to these questions would help to evaluate the recommendation.

수년 전 Groveton 대학은, 학생들에게 학업에서 부정행위를 하지 않겠다고 동의를 하고, 만일 다른 학생이 부정행위를 했다는 의심이 드는 경우 교직원에게 알리는 것을 요구하는 아너코드를 도입했다. Groveton의 아너코드는 교사들이 가까이에서 학생들을 감시하는 구제도를 폐지했다. 그 제도(구제도)하에서, 교사들은 연간 평균 30건의 부정행위를 보고했다. 아너코드는 훨씬 더 성공적인 것으로 판명되었다. 부연하자면 시행 첫해에 학생들은 21건의 부정행위를 보고했고 5년 후에는 이 수치가 14건으로 감소했다. 더욱이 최근의 조사에서 Groveton의 학생 대다수는 아너코드가 있을 때가 없을 때보다 부정행위를 줄이는 것 같다고 말했다. 이러한 증거들은 모든 대학들이 Groveton의 것과 유사한 아너코드를 도입해야 한다는 것을 시사한다. 이러한 변화가 틀림없이 대학생들 사이에서의 부정행위를 현저히 줄이는 결과를 가져올 것이다.

Recommendation   All colleges and universities should adopt honor codes similar to Groveton's.

138. The following appeared as an editorial in the student newspaper of Groveton College.

"To combat the recently reported dramatic rise in cheating among college students, colleges and universities should adopt honor codes similar to Groveton's, which calls for students to agree not to cheat in their academic endeavors and to notify a faculty member if they suspect that others have cheated. Groveton's honor code replaced an old-fashioned system in which teachers closely monitored students. Under that system, teachers reported an average of thirty cases of cheating per year. The honor code has proven far more successful: in the first year it was in place, students reported twenty-one cases of cheating; five years later, this figure had dropped to fourteen. Moreover, in a recent survey conducted by the Groveton honor council, a majority of students said that they would be less likely to cheat with an honor code in place than without." [Old version 242]

Write a response in which you discuss what specific evidence is needed to evaluate the argument and explain how the evidence would weaken or strengthen the argument.

최근 보고된 대학생들 사이에서의 엄청난 부정행위 증가를 근절하기 위해서, 대학들은 Groveton의 것과 유사한 아너코드를 도입해야 하는데, 이것은 학생들이 부정행위를 하지 않을 것에 동의하고 만일 다른 학생이 부정행위를 했다는 의심이 드는 경우 교직원에게 알리는 것을 요구하는 것이다. Groveton의 아너코드는 교사들이 가까이서 학생들을 감시하는 구제도를 대체했다. 그 제도(구제도)하에서, 교사들은 연간 평균 30건의 부정행위를 보고했다. 아너코드는 아주 성공적이었던 것으로 나타났다. 부연하면 시행 첫해에 학생들은 21건의 부정행위를 보고했고 5년 후에는 이 수치가 14건으로 감소했다. 더욱이 Groveton 아너위원회가 실시한 최근 조사에서 대다수의 학생들은 아너코드가 있을 때가 없을 때보다 부정행위를 줄이는 것 같다고 말했다.

❘ Argument　Colleges and universities should adopt honor codes similar to Groveton's.

24. A recently issued twenty-year study on headaches suffered by the residents of Mentia investigated the possible therapeutic effect of consuming salicylates. Salicylates are members of the same chemical family as aspirin, a medicine used to treat headaches. Although many foods are naturally rich in salicylates, food-processing companies also add salicylates to foods as preservatives. The twenty-year study found a correlation between the rise in the commercial use of salicylates and a steady decline in the average number of headaches reported by study participants. At the time when the study concluded, food-processing companies had just discovered that salicylates can also be used as flavor additives for foods, and, as a result, many companies plan to do so. Based on these study results, some health experts predict that residents of Mentia will suffer even fewer headaches in the future.

Write a response in which you discuss what questions would need to be answered in order to decide whether the prediction and the argument on which it is based are reasonable. Be sure to explain how the answers to these questions would help to evaluate the prediction.

최근에 발표된 Mentia 주민들이 겪고 있는 두통에 관한 20년간의 연구는 살리실산염 섭취의 치료적 효과에 대한 가능성을 조사했다. 살리실산염은 아스피린과 같은 동일 화학물질 계열로서, 두통을 치료하는 데 사용되는 의약품이다. 많은 음식에 살리실산염이 풍부하게 함유되어 있지만, 식품가공 업체들 역시 식품에 살리실산염을 방부제로 첨가해 왔다. 20년간의 연구는 살리실산염의 상업적 이용 증가와 연구에 참여한 사람들에 의해서 보고된 평균 두통 횟수의 꾸준한 감소 사이에 상관관계가 있음을 밝혀냈다. 연구 결과가 나왔을 때, 식품가공 회사들은 살리실산염이 식품의 향료 첨가물로 사용될 수도 있음을 발견했고, 그 결과, 많은 회사들이 그렇게 할 계획이다. 이 연구 결과를 바탕으로, 일부 건강 전문가들은 Mentia 주민들이 앞으로는 두통을 덜 겪게될 것이라고 예측한다.

Prediction　With this new use for salicylates, residents of Mentia will suffer even fewer headaches in the future.

26. The following appeared in the summary of a study on headaches suffered by the residents of Mentia.

"Salicylates are members of the same chemical family as aspirin, a medicine used to treat headaches. Although many foods are naturally rich in salicylates, for the past several decades, food-processing companies have also been adding salicylates to foods as preservatives. This rise in the commercial use of salicylates has been found to correlate with a steady decline in the average number of headaches reported by participants in our twenty-year study. Recently, food-processing companies have found that salicylates can also be used as flavor additives for foods. With this new use for salicylates, we can expect a continued steady decline in the number of headaches suffered by the average citizen of Mentia." [Old version 35]

Write a response in which you discuss what specific evidence is needed to evaluate the argument and explain how the evidence would weaken or strengthen the argument.

다음은 Mentia 지역 주민들이 겪고 있는 두통에 대한 연구 자료를 요약한 내용이다.

"살리실산염은 아스피린과 같은 동일 화학물질 계열로써, 두통을 치료하는 데 사용되는 의약품이다. 많은 음식에 살리실산염이 풍부하게 함유되어 있지만, 지난 수십 년간 식품가공 업체들 역시 방부제로 식품물에 살리실산염을 첨가해 왔다. 이러한 살리실산염의 상업적 사용 증가는, 20년간 연구에 참여한 사람들에 의해서 보고된 평균 두통 횟수를 꾸준히 감소시키는 것과 관련이 있는 것으로 밝혀졌다. 최근, 식품가공 회사들은 살리실산염이 식품의 향료 첨가물로 사용될 수도 있음을 발견했다. 실리실산염의 이러한 새로운 용도로, Mentia에 사는 보통 시민들이 겪고 있는 두통의 횟수는 지속적으로 꾸준히 감소할 것으로 보인다."

| Argument | With this new use for salicylates, we can expect a continued steady decline in the number of headaches suffered by the average citizen of Mentia. |

28. The following appeared in the summary of a study on headaches suffered by the residents of Mentia.

"Salicylates are members of the same chemical family as aspirin, a medicine used to treat headaches. Although many foods are naturally rich in salicylates, for the past several decades, food-processing companies have also been adding salicylates to foods as preservatives. This rise in the commercial use of salicylates has been found to correlate with a steady decline in the average number of headaches reported by participants in our twenty-year study. Recently, food-processing companies have found that salicylates can also be used as flavor additives for foods. With this new use for salicylates, we can expect a continued steady decline in the number of headaches suffered by the average citizen of Mentia."

Write a response in which you examine the stated and/or unstated assumptions of the argument. Be sure to explain how the argument depends on these assumptions and what the implications are for the argument if the assumptions prove unwarranted.

[26]번과 동일한 지문으로, Instruction만 다름.

Argument   With this new use for salicylates, we can expect a continued steady decline in the number of headaches suffered by the average citizen of Mentia.

25. The following was written as a part of an application for a small-business loan by a group of developers in the city of Monroe.

"A jazz music club in Monroe would be a tremendously profitable enterprise. Currently, the nearest jazz club is 65 miles away; thus, the proposed new jazz club in Monroe, the C-Note, would have the local market all to itself. Plus, jazz is extremely popular in Monroe: over 100,000 people attended Monroe's annual jazz festival last summer; several well-known jazz musicians live in Monroe; and the highest-rated radio program in Monroe is 'Jazz Nightly,' which airs every weeknight at 7 P.M. Finally, a nationwide study indicates that the typical jazz fan spends close to $1,000 per year on jazz entertainment." [Old version 6]

Write a response in which you discuss what specific evidence is needed to evaluate the argument and explain how the evidence would weaken or strengthen the argument.

다음은 Monroe시에 있는 한 개발업자 그룹의 중소기업 대부 신청서 일부에 기록된 내용이다.

"Monroe시에 있는 재즈 클럽은 엄청나게 수익성이 좋은 사업이다. 현재, 가장 가까운 클럽은 65마일 밖에 있다. 그래서 Monroe에 제안된 새로운 재즈 클럽, C Note는, 그 자체로 지역상권을 석권할 것이다. 더구나 재즈는 Monroe에서 아주 인기가 있다. 10만 명 이상의 사람들이 지난여름 Monroe의 연래 재즈 축제에 참석했고, 몇몇 유명한 재즈 음악가들이 Monroe에 살고 있으며, Monroe에서 최고 시청률의 라디오 프로그램은 매일 주중 오후 7시에 방영되는 'Jazz Nightly' 이다. 마지막으로 전국 조사에서도 일반적인 재즈 팬들은 재즈 오락물에 연간 1,000달러 가까이 지출하고 있는 것으로 보고되고 있다."

> Argument   A jazz music club in Monroe would be a tremendously profitable enterprise.

100. The following was written as a part of an application for a small-business loan by a group of developers in the city of Monroe.

"Jazz music is extremely popular in the city of Monroe: over 100,000 people attended Monroe's annual jazz festival last summer, and the highest-rated radio program in Monroe is 'Jazz Nightly,' which airs every weeknight. Also, a number of well-known jazz musicians own homes in Monroe. Nevertheless, the nearest jazz club is over an hour away. Given the popularity of jazz in Monroe and a recent nationwide study indicating that the typical jazz fan spends close to $1,000 per year on jazz entertainment, a jazz music club in Monroe would be tremendously profitable."

Write a response in which you examine the stated and/or unstated assumptions of the argument. Be sure to explain how the argument depends on these assumptions and what the implications are for the argument if the assumptions prove unwarranted.

[25]번과 거의 동일한 지문이나 instruction이 다름.

> Argument   A jazz music club in Monroe would be a tremendously profitable enterprise.

102. The following was written as a part of an application for a small-business loan by a group of developers in the city of Monroe.

"Jazz music is extremely popular in the city of Monroe: over 100,000 people attended Monroe's annual jazz festival last summer, and the highest-rated radio program in Monroe is 'Jazz Nightly,' which airs every weeknight. Also, a number of well-known jazz musicians own homes in Monroe. Nevertheless, the nearest jazz club is over an hour away. Given the popularity of jazz in Monroe and a recent nationwide study indicating that the typical jazz fan spends close to $1,000 per year on jazz entertainment, we predict that our new jazz music club in Monroe will be a tremendously profitable enterprise."

Write a response in which you discuss what questions would need to be answered in order to decide whether the prediction and the argument on which it is based are reasonable. Be sure to explain how the answers to these questions would help to evaluate the prediction.

[25]번과 거의 동일한 지문이나 instruction이 다름.

Prediction   Our new jazz music club in Monroe will be a tremendously profitable enterprise.

164. The following was written by a group of developers in the city of Monroe.

"A jazz music club in Monroe would be a tremendously profitable enterprise. At present, the nearest jazz club is over 60 miles away from Monroe; thus, our proposed club, the C Note, would have the local market all to itself. In addition, there is ample evidence of the popularity of jazz in Monroe: over 100,000 people attended Monroe's jazz festival last summer, several well-known jazz musicians live in Monroe, and the highest-rated radio program in Monroe is 'Jazz Nightly.' Finally, a nationwide study indicates that the typical jazz fan spends close to $1,000 per year on jazz entertainment. We therefore predict that the C Note cannot help but make money."

Write a response in which you discuss what questions would need to be answered in order to decide whether the prediction and the argument on which it is based are reasonable. Be sure to explain how the answers to these questions would help to evaluate the prediction.

[25]번과 거의 동일한 지문이나 Instruction이 다름.

| Prediction   The C Note, our proposed club, cannot help but make money.

27. The following appeared in a letter to the editor of a local newspaper.

"Commuters complain that increased rush-hour traffic on Blue Highway between the suburbs and the city center has doubled their commuting time. The favored proposal of the motorists' lobby is to widen the highway, adding an additional lane of traffic. But last year's addition of a lane to the nearby Green Highway was followed by a worsening of traffic jams on it. A better alternative is to add a bicycle lane to Blue Highway. Many area residents are keen bicyclists. A bicycle lane would encourage them to use bicycles to commute, and so would reduce rush-hour traffic rather than fostering an increase." [Old version 55]

Write a response in which you discuss what specific evidence is needed to evaluate the argument and explain how the evidence would weaken or strengthen the argument.

다음은 한 지역 신문사 편집장에게 보낸 편지의 내용이다.

"통근자들은 Blue Highway상 교외 지역과 시내 중심 사이에서의 러시아워 교통량이 그들의 통근 시간을 2배로 만든다고 불평한다. 운전자들의 압력단체가 선호하는 제안은 고속도로의 폭을 확장해서 추가 차선을 만드는 것이다. 그러나 작년에 근처의 Green Highway에 증설한 추가 차선으로 그곳의 교통체증은 더 나빠졌다. 더 나은 대안은 Blue Highway에 자전거 전용로를 추가하는 것이다. 많은 지역 주민들은 자전거 애호가들이다. 자전거 전용로는 그들이 자전거를 타고 통근을 하도록 유도할 것이고, 그래서 러시아워 교통체증을 조장하기보다는 줄일 것이다."

| Argument | To reduce rush-hour traffic on Blue highway, a bicycle lane should be added instead of a traffic lane. |

29. The following appeared in an editorial in a local newspaper.

"Commuters complain that increased rush-hour traffic on Blue Highway between the suburbs and the city center has doubled their commuting time. The favored proposal of the motorists' lobby is to widen the highway, adding an additional lane of traffic. Opponents note that last year's addition of a lane to the nearby Green Highway was followed by a worsening of traffic jams on it. Their suggested alternative proposal is adding a bicycle lane to Blue Highway. Many area residents are keen bicyclists. A bicycle lane would encourage them to use bicycles to commute, it is argued, thereby reducing rush-hour traffic."

Write a response in which you discuss what questions would need to be answered in order to decide whether the recommendation and the argument on which it is based are reasonable. Be sure to explain how the answers to these questions would help to evaluate the recommendation.

[27]번과 거의 동일한 지문이나 Instruction이 다름.

> Recommendation To reduce rush-hour traffic on Blue highway, a bicycle lane should be added instead of a traffic lane.

30. The following appeared as a recommendation by a committee planning a ten-year budget for the city of Calatrava.

"The birthrate in our city is declining: in fact, last year's birthrate was only one-half that of five years ago. Thus the number of students enrolled in our public schools will soon decrease dramatically, and we can safely reduce the funds budgeted for education during the next decade. At the same time, we can reduce funding for athletic playing fields and other recreational facilities. As a result, we will have sufficient money to fund city facilities and programs used primarily by adults, since we can expect the adult population of the city to increase." [New]

Write a response in which you discuss what specific evidence is needed to evaluate the argument and explain how the evidence would weaken or strengthen the argument.

다음은 Calatrava시의 10개년 예산 기획위원회의 권고사항이다.

"우리 시의 출산율이 감소하고 있다. 실제로 작년도 출산율은 5년 전의 출산율에 비해 겨우 5분지 1에 불과했다. 따라서 공립 학교에 등록하는 학생 수도 곧 급격하게 감소할 것이고, 우리는 앞으로 10년 동안 교육을 위한 예산을 안심하고 줄일 수 있다. 동시에, 육상 경기장과 기타 오락시설을 위한 자금도 줄일 수 있다. 결과적으로 시의 성인 인구가 증가할 것으로 기대하기 때문에, 우리는 주로 성인들이 이용하는 시의 시설과 프로그램을 지원할 충분한 자금을 가지게 될 것이다."

Argument We should reduce the funds budgeted for education during the next decade and increase the money to fund city facilities and programs used primarily by adults.

31. The following appeared in a letter to the editor of Parson City's local newspaper.

"In our region of Trillura, the majority of money spent on the schools that most students attend — the city-run public schools — comes from taxes that each city government collects. The region's cities differ, however, in the budgetary priority they give to public education. For example, both as a proportion of its overall tax revenues and in absolute terms, Parson City has recently spent almost twice as much per year as Blue City has for its public schools — even though both cities have about the same number of residents. Clearly, Parson City residents place a higher value on providing a good education in public schools than Blue City residents do." [Old version 214]

Write a response in which you discuss what specific evidence is needed to evaluate the argument and explain how the evidence would weaken or strengthen the argument.

다음은 Parson City의 지역신문사 편집장에게 보낸 편지 내용이다.

"우리 Trillura 지역에서, 대부분 학생들이 다니는 학교 - 시립학교들-에 쓰는 돈의 대부분은 각 시 정부가 거두는 세금에서 나온다. 하지만 그들이 공교육에 쓰는 예산의 우선순위는 지역의 시마다 다르다. 예를 들어, 두 시의 주민 수는 거의 비슷한데도, 전체적인 세수에서 차지하는 비율과 절대치 모두에서, Parson City는 연간 Blue City가 공교육에 쓰는 돈의 거의 2배를 썼다. 확실히, Parson City의 주민들이 Blue City의 주민들보다 질 좋은 공교육을 제공하는 데 더 높은 가치를 두고 있다."

Argument	Parson City residents place a higher value on providing a good education in public schools than Blue City residents do.

32. The following appeared in a memo from a vice president of Quiot Manufac turing.

"During the past year, Quiot Manufacturing had 30 percent more on-the-job accidents than at the nearby Panoply Industries plant, where the work shifts are one hour shorter than ours. Experts say that significant contributing factors in many on-the-job accidents are fatigue and sleep deprivation among workers. Therefore, to reduce the number of on-the-job accidents at Quiot and thereby increase productivity, we should shorten each of our three work shifts by one hour so that employees will get adequate amounts of sleep." [Old version 12]

Write a response in which you examine the stated and/or unstated assumptions of the argument. Be sure to explain how the argument depends on these assumptions and what the implications are for the argument if the assumptions prove unwarranted.

다음은 Alta 제조업체 부사장의 메모에 있는 내용이다.

"지난해 동안, Quiot 제조사는 인근 Panoply Industries보다 업무상 재해가 30%나 더 많았는데, Panoply Industries는 교대시간이 우리보다 1시간 짧다. 전문가들은 대부분 업무상 재해에 있어서 가장 중요한 요인은 근로자들의 과로와 수면 부족이라고 한다. 따라서 Quiot에서 높은 산업 재해율을 줄이고, 그렇게 함으로써 생산성을 높이기 위해서는, 근로자들이 적당한 수면을 취할 수 있도록 각 3교대의 (근무) 시간을 1시간씩 줄여야 한다."

| Argument | To reduce the number of on-the-job accidents at Quiot, we should shorten each of our three work shifts by one hour. |

104. The following appeared in a memo from a vice president of a manufacturing company.

"During the past year, workers at our newly opened factory reported 30 percent more on-the-job accidents than workers at nearby Panoply Industries. Panoply produces products very similar to those produced at our factory, but its work shifts are one hour shorter than ours. Experts say that fatigue and sleep deprivation among workers are significant contributing factors in many on-the-job accidents. Panoply's superior safety record can therefore be attributed to its shorter work shifts, which allow its employees to get adequate amounts of rest."

Write a response in which you discuss one or more alternative explanations that could rival the proposed explanation and explain how your explanation(s) can plausibly account for the facts presented in the argument.

[32]번과 거의 동일한 지문이나 Instruction이 다름.

Argument   Panoply's superior safety record can therefore be attributed to its shorter work shifts.

105. The following appeared in a memo from the vice president of Butler Manufacturing.

"During the past year, workers at Butler Manufacturing reported 30 percent more on-the-job accidents than workers at nearby Panoply Industries, where the work shifts are one hour shorter than ours. A recent government study reports that fatigue and sleep deprivation among workers are significant contributing factors in many on-the-job accidents. If we shorten each of our work shifts by one hour, we can improve Butler Manufacturing's safety record by ensuring that our employees are adequately rested."

Write a response in which you discuss what specific evidence is needed to evaluate the argument and explain how the evidence would weaken or strengthen the argument.

[32]번과 거의 동일한 지문이나 Instruction이 다름.

Argument　If we shorten each of our work shifts by one hour, we can improve Butler Manufacturing's safety record.

106. The following appeared in a memo from the Board of Directors of Butler Manufacturing.

"During the past year, workers at Butler Manufacturing reported 30 percent more on-the-job accidents than workers at nearby Panoply Industries, where the work shifts are one hour shorter than ours. A recent government study reports that fatigue and sleep deprivation among workers are significant contributing factors in many on-the-job accidents. Therefore, we recommend that Butler Manufacturing shorten each of its work shifts by one hour. Shorter shifts will allow Butler to improve its safety record by ensuring that its employees are adequately rested."

Write a response in which you discuss what questions would need to be answered in order to decide whether the recommendation is likely to have the predicted result. Be sure to explain how the answers to these questions would help to evaluate the recommendation.

[32]번과 거의 동일한 지문이나 Instruction이 다름.

| Recommendation | Butler Manufacturing should shorten each of its work shifts by one hour to improve its safety record. |

167. The following appeared in a memo from a vice president of Alta Manufacturing.

"During the past year, Alta Manufacturing had thirty percent more on-the-job accidents than nearby Panoply Industries, where the work shifts are one hour shorter than ours. Experts believe that a significant contributing factor in many accidents is fatigue caused by sleep deprivation among workers. Therefore, to reduce the number of on-the-job accidents at Alta, we recommend shortening each of our three work shifts by one hour. If we do this, our employees will get adequate amounts of sleep."

Write a response in which you discuss what questions would need to be answered in order to decide whether the recommendation and the argument on which it is based are reasonable. Be sure to explain how the answers to these questions would help to evaluate the recommendation.

[32]번과 거의 동일한 지문이나 Instruction이 다름.

Recommendation   To reduce the number of on-the-job accidents at Alta, we recommend shortening each of our three work shifts by one hour.

33. The following appeared in a memorandum from the planning department of an electric power company.

"Several recent surveys indicate that home owners are increasingly eager to conserve energy. At the same time, manufacturers are now marketing many home appliances, such as refrigerators and air conditioners, that are almost twice as energy efficient as those sold a decade ago. Also, new technologies for better home insulation and passive solar heating are readily available to reduce the energy needed for home heating. Therefore, the total demand for electricity in our area will not increase — and may decline slightly. Since our three electric generating plants in operation for the past twenty years have always met our needs, construction of new generating plants will not be necessary." [Old version 208]

Write a response in which you examine the stated and/or unstated assumptions of the argument. Be sure to explain how the argument depends on these assumptions and what the implications are for the argument if the assumptions prove unwarranted.

다음은 한 전력 회사 기획부가 작성한 메모 내용이다.

"최근 몇몇 조사에 따르면, 주택 소유자들은 점점 더 에너지를 절약하려는 노력을 기울이고 있다고 한다. 동시에 제조 회사들이 요즘 파는 냉장고나 에어컨과 같은 가전제품들은, 10년 전에 팔린 것들에 비해 에너지 효율이 거의 2배나 된다. 또한, 주택 단열재와 자연형 태양열 난방에 대한 신기술들은 가정 난방에 소요되는 에너지를 줄이기 위해서 쉽게 사용될 수 있다. 그러므로 우리 지역에서 전체 전기 수요는 증가하지 않을 것이고, 다소 줄어들 수 있다. 지난 20여 년 동안 가동 중인 3개의 발전소들이 항상 필요한 전기수요를 충족시켜 왔기 때문에, 새로운 발전소 건설은 필요하지 않다."

Argument Since our three electric generating plants in operation for the past twenty years have always met our needs, construction of new generating plants will not be necessary.

A r g u e   Groups

34. The vice president of human resources at Climpson Industries sent the following recommendation to the company's president.

"In an effort to improve our employees' productivity, we should implement electronic monitoring of employees' Internet use from their workstations. Employees who use the Internet from their workstations need to be identified and punished if we are to reduce the number of work hours spent on personal or recreational activities, such as shopping or playing games. By installing software to detect employees' Internet use on company computers, we can prevent employees from wasting time, foster a better work ethic at Climpson, and improve our overall profits." [Old version 127]

Write a response in which you examine the stated and/or unstated assumptions of the argument. Be sure to explain how the argument depends on these assumptions and what the implications are for the argument if the assumptions prove unwarranted.

Climpson Industries의 인사부 부사장이 회사 사장에게 보낸 권고 내용이다.

"당사 종업원들의 생산성을 향상시키기 위한 일환으로, 직원들이 작업장에서 인터넷을 사용하는 것에 대해 전자 감시를 실시해야 합니다. 쇼핑과 게임 같은 개인적 또는 오락활동에 낭비되는 작업 시간을 줄이려면, 자기 자리에서 인터넷을 사용하는 직원들을 확인해서 제재를 해야 합니다. 회사 컴퓨터에 인터넷 사용을 감시하는 소프트웨어를 설치해서, 직원들이 시간을 낭비하는 것을 막을 수 있고, 근무 윤리를 고무할 수 있으며, 전체적인 수익도 향상시킬 수 있습니다."

| Argument | In an effort to improve our employees' productivity, we should implement electronic monitoring of employees' Internet use from their workstations. |

426

58. The vice president for human resources at Climpson Industries sent the following recommendation to the company's president.

"In an effort to improve our employees' productivity, we should implement electronic monitoring of employees' Internet use from their workstations. Employees who use the Internet inappropriately from their workstations need to be identified and punished if we are to reduce the number of work hours spent on personal or recreational activities, such as shopping or playing games. Installing software on company computers to detect employees' Internet use is the best way to prevent employees from wasting time on the job. It will foster a better work ethic at Climpson and improve our overall profits."

Write a response in which you discuss what specific evidence is needed to evaluate the argument and explain how the evidence would weaken or strengthen the argument.

[34]번과 거의 동일한 지문이나 Instruction이 다름.

| Argument | In an effort to improve our employees' productivity, we should implement electronic monitoring of employees' Internet use from their workstations. |

94. The vice president of human resources at Climpson Industries sent the following recommendation to the company's president.

"A recent national survey found that the majority of workers with access to the Internet at work had used company computers for personal or recreational activities, such as banking or playing games. In an effort to improve our employees' productivity, we should implement electronic monitoring of employees' Internet use from their workstations. Using electronic monitoring software is the best way to reduce the number of hours Climpson employees spend on personal or recreational activities. We predict that installing software to monitor employees' Internet use will allow us to prevent employees from wasting time, thereby increasing productivity and improving overall profits."

Write a response in which you discuss what questions would need to be answered in order to decide whether the prediction and the argument on which it is based are reasonable. Be sure to explain how the answers to these questions would help to evaluate the prediction.

[34]번과 거의 동일한 지문이나 Instruction이 다름.

Prediction	Installing software to monitor employees' Internet use will allow us to prevent employees from wasting time, thereby increasing productivity and improving overall profits.

35. The following appeared in a letter from the owner of the Sunnyside Towers apartment complex to its manager.

"One month ago, all the shower heads in the first three buildings of the Sunnyside Towers complex were modified to restrict maximum water flow to one-third of what it used to be. Although actual readings of water usage before and after the adjustment are not yet available, the change will obviously result in a considerable savings for Sunnyside Corporation, since the corporation must pay for water each month. Except for a few complaints about low water pressure, no problems with showers have been reported since the adjustment. I predict that modifying shower heads to restrict water flow throughout all twelve buildings in the Sunnyside Towers complex will increase our profits even more dramatically." [Old version 185]

Write a response in which you discuss what questions would need to be answered in order to decide whether the prediction and the argument on which it is based are reasonable. Be sure to explain how the answers to these questions would help to evaluate the prediction.

다음은 Sunnyside Towers 아파트의 소유주가 관리인에게 보낸 편지 내용이다.

"한 달 전, Sunnyside Towers 단지 중 우선 3개 동의 모든 샤워 꼭지가 원래의 1/3 정도 수압으로 제한되도록 조정이 되었다. 아직 조정 전후의 실제 물 사용 계량 수치는 알 수 없으나 회사가 매달 수도료를 납부해야 하기 때문에, 이 조정으로 Sunnyside 회사는 분명히 상당한 비용절감을 할 것이다. 낮은 수압에 대한 소수의 불만을 제외하고는, 이 변경 후 샤워기에 대한 문제점이 보고된 적은 없었다. Sunnyside Towers 단지 내 12개 동 전체에 수압을 제한하도록 샤워 꼭지를 조정한다면, 우리들의 수익도 급격하게 늘 것이다."

> Prediction   Modifying shower heads to restrict water flow throughout all twelve buildings in the Sunnyside Towers complex will increase our profits even more dramatically.

52. The following appeared in a letter from the owner of the Sunnyside Towers apartment building to its manager.

"One month ago, all the shower heads on the first five floors of Sunnyside Towers were modified to restrict the water flow to approximately one-third of its original flow. Although actual readings of water usage before and after the adjustment are not yet available, the change will obviously result in a considerable savings for Sunnyside Corporation, since the corporation must pay for water each month. Except for a few complaints about low water pressure, no problems with showers have been reported since the adjustment. Clearly, restricting water flow throughout all the twenty floors of Sunnyside Towers will increase our profits further."

Write a response in which you discuss what questions would need to be answered in order to decide whether the recommendation is likely to have the predicted result. Be sure to explain how the answers to these questions would help to evaluate the recommendation.

[35]번과 거의 동일한 지문이나 Instruction이 다름.

Recommendation   Restricting water flow throughout all the twenty floors of Sunnyside Towers will increase our profits further.

128. The following appeared in a letter from the owner of the Sunnyside Towers apartment complex to its manager.

"One month ago, all the shower heads in the first three buildings of the Sunnyside Towers complex were modified to restrict maximum water flow to one-third of what it used to be. Although actual readings of water usage before and after the adjustment are not yet available, the change will obviously result in a considerable savings for Sunnyside Corporation, since the corporation must pay for water each month. Except for a few complaints about low water pressure, no problems with showers have been reported since the adjustment. Clearly, modifying shower heads to restrict water flow throughout all twelve buildings in the Sunnyside Towers complex will increase our profits further."

Write a response in which you discuss what specific evidence is needed to evaluate the argument and explain how the evidence would weaken or strengthen the argument.

[35]번과 거의 동일한 지문이나 Instruction이 다름.

Argument	Modifying shower heads to restrict water flow throughout all twelve buildings in the Sunnyside Towers complex will increase our profits further.

129. The following appeared in a letter from the owner of the Sunnyside Towers apartment complex to its manager.

"Last week, all the shower heads in the first three buildings of the Sunnyside Towers complex were modified to restrict maximum water flow to one-third of what it used to be. Although actual readings of water usage before and after the adjustment are not yet available, the change will obviously result in a considerable savings for Sunnyside Corporation, since the corporation must pay for water each month. Except for a few complaints about low water pressure, no problems with showers have been reported since the adjustment. Clearly, modifying shower heads to restrict water flow throughout all twelve buildings in the Sunnyside Towers complex will increase our profits further."

Write a response in which you examine the stated and/or unstated assumptions of the argument. Be sure to explain how the argument depends on these assumptions and what the implications are for the argument if the assumptions prove unwarranted.

[35]번과 거의 동일한 지문이나 Instruction이 다름.

Argument   Modifying shower heads to restrict water flow throughout all twelve buildings in the Sunnyside Towers complex will increase our profits further.

36. The following report appeared in the newsletter of the West Meria Public Health Council.

"An innovative treatment has come to our attention that promises to significantly reduce absenteeism in our schools and workplaces. A study reports that in nearby East Meria, where fish consumption is very high, people visit the doctor only once or twice per year for the treatment of colds. Clearly, eating a substantial amount of fish can prevent colds. Since colds represent the most frequently given reason for absences from school and work, we recommend the daily use of Ichthaid — a nutritional supplement derived from fish oil — as a good way to prevent colds and lower absenteeism." [Old version 38]

Write a response in which you discuss what specific evidence is needed to evaluate the argument and explain how the evidence would weaken or strengthen the argument.

다음은 서부 Meria Public Health 의회 신문에 실린 내용이다.

"학교와 직장에서의 잦은 결석과 결근을 상당히 줄일 것 같은 획기적인 치료법이 우리의 이목을 끌고 있습니다. 한 연구 조사에서, 생선 소비가 아주 높은 인근 동부 Meria 지역 주민들은 감기를 치료하기 위해 단지 연간 1~2회 정도 병원을 가는 것으로 나타났습니다. 분명히 상당한 양의 생선을 먹는 것은 감기를 예방할 수 있습니다. 감기는 학교나 직장에서 결석이나 결근의 가장 잦은 이유가 되기 때문에, 감기를 예방하고 잦은 결석을 줄일 수 있는 좋은 방법으로, 생선기름에서 추출한 건강 보충제인, Ichthaid를 매일 섭취할 것을 권장합니다."

Argument   The daily use of Ichthaid is a good way to prevent colds and lower absenteeism.

163. The following memo appeared in the newsletter of the West Meria Public Health Council.

"An innovative treatment has come to our attention that promises to significantly reduce absenteeism in our schools and workplaces. A study reports that in nearby East Meria, where consumption of the plant beneficia is very high, people visit the doctor only once or twice per year for the treatment of colds. Clearly, eating a substantial amount of beneficia can prevent colds. Since colds are the reason most frequently given for absences from school and work, we recommend the daily use of nutritional supplements derived from beneficia. We predict this will dramatically reduce absenteeism in our schools and workplaces."

Write a response in which you discuss what questions would need to be answered in order to decide whether the recommendation is likely to have the predicted result. Be sure to explain how the answers to these questions would help to evaluate the recommendation.

[36]번과 거의 동일한 지문이나 instruction이 다름.

Recommendation   We recommend the daily use of nutritional supplements derived from beneficia.

166. The following memo appeared in the newsletter of the West Meria Public Health Council.

"An innovative treatment has come to our attention that promises to significantly reduce absenteeism in our schools and workplaces. A study reports that in nearby East Meria, where fish consumption is very high, people visit the doctor only once or twice per year for the treatment of colds. This shows that eating a substantial amount of fish can clearly prevent colds. Furthermore, since colds are the reason most frequently given for absences from school and work, attendance levels will improve. Therefore, we recommend the daily use of a nutritional supplement derived from fish oil as a good way to prevent colds and lower absenteeism."

Write a response in which you discuss what questions would need to be answered in order to decide whether the recommendation and the argument on which it is based are reasonable. Be sure to explain how the answers to these questions would help to evaluate the recommendation.

[36]번과 거의 동일한 지문이나 instruction이 다름.

Recommendation   We recommend the daily use of a nutritional supplement derived from fish oil.

37. The following appeared in a recommendation from the planning department of the city of Transopolis.

"Ten years ago, as part of a comprehensive urban renewal program, the city of Transopolis adapted for industrial use a large area of severely substandard housing near the freeway. Subsequently, several factories were constructed there, crime rates in the area declined, and property tax revenues for the entire city increased. To further revitalize the city, we should now take similar action in a declining residential area on the opposite side of the city. Since some houses and apartments in existing nearby neighborhoods are currently unoccupied, alternate housing for those displaced by this action will be readily available." [Old version 230]

Write a response in which you discuss what specific evidence is needed to evaluate the argument and explain how the evidence would weaken or strengthen the argument.

다음은 Transopolis시의 기획국에서 권장 사항이다.

"10년 전, 포괄적 도시 재개발 프로그램의 일부로, Transopolis시는 고속도로 근처의 넓은 열악한 주택지역을 산업용도로 전용했다. 그 후, 여러 공장들이 그곳에 건설되었으며, 이 지역 범죄율도 줄어들었으며, 전체 도시의 재산세 수입이 증가했다. 시를 더욱 재활성화하기 위해, 도시 반대편에 있는 주거 감소 지역에 유사한 조치를 취해야 한다. 인근 지역에 있는 일부 집들과 아파트들이 현재 비어 있기 때문에, 이 조치로 인한 철거민들을 위한 대체 주택을 쉽게 사용할 수 있을 것이다."

Argument We should adapt for industrial use in a declining residential area on the opposite side of the city.

38. The following appeared in a memo from the new vice president of Sartorian, a company that manufactures men's clothing.

"Five years ago, at a time when we had difficulties in obtaining reliable supplies of high quality wool fabric, we discontinued production of our alpaca overcoat. Now that we have a new fabric supplier, we should resume production. This coat should sell very well: since we have not offered an alpaca overcoat for five years and since our major competitor no longer makes an alpaca overcoat, there will be pent-up customer demand. Also, since the price of most types of clothing has increased in each of the past five years, customers should be willing to pay significantly higher prices for alpaca overcoats than they did five years ago, and our company profits will increase." [Old version 21]

Write a response in which you discuss what specific evidence is needed to evaluate the argument and explain how the evidence would weaken or strengthen the argument.

다음은 한 남성복 제조업체인 Sartorian의 신임 부사장 메모 내용이다.

"5년 전, 고급 털직물의 안정적 공급이 어려웠을 당시, 우리는 알파카 코트의 생산을 중단했다. 지금은 새로운 직물 공급 업자를 확보했기 때문에, 생산을 재개해야만 한다. 이 코트는 아주 잘 팔릴 것으로 본다. 지난 5년간 알파카 코드를 시장에 내놓지 않은 데다가 우리의 주 경쟁업체도 알파카 코트를 만들지 않기 때문에, 참았던 고객수요가 있을 것이다. 아울러 대부분의 의류 가격이 지난 5년간 매년 상승했기 때문에, 고객들은 알파카 코트를 5년 전 그들이 지불했던 것보다 상당히 비싼 가격을 주고 살 것이며, 우리 회사의 수익도 늘어날 것이다."

▌Argument　We should resume production of alpaca overcoat.

95. The following appeared in a memo from the new vice president of Sartorian, a company that manufactures men's clothing.

"Five years ago, at a time when we had difficulty obtaining reliable supplies of high-quality wool fabric, we discontinued production of our popular alpaca overcoat. Now that we have a new fabric supplier, we should resume production. Given the outcry from our customers when we discontinued this product and the fact that none of our competitors offers a comparable product, we can expect pent-up consumer demand for our alpaca coats. This demand and the overall increase in clothing prices will make Sartorian's alpaca overcoats more profitable than ever before."

Write a response in which you examine the stated and/or unstated assumptions of the argument. Be sure to explain how the argument depends on these assumptions and what the implications are for the argument if the assumptions prove unwarranted.

[38]번과 거의 동일한 지문이나 instruction이 다름.

| Argument   We should resume production of alpaca overcoat.

96. The following appeared in a memo from the new vice president of Sartorian, a company that manufactures men's clothing.

"Five years ago, at a time when we had difficulty obtaining reliable supplies of high-quality wool fabric, we discontinued production of our popular alpaca overcoat. Now that we have a new fabric supplier, we should resume production. Given the outcry from our customers when we discontinued this product and the fact that none of our competitors offers a comparable product, we can expect pent-up consumer demand for our alpaca coats. Due to this demand and the overall increase in clothing prices, we can predict that Sartorian's alpaca overcoats will be more profitable than ever before."

Write a response in which you discuss what questions would need to be answered in order to decide whether the prediction and the argument on which it is based are reasonable. Be sure to explain how the answers to these questions would help to evaluate the prediction.

[38]번과 거의 동일한 지문이나 instruction이 다름.

┃ Prediction   Sartorian's alpaca overcoats will be more profitable than ever before.

39. A recent sales study indicates that consumption of seafood dishes in Bay City restaurants has increased by 30 percent during the past five years. Yet there are no currently operating city restaurants whose specialty is seafood. Moreover, the majority of families in Bay City are two-income families, and a nationwide study has shown that such families eat significantly fewer home-cooked meals than they did a decade ago but at the same time express more concern about healthful eating. Therefore, the new Captain Seafood restaurant that specializes in seafood should be quite popular and profitable. [Old version 23]

Write a response in which you discuss what specific evidence is needed to evaluate the argument and explain how the evidence would weaken or strengthen the argument.

최근의 매출 조사는, Bay시 식당들에서 해산물 요리의 소비가 지난 5년 동안 30% 증가했다고 한다. 아직까지 현재 해산물을 전문으로 취급하고 있는 식당은 하나도 없다. 게다가, Bay시의 대부분 가정들은 맞벌이 가정이고, 전국 조사에서 나와 있는 것처럼 이러한 가정들은 10년 전보다 가정에서 식사를 하는 것이 급격하게 줄어들었지만, 동시에 건강식에 더 많은 관심을 표한다. 그러므로 해산물을 전문으로 하는 Captain Seafood 식당은 아주 인기가 있고 수익도 많을 것이다.

Argument   The new Captain Seafood restaurant that specializes in seafood should be quite popular and profitable.

174. A recent sales study indicates that consumption of seafood dishes in Bay City restaurants has increased by 30 percent during the past five years. Yet there are no currently operating city restaurants whose specialty is seafood. Moreover, the majority of families in Bay City are two-income families, and a nationwide study has shown that such families eat significantly fewer home-cooked meals than they did a decade ago but at the same time express more concern about healthful eating. Therefore, the new Captain Seafood restaurant that specializes in seafood should be quite popular and profitable.

Write a response in which you discuss what questions would need to be addressed in order to decide whether the conclusion and the argument on which it is based are reasonable. Be sure to explain how the answers to the questions would help to evaluate the conclusion.

[39]번과 동일한 지문이나 instruction이 다름.

| Argument | The new Captain Seafood restaurant that specializes in seafood should be quite popular and profitable. |

40. Milk and dairy products are rich in vitamin D and calcium — substances essential for building and maintaining bones. Many people therefore say that a diet rich in dairy products can help prevent osteoporosis, a disease that is linked to both environmental and genetic factors and that causes the bones to weaken significantly with age. But a long-term study of a large number of people found that those who consistently consumed dairy products throughout the years of the study have a higher rate of bone fractures than any other participants in the study. Since bone fractures are symptomatic of osteoporosis, this study result shows that a diet rich in dairy products may actually increase, rather than decrease, the risk of osteoporosis. [Old version 34]

Write a response in which you discuss what specific evidence is needed to evaluate the argument and explain how the evidence would weaken or strengthen the argument.

우유와 유지방 제품에는 뼈를 형성시키고 강화시키는 데 아주 중요한 역할을 하는 비타민 D와 칼슘이 많다. 이 때문에 많은 사람들이 유지방이 풍부한 식이요법을 하면, 환경 및 유전적 요인에 의한 손상과, 노화에 의해 뼈가 심각하게 손상을 입는 질병인 골다공증을 억제하는 데 도움이 된다고 믿고 있다. 그러나 상당수의 사람을 대상으로 한 장기간 실험을 통해서 볼 때, 이들 대상자 중 실험 기간 동안 유제품을 꾸준히 섭취한 사람들은 그렇지 않은 사람에 비해 훨씬 높은 골절현상을 보였다. 골절증상은 골다공증이 원인이기 때문에, 이러한 실험 결과는 유제품을 많이 섭취하는 것은 골다공증을 줄이기보다는 오히려 증가시킨다는 것을 보여준다.

Argument   Since bone fractures are symptomatic of osteoporosis, this study result shows that a diet rich in dairy products may actually increase, rather than decrease, the risk of osteoporosis.

41. The following appeared in a health newsletter.

"A ten-year nationwide study of the effectiveness of wearing a helmet while bicycling indicates that ten years ago, approximately 35 percent of all bicyclists reported wearing helmets, whereas today that number is nearly 80 percent. Another study, however, suggests that during the same ten-year period, the number of bicycle-related accidents has increased 200 percent. These results demonstrate that bicyclists feel safer because they are wearing helmets, and they take more risks as a result. Thus, to reduce the number of serious injuries from bicycle accidents, the government should concentrate more on educating people about bicycle safety and less on encouraging or requiring bicyclists to wear helmets." [Old version 120]

Write a response in which you examine the stated and/or unstated assumptions of the argument. Be sure to explain how the argument depends on these assumptions and what the implications are for the argument if the assumptions prove unwarranted.

다음은 한 보건 신문에 실린 내용이다.

"자전거를 탈 때 헬멧을 쓰는 효과에 관한 10년간의 전국적인 연구조사에서, 10년 전에는 자전거를 타는 사람들의 35%가 헬멧을 썼다고 한 데 반해, 오늘날에는 그 수가 거의 80% 라고 한다. 하지만 또 다른 연구에서는 같은 10년 동안, 자전거 관련 사고는 200% 증가했다고 한다. 이 결과는 자전거를 타는 사람들이 헬멧을 착용했기 때문에 더 안전하다고 느끼고, 그 결과 더 위험을 감수한다는 것을 보여준다. 따라서 정부는 자전거 사고로부터 심각한 부상자 수를 줄이기 위해서 자전거의 안전성에 대한 교육에 더 집중하고, 자전거를 타는 사람들에게 헬멧 착용을 권장하거나 강제하지 말아야 한다."

Argument   The government should concentrate more on educating people about bicycle safety and less on encouraging or requiring bicyclists to wear helmets.

123. The following appeared in a health newsletter.

"A ten-year nationwide study of the effectiveness of wearing a helmet while bicycling indicates that ten years ago, approximately 35 percent of all bicyclists reported wearing helmets, whereas today that number is nearly 80 percent. Another study, however, suggests that during the same ten-year period, the number of accidents caused by bicycling has increased 200 percent. These results demonstrate that bicyclists feel safer because they are wearing helmets, and they take more risks as a result. Thus, there is clearly a call for the government to strive to reduce the number of serious injuries from bicycle accidents by launching an education program that concentrates on the factors other than helmet use that are necessary for bicycle safety."

Write a response in which you discuss what questions would need to be answered in order to decide whether the recommendation and the argument on which it is based are reasonable. Be sure to explain how the answers to these questions would help to evaluate the recommendation.

[41]번과 거의 동일한 지문이나 instruction이 다름.

Recommendation The government should launch an education program that concentrates on the factors other than helmet use that are necessary for bicycle safety.

125. The following appeared in a health newsletter.

"A ten-year nationwide study of the effectiveness of wearing a helmet while bicycling indicates that ten years ago, approximately 35 percent of all bicyclists reported wearing helmets, whereas today that number is nearly 80 percent. Another study, however, suggests that during the same ten-year period, the number of accidents caused by bicycling has increased 200 percent. These results demonstrate that bicyclists feel safer because they are wearing helmets, and they take more risks as a result. Thus there is clearly a call for the government to strive to reduce the number of serious injuries from bicycle accidents by launching an education program that concentrates on the factors other than helmet use that are necessary for bicycle safety."

Write a response in which you discuss what specific evidence is needed to evaluate the argument and explain how the evidence would weaken or strengthen the argument.

[123]번과 동일한 문장이나 instruction이 다름.

| Argument | The government should launch an education program that concentrates on the factors other than helmet use that are necessary for bicycle safety. |

42. The following is a letter to the head of the tourism bureau on the island of Tria.

"Erosion of beach sand along the shores of Tria Island is a serious threat to our island and our tourist industry. In order to stop the erosion, we should charge people for using the beaches. Although this solution may annoy a few tourists in the short term, it will raise money for replenishing the sand. Replenishing the sand, as was done to protect buildings on the nearby island of Batia, will help protect buildings along our shores, thereby reducing these buildings' risk of additional damage from severe storms. And since beaches and buildings in the area will be preserved, Tria's tourist industry will improve over the long term." [Old version 152]

Write a response in which you discuss what specific evidence is needed to evaluate the argument and explain how the evidence would weaken or strengthen the argument.

다음은 Tria섬의 관광공사 사장에게 보낸 편지이다.

"Tria섬 해안을 따라 있는 해변 모래의 침식은 우리 섬과 관광산업에 아주 심각한 위협이다. 이러한 침식을 막으려면, 이용객들에게 해변 이용료를 부과해야 한다. 이러한 방안이 단기적으로 소수의 관광객들을 짜증나게 할 수 있으나 모래를 보충하는 데 드는 돈을 모금할 수 있을 것이다. 모래를 보충하면, 인근의 Batia섬이 건물을 보호한 것처럼, 해안가에 있는 건물들을 보호할 것이고, 그렇게 해서 강풍으로 인한 이 건물들의 추가 피해의 위험을 줄일 수 있다. 그리고 이 지역의 해변과 건물들이 보존되기 때문에, Tria의 관광객 산업은 장기간에 걸쳐 향상될 것이다."

Argument   In order to stop the erosion, we should charge people for using the beaches.

43. The following appeared in a memorandum written by the chairperson of the West Egg Town Council.

"Two years ago, consultants predicted that West Egg's landfill, which is used for garbage disposal, would be completely filled within five years. During the past two years, however, the town's residents have been recycling twice as much material as they did in previous years. Next month the amount of recycled material — which includes paper, plastic, and metal — should further increase, since charges for pickup of other household garbage will double. Furthermore, over 90 percent of the respondents to a recent survey said that they would do more recycling in the future. Because of our town's strong commitment to recycling, the available space in our landfill should last for considerably longer than predicted." [Old version 11]

Write a response in which you discuss what specific evidence is needed to evaluate the argument and explain how the evidence would weaken or strengthen the argument.

다음은 West Egg Town시 의회 의장이 쓴 메모 내용이다.

"2년 전, 컨설턴트들은 쓰레기 처리장으로 사용되던, West Egg의 매립지가 5년 내에 포화상태가 될 것이라고 예측했다. 하지만 지난 2년 동안, 주민들은 과거에 했던 것보다 2배가량의 물자를 재활용해 왔다. 다음 달에는, 가정 쓰레기 수거 비용이 배가 되기 때문에 종이, 플라스틱, 그리고 금속을 포함한, 재활용 물자의 양은 더욱 증가할 것이다. 더구나 최근 조사 응답자의 90% 이상이 앞으로도 더 많은 재활용을 할 것이라고 대답했다. 재활용에 대한 우리 고장의 강력한 의지 때문에 쓰레기 매립지의 가용공간은 예상했던 것보다 상당히 오랫동안 쓸 수 있을 것이다."

Argument   Because of our town's strong commitment to recycling, the available space in our landfill should last for considerably longer than predicted.

44. The following appeared in a letter to the editor of a journal on environmental issues.

"Over the past year, the Crust Copper Company (CCC) has purchased over 10,000 square miles of land in the tropical nation of West Fredonia. Mining copper on this land will inevitably result in pollution and, since West Fredonia is the home of several endangered animal species, in environmental disaster. But such disasters can be prevented if consumers simply refuse to purchase products that are made with CCC's copper unless the company abandons its mining plans." [Old version 141]

Write a response in which you examine the stated and/or unstated assumptions of the argument. Be sure to explain how the argument depends on these assumptions and what the implications are for the argument if the assumptions prove unwarranted.

다음은 한 환경 문제 잡지의 편집장에게 보낸 편지 내용이다.

"지난 한 해 동안, Crust Copper 회사(CCC)는 열대 국가인 West Fredonia에 10,000스퀘어마일이 넘는 땅을 사들였다. 이 지역에서 구리 채광은, 필연적으로 오염을 초래할 것이고, West Fredonia가 몇몇 멸종 위기에 치힌 동물 종들의 서식지이기 때문에, 환경 재앙을 초래할 것이다.
그러나 이러한 재앙은, CCC 회사가 채광 계획을 포기하지 않는 한, 소비자들이 단순히 CCC의 구리로 제조된 제품들의 구매를 거부한다면 막을 수 있다."

Argument   Environmental disasters can be prevented if consumers simply refuse to purchase products that are made with CCC's copper unless the company abandons its mining plans.

45. The following is part of a memorandum from the president of Humana University.

"Last year the number of students who enrolled in online degree programs offered by nearby Omni University increased by 50 percent. During the same year, Omni showed a significant decrease from prior years in expenditures for dormitory and classroom space, most likely because instruction in the online programs takes place via the Internet. In contrast, over the past three years, enrollment at Humana University has failed to grow, and the cost of maintaining buildings has increased along with our budget deficit. To address these problems, Humana University will begin immediately to create and actively promote online degree programs like those at Omni. We predict that instituting these online degree programs will help Humana both increase its total enrollment and solve its budget problems." [Old version 39]

Write a response in which you discuss what questions would need to be answered in order to decide whether the prediction and the argument on which it is based are reasonable. Be sure to explain how the answers to these questions would help to evaluate the prediction.

다음은 Humana 대학 총장의 메모 내용이다.

"지난해 인근 Omni 대학에서 제공한 온라인 학위 프로그램 등록생 수가 50%나 증가했다. 같은 해 동안, Omni 대학은 전년도에 비해 기숙사와 강의실을 위한 지출이 대폭 삭감된 것으로 나타났는데, 이는 인터넷을 통한 온라인 프로그램 강의가 대신했기 때문일 것 같다. 반면에 지난 삼 년 동안, Humana 대학의 등록은 증가하지 못했고 건물 유지비는 예산 적자와 함께 증가되었다. Humana 대학은 이러한 문제점들을 다루기 위해서 Omni 대학 같은 온라인 학위 프로그램을 즉시 신설하고 적극적으로 홍보해야 한다. 이러한 온라인 학위 프로그램의 도입은 Humana 대학의 전체적인 등록율의 증가와 동시에 예산 문제 해결에 도움이 될 것으로 예측한다."

| Prediction | Instituting these online degree programs will help Humana both increase its total enrollment and solve its budget problems. |

| Argument | Humana University should begin immediately to create and actively promote online degree programs like those at Omni. |

49. The following is part of a memorandum from the president of Humana University.

"Last year the number of students who enrolled in online degree programs offered by nearby Omni University increased by 50 percent. During the same year, Omni showed a significant decrease from prior years in expenditures for dormitory and classroom space, most likely because online instruction takes place via the Internet. In contrast, over the past three years, enrollment at Humana University has failed to grow and the cost of maintaining buildings has increased. Thus, to increase enrollment and solve the problem of budget deficits at Humana University, we should initiate and actively promote online degree programs like those at Omni."

Write a response in which you examine the stated and/or unstated assumptions of the argument. Be sure to explain how the argument depends on these assumptions and what the implications are for the argument if the assumptions prove unwarranted.

[45]번과 거의 동일한 지문이나 instruction이 다름.

Argument   Humana University should initiate and actively promote online degree programs like those at Omni.

46. The following appeared in a health magazine published in Corpora.

"Medical experts say that only one-quarter of Corpora's citizens meet the current standards for adequate physical fitness, even though twenty years ago, one-half of all of Corpora's citizens met the standards as then defined. But these experts are mistaken when they suggest that spending too much time using computers has caused a decline in fitness. Since overall fitness levels are highest in regions of Corpora where levels of computer ownership are also highest, it is clear that using computers has not made citizens less physically fit. Instead, as shown by this year's unusually low expenditures on fitness-related products and services, the recent decline in the economy is most likely the cause, and fitness levels will improve when the economy does." [Old version 48]

Write a response in which you examine the stated and/or unstated assumptions of the argument. Be sure to explain how the argument depends on these assumptions and what the implications are for the argument if the assumptions prove unwarranted.

다음은 Corpora에서 발간된 건강 잡지에 실린 내용이다.

"비록 Corpora 시민의 1/4만이 현재의 적절한 체력 기준을 충족하지만, 20년 전에는 Corpora 시민의 절반이 그 당시 정한 기준을 충족했었다고 전문가들은 말한다. 그러나 이 전문가들이 컴퓨터 사용에 너무 많은 시간을 소비해서 체력이 약화된 것이라고 지적을 한 것은, 이들이 잘못 판단하고 있는 것이다. 전반적인 건강 상태가 최상인 Corpora 지역에서 컴퓨터 보유율이 가장 높기 때문에, 컴퓨터 사용으로 시민들이 약해지지 않았다는 것은 분명하다. 그 대신에 금년도에 건강관련 제품들과 서비스에 대한 지출이 현저하게 낮았던 것으로 볼 때, 최근 경제 불황이 주요인으로 보이며, 건강 상태도 경제 성장에 따라 향상될 것으로 보인다."

| Argument   Fitness levels will improve in Corpora when the economy does.

47. The following appeared in a memorandum from the owner of Movies Galore, a chain of movie-rental stores.

"Because of declining profits, we must reduce operating expenses at Movies Galore's ten movie-rental stores. Raising prices is not a good option, since we are famous for our low prices. Instead, we should reduce our operating hours. Last month our store in downtown Marston reduced its hours by closing at 6:00 p.m. rather than 9:00 p.m. and reduced its overall inventory by no longer stocking any DVD released more than five years ago. Since we have received very few customer complaints about these new policies, we should now adopt them at all other Movies Galore stores as our best strategies for improving profits." [Old version 213]

Write a response in which you discuss what specific evidence is needed to evaluate the argument and explain how the evidence would weaken or strengthen the argument.

다음은 비디오 대여점 체인인 Movies Galore의 주인이 한 메모 내용이다.

"수익이 줄고 있기 때문에, 우리는 Movies Galore 10개 체인점의 운영 비용을 줄여야만 한다. 우리는 저가로 유명하기 때문에, 가격을 올리는 것은 좋은 방안이 아니다. 그 대신, 영업시간을 줄여야 한다. 지난달 Marston 시내에 있는 가게가 저녁 9시가 아닌 6시에 문을 닫아 시간을 줄이고, 출시된 지 5년 이상 된 DVD들을 더 이상 비치하지 않음으로써 전체 재고를 줄였다. 이러한 새 정책에 대해서 극히 일부 고객들로부터 불평을 접수했으므로, 수익을 늘리기 위한 최상의 전략으로 이제 나머지 모든 Movies Galore 가게에서도 이 정책을 도입해야 한다."

| Argument | We should reduce our operating hours at all Movies Galore stores as our best strategies for improving profits. |

111. The following appeared in a memorandum from the owner of Movies Galore, a chain of movie-rental stores.

"In order to stop the recent decline in our profits, we must reduce operating expenses at Movies Galore's ten movie-rental stores. Since we are famous for our special bargains, raising our rental prices is not a viable way to improve profits. Last month our store in downtown Marston significantly decreased its operating expenses by closing at 6:00 P.M. rather than 9:00 P.M. and by reducing its stock by eliminating all movies released more than five years ago. By implementing similar changes in our other stores, Movies Galore can increase profits without jeopardizing our reputation for offering great movies at low prices."

Write a response in which you examine the stated and/or unstated assumptions of the argument. Be sure to explain how the argument depends on these assumptions and what the implications are for the argument if the assumptions prove unwarranted.

[47]번과 거의 동일한 지문이나 instruction이 다름.

Argument In order to stop the recent decline in our profits, we must reduce operating expenses at Movies Galore's ten movie-rental stores.

112. The following appeared in a memorandum from the owner of Movies Galore, a chain of movie-rental stores.

"In order to reverse the recent decline in our profits, we must reduce operating expenses at Movies Galore's ten movie-rental stores. Since we are famous for our special bargains, raising our rental prices is not a viable way to improve profits. Last month our store in downtown Marston significantly decreased its operating expenses by closing at 6:00 p.m. rather than 9:00 p.m. and by reducing its stock by eliminating all movies released more than five years ago. Therefore, in order to increase profits without jeopardizing our reputation for offering great movies at low prices, we recommend implementing similar changes in our other nine Movies Galore stores."

Write a response in which you discuss what questions would need to be answered in order to decide whether the recommendation and the argument on which it is based are reasonable. Be sure to explain how the answers to these questions would help to evaluate the recommendation.

[47]번과 거의 동일한 지문이나 instruction이 다름.

Recommendation   We should we must reduce operating expenses by closing at 6:00 p.m. rather than 9:00 p.m. and by reducing its stock by eliminating all movies released more than five years ago.

48. The following appeared in a magazine article about planning for retirement.

"Clearview should be a top choice for anyone seeking a place to retire, because it has spectacular natural beauty and a consistent climate. Another advantage is that housing costs in Clearview have fallen significantly during the past year, and taxes remain lower than those in neighboring towns. Moreover, Clearview's mayor promises many new programs to improve schools, streets, and public services. And best of all, retirees in Clearview can also expect excellent health care as they grow older, since the number of physicians in the area is far greater than the national average." [Old version 216]

Write a response in which you discuss what specific evidence is needed to evaluate the argument and explain how the evidence would weaken or strengthen the argument.

다음은 은퇴 계획에 관해 한 잡지 기사에 실린 내용이다.

"뛰어난 자연 경관과 변함없는 기후 때문에, Clearview는 은퇴할 곳을 찾는 사람들에게 최고의 곳이 될 것이다. 또 다른 이점은 Clearview의 주택가격이 지난해 상당히 떨어졌고, 이웃 지역에 비해 세금이 낮다는 것이다. 더욱이, Clearview 시장은 학교, 도로, 그리고 공공서비스를 증진시킬 많은 새로운 계획을 약속했다. 무엇보다도 이 지역 의료진 수는 전국 평균보다 훨씬 많으므로, Clearview에 사는 은퇴자들은 나이를 먹으면서 훌륭한 의료 서비스를 받을 수 있다."

Argument   Clearview should be a top choice for anyone seeking a place to retire.

50. An ancient, traditional remedy for insomnia — the scent of lavender flowers — has now been proved effective. In a recent study, 30 volunteers with chronic insomnia slept each night for three weeks on lavender-scented pillows in a controlled room where their sleep was monitored electronically. During the first week, volunteers continued to take their usual sleeping medication. They slept soundly but wakened feeling tired. At the beginning of the second week, the volunteers discontinued their sleeping medication. During that week, they slept less soundly than the previous week and felt even more tired. During the third week, the volunteers slept longer and more soundly than in the previous two weeks. Therefore, the study proves that lavender cures insomnia within a short period of time. [Old version 167]

Write a response in which you discuss what specific evidence is needed to evaluate the argument and explain how the evidence would weaken or strengthen the argument.

"불면증에 대한 고대의 한 전통 치료법이－라벤더 향－이제 아주 효과적인 것으로 입증되었다. 최근의 한 연구에서, 만성 불면증을 가진 30여 명의 자원자들이, 그들의 수면이 전자적으로 감지되는 통제된 방안에서, 3주 동안 매일 라벤더 향이 나는 베개를 베고 잤다. 첫 주에, 자원자들은 일반 수면제를 복용했다. 숙면을 취했으나 일어나서 피곤함을 느꼈다. 둘째 주부터는, 수면제 복용을 중단했다. 이 주에, 그들은 첫째 주에 비해 숙면을 취하지 못했고, 피곤함도 더 느꼈다. 셋째 주에는, 앞서의 2주간에 비해 더 오래 숙면을 취했다. 그러므로 이 연구는 짧은 기간에 라벤더가 불면증을 치료한다는 것을 입증한 것이다."

Argument The study proves that lavender cures insomnia within a short period of time.

53. The following appeared in a health magazine.

"The citizens of Forsythe have adopted more healthful lifestyles. Their responses to a recent survey show that in their eating habits they conform more closely to government nutritional recommendations than they did ten years ago. Furthermore, there has been a fourfold increase in sales of food products containing kiran, a substance that a scientific study has shown reduces cholesterol. This trend is also evident in reduced sales of sulia, a food that few of the most healthy citizens regularly eat." [Old version 201]

Write a response in which you discuss what specific evidence is needed to evaluate the argument and explain how the evidence would weaken or strengthen the argument.

다음은 건강 잡지에 실린 내용이다.

"Forsythe 시민들은 더 건강한 생활방식을 해 왔다. 최근 조사에서, 그들의 식습관이 10년 전에 비해 정부의 영양섭취 권장 사항을 더 가깝게 따른다고 응답한다. 더욱이, 과학적 연구에 의해 콜레스테롤을 떨어뜨린다고 알려진 물질인, kiran이 포함된 음식 식품의 판매가 4배 증가했다. 이러한 경향은 대부분의 건강한 시민들은 거의 먹지 않는 음식인, sulia 판매가 감소했다는 것을 보면 더욱 명확하다."

▌Argument   The citizens of Forsythe have adopted more healthful lifestyles.

144. The citizens of Forsythe have adopted more healthful lifestyles. Their responses to a recent survey show that in their eating habits they conform more closely to government nutritional recommendations than they did ten years ago. Furthermore, there has been a fourfold increase in sales of food products containing kiran, a substance that a scientific study has shown reduces cholesterol. This trend is also evident in reduced sales of sulia, a food that few of the healthiest citizens regularly eat.

Write a response in which you examine the stated and/or unstated assumptions of the argument. Be sure to explain how the argument depends on these assumptions and what the implications are for the argument if the assumptions prove unwarranted.

[53]번과 거의 동일한 지문이나 instruction이 다름.

┃ Argument   The citizens of Forsythe have adopted more healthful lifestyles.

151. Benton City residents have adopted healthier lifestyles. A recent survey of city residents shows that the eating habits of city residents conform more closely to government nutritional recommendations than they did ten years ago. During those ten years, local sales of food products containing kiran, a substance that a scientific study has shown reduces cholesterol, have increased fourfold, while sales of sulia, a food rarely eaten by the healthiest residents, have declined dramatically. Because of these positive changes in the eating habits of Benton City residents, we predict that the obesity rate in the city will soon be well below the national average.

Write a response in which you discuss what questions would need to be answered in order to decide whether the prediction and the argument on which it is based are reasonable. Be sure to explain how the answers to these questions would help to evaluate the prediction.

[53]번과 거의 동일한 지문이나 instruction이 다름.

Prediction The obesity rate in Benton City will soon be well below the national average.

54. Humans arrived in the Kaliko Islands about 7,000 years ago, and within 3,000 years most of the large mammal species that had lived in the forests of the Kaliko Islands had become extinct. Yet humans cannot have been a factor in the species' extinctions, because there is no evidence that the humans had any significant contact with the mammals. Further, archaeologists have discovered numerous sites where the bones of fish had been discarded, but they found no such areas containing the bones of large mammals, so the humans cannot have hunted the mammals. Therefore, some climate change or other environmental factor must have caused the species' extinctions. [Old version 202]

Write a response in which you examine the stated and/or unstated assumptions of the argument. Be sure to explain how the argument depends on these assumptions and what the implications are for the argument if the assumptions prove unwarranted.

인간은 약 7천 년 전에 Kaliko섬으로 왔고, 3천 년 사이에 Kaliko섬 숲속에 살았던 대부분의 거대한 포유류 종들이 멸종되었다. 그래도 인간이 멸종의 주요 원인은 아니다. 인간이 이들 포유류들과 어떠한 중요한 접촉이 있었다는 증거가 전혀 없기 때문이다. 더욱이 고고학자들은 어류의 뼈들이 버려진 여러 장소들을 발견했으나 이들 지역에서 포유류의 뼈는 발견되지 않았으니, 인간이 포유류를 사냥하지 않았을 것이다. 그러므로 어떤 기후변화나 다른 환경 요소로 인해 포유류가 멸종했을 것이다.

Argument   Some climate change or other environmental factor must have caused the species' extinctions in the Kaliko Islands.

165. Humans arrived in the Kaliko Islands about 7,000 years ago, and within 3,000 years most of the large mammal species that had lived in the forests of the Kaliko Islands were extinct. Previous archaeological findings have suggested that early humans generally relied on both fishing and hunting for food; since archaeologists have discovered numerous sites in the Kaliko Islands where the bones of fish were discarded, it is likely that the humans also hunted the mammals. Furthermore, researchers have uncovered simple tools, such as stone knives, that could be used for hunting. The only clear explanation is that humans caused the extinction of the various mammal species through excessive hunting.

Write a response in which you discuss one or more alternative explanations that could rival the proposed explanation and explain how your explanation(s) can plausibly account for the facts presented in the argument.

약 7천 년 전에 인간이 Kaliko섬으로 왔고, 3천 년 사이에 Kaliko섬 숲속에 살았던 대부분의 거대한 포유류 종들이 멸종되었다. 예전의 고고학적 발견들은 초기 인간들이 먹을 것을 위해서 주로 낚시와 사냥에 의존했다는 것을 암시한다. 고고학자들이 Kaliko섬에서 어류의 뼈들이 버려진 여러 장소들을 발견했고, 인간은 또한 포유류들을 사냥했을 것이기 때문이다. 더욱이, 연구가들은 사냥에 사용되었을 만한, 돌칼 같은 단순한 도구들을 발견했다. 인간이 과도한 포획으로 다양한 포유류의 종을 멸종하게 했다는 것만이 명쾌한 설명이다.

| Argument | The only clear explanation is that humans caused the extinction of the various mammal species through excessive hunting. |

55. The following appeared in an editorial in a business magazine.

"Although the sales of Whirlwind video games have declined over the past two years, a recent survey of video-game players suggests that this sales trend is about to be reversed. The survey asked video-game players what features they thought were most important in a video game. According to the survey, players prefer games that provide lifelike graphics, which require the most up-to-date computers. Whirlwind has just introduced several such games with an extensive advertising campaign directed at people ten to twenty-five years old, the age-group most likely to play video games. It follows, then, that the sales of Whirlwind video games are likely to increase dramatically in the next few months." [Old version 147]

Write a response in which you examine the stated and/or unstated assumptions of the argument. Be sure to explain how the argument depends on these assumptions and what the implications are for the argument if the assumptions prove unwarranted.

다음은 한 비즈니스 잡지에 실린 사설 내용이다.

"Whirlwind 비디오 게임 매출이 지난 2년 동안 계속 감소해오긴 했으나 최근 비디오 게이머에 대한 조사를 보면 이런 매출 추세가 반전될 것으로 보인다. 이 조사는, 게이머들에게 게임에서 가장 중요한 기능이 어떤 것이었는가를 묻는 것이었다. 조사에 따르면, 게이머들은 실물과 똑같은 그래픽이 지원되는 게임을 선호하며, 이러한 기능은 높은 컴퓨터 성능이 요구된다. Whirlwind사는 게임을 가장 많이 즐기는 연령대인 10세에서 25세 사이의 청소년들을 겨냥한 집중적인 광고와 함께 이런 몇 개의 비디오 게임을 출시했다. 그래서 Whirlwind 비디오 게임 매출이 앞으로 몇 달 사이에 급격하게 증가할 것으로 보인다."

Argument The sales of Whirlwind video games are likely to increase dramatically in the next few months.

56. The following appeared in a memo from the vice president of marketing at Dura-Sock, Inc.

"A recent study of our customers suggests that our company is wasting the money it spends on its patented Endure manufacturing process, which ensures that our socks are strong enough to last for two years. We have always advertised our use of the Endure process, but the new study shows that despite our socks' durability, our average customer actually purchases new Dura-Socks every three months. Furthermore, our customers surveyed in our largest market, northeastern United States cities, say that they most value Dura-Socks' stylish appearance and availability in many colors. These findings suggest that we can increase our profits by discontinuing use of the Endure manufacturing process." [Old version 111]

Write a response in which you examine the stated and/or unstated assumptions of the argument. Be sure to explain how the argument depends on these assumptions and what the implications are for the argument if the assumptions prove unwarranted.

다음은 Dura-Sock 회사의 마케팅 담당 부사장의 메모 내용이다.

"우리 소비자들에 대한 최근 조사는, 내구성 공정의 특허에 들어가는 비용이 낭비라고 말하고 있는데, 이것(특허)은 우리 양말이 2년 동안을 충분하게 견딜 수 있도록 강하게 해주는 특허이다. 우리는 항상 이 내구성 공법 사용을 광고했으나 우리 양말의 내구성에도 불구하고, 실제로 보통 고객들은 새 Dura-Socks을 석 달마다 구매하는 것으로, 새 조사에서는 나타났다. 더욱이 우리의 가장 큰 시장인, 미국의 북동부지역에서 실시한 시장조사에 응답한 고객들은, Dura-Socks의 모양과 다양한 색상을 가장 가치 있게 평했다. 이러한 결과는 우리가 내구성 공법을 중단함으로써 수익을 늘릴 수 있다는 것을 시사해 준다."

Argument We can increase our profits by discontinuing use of the Endure manufacturing process.

57. The following appeared in a memo from the vice president of marketing at Dura-Sock, Inc.

"A recent study of our customers suggests that our company is wasting the money it spends on its patented Endure manufacturing process, which ensures that our socks are strong enough to last for two years. We have always advertised our use of the Endure process, but the new study shows that despite our socks' durability, our average customer actually purchases new Dura-Socks every three months. Furthermore, our customers surveyed in our largest market, northeastern United States cities, say that they most value Dura-Socks' stylish appearance and availability in many colors. These findings suggest that we can increase our profits by discontinuing use of the Endure manufacturing process."

Write a response in which you discuss what specific evidence is needed to evaluate the argument and explain how the evidence would weaken or strengthen the argument.

[56]번과 동일한 지문이나 instruction이 다름.

Argument   We can increase our profits by discontinuing use of the Endure manufacturing process.

82. The following appeared in a memo from the vice president of marketing at Dura-Socks, Inc.

"A recent study of Dura-Socks customers suggests that our company is wasting the money it spends on its patented Endure manufacturing process, which ensures that our socks are strong enough to last for two years. We have always advertised our use of the Endure process, but the new study shows that despite the socks' durability, our customers, on average, actually purchase new Dura-Socks every three months. Furthermore, customers surveyed in our largest market — northeastern United States cities — say that they most value Dura-Socks' stylish appearance and availability in many colors. These findings suggest that we can increase our profits by discontinuing use of the Endure manufacturing process."

Write a response in which you discuss what questions would need to be answered in order to decide whether the recommendation and the argument on which it is based are reasonable. Be sure to explain how the answers to these questions would help to evaluate the recommendation.

[56]번과 동일한 지문이나 instruction이 다름.

Recommendation We can increase our profits by discontinuing use of the Endure manufacturing process.

59. The following appeared in a memo from the president of Bower Builders, a company that constructs new homes.

"A nationwide survey reveals that the two most-desired home features are a large family room and a large, well-appointed kitchen. A number of homes in our area built by our competitor Domus Construction have such features and have sold much faster and at significantly higher prices than the national average. To boost sales and profits, we should increase the size of the family rooms and kitchens in all the homes we build and should make state-of-the-art kitchens a standard feature. Moreover, our larger family rooms and kitchens can come at the expense of the dining room, since many of our recent buyers say they do not need a separate dining room for family meals." [Old version 94]

Write a response in which you examine the stated and/or unstated assumptions of the argument. Be sure to explain how the argument depends on these assumptions and what the implications are for the argument if the assumptions prove unwarranted.

다음은 한 신규 주택건설업체인, Bower Builders의 사장의 메모 내용이다.

"전국 조사에서, 가장 인기 있는 집의 구조는 넓은 거실과 잘 꾸며진 부엌으로 나타났다. 경쟁 업체인 Domus Construction이 우리 지역에 건설한 다수의 주택들은 이러한 시설들을 갖추고 있어서 훨씬 잘 팔리고, 있고, 가격도 전국 평균보다 훨씬 비싸다. 판매를 늘리고 수익을 늘리려면, 우리가 짓는 모든 주택에서 거실과 부엌의 크기를 늘리고, 최신식 부엌을 기본 사양으로 해야만 한다. 게다가, 최근의 우리 구입자들이 가족의 식사를 위해서 별도의 식당이 필요 없다고 하니, 넓은 거실과 부엌은 식당의 비용으로 충당할 수 있다."

Argument   We should increase the size of the family rooms and kitchens in all the homes we build and should make state-of-the-art kitchens a standard feature.

60. The following appeared in a letter from a firm providing investment advice for a client.

"Most homes in the northeastern United States, where winters are typically cold, have traditionally used oil as their major fuel for heating. Last heating season that region experienced 90 days with below-normal temperatures, and climate forecasters predict that this weather pattern will continue for several more years. Furthermore, many new homes are being built in the region in response to recent population growth. Because of these trends, we predict an increased demand for heating oil and recommend investment in Consolidated Industries, one of whose major business operations is the retail sale of home heating oil." [Old version 66]

Write a response in which you examine the stated and/or unstated assumptions of the argument. Be sure to explain how the argument depends on these assumptions and what the implications are for the argument if the assumptions prove unwarranted.

다음은 고객에게 투자 조언을 하는 한 회사의 편지 내용이다.

"일반적으로 겨울이 추운, 미국 북동부 지역에 있는 대부분 집들은, 전통적으로 난방의 주 연료로 기름을 사용한다. 지난해 난방철, 이 지역은 90일 간 평균 온도 이하의 날씨를 기록했고, 기상 관측자들은 앞으로도 수년간 동일한 날씨가 계속될 것이라고 내다보았다. 더구나 지난해 최근의 인구 증가에 따라 이 지역에 많은 신규 주택이 지어졌다. 이러한 추세 때문에, 우리는 난방용 기름에 대한 수요 증가를 예상하고, 가정용 난방 연료 소매를 주 사업으로 하고 있는, Consolidated Industries에 투자할 것을 추천한다."

> Argument We predict an increased demand for heating oil and recommend investment in Consolidated Industries, one of whose major business operations is the retail sale of home heating oil.

150. The following appeared in a letter from a firm providing investment advice to a client.

"Homes in the northeastern United States, where winters are typically cold, have traditionally used oil as their major fuel for heating. Last year that region experienced 90 days with below-average temperatures, and climate forecasters at Waymarsh University predict that this weather pattern will continue for several more years. Furthermore, many new homes have been built in this region during the past year. Because these developments will certainly result in an increased demand for heating oil, we recommend investment in Consolidated Industries, one of whose major business operations is the retail sale of home heating oil."

Write a response in which you discuss what questions would need to be answered in order to decide whether the recommendation and the argument on which it is based are reasonable. Be sure to explain how the answers to these questions would help to evaluate the recommendation.

[60]번과 거의 동일한 지문이나 instruction이 다름.

Recommendation   Invest in Consolidated Industries, one of whose major business operations is the retail sale of home heating oil.

154. The following appeared in a letter from a firm providing investment advice to a client.

"Homes in the northeastern United States, where winters are typically cold, have traditionally used oil as their major fuel for heating. Last year that region experienced twenty days with below-average temperatures, and local weather forecasters throughout the region predict that this weather pattern will continue for several more years. Furthermore, many new homes have been built in this region during the past year. Based on these developments, we predict a large increase in the demand for heating oil. Therefore, we recommend investment in Consolidated Industries, one of whose major business operations is the retail sale of home heating oil."

Write a response in which you discuss what questions would need to be answered in order to decide whether the recommendation and the argument on which it is based are reasonable. Be sure to explain how the answers to these questions would help to evaluate the recommendation.

[150]번과 거의 동일한 지문이며, instruction도 같음.

Recommendation   Invest in Consolidated Industries, one of whose major business operations is the retail sale of home heating oil.

155. The following appeared in a letter from a firm providing investment advice to a client.

"Homes in the northeastern United States, where winters are typically cold, have traditionally used oil as their major fuel for heating. Last year that region experienced twenty days with below-average temperatures, and local weather forecasters throughout the region predict that this weather pattern will continue for several more years. Furthermore, many new homes have been built in this region during the past year. Because of these developments, we predict an increased demand for heating oil and recommend investment in Consolidated Industries, one of whose major business operations is the retail sale of home heating oil."

Write a response in which you discuss what specific evidence is needed to evaluate the argument and explain how the evidence would weaken or strengthen the argument.

[150]번과 거의 동일한 지문이나 instruction이 다름.

Argument Invest in Consolidated Industries, one of whose major business operations is the retail sale of home heating oil.

145. The following appeared in a memo to the board of directors of a company that specializes in the delivery of heating oil.

"Most homes in the northeastern United States, where winters are typically cold, have traditionally used oil as their major fuel for heating. Last heating season, that region experienced 90 days with below-normal temperatures, and climate forecasters predict that this weather pattern will continue for several more years. Furthermore, many new homes are being built in the region in response to recent population growth. Because of these trends, we can safely predict that this region will experience an increased demand for heating oil during the next five years."

Write a response in which you discuss what questions would need to be answered in order to decide whether the prediction and the argument on which it is based are reasonable. Be sure to explain how the answers to these questions would help to evaluate the prediction.

다음은 난방용 기름 배달을 전문으로 하는 한 회사의 이사회에 보낸 메모의 내용이다.

"일반적으로 겨울이 추운, 미국 북동부 지역에 있는 대부분 집들은, 전통적으로 난방의 주 연료로 기름을 사용한다. 지난해 난방철, 이 지역은 90일간 평균 온도 이하의 날씨를 기록했고, 기상 관측자들은 앞으로도 수년간 동일한 날씨가 계속될 것이라고 예측했다. 더구나 지난해 최근의 인구 증가에 따라 이 지역에 많은 신규 주택이 지어졌다. 이러한 추세 때문에, 우리는 이 지역에서 난방용 기름에 대한 수요가 5년간은 더 지속될 것이라고 안심하고 예측할 수 있다."

Prediction We can safely predict that this region will experience an increased demand for heating oil during the next five years.

146. The following appeared in a memo to the board of directors of a company that specializes in the delivery of heating oil.

"Most homes in the northeastern United States, where winters are typically cold, have traditionally used oil as their major fuel for heating. Last heating season, that region experienced 90 days with below-normal temperatures, and climate forecasters predict that this weather pattern will continue for several more years. Furthermore, many new homes are being built in the region in response to recent population growth. Because of these trends, we can safely predict that this region will experience an increased demand for heating oil during the next five years."

Write a response in which you discuss what specific evidence is needed to evaluate the argument and explain how the evidence would weaken or strengthen the argument.

[145]번과 동일한 지문이나 instruction이 다름.

Argument We can safely predict that this region will experience an increased demand for heating oil during the next five years.

76. The following appeared in a newsletter offering advice to investors.

"Over 80 percent of the respondents to a recent survey indicated a desire to reduce their intake of foods containing fats and cholesterol, and today low-fat products abound in many food stores. Since many of the food products currently marketed by Old Dairy Industries are high in fat and cholesterol, the company's sales are likely to diminish greatly and company profits will no doubt decrease. We therefore advise Old Dairy stockholders to sell their shares, and other investors not to purchase stock in this company." [Old version 15]

Write a response in which you discuss what questions would need to be answered in order to decide whether the advice and the argument on which it is based are reasonable. Be sure to explain how the answers to these questions would help to evaluate the advice.

다음은 어느 신문에 실린 투자자들에 대한 조언의 글이다.

"최근 설문조사에 대한 응답자 중 80% 이상이 지방과 콜레스테롤이 함유된 음식의 섭취를 줄이고 싶다고 했고, 요즘은 많은 식료품가게에서 저지방 제품들을 많이 취급하고 있다. 현재 Old Dairy Industries가 판매하고 있는 많은 음식 제품들은 지방과 콜레스테롤이 높기 때문에, 이 회사의 매출이 격감할 것으로 보이며 당연히 매출이익도 줄어들 것이다. 따라서 이 회사의 주주들은 주식을 매각하고, 다른 주식 투자가들도 이 회사의 주식을 매입하지 않는 것이 좋다."

Advice　We therefore advise Old Dairy stockholders to sell their shares, and other investors not to purchase stock in this company.

61. The following appeared in an article in the Grandview Beacon.

"For many years the city of Grandview has provided annual funding for the Grandview Symphony. Last year, however, private contributions to the symphony increased by 200 percent and attendance at the symphony's concerts-in-the-park series doubled. The symphony has also announced an increase in ticket prices for next year. Given such developments, some city commissioners argue that the symphony can now be fully self-supporting, and they recommend that funding for the symphony be eliminated from next year's budget." [Old version 68]

Write a response in which you discuss what questions would need to be answered in order to decide whether the recommendation and the argument on which it is based are reasonable. Be sure to explain how the answers to these questions would help to evaluate the recommendation.

다음은 Grandview Beacon의 한 기사 내용이다.

"오랫동안 Grandview시는 Grandview 교향악단에 예산을 지원해 왔다. 하지만 작년에 교향악단에 대한 개인적 성금이 200% 증가했고, 교향악단의 야외공연 관중이 2배로 늘었다. 또한 교향악단은 내년도 공연료 인상을 발표했다. 이러한 일련의 과정들을 고려해, 일부 시 위원회의 위원들은, 이제는 교향악단이 충분히 자립할 수 있다고 주장하며, 내년도 예산에서 교향악단 지원금의 삭제를 권고한다."

Recommendation   Some city commissioners recommend that funding for the symphony be eliminated from next year's budget.

139. The following appeared in a memo from a budget planner for the city of Grandview.

"Our citizens are well aware of the fact that while the Grandview Symphony Orchestra was struggling to succeed, our city government promised annual funding to help support its programs. Last year, however, private contributions to the symphony increased by 200 percent, and attendance at the symphony's concerts-in-the-park series doubled. The symphony has also announced an increase in ticket prices for next year. Such developments indicate that the symphony can now succeed without funding from city government and we can eliminate that expense from next year's budget. Therefore, we recommend that the city of Grandview eliminate its funding for the Grandview Symphony from next year's budget. By doing so, we can prevent a city budget deficit without threatening the success of the symphony."

Write a response in which you discuss what questions would need to be answered in order to decide whether the recommendation is likely to have the predicted result. Be sure to explain how the answers to these questions would help to evaluate the recommendation.

다음은 Grandview시의 한 예산 편성자가 쓴 메모 내용이다.

"우리 시민들은, Grandview 교향악단이 성공을 위해서 발버둥치는 동안, 우리 시 정부가 교향악단의 프로그램을 지원하기 위해서 매년 자금지원을 약속했다는 것을 잘 압니다. 하지만 작년에 교향악단에 대한 개인적 성금이 200%나 증가했고, 교향악단의 야외공연 관중이 2배로 늘었습니다. 또한 교향악단은 내년도 공연료 인상을 발표했습니다. 이러한 사실들은 이제는 교향악단이 시 정부의 지원이 없이도 자립할 수 있고, 우리가 다음해 예산에서 이 비용을 삭제할 수 있다는 것을 시사합니다. 그러므로 Grandview시가 다음 해 예산에서 Grandview 교향악단에 대한 자금지원을 삭제할 것을 건의합니다. 그렇게 함으로써, 우리는 교향악단에 대한 부담 없이 시의 재정적자를 막을 수 있습니다."

Recommendation   We can prevent a city budget deficit without threatening the success of the symphony.

141. The following appeared in a memo to the board of the Grandview Symphony.

"The city of Grandview has provided annual funding for the Grandview Symphony since the symphony's inception ten years ago. Last year the symphony hired an internationally known conductor, who has been able to attract high-profile guest musicians to perform with the symphony. Since then, private contributions to the symphony have doubled and attendance at the symphony's concerts-in-the-park series has reached new highs. Now that the Grandview Symphony is an established success, it can raise ticket prices. Increased revenue from larger audiences and higher ticket prices will enable the symphony to succeed without funding from the city government."

Write a response in which you discuss what specific evidence is needed to evaluate the argument and explain how the evidence would weaken or strengthen the argument.

다음은 Grandview 교향악단의 이사회에 보낸 메모 내용이다.

"Grandview시는 10년 전 Grandview 교향악단의 창단 이래 매년 예산 지원을 해왔다. 작년에 교향악단은 국제적으로 저명한 지휘자를 영입했고, 이 지휘자는 교향악단과 함께 공연을 할 수 있도록 세간의 주목을 받는 초청 음악가들을 초빙해 왔다. 그 이후로, 교향악단에 대한 사적 성금이 2배나 되었고, 교향악단의 야외공연물 관중 수도 신기록을 세웠다. 이제 Grandview 교향악단은 자리를 잡았고, 공연료를 올릴 수 있다. 관객의 증가로 늘어난 수입과 관람료 인상으로 교향악단은 시 정부의 재정 지원 없이도 자립할 수 있을 것이다."

Argument   Increased revenue from larger audiences and higher ticket prices will enable the symphony to succeed without funding from the city government.

143. The following appeared in a memo from a budget planner for the city of Grandview.

"When the Grandview Symphony was established ten years ago, the city of Grandview agreed to provide the symphony with annual funding until the symphony became self-sustaining. Two years ago, the symphony hired an internationally known conductor, who has been able to attract high-profile guest musicians to perform with the symphony. Since then, private contributions to the symphony have tripled and attendance at the symphony's outdoor summer concert series has reached record highs. Now that the symphony has succeeded in finding an audience, the city can eliminate its funding of the symphony."

Write a response in which you examine the stated and/or unstated assumptions of the argument. Be sure to explain how the argument depends on these assumptions and what the implications are for the argument if the assumptions prove unwarranted.

[139]번과 유사한 지문이나 instruction이 다름.

Argument   Now that the symphony has succeeded in finding an audience, the city can eliminate its funding of the symphony.

162. The following appeared in a memo from a budget planner for the city of Grandview.

"It is time for the city of Grandview to stop funding the Grandview Symphony Orchestra. It is true that the symphony struggled financially for many years, but last year private contributions to the symphony increased by 200 percent and attendance at the symphony's concerts-in-the-park series doubled. In addition, the symphony has just announced an increase in ticket prices for next year. For these reasons, we recommend that the city eliminate funding for the Grandview Symphony Orchestra from next year's budget. We predict that the symphony will flourish in the years to come even without funding from the city."

Write a response in which you discuss what questions would need to be answered in order to decide whether the recommendation is likely to have the predicted result. Be sure to explain how the answers to these questions would help to evaluate the recommendation.

[139]번과 유사한 지문이나 instruction이 다름.

Recommendation We recommend that the city eliminate funding for the Grandview Symphony Orchestra from next year's budget.

62. The following appeared in a memo from the director of a large group of hospitals.

"In a laboratory study of liquid antibacterial hand soaps, a concentrated solution of UltraClean produced a 40 percent greater reduction in the bacteria population than did the liquid hand soaps currently used in our hospitals. During a subsequent test of UltraClean at our hospital in Workby, that hospital reported significantly fewer cases of patient infection than did any of the other hospitals in our group. Therefore, to prevent serious patient infections, we should supply UltraClean at all hand-washing stations throughout our hospital system." [Old version 98]

Write a response in which you examine the stated and/or unstated assumptions of the argument. Be sure to explain how the argument depends on these assumptions and what the implications are for the argument if the assumptions prove unwarranted.

다음은 한 대형 병원그룹 이사의 메모 내용이다.

"액체 항균성 비누에 관한 실험연구에서, UltraClean의 농축용액이, 현재 우리 병원에서 사용되는 액체 비누보다 무려 40%나 더 많은 박테리아를 줄였다. Workby에 있는 우리 병원에서 한 UltraClean의 그다음 실험에서도, 병원 측은 우리 그룹 내 여타 병원에서보다 환자 감염 케이스가 아주 적었다고 보고했다. 따라서 심각한 환자 감염을 예방하기 위해서는, 우리 병원 전체 손 세정기에 UltraClean을 공급해야 한다."

| Argument | To prevent serious patient infections, we should supply UltraClean at all hand-washing stations throughout our hospital system. |

121. The following appeared in a memo from the director of a large group of hospitals.

"In a controlled laboratory study of liquid hand soaps, a concentrated solution of extra strength UltraClean hand soap produced a 40 percent greater reduction in harmful bacteria than did the liquid hand soaps currently used in our hospitals. During our recent test of regular-strength UltraClean with doctors, nurses, and visitors at our hospital in Worktown, the hospital reported significantly fewer cases of patient infection (a 20 percent reduction) than did any of the other hospitals in our group. Therefore, to prevent serious patient infections, we should supply UltraClean at all hand-washing stations, including those used by visitors, throughout our hospital system."

Write a response in which you examine the stated and/or unstated assumptions of the argument. Be sure to explain how the argument depends on these assumptions and what the implications are for the argument if the assumptions prove unwarranted.

통제된 실험실에서의 액체 손 세척 비누에 관한 연구에서, 초강력 UltraClean 농축액이 현재 우리 병원에서 쓰는 액체 비누보다 유해한 박테리아를 40%나 더 줄였다. Worktown에 위치한 우리 병원에서 의사, 간호원, 그리고 내방객을 상대로 한 최근의 일반 UltraClean에 대한 테스트에서도, 우리 그룹 내 다른 어떤 병원보다 환자감염 사례가 훨씬 적었다고 한다(20% 감소). 그러므로 심각한 환자 감염을 예방하기 위해서는 내방객이 사용하는 것을 포함한, 우리 병원의 모든 손 세정기에 UltraClean을 공급해야 한다."

Argument   To prevent serious patient infections, we should supply UltraClean at all hand-washing stations, including those used by visitors, throughout our hospital system.

"In a controlled laboratory study of liquid hand soaps, a concentrated solution of extra strength UltraClean hand soap produced a 40 percent greater reduction in harmful bacteria than did the liquid hand soaps currently used in our hospitals. During our recent test of regular-strength UltraClean with doctors, nurses, and visitors at our hospital in Worktown, the hospital reported significantly fewer cases of patient infection (a 20 percent reduction) than did any of the other hospitals in our group. The explanation for the 20 percent reduction in patient infections is the use of UltraClean soap."

Write a response in which you discuss one or more alternative explanations that could rival the proposed explanation and explain how your explanation(s) can plausibly account for the facts presented in the argument.

[121]번과 거의 동일한 지문이나 instruction이 다름.

Argument The explanation for the 20 percent reduction in patient infections is the use of UltraClean soap.

124. The following appeared in a memo from the director of a large group of hospitals.

"In a controlled laboratory study of liquid hand soaps, a concentrated solution of extra strength UltraClean hand soap produced a 40 percent greater reduction in harmful bacteria than did the liquid hand soaps currently used in our hospitals. During our recent test of regular-strength UltraClean with doctors, nurses, and visitors at our hospital in Worktown, the hospital reported significantly fewer cases of patient infection (a 20 percent reduction) than did any of the other hospitals in our group. Therefore, to prevent serious patient infections, we should supply UltraClean at all hand-washing stations, including those used by visitors, throughout our hospital system."

Write a response in which you discuss what specific evidence is needed to evaluate the argument and explain how the evidence would weaken or strengthen the argument.

[121]번과 동일한 지문이나 instruction이 다름.

Argument   To prevent serious patient infections, we should supply UltraClean at all hand-washing stations, including those used by visitors, throughout our hospital system.

. The following appeared in a letter to the editor of the Parkville Daily newspaper.

"Throughout the country last year, as more and more children below the age of nine participated in youth-league sports, over 40,000 of these young players suffered injuries. When interviewed for a recent study, youth-league soccer players in several major cities also reported psychological pressure exerted by coaches and parents to win games. Furthermore, education experts say that long practice sessions for these sports take away time that could be used for academic activities. Since the disadvantages outweigh any advantages, we in Parkville should discontinue organized athletic competition for children under nine." [Old version 206]

Write a response in which you examine the stated and/or unstated assumptions of the argument. Be sure to explain how the argument depends on these assumptions and what the implications are for the argument if the assumptions prove unwarranted.

다음은 Parkville Daily 신문 편집장에게 보낸 서신이다.

"점점 더 많은 9세 이하의 어린아이들이 청소년 리그 대회에 참석하면서, 지난해 전국적으로 이 청소년 선수들 중 약 4만 명 이상이 부상을 입었다. 최근 조사된 인터뷰에 의하면, 일부 주요 시의 청소년 리그 축구 선수들은 시합에 이기도록 코치진과 부모로부터 심각한 심리적 압박도 받는다고 한다. 더군다나 교육 전문가들은 이들 경기 준비를 위한 오랜 훈련 기간은 학업에 소요될 시간을 빼앗아 간다고 한다. 단점이 장점보다 더 크기 때문에, Parkville에서는 9세 이하 어린이들의 조직적인 운동 경기를 중단해야 한다."

Argument Parkville should discontinue organized athletic competition for children under nine.

64. Collectors prize the ancient life-size clay statues of human figures made on Kali Island but have long wondered how Kalinese artists were able to depict bodies with such realistic precision. Since archaeologists have recently discovered molds of human heads and hands on Kali, we can now conclude that the ancient Kalinese artists used molds of actual bodies, not sculpting tools and techniques, to create these statues. This discovery explains why Kalinese miniature statues were abstract and entirely different in style: molds could be used only for life-size sculptures. It also explains why few ancient Kalinese sculpting tools have been found. In light of this discovery, collectors predict that the life-size sculptures will decrease in value while the miniatures increase in value. [Old version 56]

Write a response in which you discuss what questions would need to be answered in order to decide whether the prediction and the argument on which it is based are reasonable. Be sure to explain how the answers to these questions would help to evaluate the prediction.

수집상들은 Kali 섬에서 만들어진 고대 실물 크기의 점토 조각상을 높이 평가하지만, Kalinese 조각가들이 어떻게 그런 실제와 가까운 신체를 묘사할 수 있었는지 오랫동안 궁금해했다. 최근 고고학자들이 이 지역에서 인간의 머리와 손을 본 뜬 주조 틀을 발견함에 따라, 고대의 Kalinese인들이 이러한 조각들을 만들기 위해서, 조각 도구와 기술이 아니라 실제 인체의 모양을 한 주조를 사용했었다는 결론을 내릴 수 있게 되었다. 이 발견으로 Kalinese의 미니 조각상들이 추상적이고 스타일에 있어서도 완전히 달랐던 이유도 설명할 수 있게 되었다: 즉 주조는 실물 크기의 조각상에만 사용될 수 있었을 것이다. 이 발견은, 또한 조각 도구들이 적게 발견된 이유도 설명한다. 이러한 발견에 비추어 볼 때, 수집상들은 실물크기의 조각품에 대한 가치는 내려갈 것이고, 반면 미니 조각상은 가치가 올라갈 것이라고 예상한다.

Prediction The life-size sculptures will decrease in value while the miniatures increase in value.

65. When Stanley Park first opened, it was the largest, most heavily used public park in town. It is still the largest park, but it is no longer heavily used. Video cameras mounted in the park's parking lots last month revealed the park's drop in popularity: the recordings showed an average of only 50 cars per day. In contrast, tiny Carlton Park in the heart of the business district is visited by more than 150 people on a typical weekday. An obvious difference is that Carlton Park, unlike Stanley Park, provides ample seating. Thus, if Stanley Park is ever to be as popular with our citizens as Carlton Park, the town will obviously need to provide more benches, thereby converting some of the unused open areas into spaces suitable for socializing. [Old version 63]

Write a response in which you examine the stated and/or unstated assumptions of the argument. Be sure to explain how the argument depends on these assumptions and what the implications are for the argument if the assumptions prove unwarranted.

Stanley 공원이 처음 개장했을 당시에는, 가장 크고 가장 많이 이용되는 공원이었다. 아직도 이 공원은 가장 크지만, 더 이상 많이 이용되지는 않는다. 지난달 공원 주차장에 설치해 놓은 비디오카메라는 공원 인기가 떨어진 것을 보여준다. 즉, 하루 평균 겨우 50대의 차량만이 이용했다. 반면, 상업지역의 중심지에 위치한 작은 Carlton 공원은 평상시 주중에 150여 명 이상이 이용하고 있다. 분명한 차이는, Stanley 공원과는 달리, Carlton 공원에는 충분한 의자가 있다는 것이다. 따라서 Stanley 공원이 Carlton 공원처럼 시민들이 자주 이용하는 공원이 되기 위해서는, 의자를 설치할 필요가 있으며, 그렇게 해서 남아도는 일부 공간을 시민들의 사교를 위한 공간으로 바꾸어야 한다.

Argument	If Stanley Park is ever to be as popular with our citizens as Carlton Park, the town will obviously need to provide more benches, thereby converting some of the unused open areas into spaces suitable for socializing.

66. The following appeared in a memo from the owner of a chain of cheese stores located throughout the United States.

"For many years all the stores in our chain have stocked a wide variety of both domestic and imported cheeses. Last year, however, all of the five best-selling cheeses at our newest store were domestic cheddar cheeses from Wisconsin. Furthermore, a recent survey by Cheeses of the World magazine indicates an increasing preference for domestic cheeses among its subscribers. Since our company can reduce expenses by limiting inventory, the best way to improve profits in all of our stores is to discontinue stocking many of our varieties of imported cheese and concentrate primarily on domestic cheeses." [Old version 65]

Write a response in which you discuss what questions would need to be answered in order to decide whether the recommendation is likely to have the predicted result. Be sure to explain how the answers to these questions would help to evaluate the recommendation.

다음은 미국 전역에 있는 한 치즈 체인점 주인의 메모 내용이다.

"수년 동안, 우리 체인점은 국내산 및 수입산 치즈를 상당량 확보해 놓았다. 그러나 지난해 신규로 개장한 체인점에서 최고로 잘 팔리는 5가지 치즈들은 모두 위스콘신 산 국산 체다 치즈였다. 더욱이, 세계의 치즈라는 잡지의 최근 조사에서, 구독자들 가운데 국내산 치즈에 대한 선호도가 증가하고 있다고 나타났다. 우리 회사는 재고를 줄여서 비용을 절감할 수 있기 때문에, 모든 우리 가게들이 이익을 늘릴 수 있는 최상의 방법은 다양한 수입산 치즈의 비축을 중단하고 주로 국산 치즈를 확보하는 것이다."

Recommendation   The best way to improve profits in all of our stores is to discontinue stocking many of our varieties of imported cheese and concentrate primarily on domestic cheeses.

107. The following appeared in a memo from the business manager of a chain of cheese stores located throughout the United States.

"For many years all the stores in our chain have stocked a wide variety of both domestic and imported cheeses. Last year, however, all of the five best-selling cheeses at our newest store were domestic cheddar cheeses from Wisconsin. Furthermore, a recent survey by Cheeses of the World magazine indicates an increasing preference for domestic cheeses among its subscribers. Since our company can reduce expenses by limiting inventory, the best way to improve profits in all of our stores is to discontinue stocking many of our varieties of imported cheese and concentrate primarily on domestic cheeses."

Write a response in which you examine the stated and/or unstated assumptions of the argument. Be sure to explain how the argument depends on these assumptions and what the implications are for the argument if the assumptions prove unwarranted.

[66]번과 동일한 지문이나 instruction이 다름.

Argument	The best way to improve profits in all of our stores is to discontinue stocking many of our varieties of imported cheese and concentrate primarily on domestic cheeses.

108. The following appeared in a memo from the owner of a chain of cheese stores located throughout the United States.

"For many years all the stores in our chain have stocked a wide variety of both domestic and imported cheeses. Last year, however, all of the five best-selling cheeses at our newest store were domestic cheddar cheeses from Wisconsin. Furthermore, a recent survey by Cheeses of the World magazine indicates an increasing preference for domestic cheeses among its subscribers. Since our company can reduce expenses by limiting inventory, the best way to improve profits in all of our stores is to discontinue stocking many of our varieties of imported cheese and concentrate primarily on domestic cheeses."

Write a response in which you discuss what specific evidence is needed to evaluate the argument and explain how the evidence would weaken or strengthen the argument.

[66]번과 동일한 지문이나 instruction이 다름.

| Argument | The best way to improve profits in all of our stores is to discontinue stocking many of our varieties of imported cheese and concentrate primarily on domestic cheeses. |

67. The following appeared as part of a business plan developed by the manager of the Rialto Movie Theater.

"Despite its downtown location, the Rialto Movie Theater, a local institution for five decades, must make big changes or close its doors forever. It should follow the example of the new Apex Theater in the mall outside of town. When the Apex opened last year, it featured a video arcade, plush carpeting and seats, and a state-of-the-art sound system. Furthermore, in a recent survey, over 85 percent of respondents reported that the high price of newly released movies prevents them from going to the movies more than five times per year. Thus, if the Rialto intends to hold on to its share of a decreasing pool of moviegoers, it must offer the same features as Apex." [Old version 43]

Write a response in which you discuss what questions would need to be answered in order to decide whether the recommendation is likely to have the predicted result. Be sure to explain how the answers to these questions would help to evaluate the recommendation.

다음은 Rialto 극장 관리인이 작성한 사업안 일부이다.

"시내에 위치하고 있음에도 불구하고, 50여 년간 지역 시설이었던 Rialto 극장은, 이제 커다란 변화를 꾀하든지 아니면 영원히 문을 닫아야 한다. 이 극장은 시외 쇼핑타운에 새로 들어선 Apex 극장의 사례를 따라야 한다. Apex가 지난해 개업했을 당시, 이 극장은 비디오 아케이드, 고급 카펫과 좌석, 그리고 최신 음향시설을 갖추었다. 더군다나 최근 조사에서 응답자의 85% 이상이 새로 개봉된 영화들의 비싼 가격 탓으로 일 년에 다섯 번 이상 영화구경을 갈 수 없다고 했다. 따라서 Rialto 극장이 줄어들고 있는 관람객의 지분을 유지하려면, Apex와 같은 시설들을 갖추어야 한다."

Recommendation   If the Rialto intends to hold on to its share of a decreasing pool of moviegoers, it must offer the same features as Apex.

68. A recent study reported that pet owners have longer, healthier lives on average than do people who own no pets. Specifically, dog owners tend to have a lower incidence of heart disease. In light of these findings, Sherwood Hospital should form a partnership with Sherwood Animal Shelter to institute an adopt-a-dog program. The program would encourage dog ownership for patients recovering from heart disease, which should reduce these patients' chance of experiencing continuing heart problems and also reduce their need for ongoing treatment. As a further benefit, the publicity about the program would encourage more people to adopt pets from the shelter. And that will reduce the incidence of heart disease in the general population. [Old version 129]

Write a response in which you examine the stated and/or unstated assumptions of the argument. Be sure to explain how the argument depends on these assumptions and what the implications are for the argument if the assumptions prove unwarranted.

최근의 한 조사는, 애완동물 주인들이 애완동물이 없는 사람들보다 평균적으로 더 오래, 건강하게 산다고 밝혔다. 분명히, 개 주인들은 심장 질환 발생이 낮은 경향이 있다. 이러한 측면에서, Sherwood 병원은 애완견 분양 프로그램을 시적하기 위해서 Sherwood 동물보호센터와 파트너십을 구축해야 한다. 이 프로그램은 환자들이 개를 키우도록 장려해서, 이런 환자들이 지속적인 심장질환을 겪을 가능성을 것을 줄여주고 진행 중인 치료에 대한 필요를 줄여줄 것이다. 더 많은 이점은, 이 프로그램에 대한 여론이 더 많은 사람들이 보호센터에서 개를 데려올 것이다. 그래서 일반 대중의 심장질환 발생을 줄여줄 것이다.

Argument Sherwood Hospital should form a partnership with Sherwood Animal Shelter to institute an adopt-a-dog program to reduce the incidence of heart disease in the general population.

69. The following appeared in a memo from a vice president of a large, highly diversified company.

"Ten years ago our company had two new office buildings constructed as regional headquarters for two regions. The buildings were erected by different construction companies — Alpha and Zeta. Although the two buildings had identical floor plans, the building constructed by Zeta cost 30 percent more to build. However, that building's expenses for maintenance last year were only half those of Alpha's. In addition, the energy consumption of the Zeta building has been lower than that of the Alpha building every year since its construction. Given these data, plus the fact that Zeta has a stable workforce with little employee turnover, we recommend using Zeta rather than Alpha for our new building project, even though Alpha's bid promises lower construction costs." [Old version 93]

Write a response in which you discuss what questions would need to be answered in order to decide whether the recommendation and the argument on which it is based are reasonable. Be sure to explain how the answers to these questions would help to evaluate the recommendation.

다음은 한 거대한 다각화사업 회사 부사장의 메모 내용이다.

"10년 전, 우리 회사는 두 지역에 지역 사옥으로 신축된 2개의 건물을 소유하고 있었다. 이 건물들은 각각 Alpha 건축회사와 Zeta 건축회사가 건축했다. 두 빌딩은 평면도가 똑같았지만 Zeta 회사에서 지은 건물이 건설비가 30% 더 비쌌다. 하지만 지난해 건물 유지보수 비용은 Alpha 회사가 지은 건물의 절반에 불과했다. 게다가 신축 이후 매년 Zeta 회사에서 지은 건물의 에너지 소비가 Alpha가 지은 건물보다 적었다. 이런 자료들을 고려하고, Zeta 회사가 직원들의 이직률이 적어서 안정적인 직원들을 보유하고 있다는 점을 감안하면, 비록 Alpha 회사가 입찰에서 낮은 건축비를 제시하더라도 신규 건축 프로젝트는 Alpha 회사보다는 Zeta 회사를 이용할 것을 추천한다."

Recommendation   We recommend using Zeta rather than Alpha for our new building project, even though Alpha's bid promises lower construction costs.

70. The following appeared in a memo from a vice president of a large, highly diversified company.

"Ten years ago our company had two new office buildings constructed as regional headquarters for two regions. The buildings were erected by different construction companies — Alpha and Zeta. Although the two buildings had identical floor plans, the building constructed by Zeta cost 30 percent more to build. However, that building's expenses for maintenance last year were only half those of Alpha's. Furthermore, the energy consumption of the Zeta building has been lower than that of the Alpha building every year since its construction. Such data indicate that we should use Zeta rather than Alpha for our contemplated new building project, even though Alpha's bid promises lower construction costs."

Write a response in which you discuss what specific evidence is needed to evaluate the argument and explain how the evidence would weaken or strengthen the argument.

[69]번과 거의 동일한 지문이나 instruction이 다름.

| Argument | We recommend using Zeta rather than Alpha for our new building project, even though Alpha's bid promises lower construction costs. |

115. The following appeared in a memo from a vice president of a large, highly diversified company.

"Ten years ago our company had two new office buildings constructed as regional headquarters for two different regions. The buildings were erected by two different construction companies — Alpha and Zeta. Even though the two buildings had identical floor plans, the building constructed by Zeta cost 30 percent more to build, and its expenses for maintenance last year were twice those of the building constructed by Alpha. Furthermore, the energy consumption of the Zeta building has been higher than that of the Alpha building every year since its construction. Such data, plus the fact that Alpha has a stable workforce with little employee turnover, indicate that we should use Alpha rather than Zeta for our contemplated new building project."

Write a response in which you examine the stated and/or unstated assumptions of the argument. Be sure to explain how the argument depends on these assumptions and what the implications are for the argument if the assumptions prove unwarranted.

[69]번과 거의 동일한 지문이나 instruction이 다름.

Argument We recommend using Zeta rather than Alpha for our new building project, even though Alpha's bid promises lower construction costs.

71. The following is a letter to the editor of the Waymarsh Times.

"Traffic here in Waymarsh is becoming a problem. Although just three years ago a state traffic survey showed that the typical driving commuter took 20 minutes to get to work, the commute now takes closer to 40 minutes, according to the survey just completed. Members of the town council already have suggested more road building to address the problem, but as well as being expensive, the new construction will surely disrupt some of our residential neighborhoods. It would be better to follow the example of the nearby city of Garville. Last year Garville implemented a policy that rewards people who share rides to work, giving them coupons for free gas. Pollution levels in Garville have dropped since the policy was implemented, and people from Garville tell me that commuting times have fallen considerably. There is no reason why a policy like Garville's shouldn't work equally well in Waymarsh." [Old version 119]

Write a response in which you discuss what specific evidence is needed to evaluate the argument and explain how the evidence would weaken or strengthen the argument.

다음은 Waymarsh Times의 편집장에게 보낸 편지이다.

"Waymarch 지역 교통은 심각한 문제가 되고 있다. 불과 3년 전 교통 설문조사는 직장에 가기 위해서 출퇴근 시간이 보통 20분 정도 걸렸다고 밝혔지만, 얼마 전 끝낸 조사에 따르면, 이제는 40분 가까이 걸린다고 한다. 시 의회 의원들은 문제를 시정하기 위해서 더 많은 도로건설을 제안해 왔으나 신규 건설은, 비용이 많이 들뿐만 아니라, 일부 주거 지역에 분명히 지장을 줄 것이다. 이웃 Gearsville시의 사례를 본받는 것이 더 나을 것이다. 지난해 Gearsville시는 출근 시 합승을 하는 사람들에게 무료 주유 쿠폰을 지급하는 정책을 실시했다. 정책 실시 이후 Garville의 오염 수치가 떨어졌으며, Garville 사람들은 나에게 출퇴근 시간이 현저하게 빨라졌다고 말한다. Gearsville시와 같은 정책이 Waymarsh에서 동일한 효력을 발하지 않을 것이라는 이유가 없다."

> Argument   To solve traffic problem in Waymarsh, it would be better to implement a policy that rewards people who share rides to work, giving them coupons for free gas.

72. The following appeared as a letter to the editor of a national newspaper.

"Your recent article on corporate downsizing* in Elthyria maintains that the majority of competent workers who have lost jobs as a result of downsizing face serious economic hardship, often for years, before finding other suitable employment. But this claim is undermined by a recent report on the Elthyrian economy, which found that since 1999 far more jobs have been created than have been eliminated, bringing the unemployment rate in Elthyria to its lowest level in decades. Moreover, two-thirds of these newly created jobs have been in industries that tend to pay above-average wages, and the vast majority of these jobs are full-time." [Old version 143]

* Downsizing is the process whereby corporations deliberately make themselves smaller, reducing the number of their employees.

Write a response in which you discuss what specific evidence is needed to evaluate the argument and explain how the evidence would weaken or strengthen the argument.

다음은 한 전국지 신문사의 편집장에게 보낸 편지이다.

"Elthyria의 기업 감원에 관한 귀사의 최근 기사는, 감원으로 인해 실직한 대부분의 능력 있는 근로자들이, 다른 적당한 재취업을 하기 전까지, 종종 수년간, 심각한 경제적인 어려움을 겪고 있다고 주장합니다. 그러나 그러한 주장은 1992년 이후 없어진 직업보다 창출된 직업의 수가 훨씬 더 많아서 10여 년간 Elthyria의 실업률이 최저수준이었다는, Elthyrian 경제에 대한 최근 보고서를 볼 때 별 설득력이 없습니다. 더욱이 새로이 창출된 직업의 2/3가 평균 임금 이상인 산업에 있고 이들 대부분이 정규직입니다."

> **Argument** The article that the majority of competent workers who have lost jobs as a result of downsizing face serious economic hardship is undermined.

73. The following appeared on the Mozart School of Music Web site.

"The Mozart School of Music should be the first choice for parents considering enrolling their child in music lessons. First of all, the Mozart School welcomes youngsters at all ability and age levels; there is no audition to attend the school. Second, the school offers instruction in nearly all musical instruments as well a wide range of styles and genres from classical to rock. Third, the faculty includes some of the most distinguished musicians in the area. Finally, many Mozart graduates have gone on to become well-known and highly paid professional musicians." [Old version 172]

Write a response in which you examine the stated and/or unstated assumptions of the argument. Be sure to explain how the argument depends on these assumptions and what the implications are for the argument if the assumptions prove unwarranted.

다음은 음악 웹사이트의 Mozart 음악학교에 관한 글이다.

"Mozart 음악학교는 자녀들에게 음악교육을 시키려는 부모들이 등록을 고려하면서 가장 우선적으로 선택하는 학교이다. 우선 Mozart 학교는 자실이 있는 모든 나이대의 아동들을 환영한다. 즉, 입학하는 데 오디션이 없다. 둘째, 거의 모든 악기는 물론 클래식부터 록에 이르는 다양한 형식과 장르를 지도한다. 셋째, 교사 중에는 이 지역에서 가장 이름난 음악가들도 몇 명 있다. 마지막으로, Mozart 졸업생들은 명성과 고소득을 올리는 전문 음악가들이 되고 있다."

Argument	The Mozart School of Music should be the first choice for parents considering enrolling their child in music lessons.

74. The president of Grove College has recommended that the college abandon its century-old tradition of all-female education and begin admitting men. Pointing to other all-female colleges that experienced an increase in applications after adopting coeducation, the president argues that coeducation would lead to a significant increase in applications and enrollment. However, the director of the alumnae association opposes the plan. Arguing that all-female education is essential to the very identity of the college, the director cites annual surveys of incoming students in which these students say that the school's all-female status was the primary reason they selected Grove. The director also points to a survey of Grove alumnae in which a majority of respondents strongly favored keeping the college all female. [Old version 174]

Write a response in which you discuss what questions would need to be answered in order to decide whether the recommendation and the argument on which it is based are reasonable. Be sure to explain how the answers to these questions would help to evaluate the recommendation.

Grove 대학의 총장은 이 대학이 1세기 동안 전통으로 삼아온 여성전용교육을 포기하고 남성의 입학을 허용할 것을 권고합니다. 남녀공학을 채택한 후 지원서가 증가한 다른 여자 대학들을 지적하면서, 총장은 남녀공학이 지원과 등록을 현저히 늘릴 것이라고 주장합니다. 하지만 동창회 사무국장은 그 계획에 반대합니다. 여성전용교육은 대학의 정체성에 꼭 필요하다고 주장하면서, 이 사무국장은 신입생들이 Grove를 선택하는 주된 이유가 여성전용교육이라고 하는 연례 설문조사를 인용합니다. 이 사무국장은 또한 Grove의 동창회의 대분의 응답자들이 여성전용대학으로 유지되기를 강력하게 선호한다는 점도 지적합니다.

| Recommendation | The president of Grove College has recommended that the college abandon its century-old tradition of all-female education and begin admitting men. |

147. The following recommendation was made by the president and administrative staff of Grove College, a private institution, to the college's governing committee.

"We recommend that Grove College preserve its century-old tradition of all-female education rather than admit men into its programs. It is true that a majority of faculty members voted in favor of coeducation, arguing that it would encourage more students to apply to Grove. But 80 percent of the students responding to a survey conducted by the student government wanted the school to remain all female, and over half of the alumnae who answered a separate survey also opposed coeducation. Keeping the college all female will improve morale among students and convince alumnae to keep supporting the college financially."

Write a response in which you discuss what specific evidence is needed to evaluate the argument and explain how the evidence would weaken or strengthen the argument.

다음은 한 사립학교인, Grove 대학의 총장과 교직원들이 재단 이사회에 한 권고이다.

"우리는 Grove 대학이 남성의 입학을 허용하는 대신에 1세기 동안 전통을 지켜온 여성 전용 교육을 지켜야 한다고 권합니다. 대부분의 교직원들이, 그래야 더 많은 학생들이 Grove에 지원한다고 주장하면서 남녀공학을 선호하는 투표를 한 것은 사실입니다. 그러나 학생회가 실시한 설문조사에서 80% 이상의 학생들이 이 학교가 여자대학으로 남기를 바란다고 응답했고, 별도의 설문조사에 응답한 동문들의 과반수도 남녀공학을 반대했습니다. 여자대학으로 남아 있는 것이 학생들의 사기도 진작시킬 것이고 동문들이 재정지원을 계속할 수 있도록 납득시킬 것입니다."

Argument   Grove College should preserve its century-old tradition of all-female education.

148. The following recommendation was made by the president and administrative staff of Grove College, a private institution, to the college's governing committee.

"We recommend that Grove College preserve its century-old tradition of all-female education rather than admit men into its programs. It is true that a majority of faculty members voted in favor of coeducation, arguing that it would encourage more students to apply to Grove. But 80 percent of the students responding to a survey conducted by the student government wanted the school to remain all female, and over half of the alumnae who answered a separate survey also opposed coeducation. Keeping the college all female will improve morale among students and convince alumnae to keep supporting the college financially."

Write a response in which you examine the stated and/or unstated assumptions of the argument. Be sure to explain how the argument depends on these assumptions and what the implications are for the argument if the assumptions prove unwarranted.

[147]번과 동일한 지문이나 instruction이 다름.

Argument   Grove College should preserve its century-old tradition of all-female education.

149. The following recommendation was made by the president and administrative staff of Grove College, a private institution, to the college's governing committee.

"We recommend that Grove College preserve its century-old tradition of all-female education rather than admit men into its programs. It is true that a majority of faculty members voted in favor of coeducation, arguing that it would encourage more students to apply to Grove. But 80 percent of the students responding to a survey conducted by the student government wanted the school to remain all female, and over half of the alumnae who answered a separate survey also opposed coeducation. Keeping the college all female will improve morale among students and convince alumnae to keep supporting the college financially."

Write a response in which you discuss what questions would need to be answered in order to decide whether the recommendation is likely to have the predicted result. Be sure to explain how the answers to these questions would help to evaluate the recommendation.

[147]번과 동일한 지문이나 instruction이 다름.

Recommendation   Grove College should preserve its century-old tradition of all-female education.

156. The following recommendation was made by the president and administrative staff of Grove College, a private institution, to the college's governing committee.

"Recently, there have been discussions about ending Grove College's century-old tradition of all-female education by admitting male students into our programs. At a recent faculty meeting, a majority of faculty members voted in favor of coeducation, arguing that it would encourage more students to apply to Grove. However, Grove students, both past and present, are against the idea of coeducation. Eighty percent of the students responding to a survey conducted by the student government wanted the school to remain all female, and over half of the alumnae who answered a separate survey also opposed coeducation. Therefore, we recommend maintaining Grove College's tradition of all-female education. We predict that keeping the college all-female will improve morale among students and convince alumnae to keep supporting the college financially."

Write a response in which you discuss what questions would need to be answered in order to decide whether the recommendation is likely to have the predicted result. Be sure to explain how the answers to these questions would help to evaluate the recommendation.

[147]번과 유사한 지문이나 instruction이 다름.

Argue Groups

75. The following appeared in a letter to the editor of a Batavia newspaper.

"The department of agriculture in Batavia reports that the number of dairy farms throughout the country is now 25 percent greater than it was 10 years ago. During this same time period, however, the price of milk at the local Excello Food Market has increased from \$1.50 to over \$3.00 per gallon. To prevent farmers from continuing to receive excessive profits on an apparently increased supply of milk, the Batavia government should begin to regulate retail milk prices. Such regulation is necessary to ensure fair prices for consumers." [Old version 10]

Write a response in which you discuss what questions would need to be answered in order to decide whether the recommendation is likely to have the predicted result. Be sure to explain how the answers to these questions would help to evaluate the recommendation.

다음은 Batvia 신문의 편집장에게 보낸 서신의 내용이다.

"Batavia 농림부의 보고에 따르면, 전국적으로 낙농업자의 숫자가 과거 10년 전에 비해 25%나 증가했다고 한다. 그러나 같은 기간 동안, 이 지역에 있는 Excello Food Market에서 우유의 가격은 갤런당 1.5달러에서 3달러 이상으로 올랐다. 분명한 우유 공급 증가에 따른 지속적인 낙농업자들의 과다한 이윤을 막기 위해, Batavia 정부는 우유의 소매가격을 규제해야 한다. 이런 규제는 소비자에게 공정한 가격을 보장해주기 위해서 필요하다."

Recommendation To prevent farmers from continuing to receive excessive profits on an apparently increased supply of milk, the Batavia government should begin to regulate retail milk prices.

77. The following recommendation appeared in a memo from the mayor of the town of Hopewell.

"Two years ago, the nearby town of Ocean View built a new municipal golf course and resort hotel. During the past two years, tourism in Ocean View has increased, new businesses have opened there, and Ocean View's tax revenues have risen by 30 percent. Therefore, the best way to improve Hopewell's economy — and generate additional tax revenues — is to build a golf course and resort hotel similar to those in Ocean View." [Old version 25]

Write a response in which you examine the stated and/or unstated assumptions of the argument. Be sure to explain how the argument depends on these assumptions and what the implications are for the argument if the assumptions prove unwarranted.

다음은 Hopewell 시장의 메모에 나타난 권장 사항이다.

"2년 전, 인근 Ocean View시는 시립 골프장과 휴양지 호텔을 건설했다. 지난 2년 동안 Ocean View의 관광객이 증가했으며, 그곳에 새로운 사업들이 생겨났고, Ocean View의 세수도 30%나 증가했다. 그러므로 Hopewell의 경제를 향상시킬 수 있는 — 그리고 추가적 세수를 늘릴 수 있는 — 가장 좋은 방법은 Ocean View의 것과 유사한 골프 시설과 휴양지 호텔을 건설하는 것이다."

Argument The best way to improve Hopewell's economy — and generate additional tax revenues — is to build a golf course and resort hotel similar to those in Ocean View.

169. The following appeared in a memo from the mayor of Brindleburg to the city council.

"Two years ago, the town of Seaside Vista opened a new municipal golf course and resort hotel. Since then, the Seaside Vista Tourism Board has reported a 20% increase in visitors. In addition, local banks reported a steep rise in the number of new business loan applications they received this year. The amount of tax money collected by Seaside Vista has also increased, allowing the town to announce plans to improve Seaside Vista's roads and bridges. We recommend building a similar golf course and resort hotel in Brindleburg. We predict that this project will generate additional tax revenue that the city can use to fund much-needed public improvements."

Write a response in which you discuss what questions would need to be answered in order to decide whether the recommendation is likely to have the predicted result. Be sure to explain how the answers to these questions would help to evaluate the recommendation.

[77]번과 유사한 지문이나 instruction이 다름.

Recommendation   We recommend building a similar golf course and resort hotel in Brindleburg.

Predicted result   This project will generate additional tax revenue that the city can use to fund much-needed public improvements.

78. The following appeared in a memo from the vice president of a food distribution company with food storage warehouses in several cities.

"Recently, we signed a contract with the Fly-Away Pest Control Company to provide pest control services at our fast-food warehouse in Palm City, but last month we discovered that over $20,000 worth of food there had been destroyed by pest damage. Meanwhile, the Buzzoff Pest Control Company, which we have used for many years, continued to service our warehouse in Wintervale, and last month only $10,000 worth of the food stored there had been destroyed by pest damage. Even though the price charged by Fly-Away is considerably lower, our best means of saving money is to return to Buzzoff for all our pest control services." [Old version 41]

Write a response in which you discuss what specific evidence is needed to evaluate the argument and explain how the evidence would weaken or strengthen the argument.

다음은 몇몇 시에 식품 저장창고를 보유한 식품 유통회사 부사장의 메모 내용이다.

"최근 우리 회사는 Palm시에 있는 패스트푸드 저장창고에 병충해 방지 서비스를 하기 위해서 Fly-Away Pest-Control 회사와 계약을 했으나 지난달 이곳에서 2만 달러 이상의 식품이 병충해로 폐기되었다는 것을 알았다. 그러나 우리 회사 가 수년간 거래해 온 Buzzoff Pest-Control 회사는 Wintervale에 있는 저장창고에서 서비스를 계속해 왔는데 거기서는 지난달에 겨우 1만 달러어치의 식료품이 병충해로 폐기처분 되었다. 비록 Fly-Away 회사가 책정한 가격이 상당히 낮으 나 돈을 절약하는 최선의 방법은 우리의 모든 병충해 방지 서비스를 Buzzoff 회사에게 다시 맡기는 것이다."

> Argument   Our best means of saving money is to return to Buzzoff for all our pest control services.

114. The following appeared in a memo from the vice president of a food distribution company with food storage warehouses in several cities.

"Recently, we signed a contract with the Fly-Away Pest Control Company to provide pest control services at our warehouse in Palm City, but last month we discovered that over $20,000 worth of food there had been destroyed by pest damage. Meanwhile, the Buzzoff Pest Control Company, which we have used for many years in Palm City, continued to service our warehouse in Wintervale, and last month only $10,000 worth of the food stored there had been destroyed by pest damage. Even though the price charged by Fly-Away is considerably lower, our best means of saving money is to return to Buzzoff for all our pest control services." [Old version 41]

Write a response in which you discuss what questions would need to be answered in order to decide whether the recommendation and the argument on which it is based are reasonable. Be sure to explain how the answers to these questions would help to evaluate the recommendation.

[78]번과 거의 동일한 지문이나 instruction이 다름.

Recommendation   Our best means of saving money is to return to Buzzoff for all our pest control services.

116. The following appeared in a memo from the vice president of a food distribution company with food storage warehouses in several cities.

"Recently, we signed a contract with the Fly-Away Pest Control Company to provide pest control services at our warehouse in Palm City, but last month we discovered that over $20,000 worth of food there had been destroyed by pest damage. Meanwhile, the Buzzoff Pest Control Company, which we have used for many years in Palm City, continued to service our warehouse in Wintervale, and last month only $10,000 worth of the food stored there had been destroyed by pest damage. This difference in pest damage is best explained by the negligence of Fly-Away."

Write a response in which you discuss one or more alternative explanations that could rival the proposed explanation and explain how your explanation(s) can plausibly account for the facts presented in the argument.

[78]번과 유사한 지문이나 instruction이 다름.

Argument   This difference in pest damage is best explained by the negligence of Fly-Away.

117. The following appeared in a memo from the vice president of a food distribution company with food storage warehouses in several cities.

"Recently, we signed a contract with the Fly-Away Pest Control Company to provide pest control services at our warehouse in Palm City, but last month we discovered that over $20,000 worth of food there had been destroyed by pest damage. Meanwhile, the Buzzoff Pest Control Company, which we have used for many years in Palm City, continued to service our warehouse in Wintervale, and last month only $10,000 worth of the food stored there had been destroyed by pest damage. Even though the price charged by Fly-Away is considerably lower, our best means of saving money is to return to Buzzoff for all our pest control services."

Write a response in which you examine the stated and/or unstated assumptions of the argument. Be sure to explain how the argument depends on these assumptions and what the implications are for the argument if the assumptions prove unwarranted.

[78]번과 유사한 지문이나 instruction이 다름.

Argument   Our best means of saving money is to return to Buzzoff for all our pest control services.

79. Since those issues of Newsbeat magazine that featured political news on their front cover were the poorest-selling issues over the past three years, the publisher of Newsbeat has recommended that the magazine curtail its emphasis on politics to focus more exclusively on economics and personal finance. She points to a recent survey of readers of general interest magazines that indicates greater reader interest in economic issues than in political ones. Newsbeat's editor, however, opposes the proposed shift in editorial policy, pointing out that very few magazines offer extensive political coverage anymore. [Old version 173]

Write a response in which you discuss what questions would need to be answered in order to decide whether the recommendation and the argument on which it is based are reasonable. Be sure to explain how the answers to these questions would help to evaluate the recommendation.

표지에 국제뉴스를 다룬 Newsbeat 잡지들이 지난 3년간 가장 잘 팔리지 않는 잡지들이였기 때문에, Newsbeat의 발행인은 잡지가 오로지 경제와 개인금융에 좀 더 집중하기 위해서는 정치를 중시하는 것을 축소해야 한다고 권고하고 있다. 그녀는 독자들의 관심사는 정치적인 것보다는 경제적 문제에 더 있다는 것을 보여주는 독자들의 일반적인 관심사를 묻는 최근의 한 설문조사를 지적한다. 하지만 Newsbeat의 편집장은 이런 편집 정책의 변경에 반대하며, 더 이상 폭넓게 정치를 다루는 잡지들이 거의 없다는 점을 지적한다.

Recommendation The magazine curtail its emphasis on politics to focus more exclusively on economics and personal finance.

80. The following is taken from a memo from the advertising director of the Super Screen Movie Production Company.

"According to a recent report from our marketing department, during the past year, fewer people attended Super Screen-produced movies than in any other year. And yet the percentage of positive reviews by movie reviewers about specific Super Screen movies actually increased during the past year. Clearly, the contents of these reviews are not reaching enough of our prospective viewers. Thus, the problem lies not with the quality of our movies but with the public's lack of awareness that movies of good quality are available. Super Screen should therefore allocate a greater share of its budget next year to reaching the public through advertising." [New]

Write a response in which you discuss what questions would need to be answered in order to decide whether the recommendation and the argument on which it is based are reasonable. Be sure to explain how the answers to these questions would help to evaluate the recommendation.

다음은 Super Screen 영화 제작사의 홍보 담당 이사의 메모에서 발췌한 것이다.

"영업 담당 부서의 최근 보고에 따르면, 지난해 Super Screen이 제작한 영화를 보는 관람객 수가 그 어느 해보다 적었다. 그래도 특정한 Super Screen 영화에 대한 영화 비평가들의 긍정적 비평 비율은 실제 늘었다. 분명히 이러한 비평 내용들은 우리 잠재적 관객들한테 충분치 않다. 따라서 문제는 영화의 질에 있는 것이 아니고 좋은 영화들이 있다는 것을 대중이 모른다는 데 있다. 그러므로 Super Screen은 내년도 예산의 상당 부분을 광고를 통해서 대중한테 접근하도록 할당해야 한다."

Recommendation   Super Screen should therefore allocate a greater share of its budget next year to reaching the public through advertising.

97. The following appeared in an e-mail sent by the marketing director of the Classical Shakespeare Theatre of Bardville.

"Over the past ten years, there has been a 20 percent decline in the size of the average audience at Classical Shakespeare Theatre productions. In spite of increased advertising, we are attracting fewer and fewer people to our shows, causing our profits to decrease significantly. We must take action to attract new audience members. The best way to do so is by instituting a 'Shakespeare in the Park' program this summer. Two years ago the nearby Avon Repertory Company started a 'Free Plays in the Park' program, and its profits have increased 10 percent since then. If we start a 'Shakespeare in the Park' program, we can predict that our profits will increase, too." [New]

Write a response in which you discuss what questions would need to be answered in order to decide whether the recommendation is likely to have the predicted result. Be sure to explain how the answers to these questions would help to evaluate the recommendation.

다음은 Bardville의 Classical Shakespeare 극장의 영업부장이 보낸 이메일 내용이다.

"지난 10년간, Classical Shakespeare 극장의 평균 관람객 수가 20%나 줄었다. 광고를 늘렸음에도 불구하고, 우리 쇼를 찾는 사람들은 점점 줄고 있고, 그래서 수익도 상당히 줄어들었다. 우리는 새로운 관객들이 흥미를 가질 만한 조치를 취해야만 한다. 최선의 방법은 이번 여름에 'Shakespeare in the Park' 프로그램을 시작하는 것이다. 2년 전, 근처의 Avon Repertory 회사가 'Free Plays in the Park' 프로그램을 시작했는데, 그 후로 이 회사의 이익이 19%나 늘었다. 우리가 'Shakespeare in the Park' 프로그램을 시작한다면, 우리 수익도 늘 것으로 전망된다."

Recommendation The best way to do so is by instituting a 'Shakespeare in the Park' program this summer.

81. The following appeared in a business magazine.

"As a result of numerous complaints of dizziness and nausea on the part of consumers of Promofoods tuna, the company requested that eight million cans of its tuna be returned for testing. Promofoods concluded that the canned tuna did not, after all, pose a health risk. This conclusion is based on tests performed on samples of the recalled cans by chemists from Promofoods; the chemists found that of the eight food chemicals most commonly blamed for causing symptoms of dizziness and nausea, five were not found in any of the tested cans. The chemists did find small amounts of the three remaining suspected chemicals but pointed out that these occur naturally in all canned foods." [Old version 165]

Write a response in which you discuss what questions would need to be addressed in order to decide whether the conclusion and the argument on which it is based are reasonable. Be sure to explain how the answers to the questions would help to evaluate the conclusion.

다음은 한 비즈니스 잡지에 실린 내용이다.

"현기증과 구역질이 난다는 일부 Promofoods 참치 소비자들의 불만에 따라, Promofoods사는 테스트를 위해 지난 해 800만 개의 참치 캔을 반품하라고 요청했다. Promofoods사는 캔 참치에 전혀 지장이 없다고 결론을 내렸다. 이 결론은 Promofoods사의 화학자들이 회수된 캔의 샘플을 상대로 한 테스트에 근거한 것이다; 화학자들은 주로 현기증과 구역질 증상의 원인이 되는 8가지 식품 화학물질을 발견했으나 실험된 캔에서는 5가지가 발견되지 않았다. 화학자들은 3가지 남아 있는 의심스러운 화학물질을 소량 발견했지만, 이것은 모든 캔 식료품에서 자연스럽게 발견되는 것이라고 지적했다."

> Argument Promofoods concluded that the canned tuna did not, after all, pose a health risk.

83. The following is a letter to the editor of an environmental magazine.

"In 1975 a wildlife census found that there were seven species of amphibians in Xanadu National Park, with abundant numbers of each species. However, in 2002 only four species of amphibians were observed in the park, and the numbers of each species were drastically reduced. There has been a substantial decline in the numbers of amphibians worldwide, and global pollution of water and air is clearly implicated. The decline of amphibians in Xanadu National Park, however, almost certainly has a different cause: in 1975, trout — which are known to eat amphibian eggs — were introduced into the park." [Old version 150]

Write a response in which you discuss what specific evidence is needed to evaluate the argument and explain how the evidence would weaken or strengthen the argument.

다음은 한 환경잡지 편집장에게 보낸 편지이다.

"1975년 야생동물 조사에 의하면 제나두 국립공원에는 7종류의 양서류가 있었고, 각 종의 개체수도 많았다. 하지만 2002년도에는 겨우 4종류의 양서류만이 목격되었고, 각 종의 개체수도 급격하게 줄었다. 전 세계적으로 양서류들의 수가 현저하게 줄어들고 있는데, 이는 분명히 세계적인 물과 공기의 오염이 그 원인으로 보인다. 하지만 제나두 국립공원에서 양서류가 감소하는 것은 다른 원인이 있음이 거의 확실하다. 즉, 1975년에 송어 — 양서류의 알을 먹는 것으로 알려진— 가 이 공원에서 발견되었기 때문이다."

| Argument | The decline of amphibians in Xanadu National Park has a different cause because trout — which are known to eat amphibian eggs — were introduced into the park. |

84. The following is a letter to the editor of an environmental magazine.

"Two studies of amphibians in Xanadu National Park confirm a significant decline in the numbers of amphibians. In 1975 there were seven species of amphibians in the park, and there were abundant numbers of each species. However, in 2002 only four species of amphibians were observed in the park, and the numbers of each species were drastically reduced. One proposed explanation is that the decline was caused by the introduction of trout into the park's waters, which began in 1975. (Trout are known to eat amphibian eggs.)"

Write a response in which you discuss one or more alternative explanations that could rival the proposed explanation and explain how your explanation(s) can plausibly account for the facts presented in the argument.

[83]번과 유사한 지문이나 instruction이 다름.

Argument　The decline of amphibians in Xanadu National Park was caused by the introduction of trout into the park's waters, which began in 1975.

83번과 84번은 동일한 연구 결과를 가지고 서로 다른 결론을 내린 지문이다. 즉, 83번은 양서류의 알을 먹는 송어가 발견되었으니 양서류의 감소 원인이 물과 공기의 오염이 아닌 다른 데 있을 것이란 주장이고, 84번은 양서류의 감소 원인은 양서류의 알을 먹는 송어 때문이라는 주장이다.

85. In a study of the reading habits of Waymarsh citizens conducted by the University of Waymarsh, most respondents said that they preferred literary classics as reading material. However, a second study conducted by the same researchers found that the type of book most frequently checked out of each of the public libraries in Waymarsh was the mystery novel. Therefore, it can be concluded that the respondents in the first study had misrepresented their reading habits. [Old version 161]

Write a response in which you discuss what specific evidence is needed to evaluate the argument and explain how the evidence would weaken or strengthen the argument.

Waymarsh 대학에서 실시한 Waymarsh 주민들의 독서습관에 대한 조사에서, 대부분 응답자는 독서로 고전문학을 선호한다고 응답했다. 그러나 같은 연구팀이 두 번째 실시한 조사에서는 Waymarsh에 있는 각 도서관에서 가장 빈번하게 대여된 책의 종류는 추리소설이라고 조사되었다. 그러므로 처음에 한 조사에서 응답자들은 자신들의 독서 습관을 잘못 전했다고 결론지을 수 있다.

| Argument | It can be concluded that the respondents in the first study had misrepresented their reading habits. |

87. In a study of the reading habits of Waymarsh citizens conducted by the University of Waymarsh, most respondents said they preferred literary classics as reading material. However, a second study conducted by the same researchers found that the type of book most frequently checked out of each of the public libraries in Waymarsh was the mystery novel. Therefore, it can be concluded that the respondents in the first study had misrepresented their reading preferences.

Write a response in which you examine the stated and/or unstated assumptions of the argument. Be sure to explain how the argument depends on these assumptions and what the implications are for the argument if the assumptions prove unwarranted.

[85]번과 동일한 지문이나 instruction이 다름.

Argument   It can be concluded that the respondents in the first study had misrepresented their reading preferences.

86. The following appeared in a memo at XYZ company.

"When XYZ lays off employees, it pays Delany Personnel Firm to offer those employees assistance in creating réumé and developing interviewing skills, if they so desire. Laid-off employees have benefited greatly from Delany's services: last year those who used Delany found jobs much more quickly than did those who did not. Recently, it has been proposed that we use the less expensive Walsh Personnel Firm in place of Delany. This would be a mistake because eight years ago, when XYZ was using Walsh, only half of the workers we laid off at that time found jobs within a year. Moreover, Delany is clearly superior, as evidenced by its bigger staff and larger number of branch offices. After all, last year Delany's clients took an average of six months to find jobs, whereas Walsh's clients took nine." [Old version 241]

Write a response in which you discuss what specific evidence is needed to evaluate the argument and explain how the evidence would weaken or strengthen the argument.

다음은 XYZ 회사의 메모이다.

"XYZ사가 직원들을 해고했을 때, Delaney Personnel 회사를 고용해서, 원한다면, 이 직원들의 이력서 작성과 인터뷰 능력을 향상시킬 수 있도록 지원했다. 해직자들은 Delany사의 서비스로 도움을 많이 받았다: 즉, 지난해 이 회사로부터 도움을 받은 사람들은 그렇지 않은 사람들에 비해 훨씬 빨리 직장을 구했다. 최근에, Delany 대신에 비교적 비용이 저렴한 Walsh Personnel 회사를 이용하자는 제안이 있었다. 8년 전 XYZ사가 Walsh사를 이용했을 때, 해직 근로자의 절반만이 1년 내 직장을 구했던 점으로 보아, 이 제안은 잘못된 것이다. 더구나 Delany사는 입증된 바와 같이 많은 직원과 대규모 지사들을 보유하고 있는 아주 훌륭한 회사이다. 결국, 지난해에 Walsh사의 고객들이 구직하는 기간이 9개월이었던 반면, Delany사의 고객들은 평균 6개월 만에 직업을 구했다."

Argument   The proposal for using Walsh Personnel Firm in place of Delany would be a mistake.

89. The following appeared in a memo at XYZ company.

"When XYZ lays off employees, it pays Delany Personnel Firm to offer those employees assistance in creating réumé and developing interviewing skills, if they so desire. Laid-off employees have benefited greatly from Delany's services: last year those who used Delany found jobs much more quickly than did those who did not. Recently, it has been proposed that we use the less expensive Walsh Personnel Firm in place of Delany. This would be a mistake because eight years ago, when XYZ was using Walsh, only half of the workers we laid off at that time found jobs within a year. Moreover, Delany is clearly superior, as evidenced by its bigger staff and larger number of branch offices. After all, last year Delany's clients took an average of six months to find jobs, whereas Walsh's clients took nine."

Write a response in which you examine the stated and/or unstated assumptions of the argument. Be sure to explain how the argument depends on these assumptions and what the implications are for the argument if the assumptions prove unwarranted.

[86]번과 동일한 지문이나 instruction이 다름.

| Argument | The proposal for using Walsh Personnel Firm in place of Delany would be a mistake. |

91. Three years ago, because of flooding at the Western Palean Wildlife Preserve, 100 lions and 100 western gazelles were moved to the East Palean Preserve, an area that is home to most of the same species that are found in the western preserve, though in larger numbers, and to the eastern gazelle, a close relative of the western gazelle. The only difference in climate is that the eastern preserve typically has slightly less rainfall. Unfortunately, after three years in the eastern preserve, the imported western gazelle population has been virtually eliminated. Since the slight reduction in rainfall cannot be the cause of the virtual elimination of western gazelle, their disappearance must have been caused by the larger number of predators in the eastern preserve. [New]

Write a response in which you discuss what specific evidence is needed to evaluate the argument and explain how the evidence would weaken or strengthen the argument.

3년 전, Western Palean 야생동물 보호지역의 홍수로, 100마리의 사자와 100마리의 서부 영양이, 서부 보호지역에서 발견되는 대부분의 동일종들이 사는 East Palean 보호구역으로 옮겨졌는데, 이곳은 서부 영양과 비슷한 종인 동부 영양들이 많이 살고 있다. 기후의 차이는 단지 동부 보호지역의 강우량이 일반적으로 다소 적다는 것이다. 유감스럽게도 3년 후, 옮겨진 서부 영양이 동부 보호지역에서 거의 사라졌다. 서부 영양이 없어진 이유가 근소한 강우량의 감소 때문은 아닐 것이므로, 이들이 사라진 이유는 틀림없이 동부 보호지역에 사는 수많은 천적들 때문일 것이다.

Argument   The disappearance of western gazelle must have been caused by the larger number of predators in the eastern preserve.

92. Workers in the small town of Leeville take fewer sick days than workers in the large city of Masonton, 50 miles away. Moreover, relative to population size, the diagnosis of stress-related illness is proportionally much lower in Leeville than in Masonton. According to the Leeville Chamber of Commerce, these facts can be attributed to the health benefits of the relatively relaxed pace of life in Leeville.

Write a response in which you discuss one or more alternative explanations that could rival the proposed explanation and explain how your explanation(s) can plausibly account for the facts presented in the argument.

소도시 Leeville에 사는 근로자들이 50마일 떨어진 대도시 Masonton에 사는 근로자들보다 병가를 덜 낸다. 더구나 인구에 비해서, 스트레스 관련 질병의 진단은 Leeville이 Masonton보다 훨씬 적다. Leeville 상공회의소에 따르면, 이런 사실은 Leeville에서의 상대적으로 여유로운 생활에서 오는 건강상의 이점 때문이라고 한다.

Argument   The fewer sick days and the lower diagnosis of stress-related illness in Leeville can be attributed to the health benefits of the relatively relaxed pace of life in Leeville.

101. There is now evidence that the relaxed pace of life in small towns promotes better health and greater longevity than does the hectic pace of life in big cities. Businesses in the small town of Leeville report fewer days of sick leave taken by individual workers than do businesses in the nearby large city of Masonton. Furthermore, Leeville has only one physician for its one thousand residents, but in Masonton the proportion of physicians to residents is five times as high. Finally, the average age of Leeville residents is significantly higher than that of Masonton residents. These findings suggest that people seeking longer and healthier lives should consider moving to small communities. [Old version 234]

Write a response in which you examine the stated and/or unstated assumptions of the argument. Be sure to explain how the argument depends on these assumptions and what the implications are for the argument if the assumptions prove unwarranted.

작은 도시에서의 여유로운 생활이 바쁜 대도시 생활보다 더 나은 건강과 긴 수명을 촉진시킨다는 증거가 있다. 소도시 Leeville에 있는 사업체에서 개별 근로자들이 내는 병가 일수가 근처의 대도시 Masonton의 그것보다 적다는 보고가 있다. 더구나 Leeville은 1,000명당 1명의 의사가 있지만, Masonton의 주민당 의사 비율은 5배나 많다. 마지막으로, Leeville 주민들의 평균 나이는 Masonton 주민들보다 상당히 높다. 이러한 결과들은 오래 건강한 삶을 찾는 사람들은 작은 지역사회로 이사하는 것을 고려해야만 한다는 것을 시사해 주고 있다.

Argument People seeking longer and healthier lives should consider moving to small communities.

103. There is now evidence that the relaxed pace of life in small towns promotes better health and greater longevity than does the hectic pace of life in big cities. Businesses in the small town of Leeville report fewer days of sick leave taken by individual workers than do businesses in the nearby large city of Masonton. Furthermore, Leeville has only one physician for its one thousand residents, but in Masonton the proportion of physicians to residents is five times as high. Finally, the average age of Leeville residents is significantly higher than that of Masonton residents. These findings suggest that the relaxed pace of life in Leeville allows residents to live longer, healthier lives.

Write a response in which you discuss one or more alternative explanations that could rival the proposed explanation and explain how your explanation(s) can plausibly account for the facts presented in the argument.

[101]번과 거의 동일한 지문이나 결론과 instruction이 다름.

| Argument | These findings suggest that the relaxed pace of life in Leeville allows residents to live longer, healthier lives. |

113. The following is a recommendation from the personnel director to the president of Acme Publishing Company.

"Many other companies have recently stated that having their employees take the Easy Read Speed-Reading Course has greatly improved productivity. One graduate of the course was able to read a 500-page report in only two hours; another graduate rose from an assistant manager to vice president of the company in under a year. Obviously, the faster you can read, the more information you can absorb in a single workday. Moreover, Easy Read would cost Acme only $500 per employee — a small price to pay when you consider the benefits. Included in this fee is a three-week seminar in Spruce City and a lifelong subscription to the Easy Read newsletter. Clearly, to improve productivity, Acme should require all of our employees to take the Easy Read course."
[Old version 180]

Write a response in which you discuss what questions would need to be answered in order to decide whether the advice and the argument on which it is based are reasonable. Be sure to explain how the answers to these questions would help to evaluate the advice.

다음은 Acme 출판사의 인사 부장이 회사 사장에게 추천한 내용이다.

"많은 타 회사들은 최근 직원들에게 Easy Read 속독 과정을 받도록 한 뒤 생산성 향상을 가져왔다고 합니다. 이 교육을 받은 어느 직원은 단 2시간에 500페이지 분량의 보고서를 읽을 수 있었고; 또 다른 직원은 1년 이내에 부 부서장에서 부사장으로 승진했습니다. 분명히, 속독을 할수록, 하루에 더 많은 정보를 얻을 수 있습니다. 더구나 Easy Read 직원당 비용은 고작 5백 달러로, 이 점을 고려해 볼 때 아주 작은 비용입니다. 이 비용에는 Spruce시에서 3주간 세미나와 Easy Read 소식지의 평생 구독권입니다. 분명히, 생산성 향상을 위해서, Acme은 전 직원이 Easy Read 과정을 이수하도록 해야 합니다."

> Argument To improve productivity, Acme should require all of our employees to take the Easy Read course.

126. The following is a recommendation from the personnel director to the president of Acme Publishing Company.

"Many other companies have recently stated that having their employees take the Easy Read Speed-Reading Course has greatly improved productivity. One graduate of the course was able to read a 500-page report in only two hours; another graduate rose from an assistant manager to vice president of the company in under a year. Obviously, the faster you can read, the more information you can absorb in a single workday. Moreover, Easy Read would cost Acme only $500 per employee — a small price to pay when you consider the benefits. Included in this fee is a three-week seminar in Spruce City and a lifelong subscription to the Easy Read newsletter. Clearly, Acme would benefit greatly by requiring all of our employees to take the Easy Read course."

Write a response in which you discuss what specific evidence is needed to evaluate the argument and explain how the evidence would weaken or strengthen the argument.

[113]번과 거의 동일한 지문이나 instruction이 다름.

Argument   Acme would benefit greatly by requiring all of our employees to take the Easy Read course.

127. The following is a recommendation from the personnel director to the president of Acme Publishing Company.

"Many other companies have recently stated that having their employees take the Easy Read Speed-Reading Course has greatly improved productivity. One graduate of the course was able to read a 500-page report in only two hours; another graduate rose from an assistant manager to vice president of the company in under a year. Obviously, the faster you can read, the more information you can absorb in a single workday. Moreover, Easy Read would cost Acme only $500 per employee — a small price to pay when you consider the benefits. Included in this fee is a three-week seminar in Spruce City and a lifelong subscription to the Easy Read newsletter. Clearly, to improve overall productivity, Acme should require all of our employees to take the Easy Read course."

Write a response in which you discuss what questions would need to be answered in order to decide whether the recommendation and the argument on which it is based are reasonable. Be sure to explain how the answers to these questions would help to evaluate the recommendation.

[113]번과 거의 동일한 지문이나 instruction이 다름.

Argument To improve overall productivity, Acme should require all of our employees to take the Easy Read course.

Argue Groups

161. The following is a recommendation from the personnel director to the president of Acme Publishing Company.

"Many other companies have recently stated that having their employees take the Easy Read Speed-Reading Course has greatly improved productivity. One graduate of the course was able to read a 500-page report in only two hours; another graduate rose from an assistant manager to vice president of the company in under a year. Obviously, the faster you can read, the more information you can absorb in a single workday. Moreover, Easy Read would cost Acme only $500 per employee — a small price to pay when you consider the benefits. Included in this fee is a three-week seminar in Spruce City and a lifelong subscription to the Easy Read newsletter. Clearly, Acme would benefit greatly by requiring all of our employees to take the Easy Read course."

Write a response in which you examine the stated and/or unstated assumptions of the argument. Be sure to explain how the argument depends on these assumptions and what the implications are for the argument if the assumptions prove unwarranted.

[113]번과 거의 동일한 지문이나 instruction이 다름.

| Argument | Acme would benefit greatly by requiring all of our employees to take the Easy Read course. |

The following appeared in a letter to the school board in the town of Centerville.

"All students should be required to take the driver's education course at Centerville High School. In the past two years, several accidents in and around Centerville have involved teenage drivers. Since a number of parents in Centerville have complained that they are too busy to teach their teenagers to drive, some other instruction is necessary to ensure that these teenagers are safe drivers. Although there are two driving schools in Centerville, parents on a tight budget cannot afford to pay for driving instruction. Therefore an effective and mandatory program sponsored by the high school is the only solution to this serious problem." [Old version 175]

Write a response in which you examine the stated and/or unstated assumptions of the argument. Be sure to explain how the argument depends on these assumptions and what the implications are for the argument if the assumptions prove unwarranted.

다음은 Centerville시의 교육위원회에 보낸 편지 내용이다.

"모든 학생들은 Centervile 고등학교에서 운전 교육을 받도록 해야 한다. 지난 2년 동안 Centerville 인근에서 일어난 몇 건의 사고는 10대 운전자들이 관련되어 있다. Centerville의 많은 부모들은 시간상 자녀들 운전교육을 할 수 없다고 불평하기 때문에, 아이들이 안전 운전자가 되도록 하는 다른 조치가 필요하다. Centerville에는 2곳의 운전학원이 있지만, 생계가 빠듯한 부모들은 강습료를 감당하기 힘들다. 그러므로 고등학교에서 지원하는 효과적이면서 의무적인 프로그램만이 이러한 심각한 문제를 해결할 수 있다."

Argument   All students should be required to take the driver's education course at Centerville High School.

134. The following appeared in a letter to the school board in the town of Centerville.

"All students should be required to take the driver's education course at Centerville High School. In the past two years, several accidents in and around Centerville have involved teenage drivers. Since a number of parents in Centerville have complained that they are too busy to teach their teenagers to drive, some other instruction is necessary to ensure that these teenagers are safe drivers. Although there are two driving schools in Centerville, parents on a tight budget cannot afford to pay for driving instruction. Therefore an effective and mandatory program sponsored by the high school is the only solution to this serious problem."

Write a response in which you discuss what specific evidence is needed to evaluate the argument and explain how the evidence would weaken or strengthen the argument.

[132]번과 동일한 지문이나 instruction이 다름.

Argument   All students should be required to take the driver's education course at Centerville High School.

136. The following appeared in a letter to the school board in the town of Centerville.

"All students should be required to take the driver's education course at Centerville High School. In the past two years, several accidents in and around Centerville have involved teenage drivers. Since a number of parents in Centerville have complained that they are too busy to teach their teenagers to drive, some other instruction is necessary to ensure that these teenagers are safe drivers. Although there are two driving schools in Centerville, parents on a tight budget cannot afford to pay for driving instruction. Therefore an effective and mandatory program sponsored by the high school is the only solution to this serious problem."

Write a response in which you discuss what questions would need to be answered in order to decide whether the recommendation and the argument on which it is based are reasonable. Be sure to explain how the answers to these questions would help to evaluate the recommendation.

[132]번과 동일한 지문이나 instruction이 다름.

| Argument | All students should be required to take the driver's education course at Centerville High School. |

135. The data from a survey of high school math and science teachers show that in the district of Sanlee many of these teachers reported assigning daily homework, whereas in the district of Marlee, most science and math teachers reported assigning homework no more than two or three days per week. Despite receiving less frequent homework assignments, Marlee students earn better grades overall and are less likely to be required to repeat a year of school than are students in Sanlee. These results call into question the usefulness of frequent homework assignments. Most likely the Marlee students have more time to concentrate on individual assignments than do the Sanlee students who have homework every day. Therefore teachers in our high schools should assign homework no more than twice a week.

Write a response in which you discuss what specific evidence is needed to evaluate the argument and explain how the evidence would weaken or strengthen the argument.

고등학교 수학과 과학 교사들을 대상으로 한 조사에서, Sanlee 교육국 내 많은 교사들이 매일 숙제를 내준다고 한 반면, Marlee 교육국 내 대다수 수학과 과학 교사들은 일주일에 2~3번 정도의 숙제를 내준다고 했다. 숙제가 적었음에도 불구하고, Marlee 교육구 학생들이 Sanlee 교육구 학생들보다 전반적으로 더 좋은 성적을 얻고 유급도 적은 것 같다. 이러한 결과는 잦은 숙제에 대한 효용성에 의구심을 불러일으킨다. 아마도 Marlee 교육구 학생들은 매일 숙제가 있는 Sanlee 교육구 학생들보다 개인적인 일에 더 많은 시간을 집중할 것이다. 그러므로 우리 고등학교 교사들은 일주일에 2번 이상 숙제를 내줘서는 안 된다.

Argument   Therefore teachers in our high schools should assign homework no more than twice a week.

137. While the Department of Education in the state of Attra recommends that high school students be assigned homework every day, the data from a recent statewide survey of high school math and science teachers give us reason to question the usefulness of daily homework. In the district of Sanlee, 86 percent of the teachers reported assigning homework three to five times a week, whereas in the district of Marlee, less than 25 percent of the teachers reported assigning homework three to five times a week. Yet the students in Marlee earn better grades overall and are less likely to be required to repeat a year of school than are the students in Sanlee. Therefore, all teachers in our high schools should assign homework no more than twice a week.

Write a response in which you examine the stated and/or unstated assumptions of the argument. Be sure to explain how the argument depends on these assumptions and what the implications are for the argument if the assumptions prove unwarranted.

Attra주의 교육부는 고등학교 학생들에게 매일 숙제를 내줄 것을 권고하나 반면, 최근 주 전체 고등학교 수학과 과학 교사들을 대상으로 한 조사에서는, 매일 숙제를 내주는 것에 대한 효율성에 대해 이의를 제기했다. Marlee 관할 내의 교사 중 25% 미만이 주당 3~5회 정도 숙제를 내준다고 한 반면, Sanlee 관할 내의 교사 중 86%가 3~5회 정도 숙제를 내준다고 했다. 그러나 Marlee 관할 내에 있는 학생들은 전체적으로 성적이 좋으며, Sanlee 관할 내의 학생들보다 유급이 적은 편이다. 따라서 우리의 모든 고등학교 교사들은 주당 2회 이하로 숙제를 내주어야 한다.

> Argument Therefore, all teachers in our high schools should assign homework no more than twice a week.

140. While the Department of Education in the state of Attra suggests that high school students be assigned homework every day, the data from a recent statewide survey of high school math and science teachers give us reason to question the usefulness of daily homework. In the district of Sanlee, 86 percent of the teachers reported assigning homework three to five times a week, whereas in the district of Marlee, less than 25 percent of the teachers reported assigning homework three to five times a week. Yet the students in Marlee earn better grades overall and are less likely to be required to repeat a year of school than are the students in Sanlee. Therefore, we recommend that all teachers in our high schools should assign homework no more than twice a week.

Write a response in which you discuss what questions would need to be answered in order to decide whether the recommendation and the argument on which it is based are reasonable. Be sure to explain how the answers to these questions would help to evaluate the recommendation.

[137]번과 거의 동일한 지문이나 instruction이 다름.

| Argument | Therefore, we recommend that all teachers in our high schools should assign homework no more than twice a week.

142. Hospital statistics regarding people who go to the emergency room after roller-skating accidents indicate the need for more protective equipment. Within that group of people, 75 percent of those who had accidents in streets or parking lots had not been wearing any protective clothing (helmets, knee pads, etc.) or any light-reflecting material (clip-on lights, glow-in-the-dark wrist pads, etc.). Clearly, the statistics indicate that by investing in high-quality protective gear and reflective equipment, roller skaters will greatly reduce their risk of being severely injured in an accident. [New]

Write a response in which you examine the stated and/or unstated assumptions of the argument. Be sure to explain how the argument depends on these assumptions and what the implications are for the argument if the assumptions prove unwarranted.

롤러스케이트를 타다 사고가 나서 응급실을 찾는 사람들에 대한 병원 통계는 더 많은 보호장비가 필요하다는 것을 보여준다. 이 사람들 중, 길거리나 주차장에서 사고를 낸 사람들의 75%가 아무런 보호복(헬멧, 무릎 보호대 등)이나 빛 반사용 기구(클립식 라이트, 야광 손목 보호대 등)를 착용하지 않았다. 분명히, 이 통계는 질 좋은 보호 장비와 반사기구에 투자를 함으로써 롤러스케이트를 타는 사람들이 사고 시 심한 부상을 당하는 위험을 상당히 줄일 것이란 점을 시사한다.

Argument Roller skaters will greatly reduce their risk of being severely injured in an accident by investing in high-quality protective gear and reflective equipment.

152. The following appeared in a memo to the board of directors of Bargain Brand Cereals.

"One year ago we introduced our first product, Bargain Brand breakfast cereal. Our very low prices quickly drew many customers away from the top-selling cereal companies. Although the companies producing the top brands have since tried to compete with us by lowering their prices and although several plans to introduce their own budget brands, not once have we needed to raise our prices to continue making a profit. Given our success in selling cereal, we recommend that Bargain Brand now expand its business and begin marketing other low-priced food products as quickly as possible." [Old version 171]

Write a response in which you discuss what questions would need to be answered in order to decide whether the recommendation and the argument on which it is based are reasonable. Be sure to explain how the answers to these questions would help to evaluate the recommendation.

다음은 Bargain Brand Cereals 회사의 이사회에 보낸 메모이다.

"1년 전 우리 회사는 우리의 첫 제품인 Bargain Brand라는 아침식사용 시리얼을 출시했었다. 이 제품의 값싼 가격 때문에 가장 잘 팔리는 시리얼 회사들의 고객들을 단번에 끌어왔다. 그간 최고 제품을 가지고 있던 이들 회사들이 가격을 낮추면서 우리와 경쟁을 해왔고, 심지어 수차례에 걸쳐 저가상품을 출시했으나 지속적인 수익을 내기 위해서 한 번도 가격을 올릴 필요는 없었다. 성공적인 시리얼 판매에 따라서 이제 Bargain Brand의 사업을 확장하고 가능한 또 다른 저가 식품을 빨리 출시해야 한다."

Rcommendation   Bargain Brand now should expand its business and begin marketing other low-priced food products as quickly as possible.

153. The following appeared in a memo to the board of directors of Bargain Brand Cereals.

"One year ago we introduced our first product, Bargain Brand breakfast cereal. Our very low prices quickly drew many customers away from the top-selling cereal companies. Although the companies producing the top brands have since tried to compete with us by lowering their prices and although several plan to introduce their own budget brands, not once have we needed to raise our prices to continue making a profit. Given our success in selling cereal, we recommend that Bargain Brand now expand its business and begin marketing other low-priced food products as quickly as possible."

Write a response in which you examine the stated and/or unstated assumptions of the argument. Be sure to explain how the argument depends on these assumptions and what the implications are for the argument if the assumptions prove unwarranted.

[152]번과 동일한 지문이나 instruction이 다름.

Argument Bargain Brand now should expand its business and begin marketing other low-priced food products as quickly as possible.

157. The following appeared in a memo from the marketing director of Top Dog Pet Stores.

"Five years ago Fish Emporium started advertising in the magazine Exotic Pets Monthly. Their stores saw sales increase by 15 percent after their ads began appearing in the magazine. The three Fish Emporium stores in Gulf City saw an even greater increase than that. Because Top Dog Pet Stores is based in Gulf City, it seems clear that we should start placing our own ads in Exotic Pets Monthly. If we do so, we will be sure to reverse the recent trend of declining sales and start making a profit again."
[New]

Write a response in which you examine the stated and/or unstated assumptions of the argument. Be sure to explain how the argument depends on these assumptions and what the implications are for the argument if the assumptions prove unwarranted.

다음은 Top Dog Pet 가게의 영업 담당 이사가 한 메모 내용이다.

"5년 전, Fish Emporium은 Fxotic Pets Monthly라는 월간잡지에 광고를 시작했다. 광고가 잡지에 나간 후, 그들의 가게들은 15%나 매출이 증가했다. Gulf City에 있는 세 개의 Fish Emporium 가게들은 그보다도 매출이 더 많이 늘었다. Top Dog Pet 가게들도 Gulf City에 있기 때문에, 우리도 Exotic Pets Monthly 월간지에 광고를 시작해야 한다는 것은 자명하다. 그렇게 한다면, 최근의 매출감소 추세를 반전시키고 다시 수익을 낼 것이다."

| Argument | We should start placing our own ads in Exotic Pets Monthly to reverse the recent trend of declining sales and start making a profit again.

158. The following appeared in a memo from the marketing director of Top Dog Pet Stores.

"Five years ago, Fish Emporium started advertising in the magazine Exotic Pets Monthly. Their stores saw sales increase by 15 percent. The three Fish Emporium stores in Gulf City saw an even greater increase than that. Because Top Dog has some of its largest stores in Gulf City, it seems clear that we should start placing our own ads in Exotic Pets Monthly. If we do so, we will be sure to reverse the recent trend of declining sales and start making a profit again."

Write a response in which you discuss what specific evidence is needed to evaluate the argument and explain how the evidence would weaken or strengthen the argument.

[157]번과 거의 동일한 지문이나 instruction이 다름.

Argument We should start placing our own ads in Exotic Pets Monthly to reverse the recent trend of declining sales and start making a profit again.

160. The following appeared in a recommendation from the President of the Amburg Chamber of Commerce.

"Last October, the city of Belleville installed high-intensity lighting in its central business district, and vandalism there declined almost immediately. The city of Amburg, on the other hand, recently instituted police patrols on bicycles in its business district. However, the rate of vandalism here remains constant. Since high-intensity lighting is clearly the most effective way to combat crime, we recommend using the money that is currently being spent on bicycle patrols to install such lighting throughout Amburg. If we install this high-intensity lighting, we will significantly reduce crime rates in Amburg." [Old version 205]

Write a response in which you discuss what questions would need to be answered in order to decide whether the recommendation is likely to have the predicted result. Be sure to explain how the answers to these questions would help to evaluate the recommendation.

다음은 Amburg 상공회의소 회장의 권고이다.

"지난 10월, Belleville시는 중심 상업지역에 고강도 조명을 설치했고, 기물파손 행위는 즉시 줄어들었다. 반면, Amburg시는 최근 상업지역에 자전거 순찰을 시작했다. 그러나 기물파손 행위는 여전했다. 고강도 조명은 확실히 범죄와의 전쟁에서 가장 효과적인 방법이기 때문에, 현재 자전거 순찰에 쓰는 돈을 Amburg시 전체에 이러한 조명등을 설치하는 데 사용할 것을 건의한다. 우리가 이런 고강도 조명을 설치한다면, Amburg시에서의 범죄율은 상당히 감소할 것이다."

Recommendation   We should use the money that is currently being spent on bicycle patrols to install such lighting throughout Amburg to reduce crime rates.

172. The following appeared in a recommendation from the president of Amburg's Chamber of Commerce.

"Last October the city of Belleville installed high-intensity lighting in its central business district, and vandalism there declined within a month. The city of Amburg has recently begun police patrols on bicycles in its business district, but the rate of vandalism there remains constant. We should install high-intensity lighting throughout Amburg, then, because doing so is a more effective way to combat crime. By reducing crime in this way, we can revitalize the declining neighborhoods in our city."

Write a response in which you discuss what specific evidence is needed to evaluate the argument and explain how the evidence would weaken or strengthen the argument.

[160]번과 거의 동일한 지문이나 instruction이 다름.

Argument	We should install high-intensity lighting throughout Amburg to revitalize the declining neighborhoods in our city.

168. The following is a letter that recently appeared in the Oak City Gazette, a local newspaper.

"The primary function of the Committee for a Better Oak City is to advise the city government on how to make the best use of the city's limited budget. However, at some of our recent meetings we failed to make important decisions because of the foolish objections raised by committee members who are not even residents of Oak City. People who work in Oak City but who live elsewhere cannot fully understand the business and politics of the city. After all, only Oak City residents pay city taxes, and therefore only residents understand how that money could best be used to improve the city. We recommend, then, that the Committee for a Better Oak City vote to restrict its membership to city residents only. We predict that, without the interference of non-residents, the committee will be able to make Oak City a better place in which to live and work." [Old version 177]

Write a response in which you discuss what questions would need to be answered in order to decide whether the recommendation is likely to have the predicted result. Be sure to explain how the answers to these questions would help to evaluate the recommendation.

다음은 한 지역 신문인 Oak City Gazette지에 최근 실린 글이다.

"Better Oak시 위원회의 주 기능은 한정된 시의 예산을 어떻게 쓰는 것이 최선인지에 대해서 시 정부에 자문을 하는 것이다. 하지만 최근의 회의에서 Oak시의 주민도 아닌 위원회 위원들이 제기한 어리석은 반대로 우리는 중요한 결정을 내리지 못했다. Oak시에서 근무를 하지만 Oak시에 살지 않는 사람들은 시의 사업과 정치를 완전하게 이해할 수 없다. 결국, Oak시의 주민들만 시의 세금을 내기 때문에, 주민들만이 시를 발전시키기기 위해서 어떻게 그 돈을 써야 하는지 알 수 있다. 그래서 우리는 Better Oak시의 위원회가 그 회원 자격을 시의 주민들에 한정하는 투표를 할 것을 권한다. 우리는, 비주민들의 간섭 없이, 이 위원회가 Oak시를 살기 좋고 일하기 좋은 곳으로 만들 것이라고 믿는다."

Recommendation   The Committee for a Better Oak City vote to restrict its membership to city residents only.

170. The following appeared in a memo from the vice president of a company that builds shopping malls around the country.

"The surface of a section of Route 101, paved just two years ago by Good Intentions Roadways, is now badly cracked with a number of dangerous potholes. In another part of the state, a section of Route 40, paved by Appian Roadways more than four years ago, is still in good condition. In a demonstration of their continuing commitment to quality, Appian Roadways recently purchased state-of-the-art paving machinery and hired a new quality-control manager. Therefore, I recommend hiring Appian Roadways to construct the access roads for all our new shopping malls. I predict that our Appian access roads will not have to be repaired for at least four years." [Old version 233]

Write a response in which you discuss what questions would need to be answered in order to decide whether the recommendation is likely to have the predicted result. Be sure to explain how the answers to these questions would help to evaluate the recommendation.

다음은 전국에 걸쳐 쇼핑몰을 건설하는 회사 부사장 메모 내용이다.

"Good Intentions Roadways가 겨우 2년 전에 포장한, 101번 도로 구간의 표면이, 심하게 금이 가면서 위험한 작은 웅덩이들이 생겼다. 4년 전 Appian Roadways사가 포장한, 주의 다른 쪽 40번 도로 구간은, 여전히 상태가 좋다. 변함없는 품질보장을 보여주는 방편으로, Appian Roadways은 최근 최고의 포장 기계를 구매를 했고, 새로운 품질관리 담당자를 고용했다. 그러므로 나는 우리의 신규 쇼핑몰 진입로 건설에 Appian Roadway사를 고용할 것을 추천한다. 난 Appian이 건설한 진입로가 최소한 4년간은 보수가 필요 없을 것이라고 예측한다."

| Recommendation | We should hire Appian Roadways to construct the access roads for all our new shopping malls. |

Argue

Questions by ETS

ETS가 발표한 아규 에세이 순서

This page contains the Argument topics for the Analytical Writing section of the GRE ® revised General Test. When you take the test, you will be presented with one Argument topic from this pool.

Each Argument topic consists of a passage that presents an argument followed by specific task instructions that tell you how to analyze the argument. The wording of some topics in the test might vary slightly from what is presented here. Also, because there may be multiple versions of some topics with similar or identical wording but with different task instructions, it is very important to read your test topic and its specific task directions carefully and respond to the wording as it appears in the actual test.

---

1. Woven baskets characterized by a particular distinctive pattern have previously been found only in the immediate vicinity of the prehistoric village of Palea and therefore were believed to have been made only by the Palean people. Recently, however, archaeologists discovered such a "Palean" basket in Lithos, an ancient village across the Brim River from Palea. The Brim River is very deep and broad, and so the ancient Paleans could have crossed it only by boat, and no Palean boats have been found. Thus it follows that the so-called Palean baskets were not uniquely Palean.

Write a response in which you discuss what specific evidence is needed to evaluate the argument and explain how the evidence would weaken or strengthen the argument.

---

2. The following appeared as part of a letter to the editor of a scientific journal.

"A recent study of eighteen rhesus monkeys provides clues as to the effects of birth order on an individual's levels of stimulation. The study showed that in stimulating situations (such as an encounter with an unfamiliar monkey), firstborn infant monkeys produce up to twice as much of the hormone cortisol, which primes the body for increased activity levels, as do their younger siblings. Firstborn humans also produce relatively high levels of cortisol in stimulating situations (such as the return of a parent after an absence). The study also found that during pregnancy, first-time mother monkeys had higher levels of cortisol than did those who had had several offspring." [New]

Write a response in which you discuss one or more alternative explanations that could rival the proposed explanation and explain how your explanation(s) can plausibly account for the facts presented in the argument.

---

3. The following appeared as a letter to the editor from a Central Plaza store owner.

"Over the past two years, the number of shoppers in Central Plaza has been steadily decreasing while the popularity of skateboarding has increased dramatically. Many Central Plaza store owners believe that the decrease in their business is due to the number of skateboard users in the plaza. There has also been a dramatic increase in the amount of litter and vandalism throughout the plaza. Thus, we recommend that the city prohibit skateboarding in Central Plaza. If skateboarding is prohibited here, we predict that business in Central Plaza will return to its previously high levels."

Write a response in which you discuss what questions would need to be answered in order to decide whether the recommendation is likely to have the predicted result. Be sure to explain how the answers to these questions would help to evaluate the recommendation.

4. The following appeared in a letter from a homeowner to a friend.

"Of the two leading real estate firms in our town — Adams Realty and Fitch Realty — Adams Realty is clearly superior. Adams has 40 real estate agents; in contrast, Fitch has 25, many of whom work only part-time. Moreover, Adams' revenue last year was twice as high as that of Fitch and included home sales that averaged $168,000, compared to Fitch's $144,000. Homes listed with Adams sell faster as well: ten years ago I listed my home with Fitch, and it took more than four months to sell; last year, when I sold another home, I listed it with Adams, and it took only one month. Thus, if you want to sell your home quickly and at a good price, you should use Adams Realty."

Write a response in which you examine the stated and/or unstated assumptions of the argument. Be sure to explain how the argument depends on these assumptions and what the implications are for the argument if the assumptions prove unwarranted.

5. The following appeared in a letter to the editor of the Balmer Island Gazette.

"On Balmer Island, where mopeds serve as a popular form of transportation, the population increases to 100,000 during the summer months. To reduce the number of accidents involving mopeds and pedestrians, the town council of Balmer Island should limit the number of mopeds rented by the island's moped rental companies from 50 per day to 25 per day during the summer season. By limiting the number of rentals, the town council will attain the 50 percent annual reduction in moped accidents that was achieved last year on the neighboring island of Seaville, when Seaville's town council enforced similar limits on moped rentals."

Write a response in which you discuss what questions would need to be answered in order to decide whether the recommendation is likely to have the predicted result.

Be sure to explain how the answers to these questions would help to evaluate the recommendation.

---

6. Arctic deer live on islands in Canada's arctic regions. They search for food by moving over ice from island to island during the course of the year. Their habitat is limited to areas warm enough to sustain the plants on which they feed and cold enough, at least some of the year, for the ice to cover the sea separating the islands, allowing the deer to travel over it. Unfortunately, according to reports from local hunters, the deer populations are declining. Since these reports coincide with recent global warming trends that have caused the sea ice to melt, we can conclude that the purported decline in deer populations is the result of the deer's being unable to follow their age-old migration patterns across the frozen sea.

Write a response in which you discuss what specific evidence is needed to evaluate the argument and explain how the evidence would weaken or strengthen the argument.

---

7. The following is a recommendation from the Board of Directors of Monarch Books.

"We recommend that Monarch Books open a café in its store. Monarch, having been in business at the same location for more than twenty years, has a large customer base because it is known for its wide selection of books on all subjects. Clearly, opening the café would attract more customers. Space could be made for the café by discontinuing the children's book section, which will probably become less popular given that the most recent national census indicated a significant decline in the percentage of the population under age ten. Opening a café will allow Monarch to attract more customers and better compete with Regal Books, which recently opened its own café"

Write a response in which you discuss what questions would need to be answered in order to decide whether the recommendation is likely to have the predicted result. Be sure to explain how the answers to these questions would help to evaluate the recommendation.

---

8. The following appeared in a memo from the director of student housing at Buckingham College.

"To serve the housing needs of our students, Buckingham College should build a number of new dormitories. Buckingham's enrollment is growing and, based on current trends, will double over the next 50 years, thus making existing dormitory space inadequate. Moreover, the average rent for an apartment in our town has risen in recent years. Consequently, students will find it increasingly difficult to afford off-campus housing. Finally, attractive new dormitories would make prospective students more likely to enroll at Buckingham."

Write a response in which you discuss what specific evidence is needed to evaluate the argument and explain how the evidence would weaken or strengthen the argument.

---

9. Nature's Way, a chain of stores selling health food and other health-related products, is opening its next franchise in the town of Plainsville. The store should prove to be very successful: Nature's Way franchises tend to be most profitable in areas where residents lead healthy lives, and clearly Plainsville is such an area. Plainsville merchants report that sales of running shoes and exercise clothing are at all-time highs. The local health club has more members than ever, and the weight training and aerobics classes are always full. Finally, Plainsville's schoolchildren

represent a new generation of potential customers: these schoolchildren are required to participate in a fitness-for-life program, which emphasizes the benefits of regular exercise at an early age.

Write a response in which you examine the stated and/or unstated assumptions of the argument. Be sure to explain how the argument depends on these assumptions and what the implications are for the argument if the assumptions prove unwarranted.

---

10. Twenty years ago, Dr. Field, a noted anthropologist, visited the island of Tertia. Using an observation-centered approach to studying Tertian culture, he concluded from his observations that children in Tertia were reared by an entire village rather than by their own biological parents. Recently another anthropologist, Dr. Karp, visited the group of islands that includes Tertia and used the interview-centered method to study child-rearing practices. In the interviews that Dr. Karp conducted with children living in this group of islands, the children spent much more time talking about their biological parents than about other adults in the village. Dr. Karp decided that Dr. Field's conclusion about Tertian village culture must be invalid. Some anthropologists recommend that to obtain accurate information on Tertian child-rearing practices, future research on the subject should be conducted via the interview-centered method.

Write a response in which you discuss what questions would need to be answered in order to decide whether the recommendation and the argument on which it is based are reasonable. Be sure to explain how the answers to these questions would help to evaluate the recommendation.

11. The council of Maple County, concerned about the county's becoming overdeveloped, is debating a proposed measure that would prevent the development of existing farmland in the county. But the council is also concerned that such a restriction, by limiting the supply of new housing, could lead to significant increases in the price of housing in the county. Proponents of the measure note that Chestnut County established a similar measure ten years ago, and its housing prices have increased only modestly since. However, opponents of the measure note that Pine County adopted restrictions on the development of new residential housing fifteen years ago, and its housing prices have since more than doubled. The council currently predicts that the proposed measure, if passed, will result in a significant increase in housing prices in Maple County.

Write a response in which you discuss what questions would need to be answered in order to decide whether the prediction and the argument on which it is based are reasonable. Be sure to explain how the answers to these questions would help to evaluate the prediction.

12. Fifteen years ago, Omega University implemented a new procedure that encouraged students to evaluate the teaching effectiveness of all their professors. Since that time, Omega professors have begun to assign higher grades in their classes, and overall student grade averages at Omega have risen by 30 percent. Potential employers, looking at this dramatic rise in grades, believe that grades at Omega are inflated and do not accurately reflect student achievement; as a result, Omega graduates have not been as successful at getting jobs as have graduates from nearby Alpha University. To enable its graduates to secure better jobs, Omega University should terminate student evaluation of professors.

Write a response in which you discuss what specific evidence is needed to evaluate the argument and explain how the evidence would weaken or strengthen the argument.

---

13. In an attempt to improve highway safety, Prunty County last year lowered its speed limit from 55 to 45 miles per hour on all county highways. But this effort has failed: the number of accidents has not decreased, and, based on reports by the highway patrol, many drivers are exceeding the speed limit. Prunty County should instead undertake the same kind of road improvement project that Butler County completed five years ago: increasing lane widths, resurfacing rough highways, and improving visibility at dangerous intersections. Today, major Butler County roads still have a 55 mph speed limit, yet there were 25 percent fewer reported accidents in Butler County this past year than there were five years ago. [18]

Write a response in which you discuss what specific evidence is needed to evaluate the argument and explain how the evidence would weaken or strengthen the argument.

---

14. The following appeared as part of an article in a business magazine. [New]

"A recent study rating 300 male and female Mentian advertising executives according to the average number of hours they sleep per night showed an association between the amount of sleep the executives need and the success of their firms. Of the advertising firms studied, those whose executives reported needing no more than 6 hours of sleep per night had higher profit margins and faster growth. These results suggest that if a business wants to prosper, it should hire only people who need less than 6 hours of sleep per night."

Write a response in which you examine the stated and/or unstated assumptions of the argument. Be sure to explain how the argument depends on these assumptions and what the implications are for the argument if the assumptions prove unwarranted.

---

15. The following memorandum is from the business manager of Happy Pancake House restaurants.

"Recently, butter has been replaced by margarine in Happy Pancake House restaurants throughout the southwestern United States. This change, however, has had little impact on our customers. In fact, only about 2 percent of customers have complained, indicating that an average of 98 people out of 100 are happy with the change. Furthermore, many servers have reported that a number of customers who ask for butter do not complain when they are given margarine instead. Clearly, either these customers do not distinguish butter from margarine or they use the term 'butter' to refer to either butter or margarine."

Write a response in which you discuss one or more alternative explanations that could rival the proposed explanation and explain how your explanation(s) can plausibly account for the facts presented in the argument.

---

16. In surveys Mason City residents rank water sports (swimming, boating, and fishing) among their favorite recreational activities. The Mason River flowing through the city is rarely used for these pursuits, however, and the city park department devotes little of its budget to maintaining riverside recreational facilities. For years there have been complaints from residents about the quality of the river's water and the river's smell. In response, the state has recently announced plans to clean up Mason River. Use of the river for water sports is, therefore, sure to

increase. The city government should for that reason devote more money in this year's budget to riverside recreational facilities.

Write a response in which you examine the stated and/or unstated assumptions of the argument. Be sure to explain how the argument depends on these assumptions and what the implications are for the argument if the assumptions prove unwarranted.

---

17. The following appeared in a memorandum from the manager of WWAC radio station.

"To reverse a decline in listener numbers, our owners have decided that WWAC must change from its current rock-music format. The decline has occurred despite population growth in our listening area, but that growth has resulted mainly from people moving here after their retirement. We must make listeners of these new residents. We could switch to a music format tailored to their tastes, but a continuing decline in local sales of recorded music suggests limited interest in music. Instead we should change to a news and talk format, a form of radio that is increasingly popular in our area."

Write a response in which you discuss what specific evidence is needed to evaluate the argument and explain how the evidence would weaken or strengthen.

---

18. The following is a memorandum from the business manager of a television station.

"Over the past year, our late-night news program has devoted increased time to national news and less time to weather and local news. During this period, most of the complaints received from viewers were concerned with our station's coverage of weather and local news. In addition, local businesses that used to advertise during our late-night news program have canceled their advertising contracts with us. Therefore, in order to attract more viewers to our news programs and to avoid losing any further advertising revenues, we should expand our coverage of weather and local news on all our news programs."

Write a response in which you examine the stated and/or unstated assumptions of the argument. Be sure to explain how the argument depends on these assumptions and what the implications are for the argument if the assumptions prove unwarranted.

---

19. Two years ago, radio station WCQP in Rockville decided to increase the number of call-in advice programs that it broadcast; since that time, its share of the radio audience in the Rockville listening area has increased significantly. Given WCQP's recent success with call-in advice programming, and citing a nationwide survey indicating that many radio listeners are quite interested in such programs, the station manager of KICK in Medway recommends that KICK include more call-in advice programs in an attempt to gain a larger audience share in its listening area. [New]

Write a response in which you discuss what questions would need to be answered in order to decide whether the recommendation and the argument on which it is based are reasonable. Be sure to explain how the answers to these questions would help to evaluate the recommendation.

---

20. The following is a memorandum from the business manager of a television station.

"Over the past year, our late-night news program has devoted increased time to national news and less time to weather and local news. During this time period, most of the complaints received from viewers were concerned with our station's coverage of weather and local news. In addition, local businesses that used to advertise during our late-night news program have just canceled their advertising contracts with us. Therefore, in order to attract more viewers to the program and to avoid losing any further advertising revenues, we should restore the time devoted to weather and local news to its former level."

Write a response in which you discuss what specific evidence is needed to evaluate the argument and explain how the evidence would weaken or strengthen the argument.

---

21. The following appeared in an article written by Dr. Karp, an anthropologist.

"Twenty years ago, Dr. Field, a noted anthropologist, visited the island of Tertia and concluded from his observations that children in Tertia were reared by an entire village rather than by their own biological parents. However, my recent interviews with children living in the group of islands that includes Tertia show that these children spend much more time talking about their biological parents than about other adults in the village. This research of mine proves that Dr. Field's conclusion about Tertian village culture is invalid and thus that the observation-centered approach to studying cultures is invalid as well. The interview-centered method that my team of graduate students is currently using in Tertia will establish a much more accurate understanding of child-rearing traditions there and in other island cultures."

Write a response in which you discuss what specific evidence is needed to evaluate the argument and explain how the evidence would weaken or strengthen the argument.

22. According to a recent report, cheating among college and university students is on the rise. However, Groveton College has successfully reduced student cheating by adopting an honor code, which calls for students to agree not to cheat in their academic endeavors and to notify a faculty member if they suspect that others have cheated. Groveton's honor code replaced a system in which teachers closely monitored students; under that system, teachers reported an average of thirty cases of cheating per year. In the first year the honor code was in place, students reported twenty-one cases of cheating; five years later, this figure had dropped to fourteen. Moreover, in a recent survey, a majority of Groveton students said that they would be less likely to cheat with an honor code in place than without. Thus, all colleges and universities should adopt honor codes similar to Groveton's in order to decrease cheating among students.

Write a response in which you discuss what questions would need to be answered in order to decide whether the recommendation and the argument on which it is based are reasonable. Be sure to explain how the answers to these questions would help to evaluate the recommendation.

23. The following appeared in an article written by Dr. Karp, an anthropologist.

"Twenty years ago, Dr. Field, a noted anthropologist, visited the island of Tertia and concluded from his observations that children in Tertia were reared by an entire village rather than by their own biological parents. However, my recent interviews with children living in the group of islands that includes Tertia show that these children spend much more time talking about their biological parents than about other adults in the village. This research of mine proves that Dr. Field's conclusion about Tertian village culture is invalid and thus that the observation-centered approach to studying cultures is invalid as well. The interview-centered method that my team of graduate students is currently using in Tertia will establish a much more accurate understanding of child-rearing traditions there and in other island cultures."

Write a response in which you examine the stated and/or unstated assumptions of the argument. Be sure to explain how the argument depends on these assumptions and what the implications are for the argument if the assumptions prove unwarranted.

---

24. A recently issued twenty-year study on headaches suffered by the residents of Mentia investigated the possible therapeutic effect of consuming salicylates. Salicylates are members of the same chemical family as aspirin, a medicine used to treat headaches. Although many foods are naturally rich in salicylates, food-processing companies also add salicylates to foods as preservatives. The twenty-year study found a correlation between the rise in the commercial use of salicylates and a steady decline in the average number of headaches reported by study participants. At the time when the study concluded, food-processing companies had just discovered that salicylates can also be used as flavor additives for foods, and, as a result, many companies plan to do so. Based on these study results, some health experts predict that residents of Mentia will suffer even fewer headaches in the future.

Write a response in which you discuss what questions would need to be answered in order to decide whether the prediction and the argument on which it is based are reasonable. Be sure to explain how the answers to these questions would help to evaluate the prediction.

---

25. The following was written as a part of an application for a small-business loan

by a group of developers in the city of Monroe.

"A jazz music club in Monroe would be a tremendously profitable enterprise. Currently, the nearest jazz club is 65 miles away; thus, the proposed new jazz club in Monroe, the C-Note, would have the local market all to itself. Plus, jazz is extremely popular in Monroe: over 100,000 people attended Monroe's annual jazz festival last summer; several well-known jazz musicians live in Monroe; and the highest-rated radio program in Monroe is 'Jazz Nightly,' which airs every weeknight at 7 P.M. Finally, a nationwide study indicates that the typical jazz fan spends close to $1,000 per year on jazz entertainment."

Write a response in which you discuss what specific evidence is needed to evaluate the argument and explain how the evidence would weaken or strengthen the argument.

---

26. The following appeared in the summary of a study on headaches suffered by the residents of Mentia.

"Salicylates are members of the same chemical family as aspirin, a medicine used to treat headaches. Although many foods are naturally rich in salicylates, for the past several decades, food-processing companies have also been adding salicylates to foods as preservatives. This rise in the commercial use of salicylates has been found to correlate with a steady decline in the average number of headaches reported by participants in our twenty-year study. Recently, food-processing companies have found that salicylates can also be used as flavor additives for foods. With this new use for salicylates, we can expect a continued steady decline in the number of headaches suffered by the average citizen of Mentia."

Write a response in which you discuss what specific evidence is needed to evaluate the argument and explain how the evidence would weaken or strengthen the argument.

---

27. The following appeared in a letter to the editor of a local newspaper.

"Commuters complain that increased rush-hour traffic on Blue Highway between the suburbs and the city center has doubled their commuting time. The favored proposal of the motorists' lobby is to widen the highway, adding an additional lane of traffic. But last year's addition of a lane to the nearby Green Highway was followed by a worsening of traffic jams on it. A better alternative is to add a bicycle lane to Blue Highway. Many area residents are keen bicyclists. A bicycle lane would encourage them to use bicycles to commute, and so would reduce rush-hour traffic rather than fostering an increase."

Write a response in which you discuss what specific evidence is needed to evaluate the argument and explain how the evidence would weaken or strengthen the argument.

---

28. The following appeared in the summary of a study on headaches suffered by the residents of Mentia.

"Salicylates are members of the same chemical family as aspirin, a medicine used to treat headaches. Although many foods are naturally rich in salicylates, for the past several decades, food-processing companies have also been adding salicylates to foods as preservatives. This rise in the commercial use of salicylates has been found to correlate with a steady decline in the average number of headaches reported by participants in our twenty-year study. Recently, food-processing companies have found that salicylates can also be used as flavor additives for foods. With this new use for salicylates, we can expect a continued steady decline in the number of headaches suffered by the average citizen of Mentia."

Write a response in which you examine the stated and/or unstated assumptions of the argument. Be sure to explain how the argument depends on these assumptions and what the implications are for the argument if the assumptions prove unwarranted.

---

29. The following appeared in an editorial in a local newspaper.

"Commuters complain that increased rush-hour traffic on Blue Highway between the suburbs and the city center has doubled their commuting time. The favored proposal of the motorists' lobby is to widen the highway, adding an additional lane of traffic. Opponents note that last year's addition of a lane to the nearby Green Highway was followed by a worsening of traffic jams on it. Their suggested alternative proposal is adding a bicycle lane to Blue Highway. Many area residents are keen bicyclists. A bicycle lane would encourage them to use bicycles to commute, it is argued, thereby reducing rush-hour traffic."

Write a response in which you discuss what questions would need to be answered in order to decide whether the recommendation and the argument on which it is based are reasonable. Be sure to explain how the answers to these questions would help to evaluate the recommendation.

---

30. The following appeared as a recommendation by a committee planning a ten-year budget for the city of Calatrava. [New]

"The birthrate in our city is declining: in fact, last year's birthrate was only one-half that of five years ago. Thus the number of students enrolled in our public schools will soon decrease dramatically, and we can safely reduce the funds budgeted for education during the next decade. At the same time, we can reduce funding for athletic playing fields and other recreational facilities. As a result, we will have sufficient money to fund city facilities and programs used primarily by adults, since we can expect the adult population of the city to increase."

Write a response in which you discuss what specific evidence is needed to evaluate the argument and explain how the evidence would weaken or strengthen the argument.

---

31. The following appeared in a letter to the editor of Parson City's local newspaper.

"In our region of Trillura, the majority of money spent on the schools that most students attend — the city-run public schools — comes from taxes that each city government collects. The region's cities differ, however, in the budgetary priority they give to public education. For example, both as a proportion of its overall tax revenues and in absolute terms, Parson City has recently spent almost twice as much per year as Blue City has for its public schools — even though both cities have about the same number of residents. Clearly, Parson City residents place a higher value on providing a good education in public schools than Blue City residents do."

Write a response in which you discuss what specific evidence is needed to evaluate the argument and explain how the evidence would weaken or strengthen the argument.

---

32. The following appeared in a memo from a vice president of Quiot Manufacturing.

"During the past year, Quiot Manufacturing had 30 percent more on-the-job accidents than at the nearby Panoply Industries plant, where the work shifts are one hour shorter than ours. Experts say that significant contributing factors in many on-the-job accidents are fatigue and sleep deprivation among workers. Therefore, to reduce the number of on-the-job accidents at Quiot and thereby increase productivity, we should shorten each of our three work shifts by one hour so that employees will get adequate amounts of sleep."

Write a response in which you examine the stated and/or unstated assumptions of the argument. Be sure to explain how the argument depends on these assumptions and what the implications are for the argument if the assumptions prove unwarranted.

33. The following appeared in a memorandum from the planning department of an electric power company.

"Several recent surveys indicate that home owners are increasingly eager to conserve energy. At the same time, manufacturers are now marketing many home appliances, such as refrigerators and air conditioners, that are almost twice as energy efficient as those sold a decade ago. Also, new technologies for better home insulation and passive solar heating are readily available to reduce the energy needed for home heating. Therefore, the total demand for electricity in our area will not increase — and may decline slightly. Since our three electric generating plants in operation for the past twenty years have always met our needs, construction of new generating plants will not be necessary."

Write a response in which you examine the stated and/or unstated assumptions of the argument. Be sure to explain how the argument depends on these assumptions and what the implications are for the argument if the assumptions prove unwarranted.

34. The vice president of human resources at Climpson Industries sent the following recommendation to the company's president.

"In an effort to improve our employees' productivity, we should implement electronic monitoring of employees' Internet use from their workstations. Employees who use the Internet from their workstations need to be identified and punished if we are to reduce the number of work hours spent on personal or recreational activities, such as shopping or playing games. By installing software to detect employees' Internet use on company computers, we can prevent employees from wasting time, foster a better work ethic at Climpson, and improve our overall profits."

Write a response in which you examine the stated and/or unstated assumptions of the argument. Be sure to explain how the argument depends on these assumptions and what the implications are for the argument if the assumptions prove unwarranted.

35. The following appeared in a letter from the owner of the Sunnyside Towers apartment complex to its manager.

"One month ago, all the shower heads in the first three buildings of the Sunnyside Towers complex were modified to restrict maximum water flow to one-third of what it used to be. Although actual readings of water usage before and after the adjustment are not yet available, the change will obviously result in a considerable savings for Sunnyside Corporation, since the corporation must pay for water each month. Except for a few complaints about low water pressure, no problems with showers have been reported since the adjustment. I predict that modifying shower heads to restrict water flow throughout all twelve buildings in the Sunnyside Towers complex will increase our profits even more dramatically."

Write a response in which you discuss what questions would need to be answered

in order to decide whether the prediction and the argument on which it is based are reasonable. Be sure to explain how the answers to these questions would help to evaluate the prediction.

---

36. The following report appeared in the newsletter of the West Meria Public Health Council.

"An innovative treatment has come to our attention that promises to significantly reduce absenteeism in our schools and workplaces. A study reports that in nearby East Meria, where fish consumption is very high, people visit the doctor only once or twice per year for the treatment of colds. Clearly, eating a substantial amount of fish can prevent colds. Since colds represent the most frequently given reason for absences from school and work, we recommend the daily use of Ichthaid — a nutritional supplement derived from fish oil — as a good way to prevent colds and lower absenteeism."

Write a response in which you discuss what specific evidence is needed to evaluate the argument and explain how the evidence would weaken or strengthen the argument.

---

37. The following appeared in a recommendation from the planning department of the city of Transopolis.

"Ten years ago, as part of a comprehensive urban renewal program, the city of Transopolis adapted for industrial use a large area of severely substandard housing near the freeway. Subsequently, several factories were constructed there, crime rates in the area declined, and property tax revenues for the entire city increased. To further revitalize the city, we should now take similar action in a declining residential area on the opposite side of the city. Since some houses and apartments in existing nearby neighborhoods are currently unoccupied, alternate housing for those displaced by this action will be readily available."

Write a response in which you discuss what specific evidence is needed to evaluate the argument and explain how the evidence would weaken or strengthen the argument.

---

38. The following appeared in a memo from the new vice president of Sartorian, a company that manufactures men's clothing.

"Five years ago, at a time when we had difficulties in obtaining reliable supplies of high quality wool fabric, we discontinued production of our alpaca overcoat. Now that we have a new fabric supplier, we should resume production. This coat should sell very well: since we have not offered an alpaca overcoat for five years and since our major competitor no longer makes an alpaca overcoat, there will be pent-up customer demand. Also, since the price of most types of clothing has increased in each of the past five years, customers should be willing to pay significantly higher prices for alpaca overcoats than they did five years ago, and our company profits will increase."

Write a response in which you discuss what specific evidence is needed to evaluate the argument and explain how the evidence would weaken or strengthen the argument.

---

39. A recent sales study indicates that consumption of seafood dishes in Bay City restaurants has increased by 30 percent during the past five years. Yet there are no currently operating city restaurants whose specialty is seafood. Moreover, the majority of families in Bay City are two-income families, and a nationwide study has shown that such families eat significantly fewer home-cooked meals than they

did a decade ago but at the same time express more concern about healthful eating. Therefore, the new Captain Seafood restaurant that specializes in seafood should be quite popular and profitable.

Write a response in which you discuss what specific evidence is needed to evaluate the argument and explain how the evidence would weaken or strengthen the argument.

40. Milk and dairy products are rich in vitamin D and calcium — substances essential for building and maintaining bones. Many people therefore say that a diet rich in dairy products can help prevent osteoporosis, a disease that is linked to both environmental and genetic factors and that causes the bones to weaken significantly with age. But a long-term study of a large number of people found that those who consistently consumed dairy products throughout the years of the study have a higher rate of bone fractures than any other participants in the study. Since bone fractures are symptomatic of osteoporosis, this study result shows that a diet rich in dairy products may actually increase, rather than decrease, the risk of osteoporosis.

Write a response in which you discuss what specific evidence is needed to evaluate the argument and explain how the evidence would weaken or strengthen the argument.

41. The following appeared in a health newsletter.

"A ten-year nationwide study of the effectiveness of wearing a helmet while bicycling indicates that ten years ago, approximately 35 percent of all bicyclists reported wearing helmets, whereas today that number is nearly 80 percent. Another study, however, suggests that during the same ten-year period, the number of bicycle-related accidents has increased 200 percent. These results demonstrate that bicyclists feel safer because they are wearing helmets, and they take more risks as a result. Thus, to reduce the number of serious injuries from bicycle accidents, the government should concentrate more on educating people about bicycle safety and less on encouraging or requiring bicyclists to wear helmets."

Write a response in which you examine the stated and/or unstated assumptions of the argument. Be sure to explain how the argument depends on these assumptions and what the implications are for the argument if the assumptions prove unwarranted.

---

42. The following is a letter to the head of the tourism bureau on the island of Tria.

"Erosion of beach sand along the shores of Tria Island is a serious threat to our island and our tourist industry. In order to stop the erosion, we should charge people for using the beaches. Although this solution may annoy a few tourists in the short term, it will raise money for replenishing the sand. Replenishing the sand, as was done to protect buildings on the nearby island of Batia, will help protect buildings along our shores, thereby reducing these buildings' risk of additional damage from severe storms. And since beaches and buildings in the area will be preserved, Tria's tourist industry will improve over the long term."

Write a response in which you discuss what specific evidence is needed to evaluate the argument and explain how the evidence would weaken or strengthen the argument.

43. The following appeared in a memorandum written by the chairperson of the West Egg Town Council.

"Two years ago, consultants predicted that West Egg's landfill, which is used for garbage disposal, would be completely filled within five years. During the past two years, however, the town's residents have been recycling twice as much material as they did in previous years. Next month the amount of recycled material — which includes paper, plastic, and metal — should further increase, since charges for pickup of other household garbage will double. Furthermore, over 90 percent of the respondents to a recent survey said that they would do more recycling in the future. Because of our town's strong commitment to recycling, the available space in our landfill should last for considerably longer than predicted."

Write a response in which you discuss what specific evidence is needed to evaluate the argument and explain how the evidence would weaken or strengthen the argument.

44. The following appeared in a letter to the editor of a journal on environmental issues.

"Over the past year, the Crust Copper Company (CCC) has purchased over 10,000 square miles of land in the tropical nation of West Fredonia. Mining copper on this land will inevitably result in pollution and, since West Fredonia is the home of several endangered animal species, in environmental disaster. But such disasters can be prevented if consumers simply refuse to purchase products that are made with CCC's copper unless the company abandons its mining plans."

Write a response in which you examine the stated and/or unstated assumptions of the argument. Be sure to explain how the argument depends on these assumptions and what the implications are for the argument if the assumptions prove unwarranted.

---

45. The following is part of a memorandum from the president of Humana University.

"Last year the number of students who enrolled in online degree programs offered by nearby Omni University increased by 50 percent. During the same year, Omni showed a significant decrease from prior years in expenditures for dormitory and classroom space, most likely because instruction in the online programs takes place via the Internet. In contrast, over the past three years, enrollment at Humana University has failed to grow, and the cost of maintaining buildings has increased along with our budget deficit. To address these problems, Humana University will begin immediately to create and actively promote online degree programs like those at Omni. We predict that instituting these online degree programs will help Humana both increase its total enrollment and solve its budget problems."

Write a response in which you discuss what questions would need to be answered in order to decide whether the prediction and the argument on which it is based are reasonable. Be sure to explain how the answers to these questions would help to evaluate the prediction.

---

46. The following appeared in a health magazine published in Corpora.

"Medical experts say that only one-quarter of Corpora's citizens meet the current standards for adequate physical fitness, even though twenty years ago, one-half of all of Corpora's citizens met the standards as then defined. But these experts are mistaken when they suggest that spending too much time using computers has caused a decline in fitness. Since overall fitness levels are highest in regions of Corpora where levels of computer ownership are also highest, it is clear that using computers has not made citizens less physically fit. Instead, as shown by this year's unusually low expenditures on fitness-related products and services, the recent decline in the economy is most likely the cause, and fitness levels will improve when the economy does."

Write a response in which you examine the stated and/or unstated assumptions of the argument. Be sure to explain how the argument depends on these assumptions and what the implications are for the argument if the assumptions prove unwarranted.

---

47. The following appeared in a memorandum from the owner of Movies Galore, a chain of movie-rental stores.

"Because of declining profits, we must reduce operating expenses at Movies Galore's ten movie-rental stores. Raising prices is not a good option, since we are famous for our low prices. Instead, we should reduce our operating hours. Last month our store in downtown Marston reduced its hours by closing at 6 : 00 p.m. rather than 9 : 00 p.m. and reduced its overall inventory by no longer stocking any DVD released more than five years ago. Since we have received very few customer complaints about these new policies, we should now adopt them at all other Movies Galore stores as our best strategies for improving profits."

Write a response in which you discuss what specific evidence is needed to evaluate the argument and explain how the evidence would weaken or strengthen the argument.

---

48. The following appeared in a magazine article about planning for retirement.

"Clearview should be a top choice for anyone seeking a place to retire, because it has spectacular natural beauty and a consistent climate. Another advantage is that housing costs in Clearview have fallen significantly during the past year, and taxes remain lower than those in neighboring towns. Moreover, Clearview's mayor promises many new programs to improve schools, streets, and public services. And best of all, retirees in Clearview can also expect excellent health care as they grow older, since the number of physicians in the area is far greater than the national average."

Write a response in which you discuss what specific evidence is needed to evaluate the argument and explain how the evidence would weaken or strengthen the argument.

---

49. The following is part of a memorandum from the president of Humana University.

"Last year the number of students who enrolled in online degree programs offered by nearby Omni University increased by 50 percent. During the same year, Omni showed a significant decrease from prior years in expenditures for dormitory and classroom space, most likely because online instruction takes place via the Internet. In contrast, over the past three years, enrollment at Humana University has failed to grow and the cost of maintaining buildings has increased. Thus, to increase enrollment and solve the problem of budget deficits at Humana University, we should initiate and actively promote online degree programs like those at Omni."

Write a response in which you examine the stated and/or unstated assumptions of the argument. Be sure to explain how the argument depends on these assumptions and what the implications are for the argument if the assumptions prove unwarranted.

50. An ancient, traditional remedy for insomnia — the scent of lavender flowers — has now been proved effective. In a recent study, 30 volunteers with chronic insomnia slept each night for three weeks on lavender-scented pillows in a controlled room where their sleep was monitored electronically. During the first week, volunteers continued to take their usual sleeping medication. They slept soundly but wakened feeling tired. At the beginning of the second week, the volunteers discontinued their sleeping medication. During that week, they slept less soundly than the previous week and felt even more tired. During the third week, the volunteers slept longer and more soundly than in the previous two weeks. Therefore, the study proves that lavender cures insomnia within a short period of time. [167]

Write a response in which you discuss what specific evidence is needed to evaluate the argument and explain how the evidence would weaken or strengthen the argument.

51. The following memorandum is from the business manager of Happy Pancake House restaurants.

"Butter has now been replaced by margarine in Happy Pancake House restaurants throughout the southwestern United States. Only about 2 percent of customers have complained, indicating that 98 people out of 100 are happy with the change. Furthermore, many servers have reported that a number of customers who ask for butter do not complain when they are given margarine instead. Clearly, either these customers cannot distinguish butter from margarine or they use the term 'butter' to refer to either butter or margarine. Thus, to avoid the expense of purchasing butter and to increase profitability, the Happy Pancake House should extend this cost-saving change to its restaurants in the southeast and northeast as well."

Write a response in which you discuss what questions would need to be answered in order to decide whether the recommendation is likely to have the predicted result. Be sure to explain how the answers to these questions would help to evaluate the recommendation.

---

52. The following appeared in a letter from the owner of the Sunnyside Towers apartment building to its manager.

"One month ago, all the shower heads on the first five floors of Sunnyside Towers were modified to restrict the water flow to approximately one-third of its original flow. Although actual readings of water usage before and after the adjustment are not yet available, the change will obviously result in a considerable savings for Sunnyside Corporation, since the corporation must pay for water each month. Except for a few complaints about low water pressure, no problems with showers have been reported since the adjustment. Clearly, restricting water flow throughout all the twenty floors of Sunnyside Towers will increase our profits further."

Write a response in which you discuss what questions would need to be answered in order to decide whether the recommendation is likely to have the predicted result. Be sure to explain how the answers to these questions would help to evaluate the recommendation.

---

53. The following appeared in a health magazine.

"The citizens of Forsythe have adopted more healthful lifestyles. Their responses to a recent survey show that in their eating habits they conform more closely to government nutritional recommendations than they did ten years ago. Furthermore, there has been a fourfold increase in sales of food products containing kiran, a substance that a scientific study has shown reduces cholesterol. This trend is also evident in reduced sales of sulia, a food that few of the most healthy citizens regularly eat."

Write a response in which you discuss what specific evidence is needed to evaluate the argument and explain how the evidence would weaken or strengthen the argument.

---

54. Humans arrived in the Kaliko Islands about 7,000 years ago, and within 3,000 years most of the large mammal species that had lived in the forests of the Kaliko Islands had become extinct. Yet humans cannot have been a factor in the species' extinctions, because there is no evidence that the humans had any significant contact with the mammals. Further, archaeologists have discovered numerous sites where the bones of fish had been discarded, but they found no such areas containing the bones of large mammals, so the humans cannot have hunted the mammals. Therefore, some climate change or other environmental factor must have caused the species' extinctions.

Write a response in which you examine the stated and/or unstated assumptions of the argument. Be sure to explain how the argument depends on these assumptions and what the implications are for the argument if the assumptions prove unwarranted.

---

55. The following appeared in an editorial in a business magazine.

"Although the sales of Whirlwind video games have declined over the past two years, a recent survey of video-game players suggests that this sales trend is about to be reversed. The survey asked video-game players what features they thought were most important in a video game. According to the survey, players prefer games that provide lifelike graphics, which require the most up-to-date computers. Whirlwind has just introduced several such games with an extensive advertising campaign directed at people ten to twenty-five years old, the age-group most likely to play video games. It follows, then, that the sales of Whirlwind video games are likely to increase dramatically in the next few months."

Write a response in which you examine the stated and/or unstated assumptions of the argument. Be sure to explain how the argument depends on these assumptions and what the implications are for the argument if the assumptions prove unwarranted.

---

56. The following appeared in a memo from the vice president of marketing at Dura-Sock, Inc.

"A recent study of our customers suggests that our company is wasting the money it spends on its patented Endure manufacturing process, which ensures that our socks are strong enough to last for two years. We have always advertised our use of the Endure process, but the new study shows that despite our socks' durability, our average customer actually purchases new Dura-Socks every three months. Furthermore, our customers surveyed in our largest market, northeastern United States cities, say that they most value Dura-Socks' stylish appearance and availability in many colors. These findings suggest that we can increase our profits by discontinuing use of the Endure manufacturing process."

Write a response in which you examine the stated and/or unstated assumptions of the argument. Be sure to explain how the argument depends on these assumptions and what the implications are for the argument if the assumptions prove unwarranted.

57. The following appeared in a memo from the vice president of marketing at Dura-Sock, Inc.

"A recent study of our customers suggests that our company is wasting the money it spends on its patented Endure manufacturing process, which ensures that our socks are strong enough to last for two years. We have always advertised our use of the Endure process, but the new study shows that despite our socks' durability, our average customer actually purchases new Dura-Socks every three months. Furthermore, our customers surveyed in our largest market, northeastern United States cities, say that they most value Dura-Socks' stylish appearance and availability in many colors. These findings suggest that we can increase our profits by discontinuing use of the Endure manufacturing process."

Write a response in which you discuss what specific evidence is needed to evaluate the argument and explain how the evidence would weaken or strengthen the argument.

58. The vice president for human resources at Climpson Industries sent the following recommendation to the company's president.

"In an effort to improve our employees' productivity, we should implement electronic monitoring of employees' Internet use from their workstations. Employees who use the Internet inappropriately from their workstations need to be identified and punished if we are to reduce the number of work hours spent on personal or recreational activities, such as shopping or playing games. Installing software on company computers to detect employees' Internet use is the best way to prevent employees from wasting time on the job. It will foster a better work ethic at Climpson and improve our overall profits."

Write a response in which you discuss what specific evidence is needed to evaluate the argument and explain how the evidence would weaken or strengthen the argument.

59. The following appeared in a memo from the president of Bower Builders, a company that constructs new homes.

"A nationwide survey reveals that the two most-desired home features are a large family room and a large, well-appointed kitchen. A number of homes in our area built by our competitor Domus Construction have such features and have sold much faster and at significantly higher prices than the national average. To boost sales and profits, we should increase the size of the family rooms and kitchens in all the homes we build and should make state-of-the-art kitchens a standard feature. Moreover, our larger family rooms and kitchens can come at the expense of the dining room, since many of our recent buyers say they do not need a separate dining room for family meals."

Write a response in which you examine the stated and/or unstated assumptions of the argument. Be sure to explain how the argument depends on these assumptions and what the implications are for the argument if the assumptions prove unwarranted.

60. The following appeared in a letter from a firm providing investment advice for a client.

"Most homes in the northeastern United States, where winters are typically cold, have traditionally used oil as their major fuel for heating. Last heating season that region experienced 90 days with below-normal temperatures, and climate forecasters predict that this weather pattern will continue for several more years. Furthermore, many new homes are being built in the region in response to recent population growth. Because of these trends, we predict an increased demand for heating oil and recommend investment in Consolidated Industries, one of whose major business operations is the retail sale of home heating oil."

Write a response in which you examine the stated and/or unstated assumptions of the argument. Be sure to explain how the argument depends on these assumptions and what the implications are for the argument if the assumptions prove unwarranted.

---

61. The following appeared in an article in the Grandview Beacon.

"For many years the city of Grandview has provided annual funding for the Grandview Symphony. Last year, however, private contributions to the symphony increased by 200 percent and attendance at the symphony's concerts-in-the-park series doubled. The symphony has also announced an increase in ticket prices for next year. Given such developments, some city commissioners argue that the symphony can now be fully self-supporting, and they recommend that funding for the symphony be eliminated from next year's budget."

Write a response in which you discuss what questions would need to be answered in order to decide whether the recommendation and the argument on which it is based are reasonable. Be sure to explain how the answers to these questions would help to evaluate the recommendation.

---

62. The following appeared in a memo from the director of a large group of hospitals.

"In a laboratory study of liquid antibacterial hand soaps, a concentrated solution of UltraClean produced a 40 percent greater reduction in the bacteria population than did the liquid hand soaps currently used in our hospitals. During a subsequent test of UltraClean at our hospital in Workby, that hospital reported significantly fewer cases of patient infection than did any of the other hospitals in our group. Therefore, to prevent serious patient infections, we should supply UltraClean at all hand-washing stations throughout our hospital system."

Write a response in which you examine the stated and/or unstated assumptions of the argument. Be sure to explain how the argument depends on these assumptions and what the implications are for the argument if the assumptions prove unwarranted.

---

63. The following appeared in a letter to the editor of the Parkville Daily newspaper.

"Throughout the country last year, as more and more children below the age of nine participated in youth-league sports, over 40,000 of these young players suffered injuries. When interviewed for a recent study, youth-league soccer players in several major cities also reported psychological pressure exerted by coaches and parents to win games. Furthermore, education experts say that long practice sessions for these sports take away time that could be used for academic activities. Since the disadvantages outweigh any advantages, we in Parkville should discontinue organized athletic competition for children under nine."

Write a response in which you examine the stated and/or unstated assumptions of the argument. Be sure to explain how the argument depends on these assumptions and what the implications are for the argument if the assumptions prove unwarranted.

---

64. Collectors prize the ancient life-size clay statues of human figures made on

Kali Island but have long wondered how Kalinese artists were able to depict bodies with such realistic precision. Since archaeologists have recently discovered molds of human heads and hands on Kali, we can now conclude that the ancient Kalinese artists used molds of actual bodies, not sculpting tools and techniques, to create these statues. This discovery explains why Kalinese miniature statues were abstract and entirely different in style: molds could be used only for life-size sculptures. It also explains why few ancient Kalinese sculpting tools have been found. In light of this discovery, collectors predict that the life-size sculptures will decrease in value while the miniatures increase in value.

Write a response in which you discuss what questions would need to be answered in order to decide whether the prediction and the argument on which it is based are reasonable. Be sure to explain how the answers to these questions would help to evaluate the prediction.

---

65. When Stanley Park first opened, it was the largest, most heavily used public park in town. It is still the largest park, but it is no longer heavily used. Video cameras mounted in the park's parking lots last month revealed the park's drop in popularity: the recordings showed an average of only 50 cars per day. In contrast, tiny Carlton Park in the heart of the business district is visited by more than 150 people on a typical weekday. An obvious difference is that Carlton Park, unlike Stanley Park, provides ample seating. Thus, if Stanley Park is ever to be as popular with our citizens as Carlton Park, the town will obviously need to provide more benches, thereby converting some of the unused open areas into spaces suitable for socializing.

Write a response in which you examine the stated and/or unstated assumptions of the argument. Be sure to explain how the argument depends on these assumptions and what the implications are for the argument if the assumptions prove unwarranted.

---

66. The following appeared in a memo from the owner of a chain of cheese stores located throughout the United States.

"For many years all the stores in our chain have stocked a wide variety of both domestic and imported cheeses. Last year, however, all of the five best-selling cheeses at our newest store were domestic cheddar cheeses from Wisconsin. Furthermore, a recent survey by Cheeses of the World magazine indicates an increasing preference for domestic cheeses among its subscribers. Since our company can reduce expenses by limiting inventory, the best way to improve profits in all of our stores is to discontinue stocking many of our varieties of imported cheese and concentrate primarily on domestic cheeses."

Write a response in which you discuss what questions would need to be answered in order to decide whether the recommendation is likely to have the predicted result. Be sure to explain how the answers to these questions would help to evaluate the recommendation.

---

67. The following appeared as part of a business plan developed by the manager of the Rialto Movie Theater.

"Despite its downtown location, the Rialto Movie Theater, a local institution for five decades, must make big changes or close its doors forever. It should follow the example of the new Apex Theater in the mall outside of town. When the Apex opened last year, it featured a video arcade, plush carpeting and seats, and a state-of-the-art sound system. Furthermore, in a recent survey, over 85 percent of respondents reported that the high price of newly released movies prevents them from going to the movies more than five times per year. Thus, if the Rialto intends to hold on to its share of a decreasing pool of moviegoers, it must offer the same features as Apex."

Write a response in which you discuss what questions would need to be answered in order to decide whether the recommendation is likely to have the predicted result. Be sure to explain how the answers to these questions would help to evaluate the recommendation.

68. A recent study reported that pet owners have longer, healthier lives on average than do people who own no pets. Specifically, dog owners tend to have a lower incidence of heart disease. In light of these findings, Sherwood Hospital should form a partnership with Sherwood Animal Shelter to institute an adopt-a-dog program. The program would encourage dog ownership for patients recovering from heart disease, which should reduce these patients' chance of experiencing continuing heart problems and also reduce their need for ongoing treatment. As a further benefit, the publicity about the program would encourage more people to adopt pets from the shelter. And that will reduce the incidence of heart disease in the general population.

Write a response in which you examine the stated and/or unstated assumptions of the argument. Be sure to explain how the argument depends on these assumptions and what the implications are for the argument if the assumptions prove unwarranted.

69. The following appeared in a memo from a vice president of a large, highly diversified company.

"Ten years ago our company had two new office buildings constructed as regional headquarters for two regions. The buildings were erected by different construction companies — Alpha and Zeta. Although the two buildings had identical floor plans, the building constructed by Zeta cost 30 percent more to build. However, that building's expenses for maintenance last year were only half those of Alpha's. In addition, the energy consumption of the Zeta building has been lower than that of the Alpha building every year since its construction. Given these data, plus the fact that Zeta has a stable workforce with little employee turnover, we recommend using Zeta rather than Alpha for our new building project, even though Alpha's bid promises lower construction costs."

Write a response in which you discuss what questions would need to be answered in order to decide whether the recommendation and the argument on which it is based are reasonable. Be sure to explain how the answers to these questions would help to evaluate the recommendation.

---

70. The following appeared in a memo from a vice president of a large, highly diversified company.

"Ten years ago our company had two new office buildings constructed as regional headquarters for two regions. The buildings were erected by different construction companies — Alpha and Zeta. Although the two buildings had identical floor plans, the building constructed by Zeta cost 30 percent more to build. However, that building's expenses for maintenance last year were only half those of Alpha's. Furthermore, the energy consumption of the Zeta building has been lower than that of the Alpha building every year since its construction. Such data indicate that we should use Zeta rather than Alpha for our contemplated new building project, even though Alpha's bid promises lower construction costs."

Write a response in which you discuss what specific evidence is needed to evaluate the argument and explain how the evidence would weaken or strengthen the argument.

---

71. The following is a letter to the editor of the Waymarsh Times.

"Traffic here in Waymarsh is becoming a problem. Although just three years ago a state traffic survey showed that the typical driving commuter took 20 minutes to get to work, the commute now takes closer to 40 minutes, according to the survey just completed. Members of the town council already have suggested more road building to address the problem, but as well as being expensive, the new construction will surely disrupt some of our residential neighborhoods. It would be better to follow the example of the nearby city of Garville. Last year Garville implemented a policy that rewards people who share rides to work, giving them coupons for free gas. Pollution levels in Garville have dropped since the policy was implemented, and people from Garville tell me that commuting times have fallen considerably. There is no reason why a policy like Garville's shouldn't work equally well in Waymarsh."

Write a response in which you discuss what specific evidence is needed to evaluate the argument and explain how the evidence would weaken or strengthen the argument.

---

72. The following appeared as a letter to the editor of a national newspaper.

"Your recent article on corporate downsizing* in Elthyria maintains that the majority of competent workers who have lost jobs as a result of downsizing face serious economic hardship, often for years, before finding other suitable employment. But this claim is undermined by a recent report on the Elthyrian economy, which found that since 1999 far more jobs have been created than have been eliminated, bringing the unemployment rate in Elthyria to its lowest level in decades. Moreover, two-thirds of these newly created jobs have been in industries that tend to pay above-average wages, and the vast majority of these jobs are full-time."

* Downsizing is the process whereby corporations deliberately make themselves smaller, reducing the number of their employees.

Write a response in which you discuss what specific evidence is needed to evaluate the argument and explain how the evidence would weaken or strengthen the argument.

---

73. The following appeared on the Mozart School of Music Web site.

"The Mozart School of Music should be the first choice for parents considering enrolling their child in music lessons. First of all, the Mozart School welcomes youngsters at all ability and age levels; there is no audition to attend the school. Second, the school offers instruction in nearly all musical instruments as well a wide range of styles and genres from classical to rock. Third, the faculty includes some of the most distinguished musicians in the area. Finally, many Mozart graduates have gone on to become well-known and highly paid professional musicians."

Write a response in which you examine the stated and/or unstated assumptions of the argument. Be sure to explain how the argument depends on these assumptions and what the implications are for the argument if the assumptions prove unwarranted.

---

74. The president of Grove College has recommended that the college abandon

its century-old tradition of all-female education and begin admitting men. Pointing to other all-female colleges that experienced an increase in applications after adopting coeducation, the president argues that coeducation would lead to a significant increase in applications and enrollment. However, the director of the alumnae association opposes the plan. Arguing that all-female education is essential to the very identity of the college, the director cites annual surveys of incoming students in which these students say that the school's all-female status was the primary reason they selected Grove. The director also points to a survey of Grove alumnae in which a majority of respondents strongly favored keeping the college all female. [174]

Write a response in which you discuss what questions would need to be answered in order to decide whether the recommendation and the argument on which it is based are reasonable. Be sure to explain how the answers to these questions would help to evaluate the recommendation.

---

75. The following appeared in a letter to the editor of a Batavia newspaper.

"The department of agriculture in Batavia reports that the number of dairy farms throughout the country is now 25 percent greater than it was 10 years ago. During this same time period, however, the price of milk at the local Excello Food Market has increased from $1.50 to over $3.00 per gallon. To prevent farmers from continuing to receive excessive profits on an apparently increased supply of milk, the Batavia government should begin to regulate retail milk prices. Such regulation is necessary to ensure fair prices for consumers."

Write a response in which you discuss what questions would need to be answered in order to decide whether the recommendation is likely to have the predicted result.

Be sure to explain how the answers to these questions would help to evaluate the recommendation.

---

76. The following appeared in a newsletter offering advice to investors.

"Over 80 percent of the respondents to a recent survey indicated a desire to reduce their intake of foods containing fats and cholesterol, and today low-fat products abound in many food stores. Since many of the food products currently marketed by Old Dairy Industries are high in fat and cholesterol, the company's sales are likely to diminish greatly and company profits will no doubt decrease. We therefore advise Old Dairy stockholders to sell their shares, and other investors not to purchase stock in this company."

Write a response in which you discuss what questions would need to be answered in order to decide whether the advice and the argument on which it is based are reasonable. Be sure to explain how the answers to these questions would help to evaluate the advice.

---

77. The following recommendation appeared in a memo from the mayor of the town of Hopewell.

"Two years ago, the nearby town of Ocean View built a new municipal golf course and resort hotel. During the past two years, tourism in Ocean View has increased, new businesses have opened there, and Ocean View's tax revenues have risen by 30 percent. Therefore, the best way to improve Hopewell's economy — and generate additional tax revenues — is to build a golf course and resort hotel similar to those in Ocean View."

Write a response in which you examine the stated and/or unstated assumptions of the argument. Be sure to explain how the argument depends on these assumptions and what the implications are for the argument if the assumptions prove unwarranted.

---

78. The following appeared in a memo from the vice president of a food distribution company with food storage warehouses in several cities.

"Recently, we signed a contract with the Fly-Away Pest Control Company to provide pest control services at our fast-food warehouse in Palm City, but last month we discovered that over $20,000 worth of food there had been destroyed by pest damage. Meanwhile, the Buzzoff Pest Control Company, which we have used for many years, continued to service our warehouse in Wintervale, and last month only $10,000 worth of the food stored there had been destroyed by pest damage. Even though the price charged by Fly-Away is considerably lower, our best means of saving money is to return to Buzzoff for all our pest control services."

Write a response in which you discuss what specific evidence is needed to evaluate the argument and explain how the evidence would weaken or strengthen the argument.

---

79. Since those issues of Newsbeat magazine that featured political news on their front cover were the poorest-selling issues over the past three years, the publisher of Newsbeat has recommended that the magazine curtail its emphasis on politics to focus more exclusively on economics and personal finance. She points to a recent survey of readers of general interest magazines that indicates greater reader interest in economic issues than in political ones. Newsbeat's editor, however, opposes the proposed shift in editorial policy, pointing out that very few magazines offer extensive political coverage anymore.

Write a response in which you discuss what questions would need to be answered in order to decide whether the recommendation and the argument on which it is based are reasonable. Be sure to explain how the answers to these questions would help to evaluate the recommendation.

---

80. The following is taken from a memo from the advertising director of the Super Screen Movie Production Company. [New]

"According to a recent report from our marketing department, during the past year, fewer people attended Super Screen-produced movies than in any other year. And yet the percentage of positive reviews by movie reviewers about specific Super Screen movies actually increased during the past year. Clearly, the contents of these reviews are not reaching enough of our prospective viewers. Thus, the problem lies not with the quality of our movies but with the public's lack of awareness that movies of good quality are available. Super Screen should therefore allocate a greater share of its budget next year to reaching the public through advertising."

Write a response in which you discuss what questions would need to be answered in order to decide whether the recommendation and the argument on which it is based are reasonable. Be sure to explain how the answers to these questions would help to evaluate the recommendation.

---

81. The following appeared in a business magazine.

"As a result of numerous complaints of dizziness and nausea on the part of consumers of Promofoods tuna, the company requested that eight million cans of its tuna be returned for testing. Promofoods concluded that the canned tuna did not, after all, pose a health risk. This conclusion is based on tests performed on samples of the recalled cans by chemists from Promofoods; the chemists found that of the eight food chemicals most commonly blamed for causing symptoms of dizziness and nausea, five were not found in any of the tested cans. The chemists did find small amounts of the three remaining suspected chemicals but pointed out that these occur naturally in all canned foods."

Write a response in which you discuss what questions would need to be addressed in order to decide whether the conclusion and the argument on which it is based are reasonable. Be sure to explain how the answers to the questions would help to evaluate the conclusion.

---

82. The following appeared in a memo from the vice president of marketing at Dura-Socks, Inc.

"A recent study of Dura-Socks customers suggests that our company is wasting the money it spends on its patented Endure manufacturing process, which ensures that our socks are strong enough to last for two years. We have always advertised our use of the Endure process, but the new study shows that despite the socks' durability, our customers, on average, actually purchase new Dura-Socks every three months. Furthermore, customers surveyed in our largest market — northeastern United States cities — say that they most value Dura-Socks' stylish appearance and availability in many colors. These findings suggest that we can increase our profits by discontinuing use of the Endure manufacturing process."

Write a response in which you discuss what questions would need to be answered in order to decide whether the recommendation and the argument on which it is based

are reasonable. Be sure to explain how the answers to these questions would help to evaluate the recommendation.

---

83. The following is a letter to the editor of an environmental magazine.

"In 1975 a wildlife census found that there were seven species of amphibians in Xanadu National Park, with abundant numbers of each species. However, in 2002 only four species of amphibians were observed in the park, and the numbers of each species were drastically reduced. There has been a substantial decline in the numbers of amphibians worldwide, and global pollution of water and air is clearly implicated. The decline of amphibians in Xanadu National Park, however, almost certainly has a different cause: in 1975, trout — which are known to eat amphibian eggs — were introduced into the park."

Write a response in which you discuss what specific evidence is needed to evaluate the argument and explain how the evidence would weaken or strengthen the argument.

---

84. The following is a letter to the editor of an environmental magazine.

"Two studies of amphibians in Xanadu National Park confirm a significant decline in the numbers of amphibians. In 1975 there were seven species of amphibians in the park, and there were abundant numbers of each species. However, in 2002 only four species of amphibians were observed in the park, and the numbers of each species were drastically reduced. One proposed explanation is that the decline was caused by the introduction of trout into the park's waters, which began in 1975. (Trout are known to eat amphibian eggs.)"

Write a response in which you discuss one or more alternative explanations that could rival the proposed explanation and explain how your explanation(s) can plausibly account for the facts presented in the argument.

---

85. In a study of the reading habits of Waymarsh citizens conducted by the University of Waymarsh, most respondents said that they preferred literary classics as reading material. However, a second study conducted by the same researchers found that the type of book most frequently checked out of each of the public libraries in Waymarsh was the mystery novel. Therefore, it can be concluded that the respondents in the first study had misrepresented their reading habits.

Write a response in which you discuss what specific evidence is needed to evaluate the argument and explain how the evidence would weaken or strengthen the argument.

---

86. The following appeared in a memo at XYZ company.

"When XYZ lays off employees, it pays Delany Personnel Firm to offer those employees assistance in creating réumé and developing interviewing skills, if they so desire. Laid-off employees have benefited greatly from Delany's services: last year those who used Delany found jobs much more quickly than did those who did not. Recently, it has been proposed that we use the less expensive Walsh Personnel Firm in place of Delany. This would be a mistake because eight years ago, when XYZ was using Walsh, only half of the workers we laid off at that time found jobs within a year. Moreover, Delany is clearly superior, as evidenced by its bigger staff and larger number of branch offices. After all, last year Delany's clients took an average of six months to find jobs, whereas Walsh's clients took nine."

Write a response in which you discuss what specific evidence is needed to evaluate the argument and explain how the evidence would weaken or strengthen the argument.

---

87. In a study of the reading habits of Waymarsh citizens conducted by the University of Waymarsh, most respondents said they preferred literary classics as reading material. However, a second study conducted by the same researchers found that the type of book most frequently checked out of each of the public libraries in Waymarsh was the mystery novel. Therefore, it can be concluded that the respondents in the first study had misrepresented their reading preferences.

Write a response in which you examine the stated and/or unstated assumptions of the argument. Be sure to explain how the argument depends on these assumptions and what the implications are for the argument if the assumptions prove unwarranted.

---

88. The following appeared in a memorandum written by the vice president of Health Naturally, a small but expanding chain of stores selling health food and other health-related products.

"Our previous experience has been that our stores are most profitable in areas where residents are highly concerned with leading healthy lives. We should therefore build one of our new stores in Plainsville, which clearly has many such residents. Plainsville merchants report that sales of running shoes and exercise equipment are at all-time highs. The local health club, which nearly closed five years ago due to lack of business, has more members than ever, and the weight-training and aerobics classes are always full. We can even anticipate a new generation of customers: Plainsville's schoolchildren are required to participate in a program called Fitness for Life, which emphasizes the benefits of regular exercise at an early age."

Write a response in which you discuss what specific evidence is needed to evaluate the argument and explain how the evidence would weaken or strengthen the argument.

---

89. The following appeared in a memo at XYZ company.

"When XYZ lays off employees, it pays Delany Personnel Firm to offer those employees assistance in creating réumé and developing interviewing skills, if they so desire. Laid-off employees have benefited greatly from Delany's services: last year those who used Delany found jobs much more quickly than did those who did not. Recently, it has been proposed that we use the less expensive Walsh Personnel Firm in place of Delany. This would be a mistake because eight years ago, when XYZ was using Walsh, only half of the workers we laid off at that time found jobs within a year. Moreover, Delany is clearly superior, as evidenced by its bigger staff and larger number of branch offices. After all, last year Delany's clients took an average of six months to find jobs, whereas Walsh's clients took nine."

Write a response in which you examine the stated and/or unstated assumptions of the argument. Be sure to explain how the argument depends on these assumptions and what the implications are for the argument if the assumptions prove unwarranted.

---

90. The following appeared in a memorandum written by the vice president of Health Naturally, a small but expanding chain of stores selling health food and other health-related products.

"Our previous experience has been that our stores are most profitable in areas where residents are highly concerned with leading healthy lives. We should therefore build one of our new stores in Plainsville, which clearly has many such residents. Plainsville merchants report that sales of running shoes and exercise equipment are at all-time highs. The local health club, which nearly closed five years ago due to lack of business, has more members than ever, and the weight-training and aerobics classes are always full. We can even anticipate a new generation of customers: Plainsville's schoolchildren are required to participate in a program called Fitness for Life, which emphasizes the benefits of regular exercise at an early age."

Write a response in which you examine the stated and/or unstated assumptions of the argument. Be sure to explain how the argument depends on these assumptions and what the implications are for the argument if the assumptions prove unwarranted.

---

91. Three years ago, because of flooding at the Western Palean Wildlife Preserve, 100 lions and 100 western gazelles were moved to the East Palean Preserve, an area that is home to most of the same species that are found in the western preserve, though in larger numbers, and to the eastern gazelle, a close relative of the western gazelle. The only difference in climate is that the eastern preserve typically has slightly less rainfall. Unfortunately, after three years in the eastern preserve, the imported western gazelle population has been virtually eliminated. Since the slight reduction in rainfall cannot be the cause of the virtual elimination of western gazelle, their disappearance must have been caused by the larger number of predators in the eastern preserve. [New]

Write a response in which you discuss what specific evidence is needed to evaluate the argument and explain how the evidence would weaken or strengthen the argument.

92. Workers in the small town of Leeville take fewer sick days than workers in the large city of Masonton, 50 miles away. Moreover, relative to population size, the diagnosis of stress-related illness is proportionally much lower in Leeville than in Masonton. According to the Leeville Chamber of Commerce, these facts can be attributed to the health benefits of the relatively relaxed pace of life in Leeville.

Write a response in which you discuss one or more alternative explanations that could rival the proposed explanation and explain how your explanation(s) can plausibly account for the facts presented in the argument.

93. The following appeared in a memorandum from the manager of WWAC radio station.

"WWAC must change from its current rock-music format because the number of listeners has been declining, even though the population in our listening area has been growing. The population growth has resulted mainly from people moving to our area after their retirement, and we must make listeners of these new residents. But they seem to have limited interest in music: several local stores selling recorded music have recently closed. Therefore, just changing to another kind of music is not going to increase our audience. Instead, we should adopt a news-and-talk format, a form of radio that is increasingly popular in our area."

Write a response in which you discuss what questions would need to be answered in order to decide whether the recommendation and the argument on which it is based are reasonable. Be sure to explain how the answers to these questions would help to evaluate the recommendation.

94. The vice president of human resources at Climpson Industries sent the following recommendation to the company's president.

"A recent national survey found that the majority of workers with access to the Internet at work had used company computers for personal or recreational activities, such as banking or playing games. In an effort to improve our employees' productivity, we should implement electronic monitoring of employees' Internet use from their workstations. Using electronic monitoring software is the best way to reduce the number of hours Climpson employees spend on personal or recreational activities. We predict that installing software to monitor employees' Internet use will allow us to prevent employees from wasting time, thereby increasing productivity and improving overall profits."

Write a response in which you discuss what questions would need to be answered in order to decide whether the prediction and the argument on which it is based are reasonable. Be sure to explain how the answers to these questions would help to evaluate the prediction.

95. The following appeared in a memo from the new vice president of Sartorian, a company that manufactures men's clothing.

"Five years ago, at a time when we had difficulty obtaining reliable supplies of high-quality wool fabric, we discontinued production of our popular alpaca overcoat. Now that we have a new fabric supplier, we should resume production. Given the outcry from our customers when we discontinued this product and the fact that none of our competitors offers a comparable product, we can expect pent-up consumer demand for our alpaca coats. This demand and the overall increase in clothing prices will make Sartorian's alpaca overcoats more profitable than ever before."

Write a response in which you examine the stated and/or unstated assumptions of the argument. Be sure to explain how the argument depends on these assumptions and what the implications are for the argument if the assumptions prove unwarranted.

---

96. The following appeared in a memo from the new vice president of Sartorian, a company that manufactures men's clothing.

"Five years ago, at a time when we had difficulty obtaining reliable supplies of high-quality wool fabric, we discontinued production of our popular alpaca overcoat. Now that we have a new fabric supplier, we should resume production. Given the outcry from our customers when we discontinued this product and the fact that none of our competitors offers a comparable product, we can expect pent-up consumer demand for our alpaca coats. Due to this demand and the overall increase in clothing prices, we can predict that Sartorian's alpaca overcoats will be more profitable than ever before."

Write a response in which you discuss what questions would need to be answered in order to decide whether the prediction and the argument on which it is based are reasonable. Be sure to explain how the answers to these questions would help to evaluate the prediction.

---

97. The following appeared in an e-mail sent by the marketing director of the Classical Shakespeare Theatre of Bardville. [New]

"Over the past ten years, there has been a 20 percent decline in the size of the average audience at Classical Shakespeare Theatre productions. In spite of increased advertising, we are attracting fewer and fewer people to our shows, causing our profits to decrease significantly. We must take action to attract new audience members. The best way to do so is by instituting a 'Shakespeare in the Park' program this summer. Two years ago the nearby Avon Repertory Company started a 'Free Plays in the Park' program, and its profits have increased 10 percent since then. If we start a 'Shakespeare in the Park' program, we can predict that our profits will increase, too."

Write a response in which you discuss what questions would need to be answered in order to decide whether the recommendation is likely to have the predicted result. Be sure to explain how the answers to these questions would help to evaluate the recommendation.

---

98. The following is a recommendation from the business manager of Monarch Books.

"Since its opening in Collegeville twenty years ago, Monarch Books has developed a large customer base due to its reader-friendly atmosphere and wide selection of books on all subjects. Last month, Book and Bean, a combination bookstore and coffee shop, announced its intention to open a Collegeville store. Monarch Books should open its own in-store café in the space currently devoted to children's books. Given recent national census data indicating a significant decline in the percentage of the population under age ten, sales of children's books are likely to decline. By replacing its children's books section with a café Monarch Books can increase profits and ward off competition from Book and Bean."

Write a response in which you examine the stated and/or unstated assumptions of the argument. Be sure to explain how the argument depends on these assumptions and what the implications are for the argument if the assumptions prove unwarranted.

99. The following is a recommendation from the business manager of Monarch Books.

"Since its opening in Collegeville twenty years ago, Monarch Books has developed a large customer base due to its reader-friendly atmosphere and wide selection of books on all subjects. Last month, Book and Bean, a combination bookstore and coffee shop, announced its intention to open a Collegeville store. Monarch Books should open its own in-store café in the space currently devoted to children's books. Given recent national census data indicating a significant decline in the percentage of the population under age ten, sales of children's books are likely to decline. By replacing its children's books section with a café Monarch Books can increase profits and ward off competition from Book and Bean."

Write a response in which you discuss what specific evidence is needed to evaluate the argument and explain how the evidence would weaken or strengthen the argument.

100. The following was written as a part of an application for a small-business loan by a group of developers in the city of Monroe.

"Jazz music is extremely popular in the city of Monroe: over 100,000 people attended Monroe's annual jazz festival last summer, and the highest-rated radio program in Monroe is 'Jazz Nightly,' which airs every weeknight. Also, a number of well-known jazz musicians own homes in Monroe. Nevertheless, the nearest jazz club is over an hour away. Given the popularity of jazz in Monroe and a recent nationwide study indicating that the typical jazz fan spends close to $1,000 per year on jazz entertainment, a jazz music club in Monroe would be tremendously profitable."

Write a response in which you examine the stated and/or unstated assumptions of the argument. Be sure to explain how the argument depends on these assumptions and what the implications are for the argument if the assumptions prove unwarranted.

---

101. There is now evidence that the relaxed pace of life in small towns promotes better health and greater longevity than does the hectic pace of life in big cities. Businesses in the small town of Leeville report fewer days of sick leave taken by individual workers than do businesses in the nearby large city of Masonton. Furthermore, Leeville has only one physician for its one thousand residents, but in Masonton the proportion of physicians to residents is five times as high. Finally, the average age of Leeville residents is significantly higher than that of Masonton residents. These findings suggest that people seeking longer and healthier lives should consider moving to small communities.

Write a response in which you examine the stated and/or unstated assumptions of the argument. Be sure to explain how the argument depends on these assumptions and what the implications are for the argument if the assumptions prove unwarranted.

---

102. The following was written as a part of an application for a small-business loan by a group of developers in the city of Monroe.

"Jazz music is extremely popular in the city of Monroe: over 100,000 people attended Monroe's annual jazz festival last summer, and the highest-rated radio program in Monroe is 'Jazz Nightly,' which airs every weeknight. Also, a number of well-known jazz musicians own homes in Monroe. Nevertheless, the nearest jazz club is over an hour away. Given the popularity of jazz in Monroe and a recent nationwide study indicating that the typical jazz fan spends close to $1,000 per year on jazz entertainment, we predict that our new jazz music club in Monroe will be a tremendously profitable enterprise."

Write a response in which you discuss what questions would need to be answered in order to decide whether the prediction and the argument on which it is based are reasonable. Be sure to explain how the answers to these questions would help to evaluate the prediction.

---

103. There is now evidence that the relaxed pace of life in small towns promotes better health and greater longevity than does the hectic pace of life in big cities. Businesses in the small town of Leeville report fewer days of sick leave taken by individual workers than do businesses in the nearby large city of Masonton. Furthermore, Leeville has only one physician for its one thousand residents, but in Masonton the proportion of physicians to residents is five times as high. Finally, the average age of Leeville residents is significantly higher than that of Masonton residents. These findings suggest that the relaxed pace of life in Leeville allows residents to live longer, healthier lives.

Write a response in which you discuss one or more alternative explanations that could rival the proposed explanation and explain how your explanation(s) can plausibly account for the facts presented in the argument.

---

104. The following appeared in a memo from a vice president of a manufacturing company.

"During the past year, workers at our newly opened factory reported 30 percent more on-the-job accidents than workers at nearby Panoply Industries. Panoply produces products very similar to those produced at our factory, but its work shifts are one hour shorter than ours. Experts say that fatigue and sleep deprivation among workers are significant contributing factors in many on-the-job accidents. Panoply's superior safety record can therefore be attributed to its shorter work shifts, which allow its employees to get adequate amounts of rest."

Write a response in which you discuss one or more alternative explanations that could rival the proposed explanation and explain how your explanation(s) can plausibly account for the facts presented in the argument.

---

105. The following appeared in a memo from the vice president of Butler Manufacturing.

"During the past year, workers at Butler Manufacturing reported 30 percent more on-the-job accidents than workers at nearby Panoply Industries, where the work shifts are one hour shorter than ours. A recent government study reports that fatigue and sleep deprivation among workers are significant contributing factors in many on-the-job accidents. If we shorten each of our work shifts by one hour, we can improve Butler Manufacturing's safety record by ensuring that our employees are adequately rested."

Write a response in which you discuss what specific evidence is needed to evaluate the argument and explain how the evidence would weaken or strengthen the argument.

---

106. The following appeared in a memo from the Board of Directors of Butler Manufacturing.

"During the past year, workers at Butler Manufacturing reported 30 percent more on-the-job accidents than workers at nearby Panoply Industries, where the work shifts are one hour shorter than ours. A recent government study reports that fatigue and sleep deprivation among workers are significant contributing factors in many on-the-job accidents. Therefore, we recommend that Butler Manufacturing shorten each of its work shifts by one hour. Shorter shifts will allow Butler to improve its safety record by ensuring that its employees are adequately rested."

Write a response in which you discuss what questions would need to be answered in order to decide whether the recommendation is likely to have the predicted result. Be sure to explain how the answers to these questions would help to evaluate the recommendation.

---

107. The following appeared in a memo from the business manager of a chain of cheese stores located throughout the United States.

"For many years all the stores in our chain have stocked a wide variety of both domestic and imported cheeses. Last year, however, all of the five best-selling cheeses at our newest store were domestic cheddar cheeses from Wisconsin. Furthermore, a recent survey by Cheeses of the World magazine indicates an increasing preference for domestic cheeses among its subscribers. Since our company can reduce expenses by limiting inventory, the best way to improve profits in all of our stores is to discontinue stocking many of our varieties of imported cheese and concentrate primarily on domestic cheeses."

Write a response in which you examine the stated and/or unstated assumptions of the argument. Be sure to explain how the argument depends on these assumptions and what the implications are for the argument if the assumptions prove unwarranted.

108. The following appeared in a memo from the owner of a chain of cheese stores located throughout the United States.

"For many years all the stores in our chain have stocked a wide variety of both domestic and imported cheeses. Last year, however, all of the five best-selling cheeses at our newest store were domestic cheddar cheeses from Wisconsin. Furthermore, a recent survey by Cheeses of the World magazine indicates an increasing preference for domestic cheeses among its subscribers. Since our company can reduce expenses by limiting inventory, the best way to improve profits in all of our stores is to discontinue stocking many of our varieties of imported cheese and concentrate primarily on domestic cheeses."

Write a response in which you discuss what specific evidence is needed to evaluate the argument and explain how the evidence would weaken or strengthen the argument.

109. The following appeared in a memorandum from the general manager of KNOW radio station.

"Several factors indicate that radio station KNOW should shift its programming from rock-and-roll music to a continuous news format. Consider, for example, that the number of people in our listening area over fifty years of age has increased dramatically, while our total number of listeners has declined. Also, music stores in our area report decreased sales of recorded music. Finally, continuous news stations in neighboring cities have been very successful. The switch from rock-and-roll music to 24-hour news will attract older listeners and secure KNOW radio's future."

Write a response in which you examine the stated and/or unstated assumptions of the argument. Be sure to explain how the argument depends on these assumptions and what the implications are for the argument if the assumptions prove unwarranted.

---

110. The following appeared in a memorandum from the manager of KNOW radio station.

"Several factors indicate that KNOW radio can no longer succeed as a rock-and-roll music station. Consider, for example, that the number of people in our listening area over fifty years of age has increased dramatically, while our total number of listeners has declined. Also, music stores in our area report decreased sales of rock-and-roll music. Finally, continuous news stations in neighboring cities have been very successful. We predict that switching KNOW radio from rock-and-roll music to 24-hour news will allow the station to attract older listeners and make KNOW radio more profitable than ever."

Write a response in which you discuss what questions would need to be answered in order to decide whether the prediction and the argument on which it is based are reasonable. Be sure to explain how the answers to these questions would help to evaluate the prediction.

---

111. The following appeared in a memorandum from the owner of Movies Galore, a chain of movie-rental stores.

"In order to stop the recent decline in our profits, we must reduce operating expenses at Movies Galore's ten movie-rental stores. Since we are famous for our special bargains, raising our rental prices is not a viable way to improve profits. Last month our store in downtown Marston significantly decreased its operating expenses by closing at 6:00 P.M. rather than 9:00 P.M. and by reducing its stock by eliminating all movies released more than five years ago. By implementing similar changes in our other stores, Movies Galore can increase profits without jeopardizing our reputation for offering great movies at low prices."

Write a response in which you examine the stated and/or unstated assumptions of the argument. Be sure to explain how the argument depends on these assumptions and what the implications are for the argument if the assumptions prove unwarranted.

---

112. The following appeared in a memorandum from the owner of Movies Galore, a chain of movie-rental stores.

"In order to reverse the recent decline in our profits, we must reduce operating expenses at Movies Galore's ten movie-rental stores. Since we are famous for our special bargains, raising our rental prices is not a viable way to improve profits. Last month our store in downtown Marston significantly decreased its operating expenses by closing at 6:00 p.m. rather than 9:00 p.m. and by reducing its stock by eliminating all movies released more than five years ago. Therefore, in order to increase profits without jeopardizing our reputation for offering great movies at low prices, we recommend implementing similar changes in our other nine Movies Galore stores."

Write a response in which you discuss what questions would need to be answered in order to decide whether the recommendation and the argument on which it is based are reasonable. Be sure to explain how the answers to these questions would help to evaluate the recommendation.

---

113. The following is a recommendation from the personnel director to the president of Acme Publishing Company.

"Many other companies have recently stated that having their employees take the

Easy Read Speed-Reading Course has greatly improved productivity. One graduate of the course was able to read a 500-page report in only two hours; another graduate rose from an assistant manager to vice president of the company in under a year. Obviously, the faster you can read, the more information you can absorb in a single workday. Moreover, Easy Read would cost Acme only $500 per employee — a small price to pay when you consider the benefits. Included in this fee is a three-week seminar in Spruce City and a lifelong subscription to the Easy Read newsletter. Clearly, to improve productivity, Acme should require all of our employees to take the Easy Read course."

Write a response in which you discuss what questions would need to be answered in order to decide whether the advice and the argument on which it is based are reasonable. Be sure to explain how the answers to these questions would help to evaluate the advice.

---

114. The following appeared in a memo from the vice president of a food distribution company with food storage warehouses in several cities.

"Recently, we signed a contract with the Fly-Away Pest Control Company to provide pest control services at our warehouse in Palm City, but last month we discovered that over $20,000 worth of food there had been destroyed by pest damage. Meanwhile, the Buzzoff Pest Control Company, which we have used for many years in Palm City, continued to service our warehouse in Wintervale, and last month only $10,000 worth of the food stored there had been destroyed by pest damage. Even though the price charged by Fly-Away is considerably lower, our best means of saving money is to return to Buzzoff for all our pest control services."

Write a response in which you discuss what questions would need to be answered in order to decide whether the recommendation and the argument on which it is based

are reasonable. Be sure to explain how the answers to these questions would help to evaluate the recommendation.

---

115. The following appeared in a memo from a vice president of a large, highly diversified company.

"Ten years ago our company had two new office buildings constructed as regional headquarters for two different regions. The buildings were erected by two different construction companies — Alpha and Zeta. Even though the two buildings had identical floor plans, the building constructed by Zeta cost 30 percent more to build, and its expenses for maintenance last year were twice those of the building constructed by Alpha. Furthermore, the energy consumption of the Zeta building has been higher than that of the Alpha building every year since its construction. Such data, plus the fact that Alpha has a stable workforce with little employee turnover, indicate that we should use Alpha rather than Zeta for our contemplated new building project."

Write a response in which you examine the stated and/or unstated assumptions of the argument. Be sure to explain how the argument depends on these assumptions and what the implications are for the argument if the assumptions prove unwarranted.

---

116. The following appeared in a memo from the vice president of a food distribution company with food storage warehouses in several cities.

"Recently, we signed a contract with the Fly-Away Pest Control Company to provide pest control services at our warehouse in Palm City, but last month we discovered that over $20,000 worth of food there had been destroyed by pest damage. Meanwhile, the Buzzoff Pest Control Company, which we have used for many years in Palm City, continued to service our warehouse in Wintervale, and last month only $10,000 worth of the food stored there had been destroyed by pest damage. This difference in pest damage is best explained by the negligence of Fly-Away."

Write a response in which you discuss one or more alternative explanations that could rival the proposed explanation and explain how your explanation(s) can plausibly account for the facts presented in the argument.

---

117. The following appeared in a memo from the vice president of a food distribution company with food storage warehouses in several cities.

"Recently, we signed a contract with the Fly-Away Pest Control Company to provide pest control services at our warehouse in Palm City, but last month we discovered that over $20,000 worth of food there had been destroyed by pest damage. Meanwhile, the Buzzoff Pest Control Company, which we have used for many years in Palm City, continued to service our warehouse in Wintervale, and last month only $10,000 worth of the food stored there had been destroyed by pest damage. Even though the price charged by Fly-Away is considerably lower, our best means of saving money is to return to Buzzoff for all our pest control services."

Write a response in which you examine the stated and/or unstated assumptions of the argument. Be sure to explain how the argument depends on these assumptions and what the implications are for the argument if the assumptions prove unwarranted.

---

118. The following appeared as part of an article in a business magazine. [New]

"A recent study rating 300 male and female advertising executives according to the average number of hours they sleep per night showed an association between the amount of sleep the executives need and the success of their firms. Of the advertising firms studied, those whose executives reported needing no more than six hours of sleep per night had higher profit margins and faster growth. On the basis of this study, we recommend that businesses hire only people who need less than six hours of sleep per night."

Write a response in which you discuss what questions would need to be answered in order to decide whether the recommendation and the argument on which it is based are reasonable. Be sure to explain how the answers to these questions would help to evaluate the recommendation.

119. Evidence suggests that academic honor codes, which call for students to agree not to cheat in their academic endeavors and to notify a faculty member if they suspect that others have cheated, are far more successful than are other methods at deterring cheating among students at colleges and universities. Several years ago, Groveton College adopted such a code and discontinued its old-fashioned system in which teachers closely monitored students. Under the old system, teachers reported an average of thirty cases of cheating per year. In the first year the honor code was in place, students reported twenty-one cases of cheating; five years later, this figure had dropped to fourteen. Moreover, in a recent survey, a majority of Groveton students said that they would be less likely to cheat with an honor code in place than without.

Write a response in which you discuss one or more alternative explanations that could rival the proposed explanation and explain how your explanation(s) can plausibly account for the facts presented in the argument.

120. Several years ago, Groveton College adopted an honor code, which calls for

students to agree not to cheat in their academic endeavors and to notify a faculty member if they suspect that others have cheated. Groveton's honor code replaced a system in which teachers closely monitored students. Under that system, teachers reported an average of thirty cases of cheating per year. The honor code has proven far more successful: in the first year it was in place, students reported twenty-one cases of cheating; five years later, this figure had dropped to fourteen. Moreover, in a recent survey, a majority of Groveton students said that they would be less likely to cheat with an honor code in place than without. Such evidence suggests that all colleges and universities should adopt honor codes similar to Groveton's. This change is sure to result in a dramatic decline in cheating among college students.

Write a response in which you discuss what questions would need to be answered in order to decide whether the recommendation is likely to have the predicted result. Be sure to explain how the answers to these questions would help to evaluate the recommendation.

---

121. The following appeared in a memo from the director of a large group of hospitals.

"In a controlled laboratory study of liquid hand soaps, a concentrated solution of extra strength UltraClean hand soap produced a 40 percent greater reduction in harmful bacteria than did the liquid hand soaps currently used in our hospitals. During our recent test of regular-strength UltraClean with doctors, nurses, and visitors at our hospital in Worktown, the hospital reported significantly fewer cases of patient infection (a 20 percent reduction) than did any of the other hospitals in our group. Therefore, to prevent serious patient infections, we should supply UltraClean at all hand-washing stations, including those used by visitors, throughout our hospital system."

Write a response in which you examine the stated and/or unstated assumptions of the argument. Be sure to explain how the argument depends on these assumptions and what the implications are for the argument if the assumptions prove unwarranted.

122. The following appeared in a memo from the director of a large group of hospitals

"In a controlled laboratory study of liquid hand soaps, a concentrated solution of extra strength UltraClean hand soap produced a 40 percent greater reduction in harmful bacteria than did the liquid hand soaps currently used in our hospitals. During our recent test of regular-strength UltraClean with doctors, nurses, and visitors at our hospital in Worktown, the hospital reported significantly fewer cases of patient infection (a 20 percent reduction) than did any of the other hospitals in our group. The explanation for the 20 percent reduction in patient infections is the use of UltraClean soap."

Write a response in which you discuss one or more alternative explanations that could rival the proposed explanation and explain how your explanation(s) can plausibly account for the facts presented in the argument.

123. The following appeared in a health newsletter.

"A ten-year nationwide study of the effectiveness of wearing a helmet while bicycling indicates that ten years ago, approximately 35 percent of all bicyclists reported wearing helmets, whereas today that number is nearly 80 percent. Another study, however, suggests that during the same ten-year period, the number of accidents caused by bicycling has increased 200 percent. These results demonstrate that bicyclists feel safer because they are wearing helmets, and they take more risks as a result. Thus, there is clearly a call for the government to strive to reduce the number of serious injuries from bicycle accidents by launching an education program that concentrates on the factors other than helmet use that are necessary for bicycle safety."

Write a response in which you discuss what questions would need to be answered in order to decide whether the recommendation and the argument on which it is based are reasonable. Be sure to explain how the answers to these questions would help to evaluate the recommendation.

---

124. The following appeared in a memo from the director of a large group of hospitals.

"In a controlled laboratory study of liquid hand soaps, a concentrated solution of extra strength UltraClean hand soap produced a 40 percent greater reduction in harmful bacteria than did the liquid hand soaps currently used in our hospitals. During our recent test of regular-strength UltraClean with doctors, nurses, and visitors at our hospital in Worktown, the hospital reported significantly fewer cases of patient infection (a 20 percent reduction) than did any of the other hospitals in our group. Therefore, to prevent serious patient infections, we should supply UltraClean at all hand-washing stations, including those used by visitors, throughout our hospital system."

Write a response in which you discuss what specific evidence is needed to evaluate the argument and explain how the evidence would weaken or strengthen the argument.

125. The following appeared in a health newsletter.

"A ten-year nationwide study of the effectiveness of wearing a helmet while bicycling indicates that ten years ago, approximately 35 percent of all bicyclists reported wearing helmets, whereas today that number is nearly 80 percent. Another study, however, suggests that during the same ten-year period, the number of accidents caused by bicycling has increased 200 percent. These results demonstrate that bicyclists feel safer because they are wearing helmets, and they take more risks as a result. Thus there is clearly a call for the government to strive to reduce the number of serious injuries from bicycle accidents by launching an education program that concentrates on the factors other than helmet use that are necessary for bicycle safety."

Write a response in which you discuss what specific evidence is needed to evaluate the argument and explain how the evidence would weaken or strengthen the argument.

126. The following is a recommendation from the personnel director to the president of Acme Publishing Company.

"Many other companies have recently stated that having their employees take the Easy Read Speed-Reading Course has greatly improved productivity. One graduate of the course was able to read a 500-page report in only two hours; another graduate rose from an assistant manager to vice president of the company in under a year. Obviously, the faster you can read, the more information you can absorb in a single workday. Moreover, Easy Read would cost Acme only $500 per employee — a small price to pay when you consider the benefits. Included in this fee is a three-week seminar in Spruce City and a lifelong subscription to the Easy Read newsletter. Clearly, Acme would benefit greatly by requiring all of our employees to take the Easy Read course."

Write a response in which you discuss what specific evidence is needed to evaluate the argument and explain how the evidence would weaken or strengthen the argument.

---

127. The following is a recommendation from the personnel director to the president of Acme Publishing Company.

"Many other companies have recently stated that having their employees take the Easy Read Speed-Reading Course has greatly improved productivity. One graduate of the course was able to read a 500-page report in only two hours; another graduate rose from an assistant manager to vice president of the company in under a year. Obviously, the faster you can read, the more information you can absorb in a single workday. Moreover, Easy Read would cost Acme only $500 per employee — a small price to pay when you consider the benefits. Included in this fee is a three-week seminar in Spruce City and a lifelong subscription to the Easy Read newsletter. Clearly, to improve overall productivity, Acme should require all of our employees to take the Easy Read course."

Write a response in which you discuss what questions would need to be answered in order to decide whether the recommendation and the argument on which it is based are reasonable. Be sure to explain how the answers to these questions would help to evaluate the recommendation.

---

128. The following appeared in a letter from the owner of the Sunnyside Towers apartment complex to its manager.

"One month ago, all the shower heads in the first three buildings of the Sunnyside Towers complex were modified to restrict maximum water flow to one-third of what it used to be. Although actual readings of water usage before and after the adjustment are not yet available, the change will obviously result in a considerable savings for Sunnyside Corporation, since the corporation must pay for water each month. Except for a few complaints about low water pressure, no problems with showers have been reported since the adjustment. Clearly, modifying shower heads to restrict water flow throughout all twelve buildings in the Sunnyside Towers complex will increase our profits further."

Write a response in which you discuss what specific evidence is needed to evaluate the argument and explain how the evidence would weaken or strengthen the argument.

---

129. The following appeared in a letter from the owner of the Sunnyside Towers apartment complex to its manager.

"Last week, all the shower heads in the first three buildings of the Sunnyside Towers complex were modified to restrict maximum water flow to one-third of what it used to be. Although actual readings of water usage before and after the adjustment are not yet available, the change will obviously result in a considerable savings for Sunnyside Corporation, since the corporation must pay for water each month. Except for a few complaints about low water pressure, no problems with showers have been reported since the adjustment. Clearly, modifying shower heads to restrict water flow throughout all twelve buildings in the Sunnyside Towers complex will increase our profits further."

Write a response in which you examine the stated and/or unstated assumptions of the argument. Be sure to explain how the argument depends on these assumptions and what the implications are for the argument if the assumptions prove unwarranted.

130. The following memorandum is from the business manager of Happy Pancake House restaurants.

"Butter has now been replaced by margarine in Happy Pancake House restaurants throughout the southwestern United States. Only about 2 percent of customers have filed a formal complaint, indicating that an average of 98 people out of 100 are happy with the change. Furthermore, many servers have reported that a number of customers who ask for butter do not complain when they are given margarine instead. Clearly, either these customers cannot distinguish butter from margarine or they use the term 'butter' to refer to either butter or margarine. Thus, to avoid the expense of purchasing butter, the Happy Pancake House should extend this cost-saving change to its restaurants throughout the rest of the country."

Write a response in which you examine the stated and/or unstated assumptions of the argument. Be sure to explain how the argument depends on these assumptions and what the implications are for the argument if the assumptions prove unwarranted.

131. The following memorandum is from the business manager of Happy Pancake House restaurants.

"Butter has now been replaced by margarine in Happy Pancake House restaurants throughout the southwestern United States. Only about 2 percent of customers have complained, indicating that an average of 98 people out of 100 are happy with the change. Furthermore, many servers have reported that a number of customers who ask for butter do not complain when they are given margarine instead. Clearly, either these customers cannot distinguish butter from margarine or they use the term 'butter' to refer to either butter or margarine. Thus, we predict that Happy Pancake House will be able to increase profits dramatically if we extend this cost-saving change to all our restaurants in the southeast and northeast as well."

Write a response in which you discuss what questions would need to be answered in order to decide whether the prediction and the argument on which it is based are reasonable. Be sure to explain how the answers to these questions would help to evaluate the prediction.

132. The following appeared in a letter to the school board in the town of Centerville.

"All students should be required to take the driver's education course at Centerville High School. In the past two years, several accidents in and around Centerville have involved teenage drivers. Since a number of parents in Centerville have complained that they are too busy to teach their teenagers to drive, some other instruction is necessary to ensure that these teenagers are safe drivers. Although there are two driving schools in Centerville, parents on a tight budget cannot afford to pay for driving instruction. Therefore an effective and mandatory program sponsored by the high school is the only solution to this serious problem."

Write a response in which you examine the stated and/or unstated assumptions of the argument. Be sure to explain how the argument depends on these assumptions and what the implications are for the argument if the assumptions prove unwarranted.

133. The following memorandum is from the business manager of Happy Pancake House restaurants.

"Butter has now been replaced by margarine in Happy Pancake House restaurants throughout the southwestern United States. Only about 2 percent of customers have complained, indicating that an average of 98 people out of 100 are happy with the change. Furthermore, many servers have reported that a number of customers who ask for butter do not complain when they are given margarine instead. Clearly, either these customers cannot distinguish butter from margarine or they use the term 'butter' to refer to either butter or margarine. Thus, to avoid the expense of purchasing butter and to increase profitability, the Happy Pancake House should extend this cost-saving change to its restaurants in the southeast and northeast as well."

Write a response in which you discuss what specific evidence is needed to evaluate the argument and explain how the evidence would weaken or strengthen the argument.

---

134. The following appeared in a letter to the school board in the town of Centerville.

"All students should be required to take the driver's education course at Centerville High School. In the past two years, several accidents in and around Centerville have involved teenage drivers. Since a number of parents in Centerville have complained that they are too busy to teach their teenagers to drive, some other instruction is necessary to ensure that these teenagers are safe drivers. Although there are two driving schools in Centerville, parents on a tight budget cannot afford to pay for driving instruction. Therefore an effective and mandatory program sponsored by the high school is the only solution to this serious problem."

Write a response in which you discuss what specific evidence is needed to evaluate the argument and explain how the evidence would weaken or strengthen the argument.

---

135. The data from a survey of high school math and science teachers show that

in the district of Sanlee many of these teachers reported assigning daily homework, whereas in the district of Marlee, most science and math teachers reported assigning homework no more than two or three days per week. Despite receiving less frequent homework assignments, Marlee students earn better grades overall and are less likely to be required to repeat a year of school than are students in Sanlee. These results call into question the usefulness of frequent homework assignments. Most likely the Marlee students have more time to concentrate on individual assignments than do the Sanlee students who have homework every day. Therefore teachers in our high schools should assign homework no more than twice a week. [193]

Write a response in which you discuss what specific evidence is needed to evaluate the argument and explain how the evidence would weaken or strengthen the argument.

136. The following appeared in a letter to the school board in the town of Centerville.

"All students should be required to take the driver's education course at Centerville High School. In the past two years, several accidents in and around Centerville have involved teenage drivers. Since a number of parents in Centerville have complained that they are too busy to teach their teenagers to drive, some other instruction is necessary to ensure that these teenagers are safe drivers. Although there are two driving schools in Centerville, parents on a tight budget cannot afford to pay for driving instruction. Therefore an effective and mandatory program sponsored by the high school is the only solution to this serious problem."

Write a response in which you discuss what questions would need to be answered in order to decide whether the recommendation and the argument on which it is based

are reasonable. Be sure to explain how the answers to these questions would help to evaluate the recommendation.

---

137. While the Department of Education in the state of Attra recommends that high school students be assigned homework every day, the data from a recent statewide survey of high school math and science teachers give us reason to question the usefulness of daily homework. In the district of Sanlee, 86 percent of the teachers reported assigning homework three to five times a week, whereas in the district of Marlee, less than 25 percent of the teachers reported assigning homework three to five times a week. Yet the students in Marlee earn better grades overall and are less likely to be required to repeat a year of school than are the students in Sanlee. Therefore, all teachers in our high schools should assign homework no more than twice a week. [193]

Write a response in which you examine the stated and/or unstated assumptions of the argument. Be sure to explain how the argument depends on these assumptions and what the implications are for the argument if the assumptions prove unwarranted.

---

138. The following appeared as an editorial in the student newspaper of Groveton College.

"To combat the recently reported dramatic rise in cheating among college students, colleges and universities should adopt honor codes similar to Groveton's, which calls for students to agree not to cheat in their academic endeavors and to notify a faculty member if they suspect that others have cheated. Groveton's honor code replaced an old-fashioned system in which teachers closely monitored students. Under that system, teachers reported an average of thirty cases of cheating per year. The honor code has proven far more successful: in the first year it was in place, students reported twenty-one cases of cheating; five years later, this figure had dropped to fourteen. Moreover, in a recent survey conducted by the Groveton honor council, a majority of students said that they would be less likely to cheat with an honor code in place than without."

Write a response in which you discuss what specific evidence is needed to evaluate the argument and explain how the evidence would weaken or strengthen the argument.

---

139. The following appeared in a memo from a budget planner for the city of Grandview.

"Our citizens are well aware of the fact that while the Grandview Symphony Orchestra was struggling to succeed, our city government promised annual funding to help support its programs. Last year, however, private contributions to the symphony increased by 200 percent, and attendance at the symphony's concerts-in-the-park series doubled. The symphony has also announced an increase in ticket prices for next year. Such developments indicate that the symphony can now succeed without funding from city government and we can eliminate that expense from next year's budget. Therefore, we recommend that the city of Grandview eliminate its funding for the Grandview Symphony from next year's budget. By doing so, we can prevent a city budget deficit without threatening the success of the symphony."

Write a response in which you discuss what questions would need to be answered in order to decide whether the recommendation is likely to have the predicted result. Be sure to explain how the answers to these questions would help to evaluate the recommendation.

140. While the Department of Education in the state of Attra suggests that high school students be assigned homework every day, the data from a recent statewide survey of high school math and science teachers give us reason to question the usefulness of daily homework. In the district of Sanlee, 86 percent of the teachers reported assigning homework three to five times a week, whereas in the district of Marlee, less than 25 percent of the teachers reported assigning homework three to five times a week. Yet the students in Marlee earn better grades overall and are less likely to be required to repeat a year of school than are the students in Sanlee. Therefore, we recommend that all teachers in our high schools should assign homework no more than twice a week.

Write a response in which you discuss what questions would need to be answered in order to decide whether the recommendation and the argument on which it is based are reasonable. Be sure to explain how the answers to these questions would help to evaluate the recommendation.

141. The following appeared in a memo to the board of the Grandview Symphony.

"The city of Grandview has provided annual funding for the Grandview Symphony since the symphony's inception ten years ago. Last year the symphony hired an internationally known conductor, who has been able to attract high-profile guest musicians to perform with the symphony. Since then, private contributions to the symphony have doubled and attendance at the symphony's concerts-in-the-park series has reached new highs. Now that the Grandview Symphony is an established success, it can raise ticket prices. Increased revenue from larger audiences and higher ticket prices will enable the symphony to succeed without funding from the city government."

Write a response in which you discuss what specific evidence is needed to evaluate the argument and explain how the evidence would weaken or strengthen the argument.

142. Hospital statistics regarding people who go to the emergency room after roller-skating accidents indicate the need for more protective equipment. Within that group of people, 75 percent of those who had accidents in streets or parking lots had not been wearing any protective clothing (helmets, knee pads, etc.) or any light-reflecting material (clip-on lights, glow-in-the-dark wrist pads, etc.). Clearly, the statistics indicate that by investing in high-quality protective gear and reflective equipment, roller skaters will greatly reduce their risk of being severely injured in an accident. [New]

Write a response in which you examine the stated and/or unstated assumptions of the argument. Be sure to explain how the argument depends on these assumptions and what the implications are for the argument if the assumptions prove unwarranted.

143. The following appeared in a memo from a budget planner for the city of Grandview.

"When the Grandview Symphony was established ten years ago, the city of Grandview agreed to provide the symphony with annual funding until the symphony became self-sustaining. Two years ago, the symphony hired an internationally known conductor, who has been able to attract high-profile guest musicians to perform with the symphony. Since then, private contributions to the symphony have tripled and attendance at the symphony's outdoor summer concert series has reached record highs. Now that the symphony has succeeded in finding an audience, the city can eliminate its funding of the symphony."

Write a response in which you examine the stated and/or unstated assumptions of the argument. Be sure to explain how the argument depends on these assumptions and what the implications are for the argument if the assumptions prove unwarranted.

---

144. The citizens of Forsythe have adopted more healthful lifestyles. Their responses to a recent survey show that in their eating habits they conform more closely to government nutritional recommendations than they did ten years ago. Furthermore, there has been a fourfold increase in sales of food products containing kiran, a substance that a scientific study has shown reduces cholesterol. This trend is also evident in reduced sales of sulia, a food that few of the healthiest citizens regularly eat.

Write a response in which you examine the stated and/or unstated assumptions of the argument. Be sure to explain how the argument depends on these assumptions and what the implications are for the argument if the assumptions prove unwarranted.

---

145. The following appeared in a memo to the board of directors of a company that specializes in the delivery of heating oil.

"Most homes in the northeastern United States, where winters are typically cold, have traditionally used oil as their major fuel for heating. Last heating season, that region experienced 90 days with below-normal temperatures, and climate forecasters predict that this weather pattern will continue for several more years. Furthermore, many new homes are being built in the region in response to recent population growth. Because of these trends, we can safely predict that this region will experience an increased demand for heating oil during the next five years."

Write a response in which you discuss what questions would need to be answered in order to decide whether the prediction and the argument on which it is based are reasonable. Be sure to explain how the answers to these questions would help to evaluate the prediction.

---

146. The following appeared in a memo to the board of directors of a company that specializes in the delivery of heating oil.

"Most homes in the northeastern United States, where winters are typically cold, have traditionally used oil as their major fuel for heating. Last heating season, that region experienced 90 days with below-normal temperatures, and climate forecasters predict that this weather pattern will continue for several more years. Furthermore, many new homes are being built in the region in response to recent population growth. Because of these trends, we can safely predict that this region will experience an increased demand for heating oil during the next five years."

Write a response in which you discuss what specific evidence is needed to evaluate the argument and explain how the evidence would weaken or strengthen the argument.

---

147. The following recommendation was made by the president and administrative staff of Grove College, a private institution, to the college's governing committee.

"We recommend that Grove College preserve its century-old tradition of all-female education rather than admit men into its programs. It is true that a majority of faculty members voted in favor of coeducation, arguing that it would encourage more students to apply to Grove. But 80 percent of the students responding to a survey conducted by the student government wanted the school to remain all female, and over half of the alumnae who answered a separate survey also opposed coeducation. Keeping the college all female will improve morale among students and convince alumnae to keep supporting the college financially."

Write a response in which you discuss what specific evidence is needed to evaluate the argument and explain how the evidence would weaken or strengthen the argument.

---

148. The following recommendation was made by the president and administrative staff of Grove College, a private institution, to the college's governing committee.

"We recommend that Grove College preserve its century-old tradition of all-female education rather than admit men into its programs. It is true that a majority of faculty members voted in favor of coeducation, arguing that it would encourage more students to apply to Grove. But 80 percent of the students responding to a survey conducted by the student government wanted the school to remain all female, and over half of the alumnae who answered a separate survey also opposed coeducation. Keeping the college all female will improve morale among students and convince alumnae to keep supporting the college financially."

Write a response in which you examine the stated and/or unstated assumptions of the argument. Be sure to explain how the argument depends on these assumptions and what the implications are for the argument if the assumptions prove unwarranted.

---

149. The following recommendation was made by the president and administrative staff of Grove College, a private institution, to the college's governing committee.

"We recommend that Grove College preserve its century-old tradition of all-female education rather than admit men into its programs. It is true that a majority of faculty members voted in favor of coeducation, arguing that it would encourage more students to apply to Grove. But 80 percent of the students responding to a survey conducted by the student government wanted the school to remain all female, and over half of the alumnae who answered a separate survey also opposed coeducation. Keeping the college all female will improve morale among students and convince alumnae to keep supporting the college financially."

Write a response in which you discuss what questions would need to be answered in order to decide whether the recommendation is likely to have the predicted result. Be sure to explain how the answers to these questions would help to evaluate the recommendation.

---

150. The following appeared in a letter from a firm providing investment advice to a client.

"Homes in the northeastern United States, where winters are typically cold, have traditionally used oil as their major fuel for heating. Last year that region experienced 90 days with below-average temperatures, and climate forecasters at Waymarsh University predict that this weather pattern will continue for several more years. Furthermore, many new homes have been built in this region during the past year. Because these developments will certainly result in an increased demand for heating oil, we recommend investment in Consolidated Industries, one of whose major business operations is the retail sale of home heating oil."

Write a response in which you discuss what questions would need to be answered in order to decide whether the recommendation and the argument on which it is based

are reasonable. Be sure to explain how the answers to these questions would help to evaluate the recommendation.

---

151. Benton City residents have adopted healthier lifestyles. A recent survey of city residents shows that the eating habits of city residents conform more closely to government nutritional recommendations than they did ten years ago. During those ten years, local sales of food products containing kiran, a substance that a scientific study has shown reduces cholesterol, have increased fourfold, while sales of sulia, a food rarely eaten by the healthiest residents, have declined dramatically. Because of these positive changes in the eating habits of Benton City residents, we predict that the obesity rate in the city will soon be well below the national average.

Write a response in which you discuss what questions would need to be answered in order to decide whether the prediction and the argument on which it is based are reasonable. Be sure to explain how the answers to these questions would help to evaluate the prediction.

---

152. The following appeared in a memo to the board of directors of Bargain Brand Cereals.

"One year ago we introduced our first product, Bargain Brand breakfast cereal. Our very low prices quickly drew many customers away from the top-selling cereal companies. Although the companies producing the top brands have since tried to compete with us by lowering their prices and although several plan to introduce their own budget brands, not once have we needed to raise our prices to continue making a profit. Given our success in selling cereal, we recommend that Bargain Brand now expand its business and begin marketing other low-priced food products as quickly as possible."

Write a response in which you discuss what questions would need to be answered in order to decide whether the recommendation and the argument on which it is based are reasonable. Be sure to explain how the answers to these questions would help to evaluate the recommendation.

---

153. The following appeared in a memo to the board of directors of Bargain Brand Cereals.

"One year ago we introduced our first product, Bargain Brand breakfast cereal. Our very low prices quickly drew many customers away from the top-selling cereal companies. Although the companies producing the top brands have since tried to compete with us by lowering their prices and although several plan to introduce their own budget brands, not once have we needed to raise our prices to continue making a profit. Given our success in selling cereal, we recommend that Bargain Brand now expand its business and begin marketing other low-priced food products as quickly as possible."

Write a response in which you examine the stated and/or unstated assumptions of the argument. Be sure to explain how the argument depends on these assumptions and what the implications are for the argument if the assumptions prove unwarranted.

---

154. The following appeared in a letter from a firm providing investment advice to a client.

"Homes in the northeastern United States, where winters are typically cold, have traditionally used oil as their major fuel for heating. Last year that region experienced twenty days with below-average temperatures, and local weather forecasters throughout the region predict that this weather pattern will continue for several more years. Furthermore, many new homes have been built in this region during the past year. Based on these developments, we predict a large increase in the demand for heating oil. Therefore, we recommend investment in Consolidated Industries, one of whose major business operations is the retail sale of home heating oil."

Write a response in which you discuss what questions would need to be answered in order to decide whether the recommendation and the argument on which it is based are reasonable. Be sure to explain how the answers to these questions would help to evaluate the recommendation.

---

155. The following appeared in a letter from a firm providing investment advice to a client.

"Homes in the northeastern United States, where winters are typically cold, have traditionally used oil as their major fuel for heating. Last year that region experienced twenty days with below-average temperatures, and local weather forecasters throughout the region predict that this weather pattern will continue for several more years. Furthermore, many new homes have been built in this region during the past year. Because of these developments, we predict an increased demand for heating oil and recommend investment in Consolidated Industries, one of whose major business operations is the retail sale of home heating oil."

Write a response in which you discuss what specific evidence is needed to evaluate the argument and explain how the evidence would weaken or strengthen the argument.

156. The following recommendation was made by the president and administrative staff of Grove College, a private institution, to the college's governing committee.

"Recently, there have been discussions about ending Grove College's century-old tradition of all-female education by admitting male students into our programs. At a recent faculty meeting, a majority of faculty members voted in favor of coeducation, arguing that it would encourage more students to apply to Grove. However, Grove students, both past and present, are against the idea of coeducation. Eighty percent of the students responding to a survey conducted by the student government wanted the school to remain all female, and over half of the alumnae who answered a separate survey also opposed coeducation. Therefore, we recommend maintaining Grove College's tradition of all-female education. We predict that keeping the college all-female will improve morale among students and convince alumnae to keep supporting the college financially."

Write a response in which you discuss what questions would need to be answered in order to decide whether the recommendation is likely to have the predicted result. Be sure to explain how the answers to these questions would help to evaluate the recommendation.

157. The following appeared in a memo from the marketing director of Top Dog Pet Stores.

"Five years ago Fish Emporium started advertising in the magazine Exotic Pets Monthly. Their stores saw sales increase by 15 percent after their ads began appearing in the magazine. The three Fish Emporium stores in Gulf City saw an even greater increase than that. Because Top Dog Pet Stores is based in Gulf City, it seems clear that we should start placing our own ads in Exotic Pets Monthly. If we do so, we will be sure to reverse the recent trend of declining sales and start making a profit again."

Write a response in which you examine the stated and/or unstated assumptions of the argument. Be sure to explain how the argument depends on these assumptions and what the implications are for the argument if the assumptions prove unwarranted.

---

158. The following appeared in a memo from the marketing director of Top Dog Pet Stores.

"Five years ago, Fish Emporium started advertising in the magazine Exotic Pets Monthly. Their stores saw sales increase by 15 percent. The three Fish Emporium stores in Gulf City saw an even greater increase than that. Because Top Dog has some of its largest stores in Gulf City, it seems clear that we should start placing our own ads in Exotic Pets Monthly. If we do so, we will be sure to reverse the recent trend of declining sales and start making a profit again."

Write a response in which you discuss what specific evidence is needed to evaluate the argument and explain how the evidence would weaken or strengthen the argument.

---

159. The following appeared in a letter to the editor of the Balmer Island Gazette.

"The population on Balmer Island increases to 100,000 during the summer months. To reduce the number of accidents involving mopeds and pedestrians, the town council of Balmer Island plans to limit the number of mopeds rented by each of the island's six moped rental companies from 50 per day to 30 per day during the summer season. Last year, the neighboring island of Torseau enforced similar limits on moped rentals and saw a 50 percent reduction in moped accidents. We predict that putting these limits into effect on Balmer Island will result in the same reduction in moped accidents."

Write a response in which you discuss what questions would need to be answered in order to decide whether the prediction and the argument on which it is based are reasonable. Be sure to explain how the answers to these questions would help to evaluate the prediction.

---

160. The following appeared in a recommendation from the President of the Amburg Chamber of Commerce.

"Last October, the city of Belleville installed high-intensity lighting in its central business district, and vandalism there declined almost immediately. The city of Amburg, on the other hand, recently instituted police patrols on bicycles in its business district. However, the rate of vandalism here remains constant. Since high-intensity lighting is clearly the most effective way to combat crime, we recommend using the money that is currently being spent on bicycle patrols to install such lighting throughout Amburg. If we install this high-intensity lighting, we will significantly reduce crime rates in Amburg."

Write a response in which you discuss what questions would need to be answered in order to decide whether the recommendation is likely to have the predicted result. Be sure to explain how the answers to these questions would help to evaluate the recommendation.

---

161. The following is a recommendation from the personnel director to the president of Acme Publishing Company.

"Many other companies have recently stated that having their employees take the Easy Read Speed-Reading Course has greatly improved productivity. One graduate of the course was able to read a 500-page report in only two hours; another graduate rose from an assistant manager to vice president of the company in under a year. Obviously, the faster you can read, the more information you can absorb in a single workday. Moreover, Easy Read would cost Acme only $500 per employee — a small price to pay when you consider the benefits. Included in this fee is a three-week seminar in Spruce City and a lifelong subscription to the Easy Read newsletter. Clearly, Acme would benefit greatly by requiring all of our employees to take the Easy Read course."

Write a response in which you examine the stated and/or unstated assumptions of the argument. Be sure to explain how the argument depends on these assumptions and what the implications are for the argument if the assumptions prove unwarranted.

---

162. The following appeared in a memo from a budget planner for the city of Grandview.

"It is time for the city of Grandview to stop funding the Grandview Symphony Orchestra. It is true that the symphony struggled financially for many years, but last year private contributions to the symphony increased by 200 percent and attendance at the symphony's concerts-in-the-park series doubled. In addition, the symphony has just announced an increase in ticket prices for next year. For these reasons, we recommend that the city eliminate funding for the Grandview Symphony Orchestra from next year's budget. We predict that the symphony will flourish in the years to come even without funding from the city."

Write a response in which you discuss what questions would need to be answered in order to decide whether the recommendation is likely to have the predicted result. Be sure to explain how the answers to these questions would help to evaluate the recommendation.

163. The following memo appeared in the newsletter of the West Meria Public Health Council.

"An innovative treatment has come to our attention that promises to significantly reduce absenteeism in our schools and workplaces. A study reports that in nearby East Meria, where consumption of the plant beneficia is very high, people visit the doctor only once or twice per year for the treatment of colds. Clearly, eating a substantial amount of beneficia can prevent colds. Since colds are the reason most frequently given for absences from school and work, we recommend the daily use of nutritional supplements derived from beneficia. We predict this will dramatically reduce absenteeism in our schools and workplaces."

Write a response in which you discuss what questions would need to be answered in order to decide whether the recommendation is likely to have the predicted result. Be sure to explain how the answers to these questions would help to evaluate the recommendation.

164. The following was written by a group of developers in the city of Monroe.

"A jazz music club in Monroe would be a tremendously profitable enterprise. At present, the nearest jazz club is over 60 miles away from Monroe; thus, our proposed club, the C Note, would have the local market all to itself. In addition, there is ample evidence of the popularity of jazz in Monroe: over 100,000 people attended Monroe's jazz festival last summer, several well-known jazz musicians live in Monroe, and the highest-rated radio program in Monroe is 'Jazz Nightly.' Finally, a nationwide study indicates that the typical jazz fan spends close to $1,000 per year on jazz entertainment. We therefore predict that the C Note cannot help but make money."

Write a response in which you discuss what questions would need to be answered

in order to decide whether the prediction and the argument on which it is based are reasonable. Be sure to explain how the answers to these questions would help to evaluate the prediction.

---

165. Humans arrived in the Kaliko Islands about 7,000 years ago, and within 3,000 years most of the large mammal species that had lived in the forests of the Kaliko Islands were extinct. Previous archaeological findings have suggested that early humans generally relied on both fishing and hunting for food; since archaeologists have discovered numerous sites in the Kaliko Islands where the bones of fish were discarded, it is likely that the humans also hunted the mammals. Furthermore, researchers have uncovered simple tools, such as stone knives, that could be used for hunting. The only clear explanation is that humans caused the extinction of the various mammal species through excessive hunting.

Write a response in which you discuss one or more alternative explanations that could rival the proposed explanation and explain how your explanation(s) can plausibly account for the facts presented in the argument.

---

166. The following memo appeared in the newsletter of the West Meria Public Health Council.

"An innovative treatment has come to our attention that promises to significantly reduce absenteeism in our schools and workplaces. A study reports that in nearby East Meria, where fish consumption is very high, people visit the doctor only once or twice per year for the treatment of colds. This shows that eating a substantial amount of fish can clearly prevent colds. Furthermore, since colds are the reason most frequently given for absences from school and work, attendance levels will improve. Therefore, we recommend the daily use of a nutritional supplement derived from fish oil as a good way to prevent colds and lower absenteeism."

Write a response in which you discuss what questions would need to be answered in order to decide whether the recommendation and the argument on which it is based are reasonable. Be sure to explain how the answers to these questions would help to evaluate the recommendation.

167. The following appeared in a memo from a vice president of Alta Manufacturing.

"During the past year, Alta Manufacturing had thirty percent more on-the-job accidents than nearby Panoply Industries, where the work shifts are one hour shorter than ours. Experts believe that a significant contributing factor in many accidents is fatigue caused by sleep deprivation among workers. Therefore, to reduce the number of on-the-job accidents at Alta, we recommend shortening each of our three work shifts by one hour. If we do this, our employees will get adequate amounts of sleep."

Write a response in which you discuss what questions would need to be answered in order to decide whether the recommendation and the argument on which it is based are reasonable. Be sure to explain how the answers to these questions would help to evaluate the recommendation.

168. The following is a letter that recently appeared in the Oak City Gazette, a local newspaper.

"The primary function of the Committee for a Better Oak City is to advise the city government on how to make the best use of the city's limited budget. However, at some of our recent meetings we failed to make important decisions because of the foolish objections raised by committee members who are not even residents of Oak City. People who work in Oak City but who live elsewhere cannot fully understand the business and politics of the city. After all, only Oak City residents pay city taxes, and therefore only residents understand how that money could best be used to improve the city. We recommend, then, that the Committee for a Better Oak City vote to restrict its membership to city residents only. We predict that, without the interference of non-residents, the committee will be able to make Oak City a better place in which to live and work."

Write a response in which you discuss what questions would need to be answered in order to decide whether the recommendation is likely to have the predicted result. Be sure to explain how the answers to these questions would help to evaluate the recommendation.

---

169. The following appeared in a memo from the mayor of Brindleburg to the city council.

"Two years ago, the town of Seaside Vista opened a new municipal golf course and resort hotel. Since then, the Seaside Vista Tourism Board has reported a 20 % increase in visitors. In addition, local banks reported a steep rise in the number of new business loan applications they received this year. The amount of tax money collected by Seaside Vista has also increased, allowing the town to announce plans to improve Seaside Vista's roads and bridges. We recommend building a similar golf course and resort hotel in Brindleburg. We predict that this project will generate additional tax revenue that the city can use to fund much-needed public improvements."

Write a response in which you discuss what questions would need to be answered in order to decide whether the recommendation is likely to have the predicted result. Be sure to explain how the answers to these questions would help to evaluate the recommendation.

---

170. The following appeared in a memo from the vice president of a company that builds shopping malls around the country.

"The surface of a section of Route 101, paved just two years ago by Good Intentions Roadways, is now badly cracked with a number of dangerous potholes. In another part of the state, a section of Route 40, paved by Appian Roadways more than four years ago, is still in good condition. In a demonstration of their continuing commitment to quality, Appian Roadways recently purchased state-of-the-art paving machinery and hired a new quality-control manager. Therefore, I recommend hiring Appian Roadways to construct the access roads for all our new shopping malls. I predict that our Appian access roads will not have to be repaired for at least four years."

Write a response in which you discuss what questions would need to be answered in order to decide whether the recommendation is likely to have the predicted result. Be sure to explain how the answers to these questions would help to evaluate the recommendation.

---

171. The following appeared as a letter to the editor from the owner of a skate shop in Central Plaza.

"Two years ago the city voted to prohibit skateboarding in Central Plaza. They claimed that skateboard users were responsible for the litter and vandalism that were keeping other visitors from coming to the plaza. In the past two years, however, there has only been a small increase in the number of visitors to Central Plaza, and litter and vandalism are still problematic. Skateboarding is permitted in Monroe Park, however, and there is no problem with litter or vandalism there. In order to restore Central Plaza to its former glory, then, we recommend that the city lift its prohibition on skateboarding in the plaza."

Write a response in which you discuss what questions would need to be answered in order to decide whether the recommendation and the argument on which it is based are reasonable. Be sure to explain how the answers to these questions would help to evaluate the recommendation.

---

172. The following appeared in a recommendation from the president of Amburg's Chamber of Commerce.

"Last October the city of Belleville installed high-intensity lighting in its central business district, and vandalism there declined within a month. The city of Amburg has recently begun police patrols on bicycles in its business district, but the rate of vandalism there remains constant. We should install high-intensity lighting throughout Amburg, then, because doing so is a more effective way to combat crime. By reducing crime in this way, we can revitalize the declining neighborhoods in our city."

Write a response in which you discuss what specific evidence is needed to evaluate the argument and explain how the evidence would weaken or strengthen the argument.

---

173. The following appeared in a letter to the editor of the Balmer Island Gazette.

"The population on Balmer Island doubles during the summer months. During the summer, then, the town council of Balmer Island should decrease the maximum number of moped rentals allowed at each of the island's six moped and bicycle rental companies from 50 per day to 30 per day. This will significantly reduce the number of summertime accidents involving mopeds and pedestrians. The neighboring island of

Torseau actually saw a 50 percent reduction in moped accidents last year when Torseau's town council enforced similar limits on moped rentals. To help reduce moped accidents, therefore, we should also enforce these limitations during the summer months."

Write a response in which you examine the stated and/or unstated assumptions of the argument. Be sure to explain how the argument depends on these assumptions and what the implications are for the argument if the assumptions prove unwarranted.

---

174. A recent sales study indicates that consumption of seafood dishes in Bay City restaurants has increased by 30 percent during the past five years. Yet there are no currently operating city restaurants whose specialty is seafood. Moreover, the majority of families in Bay City are two-income families, and a nationwide study has shown that such families eat significantly fewer home-cooked meals than they did a decade ago but at the same time express more concern about healthful eating. Therefore, the new Captain Seafood restaurant that specializes in seafood should be quite popular and profitable.

Write a response in which you discuss what questions would need to be addressed in order to decide whether the conclusion and the argument on which it is based are reasonable. Be sure to explain how the answers to the questions would help to evaluate the conclusion.

부록

SOP

석박사 통합 과정에 비용과 시간은 얼마나 드나?

　미국 대학에 유학해 석박사 과정을 밟고자 하는 학생들이 하는 가장 큰 고민은, 5년간 지불해야 할 학비와 생활비가 우리나라에서 작은 아파트 하나를 살 만한 3억여 원이라는 점일 것이다. 1년에 4~5만 달러 이르는 학비와 달마다 최소 생활비로 쓸 약 2000달러를 합하면 최소 6만 달러가 매년 필요하다. 그런데 6만 달러는 주립대학의 경우이고, 사립대학은 프로그램에 따라 약 8만 달러에서 10만 달러를 지불해야 한다.

　좋은 소식은 이러한 비용을 학비와 생활비 모두 입학허가서와 동시에 허락을 받고 갈 수 있는 석박사 과정 프로그램이 다수 있다는 사실이다. 물론 모두 자료공학, 화학공학 전자공학, 생명공학 등 Engineering School에서는 funding을 보장해 주는 유명한 교수들이 다수 있고 이러한 교수는 매년 입학 허가 신청서가 올라오자마자 석박사 과정에서 자신이 운영하는 프로그램이나 연구소에서 일할 도움이 될 만한 학생들을 리크루트하려고 매우 바쁘게 움직인다.

석박사과정 합격 평점은?

　최적의 석박사 과정 학생을 선발하기 위해 SOP(The Statement of Purpose), Resume, Writing sample, 추천서에 적힌 내용을 분석·평가하는 과정을 거친다. 교수는 자신의 연구소 팀에서 현재 진행하는 연구에 투입할 경우 가장 잘 맞는 필요한 학생을 선택한다. 1) 학사 과정이나 석사 과정에서 필수과목을 적어도 B+ 이상의 점수로 이수하고 자기 분야에서 실험이나 활동을 꾸준히 하면서 4년제 대학을 우수한 성적으로 졸업한 학생인지를 확인한다. 석박사 과정은 평균 학점 3.7 이상이면 무난하다. 하지만 평균 학점이 3.7에 미치지 못하더라도 GRE subject test에서 90% 이상의 점수를 얻으면 학점이 낮은 이유를 소명하는 방식으로 허가를 받을 수 있다. 가령 6개 필수과목 중 5개 과목에서 A를 받고 한 과목에서 B-나 C+가 있을 때 소명서를 제출하면 합격 가능성이 높아진다.

전공필수 이수한 선수과목 수와 평점은?

석박사 과정 어드미션의 경우에는 대학 1, 2학년 평점보다 3, 4학년 전공과목의 성적을 더 중시해 본다. 교양과목에서 혹 C 학점이 있다 해도 전공과목인 math, physics, fluid dynamics 등에서 A 학점을 받았다면 교양과목 학점으로 고민하지 않아도 된다. 최근에는 컴퓨터공학 박사 과정 합격이 좀 더 어려워졌다. 그 이유는 우리나라 학부 과정에서 필수로 요구하는 수학이나 물리 과목이 미국 대학에서 요구하는 선수 과목의 수보다 적기 때문이다. 미국에서는 학비를 아끼고자 1, 2학년 교양과목을 커뮤니티 칼리지에서 이수하는 학생들도 많이 있다. 일반 커뮤니티 칼리지에서 컴퓨터공학과 3학년으로 편입하려면 다음과 같은 선수 과목을 반드시 이수해야 한다. 컴퓨터공학과의 경우 취업률이 좋다 보니 편입하려면 다음과 같은 과목에서 3.0 이상의 평점을 취득해야 하는 것이 현실이다.

Introduction to programming (computer science I)

Data structures (computer science II)

Computer organization and assembly language

Single variable calculus for STEM majors (one-year sequence)

Multivariable calculus

Discrete mathematics

Linear algebra

Differential equations

Calculus-based physics (one-year sequence with labs; topics covered must include mechanics and electromagnetism)

SOP

낮은 평점으로 입학이 가능한 예외의 경우도 있는가?

지원자 본인이 전문 기관이나 삼성과 같은 대기업 직원으로, 회사 장학금을 받아서 스스로 학비를 부담하는 경우에는 학점이 다소 낮아도 무리 없이 어드미션을 준다. 왜냐하면 대학에서 학생에게 월급을 지급하지 않고 학생 스스로가 학비 등을 충당하기 때문에 학점 기준이 다소 낮아도 지원하면 입학 허가를 받는다. 예를 들면 행정고시에 합격해 정부 기관 추천으로 대한민국 국비로 유학을 간다면 다소 어드미션이 어려운 학교도 GPA와 다소 무관하게 예외적으로 허가한다. 그렇다고 하더라도 학점이 최저 석박사 과정 학점인 3.0 미만인 경우에는 합격 가능성이 매우 낮아진다. 우스갯소리로 국적은 바꿔도 학적은 바꿀 수 없으니 성실하게 4.0/4.0을 취득할 수 있도록 최선을 다하는 것이 좋다.

GRE, Subject test, IBT 토플 점수 합격선은?

학점 다음으로 어드미션 커미티에서 보는 것이 GRE(Graduate Record Exam)와 IBT 토플 점수이다. GRE는 Verbal과 Quantitative로 구성된 일반 GRE뿐 아니라 전공에 따라서는 subject test 점수도 중요시한다. 공대의 경우에는 Quant는 167점(93%), Verbal은 160점(90%) 정도 취득하면 합격에 용이하다. 그러나 인문계의 경우에는 Quant 점수가 그다지 높지 않아도 합격할 수 있다. 그렇다고 해도 적어도 159 정도는 되어야 경쟁력이 있다. 상대적으로 인문계는 높은 Verbal 점수를 요구한다. 157점(75%)으로 합격한 학생도 과거에 있었다(물론 이 학생의 경우에는 라이팅 샘플 아이디어가 교수의 관심을 받기에 충분했다).

처음 대하는 단어가 매우 어려워 힘들어하는 지원자도 있으나 온라인 사이트나 학원 등에서 2달 정도 암기하고 반복하며 온라인에 후기와 함께 올려놓은 문제들을 풀어보고 임하는 것이 고득점 요령이다. 그러나 높은 점수를 얻지 못한다 해도 지원을 포기하면 안 된다. 어드미션에서는 전체적 평가를 하기 때문에 시험 점수보다 중요한 것은 라이팅 샘플이나 논문의 내용에 따라서도 결정되기 때문이다.

아비티는 영어로 2년 이상 수학한 이력이 있으면 대부분 면제이지만, 퍼듀 대학 경영학과 같은 곳은 영어를 모국어로 하지 않는 국가의 학생에게 반드시 아비티 점수를 요구한다. 미국 내 대학 순위 20위 정도의 대학원 과정에서는 대체로 토플은 100점 이상, 영역별로 25점 이상을 요구하는 곳이 대부분이다. 이보다 점수에 유연한 학교라고 할지라도 90점 이상은 대체로 요구한다. 물론 토플 하한 점수를 사이트에 79점으로 밝힌 학교도 있으나, 이는 한국인보다는 제3지대에서 오는 소수의 외국인을 배려한 점수로 봐야 한다.

컴퓨터나 수학 subject의 경우 87% 이상 받으면 대체로 경쟁력을 갖출 수 있다. 어드미션 자격 조건에 subject test를 recommend한다는 의미는 subject test를 제출하는 것이 유리하다는 것이다. 추천한다고 해서 봐도 되고 안 봐도 되는 것으로 오해가 없어야 한다. 펀드(funding) 제공 조건으로 아비티 토플 스피킹 26점 이상을 요구하는 학교도 있다. 이 경우에는 지원할 시 점수가 25점 미만이라도 application을 제출한 후에라도 26점을 받아서 다시 제출하는 것도 가능하다. 스피킹 연습은 혼자 하는 것보다는 네이티브 파트너를 구해서 함께하는 것이 점수를 올리기 쉽다. 영어가 발목을 잡지 않도록 부단히 영어 실력을 쌓는다면 원어민보다 더 능숙하게 영어를 구사할 수 있을 것이다. 시험 점수를 위한 시험이라기보다는 석박사 과정에 쉽게 적응하고 학위를 예정 시간 내에 취득할 수 있도록 영어 실력을 부단히 쌓아야 한다.

그리고 에세이 라이팅 점수는 대체로 4.0 이상은 되어야 합격 가능성이 높아진다. 전공에 따라서 4.5 이상을 요구하는 곳도 있다. 적어도 3.5는 받아야 합격할 수 있으나, 보통은 Verbal 점수보다는 라이팅 점수가 좋은 학생을 선호하는 석박사 과정이 대다수이다. AI tool로 1차 점수를 확인하므로 주어 및 동사와 수의 일치, 대명사 일치, 시제 일치, 전치사, 수동태 오류, 수사법적 표현에서 감점을 받지 않도록 완성도 높은 문장으로 에세이를 써야만 5.0을 노릴 수 있다. 부단히 연습해 History 전공으로 5.5를 받는다면 Fulbright 장학금 경쟁에서도 유리해진다.

SOP

입학 신청서 마감일은?

합격률을 높이려면 지원 신청서 작업창이 열리자마자 신속하게 지원해야 한다. 지원창은 8월 30일 지나 9월부터 지원 가능하도록 창이 열린다. 10월이 되면 대부분의 대학에서 지원창이 열려 지원 서류를 받는다. 마감일은 대개 11월 15일에서부터 이듬해 1월 30일까지이다. 석박사 과정은 늦게 지원하면 펀드를 딸 수 있는 확률이 매우 낮아진다. 합격 결과는 빠르면 1월 초부터 늦게는 4월 초까지 이메일이나 우편으로 배달된다. 그러므로 인적 사항을 적을 때 우편번호를 반드시 적어야 분실 없이 신속하게 받아볼 수 있다. 혹 mailing address에 미국 내 주소를 적는다면 조금은 더 빨리 결과를 알 수 있다.

SOP, Resume, Writing Sample, 추천서 내용이 일관성이 있는가?

다음으로 어드미션 커미티는 추천서에 적힌 내용과 SOP, resume와 writing sample를 cross check up하는 과정을 통해 지원자가 과거로부터 지금까지 계속해서 일관된 학업 목적과 계획이 있었는지를 확인한다. 지원한 학생이 학업 계획을 성취할 수 있는 기량이 있는지를 평가한다. SOP을 작성할 때는 자신의 관심 연구 분야가 지원하는 특정 교수의 분야와 부합하는지 또한 그 교수가 현재 운영 중인 팀의 연구 과제 및 목적, 내용과 부합하는지를 논하고 그 내용을 뒷받침해 줄 근거로는 writing sample을 제시해야 한다.

과거 몇 명의 학생을 추천한 이력이 있는지, 그리고 추천한 학생들의 학업 성적이 좋은지를 평가하는, 추천인 평가 등급 점수가 있다. 추천하는 교수가 노벨상 수여자라면 그가 추천하는 학생은 최우선으로 합격이 가능하다. 우리나라 교수의 경우에는 일단 논문 점수가 높은 교수가 추천을 하면 가산점이 붙는다. 학생들만 평점이 있는 것이 아니고 교수 추천도 데이터베이스화되어 있다. 추천하는 교수가, 지원하는 학교의 박사 출신일 경우에도 가산점이 붙는다. 교수에게 추천서를 부탁할 때는 이메일로 성적표, 자소서, 이력서, 논문 등을 함께 부치고, 간단하게 자신이 언제 어떤 과목을 이수했고 학점은 몇 점이었는지, 그리고 친밀감을 보일 수 있는 에피소드를 간략히 적어 부탁드린다. 만약 연구실에서 매일 뵙는 교수님이라면 직접 말씀 드리는 편이 바람직하다.

라이팅 샘플도 점수를 매기는데, 기재한 논문집 점수에 따라서 결정된다. 이른바 NATURE/SCIENCE/CELL에 대한 IF(임팩트 팩터)는 30점에서 42점 정도이다. IF는 논문 관련 정보 사이트인 Clarivate에서 알아볼 수 있다. 요즈음은 Google scholar에서 본인의 논문 내용이 누구 어떤 논문에서 몇 번이나 quote되었는지 검색할 수 있다. 라이팅 샘플이 없는 경우에는 라이팅 샘플을 써서 working paper로 제출하면 된다. 어디에도 출판된 적은 없으나 논문의 내용이 참신하다면 오히려 교수들이 경쟁적으로 이 학생을 리쿠르트하려고 할 것이다. 라이팅 샘플의 내용이 합격과 직접적으로 연관이 되는 결정적 요소인 것이다.

Resume에서 제일 중요시 보는 부분은 working paper와 출판한 논문이다. 만약에 자신이 펀드를 따고자 하는 교수 아래에서 일을 하고자 한다면, 그 교수를 자신의 논문 previous research에서 언급하거나 그 교수의 이론을 기조로 한 논문을 준비하는 것이 합격 요령이다. 박사 과정에 입학하기 전, 이와 같은 지원 과정을 통해 각 학교 교수들 간의 관계망을 그려볼 수 있는데, 이는 차후 공동 연구 과제를 딸 때 도움이 된다.

Contact Letter를 반드시 보내야 하는가?

지원서 파일을 업로드하지도 않은 채 Contact Letter를 보내는 것은 바람직하지는 않다. 일정이 많은 교수들이 지원서도 넣지 않는 학생에게 이메일을 보내지 않는 것은 통례이다. 모든 서류가 완성되었다면 콘택트 이메일 쓰는 것은 두려워할 필요가 없다. 물론 이때 콩글리시 어조로 이메일 보낸다면 이는 상당한 마이너스 요인이 될 수 있다. 영어로 쓴 이메일 커뮤니케이션을 통해 자연스럽게 아카데미 커뮤니티의 일원이 될 수 있는 유연하면서도 Formal한 자질을 보일 수 있다. 영어로 소통하는 것이 처음인 지원자는 반드시 영문 글쓰기를 잘하는 지인에게 확인을 받고 보내야 한다. 물론 첨부한 SOP, resume와 writing sample 등과 이메일이 인상적이라면 콘택트 편지를 보내자마자 교수로부터 "Love Call"을 받을 수 있다.

다만 이메일을 포함해 모든 글을 수정·보완해 줄 수 있는 멘토가 있다면 이는 말할 수 없는 자산이 된다. 네이티브 스피커가 아닌 이상 반드시 원어민이면서 자신이 지원한 전공 분야에 사전 지식이 있는 전문가의 도움을 받는 것을 추천한다. 멘토를 모델 삼아 영어 실력이 효율적으로 발전할 수 있기 때문이다. 외국인이기 때문에 영어를 모국어처럼 할 수 없다는 생각은 틀린 생각이라는 것을 분명하게 지적한다. 이런 잘못된 선입견과 자세가 이중 언어 구사자로 가는 길에서 발목을 잡을 수 있기 때문이다. 두 가지 다른 언어로 세상을 경험하는 사람과 오로지 국어로만 소통하는 사람이 보고 생각할 수 있는 focus와 boundary는 결코 동일할 수 없을 것이다.

영미권 대학 석박사 학위 과정 입학의 장점

1) 자신이 하고자 하는 연구를 계속하고 논문을 출판함으로써 연구 분야에 데뷔할 수 있다.
2) 학위를 취득하면 평사원으로 입사했을 경우 8년가량 소요되는 과장으로 입사할 수 있다.
3) 미국 대학의 경우 박사 과정 동안 펀딩을 받으며 경제적 문제 없이 5년간 학업에 정진할 수 있다.
4) 언어 장벽을 넘어 한국식 시각에서 벗어나 다양한 문화 이해를 바탕으로 새로운 지식 탐구 방법과 조직 운영에서 문제 해결 방법을 체화할 수 있다.

다음은 지난 10여 년간 석박사 과정에 지원해 합격하고 펀딩을 딴 학생 제출한 SOP 샘플과 라이팅 샘플이다. 이를 참고해 지원하고자 하는 학교에 합격할 수 있기를 바란다. 지식과 정보는 나누면 나눌수록 커진다고 한다. 그러므로 지원 전에 더욱더 정확한 정보로 유학을 준비하고, 먼저 유학한 친구나 선배들에게 도움을 받는다면 박사 과정 합격 스토리가 나의 이야기가 될 수 있다.

다음 에세이는 Bio-Chem 박사에게 지원한 학생의 에세이이다. 이공계에서 대부분 요구하는 500자 에세이는 연구 중심으로 군더더기 없이 써야 한다. 이공계 박사 과정의 경우에는 SOP와 더불어 research history의 제출을 요구하는 대학도 있다. SOP가 연구 계획이라면 research summary는 경력을 뜻한다.

다음은 전형적인 석박사 과정 SOP 질문이다.

"Please upload a statement of 500-1,000 words explaining why you are applying to 지원 대학 for graduate study. Describe your research interests and preparation for your intended field(s) of study, including prior research and other relevant experiences. Relate how the faculty, research, and resources at 지원 대학 would contribute to your future goals."

I am particularly interested in developing anti-inflammatory-inducing biomaterial and novel bio-inert scaffolds for tissue engineering. My current job at 대학 이름 University is fabricating a dual surface modification of nano/micro patterns with nonbiodegradable polymer layer-by-layer (LbL) deposition to control host responses and injectable 3D porous scaffold for biosensors and treatment of diseases and cancers. My research foci are three folds: (1) Advancing the method capable of direct investigation of cell-biomaterial interactions and in-depth research on the modulating M1-M2 macrophage polarization and differentiation of fibroblast to myofibroblast to control host inflammatory response to the implanted biomaterial; (2) Improving the scaffolds with a controlled and sustained biomolecules release system for bone regeneration and confirming them in vitro and long-term in vivo studies; (3) Developing a new miniaturized injectable scaffold with versatile functions including drug and cell delivery for tissue repair.

Over the past 2 years, I have been working for suppressing foreign body reactions by modifying the surface of silicone with anti-fouling materials, layer-by-layer deposition of hydrophilic polymers, and morphological cues to reduce capsular contracture to improve the medical device. The results of this research showed that microtexture surface with PLL/HA layer-by-layer deposition suppressed cell-cell interactions and inhibited fibroblast aggregation which promoted differentiation to myofibroblast, thus reducing foreign body reaction.

In an extension of that research, I provided chemical cue and topographical cue in a one-step process by comparing two topographically different 100-um-sized patterns, hole, and stripe, fabricated by the hydrophilic poly(acrylic acid) brushes on the PDMS surface using the photo-induced graft polymerization technique. In the research, stripe pattern with PAA brush showed a better performance in reducing foreign body reaction due to the synergistic effect of hydrophilic polymer − with less cell adhesion in the early inflammation stage − and stripe morphology − reduced cell adhesion, controlled cell shape and phenotype and cell aggregation −, and then I confirmed it by in vitro and in vivoexperiments.

Another interesting research I was involved in was developing a cancer therapy targeting M2 macrophages with a gold nanoparticle. We synthesized the uniform silica-coated 50 nm-gold nanoparticles with conjugation of the M2 macrophage marker, CD163, to target tumor-associated macrophages in the tumor microenvironment. We found the following results: targeting pro-wound healing M2 macrophage with radiotherapy reduced hypoxic regions of the tumor mass as well as total tumor mass; 50 nm thickness of silica shell enhanced the fluorescence(CD163 conjugated with Alexa 594) intensity to 4.5 fold due to metal enhanced fluorescence (MEF) effect.

This enthralling research encouraged me to seek a research opportunity with Prof. 교수 이름. His/her research work has given me new insight into my project so I am eager to obtain a Ph.D. admission to 프로그램 offered by 대학. My ultimate career goal is to hold a teaching and research position at a university where I could continue working on the research topics I care about most in collaboration with young scholars and researchers. [481]

2. Sample SOP

서울 소재 대학에서 경제학으로 학사 취득 후 국내 기업에서 HR 근무 5년차에 코넬 대학 경영학 석사 입학, 석사 2년차에 박사 과정에 지원해 합격한 자소서이다.
GRE V160 Q167 W4.0, 학부 GPA 3.7/4.0, 대학원 3.8/4.0

I intend to pursue a Ph.D. degree in Operation and Management in the 지원 대학 School of Management because it is the best setting for my pursuit of career goals. My research interests are well associated with the scholarship of Professor 교수 이름. I am deeply impressed by one of his publications on "misperceptions of economic and social inequality". The gap between the labor class and the meritocracy class has become larger since the outbreak of COVID-19, and this trend will continue to place workers into less fair social opportunities. What I learned in economics and industrial and labor relations helped me to study social issues from both micro and macro views.

I am attracted to the keyword, misperception, discussed by Prof. 교수 이름 because I understood how biased psychological roots will prevent minorities from climbing the social ladder. I am also interested in Prof. 교수 이름's work on racial and gender biases. The Whites' ambivalent attitudes toward Blacks display the indirect form of discrimination (Cydney H. Dupree et al., 2020) and America's struggle on its leadership in boosting the values of humanity gave rise to the question: How do minorities adapt to such subtle discrimination? How will it affect their adjusted identity/impression management strategy and the dominant group members' perception of racial equality?

SOP

Given a research opportunity, I am eager to work for my publications that trigger changes in the established social dialogue and the context in which minorities find their position and boundary.

I was involved in several organizational behavior projects in my graduate studies at C. ILR School. My recent qualitative work is about "Onboarding Challenging During COVID-19", in which I performed the research ranging from creating survey questions to making data analysis using Excel to verify if the frequencies of alumni activities/events affects the indicator showing their participation rate. As a result, we found alumni are less likely to participate in home school activities unless their articulated values are not well converged with those of the graduates' interests.

The frustration I struggled with at the HR office at 일했던 회사 pushed me toward more in-depth knowledge and research skills in organizational behavior research. Under the supervision of Dr. 이름 at 연구부서 we found the factors that determined the employee turnover rates to make a better result in our negotiation with the labor union. I regularly visited my professors at 산학협동 대학 to seek their advice on data analysis. I stayed up late at the 연구소 office to run statistical tests (mostly T-test and F-test) and establish regression equations describing the correlation between absenteeism and work productivity. Using the R Program, I analyzed the absenteeism of approximately 21,000 assembly line workers and found a seasonal pattern in employee cases and a particular set of conditions including the length of working hours and the number of night shifts they took. I supported the 임원 officials with data explaining that the overtime policy needs to change to 52 hours a week maximum. My effort was rewarded with the Employee of the Year award.

This experience attracted me to the ongoing research at 대학 연구소: the impacts of mental illness stigma in the workplace in view of work productivity or creativity. To deepen my understanding of the workforce with mental illness or distress, while reviewing 60 articles, I sorted the types of social discrimination using the keywords of the preference for identity disclosure and the mental disorders of psychiatric disability. It is intriguing to see that social bias on mental illness will prevent a corporation from increasing its products as much as other types of discrimination on employment. Without removing the organizational barriers that prevent employees with various mental distress or disorder from being a part of or a contributor to the business operation (Kayla B. et al., 2018), both government and corporations would pay costs that exceed billions of dollars per year (Greenberg et al., 2015). I came up with the following research topics: (1) The possibility that the supervisor's pre-knowledge contributes to impartial evaluations of the employees with psychiatric disorders; (2) the new dynamics between disclosure recipients and identity disclosure informants.

Along with my strong analytical skills, my 5-year of work experience in the HR/ER fields at 취업했던 회사, and my graduate education qualified me as a competitive doctorate student. Through the academic and field training I came to have keen eyes to observe organizational issues with a more comprehensive perception. I will continue working to establish meaningful models effective to determine the causal relations between individuals' behaviors and business practices or organizational structures. I am sure that the experiences I gained as project manager will help me become a researcher and teacher capable of handling multiple projects, lectures, and administration work more efficiently.

A close examination of recent publication topics at the 지원 대학 School of Management indicated that I could have the autonomy to take on projects that are quite ambitious in scope. My intellectual curiosity and professional experiences have imbued me with the depth and maturity your program demands. My ultimate career goal is to hold a teaching and research position at an academic or a research organization. I am therefore applying for the 지원 대학 School of Management doctoral program with a teaching or research assistantship option. Given a research opportunity, I will be a valuable member to your department and community. [917]

3. Sample SOP

8학년에 조기 유학해 버클리 음대를 졸업하고 코넬 법과대학에 입학한 학생의 자소서이다. 이 학생은 LSAT 770, 학부 GPA 3.9/4.0이었다. 법대는 https://www.lsac.org/에서 지원한다. 통합 에세이 이외 diversity essays를 요구하는 대학도 있다.

"Tell an interesting, informative story and personal story about yourself in 700-1400 words."

The first moment I became conscious of legal identification in my life was when I left home to study at the Alexander Graham Bell Public School as an 8th grader. My mother made it sure so many times to keep my passport in safe and I-20 at hand to enter Canada. Such consciousness helped me stay at the B. K. College of Music without a deportation issue. I always paid close attention to the expiration date stamped on my F1 visa noticing some of my friends got into trouble with their illegal status in the U.S.

Whether I wanted or not, I was involved in a legal fight over the copyright of the music Album we produced together as a group at B. K. College of Music. This event allowed me to study what the English words, "I will sue you." really means at the court. The conflict between 갑 and 을 aroused much controversy when 을 found out 갑 registered the copyrights of the album, which 을 co-produced with 갑, at the Korea Music Copyright Association under 갑's sole ownership. 갑 claimed since the originality of the lyrics came from his own life story, he has to be the one who deserved for the copyright ownership.

However, 을 argued that he should have the right because he is the one who played a key role in creating the album, Aliens, as the lead singer of the band, Dynamine and the composer of the lyrics and melodies from the scratch in the arrangement of the other four songs' melody and chords. The false promise that 갑 made to 을 that he would take care of all the payments that occurred in the recording session without any condition seems to weaken 을's position for profit share. As 을 was at the stake of losing his rights as co-producer, co-writer, lyricist, and vocalist, our friendships fell apart.

I had to return home when I was about to lose my F1 status in the U.S. soon after I graduated from B. K. College of Music. Although I found a drummer job at the 회사 이름 entertainment company, I had to work to pay my bills at my cousin's new restaurant, 레스토랑 이름, as well. I did a wide range of jobs for the boss from serving customers to interviewing new employees and to doing accounting jobs. I even looked for employment regulations from the Korean Labor Standards Act online to create employment contracts. Through this experience, I learned employment contracts should be designed to safeguard the interests of employees. For example, employers must give employees a written notice of dismissal at least 30 days in advance before the dismissal; a retirement allowance must be given to the employee who has continuously worked for at least one year.

A turning point in my career came when I met 변호사 이름, who is a good friend of J. P. and a lawyer at a Korean law firm (로펌 이름), often came to the restaurant. An unexpected job opportunity came to me when 변호사 이름 offered me a translation job at his law office. He was looking for someone bilingual in English and Korean to edit and proofread legal documents at the firm. I began working as a part-time assistant to Lawyer 이름. The first task assigned to me was a project which was to translate the 13 pages long license agreement between two large corporations from Korean to English in only three days. I spent all morning and evening looking up countless translated agreements in search of exact legal phrases and expressions. It was interesting to see how a legal agreement is structured and how the legal terms are different from the common vocabulary. When I presented the final product, the attorneys at the firm were satisfied with the quality of my translation, and they gave a compliment saying my translation is almost perfect to the degree only minor changes are necessary. Because of this experience, I found my writing capability other than my talents in music.

Three days later having submitted my translation work, I was offered a paralegal job from 로펌 이름 Intellectual Property Group. At first, it was not easy to grasp various subjects such as patents, copyright, trademark, design, unfair competition, and IP transactions in a short time. Although it took me a while to become familiar with the legal terms used in automotive technology, chemistry, biology, and pharmacy, I studied not only legal terms using a Patent search database called KIPRIS but the legal template designed for effective legal writing. Having been surrounded by experienced lawyers on the job, I became determined to change my career path from a drummer to a lawyer. Many would question how a musician would challenge a lawyer job, however, I found some common ground between the seemingly different fields of study, just follow the rules as I play the rhythm.

To accomplish this career, I spent about six months to prepare the LSAT. While studying for it, I was able to enhance practical skills such as how to draw reasonable, logical conclusions or assumptions from limited information and how to write to be persuasive enough to be read by others. I believe the top lawyers are not the ones with only logical and analytical thinking skills, but those who display great creativity in their problem-solving. [878]

다음은 서울에서 학사를 받고 미국 경영학부 산업조직심리로 박사 과정에 합격한 지원자의 에 세이이다.

The dual BA degrees in Business Administration and Psychology from 대학 이름 University helped me find my first job at 회사 이름, a start-up company. I was impressed by its idealistic vision to raise community awareness and promote public support for environmental protection and energy conservation. As a fledgling, I was happy in the win-win situation where I could enhance my data reading and analysis skills while contributing to environmental protection. However, soon I learned there were quite a few dissatisfied workers in my team. I questioned what would account for the high turnover rate at 회사. Having unofficial interviews with several coworkers there, I learned that their dissatisfaction was due to the 회사 culture and ethics, not the salary amount itself. They complained that how the company operates is not so transparent that they are skeptical about securing their future position. After I joined three farewell parties for the employees in the department, I decided to return to school.

Over the past two years, I studied various factors determining prospective and current employees' job attitudes and behavior. I focused on "job satisfaction, work engagement, and turnover" to provide answers to what could be the antecedents of emerging adults' career calling that affect occupational commitment, work engagement, and job satisfaction. I employed Structural Equation Modeling and Latent Growth Modeling to show the correlation between the keywords and statistical packages such as SPSS, Amos, and Mplus to verify the assumptions' reliability. I hypothesized that an autonomous parenting attitude affects the undergraduate student's calling, mediated by career decision-self efficacy and moderated by parent transcendent value orientation. For method, structural equation modeling to investigate both direct and indirect effects of parenting attitude on career calling and multiple hierarchical regression modeling to examine the moderation effect of parents' transcendent value orientation were employed. The results show that Korean parents play a pivotal role in their children's career decision-making processes through various pathways. In conclusion, their influence is effective for college students to build work value.

I also presented posters at the conferences (two posters as the first authors) about calling. I investigated (1) the correlation between the supervisor's calling and followers' organizational commitment in the organizational setting; (2) the mediation effect of career preparation behaviors on the relationship between autonomous child-rearing attitude and the career calling of their children; (3) the moderation effect of applicants' calling on the relationship between the shared value that corporates create and the intention-to-apply. It was an invaluable experience to share my research ideas with other scholars, accept criticism, and defend my arguments.

In addition to writing my papers, I also participated in a government project funded by the Korean Railroad Corporation to develop the aptitude test for current and prospective employees of locomotive engineers and railroad controllers. For this project, my job was reviewing previous literature and cases overseas to extract relevant constructs to assess from job descriptions and employee interviews, designing and validating the assessment through preliminary tests and standardized tests with more than 700 participants. Through this experience I learned how and what to do for qualitative and quantitative research.

While reviewing the previous literature, I became more curious about the following questions: (1) the interaction of situational and personal factors that may impact employee turnover; (2) research methods and statistical modeling. Given a research opportunity at 지원 대학, I am passionate about how to enhance workers' engagement and discourage their turnover.; Is it possible that understanding cultural differences, individual personalities or work values, and organizational climate contribute to increasing productivity.

During my graduate years, I concluded that my research interests are well aligned with those of 관심 교수 이름 because I saw the potential to build on the ongoing research at 대학 연구소. It is impressive to find reasons for leave and the difference between voluntary versus involuntary turnover. More importantly, loyalty to a lifetime job is no longer as valued as before. The experts in the fields of engineering field and business often think it can be another step in their career development, particularly those with boundaryless and protean career orientation. Given a research opportunity, I want to immerse myself in making analyses to find if the boundaryless and protean career orientation may mediate the relationship between openness and turnover. And the antecedents of turnover rates are different between those who consider their job as means of monetary reward and those who do not. I assume that work values are less likely to be affected by distributional justice than moral justice. I believe moral justice gives more leverage to the worker motivation to seek meaningfulness in their roles and position, particularly in management.

Another professor who attracted me to 프로그램 이름 is Prof. 교수 이름. Upon reviewing her papers on the person-environment fit and vocational intriguing to me. It is impressive to see the weak relationship between vocational interest and job satisfaction, contradictory to common sense. The results that vocational interest is correlated more strongly with intrinsic satisfaction than extrinsic satisfaction indicate that the construct of 'job satisfaction' is compounded. It would be my honor if I could investigate which contextual or individual factors can strengthen or weaken the relationship between vocational interest and job satisfaction. My question is if collectivistic self-construal mitigates the relationship more than individualistic self-construal.

In hope of becoming an Industrial and Organizational psychologist who will contribute to improving the psychological well-being of workers and productivity.

I am eager to seek admission to a Ph. D. degree in Psychology with a specialization in Industrial-Organizational Psychology. My career goal is to hold a teaching and research position at a university or college. I am open to any possible Ph. D. research available in your school and anxious to strengthen my research skills and methodological capacities through the enriched academic program offered by 대학 연구소 or 프로그램. [1001]

5. Sample SOP

영어영문과에서 학부 생활을 하고, 서울에서 하이브리드 프로그램으로 석사를 준비해서 컬럼비아 대학교 아시안 스터디 박사 과정에 입학한 학생의 자소서이다.

Last year, the "MeToo" movement widely spread out in my country, calling for the importance of women's position and their opportunities to build a better society. This movement captures the essence of my principal academic interest, revealing the social frame disguised by Confucian virtues in modern Korea. Such motivation conveys the basis of my attraction to the research and publication of Prof. 교수 이름 at 대학 이름. My desire to have a research opportunity in collaboration with her/him is a primary reason for me to apply to the doctoral degree program of the 지원 학과 at the 대학 이름.

Working at 회사 이름 at Nanjing in China as a translator and interpreter first allowed me to know about the Chinese social system. With a motivation to become a fluent translator in English and Chinese, I entered the joint MA program of translation and interpreting program offered by KUMU program but, as my transcript suggests, although this program helped me hone my skills in translation, it housed few courses related to East Asian literature, history, and culture. So taking relevant courses would be crucial for me to write a thesis in less than 2 years and a dissertation in less than 5 years at 대학 이름.

Through the program, I am enthusiastic about analyzing the previous literature regarding the relationship between social and literary forms, with questions of colonial literature, issues of gender and nationalism, the relationship between social frame and literature in the modern period before publishing my work. My research foci are three folds: (1) What are the explanations for dismantling the class stratification in premodern and modern Korea ?; (2) Why and how are the women's contributions to the progress of modernization of Korea overshadowed by the cost of the independent movement?; (3) What efforts did the modern Korean society make to encourage women to reconstruct the social hierarchy?

In the second semester of the 학부 program, I studied the notion of equivalence in different theoretical approaches to translations and learned without reflecting cultural colors and ideological differences in translation, any translation job can be considered incomplete. As Sherry Simon pointed out, translator jobs have been considered more suitable one to women. Such prejudice prompted me to look into the difference that appeared between the translation works done by women and those by men. For this, I investigated the gender differences in translation by analyzing several British and American poems translated in the Korean colonial period. [503]

다음은 Diversity 에세이이다. 다양성과 인본주의 가치를 추구하는 미국 대학에서 전공 분야

지식 이외에 학생의 인성을 보기 위해 요구하는 에세이이다. 진솔하게 자신만의 에세이를 적어야 한다.

Diversity Essay

1. Sample Optional Diversity Essay

Ideology and North Korean defectors

It is said, "Blood is thicker than water." but I saw "Ideology is thicker than blood." as a citizen of South Korea, the only divided nation in the world. It was the ideology war that divided my grandparents' family for more than 6 decades. My grandparents had to flee from persecution without knowing if their parents or siblings were dead or alive. I listened to this movie-like story so many times that it is deeply engraved in my memory. It was about the two Koreas, the Korean people, and my family.

My grandparents's story begins in their hometown, Yeongbyeon in 1946. Soon after the Japanese ownership system became void, my great-grandparents held their property ownership over the land they cultivated with their parents, brothers, sisters, uncles, aunts, and cousins. However, the rise of the communist party led not only to seize the land under the Land Reform Law(1946) but, forced them to leave their home and land with only a few things in their hands.

My grandfather told me they swam across the Imjin River running through the demilitarized zone, carrying my older uncle on his back in the dark. What more troubles them was not the deep and wide river but the guards in patrol. If they were caught, they would have been sent to a concentration camp. In a worst-case scenario, they might have been shot right there. I admire my grandparents who dared to run away to South from North for the freedom of choice.

It must have been their drama-like story that led my attention to the political column more than any other section of the newspaper. History repeats today in Seoul where more than 30,000 North Korean defectors are struggling to adapt to a new life of capitalism. While volunteering in the Somyeong Middle School, I learned what prevents many North Korean defectors from achieving success in South Korean society is its deeply rooted prejudice and pride. I have witnessed that many defectors are reluctant to reveal their past for fear of discrimination, although we all look alike in the eyes of westerners.

While studying at 대학 이름, I saw the importance of diversity in understanding other people's ideas, cultures, and music. Although a soloist's singing Aria is so attractive, it sounds even more overwhelming when playing with other opera singers being accompanied by the orchestra. There could be revolutionary individuals but their new ideas will bloom only when others are determined to support their new ideas. As a member of society, we should work together to reform the patriarchal system that consider women as a minor gender. When our years are well trained to hear the voices from the socio-politically disadvantaged class. [790]

2. Sample Optional Diversity Essay

Technology and Humanitarian Work

I have three different first names: Dong-woo is my Korean name, and Chuck in English, other than these two names, I have another, Aquasi, which indicates a boy born on Sunday in the Chwi language. My life in Ghana is something that I will never forget. Although I am away from its plain and lake, I am still a member of their community. I have been sponsoring the World Vision organization to support their education.

In my freshman, I saw a photo in which a black child was waiting in line for food. His big eyes looked like shining stars next to some women in frustration. In June 2003, I took my first trip to Ghana, Africa as a volunteer member of the UNDP organization. The streets of Kumasi were full of armed soldiers driving whacked cars emitting fumes, full of rubble and dust. In contrast, children playing with cows, soil, grass, and rocks looked happy.

I taught children how to use computers at the New Road School that the sister of the chief of the Chwi tribe was the principal. To my surprise, I found only one computer machine was placed on the teacher's desk without the Internet connection. I showed them how the Internet line works for searching for information and checking emails by drawing pictures on the blackboard.

To install a cable line close to the school, I raised funds with college friends in Seoul and, luckily one of my schoolmates heard of this news and donated 100,000 dollars to cover the Internet line installation.

I experienced the segregated society similar to the 1950's at Montgomery. When I was getting in a bus, the black driver identified me as a White and asked me to take a seat in the front. Once young children who watched my washing dishes said, "Mai ohoro kungkungt," which means that why a White guy is cleaning dishes in the Chwi language. I approached the boy and explained that I am not a White but Asian, and it is not right to divide people White and Black instead, we should learn how to respect differences in others.

Soon I could gain a reputation as a good teacher and technician in the community. With other volunteers, I dug a well and water pump it for fresh water and showed them how to filter water so they could drink fresh water. We taught them how to use resources to provide them with clean water by demonstrating how to build a filtering system made of layers of pebbles and charcoals. When the generator was out of order, I could fix it with the knowledge and skills I learned in the military. I was more than welcomed at the community of Chwi because I could gain their respect by helping them to get fresh water daily.

Among 50 indigenous languages the five major ones are Akan, Ewe, Ga, Dagaare, and Dagbani, but Chwi use English officially. I learned Chwi but, is not one of the major indigenous language. But I studied their language by figuring out their vowel sounds; it has a five vowel system, 'a, e, i, o, u'. I also learned that Chwi have stop, fricative, nasal, and improvise consonants and interestingly 'tap r'. Its word order is not SVO but SOV like Korean language. I used English most of time but, they were more delighted with my Chwi accent.

Before I travelled to Ghana. I believe we were doing humanitarian work to help others so we need philanthropists' supports to help the socio-economically disadvantaged, however, through my experiences in Ghana I learned what makes dramatic changes in the world is technology, if you use it appropriately, it will provide crucial solutions to the problems of poverty and famine. Now I am passionate about advancing technology that will play a pivotal role in changing the quality of life of mankind. [650]

	3. Contact Letter

　끝으로 간단한 콘택트 편지를 참고해 지원한 교수에게 모두 이메일을 보내는 편이 바람직하다. 박사 과정은 매우 개인적인 선택이 될 수 있기 때문이다. 불필요한 정보나 과도한 감사를 담아 감정적 어조로 적은 편지는 자제한다.

Dear Prof. 교수 이름

I am writing this letter to contact you and introduce myself personally.

Although I have completed submitting my application and references online, I am forwarding my SOP and resume for your reference.

If you have any questions about my application, you may contact me anytime.

Thank you for reading my email despite your busy schedule. Then I look forward to hearing from you.

Sincerely,

성명

❚지은이❚ 김문희(Michelle Seo) writingmatters@gmail.com

- 이화여자대학교 영문과 졸업
- California State University, Northridge 언어학 석사
- Holy Names College 교육대학원
- Mountain Diablo 고등학교 교사
- Glenbrook 중학교 교사
- Writing Institute Developer
- 가주국제문화대학에서 캘리포니아주 교사임용시험을 위한 analytical writing 지도

한울아카데미 2499

GRE Writing (3rd edition)

Analytical Essay

ⓒ 김문희, 2024

지은이 ∣ 김문희(Michelle Seo)
펴낸이 ∣ 김종수
펴낸곳 ∣ 한울엠플러스(주)
편집책임 ∣ 최진희

1판 1쇄 발행 ∣ 2006년 1월 11일
2판 1쇄(New GRE Writing) 발행 ∣ 2012년 7월 20일
3판 1쇄 발행 ∣ 2024년 5월 1일

주소 ∣ 10881 경기도 파주시 광인사길 153 한울시소빌딩 3층
전화 ∣ 031-955-0655
팩스 ∣ 031-955-0656
홈페이지 ∣ www.hanulmplus.kr
등록 ∣ 제406-2015-000143호

Printed in Korea.
ISBN 978-89-460-7500-9 13740